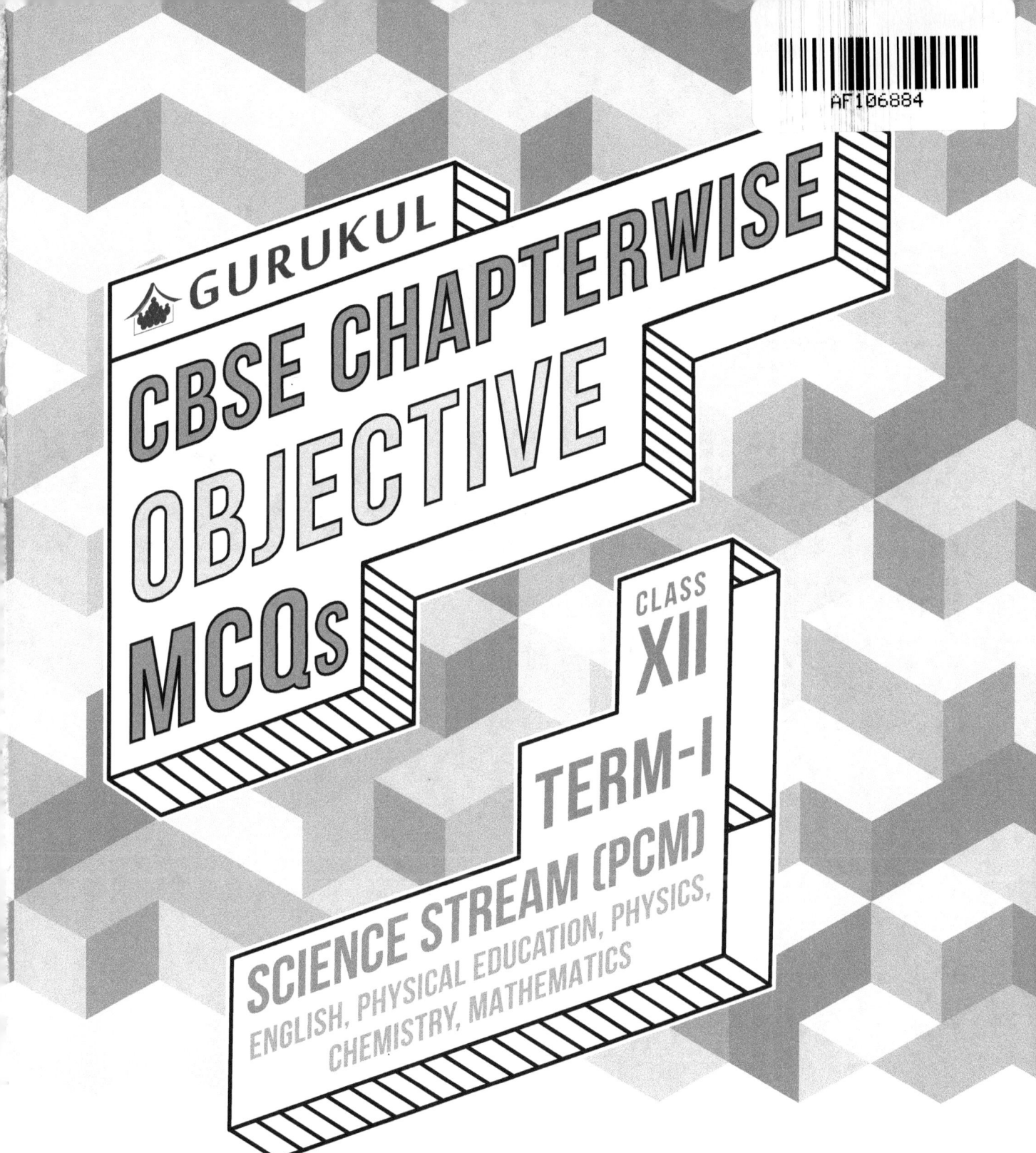

 COPYRIGHT RESERVED BY THE PUBLISHER

All rights reserved. No part of this publication may be reproduced in any form without the prior permission of the Oswal Publishers.

DISCLAIMER

With the ambition of providing standard academic resources, we have exercised extreme care in publishing the content. In case of any discrepancies in the matter, we request readers to excuse the unintentional lapse and not hold us liable for the same. Suggestions are always welcome.

EDITION : 2021

ISBN : 978-93-91184-15-5

PUBLISHED BY

GURUKUL BOOKS & PACKAGING

(Unit of Oswal Printers & Publishers Pvt. Ltd.)

 1/12, Sahitya Kunj, M.G. Road, Agra - 282002

 (0562) 2527771-4, +91 7534077222

 info@oswalpublishers.in

 www.oswalpublishers.com

The cover of this book has been designed using resources from Freepik.com

Printed At Upkar Printing Unit, Agra

PREFACE

Board exams are a crucial milestone for every student. For students to perform well in this exam, we have introduced CBSE Chapterwise Objective MCQs for the TERM I Examinations for class XII. We have designed this book, keeping in mind all the changing scenarios and exam patterns. The content of the book is strictly based on the latest circular (Acad- 51, 53 and 55) issued by the board in July, 2021 for TERM I examinations. This book will help the learners achieve the learning objectives in an easy to grasp manner.

This book contains matter compiled by highly proficient teachers and subject matter experts from across the country. Questions are segregated as per their respective chapters to facilitate easy navigation between them. Every attempt has been made to keep the language of the book crisp and accessible.

We hope you will find this book helpful in your preparations for Std. XII board examinations. We would advise you to stay calm and manage your time wisely. Don't be overwhelmed with the amount of resources and study guides available; be selective and efficient in your preparation.

—Publisher

SPECIAL HIGHLIGHTS

Questions focused on the New Objective Paper Pattern, according to the latest circular issued by the Board (Acad-51, 53 and 55) in July 2021.

Study material strictly based on the reduced syllabus issued by the Board in July 2021 for TERM I examination.

Based on the board's most recent typologies of Objective Type Questions:

Stand-Alone MCQs

1. Which one of the following is the unit of electric charge?
   (a) Coulomb   (b) Newton
   (c) Volt   (d) Coulomb/volt
2. The electric charge always resides:
   (a) at the centre of charged conductor
   (b) at the interior of charged conductor
   (c) on the outer surface of charged conductor
   (d) randomly all over the charged conductor

Assertion-Reason questions

52. **Assertion:** The charge on any body can be increased or decreased in terms of e.
    Reason: Quantization of charge means that the charge on a body is the integral multiple of e.
53. **Assertion:** The properties that the force with which two charges attract or repel each other are not affected by the presence of a third charge.
    Reason: Force on any charge due to a number of other charges is the vector sum of all the forces on that charge due to other charges, taken one at a time.

MCQs with a case study

66. Microwave oven works on the principle of torque acting on an electric dispole. The food we consume has water molecules which are permanent electric dipoles. Oven produces microwaves that are oscillating **electromagnetic fields and produce torque on the water** molecules. Due to this torque on each water molecules, the molecules rotate very fast and produce thermal energy. Thus, heat generated is used to heat the food.
    (i) An electric dipole is placed at an angle of 30° to a **uniform electric field.**
    The dipole will experience

2000+ New Chapter-wise Questions included

It consists of questions from the official CBSE Question Bank, issued in April 2021

57. Read the passage given below and answer the following questions: [CBSE Website]
    Nucleophilic substitution reaction of haloalkane can be conducted according to both S_N^1 and S_N^2 mechanisms. However, which mechanism it is based on is related to such factors as the structure of haloalkane, and properties of leaving group, nucleophilic reagent and solvent.

45. The self-inductance L of a solenoid of length l and area of cross section A, with a fixed number of turns N increases as: [NCERT Exemplar]
    (a) l and A increase.
    (b) l decreases and A increases.
    (c) l increases and A decreases.
    (d) both l and A decrease

NCERT & NCERT Exemplar questions included

20. (a) decreases directly as the distance from the centre
    Explanation: Electric Field is directly proportional to the magnitude of charge and inversely proportional to the square of the distance from the charge.
21. (c) radial, inwards
    Explanation: Electric lines of force about a negative point charge are radial, inwards.

Detailed Explanations for MCQs

Recent Years board objective questions included

46. The electric flux through a closed Gaussion Surface depend upon : [CBSE OD, Set 2, 2020]
    (a) Net charge enclosed and permitivity of the medium
    (b) Net charge enclosed, permitivity of the medium and size of the gaussion surface
    (c) Net charge enclosed only
    (d) Permitivity of the medium only

Practice Periodic Tests available on www.oswalpublishers.com

CONTENTS

English Core	9–88
SYLLABUS	11
1. Discursive Passage	13
Answers	24
2. Literary Passage	25
Answers	32
3. Case-Based Passage	34
Answers	45
4. Notice Writing	47
Answers	47
5. Advertisements	48
Answers	49
6. Letter Writing	50
Answers	51
7. Article Writing	52
Answers	53
8. Flamingo-Prose	54
Answers	64
9. Flamingo-Poetry	67
Answers	77
10. Vistas-Prose	80
Answers	87

Physical Education	89–112
SYLLABUS	91
1. Planning in Sports	93
Answers	95
2. Sports and Nutrition	97
Answers	99
5. Children and Women in Sports	101
Answers	103
6. Test and Measurement in Sports	105
Answers	107
8. Biomechanics and Sports	109
Answers	111

Physics	113–194
SYLLABUS	115
1. Electric Charges and Fields	117
Answers	123
2. Electrostatic Potential and Capacitance	128
Answers	133
3. Current Electricity	139
Answers	145
4. Moving Charges and Magnetism	151
Answers	157
5. Magnetism and Matter	164
Answers	168
6. Electromagnetic Induction	172
Answers	177
7. Alternating Current	183
Answers	188

Chemistry	195–250
SYLLABUS	197
1. Solid State	199
Answers	203
2. Solutions	207
Answers	212
7. p-Block Elements	217
Answers	221
10. Haloalkanes & Haloarenes	225
Answers	230
11. Alcohols, Phenols & Ethers	234
Answers	238

14. Biomolecules	242
Answers	*247*

Mathematics 251–328

SYLLABUS	253
1. Relations and Functions	255
Answers	*259*
2. Inverse Trigonometric Functions	265
Answers	*267*
3. Matrices	272
Answers	*277*
4. Determinants	283
Answers	*287*
5. Continuity and Differentiability	294
Answers	*298*
6. Applications of Derivative	309
Answers	*313*
7. Linear Programming	321
Answers	*326*

ENGLISH CORE

SYLLABUS
English Core (Code No. 301)

SECTION	Term – I	WEIGHTAGE (IN MARKS)
A	**Reading Comprehension:** (Two Passages) • Unseen passage (factual, descriptive or literary/discursive or persuasive) • Case Based Unseen (Factual) Passage	14 (8 + 6 Marks)
B	**Creative Writing Skills:** <u>Short Writing Tasks</u> • Notice Writing • Classified Advertisements <u>Long Writing Tasks (One)</u> • Letter to an Editor (giving suggestions or opinion on issues of public interest) • Article Writing	3 + 5 Marks Total = 08
C	**Literature:** Literary-prose/poetry extracts (seen-texts) to assess comprehension and appreciation, analysis, inference, extrapolation Questions Based on Texts to assess comprehension and appreciation, analysis, inference, extrapolation. <u>Book-Flamingo (Prose)</u> • The Last Lesson • Lost Spring • Deep Water <u>Book-Flamingo (Poetry)</u> • My Mother at Sixty-Six • An Elementary School Classroom in a Slum • Keeping Quiet <u>Book-Vistas (Prose)</u> • The Third Level • The Enemy	11 Marks for Flamingo + 7 Marks for Vistas = 18 Marks
	TOTAL	40
	ASL	10
	Grand Total	40 + 10 = 50

Prescribed Books:

1. **Flamingo:** English Reader published by National Council of Education Research and Training, New Delhi.
2. **Vistas:** Supplementary Reader published by National Council of Education Research and Training, New Delhi

Discursive Passage

1. Read the passage carefully:

1. There were hundreds of us in the lecture hall, watching the descent of the Vikram Lander, with the Pragyan rover, descending on the lunar surface, its thrusters in full force, slowing down the free fall of the delicate component of the Chandrayaan-2 spacecraft, all 1498 kg of it hurtling down, pulled by the gravity of Moon. It had separated from the rest of the spacecraft four days ago, leaving the orbiter in its path about 100 km above the lunar surface, where it is going to spend at least 7 years, with its eight excellent instruments sending back crucial scientific information about the Moon, its environment and even the Sun.

2. We were applauding as the green dot on the plot of the landing trajectory, showing the altitude and the range of the lander, reached about two km above the surface, at that point its speed was about 50 m/s. Far too high still, we thought- it had to come well below 5 m/s for a soft landing as it reached the ground. Then our spirits fell as it deviated from the expected course, and got stuck, indicating that we had lost communication. This is the phase, which the ISRO Chairperson Dr. K. Sivan had described as the, "15 minutes of terror". We still haven't recovered communication, but thermal imaging from the orbiter's cameras has located the site of the landing on Sunday. The extent of the damage to Vikram is still being assessed. If things had gone according to plan, India would have joined the elite club of three other nations that have landed in one piece on an extra-terrestrial surface–the Moon, Mars or an asteroid. If the Rover had been out on its 14 days prowl, we would have learnt about the traces of gaseous elements near the surface of the Moon and also about the low level Moonquakes from the embedded seismometer.

3. Chandrayaan-2 was launched in July on the GSLV-3, taking a complicated, fuel efficient path to the Moon lasting over 40 days. In contrast with the Apollo missions being launched on the more powerful Saturn-V launchers in the 1960s, this mission was kept affordable, but sent the mission on a long journey fraught with possible pitfalls. Till the last minute, the entire manoeuvre had worked like clockwork, showing the high level of sophistication that ISRO is capable of in its planning, design, fabrication and execution. This in my mind is the major success story of ISRO so far in this mission.

4. We are now hopeful that we will gain contact with Vikram, lovingly named after the founder of ISRO in its birth centenary year. Even if some of the instruments can be made to work, we would have valuable information and images close to the lunar surface and learn more about what to do and what not to in our next attempt. It is also time to look beyond the landing event. Chandrayaan-2 is so much more than the landing event, which seemed to have caught most of the attention of the public and the media. On the rest of the vehicle in orbit, we have two very sophisticated imagers. The high-resolution Orbiter Camera photographs the lunar surface to a resolution of 0.3 m, the best in any Moon mission so far, by any nation. Another terrain-mapping camera takes photos in multiple colours. Since all previous missions had concentrated on the equatorial region and northern hemisphere of the Moon, Chandrayaan-2's work in the southern polar region will be unique.

5. The CLASS instrument on the orbiter will quantify the amount of calcium, magnesium, iron, sodium and other useful elements on or below the lunar surface through X-ray fluorescence. The IIRS instrument, also on the orbiter, will tell us about water and minerals under the surface. In addition to detecting them, it can also help us quantify and tell us about how hard they would be to extract. Why do we need this information? It is inevitable that one day humans will have to go out into the solar system to look for resources, and even for habitation. India being one of the most populous nation of the Earth will have to play a major role.

6. Even if we choose not to live on the Moon, we need a Moon base, as a refuelling station, or as an assembly or service station. We have to know what resources are available on the Moon. What if a small part of this mission is not successful? In my mind, the journey of ISRO team that has brought the mission to where it is now, is more important than the task that will be performed. Similarly, the complicated journey of the spacecraft from the Earth to and around the Moon has adequately demonstrated what Indian technology can achieve.

1.1. On the basis of your understanding of the passage, answer any ten of the following questions by choosing the most appropriate option:

(a) How many days ago was Vikram Lander separated from the spacecraft?
 (i) one day
 (ii) two days
 (iii) three days
 (iv) four days

(b) For how long it is supposed to remain upon the lunar surface?
   (i) 5 years (ii) 6 years
   (iii) 7 years (iv) 8 years

(c) Based on your understanding of the passage, choose the option that lists the CORRECT order of the sentences.
   1. The extent of the damage to Vikram is still being assessed.
   2. The IIRS instrument, also on the orbiter, will tell us about water and minerals under the surface.
   3. Vikram Lander deviated from the expected course, and got stuck, indicating that we had lost communication.
   4. Chandrayaan-2 was launched in July on the GSLV-3.
   (i) 1, 2, 4, 3 (ii) 3, 1, 4, 2
   (iii) 3, 2, 4, 1 (iv) 2, 3, 4, 1

(d) Chandrayaan-2 was supposed to land on......
   (i) Southern Pole (ii) Northern Pole
   (iii) Lunar surface (iv) Equatorial region

(e) The CLASS instrument on the orbiter will quantify the amount of which of the following element?

   (1)   (2)   (3)   (4)

   (i) image 1 (ii) image 2
   (iii) image 3 (iv) image 4

(f) Chandrayaan-2 was launched in July on the...........
   (i) ALSV-5 (ii) GSLV-3
   (iii) IIRS (iv) GSLV-4 1.2

(g) Why were the scientists happy when they saw the green dot on the trajectory?
   (i) because it told about water and minerals under the surface.
   (ii) because it indicated the altitude and the range of the lander.
   (iii) because it told about the presence of gaseous elements.
   (iv) because it reached in expected course of time.

(h) What is the function of CLASS instrument on the orbiter?
   (i) It gives information about the moon.
   (ii) It shows images of the moon.
   (iii) It quantifies the amount of calcium, magnesium, iron, sodium and other useful elements on or below the lunar surface.
   (iv) It measures the air pressure on moon.

(i) Which things are available on the moon even if we don't make it our habitat?
   (i) a moon base
   (ii) a refuelling station
   (iii) a service station
   (iv) all of these

(j) Which word in the passage means same as 'distinctive'? (para 4)
   (i) concentrated (ii) unique
   (iii) valuable (iv) sophisticated

(k) Pick the option that tells the feeling of the writer when the Lander deviated from the expected course, and got stuck, indicating that it had lost communication.
   (i) frustrating (ii) provoking
   (iii) disheartening (iv) hostile

2. Read the passage carefully:

1. We sit in the last row, bumped about but free of stares. The bus rolls out of the dull crossroads of the city, and we are soon in open countryside, with fields of sunflowers as far as the eye can see, their heads all facing us. Where there is no water, the land reverts to desert. While still on level ground, we see in the distance the tall range of the Mount Bogda, abrupt like a shining prism laid horizontally on the desert surface. It is over 5,000 metres high, and the peaks are under permanent snow, in powerful contrast to the flat desert all around. Heaven Lake lies part of the way up this range about 2,000 metres above sea-level, at the foot of one of the higher snow-peaks.

2. As the bus climbs, the sky, brilliant before, grows overcast. I have brought nothing warm to wear: it is all down at the hotel in Urumqi. Rain begins to fall. The man behind me is eating overpoweringly smelly goat's cheese. The bus window leaks inhospitably but reveals a beautiful view. We have passed quickly from desert through arable land to pasture, and the ground is now green with grass, the slopes dark with pine. A few cattle drink at a clear stream flowing past moss-covered stones; it is a Constable landscape. The stream changes into a white torrent, and as we climb higher, I wish more and more that I had brought with me something warmer than the pair of shorts that have served me so well in the desert. The stream which, we are told, rises in Heaven Lake, disappears, and we continue our slow ascent. About noon, we arrive at Heaven Lake, and look for a place to stay at the foot, which is the resort area. We get a room in a small cottage, and I am happy to note that there are thick quilts on the beds.

3. Standing outside the cottage, we survey our surroundings. Heaven Lake is long, sardine-

shaped and fed by snowmelt from a stream at its head. The lake is an intense blue, surrounded on all sides by green mountain walls, dotted with distant sheep. At the head of the lake, beyond the delta of the inflowing stream, is a massive snow-capped peak which dominates the vista; it is part of a series of peaks that culminate, a little out of view, in Mount Bogda itself.

4. For those who live in the resort, there is a small mess-hall by the shore. We eat here sometimes, and sometimes buy food from the vendors outside, who sell Kabab and naan until the last buses leave. The kababs, cooked on skewers over charcoal braziers, are particularly good; highly spiced and well-done. Horse's milk is available too from the local Kazakh herdsmen, but I decline this. I am so affected by the cold that Mr. Cao, the relaxed young man who runs the mess, lends me a spare pair of trousers, several sizes too large but more than comfortable. Once I am warm again, I feel a pre-dinner spurt of energy— dinner will be long in coming—and I ask him whether the lake is good for swimming in. "Swimming?" Mr. Cao says, "You aren't thinking of swimming, are you?"

5. "I thought I might," I confess. "What's the water like?" He doesn't answer me immediately, turning instead to examine some receipts with exaggerated interest. Mr. Cao, with great off-handedness, addresses the air. "People are often drowned here", he says. After a pause, he continues. "When was the last one?" This question is directed at the cook, who is preparing a tray of "mantou" (squat, white steamed bread rolls), and who now appears, wiping his doughy hand across his forehead. "Was it the Beijing athlete?" asks Mr. Cao.

2.1. On the basis of your understanding of the passage, answer any ten of the following questions by choosing the most appropriate option:

(a) One benefit of sitting in the last row of the bus was that......
   (i) the narrator enjoyed the bumps
   (ii) no one stared at him
   (iii) he could see the sunflowers
   (iv) he avoided the dullness of the city

(b) The narrator was travelling to.......
   (i) Mount Bogda
   (ii) Heaven Lake
   (iii) a 2,000-metre high snow-peak
   (iv) Urumqi

(c) Based on your understanding of the passage, choose the option that lists the CORRECT sequence of the process.
   1. As the bus climbs, the sky, brilliant before, grows overcast
   2. The kababs, cooked on skewers over charcoal braziers, are particularly good; highly spiced and well-done.
   3. The bus rolls out of the dull crossroads of the city, and we are soon in open countryside
   4. We get a room in a small cottage, and I am happy to note that there are thick quilts on the beds
   (i) 1, 3, 4, 2   (ii) 2,3,4,1
   (iii) 3, 1, 4, 2   (iv) 4,3,1,2

(d) Mount Bogda is compared to.......
   (i) a horizontal desert surface
   (ii) a shining prism
   (iii) a constable landscape
   (iv) the overcast sky

(e) Which option represents the shape of the 'Heaven Lake'?

(1)   (2)

(3)   (4)

   (i) image 1   (ii) image 2
   (iii) image 3   (iv) image 4

(f) The man behind the narrator was eating overpoweringly.......
   (i) smelly goat's cheese
   (ii) smelly pickles
   (iii) fragrant fruits
   (iv) none of these

(g) What did the narrator see at distance from the bus when they were still on ground?
   (i) the tall range of the Mount Bogda
   (ii) the wide range of forests
   (iii) snow-covered hills
   (iv) sheep and goats mounting the hills

(h) Where has the narrator left his warm clothes?
   (i) at home
   (ii) in the bus
   (iii) in the hotel
   (iv) at his friend's house

(i) What is 'Mantou'?
   (i) a thick hamburger
   (ii) a squat, garlic bread
   (iii) a squat, white steamed bread roll
   (iv) a squat, hotdog

(j) Which word in the passage means same as 'terminate'? (para 3)
   (i) culminate   (ii) intense
   (iii) dominate   (iv) distant

(k) As the bus climbs up while heading towards Mount Bogda, how did the weather begin to change?
1. It was becoming warmer.
2. It was becoming cooler.
3. It began raining.
4. The snow started falling down.
(i) 1 and 2   (ii) 2 and 3
(iii) 1 and 3   (iv) 3 and 4

3. Read the passage carefully:

1. Swami Vivekananda was a Hindu monk and one of the most celebrated spiritual leaders of India. He was more than just a spiritual mind; he was a prolific thinker, great orator and passionate patriot. He carried forward the free-thinking philosophy of his guru, Ramakrishna Paramhansa into a new paradigm. He worked tirelessly towards betterment of the society, in servitude of the poor and needy, dedicating his all for his country. He was responsible for the revival of Hindu spiritualism and established Hinduism as a revered religion on world stage. His message of universal brotherhood and self-awakening remains relevant especially in the current backdrop of widespread political turmoil around the world.

2. The young monk and his teachings have been an inspiration to many and his words have become goals of self-improvement especially for the youth of the country. For this very reason, his birthday, January 12, is celebrated as the National Youth Day in India. Born as Narendranath Dutta, into an affluent Bengali family in Calcutta, Vivekananda was one of the eight children of Vishwanath Dutta and Bhuvaneshwari Devi. He was born on January 12, 1863. Father Vishwanath was a successful attorney with considerable influence in society. Narendranath's mother Bhuvaneshwari was a woman endowed with a strong, God-fearing mind who had a great impact on her son.

3. As a young boy, Narendranath displayed sharp intellect. He was mischievous by nature but also had interest in music, both instrumental as well as vocal. He excelled in his studies as well, first at the Metropolitan institution, and later at the Presidency College in Calcutta. By the time he graduated from the college, he had acquired a vast knowledge of different subjects. He was active in sports, gymnastics, wrestling and body building. He was an avid reader and read up on almost everything under the sun. He perused the Hindu scriptures like the Bhagvad Gita and the Upanishads on one hand, while on the other hand he studied western philosophy, history and spirituality by David Hume, Johann Gottlieb Fichte and Herbert Spencer.

4. Although Narendranath's mother was a devout woman and he had grown up in a religious atmosphere at home, he underwent a deep spiritual crisis at the start of his youth. His well-studied knowledge led him to question the existence of God and for some time he believed in Agnosticism. Yet he could not completely ignore the existence of a Supreme Being. He became associated with Brahmo Movement led by Keshab Chandra Sen, for some time. The Bramho Samaj recognised one God unlike the idol-worshipping, superstition-ridden Hinduism. The host of philosophical questions regarding the existence of God rolling through his mind remained unanswered. During this spiritual crisis, Vivekananda first heard about Sri Ramakrishna from William Hastie, the Principal of the Scottish Church College.

5. Earlier, to satisfy his intellectual quest for God, Narendranath visited prominent spiritual leaders from all religions, asking them a single question, "Have you seen God?" Each time he came away without a satisfying answer. He put forward the same question to Sri Ramakrishna at his residence in Dakshineshwar Kali Temple compounds. Without a moment's hesitation, Sri Ramakrishna replied: "Yes, I have. I see God as clearly as I see you, only in a much deeper sense." Vivekananda, initially unimpressed by the simplicity of Ramkrishna, was astonished with Ramakrishna's reply. Ramakrishna gradually won over this argumentative young man with his patience and love. The more Narendranath visited Dakshineshwar, the more his questions were answered.

3.1. On the basis of your understanding of the passage, answer any ten of the following questions by choosing the most appropriate option:

(a) Swami Vivekananda was a.......
(i) spiritual leader
(ii) philosopher
(iii) reader
(iv) motivational speaker

(b) Narendranath believed in Agnosticism which meant.......
(i) believing in existence of God
(ii) believing in non- existence of God
(iii) following religion strongly
(iv) not following the religion

(c) Based on your understanding of the passage, choose the option that lists the CORRECT order of the events in the life of Swami Vivekananda:
1. Narendranath was also associated with the Brahmo Movement.
2. He studied both the Hindu scriptures and western philosophy and spirituality.
3. Narendranath was born on January 12, 1863.
4. Ramkrishna's simplistic nature eventually won over Narendranath.
(i) 1, 2, 3, 4   (ii) 4, 2, 1, 3
(iii) 3, 2, 1, 4   (iv) 1, 4, 2, 3

(d) What was Vishwanatha Datta's profession?
(i) attorney   (ii) spiritual leader
(iii) teacher   (iv) none of these

(e) Which option represents INCORRECT data related to the life of Swami Vivekananda?

(i) Swami Vivekananda preached the message of universal brotherhood.
(ii) Swami Vivekananda showed more interest in music than in academics.
(iii) In his youth, Swami Vivekananda believed in Agnosticism.
(iv) Swami Vivekananda heard about Sri Ramakrishna from the principal of the Scottish Church College.

(f) Which option represents the CORRECT traits of Swami Vivekananda?

1. Intellectual Monarchist Orator	2. Intellectual Argumentative Spiritual	3. Intellectual Patriot Atheist	4. Orator Patriot Nihilist
(1)	(2)	(3)	(4)

(i) option 1 (ii) option 2
(iii) option 3 (iv) option 4

(g) Vivekananda's birthday, January 12, is celebrated as ....
(i) The National Religious Day
(ii) The National Youth Day in India
(iii) The Youth Parliamentary Day
(iv) The Awakening Youth of India

(h) What other qualities did Vivekanand possess besides having spiritual mind?
(i) a prolific thinker
(ii) a great orator
(iii) a passionate patriot
(iv) all of these

(i) Why did Narendranath visit prominent spiritual leaders from all religions?
(i) to understand different religions properly
(ii) to get the knowledge of different faiths
(iii) to get the knowledge of whereabouts of God
(iv) to spread religious thoughts

(j) Which word in the passage is opposite to 'half-hearted'? (para 3)
(i) perused (ii) belied
(iii) affluent (iv) avid

(k) Pick the options that CORRECTLY list the feelings that Swami Vivekananda had in his youth towards God.
1. agnostic   2. confused
3. faithful   4. atheist
(i) 1 and 2   (ii) 1 and 4
(iii) 2 and 3   (iv) 1 and 3

4. **Read the passage carefully:**

1. Mahatma Gandhi, by name of Mohandas Karamchand Gandhi, (born October 2, 1869, Porbandar, India, died January 30, 1948, Delhi), Indian lawyer, politician, social activist and writer who became the leader of the nationalist movement against the British rule of India. As such, he came to be considered as the father of his country. Gandhi is internationally esteemed for his doctrine of non-violent protest (Satyagraha) to achieve political and social progress.

2. In the eyes of millions of his fellow Indians, Gandhi was the Mahatma ('Great Soul'). The unthinking adoration of the huge crowds that gathered to see him all along the route of his tours made them a severe ordeal; he could hardly work during the day or rest at night. "The woes of the Mahatmas," he wrote, "are known only to the Mahatmas." His fame spread worldwide during his lifetime and only increased after his death. The name Mahatma Gandhi is now one of the most universally recognised on Earth.

3. Gandhi was the youngest child of his father's fourth wife. His father was Karamchand Gandhi, who was the dewan (chief minister) of Porbandar, the capital of a small principality in western India (what is now in Gujarat state) under British suzerainty, did not have much in the way of a formal education. He was, however, an able administrator who knew how to steer his way between the capricious princes, their long-suffering subjects and the headstrong British political officers in power. Gandhiji's mother, Putlibai, was completely absorbed in religion, did not care much for finery or jewellery, divided her time between her home and the temple, fasted frequently and wore herself out in days and nights of nursing whenever there was sickness in the family. Mohandas grew up in a home steeped in Vaishnavism—worship of the Hindu God Vishnu, with a strong tinge of Jainism, a morally rigorous Indian religion whose chief tenets are non-violence and the belief that everything in the universe is eternal. Thus, he took for granted ahimsa (no injury to all living beings), vegetarianism, fasting for self-purification and mutual tolerance between adherents of various creeds and sects.

4. The educational facilities at Porbandar were rudimentary; in the primary school that Mohandas attended, the children wrote the alphabet in the dust with their fingers. Luckily for him, his father became dewan of Rajkot, another princely state. Though Mohandas occasionally won prizes and scholarships at the local schools, his record on the whole was mediocre. One of the terminal reports rated him as "good at English, fair in Arithmetic and weak in Geography; conduct very good, bad handwriting." He was married at the age of 13 and thus lost a year at school. A diffident child, he shone neither in the classroom nor on the playing field. He loved to go out on long solitary walks

when he was not nursing his by then ailing father (who died soon thereafter) or helping his mother with her household chores.

5. He had learned, in his words, "to carry out the orders of the elders, not to scan them." With such extreme passivity, it is not surprising that he should have gone through a phase of adolescent rebellion, marked by secret atheism, petty thefts, furtive smoking, and most shocking of all for a boy born in a Vaishnava family, meat eating. His adolescence was probably no stormier than that of most children of his age and class. What was extraordinary was the way his youthful transgressions ended. 'Never again' was his promise to himself after each escapade. And he kept his promise. Beneath an unprepossessing exterior, he concealed a burning passion for self-improvement that led him to take even the heroes of Hindu mythology, such as Prahlada and Harishchandra, legendary embodiments of truthfulness and sacrifice as living models.

6. In 1887 Mohandas scraped through the matriculation examination of the University of Bombay (now University of Mumbai) and joined Samaldas College in Bhavnagar (Bhaunagar). As he had to suddenly switch from his native language—Gujarati—to English, he found it rather difficult to follow the lectures. Meanwhile, his family was debating his future. Left to himself, he would have liked to have been a doctor. But, besides the Vaishnava prejudice against vivisection, it was clear that, if he was to keep up the family tradition of holding high office in one of the states in Gujarat, he would have to qualify as a barrister. That meant a visit to England and Mohandas, who was not too happy at Samaldas College, jumped at the proposal. His youthful imagination conceived England as "a land of philosophers and poets, the very centre of civilisation. But there were several hurdles to be crossed before the visit to England could be realised. His father had left the family little property; moreover, his mother was reluctant to expose her youngest child to unknown temptations and dangers in a distant land. But Mohandas was determined to visit England. One of his brothers raised the necessary money and his mother's doubts were allayed when he took a vow that, while away from home, he would not touch wine, women or meat. Mohandas disregarded the last obstacle, the decree of the leaders of the Modh Bania sub caste (Vaishya caste), to which the Gandhi's belonged, who forbade his trip to England as a violation of the Hindu religion and sailed in September 1888. Ten days after his arrival, he joined the Inner Temple, one of the four London law colleges (The Temple).

7. Gandhi took his studies seriously and tried to brush up on his English and Latin by taking the University of London matriculation examination. But, during the three years he spent in England, his main preoccupation was with personal and moral issues rather than with academic ambitions. The transition from the half-rural atmosphere of Rajkot to the cosmopolitan life of London was not easy for him. As he struggled painfully to adapt himself to Western food, dress and etiquette, he felt awkward. His vegetarianism became a continual source of embarrassment to him; his friends warned him that it would wreck his studies as well as his health. Fortunately for him he came across a vegetarian restaurant as well as a book providing a reasoned defence of vegetarianism, which henceforth became a matter of conviction for him, not merely a legacy of his Vaishnava background. The missionary zeal he developed for vegetarianism helped to draw the pitifully shy youth out of his shell and gave him a new poise. He became a member of the executive committee of the London Vegetarian Society, attending its conferences and contributing articles to its journal. Africa was to present Gandhi challenges and opportunities that he could hardly have conceived. In the end he would spend more than two decades there, returning to India only briefly in 1896–97. The youngest two of his four children were born there.

4.1. On the basis of your understanding of the passage, answer any ten of the following questions by choosing the most appropriate option:

(a) Gandhiji's nonviolent protest was......
    (i) against the Britishers
    (ii) to achieve political and social progress
    (iii) to achieve freedom
    (iv) to flee Britishers from India

(b) Gandhiji was brought up in a family following......
    (i) jainism   (ii) ahimsa
    (iii) buddhism (iv) vaishnavism

(c) Based on your understanding of the passage, choose the option that lists the CORRECT sequence of the given sentences.
    1. Gandhiji found transition from the half-rural atmosphere of Rajkot to the cosmopolitan life of London tough.
    2. Gandhiji joined the Inner Temple, one of the four London law colleges.
    3. Gandhiji was a diffident child, and loved to go out on long solitary walks.
    4. Gandhiji became a member of the executive committee of the London Vegetarian Society,
    (i) 1, 2, 3, 4   (ii) 2, 3, 4, 1
    (iii) 2, 1, 4, 3   (iv) 3, 2, 1, 4

(d) During his adolescence age, Gandhiji was......
    (i) like other children of his age
    (ii) different from other children
    (iii) superior to them
    (iv) below the average children

(e) Choose the option that represents INCORRECT data related to Mahatma Gandhi.
    (i) Gandhi's vegetarianism became a continual source of confidence for him.
    (ii) Gandhi developed a missionary zeal for vegetarianism which, helped to draw his

pitifully shy youth out of his shell and gave him a new poise.

(iii) Gandhi became a member of the executive committee of the London Vegetarian Society.

(iv) Gandhi felt awkward as he struggled painfully to adapt to Western food, dress, and etiquette.

(f) Gandhiji became a member of the executive committee for the:

1. Whiskey Women Meat	2. Wine Men Meat	3. Wine Money Meat	4. Wine Women Meat
(1)	(2)	(3)	(4)

(i) option 1 (ii) option 2
(iii) option 3 (iv) option 4

(h) What vow did Gandhiji take before going to London?
(i) he would not touch wine
(ii) he would not touch women
(iii) he would not touch meat
(iv) all of these

(i) What difficulty did Gandhiji face in England?
(i) food (ii) language
(iii) living place (iv) water

(j) Which word in the passage means the same as 'unpleasant'? (para 2)
(i) ordeal (ii) adoration
(iii) vows (iv) recognised

(k) Pick the option that correctly lists the qualities of Gandhi in the passage.
(i) reserved (ii) unreserved
(iii) diffident (iv) confident.

5. **Read the passage given below:**

1. "Who doesn't know how to cook rice? Cooking rice hardly takes time." said my father. So I challenged myself. I switched from news to YouTube and typed, "How to cook rice?" I took one and a half cups of rice. Since I didn't have access to a rice cooker, I put the rice in a big pot. Firstly, the rice has to be washed to get rid of dust and starch. I thought I won't be able to drain the rice and that it will fall out of the pot. I observed the chef as I swirled the rice around and used my dexterous hands to drain it, not once, not twice, but three times. I looked down at the sink and saw less than 50 grains that made their way out of the pot. Suffice to say, I was up to the mark.

2. The video stated that the key to perfect rice is equal amounts of rice and water. I have heard that professionals don't need to measure everything; they just know what the right amount is. But as this was my first time in the kitchen, I decided to experiment by not measuring the water needed for boiling the rice. I wanted the rice to be firm when bitten, just like pasta. I don't enjoy the texture of mushy rice. It has to have that chutzpah;

(i) London Vegetarian Society
(ii) Indian Vegetarian Society
(iii) US Vegetarian Society
(iv) None of the above

(g) **Which option represents the CORRECT list of vows Gandhiji promised his mother to abstain from, before sailing to England?**

it has to resist my biting power just for a bit before disintegrating.

3. After what seemed like 10 minutes, all the water disappeared. I went in to give it a good stir. To my surprise, some of the rice got stuck to the pot. I tried to scrape it off but to no avail. At the same time, there was a burning smell coming from it. I quickly turned the stove off. "What have you done to the kitchen?" shouted Mother, while coming towards the kitchen. I managed to ward her off.

4. Finally, when the time came to taste my creation, I was surprised! It wasn't bad at all. The rice had the desired consistency. Sure, a little more salt would've been better, but I just added that while eating. The experience was fairly rewarding and memorable. It taught me a new sense of respect for those who cook food on a regular basis at home or engage in gourmet creations professionally.

5.1. On the basis of your understanding of the above passage, answer any ten of the following questions by choosing the most appropriate option:

(a) Father's question to the narrator, about knowing how to cook rice, was intended to:
(i) criticize the narrator's lack of abilities
(ii) make the process sound simple
(iii) encourage the narrator to take up cooking
(iv) showcase his own expertise in cooking rice

(b) "I switched from news to YouTube...." Pick the option in which the meaning of 'switch(ed)' is NOT the same as it is in the passage.
(i) He switched on the radio to listen to the news while having dinner
(ii) "Forget these diet supplements and switch to yoga, if you want a true sense of well-being"
(iii) Mom switched to reading fiction recently because she was bored with cook-books
(iv) The company will switch the trucks to other routes to bring down city pollution

(c) Based on your understanding of the passage, choose the option that lists the CORRECT sequence of the process.
1. Use water to wash the rice.
2. Repeat the process three times.

3. Drain the water off.
4. Put rice in a utensil.
5. Swirl the water in and around the rice.
   (i) 4, 2, 1, 3, 5   (ii) 1, 3, 2, 5, 4
   (iii) 4, 1, 5, 3, 2   (iv) 5, 1, 2, 4, 3

(d) The narrator says that he has dexterous hands. He would have had a problem had it been the opposite. NOT BEING dexterous means, being:
   (i) uncomfortable   (ii) clumsy
   (iii) unclear   (iv) clueless

(e) Which option represents the correct ratio of water to rice for cooking 'perfect rice'?

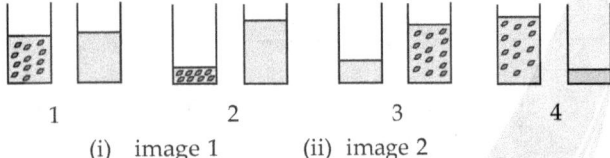

   (i) image 1   (ii) image 2
   (iii) image 3   (iv) image 4

(f) How did mother react to the burning smell?
   (i) she commented on it
   (ii) she brushed it aside
   (iii) she enquired about it
   (iv) she handled it

(g) According to the passage, the fact that the narrator risked experimentation, on his maiden attempt in the kitchen, shows that he was:
   (i) conscientious
   (ii) nervous
   (iii) presumptuous
   (iv) courteous

(h) Pick the option showing the CORRECT use of the word 'chutzpah'.
   (i) It is the court's duty to dispense chutzpah to everyone irrespective of caste or creed
   (ii) The speaker may not have much of a stage presence, but you've got to admit she's got chutzpah
   (iii) I could crack the code easily which proved me to be a chutzpah and I was the only one who could do so
   (iv) After his father's demise, the daughter took over the family's chutzpah to save it from disaster

(i) Pick the option that correctly states what DID NOT happen after the writer checked on the rice.
   (i) turning the stove off
   (ii) being taken aback at the condition of rice
   (iii) forgetting to scrape the stuck rice
   (iv) smelling the delicious aroma of cooked rice

(j) The narrator's creation was:
   (i) almost perfect to taste
   (ii) way off from what he wanted
   (iii) overly seasoned
   (iv) quite distasteful

(k) Pick the option that correctly lists the final feelings of the writer with reference to the cooking experience.

1. frustrating   2. amusing
3. satisfying   4. disillusioning
5. exacting   6. enlightening
   (i) 1 and 4   (ii) 2 and 5
   (iii) 3 and 6   (iv) 1 and 3

6. Read the passage carefully:

1. That large animals require luxuriant vegetation has been a general assumption which has passed from one work to another, but I do not hesitate to say that it is completely false and that it has vitiated the reasoning of geologists on some points of great interest in the ancient history of the world. The prejudice has probably been derived from India, and the Indian islands, where troops of elephants, noble forests, and impenetrable jungles, are associated together in everyone's mind. If, however, we refer to any work of travels through the southern parts of Africa, we shall find allusions in almost every page either to the desert character of the country or to the numbers of large animals inhabiting it. The same thing is rendered evident by the many engravings which have been published of various parts of the interior.

2. Dr. Andrew Smith, who has lately succeeded in passing the Tropic of Capricorn, informs me that, taking into consideration the whole of the southern part of Africa, there can be no doubt of its being a sterile country. On the southern coasts, there are some fine forests, but with these exceptions, the traveller may pass for days together through open plains, covered by poor and scanty vegetation. Now, if we look at the animals inhabiting these wide plains, we shall find their numbers extraordinarily great, and their bulk immense.

3. It may be supposed that although the species are numerous, the individuals of each kind are few. By the kindness of Dr. Smith, I am enabled to show that the case is very different. He informs me, that in lat. 24, in one day's march with the bullock-wagons, he saw, without wandering to any great distance on either side, between one hundred and one hundred and fifty rhinoceroses – the same day he saw several herds of giraffes, amounting together to nearly a hundred.

4. At the distance of a little more than one hour's march from their place of encampment on the previous night, his party actually killed at one spot eight hippopotamuses and saw many more. In this same river, there were likewise crocodiles. Of course, it was a case quite extraordinary, to see so many great animals crowded together, but it evidently proves that they must exist in great numbers. Dr. Smith describes the country passed through that day, as 'being thinly covered with grass, and bushes about four feet high and still more thinly with mimosa-trees.'

5. Besides these large animals, anyone least acquainted with the natural history of the Cape has read of the herds of antelopes, which can be compared only with the flocks of migratory birds. The numbers indeed of the lion, panther and hyena, and the multitude of birds of prey, plainly speak

of the abundance of the smaller quadrupeds: one evening seven lions were counted at the same time prowling round Dr. Smith's encampment. As this able naturalist remarked to me, the carnage each day in southern Africa must indeed be terrific! I confess it is truly surprising how such a number of animals can find support in a country producing so little food?

6. The larger quadrupeds no doubt roam over wide tracts in search of it; and their food chiefly consists of Underwood, which probably contains much nutriment in a small bulk. Dr. Smith also informs me that the vegetation has a rapid growth; no sooner is a part consumed, than its place is supplied by a fresh stock. There can be no doubt, however, that our ideas respecting the apparent amount of food necessary for the support of large quadrupeds are much exaggerated. The belief that where large quadrupeds exist, the vegetation must necessarily be luxuriant is the more remarkable because the converse is far from true.

7. Mr. Burchell observed to me that when entering Brazil, nothing struck him more forcibly than the splendour of the South American vegetation contrasted with that of South Africa, together with the absence of all large quadrupeds. In his travels, he has suggested that the comparison of the respective weights (if there were sufficient data) of an equal number of the largest herbivorous quadrupeds of each country would be extremely curious. If we take on the one side, the elephants, hippopotamus, giraffe, bos caffer, eland, five species of rhinoceros; and on the American side, two tapirs, the guanaco, three deer, the vicuna, peccari, capybara (after which we must choose from the monkeys to complete the number), and then place these two groups alongside each other it is not easy to conceive ranks more disproportionate in size.

8. After the above facts, we are compelled to conclude, against the anterior probability that among the Mammalia there exists no close relation between the bulk of the species and the quantity of the vegetation, in the countries which they inhabit

(Source; Voyage of the Beagle, Charles Darwin (1890)

6.1. **On the basis of your understanding of the passage, answer any ten of the following questions by choosing the most appropriate option:**

(a) **The flights of migratory birds are mentioned.**
   (i) to describe an aspect of the South African fauna
   (ii) to suggest the size of the antelope herds
   (iii) to contrast with the habits of the antelopes
   (iv) to illustrate a possible source of food for the large carnivores

(b) **According to the author, the prejudice has led.**
   (i) to incorrect assumptions on the part of geologists
   (ii) to false ideas about the animals in Africa
   (iii) to errors in the reasoning of the biologists
   (iv) to doubts in his mind

(c) **Based on your understanding of the passage, choose the option that lists the CORRECT sequence of the process.**
   1. The animals inhabiting the wide plains are large in numbers.
   2. It may be supposed that although the species are numerous, the individuals of each kind are few.
   3. On the southern coasts of Africa, there are some fine forests.
   4. The numbers indeed of the lion, panther and hyena, and the multitude of birds of prey, plainly speak of the abundance of the smaller quadrupeds.

   (i) 3, 1, 4, 2   (ii) 4, 2, 1, 3
   (iii) 3, 1, 2, 4   (iv) 1, 2, 4, 3

(d) **Burchell's observations were quoted by Darwin in order to......**
   (i) prove a hypothesis
   (ii) describe a region of great beauty
   (iii) oppose a popular misconception
   (iv) illustrate a well-known phenomenon

(e) **Which image represents the exact image of southern part of Africa according to Dr. Andrew Smith?**

1   2   3   4

(i) image 1   (ii) image 2
(iii) image 3   (iv) image 4

(f) **Who had lately succeeded in passing the Tropic of Cancer?**
   (i) Dr. Andrew Smith
   (ii) Dr. Andy Smith
   (iii) Dr. Phil Smith
   (iv) none of these

(g) **What does Dr. Smith refer to as 'carnage'?**
   (i) the vegetation with a rapid growth
   (ii) the amount of food hunted to sustain a large number of carnivorous animals
   (iii) the apparent amount of food to support large quadrupeds which is much exaggerated
   (iv) the southern part of Africa as a sterile country

(h) What struck Mr. Burchell while entering Brazil?
   (i) large animals and lush vegetation.
   (ii) the splendour of the South American vegetation contrasted with that of South Africa
   (iii) multiple species of quadrupeds
   (iv) quantity of the vegetation

(i) Which big mammal was killed by Dr. Smith's party?
   (i) hippopotamuses
   (ii) elephants
   (iii) buffalos
   (iv) rhinoceros

(j) Which word in the passage means same as 'lush'? (para 1)
   (i) impenetrable   (ii) luxuriant
   (iii) allusion   (iv) vitiated

(k) 'The belief that where large quadrupeds exist, the vegetation must necessarily be luxuriant' but the converse was far from true. For Dr. Smith, how did it occur?
   1. Incredible   2. Astonishing
   3. Exhilarating   4. Customary
   (i) 1 and 3   (ii) 1 and 2
   (iii) 2 and 3   (iv) 2 and 4

7. Read the passage carefully:

1. In ancient India, nearly 5000 years ago, there lived a young Nishada (a tribe of hunters) prince by the name of Eklavya. Even though he was a hunter by birth, being the son of the chief of hunters in the forests of Hastinapur, he aspired to become a great archer and a brave warrior. He expressed this desire to his father, "Father, I want to be an archer and become a disciple of the great Guru Dronacharya, the greatest teacher of the art of archery and the science of warfare in the kingdom. Please give me your blessings before I set out for his Gurukul." His father remained silent. Eklavya knew what was bothering his father. He said, "Father, I know we are Shudras, belonging to the hunting tribe. But the Guru is a wise and learned man. Please allow me to become his disciple." Eklavya's father was a kind man and did not wish to refuse his son. So he gave his blessings and sent his son on his way.

2. Eklavya reached the Gurukul of Guru Dronacharya, who was also the royal teacher of the Pandavas and the Kauravas. Thrilled at the prospect of finally meeting the Guru he had idolised, his eyes eagerly sought out the teacher. He soon spotted him instructing a boy, none other than the Pandava Arjun. Eklavya went to Drona and folded his hands in greeting, bowing down low to touch the sage's feet. Drona was surprised to see the stranger and asked him, "Who are you?" "Oh Guru, I am Eklavya, the son of the Chief of the Nishada tribe of hunters in the forests of Hastinapur. Please accept me as your humble shishya and teach me the art of archery and the science of warfare", replied Eklavya. Dronacharya reflected for a minute, then said, "Eklavya, if you are a Nishada hunter, then you are a Shudra, the lowest caste in the kingdom. I am a Brahmin, the highest of castes. All my students are Kshatriyas, the warrior caste. I cannot teach a Shudra boy."

3. The Pandavas stood watching the exchange. Encouraged by the Guru's words, Arjuna spoke up, "Guru Dronacharya is a royal teacher, appointed by the King to train us, the princes of the kingdom. How dare you expect to be taught by him! Leave the gurukul now. "Eklavya was surprised and hurt at the Guru's words, and stunned by Arjuna's insult. He was a chief's son, yet he had never insulted anyone. He quietly left the gurukul. Resolute in his determination to learn archery, he went back to the forest. There he built an idol of Guru Dronacharya with mud and placed it in a secluded clearing. Eklavya believed that if he practiced faithfully in front of his Guru, he would be able to master the art of archery. So every morning he would pray to the idol and practice throughout the day. After years of practicing, he became a skilled archer, even surpassing the best archer in the kingdom Arjuna.

4. One day, while practicing, a dog started barking some distance away. Its constant barking irritated Eklavya, who fired seven arrows in quick succession, filling the dog's mouth without injuring it. The dog was no longer able to bark and roamed around the forest. Thus roaming, the dog reached the Pandavas, who were practicing in the forest along with Guru Dronacharya. Drona was amazed to see such a feat of archery. He realized that only an extremely skilled archer could have done this. He, along with the Pandavas, set out to look for the archer. Soon they came across a young man, dressed in a hunter's clothes practicing archery. It was Eklavya. Dronacharya went up to him and asked, "Your aim is remarkable! Who is your teacher ?" "You, Sir," replied Eklavya. Dronacharya was stunned. "How can I be your Guru when I have never met you before ?" "I am Eklavya, the boy who came to learn archery from you at your gurukul. After you refused, I came back to the forest and made a mud idol of you. I prayed to it every day and with its blessing I was able to master the skills of archery", replied Eklavya.

5. Arjuna was angry, as he was sure of his place as the best archer in the world. Dronacharya also realised that Eklavya had the skills to surpass even Arjuna. However, as the royal teacher, Eklavya's excellence would put him in a difficult situation, as a mere Shudra hunter would surpass a Kshatriya prince under his tutelage. He devised a way out. To Eklavya he said, "Seeing that you have learnt from me, you will now have to pay guru dakshina, my gift for training you." Eklavya was overjoyed at this. A guru dakshina was the offering made to a teacher when the teacher considered the shishya to have completed his learning. He replied, "I am blessed that you have asked me for guru dakshina.

I would never refuse anything that you ask." Dronacharya seized his chance, "Eklavya, as guru dakshina, you have to give me your right thumb." Everyone was shocked, even Arjuna. Everyone knew that an archer could never shoot an arrow without his right thumb.

6. Eklavya looked steadily at Dronacharya. He realised the reason behind this demand. Nevertheless he replied, "I will never disobey your wish, Sir. I am grateful that you recognised me as your disciple even though I am a Shudra." Saying this, he took a knife and cut off his right thumb and placed it at his Guru's feet. Everyone, including Dronacharya marvelled at the boy's courage. Dronacharya was humbled and blessed Eklavya, "You will be known far and wide as a great archer, even without your thumb. Moreover, you will always be remembered as the greatest student ever for your loyalty towards your guru." So saying, Dronacharya and the Pandavas left the forest. Eklavya learnt to shoot with forefinger and middle finger and remains an example of the ideal student till today.

7.1. **On the basis of your understanding of the passage, answer any ten of the following questions by choosing the most appropriate option:**

(a) By birth, Eklavya was a......
 (i) shudra (ii) nishada
 (iii) hunter (iv) all of these

(b) Based on the above passage align the pictures below in the CORRECT sequence.

    1   2   3   4

(i) 1, 2, 3, 4 (ii) 2, 3, 1, 4
(iii) 1, 3, 4, 2 (iv) 2, 4, 3, 1

(c) Arjuna's **behaviour towards** Eklavya was......
 (i) rude (ii) polite
 (iii) friendly (iv) cruel

(d) Based on your understanding of the passage, choose the option that lists the CORRECT sequence of the given sentences.
 1. Eklavya expressed this desire of wanting to be an archer and a disciple of the great Guru Dronacharya to his father.
 2. Eklavya was a Nishada prince, a hunter by birth, and the son of the chief of hunters in the forests of Hastinapur.
 3. There he built an idol of Guru Dronacharya with mud and placed it in a secluded clearing.
 4. Dronacharya was a Brahmin, Dronacharya's students were Kshatriyas, and so, refused to accept Eklavya, who was a Shudra for his disciple.
 (i) 2, 1, 4, 3 (ii) 1, 2, 3, 4
 (iii) 2, 3, 1, 4 (iv) 4, 3, 2, 1

(e) Based on the given passage choose the option that is NOT TRUE.
 1. Arjuna was angry, as he was sure of his place as the best archer in the world.
 2. Dronacharya also realised that Eklavya would not have the skills to surpass even Arjuna.
 3. However, as the royal teacher, Arjuna's excellence would put him in a difficult situation.
 4. As a royal teacher a Shudra hunter would surpass a Kshatriya prince under his tutelage

(i) 2, 1 (ii) 2, 3
(iii) 1, 3 (iv) 4, 3

(f) Which fingers as per the picture did Eklavya use after his *'guru dakshina'* to Dronacharya?

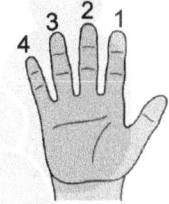

(i) 1 and 2 (ii) 2 and 3
(iii) 1 and 4 (iv) 1 and 3

(g) What was Eklavya's desire which he revealed to his father ?
 (i) he wanted to get good education
 (ii) he wanted to become Dronacharya's disciple
 (iii) he wanted to become an archer
 (iv) both (ii) and (iii)

(h) What was bothering Eklavya's father when Eklavya expressed his desire ?
 (i) they belonged to the hunting tribe
 (ii) Eklavya's inconsistency
 (iii) Eklavya's distraction
 (iv) they were too poor to pay the fee

(i) Why did Dronacharya refuse to teach Eklavya ?
 (i) he didn't like Eklavya
 (ii) Eklavya was undisciplined
 (iii) Eklavya belonged to lower caste
 (iv) Eklavya's father misbehaved with Dronacharya

(j) Which word in the passage means opposite to 'half-hearted'? (para 3)
   (i) encouraged   (ii) resolute
   (iii) determined   (iv) stunned

(k) Identify the synonym for the word 'overjoyed' in the above passage.
   (i) hurt   (ii) stunned
   (iii) surpass   (iv) thrilled

Answers

1.1. (a) (iv) four days
   (b) (iii) 7 years
   (c) (ii) 3, 1, 4, 2
   (d) (i) Southern Pole
   (e) (iv) image 4
   (f) (ii) GSLV-3
   (g) (ii) because it indicated the altitude and the range of the lander
   (h) (iii) It quantifies the amount of calcium, magnesium, iron, sodium and other useful elements on or below the lunar surface.
   (i) (iv) all of these
   (j) (ii) unique
   (k) (iii) disheartening

2.1. (a) (ii) no one stared at him
   (b) (ii) Heaven Lake
   (c) (iii) 3, 1, 4, 2
   (d) (ii) a shining prism
   (e) (ii) image 2
   (f) (i) smelly goat's cheese
   (g) (i) the tall range of Mount Bogda
   (h) (iii) in the hotel
   (i) (iii) a squat, white steamed bread roll
   (j) (i) culminate
   (k) (ii) 2 and 3

3.1. (a) (i) spiritual leader
   (b) (ii) believing in non-existence of God
   (c) (iii) 3,2,1,4
   (d) (i) attorney
   (e) (ii) Swami Vivekananda showed more interest in music than in academics.
   (f) (ii) option 2
   (g) (ii) The National Youth Day in India
   (h) (iv) all of these
   (i) (iii) to get the knowledge of whereabouts of God
   (j) (iv) avid
   (k) (i) 1 and 2

4.1. (a) (ii) to achieve political and social progress
   (b) (iv) Vaishnavism
   (c) (iv) 3, 2, 1, 4
   (d) (i) like other children of his age
   (e) (i) Gandhi's vegetarianism became a continual source of confidence for him.
   (f) (i) London vegetarian society
   (g) (iv) option 4
   (h) (iv) all of these
   (i) (i) food
   (j) (i) ordeal
   (k) (iii) diffident

5.1. (a) (ii) make the process sound simple.
   (b) (i) He switched on the radio to listen to the news while having dinner.
   (c) (iii) 4, 1, 5, 3, 2
   (d) (ii) clumsy
   (e) (i) image 1
   (f) (iii) she enquired about it
   (g) (iii) presumptuous.
   (h) (ii) The speaker may not have much of a stage presence, but you've got to admit she's got chutzpah.
   (i) (iv) smelling the delicious aroma of cooked rice.
   (j) (i) almost perfect to taste.
   (k) (iii) 3 and 6

6.1. (a) (ii) to suggest the size of the antelope herds
   (b) (i) to incorrect assumptions on the part of geologists
   (c) (iii) 3, 1, 2, 4
   (d) (iii) oppose a popular misconception
   (e) (iii) image 3
   (f) (i) Dr. Andrew Smith
   (g) (ii) the amount of food hunted to sustain a large number of carnivorous animals
   (h) (ii) the splendour of the South American vegetation contrasted with that of South Africa
   (i) (i) hippopotamuses
   (j) (ii) luxuriant
   (k) (i) 1 and 3

7.1. (a) (iv) all of these
   (b) (iv) 2, 4, 3, 1
   (c) (i) rude
   (d) (i) 2, 1, 4, 3
   (e) (ii) 2, 3
   (f) (i) 1 and 2
   (g) (iv) both (ii) and (iii)
   (h) (i) they belonged to the hunting tribe
   (i) (iii) Eklavya belonged to lower caste
   (j) (ii) resolute
   (k) (iv) thrilled

2. Literary Passage

1. Harry Potter (Excerpt)
–J.K. Rowling

October arrived, spreading a damp chill over the grounds and into the castle. Madam Pomfrey, the nurse, was kept busy by a sudden spate of colds among the staff and students. Her Pepper up potion worked instantly, though it left the drinker smoking at the ears for several hours afterwards. Ginny Weasley, who had been looking pale, was bullied into taking some by Percy. The steam pouring from under her vivid hair gave the impression that her whole head was on fire. Raindrops, the size of bullets thundered on the castle windows for days on end; the lake rose, the flower beds turned into muddy streams, and Hagrid's pumpkins swelled to the size of garden sheds.

Even aside from the rain and wind it hadn't been a happy practice session. Fred and George, who had been spying on the Slytherin team, had seen for themselves, the speed of those new Nimbus Two Thousand and Ones. They reported that the Slytherin team was no more than seven greenish blurs, shooting through the air like missiles. As Harry squelched along the deserted corridor, he came across somebody who looked just as preoccupied as he was. Nearly Headless Nick, the ghost of Gryffindor Tower, was staring morosely out of a window, muttering under his breath, "...... don't fulfill their requirements...... half an inch, if that......"

"Hello, Nick," said Harry. "Hello, hello," said Nearly Headless Nick, starting and looking round. He wore a dashing, plumed hat on his long curly hair, and a tunic with a ruff, which concealed the fact that his neck was almost completely severed. He was pale as smoke, and Harry could see right through him to the dark sky and torrential rain outside.

"You look troubled, young Potter," said Nick, folding a transparent letter as he spoke and tucking it inside his doublet. "So do you," said Harry. "Ah," Nearly Headless Nick waved an elegant hand, "a matter of no importance...... It's not as though I really wanted to join......Thought I'd apply, but apparently I 'don't fulfill requirements' -

I. On the basis of your reading of the passage given above, answer any ten of the following questions by choosing the most appropriate option:

(a) From where was the steam pouring out of Ginny Weasley's body?
 (i) Under her ears (ii) Under her hair
 (iii) Under her arm (iv) Under her nose

(b) Who was affected by the outbreak of cold?
 (i) Madam Pomfrey (ii) Staff
 (iii) Harry (iv) Nick

(c) Based on your understanding of the passage, choose the option that lists the CORRECT sequence of the given statements.
 1. Hagrid's pumpkins swelled to the size of garden sheds.
 2. The ghost of Gryffindor Tower, was staring morosely out of a window, muttering under his breath.
 3. Harry could see right through him to the dark sky and torrential rain outside.
 4. The steam pouring from under Ginny's vivid hair gave the impression that her whole head was on fire.
 (i) 2, 1, 3, 4 (ii) 3, 2, 4, 1
 (iii) 4, 1, 2, 3 (iv) 1, 4, 2, 3

(d) How did Madam Pomfrey's potion affect the staff and students?
 (i) The potion had an adverse effect on them
 (ii) The staff and the students began feeling extremely warm.
 (iii) It left the drinker smoking at the ears for several hours.
 (iv) The drinker immediately began feeling nauseate.

(e) Which image depicts the hair style of headless Nick?

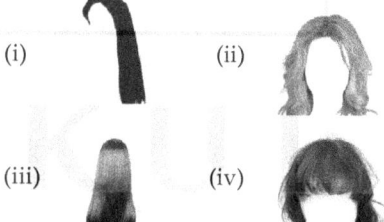

(f) What report did Fred and George give about the Slytherin team?
 (i) They told that it was a slow team.
 (ii) They reported that it was no more than seven greenish blurs.
 (iii) They reported that it was shooting through air like guns.
 (iv) They said that that the speed of the team was indescribable.

(g) What turned into muddy streams ?
 (i) The Gryffindor Tower

(ii) The flower beds
(iii) Garden
(iv) Street

(h) Why was Nearly Headless Nick unhappy?
(i) It was raining heavily outside.
(ii) He didn't fulfill the requirement to join the hunt.
(iii) Harry had scolded him.
(iv) He didn't want to join the hunt.

(i) Pick the option that tells what Nearly Headless Nick was NOT wearing which concealed the fact that his neck was almost completely severed.
(i) A dashing hat
(ii) A tunic with a ruff
(iii) A bright coloured tie
(iv) All of the above

(j) How could Harry see right through Headless Nick?
(i) Nick was wearing an invisible dress.
(ii) Nick was transparent like glass.
(iii) Nick was pale as smoke.
(iv) Nick was very lean.

(k) Pick the option that states the feelings of the Nearly Headless Nick, the ghost of Gryffindor Tower, when he was staring out of a window, muttering under his breath?
(i) Resentful   (ii) Honoured
(iii) Relaxed   (iv) Disturbed

2. Evening Star
—Edger Allan Poe

'Twas noontide of summer,
And mid-time of night;
And stars, in their orbits,
Shone pale, thro' the light

Of the brighter, cold moon,
'Mid planets her slaves,
Herself in the Heavens,
Her beam on the waves.

I gazed awhile
On her cold smile;
Too cold- too cold for me-
There pass'd, as a shroud,

A fleecy cloud,
And I turned away to thee,
Proud Evening Star,
In thy glory afar,

And dearer thy beam shall be;
For joy to my heart
Is the proud part
Thou bearest in Heaven at night,

And more I admire
Thy distant fire,
Than that colder, lowly light.

I. On the basis of your reading of the poem given above, answer any ten of the following questions by choosing the most appropriate option:

(a) By 'noontide of summer' the poet is referring to what time of the year?
(i) April and May
(ii) Middle of summer
(iii) At 12 o'clock every day
(iv) High tide at the sea

(b) The literary device used in 'Proud Evening Star' is :
(i) simile   (ii) metaphor
(iii) personification (iv) alliteration

(c) Based on your understanding of the poem, choose the option that lists the CORRECT sequence of the given lines.
1. 'Mid planets her slaves,
2. And stars, in their orbits,
3. Thou bearest in Heaven at night
4. There pass'd, as a shroud,
(i) 2,1,4,3   (ii) 3,4,1,2
(iii) 1,4,2,3   (iv) 4,3,2,1

(d) What does the poet admire about the Evening Star?
(i) Its distant fire (ii) Its cold light
(iii) Its twinkling   (iv) Its beauty

(e) According to the poem which image shows the object with which shroud is being compared to?

(i)

(ii)

(iii)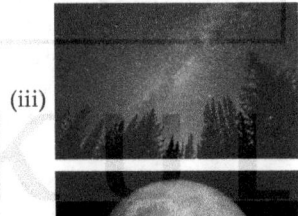

(iv)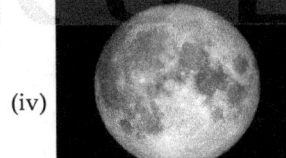

(f) What are the planets referred to?
(i) As slaves of the moon
(ii) Human forms
(iii) Celestial beings
(iv) 9 stars

(g) What does the poet say about the Evening Star?
(i) It is brighter and colder
(ii) It is warmer

(iii) It appeals to the human eye
(iv) It comes out late at night

(h) How did the stars shine in comparison to the moon?
  (i) The stars shone brighter than the moon.
  (ii) The stars do not shine at all in the light of moon.
  (iii) The stars shone in a dull manner in comparison to the moon.
  (iv) The stars shine with the help of sun.

(i) Pick the correct adjective that has NOT been used for the moon?
  (i) Cold (ii) Warm
  (iii) Bright (iv) Lowly light

(j) How does the poet describe the smile of the moon?
  (i) Welcoming (ii) Friendly
  (iii) Cruel (iv) Too cold

(k) Pick the option that tells about the poet's choice over Moon.
  (i) Planets (ii) Heaven
  (iii) The Evening star (iv) Cloud

3. The Kitemaker (Excerpt)
—Ruskin Bond

He, Mehmood the kite maker, had in the prime of his life, been well known throughout the city. Some of his more elaborate kites once sold for as much as three or four rupees each. At the request of the Nawab, he had once made a very special kind of kite, unlike any, that had been seen in the district.

It consisted of a series of small, very light paper disks trailing on a thin bamboo frame. To the end of each disc, he fixed a sprig of grass, forming a balance on both sides. The surface of the foremost disc was slightly convex, and a fantastic face was painted on it, having two eyes made of small mirrors. The discs, decreasing in size from head to tail, assumed an undulatory form and gave the kite the appearance of a crawling serpent. It required great skill to raise this cumbersome device from the ground, and only Mehmood could manage it.

Everyone had heard of the 'Dragon Kite' that Mehmood had built, and word went round that it possessed supernatural powers. A large crowd assembled in the open to watch its first public launching in the presence of the Nawab. At the first attempt, it refused to leave the ground. The discs made a plaintive, protesting sound, and the sun was trapped in the little mirrors, making of the kite a living, complaining creature.

Then the wind came from the right direction, and the Dragon Kite soared into the sky, wriggling its way higher and higher, the sun still glinting in its devil-eyes and when it went very high, it pulled fiercely on the twine, and Mehmood's young sons had to help him with the reel. Still, the kite pulled, determined to be free, to break loose, to live a life of its own. And eventually it did so. The twine snapped, the kite leaped away towards the sun, sailing on heavenwards until it was lost to view.

I. On the basis of your reading of the passage given above, answer any ten of the following questions by choosing the most appropriate option:

(a) Which option shows that Mehmood had been well known throughout the city.
  (i) He made very decorative kites.
  (ii) His kites were liked by all.
  (iii) He was Nawab's personal kitemaker.
  (iv) His kites once sold for as much as three or four rupees each.

(b) What belief did everybody bear about the 'Dragon Kite'?
  (i) It was made of dragon's wings.
  (ii) It had magical influences.
  (iii) It possessed supernatural powers.
  (iv) It would reach God.

(c) Based on your understanding of the passage, choose the option that lists the CORRECT sequence of the making of kite.
  1. The surface of the foremost disc of the kite was slightly convex.
  2. The discs, decreasing in size from head to tail, assumed an undulatory form.
  3. Mehmood had once made a very special kind of kite.
  4. A fantastic face was painted on it.
  (i) 1,4,3,2 (ii) 3,1,4,2
  (iii) 3,4,2,1 (iv) 2,4,1,3

(d) Who requested Mehmood to make the kite?
  (i) The Nawab (ii) His sons
  (iii) The public (iv) His relatives

(e) Which image depicts the appearance of the special kite made by Mehmood?

(i)  (ii)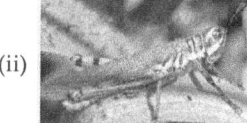

(iii)  (iv)

(f) Why did it require great skill to raise the kite from the ground?
  (i) because it had magical powers.
  (ii) because it was too bulky.
  (iii) because it was torn from the corner.
  (iv) because nobody in the city knew to fly kites.

(g) The two eyes on the face of the kite were made of which shiny material?
  (i) Gold (ii) Silver
  (iii) Mirror (iv) Foil

(h) How much did the kite maker earn for his one elaborate kite?
  (i) three or four rupees
  (ii) two rupees
  (iii) Four rupees
  (iv) one rupee

(i) Pick the option that tells what did NOT happen at the first attempt when the dragon kite was launched?
(i) It refused to leave the ground.
(ii) The Sun was trapped in little mirrors.
(iii) The discs made a lovely sound.
(iv) The kite looked like a living, complaining creature.

(j) What happened to the kite eventually when the wind came from the right direction?
(i) It did not soar very high.
(ii) It dropped down.
(iii) It was torn.
(iv) It disappeared from the view.

(k) Pick the option that states the feelings of the large crowd that assembled in the open to watch the kite's first public launching in the presence of the Nawab.
(i) Curiosity   (ii) Apathy
(iii) Anxiety   (iv) Remorse

4. Gunga Din (The regimental bhisti) (Excerpt)
—Rudyard Kipling

I sha'n't forgit the night
When I dropped be'ind the fight
With a bullet where my belt plate should 'a' been.
I was chokin' mad with thirst,

An' the man that spied me first
Was our good old grinnin', gruntin' GungaDin.
'E lifted up my 'ead,
An' he plugged me where I bled,

An' 'e guv me 'arf-a-pint o' water-green :
It was crawlin' and it stunk,
But of all the drinks I've drunk,
I'm gratefullest to one from Gunga Din.

It was "Din! Din! Din!"
'Ere's a beggar with a bullet through 'is spleen;
'E's chawin' up the ground,
An' 'e's kickin' all around :

For Gawd's sake git the water, Gunga Din!
'E carried me away
To where a dooli lay,
An' a bullet come an' drilled the beggar clean.

'E put me safe inside,
An' just before 'e died :
"I 'ope you liked your drink," sez Gunga Din.

So I'll meet 'im later on
At the place where 'e is gone—
Where it's always double drill and no canteen;
'E'll be squattin' on the coals,
Givin' drink to poor damned souls,
An' I'll get a swig in hell from Gunga Din!
Yes, Din! Din! Din!

You Lazarushian-leather Gunga Din!
Though I've belted you and flayed you,
By the living Gawd that made you,
You're a better man than I am, Gunga Din!

I. On the basis of your reading of the poem given above, answer any ten of the following questions by choosing the most appropriate option:

(a) The poem appears to be written by............
(i) a soldier   (ii) a beggar
(iii) Gunga Din   (iv) villager

(b) Gunga Din is the regimental bhishti. His job is to.............
(i) save soldiers
(ii) give his regimental soldiers water
(iii) give his regimental soldiers a drink
(iv) fight with the enemy

(c) Based on your understanding of the poem, choose the option that lists the CORRECT sequence of the given lines.
1. he plugged me where I bled.
2. a bullet come an' drilled the beggar clean.
3. By the living Gawd that made you.
4. I'm gratefullest to one from Gunga Din.
(i) 1,3,2,4   (ii) 2,4,3,1
(iii) 1,4,2,3   (iv) 3,2,1,4

(d) Who dies first?
(i) The British soldier
(ii) the enemy
(iii) Gunga Din
(iv) a villager

(e) According to the poem which among the following images gives the picture of Gunga Din?

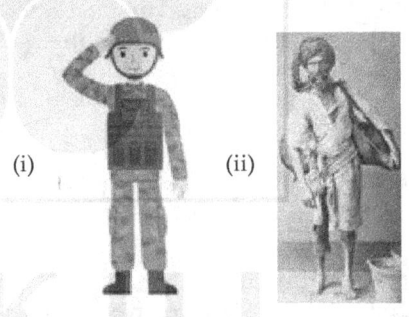

(f) Where does the poet hope to meet Gunga Din?
(i) hell
(ii) a place where he lives
(iii) his village
(iv) England

(g) What does the soldier call Gunga Din?
   (i) living God   (ii) soldier
   (iii) water man   (iv) beggar
(h) What happens to Gunga Din at the end of the poem?
   (i) He dies
   (ii) become soldier
   (iii) continued serving water
   (iv) He left the regiment
(i) Pick the option from the poem that does NOT tell the quality of water which Gunga Din gave to the soldier.
   (i) Green
   (ii) Clean
   (iii) Stinking
   (iv) Having creepy creatures
(j) What had happened to the speaker?
   (i) He fainted due to heat
   (ii) He got a stroke
   (iii) He was hit by a bullet near the belt plate
   (iv) He was dying out of hunger
(k) Pick the option that tells about how the poet depicts the British soldier?
   (i) Loud and coarse
   (ii) full of insults
   (iii) Full of threats
   (iv) All of these

5. Dynamism of India

India has been able to make the most of globalisation and has gained a pivotal role. It provides the example of an economy which has allied dynamism and equilibrium. The past year offers the two-fold satisfaction of a spectacular 7.5 per cent growth rate and inflation under control. Thanks to the size and dynamism of its domestic market, it can project itself into the future with confidence.

India is now the biggest international service provider in information technologies, and this at a time when the western countries are experiencing a real shortage of manpower in this very field. A scientific power, India, today, is also a key player in space research. Thanks to the excellence of the Indian Space Research Organization, it is the forefront of technologies for launchers and the construction of satellites.

This economic vitality has developed on the basis of a strong concern for social justice. In the face of inequalities that still remain and could be increasing, India has given priority, to poverty reduction, job creation and support of the agricultural sector. Your country has shown that economic growth and concern for the greater good are not incompatible. India, however, does not only offer an economic model. It stands as an example for nations that show due respect for cultural identities.

This represents a major challenge as globalisation has inherent in it, two-fold risk. First of all, there is the risk of domination of certain forms of thinking, of certain ways of life and expression. The diversity of cultures, religions, traditions and memories is an essential component of the richness of our world. If we are not careful, it could die one day. Then there is the risk of confrontation of identities. Lack of respect for what people stand for, can nurture claims of nationalists and fundamentalists.

I. On the basis of your reading of the passage given above, answer any ten of the following questions by choosing the most appropriate option:

(a) How is India now the biggest international service provider in information technologies?
   (i) Unemployed youth are more in number in India
   (ii) Western countries have a shortage of manpower in this very field.
   (iii) People outside India are not willing to work.
   (iv) Indian youth is more educated.

(b) How could India been able to bring inflation under control in the past year?
   (i) Due to its size and dynamism of its domestic market
   (ii) Due to its natural resources.
   (iii) Due to its geographical conditions.
   (iv) Due to its intellectual crop of youth.

(c) Based on your understanding of the passage, choose the option that lists the CORRECT sequence of the given statements.
   1. A scientific power, India, today, is also a key player in space research.
   2. The diversity of cultures, religions, traditions and memories is an essential component of the richness of our world.
   3. India provides the example of an economy which has allied dynamism and equilibrium.
   4. India stands as an example for nations that show due respect for cultural identities.
   (i) 1,4,3,2   (ii) 3,2,1,4
   (iii) 2,1,3,4   (iv) 3,1,4,2

(d) Why did the speaker thank the Indian Space Research Organization?
   (i) It is the forefront of technologies for launchers and the construction of satellites.
   (ii) The group of scientists working together are quite balanced.
   (iii) It is leading in producing rockets.
   (iv) Indian scientists are very intelligent.

(e) According to the passage which image shows India's direction of focus for development?

(i)    (ii)

(iii)    (iv)

(f) In which context did the speaker says "your country has shown that economic growth and concern for the greater good are not incompatible"?
  (i) He is complaining
  (ii) He is appreciating.
  (iii) He is finding faults
  (iv) He is comparing.

(g) In which respect has India set an example for nations?
  (i) Social equality
  (ii) Cultural identity
  (iii) Economic growth
  (iv) Religious fairness

(h) To whom does the writer shows his gratitude for placing India at the forefront of technologies for launchers and the construction of satellites?
  (i) Indian scientists
  (ii) Indian technology
  (iii) Indian Space Research Organization
  (iv) Indian Government

(i) Pick the option from the passage that tells that inspite of inequalities, India has not given priority to.........
  (i) Poverty reduction
  (ii) Job creation
  (iii) Support to the agricultural sector
  (iv) Women education

(j) What would happen to diversity of cultures, religions, traditions and memories if we do not remain careful?
  (i) They would spread fast
  (ii) They would die
  (iii) They would pass on to others
  (iv) They would not flourish

(k) Pick the option that tells about the writer's feelings when he talks about the two fold risks of globalisation?
  (i) Fear   (ii) Concern
  (iii) Anxiety   (iv) All of these

6. The Highwayman
—Alfred Noyes

The wind was a torrent of darkness among the gusty trees,
The moon was a ghostly galleon tossed upon cloudy seas,
The road was a ribbon of moonlight over the purple moor,
And the highwayman came riding—
Riding—riding—
The highwayman came riding, up to the old inn-door
He'd a French cocked-hat on his forehead, a bunch of lace at his chin,
A coat of the claret velvet, and breeches of brown doe-skin;
They fitted with never a wrinkle : his boots were up to the thigh!
And he rode with a jewelled twinkle,
His pistol butts a-twinkle,
His rapier hilt a-twinkle, under the jewelled sky.
Over the cobbles he clattered and clashed in the dark inn-yard,
And he tapped with his whip on the shutters, but all was locked and barred;
He whistled a tune to the window, and who should be waiting there
But the landlord's black-eyed daughter,
Bess, the landlord's daughter,
Plaiting a dark red love-knot into her long black hair.
And dark in the dark old inn-yard a stable-wicket creaked
Where Tim the ostler listened. His face was white and peaked.
His eyes were hollows of madness, his hair like mouldy hay,
But he loved the landlord's daughter,
The landlord's red-lipped daughter.
Dumb as a dog he listened, and he heard the robber say—
"One kiss, my bonny sweetheart, I'm after a prize to-night,
But I shall be back with the yellow gold before the morning light;
Yet, if they press me sharply, and harry me through the day,
Then look for me by moonlight,
Watch for me by moonlight,
I'll come to thee by moonlight, though hell should bar the way."

I. On the basis of your reading of the poem given above, answer any ten of the following questions by choosing the most appropriate option:

(a) How does the poet describe the road?
  (i) As a ribbon of moonlight over the purple moor
  (ii) As a dark lane
  (iii) As a road lit by the stars
  (iv) A ribbon of silk

(b) Who was waiting for the highway man?
  (i) Bess, the landlord's daughter
  (ii) The gate-keeper
  (iii) Tim, the ostler
  (iv) The Landlord

(c) Based on your understanding of the poem, choose the option that lists the CORRECT sequence of the given statements.
  1. He clattered and clashed in the dark inn-yard.
  2. His face was white and peaked.
  3. He'd a french cocked-hat on his forehead.
  4. He heard the robber say— "One kiss, my bonny sweetheart, I'm after a prize to-night.

(i) 2,1,3,4   (ii) 3,1,2,4
(iii) 1,4,2,3   (iv) 2,4,1,3

(d) **What does the poet mean by 'Under the jewelled sky'?**
  (i) The jewels in Bess's hair
  (ii) The sky that was dark
  (iii) A starry night where the stars are the jewels.
  (iv) The jewels the highway man was carrying

(e) **According to the poem which image represents the picture of highwayman?**

(i)

(ii)

(iii)

(iv)

(f) **Which literary device is used in the line 'The moon was a ghostly galleon'?**
  (i) simile   (ii) alliteration
  (iii) metaphor   (iv) repetition

(g) **Apart from the highwayman, who else loved Bess?**
  (i) The royal policeman
  (ii) Tim, the ostler
  (iii) The landlord
  (iv) The gate-keeper

(h) **How did Tim, the ostler appear?**
  (i) Smart and handsome
  (ii) His face was white and peaked and eyes were hollows of madness
  (iii) Young and sober
  (iv) Cruel and rough

(i) **Pick the option from the poem that tells which literary device is NOT used in the line "And the highwayman came riding-riding-riding" is ...**
  (i) Assonance   (ii) Onomatopoeia
  (iii) Repetition   (iv) Duplication

(j) **What sound did the Highwayman make when he found all the shutters locked?**
  (i) He tapped with his shoes
  (ii) He knocked on the door
  (iii) He stringed his guitar
  (iv) He whistled a tune

(k) **Pick the option that tells what the king's men do with Bess?**
  (i) They kept her in King's palace.
  (ii) They left her in the woods.
  (iii) Bess was captured and tortured by the king's men.
  (iv) They got her married with a pauper.

7. At Home in India
—An Interview with Ruskin Bond

There are many among us who, given the opportunity to leave India, are only too happy to go. But whenever I have had the chance to go away, I have held back. Or something has held me back. What is it that has such a hold on me, but leaves others free to where they will, sometimes never to come back? A few years ago, I was offered a well-paid job in a magazine in Hong Kong. I thought about it for weeks, worried myself to distraction, and finally, with a great sigh of relief, turned it down.

My friends thought I was crazy. They still do. Most of them would have jumped at a comparable offer, even if it had meant spending the rest of their lives far from the palm fringed coasts or pine-clad mountains of this land. Many friends have indeed gone away, never to return, except perhaps to get married, very quickly, before they are off again! Don't they feel homesick, I wonder.

I am almost paranoid at the thought of going away and then being unable to come back. This almost happened to me when, as a boy, I went to England, longed to return to India, and did not have the money for the passage. For two years I worked and saved like a miser (something I have never done since) until I had enough to bring me home. And 'home' wasn't parents and brothers and sisters. They were no longer here. Home, for me, was India. So what is it that keeps me here? My birth? I take too closely after a Nordic grandparent to pass for a typical son of the soil.

Hotel receptionists often ask me for my passport. 'Must I carry a passport to travel in my own country?' I ask. 'But you don't look like an Indian,' they protest. 'I'm a Red Indian,' I say. India is where I was born and went to school and grew to manhood. India was where my father was born and went to school and worked and died. India is where my grandfather lived and died. Surely that entitles me to a place in the Indian sun.

I. On the basis of your reading of the passage given above, answer any ten of the following questions by choosing the most appropriate option:

(a) What did the narrator do when he was offered a well-paid job in Hong Kong?
   (i) He readily accepted it.
   (ii) He refused to join it.
   (iii) He asked for more salary.
   (iv) He asked for the placement in Indian city.

(b) When author was a boy, why couldn't he come back to India from England?
   (i) His parents forbade him.
   (ii) The British government didn't permit him.
   (iii) He fell short of money.
   (iv) Due to bad climatic conditions England.

(c) Based on your understanding of the passage, choose the option that lists the CORRECT sequence of the given statements.
   1. Hotel receptionists often ask me for my passport.
   2. Author was almost paranoid at the thought of going away from India.
   3. And 'home' wasn't parents and brothers and sisters.
   4. Author's friends thought he was crazy.
   (i) 1,3,2,4   (ii) 4,2,3,1
   (iii) 3,1,2,4   (iv) 3,2,4,1

(d) What is 'Home' for the author?
   (i) Where his parents live.
   (ii) Where his friends reside.
   (iii) India
   (iv) Where he gets emotional

(e) Which image shows the picture of the place where author lives?

(i)   (ii)

(iii)   (iv)

(f) When the author turned down the job offer in Hong Kong, what did his friends think about him?
   (i) He did quite a sensible thing.
   (ii) He was crazy.
   (iii) He was impractical.
   (iv) He was a calculable person.

(g) According to the author, what holds him on to stay back in India?
   (i) The job offered didn't attract him.
   (ii) The land
   (iii) His grandparents' memories
   (iv) The fear of not returning back to India

(h) How was author so different from his friends?
   (i) Unlike his friends, the author wanted to leave India later on.
   (ii) His friends' homesickness.
   (iii) Their willingness to work abroad.
   (iv) Their inclination towards their motherland.

(i) Pick the option that mentions what does NOT make the author think that he belonged to India?
   (i) He was born in India.
   (ii) He went to school in England.
   (iii) His father worked and died in India.
   (iv) His grandfather lived in India.

(j) What did the author inherit from his Nordic grandparents?
   (i) Their brilliant mind
   (ii) Their music
   (iii) Their looks
   (iv) Their artistic quality

(k) Pick the option that states the feelings of the people when they are offered jobs outside India?
   (i) Insipidness   (ii) Tardiness
   (iii) Helplessness   (iv) Enthusiasm

Answers

1. Harry Potter (Excerpt)
–J.K. Rowling

1. (a) (ii) Under her hair
   (b) (ii) Staff
   (c) (iii) 4, 1, 2, 3
   (d) (iii) It left the drinker smoking at the ears for several hours.
   (e) (ii) image
   (f) (ii) They reported that it was no more than seven greenish blurs.
   (g) (ii) The flower beds
   (h) (ii) He didn't fulfill the requirement to join the hunt
   (i) (iii) A bright coloured tie
   (j) (iii) He was pale as smoke.
   (k) (i) Resentful

2. Evening Star
–Edger Allan Poe

2. (a) (ii) Middle of summer
   (b) (iii) personification

(c) (i) 2,1,4,3
(d) (i) Its distant fire
(e) Image (i)
(f) (i) As slaves of the moon
(g) (ii) It is warmer
(h) (iii) The stars shone in a dull manner in comparison to the moon.
(i) (ii) Warm
(j) (iv) Too cold
(k) (iii) The Evening star

3. The Kitemaker (Excerpt)
–Ruskin Bond

3. (a) (iv) His kites once sold for as much as three or four rupees each
(b) (iii) It possessed supernatural powers.
(c) (ii) 3,1,4,2
(d) (i) The Nawab
(e) (iv) Image
(f) (ii) because it was too bulky
(g) (iii) Mirror
(h) (i) three or four rupees
(i) (iii) The discs made a lovely sound.
(j) (iv) It disappeared from the view.
(k) (i) Curiosity

4. Gunga Din (The regimental bhisti) (Excerpt)
–Rudyard Kipling

4. (a) (i) a soldier
(b) (ii) give his regimental soldiers water
(c) (iii) 1,4,2,3
(d) (iii) Gunga Din
(e) (ii) Image
(f) (i) hell
(g) (iv) beggar
(h) (i) He dies
(i) (ii) Clean
(j) (iii) He was hit by a bullet near the belt plate
(k) (iv) All of these

5. Dynamism of India

5. (a) (ii) Western countries have a shortage of manpower in this very field.
(b) (i) Due to its size and dynamism of its domestic market

(c) (iv) 3,1,4,2
(d) (i) It is the forefront of technologies for launchers and the construction of satellites.
(e) (i) Image
(f) (ii) He is appreciating
(g) (ii) Cultural Identity
(h) (iii) Indian Space Research Organization
(i) (iv) Women education
(j) (ii) They would die
(k) (iv) All of these

6. The Highwayman
–Alfred Noyes

6. (a) (i) As a ribbon of moonlight over the purple moor
(b) (i) Bess, the landlord's daughter
(c) (ii) 3,1,2,4
(d) (iii) A starry night where the stars are the jewels.
(e) (i) Image
(f) (iii) Metaphor
(g) (ii) Tim, the ostler
(h) (ii) His face was white and peaked and eyes were hollows of madness
(i) (ii) Onomatopoeia
(j) (iv) He whistled a tune
(k) (iii) Bess was captured and tortured by the king's men.

7. At Home in India
–An Interview with Ruskin Bond

7. (a) (ii) He refused to join it.
(b) (iii) He fell short of money.
(c) (ii) 4,2,3,1
(d) (iii) India
(e) (i) Image
(f) (ii) He was crazy.
(g) (ii) The land
(h) (iii) Their willingness to work abroad.
(i) (ii) He went to school in England.
(j) (iii) Their looks
(k) (iv) Enthusiasm

❑❑

3

Case-Based Passage

1. **Read the passage carefully:**
   1. At least a third of the huge ice fields in Asia's towering mountain chain are doomed to melt due to climate change, according to a landmark report, with serious consequences for almost 2 billion people. Even if carbon emissions are dramatically and rapidly cut and succeed in limiting global warming to 1.5°C, 36% of the glaciers along in the Hindu Kush and Himalaya range will have gone by 2100. If emissions are not cut, the loss soars to two-thirds, the report found.
   2. The glaciers are a critical water store for the 250 million people who live in the Hindu Kush-Himalaya (HKH) region, and 1.65 billion people rely on the great rivers that flow from the peaks into India, Pakistan, China and other nations. "This is the climate crisis you haven't heard of," said Philippus Wester of the International Centre for Integrated Mountain Development (Icimod), who led the report. "In the best of possible worlds, if we get really ambitious [in tackling climate change], even then we will lose one-third of the glaciers and be in trouble. That for us was the shocking finding."
   3. Wester said that, despite being far more populous, the HKH region had received less attention than other places, such as low-lying island states and the Arctic, that are also highly vulnerable to global warming. Prof. Jemma Wadham, at the University of Bristol, said: "This is a landmark piece of work focused on a region that is a hotspot for climate change impacts."

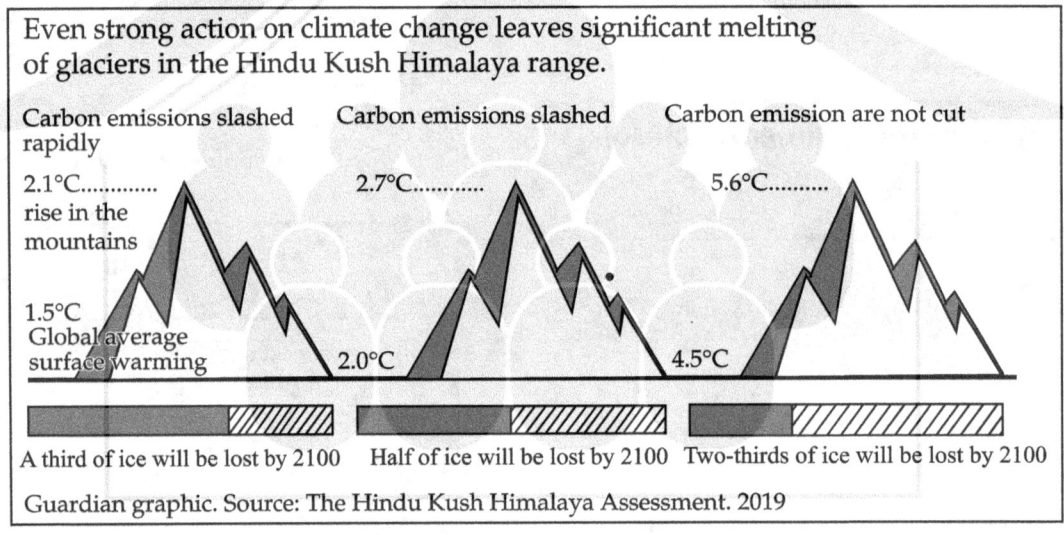

Guardian graphic. Source: The Hindu Kush Himalaya Assessment. 2019

   4. The new report, requested by the eight nations the mountains span, is intended to change that. More than 200 scientists worked on the report over five years, with another 125 experts peer reviewing their work. Until recently the impact of climate change on the ice in the HKH region was uncertain, said Wester. "But we really do know enough now to take action, and action is urgently needed," he added. The HKH region runs from Afghanistan to Myanmar and is the planet's "third pole", harbouring more ice than anywhere outside Arctic and Antarctica. Limiting the global temperature rise to 1.5°C above pre-industrial levels requires cutting emissions to zero by 2050. This is felt to be extremely optimistic by many but still sees a third of the ice lost, according to the report. If the global rise is 2°C, half of the glaciers will be projected to melt away by 2100.
   5. Since the 1970s, about 15% of the ice in the HKH region has disappeared as temperatures have risen. But the HKH range is 3,500 km long and the impact of warming is variable. Some glaciers in Afghanistan and Pakistan are stable and a few are even gaining ice, most probably due to increased cloud cover that shields the sun and changed winds that bring more snow. But even these will start melting with future warming, Wester said.
   6. The melting glaciers will increase river flows through to 2050 to 2060, he said, pushing up the risk of high-altitude lakes bursting their banks and engulfing communities. But from the 2060s, river flows will go into decline. The Indus and central Asian rivers will be most affected. "Those areas will be hard hit," said Wester. Lower flows will cut the power from the hydrodams that generate much of the region's electricity. But the most

serious impact will be on farmers in the foothills and downstream. They rely on predictable water supplies to grow the crops that feed the nations in the mountains' shadows.

But the changes to spring melting already appear to be causing the pre-monsoon river flow to fall just when farmers are planting their crops. Worse, said Wester, the monsoon is also becoming more erratic and prone to extreme downpours. "One-in-100 year floods are starting to happen every 50 years," he said.

1.1. On the basis of your understanding of the passage, answer any ten of the following questions by choosing the most appropriate option:

(a) By how much percentage will the glaciers have gone in the Hindu Kush and Himalaya range by 2100?
   (i) 32%   (ii) 34%
   (iii) 36%   (iv) 38%

(b) Pick the option that lists statements that are NOT TRUE according to the passage.
   1. 36% of the glaciers in the Hindu Kush and Himalaya range will have gone by 2100.
   2. 1.65 million people rely on the rivers that flow from the peaks into India, Pakistan and China.
   3. The Hindu Kush-Himalaya region runs from Afghanistan to Nepal.
   4. River flows will decline from 2060s.
   (i) 2 and 3   (ii) 1 and 4
   (iii) 3 and 4   (iv) 2 and 4

(c) If carbon emissions are lowered quickly then the temperature in mountains of HKH range will rise up to..........................
   (i) 1.2°C   (ii) 2.0°C
   (iii) 1.5°C   (iv) 2.1°C

(d) Based on the information given in the passage, choose the option that lists the CORRECT depiction of loss of ice if carbon emissions are slashed.

   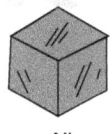

1/3rd   1/2   2/3rds   All
1   2   3   4

   (i) image 1   (ii) image 2
   (iii) image 3   (iv) image 4

(e) According to the 2019 assessment of Hindu Kush Himalaya range, which option lists the CORRECT percentage of ice that has disappeared since 1970s.

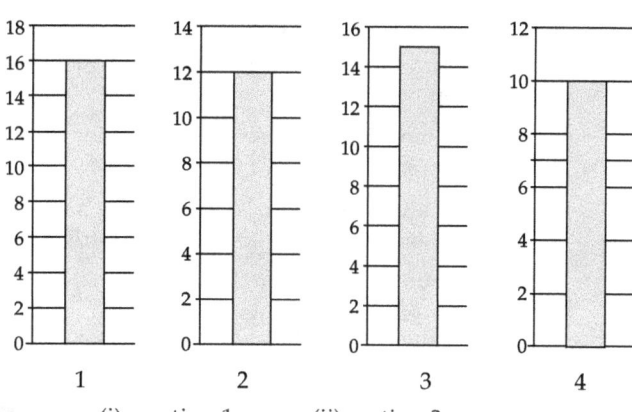

   (i) option 1   (ii) option 2
   (iii) option 3   (iv) option 4

(f) Based on the given graphical representation of data in the passage, choose the option that lists the statement that is TRUE with respect to the slashing of emissions.
   (i) If global warming is limited to 1.5°C then only a third of ice will be lost by 2100
   (ii) If global warming is limited to 2.0°C then only two thirds of ice will be lost by 2100
   (iii) If global warming is limited to 5.6°C then only two thirds of ice will be lost by 2100
   (iv) If global warming is limited to 4.5°C then only half of ice will be lost by 2100

(g) If the carbon emission is not cut at all then how much ice will be lost by 2100?
   (i) one-third   (ii) one-fourth
   (iii) two-third   (iv) three-fourth

(h) The HKH region runs from .... and is the planet's "third pole".
   (i) Afghanistan to Myanmar
   (ii) India to Pakistan
   (iii) Pakistan to China
   (iv) Myanmar to Afghanistan

(i) For how many people who live in the Hindu Kush-Himalaya (HKH) region, the glaciers are a critical water store?
   (i) 1.65 billion
   (ii) 1.65 million
   (iii) 250 million
   (iv) 250 billion

(j) Which word in the passage means same as 'promptly'? (para 1)
   (i) rapidly
   (ii) emissions
   (iii) dramatically
   (iv) soars

(k) Arrange the given statements according to the sequence in which they occur in the passage.

1. Rise in temperatures since 1970 has led to the disappearance of about 15% of ice in HKH region.
2. More than 200 scientists worked on the HKH Assessment report for over five years.
3. The Indus and central Asian rivers will be most affected by the rise in temperature.
4. If carbon emissions are left uncut then by 2100 loss of glaciers soars by two-thirds.

(i) 1, 2, 3, 4 (ii) 4, 2, 1, 3
(iii) 3, 2, 1, 4 (iv) 1, 4, 2, 3

2. Read the passage given below.

1. The present generation is well updated in the use of internet and computers. The rapid development in computer technology and increase in accessibility of the internet for academic purposes has changed the face of education for everyone associated with it. Let's look at the data arising out of a recent survey that was done to ascertain the time spent on utilisation of the computer and internet:

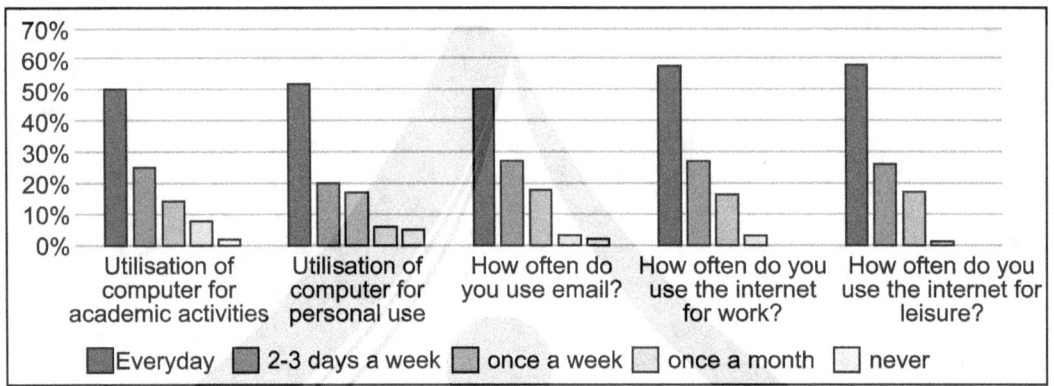

2. At present, many schools and universities have been implementing internet-based learning, as it supplements the conventional teaching methods. The internet provides a wide variety of references and information to academics as well as scientific researchers. Students often turn to it to do their academic assignments and projects.

3. However, research on the Net is very different from traditional library, and the differences can cause problems. The Net is a tremendous resources, but it must be used carefully and critically.

4. According to a 2018 Academic Student e-book Experience Survey, conducted by LJ's research department and sponsored by EBSCO, when reading for pleasure, almost 74% of respondents said they preferred print books for leisure whereas, 45% of respondents chose e-books rather than the printed versions, for research or assignments.

5. When asked what e-book features make them a favourite for research, the respondents were clear. Having page numbers to use in citations, topped the list (75%); followed by the ability to resize text to fit a device's screen (67%); the ability to bookmark pages, highlight text, or take notes for later reference (60%); downloading the entire e-book (57%); and allowing content to be transferred between devices (43%) were the varied responses.

2.1. On the basis of your understanding of the passage, answer any ten of the following questions by choosing the most appropriate option:

(a) According to the passage, one of the reason for the recent transformation of education is the:
(i) techno-efficiency of the present generation
(ii) expanse of courses on technology
(iii) simplification of the teaching and learning method
(iv) easy availability of the internet

(b) Pick the option that lists statements that are NOT TRUE according to the passage.
1. Internet-based education can only complement familiar methods of education.
2. Net-based learning will replace face-to-face education.
3. The resources that the net provides are a danger to the education system.
4. The current times has seen a rise in the convenience of using the internet for academic purposes.
(i) 1 and 2 (ii) 3 and 4
(iii) 2 and 3 (iv) 1 and 4

(c) The word 'tremendous', as used in paragraph 3, means the same as:
(i) 'expensive' (ii) 'renowned'
(iii) 'innovative' (iv) 'incredible'

(d) Based on the graphical chart in the passage, choose the option that lists the CORRECT depiction of internet usage for work and for leisure, for once a month.

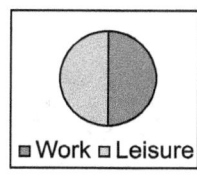  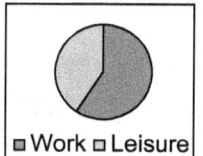 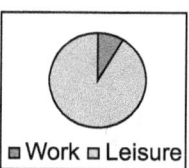

        1   2   3   4

    (i) option 1   (ii) option 2
    (iii) option 3   (iv) option 4

(e) "... but it must be used carefully and critically." The idea of being careful and critical while using the internet, is mainly a reference to:
    (i) hardware malfunction
    (ii) plagiarism
    (iii) troubleshooting
    (iv) virus threats

(f) Based on the given graphical representation of data in the passage, choose the option that lists the statements that are TRUE with respect to the usage of email.
    1. The everyday usage of email is more than the everyday usage of computer for personal use.
    2. About 18% people use email once a week.
    3. There are a smaller number of email users using it 2-3 times a week than the ones using it once a month.
    4. Less than 5% of people never use the email.
    (i) 1 and 3   (ii) 2 and 4
    (iii) 1 and 2   (iv) 3 and 4

(g) Based on the given graphical chart, pick the option that lists the area of zero response from respondents.
    (i) never using the internet for work and leisure
    (ii) daily use of the computer for academic activities
    (iii) writing and receiving emails once a week
    (iv) using the internet for personal tasks once a month

(h) In the cartoon, the student's reaction reveals that he is........................
    (i) indignant   (ii) apologetic
    (iii) obedient   (iv) inquisitive

(i) Which of the following statements is NOT substantiated by information in paragraph 4?
    (i) About three-quarters of the respondents preferred print books for recreational reading
    (ii) A little more than a 50% of the respondents voted for e-books for research or assignments
    (iii) More than 50% respondents stated enjoying both versions of books for leisure reading
    (iv) The survey was intended for understanding the e-book experience among students

(j) According to the 2018 survey, which is the option that correctly displays the features of :
    (A) page numbers for use in citation and
    (B) content transfer between devices respectively.

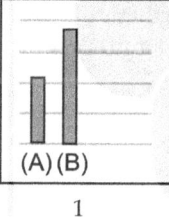 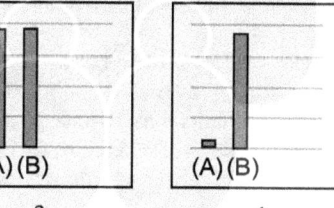

        1   2   3   4

    (i) option 1   (ii) option 2
    (iii) option 3   (iv) option 4

(k) Arrange the given e-book features preferred for research from the least favourite to the most favourite, from the following:
    1. downloading the entire e-book.
    2. choosing page numbers in critations.
    3. highlighting text.
    4. resizing text to fit screen.
    (i) 1, 3, 4, 2   (ii) 3, 2, 1, 4
    (iii) 2, 4, 3, 1   (iv) 4, 1, 2, 3

3. Read the passage carefully:

1. Over 100 persons have died in the floods in Assam so far while another 147 were killed in lightning strikes in Bihar last month. But with the monsoon season less than half way through, more loss of lives and property are expected if the trend in the past five years is anything to go by.

2. Take for instance human lives lost. In 2015, a little less than 1,000 persons died of flood and rain-related incidents, but in 2019, nearly 2,500 persons had lost their lives, according to government data. The loss of cattle also increased. While in 2015, less than 30,000 cattle died, in 2019, it was nearly 72,000.(See graphic 1)

3. To sum up the flood and its impact in the past five years, over 8,700 people were killed, over 2 lakh cattle died and more than 36 lakh houses were destroyed in floods. The cost of damage to property has also shot up in these five years. While in 2015, the damage suffered totalled ₹ 33,257 crore, in 2018, the last year for which data is available, it went up to ₹ 95,736 crore. The cost of damage is likely to be more in 2019 as over a dozen states, including Bihar, Assam, Himachal Pradesh, Kerala and Maharashtra, witnessed large-scale devastation.

4. Besides the rising damage, the cost to the exchequer towards relief work has also increased. In 2016-17, the Centre released ₹ 11,441 cr under the National Disaster Relief Fund while its share under the State Disaster Relief Fund was ₹ 8,375 crore. This increased to ₹ 14,108 cr and ₹ 10,429 cr respectively in 2019-20. (See graphic 2)

5. The flood's increasing loss of lives and property appears to make a mockery of all the expert committees, task forces and commissions the government has formed. In 1972, the Ganga Flood Control Commission was set-up in Patna to address the flood problem and erosion in the Ganga basin states. In 1980, the Brahmaputra Board came into existence to address the flood erosion problem in the northeastern states and Sikkim. (See table)

6. The government also launched a Flood Management Programme in the Eleventh Plan (2007-12) for providing financial assistance to state governments to undertake work related to river management, flood control, anti-erosion, drainage development, flood proofing, among others. The FMP was continued for three years under the Twelfth Plan from 2017-18 to 2019-20. It has subsequently been included as a component of the Flood Management and Border Areas Programme in the Ministry of Jal Shakti. But all these appear to have come to a naught as the government's approach is more reactive than proactive, according to experts. Instead of focusing on the real problem, it was only concerned about relief measures, they said.

7. They pointed out that the area affected by floods has doubled since 1950. "The flood-affected area in 1950 was 25 million hectare, now it has doubled to nearly 50 million hectare. But, what is surprising is that nobody looks concerned about the real issues. Earlier, only villages used to be affected but now cities are also getting flooded. Chennai and Patna are just examples. I had written to the government in 2015, highlighting the poor drainage system in cities," said former IIT professor Dinesh Kumar Mishra.

Himanshu Thakkar, the coordinator of the South Asia Network of Dams, Rivers and People, said effective management of dams could bring down the damage caused by floods. "We have over 5,000 dams. Every dam can help moderate floods in the downstream area but only if it is operated properly," Thakkar said.

Committees & commissions	Aim	Work
Ganga Flood Control Commission	Flood, erosion in Ganga basin states.	Prepared 23 comprehensive master plans.
Rashtriya Barh Aayog	To evolve coordinated, integrated approach for flood control.	Submitted report in 1980 recommending measures Brahmaputra Board.
Brahmaputra Board	Flood, erosion problems in northeastern states.	Prepared 57 master plans for implementation.
Task Force-2004	Flood management and erosion control.	Submitted report in December 2004, recommending short, long-term measures.
Flood Management Programme	To provide financial assistance for river management, flood control, erosion.	Other than allocating financial aid, it is involved in flood forecasting.

Case-Based Passage | 39

3.1. On the basis of your understanding of the passage, answer any ten of the following questions by choosing the most appropriate option:

(a) How many people were killed due to lightning in Bihar?
 (i) 142 (ii) 157
 (iii) 147 (iv) 137

(b) Pick the option from the list below that is NOT TRUE according to the passage.
 1. The floods only affect villages and not cities.
 2. The Flood Management Program continued for three years under the Twelfth Plan from 2017-18 to 2019-20.
 3. If operated properly, dams can help control floods in the downstream areas.
 4. The area affected by floods has decreased nearly by half since 1950.
 (i) 1 and 3 (ii) 2 and 4
 (iii) 3 and 4 (iv) 1 and 4

(c) The number of cattle that died due to floods in 2019 was ....

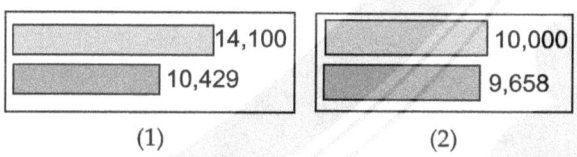

 (i) option 1 (ii) option 2
 (iii) option 3 (iv) option 4

(f) How much cost of damage to property has risen in the year 2018?
 (i) ₹ 33,257 crore (ii) ₹ 26,396 crore
 (iii) ₹ 95,736 crore (iv) ₹ 95,675 crore

(g) Which states have witnessed a large-scale devastation in the year 2019?
 (i) Bihar
 (ii) Assam
 (iii) Himachal Pradesh
 (iv) All of these

(h) The FMP was continued for three years under the Twelfth Plan for which period?
 (i) 2016-17 to 2018-19
 (ii) 2015-16 to 2017-18
 (iii) 2014-15 to 2016-17
 (iv) 2017-18 to 2019-20

(i) Examples of which two cities have been taken which have poor drainage system?
 (i) Mumbai and Patna
 (ii) Chennai and Patna
 (iii) Chennai and Mumbai
 (iv) Assam and Chennai

(j) Which word in the passage means same as 'illustration'? (para 2)
 (i) related (ii) according
 (iii) instance (iv) nearly

(k) Pick the option from the list below list that is TRUE according to the passage.
 1. The floods only affect villages and not cities.
 2. The Flood Management Program was discontinued after three years under the Twelfth Plan from 2016-17 to 2018-19.

 (i) nearly 72,000 (ii) 72,000
 (iii) 30,000 (iv) less than 30,000

(d) Arrange the following events in chronological order according to the passage.
 1. Flood Management and Border Areas Programme was added as a component to the Twelfth Plan in the Ministry of Jal Shakti.
 2. A Flood Management Plan was set-up in the Eleventh Plan to provide financial assistance to State Governments.
 3. The Ganga Flood Control Commission was set-up to address flood and erosion problems in the Ganga Basin states.
 4. The Brahmaputra Board was formed to address flood erosion problems in the north-eastern states and Sikkim.
 (i) 1, 4, 3, 2 (ii) 2, 1, 4, 3
 (iii) 3, 4, 2, 1 (iv) 1, 2, 3, 4

(e) According to the figure, which option best represents the money spent by the National Disaster Relief Fund and the State Disaster Relief Fund in the year 2019-2020?

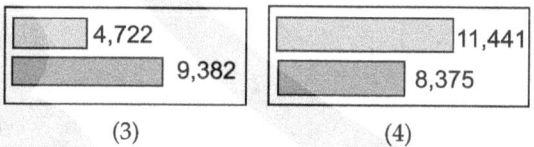

 3. The Task Force – 2004, submitted a report which recommended short and long term measures for flood management and erosion control.
 4. The area affected by floods has doubled from 25 million hectares to 50 million hectares since 1950.
 (i) 1 and 3 (ii) 2 and 4
 (iii) 3 and 4 (iv) 1 and 4

4. Read the passage carefully:
 1. Education in India is primarily provided by public schools (controlled and funded by the government at three levels: central, state and local) and private schools. Under various articles of the Indian Constitution, free and compulsory education is provided as a fundamental right to children aged 6 to 14. The approximate ratio of public schools to private schools in India is 7:5.
 2. India has made progress in increasing the attainment rate of primary education. In 2011, Approximately 75% of the population, aged between 7 and 10 years, was literate. India's improved education system is often cited as one of the main contributors to its economic development. Much of the progress, especially in higher education and scientific research, has been credited to various public institutions.
 3. At the primary and secondary level, India has a large private school system complementing the government run schools, with 29% of students receiving private education in the 6 to 14 age group. Certain post-secondary technical schools are also private. The private education market in India had a revenue of US $450 million in 2008, but is projected to be a US $40 billion market.

Education in Republic of India

Ministry of Education

Minister of Education	Ramesh Pokhriyal

National education budget

Budget	4.1% of GDP

General details

Primary languages	Indian languages, English
System type	Federal, State or Private
Established	1 April 2010
Compulsory Education	

Literacy (2011)

Total	74%
Male	82.2%
Female	69.5%

Enrollment

Total	(N/A)
Primary	95%
Secondary	69%
Post Secondary	25%

4. As per the Annual Status of Education Report (ASER) 2012, 96.5% of all rural children between the ages of 6-14 were enrolled in school. This is the fourth annual survey to report enrolment above 96%. India has maintained an average enrolment ratio of 95% for students in this age group from year 2007 to 2014. As an outcome the number of students in the age group 6-14 who are not enrolled in school has come down to 2.8% in the academic year 2018 (ASER 2018). Another report from 2013 stated that there were 229 million students enrolled in different accredited urban and rural schools of India, from Class I to XII, representing an increase of 23 lakh students over 2002 total enrolment, and a 19% increase in girl's enrolment.

5. While quantitatively India is inching closer to universal education, the quality of its education has been questioned particularly in its government run school system. While more than 95 per cent of children attend primary school, just 40 per cent of Indian adolescents attend secondary school (Grades 9-12). Since 2000, the World Bank has committed over $2 billion to education in India. Some of the reasons for the poor quality include absence of around 25% of teachers every day. States of India have introduced tests and education assessment system to identify and improve such schools.

6. Although there are private schools in India, they are highly regulated in terms of what they can teach, in what form they can operate (must be a non-profit to run any accredited educational institution) and all other aspects of operation. Hence, the differentiation of government schools and private schools can be misleading.

7. In January 2019, India had over 900 universities and 40,000 colleges. In India's higher education system, a significant number of seats are reserved under affirmative action policies for the historically disadvantaged Scheduled Castes and Scheduled Tribes and Other Backward Classes. In universities, colleges, and similar institutions affiliated to the federal government, there is a maximum 50% of reservations applicable to these disadvantaged groups, at the state level it can vary. Maharashtra had 73% reservation in 2014, which is the highest percentage of reservations in India.

4.1. On the basis of your understanding of the passage, answer any ten of the following questions by choosing the most appropriate option:

(a) The approximate ratio of public schools to private schools in India is............................
   (i) 5 : 7 (ii) 1 : 9
   (iii) 7 : 5 (iv) 9 : 7

(b) Pick the option that lists statements that are NOT TRUE according to the passage.
   1. India's improved education system is often cited as one of the main contributors to its economic development.
   2. At the primary and secondary level, India has a large private school.
   3. Report from 2013 stated that there were 329 million students enrolled in different accredited urban and rural schools of India.
   4. Maharashtra had 33% reservation in 2014, which is the lowest percentage of reservations in India.
   (i) 3 and 4 (ii) 2 and 4
   (iii) 1 and 2 (iv) 1 and 3

(c) India's improved education system is often cited as one of the main contributors to its ....
   (i) overall development
   (ii) social development
   (iii) economic development
   (iv) political development

(d) Based on the Statistical data in the passage, which option represents the correct graphical representation of enrolment rate in Primary and Secondary schools?

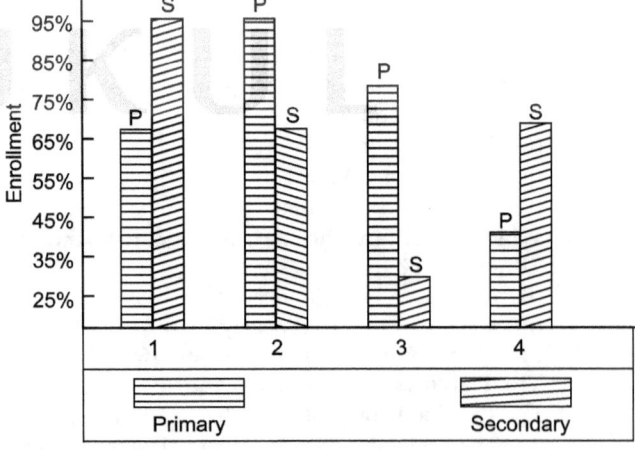

   (i) image 1 (ii) image 2
   (iii) image 3 (iv) image 4

(e) According to table, what was the literacy rate of females in the year 2011?
   (i) 74% (ii) 82.2%
   (iii) 69.5% (iv) 69%

(f) Based on the given statistical data in the passage, choose the option that lists the statements that are TRUE with respect to the education policy.
   1. Enrolment in Secondary Schools was 69%.
   2. National Education Budget passed by the ministry is 3.1% of the GDP.
   3. The literacy rate of women was 69.5% in 2011.
   4. As per 2011 census, total literacy rate was 82.2%.
   (i) 1 and 4 (ii) 2 and 4
   (iii) 3 and 4 (iv) 1 and 3

(g) Much of the progress, especially in higher education and scientific research, has been attributed to......
   (i) private institutions
   (ii) public institutions
   (iii) government institutions
   (iv) semi government institution

(h) One of the reasons for the poor quality of education in Government-run schools in India is...........
   (i) poor infrastructure
   (ii) absence of around 25% of teachers every day
   (iii) low enrolment of girls
   (iv) no aid given by the government

(i) Which State of India has the highest percentage of reservations in Universities and Colleges?
   (i) Maharashtra (ii) Odisha
   (iii) Bihar (iv) Uttar Pradesh

(j) Which word in the passage means same as 'registered'? (para 4)
   (i) survey (ii) accredited
   (iii) enrolled (iv) representing

(k) Arrange the given sentences in the sequence in which they appeared in the passage.
   1. In universities, colleges, and similar institutions, there are a maximum 50% of reservations applicable to the disadvantaged groups.
   2. Certain post-secondary technical schools are also private.
   3. The approximate ratio of public schools to private schools in India is 7:5.
   4. While more than 95 percent of children attend primary school, just 40 percent of Indian adolescents attend secondary school.
   (i) 1, 2, 4, 3 (ii) 4, 1, 2, 3
   (iii) 3, 2, 4, 1 (iv) 3, 1, 4, 2

5. Read the passage carefully:
   1. India ranks third in the list of countries with the largest number of threatened turtle and tortoise species in the world after China and Vietnam, an international report released on Thursday has revealed.

   2. The country has two of the world's 25 most threatened freshwater turtle species – Northern River Terrapin (*Batagur baska*) found in the Sundarbans, West Bengal and the Red-Crowned Roof Turtle (*Batagur kachuga*), found only within the riverine National Chambal Gharial Wildlife Sanctuary (NCGWS) in Madhya Pradesh.

   3. Another three species – South Asian Narrow-headed Softshell Turtle (*Chitra indica*) from NCGWS, Black Softshell Turtle (*Nilssonia nigricans*) from Assam, and the Arakan Forest Turtle (*Heosemys depressa*) from Mizoram, were identified under the list of top 50 most threatened species globally. This takes the tally in India to 7.4% under the world's 25 most threatened turtle species and 10% of the top 50.

   4. Additionally, the study identified the Keeled Box Turtle (*Cuora mouhotii*), Asian Giant Tortoise (*Manouria emys*) in northeast India, and the Leith's Softshell Turtle (*Nilssonia leithii*) from western India, as three other threatened species outside the top 50, assessed as critically endangered. The details were revealed in the report - Turtles in Trouble: The World's 25+ Most Endangered Tortoises and Freshwater Turtles - in Ojai, California, USA compiled by the Turtle Conservation Coalition, an international body comprising eight conservation groups including the International Union for Conservation of Nature (IUCN) and Turtle Surveillance Alliance (TSA), a group protection these species in India as well.

   5. "Our study found that Asia was facing a crisis with 63% of the top threatened tortoise and turtle species identified from the continent, followed by Africa and Latin America at 14.8% each," Rick Hudson, President and Chief Executive Officer, TSA, that released the study, told HT in a telephonic interview.

   6. The study identified 356 tortoise and freshwater turtle species globally, of which, 148 or 60.4% of those species have been included in the IUCN 2017 Red List, and 41.6% of all turtle and tortoise species are officially listed as 'Threatened' by IUCN criteria (categorised as vulnerable, endangered or critically endangered). Of this, all species identified in India are listed either under 'endangered' or 'critically endangered' categories. Yangtze Giant Softshell Turtle from China is the most threatened species worldwide.

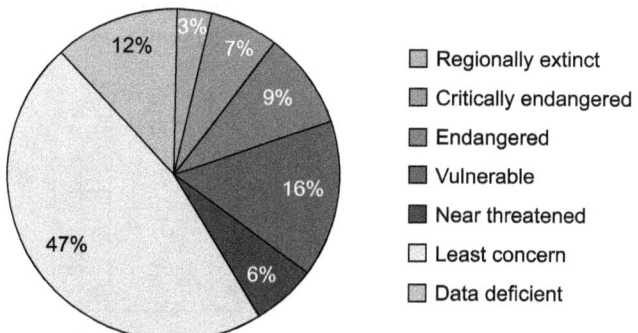

Species list for top threatened in India
Two species listed under top 25 threatened worldwide
➤ Northern River Terrapin (*Batagur baska*)
➤ Red-Crowned Roof Turtle (*Batagur kachuga*)
Five species listed under top 50 (including the two above) threatened worldwide
➤ South Asian Narrow-headed Softshell Turtle (*Chitra indica*)
➤ Black Softshell Turtle (*Nilssoni anigricans*)
➤ Arakan Forest Turtle (*Heosemys depressa*)
Three other threatened species outside the top 50 assessed as critically endangered
➤ Keeled Box Turtle (*Cuora mouhotii*)
➤ Asian Giant Tortoise (*Manouria emys*)
➤ Leith's Softshell Turtle (*Nilssonia leithii*)
[Source : eea.europa.eu]

5.1. On the basis of your understanding of the passage, answer any ten of the following questions by choosing the most appropriate option:

(a) Scientific name for the Red-Crowned Roof Turtle is...............................
 (i) *Cuora mouhotii* (ii) *Batagur baska*
 (iii) *Batagur kachuga* (iv) *Nilssonia leithii*

(b) Pick the option that lists statements that are NOT TRUE according to the passage.
 1. India has one of the world's 25 most threatened freshwater turtle species.
 2. Three species of turtle were identified under the list of top 50 most threatened species globally.
 3. Yangtze Giant Softshell Turtle from Korea is the most threatened species worldwide.
 4. Asia was facing a crisis with 63% of the top threatened tortoise and turtle species identified from the continent.
 (i) 1 and 3 (ii) 2 and 4
 (iii) 1 and 2 (iv) 2 and 3

(c) What is India's count in the percentage of the world's 50 most threatened turtle species?
 (i) 7.4% (ii) 8%
 (iii) 8.4% (iv) 10%

(d) Based on the graph given in the passage, choose the option that CORRECTLY represents the ratio of critically endangered to endangered species of turtles countrywide.

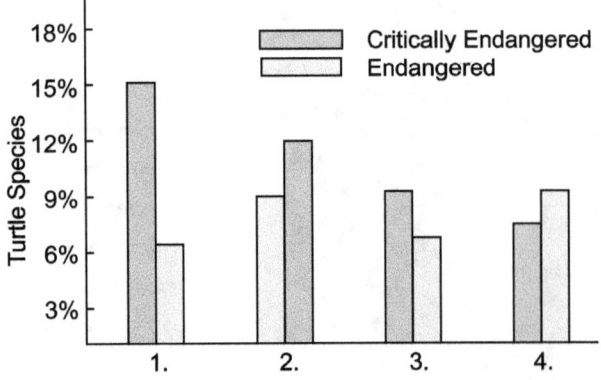

 (i) option 1 (ii) option 2
 (iii) option 3 (iv) option 4

(e) International Union for Conservation of Nature (IUCN) works for ....
 (i) the protection of turtle species
 (ii) the conservation of nature
 (iii) the conservation of turtle species
 (iv) the surveillance of turtles

(f) Based on the given graphical representation of data in the passage, choose the option that lists the statements that are TRUE with respect to the species of turtle.
 1. Scientific name of Asian Giant Tortoise is *Nilssoni anigricans*.
 2. Arakan Forest Turtle Comes under the top 50 species which are threatened worldwide.
 3. Red-Crowned Roof Turtle falls under the category of top 25 threatened species worldwide.
 4. Northern River Terrapin is found in South Africa.
 (i) 2 and 3 (ii) 1 and 2
 (iii) 2 and 4 (iv) 3 and 4

(g) Yangtze Giant Softshell Turtle which is the most threatened species worldwide is found in which country?
 (i) China (ii) Japan
 (iii) Korea (iv) Vietnam

(h) Rick Hudson, President and Chief Executive Officer, TSA, that released the study, told HT in a telephonic interview that ....
 (i) Asia was facing a crisis with 63% of the top threatened tortoise
 (ii) Turtle species identified from the continent is also included under this
 (iii) African and Latin American species comes at the second place
 (iv) All of these

(i) Turtle Conservation Coalition, an International body comprises how many conservation groups?
 (i) 7 conservation groups
 (ii) 8 conservation groups
 (iii) 9 conservation groups
 (iv) 10 conservation groups

(j) Which word in the passage means same as 'involving? (para 4)
 (i) coalition (ii) comprising
 (iii) compiled (iv) conservation

(k) Arrange the given species of turtle which are under threat from the most to the least.
 (1) regionally extinct
 (2) endangered
 (3) least concern
 (4) near threatened
 (i) 1, 2, 4, 3 (ii) 3, 2, 1, 4
 (iii) 2, 4, 3, 1 (iv) 4, 3, 2, 1

6. Read the passage carefully:

1. NSYNC singer Lance Bass can't afford the $20 million price tag for a ride into space now, he should try again, in say, a decade. But within a decade or so, even some of Bass's fans could afford a quick and safe trip to the suborbital edge of space, roughly 50-60 miles above earth, says Frank Seitzen, President of the Space Transport Association.

2. "I think you're may be 10 or 12 years away from having companies that are reliable and that can go through that process for $5,000 or $10,000," Seitzen said. There's a hungry demand from would be space tourists and a $10 million prize is inspiring designers. The Prize, created in 1994 to spur the development of new space travel technologies, has attracted at least 21 space vehicle designs from people in five countries. The non-profit X Prize Foundation, founded by a group of donors inspired by the $25,000 Orteig Prize that Charles Lindbergh won in 1927, will give the prize.

3. Each design team is hoping to develop the first reusable rocket capable of blasting a pilot and two to five passengers to a height of 62 miles. NASA awards astronaut status for flights above 50 miles. Some design contestants boast that such trips will be available by 2005, although the first few travellers will face $100,000 bills until the market matures.

4. Despite steep prices and lagging technology, Seitzen and others are convinced that a lucrative travel business awaits. Space Adventures, a travel agency that helped coordinate the first tourist trip to the International Space Station last year by US businessman Dennis Tito, claims it has collected $2 million in deposits from more than 120 would-be suborbital tourists. For client Wally Funk, who has paid her deposit, suborbital travel is a disappointing, yet feasible, alternative to decades of trying to reach space. Funk, a retired aviation safety investigator says, "I would do (a space station trip) in a heartbeat, but I can't because I'm not a millionaire."

5. Compared to Tito's groundbreaking effort last year, future suborbital flights look easy. Tito was subjected to rigid medical requirements and a gruelling six-month training course in Russia. But suborbital travellers will need only a few days of training and pending FAA approval, would have to pass a much lower bar for medical standards."We always say that if you can safely ride a rollercoaster, then you are fit for a suborbital flight," says Space Adventures spokeswoman Tereza Predescu.

6. Four commercial spaceports, which launch rockets into space like airports launch planes, are already licensed to operate by the FAA in Virginia, California, Alaska and Florida, and they are eager to welcome extra business from space tourists, negating the need to catch a ride to Russia. For those reasons, suborbital travel may represent a $1 billion in a year market, according to Space Adventures President and CEO Eric Anderson, that's 10,000 travellers paying $100,000 each during the first few years of adventure space travel.

(Source: auto.economictimes.indiatimes.com)

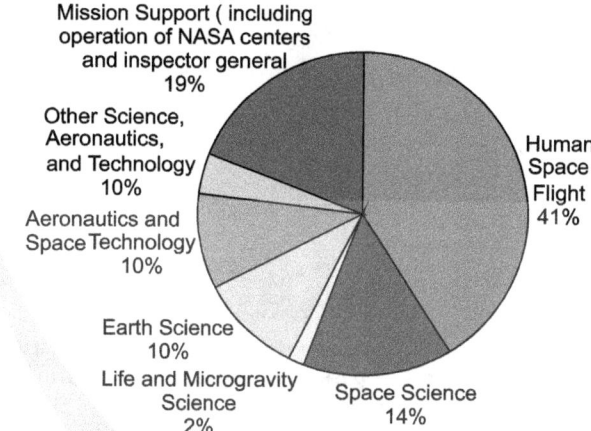

NASA budget for science-related programs and activities, FY 1997 (constant FY 1995 dollars)

6.1. On the basis of your understanding the passage, answer any ten of the following questions by choosing the most appropriate option:

(a) Space adventure claims that.....................
   (i) it is a business of less profit
   (ii) it is a lucrative business
   (iii) people don't want to go to space
   (iv) none of these

(b) Pick the option that lists statements that are NOT TRUE according to the passage.
   1. Despite steep prices and lagging technology ,Seitzen and others are convinced that a lucrative travel business awaits.
   2. Five commercial spaceports, which launch rockets into space like airports launch planes, are already licensed to operate by the FAA in Virginia, California, Alaska and Florida.
   3. Space Adventures, a travel agency, claims it has collected $ 12 million in deposits from more than 120 would-be suborbital tourists.
   4. There's a hungry demand from would be space tourists and a $10 million prize is inspiring designers.

   (i) 1 and 3   (ii) 2 and 3
   (iii) 2 and 4   (iv) 3 and 4

(c) Dennis Tito ....
   (i) underwent rigid medical checkups
   (ii) attended a six month training course
   (iii) both (i) and (ii)
   (iv) none of these

(d) Based on the graphical chart in the passage, choose the option that lists the CORRECT depiction of proposed budget for Earth Science and Human Space Flight.

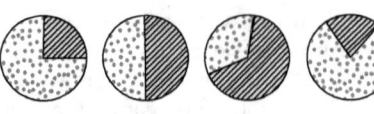

Human Space Flight
Earth Science

(1) (2) (3) (4)

(i) option 1 (ii) option 2
(iii) option 3 (iv) option 4

(e) How much amount of money is inspiring designers?
   (i) a $100 million prize
   (ii) a $10 million prize
   (iii) a $20 million prize
   (iv) a $15 million prize

(f) Based on the given graphical representation of data in the passage, choose the option that lists the statements that are TRUE.
   1. Human Science and Human Space Flight share the same percentage of budget.
   2. Aeronautical and Space Technology have the same amount of budget as that of Earth Science.
   3. The maximum budget has been kept for Mission Support.
   4. Life and Microgravity Science got the least share in budget.
   (i) 1 and 4   (ii) 2 and 3
   (iii) 3 and 4 (iv) 2 and 4

(g) NASA awards astronaut status for flights above which height?
   (i) 50 miles   (ii) 60 miles
   (iii) 70 miles (iv) 80 miles

(h) In a decade, how much fare can be reduced for a space traveller?
   (i) to $20,000 or even $15,000
   (ii) to $20,000 or even $10,000
   (iii) to $10,000 or even $5,000
   (iv) to $20,000 or even $5,000

(i) What are the prerequisites for space travelling?
   (i) the space travellers should be medically fit
   (ii) the space travellers need to get proper training.
   (iii) the one who can ride roller coaster is fit as a space traveller
   (iv) all of these

(j) Find the word in the passage which means same as 'profitable'? (para 4)
   (i) steep   (ii) lucrative
   (iii) feasible (iv) coordinate

(k) Arrange the given sentences in the correct order in which they appeared in the paragraph.
   1. The Prize, created in 1994 to spur the development of new space travel technologies, has attracted at least 21 space vehicle designs from people in five countries.
   2. Suborbital travel may represent a $1 billion a year market, according to Space Adventures President and CEO Eric Anderson.
   3. Lance Bass can't afford the $20 million price tag for a ride into space now, he should try again in, say, a decade.
   4. Tito was subjected to rigid medical requirements and a gruelling six-month training course in Russia.
   (i) 3, 2, 4, 1   (ii) 3, 1, 4, 2
   (iii) 4, 2, 3, 1 (iv) 1, 4, 3, 2

7. Read the passage carefully:

1. 1 in every 10 worker in India is a child; a child who is guaranteed protections under the Indian Law, and guaranteed an education and mid-day meals, till the age of 14. The sight of a chotu running to fetch you a chai on the train platform or at your local tea stall, isn't much of a sight in India. In fact, one could almost say that the chotu has become so ubiquitous, that him not being there would be a bit confusing for some of the regulars. It has been normalised and has become an internalised personality trait of the larger Indian society, which tacitly continues to support the chotu culture at the tea stall and within the home.

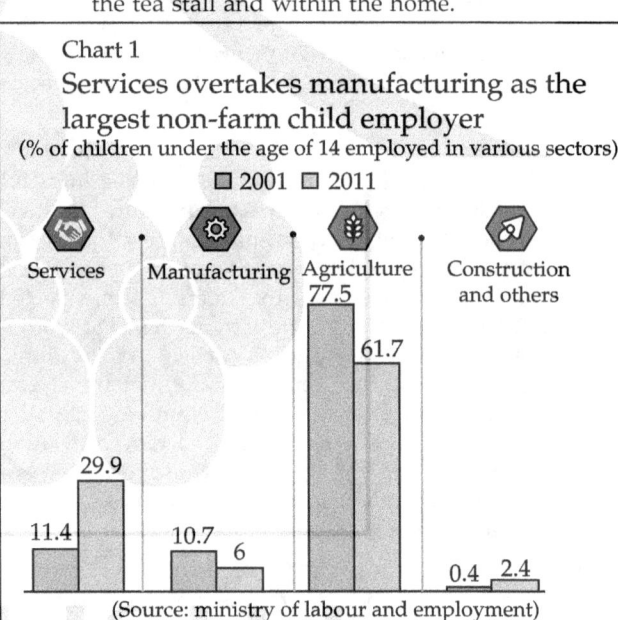

2. In fact it's become so natural that, when engaging with some of our more conscientious friend, both chotu and we, know the routine to pull off. You casually ask chotu how old he is as he cleans your table, and he, with a pail the size of his torso, responds saying he's 18. His gangly limbs and prepubescent face are a dead giveaway, but now that he's said he's 18, there's not much you can do… is there?

3. According to the UNICEF, there are about 10.1 million children employed in child labour in India today. That amounts to approximately 13% of our workforce. India has been trying to combat this blight since before it became a republic, with the passing of the Employment of Children Act, 1938.

While primitive, it was evident that even under an extractive colonial regime, it was understood that the use of children in the production process was anathema. Post–independence, the Factories Act, 1948 and the Mines Act, 1952, banned the practice of using children below the age of 14 and 18, in their respective production processes.

4. This set the tone for the Child Labour (Prohibition and Regulation) Act of 1986 which prevents the employment of children below the age of 14 years in life-threatening occupations identified in a list by the law and finally the Juvenile Justice (Care and Protection) of children Act of 2000 made the employment of children a punishable offence.

5. The JJ Act came into force shortly after India ratified the Convention on the Rights of the Child (CRC), in 1992 and made the offence punishable with imprisonment from three months to one year or with fine no less than INR 10,000–20,000 rupees or with both.

The Right to Education Act, passed in 2009, was supposed to go beyond punishing people for child labour to creating a conducive environment for building the capabilities of all Indian children, so that they could have a complete education and enter the workforce out of choice and not compulsion. However, even after all this, child labour continues to be the norm in a lot of industries.

6. Oxfam India is working on ground in the 5 poorest states in India (Uttar Pradesh, Chhattisgarh, Jharkhand, Odisha and Bihar) enrol children to schools and help them achieve their fundamental right of education as promised under the Right to Education Act (2009). Donate now to help secure the future of India's children.

7.1. On the basis of your understanding of the passage, answer any ten of the following questions by choosing the most appropriate option:

(a) The 'chotu' culture in India has been promoted silently by......................
 (i) the government
 (ii) the offices
 (iii) the family of Chotu
 (iv) Indian society

(b) List the Acts restricting Child labour in chronological order?
 1. The Factories Act
 2. The Child Labour Act
 3. The Employment of Children Act
 4. The Mines Act
 (i) 1, 3, 2, 4 (ii) 3, 1, 4, 2
 (iii) 2, 3, 1, 4 (iv) 1, 2, 3, 4

(c) What percentage of children was employed in the agriculture sector in the year 2011?
 (i) 77.5% (ii) 61.7%
 (iii) 29.9% (iv) 67.7%

(d) As per the chart given in the passage, which sector is the lowest child employer?
 (i) construction
 (ii) agriculture
 (iii) manufacturing
 (iv) services

(e) When did India ratify the Convention on the Rights of the Child (CRC)?
 (i) 1952 (ii) 1992
 (iii) 1938 (iv) 1948

(f) For which occupation does the Juvenile Justice of Children Act of 2000 made the employment of children a punishable offence?
 (i) life threatening occupation
 (ii) construction works
 (iii) factory Labour
 (iv) manufacturing sector

(g) In which year was 29.9% of children were employed in the service sector?
 (i) Year 2001 (ii) Year 2010
 (iii) Year 2011 (iv) Year 2000

(h) The JJ Act made the employment of children punishable offence with imprisonment ....
 (i) from six months to one year
 (ii) from three months to six months
 (iii) from three months to one year
 (iv) from three months to five months

(i) Employment of Children Act was passed in which year?
 (i) 1935 (ii) 1936
 (iii) 1937 (iv) 1938

(j) Which word in the passage means same as 'universal'? (para 1)
 (i) normalised (ii) ubiquitous
 (iii) internalised (iv) tacitly

(k) The Child Labour (Prohibition and Regulation) Act of 1986 prevents the employment of children below the age of 14 years in life-threatening occupations. Pick the options which relates to life-threatening occupations.
 1. working in mines
 2. working at home
 3. working in a factory
 4. working in the fields
 (i) 1, 2, 3 (ii) 2, 3, 4
 (iii) 1, 3, 4 (iv) 4, 3, 2

Answers

1.1. (a) (iii) 36%
 (b) (i) 2 and 3
 (c) (iv) 2.1°C
 (d) (ii) image 2

- (e) (iii) option 3
- (f) (i) If global warming is limited to 1.5°C then only a third of ice will be lost by 2100.
- (g) (iii) two-third
- (h) (i) Afghanistan to Myanmar
- (i) (iii) 250 million
- (j) (i) rapidly
- (k) (ii) 4, 2, 1, 3

2.1.
- (a) (iv) easy availability of the internet.
- (b) (iii) 2 and 3
- (c) (iv) 'incredible'.
- (d) (iii) option 3
- (e) (ii) plagiarism.
- (f) (ii) 2 and 4
- (g) (i) never using the internet for work and leisure
- (h) (i) indignant
- (i) (iv) The survey was intended for understanding the e-book experience among students.
- (j) (ii) option 2
- (k) (i) 1, 3, 4, 2

3.1.
- (a) (iii) 147
- (b) (iv) 1 and 4
- (c) (i) nearly 72,000
- (d) (iii) 3, 4, 2, 1
- (e) (i) option 1
- (f) (iii) 95,736 crore
- (g) (iv) All of these
- (h) (iv) 2017-18 to 2019-20
- (i) (ii) Chennai and Patna
- (j) (iii) instance
- (k) (iii) 3 and 4

4.1.
- (a) (iii) 7:5
- (b) (i) 3 and 4
- (c) (iii) economic development
- (d) (ii) image 2
- (e) (iii) 69.5%
- (f) (iv) 1 and 3
- (g) (ii) public Institutions
- (h) (ii) absence of around 25% of teachers every day
- (i) (i) Maharashtra
- (j) (iii) enrolled
- (k) (iii) 3, 2, 4, 1

5.1.
- (a) (iii) *Batagur Kachuga*
- (b) (i) 1 and 3
- (c) (iv) 10%
- (d) (iii) option 4
- (e) (ii) the conservation of nature
- (f) (i) 2 and 3
- (g) (i) China
- (h) (iv) All of these
- (i) (ii) 8 conservation groups
- (j) (ii) comprising
- (k) (i) 1, 2, 4, 3

6.1.
- (a) (ii) it is a lucrative business
- (b) (ii) 2 and 3
- (c) (iii) both (i) and (ii)
- (d) (iv) option 4
- (e) (ii) a $10 million prize
- (f) (iv) 2 and 4
- (g) (i) 50 miles
- (h) (iii) to $ 10,000 or even $5000
- (i) (iv) All of these
- (j) (ii) lucrative
- (k) (ii) 3,1,4,2

7.1.
- (a) (iv) Indian society
- (b) (ii) 3, 1, 4, 2
- (c) (ii) 61.7%
- (d) (i) construction
- (e) (ii) 1992
- (f) (i) life threatening occupation
- (g) (iii) year 2011
- (h) (iii) from three months to one year
- (i) (iv) 1938
- (j) (ii) ubiquitous
- (k) (iii) 1, 3, 4

4. Notice Writing

1. **A notice is:**
   (a) A letter
   (b) An information for large audience
   (c) A private information for a person
   (d) All of these
2. **The first thing written in a notice is:**
   (a) Name of the writer
   (b) Name of the organisation
   (c) Heading/ Title
   (d) Date
3. **Which of the following pronoun should be avoided in a notice:**
   (a) Me   (b) I
   (c) My   (d) All of these
4. **Notices are written for:**
   (a) An event   (b) A programme
   (c) A lost property (d) All of these
5. **One of the following is not a part of the notice:**
   (a) Body   (b) Date
   (c) Greetings   (d) Heading
6. **The word "Notice" is written in:**
   (a) Cursive   (b) Block letter
   (c) Calligraphy   (d) All of these
7. **The last thing written in a notice is:**
   (a) Name of the writer
   (b) Signature of the writer
   (c) Designation of the writer
   (d) Address of the writer
8. **Which among these is not a good place to display a notice?**
   (a) A school bulletin board
   (b) Outside auditoriums
   (c) Lobbies of residential complexes
   (d) Home
9. **In a notice the name is written as:**
   (a) Initials   (b) Full name
   (c) Only the first name (d) Only the last name
10. **The notice should be written in:**
    (a) 1 paragraph
    (b) 2 paragraph
    (c) 3 paragraph
    (d) As many paragraphs as required
11. **A Notice must answer which questions:**
    (a) What   (b) Where
    (c) When   (d) All of these
12. **Whose name should be written in the end of the notice?**
    (a) Authorised person (b) Invitees
    (c) Receiver   (d) Nobody's
13. **Notice should be written inside a box.**
    (a) Maybe   (b) May not be
    (c) Yes   (d) No
14. **Which among the following is not an element of a notice?**
    (a) Time   (b) Address of the sender
    (c) Catchy heading (d) Venue
15.

> School Fitness Centre
> NOTICE
> 12th February, 20XX
> Time Change
> From the end of August, the fitness centre will be closed during the weekends and evenings.
> Raj
> The Secretary

The school fitness centre will:
(a) Change its opening hours at the end of August.
(b) Open again to students at the end of August.
(c) Have shorter opening hours until the end of August.
(d) Have shorter opening hours at the end of August.

Answers

1. (b) An information for large audience
2. (b) Name of the organisation
3. (d) All of these
4. (d) All of these
5. (c) Greetings
6. (b) Block letter
7. (c) Designation of the writer
8. (d) Home
9. (b) Full name
10. (a) 1 paragraph
11. (d) All of these
12. (a) Authorised person
13. (c) Yes
14. (b) Address of the sender
15. (a) Change its opening hours at the end of August.

The format of Notice Writing has not been given by the Board. In case of any updation, the same will reflect on our website.

5. Advertisements

1. How many types of advertisements are there?
   (a) 3 (b) 4
   (c) 6 (d) 2

2. The advertisement should be written in:
   (a) 1 paragraph
   (b) 2 paragraph
   (c) 3 paragraph
   (d) As many paragraphs as required

3. The advertisement should have:
   (a) short-catchy phrases (b) very formal manner
   (c) a informal manner (d) humour

4. Arrange the correct order of "SITUATION VACANT" Advertisement.
   (i) Wanted software engineer for Ivy Software Solutions, a leading name in computers. Candidate should possess a Master's Degree in Computer Software Programming and at least 3 years experience with a known computer concern.
   (ii) Remuneration no constraint for suitable candidate.
   (iii) Apply with detailed resume within ten days to General Manager, Ivy Software Solutions, Agra Cantt, Agra. Phone 24236709, email id- generalmanager@gmail.com.
   (iv) SITUATION VACANT
       (a) i-ii-iii-iv (b) ii-iii-i-iv
       (c) iv-iii-ii-i (d) iv-i-ii-iii

5. Arrange the correct order of "FOR PURCHASE OF VEHICLE" Advertisement.
   (i) Wanted a Honda Motor cycle, 2018 or 2019 model, in excellent condition, not more than 60,000km run, average around 80-90 km per litre, complete documents.
   (ii) Interested parties to contact: S.K. Joshi-30-C, Janakpuri, New Delhi:9876543210
   (iii) Insurance paid for current year. Price not exceed ₹26,000.
   (iv) FOR PURCHASE
       (a) i-ii-iii-iv (b) iv-i-iii-ii
       (c) iv-iii-ii-i (d) ii-iii-iv-i

6. Arrange the correct order of "SALE OF VEHICLE" Advertisement.
   (i) Contact Mr.Khanna: 987612340
   (ii) Recently serviced, insurance for current year done. Expected Price not below 2.40 lacs
   (iii) FOR SALE
   (iv) Available White Maruti Swift Dzire,2018 Model in excellent working condition, 65,000 km run average 1.2km/litre, self-driven, sparingly used, music system Panasonic, black leather seat covers, all other accessories intact.
       (a) i-ii-iii-iv (b) iv-iii-ii-i
       (c) iii-iv-ii-i (d) ii-iii-i-iv

7. Arrange the correct order of "SALE OF PROPERTY" Advertisement.
   (i) Available first floor DDA flat at Ashok Nagar, two bedrooms with attached bathroom, modular kitchen, drawing/dinning with full interiors, two balconies and car parking, North/park facing,
   (ii) Located near main market, metro station at walking distance. Price negotiable.
   (iii) FOR SALE
   (iv) Interested parties contact: Jitesh Khanna, Ph.: 9999335700
       (a) i-iii-iv-ii (b) iii-i-ii-iv
       (c) iv-ii-iii-i (d) i-iii-ii-iv

8. Wanted two young and dynamic Sales Executives for our marketing division. Minimum Qualifications – M. Pharma. Work experience of at least 5 years. Proficiency in English, impressive personality & ready to travel. Good salary and other perks. Apply in confidence with complete resume till 15 March 2013 to Manager, Herbal India 6 B/247, Ashok Vihar, New Delhi-110070.

   The given advertisement is a _____ type of advertisement.
   (a) Situation Vacant (b) Educational
   (c) Sale and Purchase (d) Matrimonial

9. IIFL announces the commencement of its short-term courses in French, Chinese, Japanese, Spanish, etc. Duration – 6 months. Eligibility – Senior Secondary. Excellent faculty. Computerised training. Incentives for early birds. Ten per cent of seats free. Send in your application by the 16th May 20XX or Contact Secretary, Phone 24236709.

   The given advertisement is a _____ type of advertisement.
   (a) Situation Vacant (b) Educational
   (c) Sale and Purchase (d) Matrimonial

10. Alliance invited for a very handsome, tall and cultured IT professional 29 years, 180 cm tall NRI settled in London as CEO of a reputed firm. Exceptionally beautiful, highly educated and cultured girl between 21 and 25 and at least 5'4" tall. Only status Punjabi families. Box 867 B, The Times of India, New Delhi.

    The given advertisement is a _____ type of advertisement.

    (a) Situation Vacant (b) Educational
    (c) Sale and Purchase (d) Matrimonial

11. Lost black leather purse in DTC bus (route no. 315), while travelling between Lucknow Road and Red Fort. Besides cash, it contains some very important bills and receipts. The finder will be suitably rewarded. Please contact Anil Sood, B-67, Lucknow Road, New Delhi or Phone 27618456.

    (a) Situation Vacant (b) Educational
    (c) Sale and Purchase (d) Lost and Found

12. Available Maruti 800 DX, 2000 Model in excellent working condition. White scratchless, self driven, sparingly used. Average 18 km a liter. All accessories intact. Expected Price not below ₹ 1.40 lacs. Contact. Mr. Malhotra, 24673289.

    The given advertisement is a _____ type of advertisement.

    (a) Situation Vacant (b) Educational
    (c) Sale and Purchase (d) Lost and Found

13. Coal India, New Delhi wants suitable accommodation on rent to be used as a guest house. Minimum carpet area of 2500 sq. ft. in a posh South Delhi area preferred. Interested parties may please contact 5, Balu, G.M. Coal India, 35 Asaf Ali Road, New Delhi or Phone: 22524876.

    The given advertisement is a _____ type of advertisement.

    (a) Situation Vacant
    (b) Accommodation wanted
    (c) Sale and Purchase
    (d) Lost and Found

14. Required one accountant and two office assistants for a renowned firm. Minimum qualification: Bachelor's degree in commerce and work experience of minimum one year. Remuneration—best in the industry. Interested candidates can send their CVs by courier/speed post to Greenland Enterprises Ltd, 4436/16, Daryaganj, Delhi-110006. Contact Krishna, Secretary, Mobile no 98111XXXXX.

    The given advertisement is a _____ type of advertisement.

    (a) Situation Vacant
    (b) Accommodation wanted
    (c) Sale and Purchase
    (d) Lost and Found

15. What is missing in the given advertisement?

Available For Rent
Newly constructed flat on M.G. Road with 24 hrs. water and electricity back-up facility. Has two bedrooms with attached bathrooms, one huge drawing-cum-dining. Expected rent-Rs. 24,000 p.m. Company lease only. Contact: Mohan, Jayanagar, Bengaluru.

    (a) Date
    (b) Contact number
    (c) Category of advertisement
    (d) Address

Answers

1. (d) 2
2. (a) 1 paragraph
3. (a) short-catchy phrases
4. (d) iv-i-ii-iii
5. (b) iv-i-iii-ii
6. (c) iii-iv-ii-i
7. (b) iii-i-ii-iv
8. (a) Situation Vacant
9. (b) Educational
10. (d) Matrimonial
11. (d) Lost and Found
12. (c) Sale and Purchase
13. (b) Accommodation wanted
14. (a) Situation Vacant
15. (b) Contact number

The format of Advertisements has not been given by the Board. In case of any updation, the same will reflect on our website.

6. Letter Writing

1. What is the purpose of writing a letter to the editor?
   (a) To express one's request
   (b) To express one's opinion or give comment on a current issue
   (c) To give warning about the issue
   (d) To inform the readers about a certain issue

2. Which of the following is the correct tone for letter to the editor?
   (a) personal
   (b) formal
   (c) amusing
   (d) serious

3. How should we address the audience of the letter?
   (a) Dear Sir/Madam or Dear Editor,
   (b) To The Editor,
   (c) Sir/Madam,
   (d) To Whom it may Concern

4. One of the main parts of the letter that includes the address and date. In some cases, it is okay to just write the date.
   (a) Signature
   (b) Salutation/Greeting
   (c) Body
   (d) Heading

5. It is the main text of your letter.
   (a) Closing
   (b) Signature
   (c) Heading
   (d) Body

6. Your letter to an editor should always include _____.
   (a) A long opening paragraph
   (b) A brief opening paragraph which introduces your reason of writing
   (c) Bullet points with main reason for writing
   (d) A polite opening asking about the health.

7. The reason with which you write a letter to an editor is:
   (a) Purpose
   (b) Content
   (c) Audience
   (d) Format

8. It is one of the main part of a letter that includes a short capitalised expression such as 'sincerely' of 'love' and is followed by a comma.
   (a) Salutation
   (b) Closing
   (c) Date
   (d) Body

9. This is what you sign your name beginning directly after the closing?
   (a) Closing
   (b) Signature
   (c) Body
   (d) Salutation

10. The layout of a letter to an editor is:
    (a) Purpose
    (b) Content
    (c) Audience
    (d) Format

11. The topic of a letter to an editor is:
    (a) Purpose
    (b) Content
    (c) Audience
    (d) Format

12. A _____ is a greeting used in a letter.
    (a) date
    (b) closing
    (c) salutations
    (d) body

13. 33, Jal Vihar,
    Wazirabad,
    New Delhi–33
    The Editor,
    Hindustan Times,
    New Delhi.

    Subject: Need for people's movement for the clean Yamuna

    Dear Editor,

    I am Radha G member of NGO AWAAZ. I am writing to you in order to highlight the deteriorating condition of the river Yamuna.

    The city of Delhi is getting contaminated water from the river Yamuna. The residents are to be blamed for this. They pollute the river with garbage, sewage and filth. The river water is full of bacteria, plastic, chemicals and other waste materials. It is unfit for consumption.

    The people have been demanding a Water Treatment Plant. The authorities have not yet responded to the repeated requests.

    I request you to highlight the problem in your newspaper and arouse public interest. We all need to get together in order to get the plant set up in the area.

    What is missing in the given letter?
    (a) Body
    (b) Salutations
    (c) Date
    (d) Closing

14. I am Sakshi/ Sameer, a concerned resident of the city of Mohali. I am writing you this letter to draw your attention towards the problem of growing invasion of slums on the roadsides of Mohali. Since the last few months, slums have been multiplying in places like footpaths, empty parks, and market areas. Slums on the roadside create difficulty in the movement of traffic and cause unnecessary jams. The living conditions are also risky for those living so close to speedily passing vehicles. I request you to publish my grievance in the columns of your newspaper. This would help in making the city authorities aware of the problems faced by the city folks and they will be required to take taking necessary actions for public welfare.

What is the purpose of the given letter?
(a) Opinion on issues of public interest
(b) Giving suggestions
(c) Complaint
(d) Request

15. Shobha
4, Gandhinagar
Mumbai.

Dated: 15th March 20XX

The Editor
Hindustan News
Mumbai.

Respected Ma'am/ Sir

Through the columns of your esteemed newspaper, I would like to draw people's attention towards the valiant service extended by the cleanliness and sanitation workers of our country during the COVID-19 outbreak.

Nowadays, with a pandemic on the rise, cleanliness and hygiene has become one of our major concern. In the times when we all are sitting safely at our homes, these brave people have taken the responsibility of keeping our hospitals, roads and streets clean. They are bravely facing the risks and are doing their jobs in a dedicated manner. We should all be thankful for their precious service.

I request you to publish my letter in your newspaper so that the people realise the importance of cleanliness workers in our society and give them the respect they rightly deserve.

Yours faithfully

Manu/ Meena

What is the missing part in the given letter to an editor?
(a) Salutations   (b) Subject
(c) Closing   (d) Date

Answers

1. (b) To express one's opinion or give comment on a current issue
2. (b) formal
3. (a) Dear Sir/Madam or Dear Editor,
4. (d) Heading
5. (d) Body
6. (b) A brief opening paragraph which introduces your reason of writing
7. (a) Purpose
8. (b) Closing
9. (b) Signature
10. (d) Format
11. (b) Content
12. (c) salutations
13. (d) Closing
14. (a) Opinion on issues of public interest
15. (b) Subject

The format of Letter Writing has not been given by the Board. In case of any updation, the same will reflect on our website.

7. Article Writing

1. You can make your article more interesting by _____.
   (a) Writing long sentences the entire time.
   (b) Writing short sentences.
   (c) asking rhetorical questions
   (d) using really formal language

2. Subheadings are useful in an article because:
   (a) They help in organising ideas
   (b) They keep things fresh
   (c) They don't do anything useful
   (d) They make the article attractive

3. What should you include in your article?
   (a) Only your opinion
   (b) At least 6 rhetorical questions
   (c) A range of different techniques to argue or persuade
   (d) Lots of technical language and jargon

4. Why should the last paragraph make some reference to the opening paragraph?
   (a) To make it look neater
   (b) It should not make reference
   (c) To confuse the reader
   (d) To draw the points together and conclude

5. An article needs a headline:
   (a) Only if you can think of one
   (b) To be catchy and encourage people to read it
   (c) To be in capital letters and bold
   (d) To be long and detailed

6. What is the first part of an article?
   (a) Writer's name   (b) Heading
   (c) Conclusion   (d) Body

7. In this part of the article you can find the author's opinion.
   (a) Heading   (b) Writer's name
   (c) Body   (d) Conclusion

8. Here you will find the main part of the article.
   (a) Heading   (b) Body
   (c) Conclusion   (d) Opinion

9. The main idea of an article is for it to be published.
   (a) True
   (b) False
   (c) It is to spread the message and create awareness
   (d) To make the writer famous

10. Choose the motive to write an article.
    (a) Give advice
    (b) Summary of a movie
    (c) Invite the reader to an event
    (d) None of the above

11. In the body of the article, you should elaborate the topic and describe it:
    (a) May be   (b) May not be
    (c) Definitely   (d) Never

12. How do statistics and facts help in article?
    (a) They give the reader a chance to do some Math.
    (b) They fill up the article so that it's not too short.
    (c) They give extra information and help the reader understand what happened.
    (d) Statistics and Facts are fun- so it's good to have them in articles.

13. What is the one way to end an article?
    (a) Leave the reader with a question
    (b) Write "The End" after the last sentence
    (c) Write "Thank you" after the last sentence
    (d) An article can end with a personal statement from the writer.

14. The invention of mobile phones is one of the major advancements in human history. They have impacted the way people communicate with each other. They have created an easier platform for the spread of information from one person to another despite distances. The advantages of the mobile phones are many. However, the mobile also has its disadvantages. Adolescents and teenagers are usually in a distracted state because of mobile phones. They are seen talking and texting at all places even while on the road, while driving and even during classes. This can be detrimental as it may cause accidents and also prevent them from reaching their potential in academics. Anti-social elements are known to use mobiles for nefarious activities and terrorist acts. Research has also shown that overuse of mobile phones may cause harm to our body. Certain self-control measures over the use of mobiles will help us use them for our benefit and reduce their harmful effects.

    What is missing in the given article?
    (a) Heading   (b) Writer's name
    (c) Both (a) and (b) (d) None of these

15. In article writing a by-line is_____.
(a) An extra piece of information
(b) The name of the writer
(c) Pointless
(d) Part of a goal line

Answers

1. (c) asking rhetorical questions
2. (a) They help in organising ideas
3. (c) A range of different techniques to argue or persuade
4. (d) To draw the points together and conclude
5. (b) To be catchy and encourage people to read it
6. (b) Heading
7. (d) Conclusion
8. (b) Body
9. (c) It is to spread the message and create awareness
10. (a) Give advice
11. (c) Definitely
12. (c) They give extra information and help the reader understand what happened.
13. (d) An article can end with a personal statement from the writer.
14. (c) Both (a) and (b)
15. (b) The name of the writer

The format of Article Writing has not been given by the Board. In case of any updation, the same will reflect on our website.

Flamingo-Prose

1. The Last Lesson
—Alphonse Daudet

Read the extracts given below and answer the questions that follow.

1. *Reading the bulletin, called after me, "Don't go so fast, bub; you'll get to your school in plenty of time!" I thought he was making fun of me and reached M. Hamel's little garden all out of breath.*

   (a) Who was called 'bub'?
   - (i) M. Hamel
   - (ii) villagers
   - (iii) Franz
   - (iv) postmaster

   (b) Why was the narrator in a hurry?
   - (i) he was late to school
   - (ii) his teacher has called him immediately
   - (iii) his teacher was going away and he wanted to him one last time
   - (iv) his friends were waiting for him in school

   (c) Identify the tone in which the speaker said the words, "Don't go so fast, bub; you'll get to your school in plenty of time!"?
   - (i) sarcastic
   - (ii) humorous
   - (iii) depressive
   - (iv) cheerful

   (d) M. Hamel taught the children............................
   - (i) German
   - (ii) French
   - (iii) Russian
   - (iv) English

2. *While I was wondering about it all, M. Hamel mounted his chair, and, in the same grave and gentle tone which he had used to me, said, "My children, this is the last lesson I shall give you. The order has come from Berlin to teach only German in the schools of Alsace and Lorraine. The new master comes tomorrow. This is your last French lesson. I want you to be very attentive."*

   (a) What was the tone of M.Hamel when he was addressing his students?
   - (i) cheerful
   - (ii) excited
   - (iii) somber
   - (iv) angry

   (b) The grave and gentle tone in which M. Hamel spoke after getting the orders from Berlin was due to......
   - (i) his patriotic feeling for his country
   - (ii) his love for his mother tongue
   - (iii) the grief of not being able to teach French in future
   - (iv) All of these

   (c) When would Mr. Hamel leave?
   - (i) the same day
   - (ii) next day
   - (iii) after one week
   - (iv) after one month

   (d) What did he want from the students?
   - (i) to give him a farewell
   - (ii) to oppose the orders
   - (iii) to be attentive
   - (iv) to leave the school

3. *Poor man! It was in honour of this last lesson that he had put on his fine Sunday clothes, and now I understood why the old men of the village were sitting there in the back of the room. It was because they were sorry, too, that they had not gone to school more. It was their way of thanking our master for his forty years of faithful service and of showing their respect for the country that was theirs no more.*

   (a) Who was called 'Poor man'?
   - (i) Hauser
   - (ii) the Frenchman
   - (iii) M. Hamel
   - (iv) blacksmith

   (b) What kind of feelings were expressed by the villagers when they sat for the last class?
   - (i) remorseful
   - (ii) joyful
   - (iii) anxious
   - (iv) confused

   (c) Why did the old men come for the class?
   - (i) to honour the Hamel's services
   - (ii) to learn the French last time
   - (iii) to see the commotion in the school
   - (iv) to bid farewell to the teacher

   (d) Why did the country belong to them no more?
   - (i) because they were leaving the country
   - (ii) because Germans had taken over their country
   - (iii) because it was destroyed in the war
   - (iv) because their country was merging into some other country

4. *I heard M. Hamel say to me, "I won't scold you, little Franz; you must feel bad enough. See how it is! Everyday we have said to ourselves, 'Bah! I've plenty of time. I'll learn it tomorrow.' And now you see where we've come out. Ah, that's the great trouble with Alsace; she puts off learning till tomorrow.*

   (a) Why was M. Hamel not angry with Franz?
   - (i) as it was Hamel's last lesson
   - (ii) as it was Franz's last lesson
   - (iii) as it was the last lesson in French
   - (iv) as it was last day of school

   (b) What impression do you form of M. Hamel as a teacher when he says, "I won't scold you, little Franz; you must feel bad enough"?
   1. He is experienced
   2. He is exemplary
   3. He is strict
   4. He is gentle

     (i)   1, 2, 4   (ii) 2, 3, 4
     (iii) 1, 4, 3   (iv) all of these
   (c) What does Hamel mean by 'ourselves'?
     (i)   teachers   (ii) children
     (iii) villagers   (iv) French people
   (d) What was the problem with Alsace? Where they all have come out?
     (i)   German would be taught to them from then onwards
     (ii) they would never be able to learn French
     (iii) it was their last lesson in French
     (iv) all of these

5. *Then, from one thing to another, M. Hamel went on to talk of the French language, saying that it was the most beautiful language in the world — the clearest, the most logical; that we must guard it among us and never forget it, because when a people are enslaved, as long as they hold fast to their language it is as if they had the key to their prison. Then he opened a grammar and read us our lesson. I was amazed to see how well I understood it. All he said seemed so easy, so easy! I think, too, that I had never listened so carefully, and that he had never explained everything with so much patience.*
   (a) What is M. Hamel's language/mother tongue?
     (i)   French   (ii) German
     (iii) English   (iv) Spanish
   (b) Identify the literary device in 'from one thing to another'.
     (i)   metaphor   (ii) personification
     (iii) allusion   (iv) hyperbole
   (c) What is Hamel asking the people to do for their language?
     (i)   forget their language
     (ii) begin learning German
     (iii) guard their language
     (iv) learn their language
   (d) How could the enslaved people have the key to the prison?
     (i)   if they ask the prisoner for it
     (ii) if they do not leave their language
     (iii) if they snatch the key
     (iv) if they do not leave their country

6. Who is the author of 'The Last Lesson'?
   (a) Jane Austen
   (b) Rabindranath Tagore
   (c) Alphonse Daudet
   (d) None of the above

7. "The Last Lesson" story was written in which year?
   (a) 1869 - 1870   (b) 1870 - 1871
   (c) 1872- 1873   (d) 1870 - 1872

8. The story 'The Last Lesson' highlights which human tendency?
   (a) Male Chauvinism (b) Procrastination
   (c) Courage   (d) Cowardice

9. What does 'The Last Lesson' symbolize?
   (a) Loss
   (b) Loss of freedom
   (c) Loss of language
   (d) Loss of language and freedom

10. What does 'The Last Lesson' signify?
    (a) change of power   (b) change of Government
    (c) change in life   (d) change of teachers

11. What do the marching soldiers under the windows represent?
    (a) The Dawn of Prussia in the defeat of French people
    (b) The defeat of Prussia
    (c) The victory of French
    (d) None of these

12. What was Franz expected to be prepared for at school that day?
    (a) song   (b) dance
    (c) essay writing   (d) participles

13. What does the expression "in great dread of scolding" mean?
    (a) to be happy about it
    (b) very badly scared of scolding
    (c) to be indifferent
    (d) None of these

14. For the last two years, where did all the bad news come from?
    (a) The Bulletin Board (b) Town Hall
    (c) School   (d) M. Hamel's House

15. Don't go so fast, you will get to your school in plenty of time means _____.
    (a) getting late   (b) very early
    (c) not early   (d) early enough

16. From where did the orders come to teach only German in the districts of Alsace and Lorraine?
    (a) France   (b) Lorraine
    (c) Berlin   (d) Germany

17. Which language would the students study from the next day?
    (a) English   (b) German
    (c) French   (d) Spanish

18. What was Franz banking on to enter the class as he was late?
    (a) M.Hamel's teaching on the blackboard
    (b) commotion in the class
    (c) Hauser helping him sneak in
    (d) to quietly walk in when everyone was preoccupied with participles

19. What changed Franz's feelings about M.Hamel and school?
    (a) Police Patrolling
    (b) Orders from Berlin
    (c) Strict words from M. Hamel
    (d) old Primer

20. Franz looked for opportunities to skip school to do what?
    (a) work on mills   (b) go fishing
    (c) water the plants   (d) collect birds eggs

21. Hamel is introduced as a ruler-wielding teacher. This demonstrates that:
    (a) he is concerned
    (b) he is adamant
    (c) he is unfeeling
    (d) he is a hard taskmaster
22. Why was Franz surprised?
    (a) because of village elders
    (b) because of police patrolling
    (c) because of students' behaviour
    (d) because of M.Hamel's kind and polite behaviour
23. What did Hauser bring?
    (a) sweets   (b) children
    (c) friends   (d) old primer
24. For how many years did M. Hamel serve the school?
    (a) 20 years   (b) 35 years
    (c) 30 years   (d) 40 years
25. Why did the villagers come to meet M. Hamel in the school?
    (a) to complain   (b) to say goodbye
    (c) to gossip   (d) to show gratitude
26. What was M. Hamel wearing on the day of 'The Last Lesson'?
    (a) black silk cap (b) frilled shirt
    (c) green coat   (d) all of these
27. What did Mr. Hamel bring for his class on his last day in the school?
    (a) new pens   (b) new notebooks
    (c) new notebooks   (d) story books
28. Expression 'Thunder Clap" in the lesson means _____.
    (a) loud but not clear
    (b) loud and clear
    (c) startling and unexpected
    (d) unpleasant
29. Why was Franz feeling regretful and sad?
    (a) for reaching late
    (b) for not learning participles
    (c) for change of the Government
    (d) for not learning his mother tongue
30. Franz thinks- will they make them sing in German-even the pigeons? What could this mean?
    (a) German would use brutal force over everyone
    (b) harsh orders will be passed
    (c) when people are deprived of their essence even the surroundings are affected.
    (d) the Germans will rob France of its language.
31. Why did Hamel blame himself?
    (a) not having taught them enough French
    (b) not being strict
    (c) giving students a holiday at times
    (d) not being responsible
32. What does M. Hamel's motionless posture reflect?
    (a) the school is dismissed
    (b) sense of finality
    (c) changing order of life
    (d) feeling of nostalgia
33. Why does the author urge the reader to respect his language?
    (a) It is what makes you respect your countrymen.
    (b) It is the key to freedom.
    (c) You can express yourself.
    (d) It is unique and reflects literature and art.
34. 'Vive la France' became emotional evidence of M. Hamel's?
    (a) sadness and patriotism
    (b) finality and depression
    (c) nostalgia and emotional outburst
    (d) love for the school and teaching as a profession
35. What is the moral that the Alphonse Daudet wants to bring out?
    (a) not to put off things that one can do that day
    (b) old order changed to new
    (c) one should accept everything that happens
    (d) teachers should be respected
36. _____ asked Franz not to hurry to school.
    (a) Old Hauser
    (b) Former Mayor
    (c) Former Postmaster
    (d) Blacksmith Watcher
37. Franz find the atmosphere outside _____ as compared to 'learning rules of participles'.
    (a) boring   (b) attractive
    (c) monotonous   (d) annoying
38. _____ occupied the back benches in the class.
    (a) Weak students
    (b) Teachers
    (c) Monitors of the class
    (d) Village elders
39. M.Hamel blamed _____ for not sending students to school.
    (a) parents   (b) friends
    (c) teachers   (d) watchman
40. Franz was able to understand the grammar lesson easily because he was _____. [NCERT]
    (a) receptive   (b) appreciative
    (c) introspective (d) competitive

Find the correct statement in the following:

41. (i) For the last two years — all the good news come from there.
    (ii) Usually when school began — there was quietness.
    (iii) What a thunderclap — these words to me!
    (iv) It was in the honour of this first lesson — that he had put on his fine Sunday clothes.
42. (i) I started for school very early that morning — and was in a great dread of scolding.
    (ii) In the open field back of the sawmill — the Russian soldiers were drilling.
    (iii) Through the window — I saw my classmates already left.
    (iv) After the grammar — we had a lesson in writing.

Rearrange the sentences in the correct sequence and choose the correct option :

43. (i) While I was thinking of all this, I heard my name called.
    (ii) When I passed the town hall there was a crowd in front of the bulletin- board.
    (iii) All at once the church-clock struck twelve.
    (iv) I jumped over the bench and sat down at my desk.
    Options:
    (a) (ii)-(iv)-(i)-(iii) (b) (iii)-(i)-(ii)-(iv)
    (c) (iv)-(ii)-(i)-(iii) (d) (ii)-(i)-(iv)-(iii)

44. (i) It was their way of thanking our master for his forty years of faithful service.
    (ii) The order has come from Berlin to teach only German in the schools of Alsace and Lorraine.
    (iii) The only sound was the scratching of the pens over the paper.
    (iv) But he had the courage to hear every lesson to the last.
    Options:
    (a) (iii)-(i)-(ii)-(iv) (b) (ii)-(i)-(iv)-(iii)
    (c) (ii)-(iv)-(i)-(iii) (d) (ii)-(i)-(iii)-(iv)

45. **Assertion:** Franz was in great terror of scolding by his teacher.
    Reason: He lied to him about his parents.
    (i) Both assertion and reason are correct and reason is the correct explanation of assertion.
    (ii) Both assertion and reason are correct but reason is not the correct explanation of assertion.
    (iii) Assertion is true and reason is false
    (iv) Assertion is false and reason is true.

46. **Assertion:** There was a crowd in front of the bulletin-board at the town hall.
    Reason: There was an order from the commanding officer.
    (i) Both assertion and reason are correct and reason is the correct explanation of assertion.
    (ii) Both assertion and reason are correct but reason is not the correct explanation of assertion.
    (iii) Assertion is true and reason is false.
    (iv) Assertion is false and reason is true.

47. **Assertion:** Franz saw M. Hamel walking up and down with his terrible iron ruler.
    Reason: M. Hamel was angry with Franz for being late.
    (i) Both assertion and reason are correct and reason is the correct explanation of assertion.
    (ii) Both assertion and reason are correct but reason is not the correct explanation of assertion.
    (iii) Assertion is true and reason is false.
    (iv) Assertion is false and reason is true.

48. **Assertion:** M. Hamel had been wearing beautiful green coat, frilled shirt and silk cap.
    Reason: It was his last day in the school.
    (i) Both assertion and reason are correct and reason is the correct explanation of assertion.
    (ii) Both assertion and reason are correct but reason is not the correct explanation of assertion.
    (iii) Assertion is true and reason is false.
    (iv) Assertion is false and reason is true.

49. **Assertion:** Young men of the village were sitting in the back of the classroom.
    Reason: They were sorry because they had not gone to school.
    (i) Both assertion and reason are correct and reason is the correct explanation of assertion.
    (ii) Both assertion and reason are correct but reason is not the correct explanation of assertion.
    (iii) Assertion is true and reason is false.
    (iv) Assertion is false and reason is true.

2. Lost Spring
–Anees Jung

Read the extracts given below and answer the questions that follow.

1. *My acquaintance with the barefoot ragpickers leads me to Seemapuri, a place on the periphery of Delhi yet miles away from it, metaphorically. Those who live here are squatters who came from Bangladesh back in 1971. Saheb's family is among them. Seemapuri was then a wilderness. It still is, but it is no longer empty. In structures of mud, with roofs of tin and tarpaulin, devoid of sewage, drainage or running water, live 10,000 ragpickers. They have lived here for more than thirty years without an identity, without permits but with ration cards that get their names on voters' lists and enable them to buy grain. Food is more important for survival than an identity.*

   (a) **How did the author reach Seemapuri?**
       (i) obliged by his duty
       (ii) by official orders
       (iii) by his contact with rag pickers
       (iv) because of his friend's work

   (b) **What does the phrase "devoid of sewage, drainage or running water" help us understand about the condition of the ragpickers?**
       (i) They live in places unfit for human living
       (ii) They have made Seemapuri their home
       (iii) The ragpickers live near sewage pipes
       (iv) The ragpickers strive for their livelihood

   (c) **Which people came to reside in Seemapuri?**
       (i) refugees from Bangladesh
       (ii) refugees from Punjab
       (iii) refugees from Pakistan
       (iv) refugees from Kashmir

   (d) **How was Seemapuri earlier?**
       (i) densely populated
       (ii) uninhabited
       (iii) a sacred place
       (iv) forest area

2. *Food is more important for survival than an identity. "If at the end of the day we can feed our families and go to bed without an aching stomach, we would rather live here than in the fields that gave us no grain," say a group of women in tattered saris when I ask them why they left their beautiful land of green fields and rivers. Wherever they find food, they pitch their tents that become transit homes. Children grow up in them, becoming partners in survival. And survival in Seemapuri means rag-picking. Through the years, it has acquired the proportions of a fine art. Garbage to them is gold. It is their daily bread, a roof over their heads, even if it is a leaking roof. But for a child it is even more.*

   (a) The phrase 'transit homes' refer to the dwellings that are:
   - (i) unhygienic
   - (ii) inadequate
   - (iii) fragile
   - (iv) temporary

   (b) Identify the figure of speech used in the sentence "Garbage to them is gold".
   - (i) hyperbole
   - (ii) simile
   - (iii) synecdoche
   - (iv) personification

   (c) Choose the term which best matches the statement 'Food is more important for survival than an identity"?
   - (i) immorality
   - (ii) necessity
   - (iii) obligation
   - (iv) ambition

   (d) What does 'acquired the proportions of a fine art' mean?
   - (i) rag-picking has regained its lost status.
   - (ii) a segment of ragpickers are skilled in fine arts
   - (iii) rag-picking has attained the position of a skill.
   - (iv) only a few people are experts in rag-picking.

3. *When the older man enters, she gently withdraws behind the broken wall and brings her veil closer to her face. As custom demands, daughters-in-law must veil their faces before male elders. In this case the elder is an impoverished bangle maker. Despite long years of hard labour, first as a tailor, then a bangle maker, he has failed to renovate a house, send his two sons to school. All he has managed to do is teach them what he knows — the art of making bangles.*

   (a) Who is the old man?
   - (i) Mukesh's grandfather
   - (ii) Mukesh's father
   - (iii) a villager
   - (iv) village head

   (b) What was the woman's gesture when the old man entered?
   - (i) she hid behind the wall
   - (ii) she went out of the house
   - (iii) she went inside the kitchen
   - (iv) she brought him a cup of tea

   (c) The phrase 'impoverished bangle maker' here refers to the person who was ……………
   - (i) very old
   - (ii) penniless
   - (iii) wealthy enough
   - (iv) owner of the house

   (d) The elder was not able to ………………
   - (i) teach good lessons to his son
   - (ii) send his children to school
   - (iii) renovate his house
   - (iv) both (ii) and (iii)

4. *"It is his karam, his destiny," says Mukesh's grandmother, who has watched her own husband go blind with the dust from polishing the glass of bangles. "Can a god-given lineage ever be broken?" She implies. Born in the caste of bangle makers, they have seen nothing but bangles in the house, in the yard, in every other house, every other yard, every street in Firozabad.*

   (a) What has happened to Mukesh's grandfather?
   - (i) he suffered from asthma due to working in glass factory
   - (ii) he went blind with the dust of polishing bangles
   - (iii) he died due to suffocation in dingy cells of glass factory
   - (iv) he purchased the glass factory and became the owner

   (b) Identify the literary device in this statement 'for the children it is wrapped in wonder, for the elders it is a means of survival'.
   - (i) metaphor
   - (ii) antithesis
   - (iii) irony
   - (iv) hyperbole

   (c) Why didn't Mukesh's family stop working in glass factory?
   - (i) they were under heavy debt
   - (ii) they were born in the caste of bangle makers
   - (iii) it was their ancestral business
   - (iv) both (ii) and (iii)

   (d) Which city's every street is comprised bangle makers?
   - (i) Firozabad
   - (ii) Faridabad
   - (iii) Ghaziabad
   - (iv) Moradabad

5. *She still has bangles on her wrist, but no light in her eyes. "Ek waqt ser bhar khana bhi nahin khaya." she says, in a voice drained of joy. She has not enjoyed even one full meal in her entire lifetime-that's what she has reaped! Her husband, an old man with a flowing beard says, "I know nothing except bangles. All I have done is made a house for the family to live in." Hearing him one wonders if he has achieved what many have failed in their lifetime. He has a roof over his head! The cry of not having money to do anything except carry on the business of making bangles, not even enough to eat, rings in every home. The young men echo the lament of the elders. Little has moved with time, it seems in Firozabad, years of mind-numbing toil have killed all initiative and the ability to dream.* **[NCERT]**

   (a) 'She still has bangles on her wrist, but no light in her eyes.' This implies that:
   - (i) she is married but has lost the charm in her eyes.
   - (ii) she is a married woman who has lost her grace and beauty.
   - (iii) though she is married, her eyes are devoid of happiness.
   - (iv) she is a married woman who has lost her eyesight.

(b) 'He has a roof over his head!' The tone of the author is:
(i) pessimistic (ii) empathetic
(iii) sympathetic (iv) optimistic

(c) Choose the term which best matches the statement 'The young men echo the lament of their elders.'
(i) acceptance (ii) reflection
(iii) reiteration (iv) doubtfulness

(d) 'Years of mind-numbing toil have killed all initiative and the ability to dream'. This shows that:
(i) the bangle makers are exhausted yet they are enterprising and have dreams.
(ii) the drudgery of work has destroyed their willingness to improve their lot.
(iii) the daily grind has stolen the dreams of the bangle makers and made them dull.
(iv) the bangle makers have been working so hard that there's no time to dream.

6. Who is the author of the story, 'Lost Spring'?
(a) James Bond (b) Arundhati Roy
(c) Sudha Murthy (d) Anees Jung

7. Name the birthplace of the author.
(a) Mumbai (b) Delhi
(c) Kochi (d) Rourkela

8. What does the title 'Lost Spring' symbolise?
(a) Lost blooming childhood
(b) Autumn season
(c) Lost money
(d) Lost age

9. What does the author analyse in the story?
(a) Rich people
(b) Garbage
(c) Poor children and their exploitation
(d) Her works

10. According to the author, what was garbage for the parents?
(a) Means of entertainment
(b) Means of joy
(c) Means of sorrow
(d) Means of survival

11. According to the author, what was garbage for the children?
(a) Means of entertainment
(b) Means of timepass
(c) Means of playing
(d) A wonder

12. What is the meaning of Saheb-e-Alam?
(a) Owner (b) Rich man
(c) Poor man (d) Lord of the Universe

13. What was Saheb looking for?
(a) Eggs (b) Gold
(c) Coins (d) Toys

14. Saheb hailed from which place?
(a) Delhi
(b) Seemapuri
(c) Greenfields of Dhaka
(d) None of the above

15. What do the boys appear like to the author in the story?
(a) Morning crows (b) Evening crows
(c) Morning birds (d) Evening birds

16. Why did Saheb go through garbage dumps?
(a) To find a silver coin
(b) To find a rupee
(c) To find a ten rupee note
(d) All of these

17. Why is the author calling garbage as 'gold' in the story?
(a) Because of jewels in it
(b) Because of gems in it
(c) Because of gold in it
(d) Because of its encashment value

18. What excuse do the rag pickers give for not wearing chappals?
(a) Mothers don't give chappals to wear
(b) No interest in wearing chappals
(c) A tradition of not wearing chappals
(d) All of these

19. What did the man from Udipi pray for, when he was young?
(a) a pair of trousers
(b) a pair of shoes
(c) a few friends
(d) an opportunity to study in a school

20. What is the metaphorical symbol of Seemapuri in the lesson?
(a) Poverty (b) Exploitation
(c) Enjoyment (d) A little hell

21. Why did Saheb leave Dhaka?
(a) Because of lack of resources
(b) Because of lack of enough food
(c) Because of friends
(d) Because of parents

22. What are the reasons for the migration of people from villages to city in the lesson?
(a) Sweeping of houses and fields by storms
(b) No money
(c) Education and unemployment
(d) Safety

23. Where was Saheb employed?
(a) At a tea stall (b) At a saree shop
(c) At a jewellery shop (d) At a sweet shop

24. What change did Anees Jung see in Saheb when she saw him standing by the gate of the neighbourhood club?
(a) As if lost his freedom
(b) Lost ownership
(c) Lost joy
(d) All of these

25. What is Mukesh's dream?
    (a) To be a doctor   (b) To be a pilot
    (c) To be a rogue   (d) To be a motor-mechanic
26. Mukesh wants to learn to become a motor mechanic by:
    (a) finding a tutor
    (b) going to a garage to learn
    (c) by reading books
    (d) by joining a school
27. What efforts can help Mukesh materialise his dream of becoming a car driver?
    (a) Hard work
    (b) Going to garage
    (c) Guidance of his owner
    (d) All of these
28. How is Mukesh's attitude different from that of his family?
    (a) Being daring, firm and clear
    (b) Being a fighter
    (c) Being a coward
    (d) Not clear
29. Who employs the local families of Firozabad?
    (a) Bureaucrats
    (b) Merchants
    (c) Politicians
    (d) The glass blowing industry
30. What is the function of glass blowing industry?
    (a) To make windows
    (b) To make doors
    (c) To mould glass
    (d) To mould glass and make colourful bangles
31. What makes the working conditions of the children worst in the glass industry?
    (a) Dark dingy cells without light and air
    (b) Dazzling and sparking of welding light
    (c) High temperature
    (d) All of these
32. What compels the workers in bangle industry of Firozabad to poverty?
    (a) Caste and ancestral profession
    (b) *Karam* theory and society
    (c) Bureaucrats and politicians
    (d) All of these
33. Who are responsible for the poor condition of bangle makers in Firozabad?
    (a) Parents   (b) Society
    (c) Bureaucrats   (d) All of these
34. "One wonders if he has achieved what many have failed to achieve in their lifetime. He has a roof over his head"; these lines were said in reference to the condition of:
    (a) the elderly woman's old husband
    (b) Mukesh's father
    (c) the bangle factory owner
    (d) Mukesh's elder brother
35. What bothers the author most about the bangle makers?
    (a) the stigma of poverty and caste
    (b) the affluence of the landlords
    (c) the behaviour of the factory owners
    (d) the labour laws
36. According to the author, rag picking has become _____, over the years.
    (a) profession   (b) fine art
    (c) tradition   (d) culture
37. One day, Saheb was seen by the author, watching some young men playing _____.
    (a) cricket   (b) tennis
    (c) hockey   (d) soccer
38. Mukesh was a _____.
    (a) Student   (b) Worker
    (c) Bangle maker   (d) Ragpicker
39. Mukesh's father was _____ before he became a bangle-maker.
    (a) tailor   (b) carpenter
    (c) rag-picker   (d) Mason
40. The frail woman in Mukesh's house is his _____.
    (a) mother   (b) elder brother's wife
    (c) wife   (d) niece

Find the correct statement in the following:
41. (i) There were many storms — that swept away their fields and homes.
    (ii) I have seen men and women — walking barefoot, in cities, on village roads.
    (iii) Young boys like the son of the Principal — now wore shoes.
    (iv) Food is more important for survival — than the house.
42. (i) It is lack of money — but a tradition to stay barefoot.
    (ii) I remember a story a man — from Trichur once told me.
    (iii) They have lived here for more than thirty years — without an identity.
    (iv) Every other family in — Faridabad is engaged in making bangles.

Rearrange the sentences in the correct sequence and choose the correct option :
43. (i) On the ground, in large aluminium platters, are more chopped vegetables.
    (ii) He would stop briefly at the temple and pray for a pair of shoes.
    (iii) The young men echo the lament of their elders.
    (iv) Over the months, I have come to recognize each of them.
    Options:
    (a) (ii)-(iv)-(i)-(iii)   (b) (iii)-(i)-(ii)-(iv)
    (c) (iv)-(ii)-(i)-(iii)   (d) (ii)-(i)-(iv)-(iii)
44. (i) She still has bangles on her wrist, but no light in her eyes.
    (ii) As custom demands, daughters-in-law must veil their faces before male elders.

(iii) And daring is not part of his growing up.
(iv) Set amongst the green fields of Dhaka, his home is not even a distant memory.
Options:
(a) (ii)-(iv)-(i)-(iii) (b) (iii)-(i)-(ii)-(iv)
(c) (iv)-(ii)-(i)-(iii) (d) (ii)-(i)-(iv)-(iii)

45. **Assertion:** Every morning Saheb went out to look for gold in the garbage dump.
    Reason: There was a gold shop near the garbage dump.
    (i) Both assertion and reason are correct and reason is the correct explanation of assertion.
    (ii) Both assertion and reason are correct but reason is not the correct explanation of assertion.
    (iii) Assertion is true and reason is false.
    (iv) Assertion is false and reason is true.

46. **Assertion:** Saheb couldn't go to school.
    Reason: His parents didn't want him to go to school.
    (i) Both assertion and reason are correct and reason is the correct explanation of assertion.
    (ii) Both assertion and reason are correct but reason is not the correct explanation of assertion.
    (iii) Assertion is true and reason is false.
    (iv) Assertion is false and reason is true.

47. **Assertion:** The narrator had seen children walking barefoot in cities and on village roads.
    Reason: It is a tradition and not just lack of money.
    (i) Both assertion and reason are correct and reason is the correct explanation of assertion.
    (ii) Both assertion and reason are correct but reason is not the correct explanation of assertion.
    (iii) Assertion is true and reason is false.
    (iv) Assertion is false and reason is true.

48. **Assertion:** The rag pickers of Bangladesh left their land of green fields and rivers.
    Reason: They found jobs in the Seemapuri.
    (i) Both assertion and reason are correct and reason is the correct explanation of assertion.
    (ii) Both assertion and reason are correct but reason is not the correct explanation of assertion.
    (iii) Assertion is true and reason is false.
    (iv) Assertion is false and reason is true.

49. **Assertion:** Mukesh wanted to be a motor mechanic.
    Reason: His family was engaged in making glass bangles in Firozabad.
    (i) Both assertion and reason are correct and reason is the correct explanation of assertion.
    (ii) Both assertion and reason are correct but reason is not the correct explanation of assertion.
    (iii) Assertion is true and reason is false.
    (iv) Assertion is false and reason is true.

3. Deep Water
—William Douglas

Read the extracts given below and answer the questions that follow.

1. *My breath was gone. I was frightened. Father laughed, but there was terror in my heart at the overpowering force of the waves. My introduction to the Y.M.CA. swimming pool revived unpleasant memories and stirred childish fears. But in a little while I gathered confidence. I paddled with my new water wings, watching the other boys and trying to learn by aping them. I did this two or three times on different days and was just beginning to feel at ease in the water when the misadventure happened.* **[NCERT]**

(a) **Choose the correct option with reference to the two statements given below.**
   Statement 1: The author's father laughed to mock his son's inability to swim.
   Statement 2: The author wanted to swim just to prove to his father that he can swim.
   (i) Statement 1 is true but Statement 2 is false.
   (ii) Statement 1 is false but Statement 2 is true.
   (iii) Both Statement 1 and Statement 2 cannot be inferred.
   (iv) Both Statement 1 and Statement 2 can be inferred.

(b) **"My introduction to the Y.M.CA. swimming pool revived unpleasant memories and stirred childish fears." It can be inferred that this was a clear case of:**
   (i) suppression (ii) oppression
   (iii) depression (iv) repression

(c) **The misadventure that took place right after the author felt comfortable was that:**
   (i) the author slipped and fell into the swimming pool.
   (ii) a bully tossed him into the pool for the sake of fun.
   (iii) his coach forgot to teach him how to handle deep water.
   (iv) his father couldn't help him from drowning into the water.

(d) **Choose the option that describes the equipment used by the author while learning to swim.**

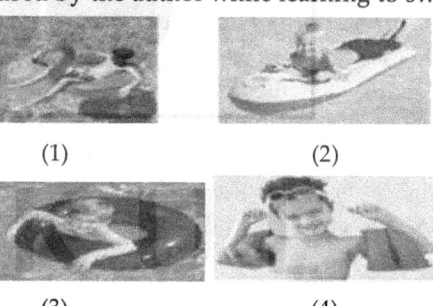

(1)   (2)

(3)   (4)
(i) option (1)   (ii) option (2)
(iii) option (3)   (iv) option (4)

2. *Then all effort ceased. I relaxed. Even my legs felt limp; and a blackness swept over my brain. It wiped out fear; it wiped out terror. There was no more panic. It was quiet and peaceful. Nothing to be afraid of. This is nice... to be drowsy... to go to sleep... no need to jump... too tired to jump... it's nice to be carried gently... to float along in space... tender arms around me... tender arms like Mother's... now I must go to sleep... I crossed to oblivion, and the curtain of life fell.*
[NCERT]

(a) Choose the correct option with reference to the two statements given below.

   Statement 1: The author tried his best to jump out of water.

   Statement 2: After a while, the author was not anxious in water.
   (i) If Statement 1 is the cause, Statement 2 is the effect.
   (ii) If Statement 1 is the effect, Statement 2 is the cause.
   (iii) Both the statements are the effects of a common cause.
   (iv) Both the statements are the effects of independent causes.

(b) The 'curtain (of life) fell' corresponds to an aspect of:
   (i) Geometry   (ii) History
   (iii) Sports   (iv) Drama

(c) The purpose of using "…" in the above passage is to:
   (i) show omission
   (ii) indicate pauses
   (iii) shorten a dialogue
   (iv) replace an idea

(d) Which option indicates that the poet lost consciousness?
   (i) 'It was quiet and peaceful.
   (ii) 'I crossed to oblivion.'
   (iii) 'Tender arms like Mother's.'
   (iv) 'It wiped out fear.'

3. *A few years later when I came to know the waters of the Cascades, I wanted to get into them. And whenever I did— whether I was wading the Tieton or Bumping River or bathing in Warm Lake of the Goat Rocks—the terror that had seized me in the pool would come back.*

   (a) Who is narrating the incident?
   (i) Douglas   (ii) instructor
   (iii) the big boy (iv) Douglas' mother

   (b) Identify the literary device used in 'the terror that had seized me in the pool would come back'.
   (i) metaphor   (ii) foreshadowing
   (iii) flashback (iv) allegory

   (c) Which terror is he talking about?
   (i) drowning in the pool
   (ii) seized by the big boy
   (iii) pushed by someone in the water
   (iv) mocked by the other trainees

   (d) In which of the following the speaker went for swimming?
   (i) Tieton River
   (ii) Water of Cascades
   (iii) Bumping River
   (iv) All of these

4. *Tiny vestiges of the old terror would return. But now I could frown and say to that terror, "Trying to scare me, eh? Well, here's to you ! Look !"*

   (a) Who is the speaker of the above lines ?
   (i) Douglas
   (ii) Douglas' trainer
   (iii) Douglas' mother
   (iv) the big boy

   (b) Which of the following word cannot be used in place of 'vestige'?
   (i) fragments   (ii) signs
   (iii) non-indication (iv) traces

   (c) What does the last line show about the speaker's attitude?
   (i) his confidence (ii) his negligence
   (iii) his rudeness (iv) his arrogance

   (d) What did he do after saying 'Look!'?
   (i) he stopped swimming
   (ii) he went down again in the pool
   (iii) he fought with the boy who bullied him
   (iv) he took up another hobby

5. Who is the author of the story 'Deep Water'?
   (a) William Shakespeare
   (b) William George Bernard Shaw
   (c) William Wordsworth
   (d) William Douglas

6. In which subject has the author graduated?
   (a) English and History
   (b) English and Science
   (c) Science and Social studies
   (d) English and Economics

7. For how many years had the author taught in high school in Yakima?
   (a) 2 years   (b) 4 years
   (c) 3 years   (d) 5 years

8. After the author was fed up with teaching, he decided to opt for which career?
   (a) Medical   (b) Gardening
   (c) Engineering (d) A legal career

9. Deep water is an excerpt from which book?
   (a) Fear of water
   (b) Of Men and Mountains
   (c) How to Swim
   (d) Fearless

10. What is the theme of the story 'Deep Water'?
    (a) Victory in facing the fear
    (b) Being fearful
    (c) To learn swimming
    (d) All of the above

11. What does 'Deep Water' signify?
    (a) Beauty   (b) Depth of Sea
    (c) Depth of Ocean (d) Fear

12. What does the story 'Deep Water' talks about?
    (a) Fear of water and the way to overcome it
    (b) Fear of people
    (c) Fear of dogs
    (d) Fear of swimming

13. What does Y.M.C.A stands for?
    (a) Young Men's Christian Authority
    (b) Young Men's Christian Association
    (c) Young Men's Christian Army
    (d) Young Men's Christopher Association
14. His mother warned him against swimming in the Yakima River because it had:
    (a) strong currents
    (b) it was meant only for boating
    (c) many people had drowned there
    (d) it had no lifeguards around
15. Where did the writer go when he was 3 or 4 years old in the story?
    (a) Washington   (b) New Zealand
    (c) California   (d) Canada
16. Why did he develop a fear of water?
    (a) Because of knocking down by waves at a beach
    (b) Because of a young boy
    (c) Because of instructor
    (d) Because of drowning at a young age
17. What haunts the author in the lesson 'Deep Water'?
    (a) Terrible experience in the pool
    (b) Ghosts
    (c) His mother's words
    (d) A push by a young boy
18. Why did Douglas hate to walk with bare legs?
    (a) because of ugly looking legs
    (b) because of fat legs
    (c) because of skin colour
    (d) because of skinny legs
19. Who threw Douglas into the swimming pool?
    (a) A young boy   (b) Instructor
    (c) Instructor   (d) Watchman
20. At first, why was the writer not much frightened when he was thrown into the pool?
    (a) Because he was sleeping
    (b) Because he was intoxicated
    (c) Because he thought that the lifeguard would come to his rescue
    (d) Because of confidence
21. What were the series of emotions and fears that Douglas experienced when he was thrown into the pool?
    (a) Fear
    (b) Confidence
    (c) Happy
    (d) Mixed feelings of confidence and fear
22. How many times did Douglas try to come to the surface of the pool?
    (a) Twice   (b) Once
    (c) Five times   (d) Thrice
23. "I crossed to oblivion, and the curtain of life fell". What does oblivion mean?
    (a) spavilion   (b) changing room
    (c) unconsciousness   (d) death
24. When he regained consciousness, he:
    (a) laughed at his experience
    (b) had 104° F fever
    (c) shook and cried and didn't eat anything
    (d) told his mother about his misadventure
25. What was the impact of the pool incident on Douglas?
    (a) Learned swimming
    (b) Became confident
    (c) Became overconfident
    (d) Hydrophobia was revived
26. What lesson did Douglas learn from his experience of drowning and then learning to swim?
    (a) Learnt swimming
    (b) Love for swimming
    (c) Swimming is not difficult
    (d) Face the fear
27. Why was Douglas determined to get over his fear of water?
    (a) because he wanted to swim in the waters of the Cascade
    (b) because his friend had challenged him
    (c) because he had a bet on it
    (d) because he wanted to win a medal
28. How did the instructor make Douglas a good swimmer?
    (a) Planning
    (b) With the help of ropes
    (c) By pushing him into the pool
    (d) With the help of ropes and belts
29. Douglas had to repeat exhaling and inhaling exercises.
    (a) hundred times   (b) forty times
    (c) fifty times   (d) ten times
30. Where is Metolius located?
    (a) New Zealand   (b) California
    (c) Oregon   (d) Japan
31. How much distance did Douglas cover while swimming across the lake Wentworth?
    (a) 4 miles   (b) 3 miles
    (c) 5 miles   (d) 2 miles
32. Where is the lake Wentworth?
    (a) New Hampshire   (b) Washington
    (c) California   (d) Washington D.C
33. Whenever terror struck again, Douglas would start.
    (a) shouting   (b) laughing
    (c) crying   (d) talking to terror
34. 'What do you think you can do to me'? These words were spoken by Douglas to:
    (a) a shark   (b) to his instructor
    (c) to his friend   (d) to terror
35. All we have to fear is fear itself. Who said these words?
    (a) Douglas   (b) his instructor
    (c) his father   (d) President Roosevelt
36. The writer decided to learn to swim when he was about _____ years old.
    (a) ten or eleven years old
    (b) fifteen or sixteen years old
    (c) twenty years old
    (d) eighteen years old

37. He practised in the pool _____ days a week.
    (a) three   (b) five
    (c) two   (d) four
38. The pool's depth at the deep end was _____.
    (a) twenty feet   (b) nine feet
    (c) six feet   (d) eight feet
39. The nine feet seemed to Douglas like _____.
    (a) hundred feet   (b) ninety feet
    (c) fifty feet   (d) twenty-five feet
40. The water in the pool had a _____ colour.
    (a) dirty yellow tinge   (b) a blue reflection
    (c) green colour   (d) no colour

    Find the correct statement in the following:
41. (i) From the beginning — I had a fascination towards water.
    (ii) My introduction to the Y.M.C.A. swimming pool revived — pleasant memories.
    (iii) I flailed at the surface of the water, — swallowed and choked.
    (iv) This handicap stayed with me — as the days rolled by.
42. (i) I went to the pool when — everyone was there.
    (ii) I struck at the water — as I went up.
    (iii) Finally one December — I decided to get an instructor and learn swim.
    (iv) A mass of yellow water — held me.

    Rearrange the sentences in the correct sequence and choose the correct option:
43. (i) I was frightened, but not frightened out of my wits.
    (ii) My lungs ached, my head throbbed.
    (iii) The water was still, and the tiled bottom was as white and clean as a bathtub.
    (iv) The next I remember I was lying on my stomach beside the pool, vomiting.
    Options:
    (a) (ii)-(iv)-(i)-(iii)   (b) (iii)-(i)-(ii)-(iv)
    (c) (iv)-(ii)-(i)-(iii)   (d) (ii)-(i)-(iv)-(iii)
44. (i) With that he picked me up and tossed me into the deep end.
    (ii) For days a haunting fear was in my heart.
    (iii) Tiny vestiges of the old terror would return.
    (iv) I imagined I would bob to the surface like a cork
    Options:
    (a) (i)-(iv)-(ii)-(iii)   (b) (iii)-(i)-(ii)-(iv)
    (c) (iv)-(ii)-(i)-(iii)   (d) (ii)-(i)-(iv)-(iii)

45. **Assertion:** Douglas' mother kept warning him about the Yakima River.
    Reason: There were many drowning incidents in the river.
    (i) Both assertion and reason are correct and reason is the correct explanation of assertion.
    (ii) Both assertion and reason are correct but reason is not the correct explanation of assertion.
    (iii) Assertion is true and reason is false.
    (iv) Assertion is false and reason is true.
46. **Assertion:** Douglas had a liking for the water from the beginning.
    Reason: The waves had knocked him down when he was very young.
    (i) Both assertion and reason are correct and reason is the correct explanation of assertion.
    (ii) Both assertion and reason are correct but reason is not the correct explanation of assertion.
    (iii) Assertion is true and reason is false.
    (iv) Assertion is false and reason is true.
47. **Assertion:** Douglas' introduction to the YMCA pool revived unpleasant memories of his childhood.
    Reason: He went into the pool when many people were there to help him.
    (i) Both assertion and reason are correct and reason is the correct explanation of assertion.
    (ii) Both assertion and reason are correct but reason is not the correct explanation of assertion.
    (iii) Assertion is true and reason is false.
    (iv) Assertion is false and reason is true.
48. **Assertion:** A big tough eighteen year old boy tossed Douglas in the pool.
    Reason: Douglas landed in a sitting position and was out of his wits.
    (i) Both assertion and reason are correct and reason is the correct explanation of assertion.
    (ii) Both assertion and reason are correct but reason is not the correct explanation of assertion.
    (iii) Assertion is true and reason is false.
    (iv) Assertion is false and reason is true.
49. **Assertion:** The swimming instructor made Douglas worse than before.
    Reason: Douglas swam across the Warm Lake to the other shore and back.
    (i) Both assertion and reason are correct and reason is the correct explanation of assertion.
    (ii) Both assertion and reason are correct but reason is not the correct explanation of assertion.
    (iii) Assertion is true and reason is false.
    (iv) Assertion is false and reason is true.

Answers

1. The Last Lesson
—Alphonse Daudet

1. (a) (iii) Franz
   (b) (i) he was late to school
   (c) (iii) depressive
   (d) (ii) French
2. (a) (iii) somber
   (b) (iv) All of these
   (c) (ii) next day
   (d) (iii) to be attentive

3. (a) (iii) M. Hamel
   (b) (i) remorseful
   (c) (i) to honour the Hamel's services
   (d) (ii) because Germans had taken over their country
4. (a) (iii) as it was the last lesson in French
   (b) (i) 1, 2, 4
   (c) (ii) children
   (d) (iv) all of these
5. (a) (i) French
   (b) (i) metaphor
   (c) (iii) guard their language
   (d) (ii) if they do not leave their language
6. (d) Alphonse Daudet
7. (b) 1870 - 1871
8. (b) Procrastination
9. (d) Loss of language and freedom
10. (c) change in life
11. (a) The Dawn of Prussia in the defeat of French people
12. (d) participles
13. (b) very badly scared of scolding
14. (a) The Bulletin Board
15. (d) early enough
16. (c) Berlin
17. (b) German
18. (b) commotion in the class
19. (b) Orders from Berlin
20. (d) collect birds eggs
21. (d) he is a hard taskmaster
22. (b) because of M.Hamel's kind and polite behaviour
23. (d) old primer
24. (d) 40 years
25. (d) to show gratitude
26. (d) all of these
27. (b) new notebooks
28. (c) startling and unexpected
29. (d) for not learning his mother tongue
30. (c) when people are deprived of their essence even the surroundings are affected.
31. (c) giving students a holiday at times
32. (b) sense of finality
33. (b) It is the key to freedom.
34. (a) sadness and patriotism
35. (a) not to put off things that one can do that day
36. (d) Blacksmith Watcher
37. (b) attractive
38. (d) Village elders
39. (a) parents
40. (a) receptive
41. (iii) What a thunderclap — these words to me!
42. (iv) After the grammar — we had a lesson in writing.
43. (a) (ii)-(iv)-(i)-(iii)
44. (a) (ii)-(i)-(iii)-(iv)
45. (iii) Assertion is true and reason is false.
46. (ii) Both assertion and reason are correct but reason is not the correct explanation of assertion.
47. (iii) Assertion is true and reason is false.
48. (i) Both assertion and reason are correct and reason is the correct explanation of assertion.
49. (v) Assertion is false and reason is true.

2. Lost Spring
–Anees Jung

1. (a) (iii) by his contact with rag pickers
   (b) (i) They live in places unfit for human living
   (c) (i) refugees from Bangladesh
   (d) (ii) uninhabited
2. (a) (iv) temporary
   (b) (i) hyperbole
   (c) (ii) necessity
   (d) (iii) rag-picking has attained the position of a skill.
3. (a) (ii) Mukesh's father
   (b) (i) she hid behind the wall
   (c) (ii) penniless
   (d) (iv) both (ii) and (iii)
4. (a) (ii) he went blind with the dust of polishing bangles
   (b) (ii) antithesis
   (c) (iv) both (ii) and (iii)
   (d) (i) Firozabad
5. (a) (iii) though she is married her eyes are devoid of happiness.
   (b) (iv) optimistic
   (c) (iii) reiteration
   (d) (ii) the drudgery of work has destroyed their willingness to improve their lot.
6. (d) Anees Jung
7. (d) Rourkela
8. (a) Lost blooming childhood
9. (c) Poor children and their exploitation
10. (d) Means of survival
11. (d) A wonder
12. (d) Lord of the Universe
13. (b) Gold
14. (c) Greenfields of Dhaka
15. (c) Morning birds
16. (d) All of these
17. (d) Because of its encashment value
18. (d) All of these
19. (b) a pair of shoes
20. (d) A little hell
21. (b) Because of lack of enough food
22. (a) Sweeping of houses and fields by storms
23. (a) At a tea stall
24. (d) All of these
25. (d) To be a motor- mechanic
26. (b) going to a garage to learn

27. (d) All of these
28. (a) Being daring, firm and clear
29. (d) The glass blowing industry
30. (d) To mould glass and make colourful bangles
31. (d) All of these
32. (d) All of these
33. (d) All of these
34. (a) the elderly woman's old husband
35. (a) the stigma of poverty and caste
36. (b) fine art
37. (b) tennis
38. (c) Bangle-maker
39. (a) tailor
40. (b) elder brother's wife
41. (i) There were many storms — that swept away their fields and homes.
42. (iii) They have lived here for more than thirty years — without an identity.
43. (a) (iv)-(ii)-(i)-(iii)
44. (c) (iv)-(ii)-(i)-(iii)
45. (iii) Assertion is true and reason is false.
46. (iii) Assertion is true and reason is false.
47. (i) Both assertion and reason are correct and reason is the correct explanation of assertion.
48. (iii) Assertion is true and reason is false.
49. (ii) Both assertion and reason are correct but reason is not the correct explanation of assertion.

3. Deep Water
—William Douglas

1. (a) (iii) Both Statement 1 and Statement 2 cannot be inferred.
   (b) (iv) repression
   (c) (ii) a bully tossed him into the pool for the sake of fun.
   (d) (iv) option (4)
2. (a) (i) If Statement 1 is the cause, Statement 2 is the effect.
   (b) (iv) Drama.
   (c) (ii) indicate pauses.
   (d) (ii) 'I crossed to oblivion.'
3. (a) (i) Douglas
   (b) (iii) flashback
   (c) (i) drowning in the pool
   (d) (iv) All of these
4. (a) (i) Douglas
   (b) (iii) non-indication
   (c) (i) his confidence
   (d) (ii) he went down again in the pool

5. (d) William Douglas
6. (d) English and Economics
7. (a) 2 years
8. (d) A legal career
9. (b) Of Men and Mountains
10. (a) Victory in facing the fear
11. (d) Fear
12. (a) Fear of water and the way to overcome it
13. (b) Young Men's Christian Association
14. (c) many people had drowned there
15. (c) California
16. (a) Because of knocking down by waves at a beach
17. (a) Terrible experience in the pool
18. (d) Because of skinny legs
19. (a) A young boy
20. (d) Because of confidence
21. (d) Mixed feelings of confidence and fear
22. (d) Thrice
23. (c) unconsciousness
24. (c) shook and cried and didn't eat anything
25. (d) Hydrophobia was revived
26. (d) Face the fear
27. (a) because he wanted to swim in the waters of the Cascade
28. (d) With the help of ropes and belts
29. (a) hundred times
30. (c) Oregon
31. (d) 2 miles
32. (a) New Hampshire
33. (d) talking to terror
34. (d) to terror
35. (d) President Roosevelt
36. (a) ten or eleven
37. (b) five
38. (b) nine feet
39. (b) ninety feet
40. (a) dirty yellow tinge
41. (iii) I flailed at the surface of the water, — swallowed and choked.
42. (iv) A mass of yellow water --- held me.
43. (a) (iii)-(i)-(ii)-(iv)
44. (a) (i)-(iv)-(ii)-(iii)
45. (i) Both assertion and reason are correct and reason is the correct explanation of assertion.
46. (ii) Assertion is false and reason is true.
47. (iii) Assertion is true and reason is false.
48. (ii) Both assertion and reason are correct but reason is not the correct explanation of assertion.
49. (iv) Assertion is false and reason is true.

9. Flamingo-Poetry

1. My Mother At Sixty-Six
—Kamala Das

Read the extracts given below and answer the questions that follow.

1. *Driving from my parent's home to Cochin last Friday morning, I saw my mother,*
   beside me, doze, open mouthed, her face ashen like that of a corpse and realized with pain that she was as old as she looked but soon put that thought away...

   [NCERT]

   (a) Choose the option that best applies to the given extract.
   (1) a conversation
   (2) an argument
   (3) a piece of advice
   (4) a strategy
   (5) a recollection
   (6) a suggestion
   (i) 1, 3 and 6   (ii) 2, 4, and 5
   (iii) Only 5   (iv) Only 1

   (b) Choose the book title that perfectly describes the condition of the poet's mother.

Title 1	You're only Old Once! —by Dr. Seuss
Title 2	The Gift of Years —by Joan Chittister
Title 3	Somewhere Towards the End —by Diana Athill
Title 4	The Book You Wish Your Parents Had Read —by Philippa Perry

   (i) Title 1   (ii) Title 2
   (iii) Title 3   (iv) Title 4

   (c) Choose the option that applies correctly to the two statements given below.

   Assertion: The poet wards off the thought of her mother getting old quickly.
   Reason: The poet didn't want to confront the inevitability of fate that was to dawn upon her mother.
   (i) Assertion can be inferred but the Reason cannot be inferred.
   (ii) Assertion cannot be inferred but the Reason can be inferred.
   (iii) Both Assertion and Reason can be inferred.
   (iv) Both Assertion and Reason cannot be inferred.

   (d) Choose the option that displays the same literary device as in the given lines of the extract.
   "her face ashen like that of a corpse..."
   (i) Just as I had this thought, she appeared and...
   (ii) My thoughts were as heavy as lead that evening when ...
   (iii) I think like everyone else who...
   (iv) I like to think aloud when...

2. *And*
   looked out at Young
   Trees sprinting, the merry children spilling out of their homes, but after the airport's security check, standing a few yards away, I looked again at her, wan, pale as a late winter's moon and felt that old familiar ache...

   [NCERT]

   (a) What is the most likely reason the poet capitalised 'Young Trees'?
   This was to:
   (i) convey a clearer meaning
   (ii) highlight the adjective noun combination.
   (iii) enhance the contrast.
   (iv) draw a connection with the title.

   (b) Choose the option that appropriately describes the relationship between the two statements given below.
   Statement 1: The poet knows her mother has aged.
   Statement 2: The poet feels the pain of separation.
   (i) Beginning – Ending
   (ii) Cause – Effect
   (iii) Question – Answer
   (iv) Introduction – Conclusion

   (c) Choose the option that completes the sentence given below.
   Just as the brightness of the winter's moon is veiled behind the haze and mist, similarly, _____.
   (i) the pain of separation has shaded mother's expression.
   (ii) age has fogged mother's youthful appearance.
   (iii) growing up has developed a seasoned maturity in the poet.
   (iv) memories warm the heart like the pale moon in winter.

(d) Choose the correct option out of the ones given below.

(1)	Simile	Metaphor
	the merry children spilling.	old familiar ache.

(2)	Metaphor	Imagery
	pale as the late writer's moon.	Young trees sprinting.

(3)	Imagery	Personification
	all I did was smile	the merry children spilling.

(4)	Personification	Simile
	Young tree sprinting.	pale as a late writer's moon.

    (i) option 1   (ii) option 2
    (iii) option 3   (iv) option 4

3. Who is the poet of poem 'My Mother at Sixty-Six'?
   (a) John Keats
   (b) Rudyard Kipling
   (c) William Wordsworth
   (d) Kamala Das

4. What is the significance of the title 'My Mother at Sixty-Six'?
   (a) Poet's fear of losing her old mother
   (b) Poet's fear of moving fast
   (c) Poet's inability to express her feelings
   (d) All of these

5. What is the main idea of the poem 'My Mother at Sixty-Six'?
   (a) Painful old age
   (b) Discolouration of skin
   (c) Carelessness of a daughter
   (d) Lack of strength

6. What is the distinctive feature of the poem?
   (a) metaphors are used
   (b) simile is used
   (c) alliteration is used
   (d) narrative style using a single sentence in a set of 14 lines

7. What does the narrative style of the poem signify?
   (a) differing thoughts
   (b) many thoughts
   (c) contrasting thoughts
   (d) a single thread of thought mixed with harsh realities

8. Who lives in Cochin?
   (a) Poet
   (b) Her parents
   (c) Both (a) and (b)
   (d) None of these

9. Name the poetic devices used in the poem.
   (a) metaphor
   (b) simile
   (c) alliteration
   (d) all of these

10. What is the kind of pain and ache that the poet feels in the poem 'My Mother at Sixty-Six'?
    (a) losing her mother
    (b) heart attack
    (c) headache
    (d) children screaming at her

11. What did the poet realise with pain?
    (a) her mother's appearance like a corpse
    (b) she is inconsiderate
    (c) old age is pleasant
    (d) she has duties

12. What is the familiar ache?
    (a) poet's childhood fear
    (b) poet's mother's weak health
    (c) poet's duties
    (d) poet's helplessness

13. What was the poet's childhood fear?
    (a) Parting from her husband
    (b) Parting from her friends
    (c) Parting from her siblings
    (d) Losing her mother

14. Which poetic device is used in "Trees sprinting-"?
    (a) Metaphor (b) Simile
    (c) Alliteration (d) Personification

15. What do the running trees signify?
    (a) fast moving appearance
    (b) speed of the moving car
    (c) fast moving change in human life from childhood to old age
    (d) None of the above

16. What does the poet notice outside the car?
    (a) sprinting trees and running children
    (b) schools and roads
    (c) other vehicles
    (d) many people on the road

17. Why has the poet used the imagery of merry children spilling out of their homes?
    (a) to show hope
    (b) to show happiness
    (c) to show youthfulness of her age
    (d) to show hope and happiness in children

18. What does the narrative single sentence style of the poem highlight?
    (a) Poet's feelings
    (b) Poet's insecurities
    (c) Poet's thoughts
    (d) Poet's intertwining thoughts

19. Which rhyming scheme is used in the poem?
    (a) coupled rhyme (b) monorhyme
    (c) Alternate rhyme (d) free verse

20. Quote an example of a simile used in the poem.
    (a) familiar ache
    (b) like that of a corpse
    (c) wan and pale
    (d) the merry children

21. Quote an example of a metaphor used in the poem.
    (a) As a late winter's moon
    (b) The merry children spilling out of their homes

(c) Driving from my parent's home
(d) None of the above

22. Quote an example of alliteration used in the poem.
    (a) like ashen
    (b) smile, smile and smile
    (c) Friday morning
    (d) None of the above

23. Quote an example of personification used in the poem.
    (a) sprinting trees
    (b) home to Cochin
    (c) airport's security check
    (d) All of these

24. How is the imagery of *'young trees and merry children'* a contrast to the mother?
    (a) mother is old in comparison to the trees and children
    (b) mother is like ash while the trees are green and children are happy
    (c) like spring and autumn season
    (d) mother's health-hopelessness and trees and merry children- youthfulness and hope

25. What was the expression of the poet's face while parting from her mother?
    (a) satirical
    (b) funny
    (c) sad
    (d) smiling

26. Why does the poet feel parted, upset and sad?
    (a) because of her fears
    (b) because she was getting late
    (c) fear of missing her flight
    (d) because of her duty towards mother and her own needs

27. Why did the poet look at her mother again?
    (a) because she was busy
    (b) because she was going away
    (c) because she wanted to stay back
    (d) because of fear and insecurity

28. What question arises from the complexity of the situation in the poem?
    (a) what to do in old age
    (b) how to take care of one's loved ones
    (c) how to drive
    (d) how to strike a balance between duties and responsibilities

29. What is the tone of the poem towards the end?
    (a) sad
    (b) hopeless
    (c) cheerful
    (d) resignation with acceptance

30. What do the parting words "See you soon Amma" signify?
    (a) her carelessness
    (b) her optimistic farewell full of cheerfulness
    (c) she bids goodbye like this
    (d) she is in a hurry

31. What does the expression smile, smile and smile signify?
    (a) poet was going home and was elated
    (b) poet was happy
    (c) poet was hopeless
    (d) poet's desperate efforts to hide her fears

32. What does the poet's smile signify in the poem?
    (a) her assurance to mother and helplessness inside
    (b) she has responsibilities
    (c) she has to do her duty first
    (d) she is a loving daughter

33. *'Smile and smile and smile'* is an_____.
    (a) anaphora
    (b) simile
    (c) alliteration
    (d) personification

34. The poetess says her mother looked pale like a_____.
    (a) corpse
    (b) ghost
    (c) malnourished child
    (d) anaemic person

35. Kamala Das is a _____.
    (a) Bengali
    (b) Punjabi
    (c) Keralite
    (d) Gujarati

36. The tone of the poet in the poem is primarily a combination of _____ and _____. [NCERT]
    1. dauntlessness   2. apprehension
    3. dejection   4. disappointment
    (a) 1 and 2
    (b) 2 and 3
    (c) 3 and 4
    (d) 1 and 4

37. The phrase *'old familiar ache'* has been used to refer to a _____.
    (a) fear
    (b) sadness
    (c) happiness
    (d) anxiety

38. **Assertion:** The poet was worried about her mother.
    Reason: Her mother was going to other city.
    (i) Both assertion and reason are correct and reason is the correct explanation of assertion.
    (ii) Both assertion and reason are correct but reason is not the correct explanation of assertion.
    (iii) Assertion is true and reason is false.
    (iv) Assertion is false and reason is true.

39. **Assertion:** Poet's mother looked very dull and lethargic.
    Reason: She was tired of her work.
    (i) Both assertion and reason are correct and reason is the correct explanation of assertion.
    (ii) Both assertion and reason are correct but reason is not the correct explanation of assertion.
    (iii) Assertion is true and reason is false.
    (iv) Assertion is false and reason is true.

40. **Assertion:** The poet looked at the young trees and playing children out of the window.
    Reason: She wanted to avoid the thought of her mother who was growing old.
    (i) Both assertion and reason are correct and reason is the correct explanation of assertion.
    (ii) Both assertion and reason are correct but reason is not the correct explanation of assertion.

(iii) Assertion is true and reason is false.
(iv) Assertion is false and reason is true.

41. **Assertion:** The smile on the poet's face was natural and the outcome of her going to Cochin.
    Reason: The poet was not confident whether she would be able to see her mother again.
    (i) Both assertion and reason are correct and reason is the correct explanation of assertion.
    (ii) Both assertion and reason are correct but reason is not the correct explanation of assertion.
    (iii) Assertion is true and reason is false.
    (iv) Assertion is false and reason is true.

42. **Assertion:** The poet's mother has been compared to the 'late winter's moon'.
    Reason: She was as beautiful as the moon in her young age.
    (i) Both assertion and reason are correct and reason is the correct explanation of assertion.
    (ii) Both assertion and reason are correct but reason is not the correct explanation of assertion.
    (iii) Assertion is true and reason is false.
    (iv) Assertion is false and reason is true.

2. An Elementary School Classroom in Slum
—Stephen Spender

Read the extracts given below and answer the questions that follow.

1. *Far far from gusty waves*
   Like rootless weeds, the hair torn round their pallor
   The tall girl with her weighed-down head. The paper-seeming
   boy, with rat's eyes. The stunted, unlucky heir

   (a) What are the children equaled with?
       (i) gusty waves (ii) rootless weeds
       (iii) rat's eyes (iv) paper
   (b) Why do you think the tall girl is sitting with a weighed down head?
       (i) because she is depressed
       (ii) due to her miserable life
       (iii) she feels embarrassed
       (iv) all of these
   (c) The literary device used by the poet in 'rat's eyes' is...............
       (i) metaphor (ii) simile
       (iii) alliteration (iv) symbol
   (d) What is the condition of the boy?
       (i) he is contented
       (ii) he is unhappy
       (iii) he is thin as paper
       (iv) he wants to revolt

2. *On sour cream walls, donations. Shakespeare's head,*
   Cloudless at dawn, civilised dome riding all cities.
   Belled, flowery, Tyrolese valley. Open-handed map
   Awarding the world its world. And yet, for these
   Children, these windows, not this map, their world,
   Where all their future's painted with a fog,

   (a) What does the expression - *sour cream walls* - suggest?
       (i) display of donated artefacts on the walls.
       (ii) badly maintained walls.
       (iii) wall-to wall furniture.
       (iv) a poor choice of paint for walls.
   (b) The map of the world in the classroom symbolises.
       (i) hopes and aspirations of the children
       (ii) travel plans of the school authorities
       (iii) a world that is unconnected to the children.
       (iv) interconnectivity within the world
   (c) The expression, *Shakespeare's head* is an example of:
       (i) pun (ii) satire
       (iii) parody (iv) irony
   (d) In the extract. *'future's painted with a fog'* suggests that the:
       (i) classroom is as foggy as the paint on the walls.
       (ii) beautiful valleys are not a part of the children's future.
       (iii) life ahead for the slum childen is as unclear and hazy as fog.
       (iv) fog often finds itself in the classrooms through broken windows.

3. *Surely, Shakespeare is wicked, the map a bad example,*
   With ships and sun and love tempting them to steal
   For lives that slyly turn in their cramped holes
   From fog to endless night? On their slag heap, these children

   (a) Why is Shakespeare described as wicked?
       (i) children have no idea of literary genius of Shakespeare
       (ii) he map a bad example
       (iii) children are bothered by hunger and despair
       (iv) all of these
   (b) What is the symbolic meaning of *"from fog to endless night"*?
       (i) from early morning to late night
       (ii) everyday was the same for the slum children
       (iii) from winter's long night till morning
       (iv) atmosphere without sunlight
   (c) What is the poetic device used in the words 'slag heap'?
       (i) hyperbole (ii) metaphor
       (iii) imagery (iv) symbol
   (d) Why is it called that children live in holes?
       (i) their houses look like rat's hole
       (ii) their houses are small, dirty and congested
       (iii) children live in rat holes
       (iv) none of these

4. *This map becomes their windows and these windows*
   That shut upon their lives like catacombs,

Break O break open till they break the town
And show the children to green fields, and make their world
Run azure on gold sands, and let their tongues
Run naked into books the white and green leaves open
History theirs whose language is the sun. **[NCERT]**

(a) Pick the option that is NOT TRUE according to this extract.
   (i) The children should be allowed to read books and form their opinions.
   (ii) Education without breaking the shackles of poverty, is meaningless.
   (iii) The policy makers show the reality of the real world to the children.
   (iv) The children see the world of poverty and misery through the windows.

(b) Pick the options that matches best with the phrase 'break o break open'.
   (1) break free   (2) break silence
   (3) break out   (4) break even
   (5) break through   (6) break ground
   (i) 1, 3 and 5   (ii) 2, 3 and 6
   (iii) 1, 4 and 6   (iv) 2, 3 and 5

(c) Look at the given book covers. Pick the option that reflects the meaning of 'catacomb' in the extract.

(1)   (2)   (3)   (4)

   (i) option 1   (ii) option 2
   (iii) option 3   (iv) option 4

(d) On the basis of the extract, pick the opinion that is closest to that of the poet.

 **(1)** The children should be given free time to play in the fields to develop their creativity.

 **(2)** The children must be given freedom to experience the wholesome bounties of nature.

 **(3)** The condition of the children can improve if they are shown the beautiful world out of their window.

 **(4)** The children can spread light and awareness if they become morally responsible.

   (i) option 1   (ii) option 2
   (iii) option 3   (iv) option 4

5. Who is the poet of the poem, 'An Elementary School Classroom in a Slum'?
   (a) Kipling   (b) Wordsworth
   (c) Kamlanath   (d) Stephen Spender

6. What theme did the poet concentrate on in the poem?
   (a) theme of social injustice and class inequalities
   (b) theme of children and their happiness
   (c) theme of insecurities
   (d) None of the above

7. What does the poet portray in the poem?
   (a) young minds
   (b) playfulness of the children
   (c) questions of children
   (d) the plight of young children in the slums

8. What are the poetic devices used in the poem?
   (a) alliteration and simile
   (b) metaphor and imagery
   (c) synecdoche, and irony
   (d) All of these

9. "Far far from gusty waves these children's faces. Like rootless weeds, the hair torn round their pallor": what do these words express?
   (a) poor state of the classroom
   (b) poor plight of children's homes
   (c) poor plight of teachers
   (d) poor plight of the slum children

10. Why is the head of the tall girl 'weighed down'?
    (a) by the burden of studies
    (b) by the burden of work
    (c) by the burden of her world
    (d) All of these

11. What is the meaning of 'The paper seeming boy, with rat eyes'?
    (a) rich people
    (b) rich children
    (c) powerful people and their influence
    (d) weak and malnutrition boy

12. What does paper-seeming boy mean?
    (a) had a paper in his hand
    (b) was as thin as a sheet of paper
    (c) was white in colour like a sheet of paper
    (d) All of these

13. What is the stunted boy reciting?
    (a) a happy song from his seat
    (b) a religious song in a group
    (c) a sad song from the front of the class
    (d) a lesson from his desk

14. Who is the unlucky heir and what has he inherited?
    (a) a fat boy, has inherited obesity from his mother
    (b) a short, thin boy, has inherited stunted growth from his family

(c) an intelligent boy, has inherited intelligence
(d) thin boy with rat's eyes, has inherited a deformed body from his father

15. "*His eyes live in a dream*"- what is the dream?
    (a) watching a movie
    (b) going abroad
    (c) eating ice cream
    (d) dream of better times with games and open spaces

16. What other freedom does the poet wants the slum children to enjoy?
    (a) freedom of roaming
    (b) freedom to spend money
    (c) freedom to eat
    (d) freedom of knowledge, wisdom and expression

17. What does the poet compare the colour of walls with?
    (a) rotten fruits
    (b) stale chapatis
    (c) rotten vegetables
    (d) sour cream

18. What does the colour of the classroom walls point out?
    (a) happy and poor state
    (b) happy and rich state
    (c) poor condition of the slum
    (d) None of these

19. In what sense are the slum children different?
    (a) their IQ
    (b) their wisdom
    (c) their dresses
    (d) because of no access to hope and openness of the world

20. Mention any two images used to explain the plight of the slum children.
    (a) open handed map and rootless weeds
    (b) from his desk and rat's eyes
    (c) belled and flowery
    (d) foggy slums and bottle bits on stones

21. What do the faces of children in the slum areas reflect?
    (a) happiness
    (b) their aspirations
    (c) their energy
    (d) sadness and lack of enthusiasm

22. What is the Tree Room in the poem?
    (a) A tree - shaped room
    (b) A room on a tree where squirrels play
    (c) A room on a tree where rats play
    (d) A room on a tree where pigeons play

23. What is ironical about the wall hangings and donations in the classroom?
    (a) set up in very clean environment
    (b) completely opposite to the needs of the children in the classroom
    (c) set up in happy environment
    (d) set up in gloomy set up

24. Why are the pictures and maps meaningless?
    (a) they are fake and show a false thing
    (b) they are old and have faded away
    (c) they show vastness which is opposite to the world and needs of the children in the classroom
    (d) All of these

25. What does the poet wish for the children of the slums?
    (a) He wishes them to be happy and healthy
    (b) He wishes a good change for them
    (c) He wants them to enjoy the bounties of nature
    (d) All of these

26. What does the expression 'Open handed map " show?
    (a) power of the poor
    (b) the poor can not access the world
    (c) the poor are powerless
    (d) maps are open to all, they reveal everything

27. What do the words "Their future is painted with fog" convey?
    (a) no love and care
    (b) no warmth
    (c) no hard work
    (d) no hope of improvement

28. What do Catacombs signify?
    (a) relevance of the map hanging on the wall of the classroom
    (b) confinement to the slums, the maps being irrelevant
    (c) importance of the school
    (d) death

29. What have the windows done to the children's lives in the poem?
    (a) shut the doors
    (b) blocked the passage
    (c) clocked the Sunlight
    (d) have shut the children inside and blocked their growth

30. What does the expression 'Break O break open' suggest?
    (a) barriers on the road
    (b) barriers of garbage heap
    (c) barriers of dirty environment must be broken
    (d) None of the above

31. What do the words 'From fog to endless night' mean?
    (a) bright light outside
    (b) bright future
    (c) hopelessness
    (d) dark and uncertain future of slum children from birth to death

32. 'Awarding the world its world' what do these words express?
    (a) the world is ours
    (b) the world is yours
    (c) the world belong to the poor
    (d) the world belongs to the rich

33. What do the 'governor, inspector, visitor' in the poem depict?
    (a) Higher officials

(b) Government officials
(c) Political people
(d) Powerful and influential people

34. **How can powerful people help the poor children?**
    (a) by fighting with the government
    (b) by fighting with the powerful
    (c) by bridging gaps of inequalities and injustice
    (d) by fighting with the rich

35. **The literary device in 'slums as big as doom is_____.**
    (a) simile   (b) metaphor
    (c) alliteration   (d) personification

36. **The literary device in 'whose language is the sun' is _____.**
    (a) simile   (b) metaphor
    (c) alliteration   (d) personification

37. **The literary device in 'spectacles of steel' is _____.**
    (a) simile   (b) metaphor
    (c) alliteration   (d) personification

38. **The last stanza is unlike the rest of the poem _____.**
    (a) long   (b) short
    (c) optimistic   (d) pessimistic

39. **Shakespeare is wicked because he_____ the children.**
    (a) educates   (b) tempts
    (c) loves   (d) hates

40. **Assertion:** Shakespeare has been described as wicked in the poem.
    Reason: He has made the lives of the slum children horrible.
    (i) Both assertion and reason are correct and reason is the correct explanation of assertion.
    (ii) Both assertion and reason are correct but reason is not the correct explanation of assertion.
    (iii) Assertion is true and reason is false.
    (iv) Assertion is false and reason is true.

41. **Assertion:** The walls of the elementary school classroom in slum are beautifully decorated.
    Reason: As they have not been painted recently.
    (i) Both assertion and reason are correct and reason is the correct explanation of assertion.
    (ii) Both assertion and reason are correct but reason is not the correct explanation of assertion.
    (iii) Assertion is true and reason is false.
    (iv) Assertion is false and reason is true.

42. **Assertion:** The poet wants that the children of the slum school should be given basic facilities.
    Reason: He appeals to the people in power.
    (i) Both assertion and reason are correct and reason is the correct explanation of assertion.
    (ii) Both assertion and reason are correct but reason is not the correct explanation of assertion.
    (iii) Assertion is true and reason is false.
    (iv) Assertion is false and reason is true.

43. **Assertion:** The children of the elementary school lead wretched lives.
    Reason: They are deprived of the rights they are entitled to.
    (i) Both assertion and reason are correct and reason is the correct explanation of assertion.
    (ii) Both assertion and reason are correct but reason is not the correct explanation of assertion.
    (iii) Assertion is true and reason is false.
    (iv) Assertion is false and reason is true.

44. **Assertion:** The future of the slum children is painted with fog.
    Reason: They live in cold places with dark rooms.
    (i) Both assertion and reason are correct and reason is the correct explanation of assertion.
    (ii) Both assertion and reason are correct but reason is not the correct explanation of assertion.
    (iii) Assertion is true and reason is false.
    (iv) Assertion is false and reason is true.

3. Keeping Quite
—Pablo Neruda

Read the extracts given below and answer the questions that follow.

1. *For once on the face of the Earth
   let's not speak in any language,
   let's stop for one second,
   and not move our arms so much.
   It would be an exotic moment
   without rush, without engines,
   we would all be together
   in a sudden strangeness.* [NCERT]

   (a) The poet uses the word "let's" to _____.
       (i) initiate a conversation between the poet and the readers.
       (ii) invite readers as part of the poem's larger call to humanity.
       (iii) welcome readers into the world of the poem and its subject.
       (iv) address readers as fellow members of the human race.

   (b) Margaret Atwood said, "Language divides us into fragments, I wanted to be whole."
       Choose the option that correctly comments on the relationship between Margaret Atwood's words and the line from the above extract – "let's not speak in any language"
       (i) Atwood endorses Neruda's call to not speak in any language.
       (ii) Atwood justifies Neruda's request to not engage in any speaking.
       (iii) Atwood undermines Neruda's intent to stop and not speak in any language.
       (iv) Atwood surrenders to Neruda's desire for silence and not speak in any language.

(c) Why do you think the poet employs words like "exotic" and "strangeness"?
   (i) To highlight the importance of everyone being together suddenly for once.
   (ii) To emphasize the frenetic activity and chaos that usually envelops human life.
   (iii) To indicate the unfamiliarity of a sudden moment without rush or without engine.
   (iv) To direct us towards keeping quiet and how we would all be together in that silence.

(d) Choose the option that correctly matches the idioms given in Column A with their meanings in Column B.

Column - A	Column - B
1. On the face of the earth	(a) In existence
2. What on earth	(b) To do all possible to accomplish something
3. Move heaven and earth	(c) To express surprise or shock
4. The salt of the earth	(d) To be good and worthy

   (a) 1-a, 2-d, 3-c, 4-b   (b) 1-a, 2-c, 3-b, 4-d
   (c) 1-b, 2-a, 3-d, 4-c   (d) 1-d, 2-b, 3-c, 4-a

2. *Those who prepare green wars,*
   wars with gas, wars with fire,
   Victory with no survivors,
   would put on clean clothes
   and walk about with their brothers
   in the shade, doing nothing.

   (a) Who are 'those' in line 1?
       (i) politicians   (ii) scientists
       (iii) statesman   (iv) all of these
   (b) What are 'green wars'?
       (i) war with the trees
       (ii) war with the vegetables
       (iii) war against nature
       (iv) war for nature
   (c) Identify the figure of speech used in 'clean clothes'
       (i) personification (ii) alliteration
       (iii) metaphor   (iv) hyperbole
   (d) What does the poet expect from the men?
       (i) to indulge in Chemical wars rather than fire arms
       (ii) to fight harmoniously
       (iii) co-exist in peaceful atmosphere
       (iv) to spare atmosphere and then fight

3. *If we were not so single-minded*
   about keeping our lives moving,
   and for once could do nothing,
   perhaps a huge silence
   might interrupt this sadness
   of never understanding ourselves
   and of threatening ourselves with death.

   (a) Whom does 'we' refer to in the above lines?
       (i) army men   (ii) human beings
       (iii) citizens of US (iv) men
   (b) Why does the poet want us to 'do nothing' for once?
       (i) to give rest to our body
       (ii) to experience the freedom
       (iii) to enjoy the leisure time
       (iv) to analyse our actions
   (c) Which figure of speech is used in the first line?
       (i) personification   (ii) allegory
       (iii) alliteration   (iv) repetition
   (d) How can a huge silence do good to us?
       (i) we can achieve peace in this silence only
       (ii) it helps us in analysing ourselves
       (iii) interrupts the sadness of threatening ourselves with death.
       (iv) all of these

4. *Perhaps the Earth can teach us*
   as when everything seems dead
   and later proves to be alive
   Now I'll count upto twelve
   and you keep quiet and I will go.

   (a) What does the Earth teach us?
       (i) that people should live in harmony
       (ii) that there is life under stillness
       (iii) that people should not indulge in war
       (iv) that all people are its children
   (b) What does the poet mean to achieve by counting up to twelve?
       (i) peace by introspecting
       (ii) experience happiness
       (iii) knowledge of controlling anger
       (iv) achieving power
   (c) From the above lines, what do you guess about the poet's thought process?
       (i) he is hypothetical
       (ii) he is practical
       (iii) he is philosophical
       (iv) he is emotional
   (d) What is always alive, even when everything seems to be dead?
       (i) our deeds
       (ii) our memories
       (iii) people's behaviour
       (iv) activities beneath the earth's surface

5. **What is the pen name of the poet of the poem 'Keeping Quiet'?**

(a) Neruda (b) Pable
(c) Pablo (d) Pablo Neruda

6. What does the poem 'Keeping Quiet' speak about?
   (a) the necessity to be happy
   (b) the necessity to introspect, understand and have feelings of brotherhood
   (c) the necessity to work quietly
   (d) None of above

7. What is the essence or message of the poem?
   (a) introspection and retrospection to be more peaceful and be in harmony
   (b) to prosper
   (c) to be happier
   (d) to reach out more people

8. What is the rhyming scheme used in the poem 'Keeping Quite'?
   (a) enclosed rhyme (b) Monorhyme
   (c) Sonnet (d) Free verse

9. What does the poet feel is needed to be at peace?
   (a) meeting with people
   (b) talking with people
   (c) interaction with the people
   (d) soul searching

10. How will counting upto 12 help?
    (a) improve our maths
    (b) helps in knowing months of a year
    (c) it will help to create peace and harmony
    (d) All of the above

11. According to the poet what creates barriers?
    (a) interactions (b) reactions
    (c) fighting (d) languages

12. What does the style of the poem symbolise?
    (a) desires (b) happiness
    (c) hope (d) desire and hope

13. How is keeping quiet related to life and can change attitude?
    (a) it helps to think and search soul
    (b) helps to scratch one's soul
    (c) helps to develop new thinking process
    (d) All of the above

14. What does the poem 'Keeping Quiet' teach us?
    (a) how to maintain silence
    (b) not to make noise
    (c) speaking creates noise
    (d) to be peaceful, thoughtful and have feelings of brotherhood

15. Why is silence treated as a big issue?
    (a) it helps to search our soul
    (b) helps us to analyse our actions
    (c) helps us to be thoughtful and find our true self
    (d) All of the above

16. What is the sadness in the poem that the poet speaks about?
    (a) violence because of unthoughtfulness of the people
    (b) unnecessary movements
    (c) speaking aloud
    (d) fighting

17. What does the poet want people to do for one second?
    (a) to sing
    (b) to close eyes
    (c) to stand quietly
    (d) to be silent and motionless

18. How does the poet perceive life?
    (a) as stillness
    (b) as silence
    (c) a noisy place
    (d) a continuous evolution of nature

19. Not move our arms' what does this expression refer to?
    (a) sit quietly
    (b) stand quietly
    (c) to be inactive
    (d) sitting still without any movement

20. What would everyone feel at that exotic moment?
    (a) happy
    (b) content
    (c) dancing
    (d) strange blissful oneness

21. Why is the moment of silence called Exotic?
    (a) because of the beautiful scenery around
    (b) because of the small gathering
    (c) because of large gathering
    (d) because of perfect peace and harmony

22. What is the poet expecting from fishermen?
    (a) to find more fish
    (b) to go deeper into the sea
    (c) to think and stop harming the fish
    (d) None of the above

23. While gathering salt, what will happen to the man if he keep silent for a moment?
    (a) he will stop dropping it
    (b) he will look at the ground
    (c) he will walk carefully
    (d) he will think of the harm the salt is doing to his hands

24. What does hurt hand refer to?
    (a) growing needs of the man
    (b) growing greed of man
    (c) unfulfilled desires
    (d) growing insensitivity of man to pain

25. Which images in the poem show that the poet condemns or hate violence?
    (a) fishermen not harming whales
    (b) wars leaving behind no survivors to celebrate
    (c) poet's refusal to deal with death
    (d) All of the above
26. What does the poet say that the people who prepare for war will do, when they keep quiet?
    (a) put on clean clothes
    (b) walk about with their brothers
    (c) do nothing
    (d) all of these
27. What are the different kinds of wars mentioned in the poem?
    (a) War against humanity
    (b) War against nature
    (c) War with gases and fire
    (d) All of the above
28. What can be a cure or an antidote to violent actions?
    (a) speaking practice   (b) wise words
    (c) polished language   (d) practice of silence
29. What will happen if there are no engines and no crowd?
    (a) noise will be lessened
    (b) no crowd on roads
    (c) no traffic rush
    (d) it will create a perfect, happy moment
30. What should not be confused with total inactivity or death?
    (a) no movement
    (b) a statue
    (c) talking people
    (d) stillness and silence
31. How can the moments of no activity help people?
    (a) they will be healthy
    (b) they will be happy
    (c) they will work easily
    (d) to relax and be more thoughtful
32. What does the Earth symbolise?
    (a) perseverance and new beginning from seemingly stillness
    (b) stillness
    (c) greenery
    (d) prosperity
33. How will silence benefit the man and nature?
    (a) both will be friends
    (b) man will know nature better
    (c) man will be healthy
    (d) man will stop hurting nature and both will heal themselves
34. What is destroying the environment?
    (a) unthoughtful actions
    (b) violent actions
    (c) speaking without thinking
    (d) All of the above
35. How will keeping quiet protect our environment?
    (a) by creating peace and brotherhood feelings
    (b) no noise will be there
    (c) people will not fight
    (d) None of the above
36. Man needs to learn a lesson from _____.
    (a) Moon   (b) Stars
    (c) Earth   (d) Sun
37. According to the poet wars that are fought have no _____.
    (a) soldiers   (b) weapons
    (c) fighter planes (d) survivors
38. 'Cold sea' is a _____ poetic device.
    (a) personification   (b) transferred epithet
    (c) metaphor   (d) alliteration
39. 'Without rush, without engines' refers to _____.
    (a) no noise
    (b) no hurry to go to the office
    (c) no travelling
    (d) no holidaying
40. Man threatens himself with _____.
    (a) death   (b) birth
    (c) robbery   (d) suicide
41. **Assertion:** The self-introspection is necessary for all literary persons.
    Reason: Then only they will be able to meditate and save mankind from destruction.
    (i) Both assertion and reason are correct and reason is the correct explanation of assertion.
    (ii) Both assertion and reason are correct but reason is not the correct explanation of assertion.
    (iii) Assertion is true and reason is false.
    (iv) Assertion is false and reason is true.
42. **Assertion:** The poet wants everyone to remain quiet for some time.
    Reason: Silence will allow to listen to the voices of quiet and serene nature.
    (i) Both assertion and reason are correct and reason is the correct explanation of assertion.
    (ii) Both assertion and reason are correct but reason is not the correct explanation of assertion.
    (iii) Assertion is true and reason is false.
    (iv) Assertion is false and reason is true.
43. **Assertion:** The exercise of counting up to twelve is suggested by the poet.
    Reason: It helps to sit still and achieve a sense of togetherness.

(i) Both assertion and reason are correct and reason is the correct explanation of assertion.
(ii) Both assertion and reason are correct but reason is not the correct explanation of assertion.
(iii) Assertion is true and reason is false.
(iv) Assertion is false and reason is true.

44. **Assertion:** Pablo Neruda desires to stop inhuman activities.
    Reason: He wants to live in a peaceful atmosphere.
    (i) Both assertion and reason are correct and reason is the correct explanation of assertion.
    (ii) Both assertion and reason are correct but reason is not the correct explanation of assertion.
    (iii) Assertion is true and reason is false.
    (iv) Assertion is false and reason is true.

45. **Assertion:** The poet wants everyone to learn from the nature to create and not to destroy.
    Reason: He wants to escape from his duty towards the mankind.
    (i) Both assertion and reason are correct and reason is the correct explanation of assertion.
    (ii) Both assertion and reason are correct but reason is not the correct explanation of assertion.
    (iii) Assertion is true and reason is false.
    (iv) Assertion is false and reason is true.

Answers

1. My Mother At Sixty-Six
—Kamala Das

1. (a) (iii) Only 5
   (b) (iii) Title 3
   (c) (iii) Both Assertion and Reason can be inferred.
   (d) (ii) My thoughts were as heavy as lead that evening when …
2. (a) (iii) enhance the contrast.
   (b) (ii) Cause – Effect
   (c) (ii) age has fogged mother's youthful appearance.
   (d) (iv) option 4
3. (d) Kamala Das
4. (a) Poet's fear of losing her old mother
5. (a) Painful old age
6. (d) narrative style using a single sentence in a set of 14 lines
7. (d) a single thread of thought mixed with harsh realities
8. (a) Poet
9. (d) all of these
10. (a) losing her mother
11. (a) her mother's appearance like a corpse
12. (a) her childhood fear
13. (d) Losing her mother
14. (d) Personification
15. (c) fast moving change in human life from childhood to old age
16. (a) sprinting trees and running children
17. (d) to show hope and happiness in children
18. (d) Poet's intertwining thoughts
19. (d) free verse
20. (b) like that of a corpse
21. (b) The merry children spilling out of their homes
22. (d) None of the above
23. (a) sprinting trees
24. (d) mother's health-hopelessness and trees and merry children- youthfulness and hope
25. (d) smiling
26. (d) because of her duty towards mother and her own needs
27. (d) because of fear and insecurity
28. (d) how to strike a balance between duties and responsibilities
29. (c) cheerful
30. (b) her optimistic farewell full of cheerfulness
31. (d) poet's desperate efforts to hide her fears
32. (a) her assurance to mother and helplessness inside
33. (a) anaphora
34. (a) corpse
35. (c) Keralite
36. (b) 2 and 3
37. (a) fear
38. (iii) Assertion is true and reason is false.
39. (iii) Assertion is true and reason is false.
40. (i) Both assertion and reason are correct and reason is the correct explanation of assertion.
41. (iv) Assertion is false and reason is true.
42. (iii) Assertion is true and reason is false.

2. An Elementary School Classroom in Slum
—Stephen Spender

1. (a) (ii) rootless weeds
   (b) (iv) all of these
   (c) (i) metaphor
   (d) (iii) he is thin as paper
2. (a) (ii) badly maintained walls.
   (b) (i) hopes and aspirations of the children.
   (c) (iv) irony.
   (d) (iii) life ahead for the slum children is as unclear and hazy as fog.

3. (a) (ii) he map a bad example
   (b) (ii) from early morning to late night
   (c) (ii) metaphor
   (d) (ii) their houses are small, dirty and congested
4. (a) (iii) The policy makers show the reality of the real world to the children.
   (b) (ii) 2, 3 and 6
   (c) (iii) option 3
   (d) (ii) option 2
5. (d) Stephen Spender
6. (a) themes of social injustice and class inequalities
7. (d) the plight of young children in the slums
8. (d) All of these
9. (d) poor plight of the slum children
10. (c) by the burden of her world
11. (d) weak and malnutrition boy
12. (b) was as thin as a sheet of paper
13. (d) a lesson from his desk
14. (a) thin boy with rat's eyes, has inherited a deformed body from his father
15. (d) dream of better times with games and open spaces
16. (d) freedom of knowledge, wisdom and expression
17. (d) sour cream
18. (c) poor condition of the slum
19. (d) because of no access to hope and openness of the world
20. (d) foggy slums and bottle bits on stones
21. (d) sadness and lack of enthusiasm
22. (b) A room on a tree where squirrels play
23. (b) completely opposite to the needs of the children in the classroom
24. (c) they show vastness which is opposite to the world and needs of the children in the classroom
25. (d) All of these
26. (d) maps are open to all, they reveal everything
27. (d) no hope of improvement
28. (b) confinement to the slums, the maps being irrelevant
29. (d) have shut the children inside and blocked their growth
30. (c) barriers of dirty environment must be broken
31. (d) dark and uncertain future of slum children from birth to death
32. (d) the world belongs to the rich
33. (d) Powerful and influential people
34. (c) by bridging gaps of inequalities and injustice
35. (a) simile
36. (b) metaphor
37. (b) metaphor
38. (c) optimistic
39. (b) tempts
40. (iii) Assertion is true and reason is false.
41. (iv) Assertion is false and reason is true.
42. (i) Both assertion and reason are correct and reason is the correct explanation of assertion.
43. (i) Both assertion and reason are correct and reason is the correct explanation of assertion.
44. (iii) Assertion is true and reason is false.

3. Keeping Quite
—Pablo Neruda

1. (a) (ii) invite readers as part of the poem's larger call to humanity.
   (b) (i) Atwood endorses Neruda's call to not speak in any language.
   (c) (ii) To emphasize the frenetic activity and chaos that usually envelops human life.
   (d) (ii) 1-a, 2-c, 3-b, 4-d
2. (a) (iv) all of these
   (b) (iii) war against nature
   (c) (ii) alliteration
   (d) (iii) co-exist in peaceful atmosphere
3. (a) (ii) human beings
   (b) (iv) to analyse our actions
   (c) (iii) alliteration
   (d) (iv) all of these
4. (a) (ii) that there is life under stillness
   (b) (i) peace by introspecting
   (c) (ii) he is practical
   (d) (iv) activities beneath the earth's surface
5. (d) Pablo Neruda
6. (d) the necessity to introspect, understand and have feelings of brotherhood
7. (a) introspection and retrospection to be more peaceful and be in harmony
8. (d) Free verse
9. (d) soul searching
10. (d) it will help to create peace and harmony
11. (d) languages
12. (d) desire and hope
13. (d) All of the above
14. (d) to be peaceful, thoughtful and have feelings of brotherhood
15. (d) All of the above
16. (a) violence because of unthoughtfulness of the people
17. (d) to be silent and motionless
18. (d) a continuous evolution of nature
19. (d) sitting still without any movement
20. (d) strange blissful oneness

21. (d) because of perfect peace and harmony
22. (c) to think and stop harming the fish
23. (d) he will think of the harm the salt is doing to his hands
24. (d) growing insensitivity of man to pain
25. (d) All of the above
26. (d) all of these
27. (d) All of the above
28. (d) practice of silence
29. (d) it will create a perfect, happy moment
30. (d) stillness and silence
31. (d) to relax and be more thoughtful
32. (a) perseverance and new beginning from seemingly stillness
33. (d) man will stop hurting nature and both will heal themselves
34. (d) All of the above
35. (a) by creating peace and brotherhood feelings
36. (c) Earth
37. (d) survivors
38. (b) transferred epithet
39. (a) no noise
40. (a) death
41. (iv) Assertion is false and reason is true.
42. (iii) Assertion is true and reason is false.
43. (i) Both assertion and reason are correct and reason is the correct explanation of assertion.
44. (i) Both assertion and reason are correct and reason is the correct explanation of assertion.
45. (ii) Both assertion and reason are correct but reason is not the correct explanation of assertion.

10

Vistas-Prose

1. The Third Level
—Jack Finney

Read the extracts given below and answer the questions that follow.

1. *The presidents of the New York Central and the New York, New Haven and Hartford railroads will swear on a stack of timetables that there are only two. But I say there are three, because I've been on the third level of the Grand Central Station. Yes, I've taken the obvious step: I talked to a psychiatrist friend of mine, among others.*

    (a) How many levels are there in reality?
      (i) one level   (ii) two levels
      (iii) three levels (iv) four levels
    (b) Whose names have been taken to confirm the levels at the station?
      (i) the presidents of the New York Central and New York
      (ii) the presidents of the New Haven
      (iii) the president of Hartford
      (iv) all of these
    (c) Why is the speaker confident about the third level?
      (i) because he had seen it on television
      (ii) because he had heard it from everyone
      (iii) because he had been there himself
      (iv) because he had his house there
    (d) The statement 'But I say there are three, because I've been on the third level of the Grand Central Station' made by Charley shows that he was.............. .
      (i) fully confident
      (ii) living under illusion
      (iii) day-dreaming
      (iv) reluctant to face the truth

2. *But that's the reason, he said, and my friends all agreed. Everything points to it, they claimed. My stamp collecting, for example; that's a 'temporary refuge from reality'. Well, maybe, but my grandfather didn't need any refuge from reality; things were pretty nice and peaceful in his day, from all I hear, and he started my collection. It's a nice collection too, blocks of four of practically every U.S. issue, first-day covers, and so on.*

    (a) What did Charley's friends agree to?
      (i) that he was a brilliant person
      (ii) that he wanted to escape the harsh realities of life
      (iii) that he needed to go in the past
      (iv) that he didn't like the present scenario
    (b) Why do human beings need a 'temporary refuge from reality' as showcased in the chapter?
      (i) to get away momentarily from all the troubles
      (ii) to evade the work
      (iii) to elude from the truth
      (iv) to experience the world of fantasy
    (c) How was the time in his grandfather's days?
      (i) insecure   (ii) peaceful
      (iii) chaotic   (iv) dangerous
    (d) What type of stamps did Charley's grandfather collect?
      (i) amazing
      (ii) blocks of four of practically every U. S. issue
      (iii) first day covers
      (iv) all of these

3. *I'm just an ordinary guy named Charley, thirty-one years old, and I was wearing a tan gabardine suit and a straw hat with a fancy band; I passed a dozen men who looked just like me. And I wasn't trying to escape from anything; I just wanted to get home to Louisa, my wife. I turned into Grand Central from Vanderbilt Avenue, and went down the steps to the first level, where you take trains like the Twentieth Century. Then I walked down another flight to the second level, where the suburban trains leave from, ducked into an arched doorway heading for the subway—and got lost. That's easy to do. I've been in and out of Grand Central hundreds of times, but I'm always bumping into new doorways and stairs and corridors.*

    (a) What did Charley want to tell about himself?
      (i) that he was a simple man
      (ii) that he was wearing a Gabardine suit
      (iii) that he was escaping from the real world
      (iv) that he didn't want to go home
    (b) What is the literary device used in 'Now, I don't know why this should have happened to me'?
      (i) symbolism   (ii) metaphor
      (iii) hyperbole   (iv) alliteration
    (c) Where was Charley actually going?
      (i) out of the town
      (ii) to his office
      (iii) to his home
      (iv) to his friend's home
    (d) What did Charley mean by 'I wasn't trying to escape from anything'?
      (i) he was not in his normal state of mind
      (ii) he did not want to escape from anywhere

(iii) he wanted to leave his wife Louisa at that hour
(iv) he was more comfortable in his imagination than living the reality

4. *Sometimes I think Grand Central is growing like a tree, pushing out new corridors and staircases like roots. There's probably a long tunnel that nobody knows about feeling its way under the city right now, on its way to Times Square, and maybe another to Central Park. And maybe.......... because for so many people through the years Grand Central has been an exit, a way of escape .... maybe that's how the tunnel I got into... But I never told my psychiatrist friend about that idea.*

   (a) Why did he think that Grand Central was growing like a tree?
      (i) because it had a lot of trees in it
      (ii) because it had a lot of corridors and staircases
      (iii) because it had a lot of trees around it
      (iv) because it had a continuously been under construction
   (b) Identify the figure of speech used in the sentence 'pushing out new corridors and staircases like roots'.
      (i) metaphor   (ii) imagery
      (iii) simile   (iv) personification
   (c) Why did anybody not know about the long tunnel?
      (i) it is a secret tunnel under the city
      (ii) it is kept hidden from public
      (iii) it is a kind of magical tunnel
      (iv) because nobody went to that part
   (d) What were the speaker's feelings when he described the Grand Central?
      (i) he was shocked
      (ii) he got upset
      (iii) he got anxious
      (iv) he was fascinated

5. *Have you ever been there? It's a wonderful town still, with big old frame houses, huge lawns, and tremendous trees whose branches meet overhead and roof the streets. And in 1894, summer evenings were twice as long, and people sat out on their lawns, the men smoking cigars and talking quietly, the women waving palm-leaf fans, with the fireflies all around, in a peaceful world. To be back there with the First World War still twenty years off, and World War II over forty years in the future... I wanted two tickets for that.* **[NCERT]**

   (a) Who does 'you' refer to?
      (i) Charley's psychiatrist, Sam Weiner
      (ii) Charley's wife, Louisa
      (iii) The reader
      (iv) Nobody in particular, it is a figure of speech.
   (b) Choose the option that best describes the society represented in the above extract.
      (i) content, peace-loving
      (ii) leisurely, sentimental
      (iii) orthodox, upper class
      (iv) comfortable, ancient

   (c) Imagine that the city of Galesburg is hosting a series of conferences and workshops. In which of the following conferences or workshops are you least likely to find the description of Galesburg given in the above extract?
      (i) Gorgeous Galesburg: Archiving a Tourist Paradise
      (ii) Welcome to the home you deserve: Galesburg Realtors
      (iii) Re-imagining a Warless Future: Technology for Peace
      (iv) The Woman Question: The world of women at home
   (d) "Tremendous trees whose branches meet overhead and roof the streets" is NOT an example of:
      1. imagery   2. metaphor
      3. alliteration 4. anachronism
      (i) option (1) and (2)
      (ii) option (1) and (3)
      (iii) option (2) and (3)
      (iv) option (2) and (4)

6. Who is the author of the story, 'The Third Level'?
   (a) George Orwell   (b) Agatha Christie
   (c) James Joyce   (d) Jack Finney

7. What is the theme of the lesson?
   (a) human tendency of escapism because of the harsh realities of the present
   (b) time travelling
   (c) theory of escapism
   (d) a dialogue between a patient and a psychiatrist

8. How does the story begin?
   (a) in a jovial manner
   (b) in an aggressive manner
   (c) on a happy note
   (d) in a serious manner

9. What does the Third level signify?
   (a) a human tendency to escape from the harsh realities of the present to past happy times
   (b) a third way on Grand Central station
   (c) a third gate on Grand Central Station
   (d) None of the above

10. What was the 'Third Level'?
    (a) a third tier on the station
    (b) a third storey on the station
    (c) an imaginary discovery of the narrator's mind
    (d) None of the above

11. Why was the narrator seeing this 'Third Level'?
    (a) as a wish to visit Galesberg
    (b) wanted to meet his friends
    (c) wanted to take a break from office
    (d) as a result of stress and anxiety in his mind

12. How did Charley reach the 'Third Level'?
    (a) In his fantasy he takes a subway or a corridor faster than a bus
    (b) In a superfast train

(c) In jetways
(d) In an escalator

13. What did Charley see at the Third Level?
    (a) flickering gas lights and people with funny moustaches
    (b) brass spittoons
    (c) glint of light
    (d) All of the above

14. Where was Charley ducked on Central Station?
    (a) into a room
    (b) into an office
    (c) into an arched door
    (d) into a store

15. Who was Sam in The Third Level?
    (a) a doctor and a friend of Charley
    (b) a teacher and a friend of Charley
    (c) a psychiatrist and a friend of Charley
    (d) None of the above

16. What specific difference did Charley notice at the Third Level of Central Station?
    (a) Everything was weird
    (b) Everything was old styled and bigger in size
    (c) Everything was too big
    (d) Everything was shining

17. What is the significance of 1894 in the lesson?
    (a) It was past
    (b) Authors' parents were alive
    (c) Author's childhood time
    (d) Representing a peaceful, romantic living time

18. What is the meaning of 'Waking dream wish fulfillment"?
    (a) a pleasant wish that makes one forget the present
    (b) a pleasant wish that takes one to the future
    (c) a pleasant wish which inspires to work
    (d) a pleasant wish that makes one forget the past

19. What is 'Waking dream wish fulfilment" according to the psychiatrist in the lesson?
    (a) Charley's finding of a Third level at Grand Central Station and realisation of his wish to visit Galesberg Illinois
    (b) Charley's dream was fulfilled
    (c) Charley's escapism from realities
    (d) None of the above

20. From where did Charley turn to Grand Central?
    (a) Galesberg
    (b) Illinois
    (c) Vanderbilt Avenue
    (d) Times Square

21. Which lobby did Charley come out in, when he got into a mile long tunnel?
    (a) Roosevelt Hotel
    (b) Times Square
    (c) Vanderbilt Avenue
    (d) Galesburg

22. What happened when Charley entered the Grand Central Station?
    (a) he found a huge tree like Station
    (b) new staircases, corridors and tunnels
    (c) trees kept spreading its roots throwing rooms and windows
    (d) All of these

23. How does the story interweave fantasy and reality?
    (a) For Charley's tendency to treat harsh realities with his imaginary Third Level
    (b) It presents imagination
    (c) Imagination happens on Central Station
    (d) None of the above

24. What convinced Charley that he had reached the Third Level Grand Central Station and not the second level?
    (a) a different world of gas lights and brass spittoons
    (b) beards and moustaches of 1894
    (c) newspaper with a date June 11, 1894
    (d) All of these

25. What did the man in the booth on the 'Third Level' wore?
    (a) green eyeshade and long black sleeve protectors
    (b) tan gabardine suit
    (c) a black four-button suit
    (d) derby hat

26. Why did Charley visit Sam?
    (a) To consult the incident of the 'Third Level' at Grand Central Station
    (b) To invite him
    (c) To invite him to accompany at Galesberg
    (d) To guide him in Galesberg

27. What kind of appearances people had at Third level and why did the clerk refuse to accept money?
    (a) funny and clerk refused to accept money because it was currency of modern times
    (b) funny and clerk refused to accept money because notes were big
    (c) weird and clerk refused to accept money because notes were torn
    (d) weird and clerk refused to accept money because notes were wet

28. How would you describe Charley's vision of his grandfather's life and times? [NCERT]
    (a) wistful escapism
    (b) idealised sentimentality
    (c) nostalgic simplicity
    (d) dreamy perfection

29. Why was Louisa worried?
    (a) knowing the incident of Third Level
    (b) for not getting tickets
    (c) tickets were delayed
    (d) Sam was scaring

30. Why does Charley want to visit Galesberg?
    (a) to escape from the troublesome world
    (b) to enjoy

(c) to see the beautiful landscape
(d) to meet his old friends

31. **What is First Day Cover?**
    (a) A new stamp gets the Postmark and date
    (b) A gift
    (c) A gift wrapper
    (d) A magazine's cover page

32. **Who had sent that First Day cover and when?**
    (a) Sam's father in 1896
    (b) Sam's uncle in 1894
    (c) Sam's friend in 1896
    (d) Sam in 1894

33. **What is Sam's letter to Charley represent?**
    (a) a blend
    (b) an acceptance to visit
    (c) a proof of his fantasy
    (d) a blend of reality with fantasy

34. **What did the letter state?**
    (a) That everything is okay
    (b) That Sam is joining them
    (c) Third level do exist and Charley was advised to keep looking at this worth seeing place
    (d) None of the above

35. **What is Sam's letter testimony to in the lesson proving?**
    (a) his acceptance to travel
    (b) his refusal to travel
    (c) Sam accompanying Charley
    (d) Charley's tendency of escapism from the realities

36. **The genre of the lesson "third level" is _____.**
    (a) science fiction   (b) tragedy
    (c) fantasy   (d) historical fiction

37. **Charley's wife name was _____.**
    (a) Leena   (b) Louisa
    (c) Alexa   (d) Lisa

38. **Sam was invited for a _____ party according to the letter.**
    (a) coffee   (b) tea
    (c) bachelor's   (d) lemonade

39. **_____ signatures were there on the letter.**
    (a) Charley's teacher (b) Charley's grandfather
    (c) Sam   (d) Louisa

40. **Charley found _____ in his stamp collection.**
    (a) old addresses   (b) hair styles
    (c) old letters   (d) first day cover

    Find the correct statement in the following:

41. (i) Everybody I know wants to escape, but they don't --- wander down into any second level.
    (ii) One night last winter --- I worked late at the office.
    (iii) All I could hear was the --- empty sound of my own footsteps and I didn't pass a soul.
    (iv) There is something ---- nice about jail, even in 1894.

42. (i) And I wanted --- three tickets to Galesburg, Illinois.
    (ii) There were brass spittoons --- on the platform.
    (iii) Sometimes I think Grand Central is growing --- like a mushroom.
    (iv) The corridor I was in began angling left and slanting downward ---- and I thought that was left, but I kept walking.

    Rearrange the sentences in the correct sequence and choose the correct option :

43. (i) My stamp collecting, for example; that's a 'temporary refuge from reality
    (ii) The tunnel turned sharp left; I went down a short flight of stairs and came out on the third level at the Grand Central Station.
    (iii) But I say there are three, because I've been on the third level of the Grand Central Station.
    (iv) My friend Sam Weiner disappeared!
    Options:
    (a) (ii)-(iv)-(i)-(iii)   (b) (iii)-(i)-(ii)-(iv)
    (c) (iv)-(ii)-(i)-(iii)   (d) (ii)-(i)-(iv)-(iii)

44. (i) The lights were dim and sort of flickering.
    (ii) Another time I came up in an office building on Forty-Sixth street, three blocks away.
    (iii) I was in a hurry to get uptown to my apartment so I decided to take the subway from Grand Central because it's faster than bus.
    (iv) They're never opened; you just put blank paper in the envelope.
    Options:
    (a) (ii)-(iv)-(i)-(iii)   (b) (iii)-(ii)-(i)-(iv)
    (c) (iv)-(ii)-(i)-(iii)   (d) (ii)-(i)-(iv)-(iii)

4. The Enemy
—Pearl S. Buck

Read the extracts given below and answer the questions that follow.

1. *"Who is that?" Hana cried. She dropped Sadao's arm and they both leaned over the railing of the veranda. Now they saw him again. The man was on his hands and knees crawling. Then they saw him fall on his face and lie there.*

   (a) Why did Hana cry?
   (i) she saw a creature coming towards her
   (ii) she saw waves rising high
   (iii) she was frightened to see an animal
   (iv) she was shocked to see an injured man

   (b) Identify the figure of speech in the statement "Those islands yonder, they are the stepping-stones to the future of Japan."
   (i) simile   (ii) metaphor
   (iii) hyperbole   (iv) irony

   (c) How was the man moving?
   (i) he was moving with difficulty
   (ii) he was crawling
   (iii) he was moving with pain
   (iv) all of these

(d) What happened to the man?
  (i) he ran away through the sea
  (ii) he fell down lying flat on his face
  (iii) he stood up perfectly fine
  (iv) he attacked Dr. Sadao

2. *"A white man!" Hana whispered.*

   Yes, it was a white man. The wet cap fell away and there was his wet yellow hair, long, as though for many weeks it had not been cut and upon his young and tortured face was a rough yellow beard. He was unconscious and knew nothing that they did for him.

   (a) What did Dr. Sadao and Hana meant by 'white man'?
     (i) the man whose face appeared white due to sand
     (ii) an American
     (iii) a man having white disease
     (iv) a man wearing white dress

   (b) Hana's remark "A white man!" on seeing the white man indicated what she was feeling. Pick the option that correctly states her feelings.
     1. Horror   2. Shock
     3. Unfamiliarity   4. Annoyance
     (i) 1 and 2   (ii) 2 and 3
     (iii) 2 and 4 (iv) 1 and 4

   (c) How did the white man's face appear?
     (i) young   (ii) tortured
     (iii) fresh   (iv) both (i) and (ii)

   (d) Why didn't the man know the presence of Dr. Sadao and Hana?
     (i) as he was sleeping
     (ii) as he was unconscious
     (iii) as he was pretending to be unconscious
     (iv) Dr. Sadao and Hana were facing his back

3. *Now Sadao remembered the wound and with his expert fingers he began to search for it. Blood flowed freshly at his touch. On the right side of his lower back Sadao saw that a gun wound had been reopened. The flesh was blackened with powder. Sometime, not many days ago, the man had been shot and had not been tended. It was bad chance that the rock had struck the wound.*

   (a) Who was wounded?
     (i) Sadao   (ii) Hana
     (iii) soldier (iv) Yumi

   (b) Which word best suits 'trained' in the extract?
     (i) touch   (ii) tended
     (iii) expat   (iv) expert

   (c) What kind of wound the man had?
     (i) it was a knife stab
     (ii) it was an injury
     (iii) it was a gun shot
     (iv) it was due to spikes on rocks

   (d) How old was the wound?
     (i) few days old   (ii) a month old
     (iii) a week old   (iv) many days old

4. *"Oh, how he is bleeding!" Hana whispered again in a solemn voice. The mists screened them now completely and at this time of day no one came by. The fishermen had gone home and even the chance beachcombers would have considered the day at an end.*

   (a) 'Hana whispered again in a solemn voice', what does this indicate?
     (i) fright   (ii) serious concern
     (iii) indifference (iv) none of these

   (b) What kind of weather it was?
     (i) there was snowfall
     (ii) there was heavy mist
     (iii) there was low mist
     (iv) It was raining

   (c) How many people were there at the beach that time?
     (i) one (Hana)
     (ii) two (Hana and Dr. Sadao)
     (iii) three (Hana, Dr. Sadao and soldier)
     (iv) four (Hana, Dr. Sadao, maid and soldier)

   (d) Who are beachcombers?
     (i) people who wander near beach for enjoyment
     (ii) people who makes a living by searching beaches for articles
     (iii) people who comes to beaches for fishing
     (iv) people who clean the beaches of dirt and filth

5. *The man moaned with pain in his stupor but he did not awaken. "The best thing that we could do would be to put him back in the sea," Sadao said, answering himself. Now that the bleeding was stopped for the moment he stood up and dusted the sand from his hands. "Yes, undoubtedly that would be best," Hana said steadily. But she continued to stare down at the motionless man. "If we sheltered a white man in our house we should be arrested and if we turned him over as a prisoner, he would certainly die," Sadao said. "The kindest thing would be to put him back into the sea," Hana said. But neither of them moved. They were staring with curious repulsion upon the inert figure.* **[NCERT]**

   (a) In which of the following options can the underlined words NOT be replaced with 'stupor'?
     (i) She hung up the phone feeling as though she had woken up from a slumber.
     (ii) The manager complained about the employee's sluggishness.
     (iii) He seemed to be in a trance when the doctor called upon him last week.
     (iv) Seeing him in a daze, the lawyer decided not to place him in the witness box.

   (b) Pick the option that best describes Sadao and Hana in the passage.
     (i) Sadao: scrupulous Hana: wary
     (ii) Sadao: daring   Hana: prudent
     (iii) Sadao: prudent   Hana: suspicious
     (iv) Sadao: wary   Hana: daring

(c) **Pick the idiom that best describes the situation in which Sadao and Hana were in.**
   (i) to be like a fish out of water
   (ii) like water off a duck's back
   (iii) to be dead in the water
   (iv) to be in hot water

(d) **Choose the correct option with reference to the two statements given below.**
   Statement 1: Sadao and Hana cared about the soldier but were worried about the consequences of being considerate.
   Statement 2: Sadao and Hana wanted to shirk their responsibilities of looking after an injured soldier, who could be an American.
   (i) Statement 1 is true but Statement 2 is false.
   (ii) Statement 1 is false but Statement 2 is true.
   (iii) Both Statement 1 and Statement 2 are true.
   (iv) Both Statement 1 and Statement 2 are false.

6. **Who is the author of the lesson 'The Enemy'?**
   (a) Pearl S. Buck   (b) Dickens
   (c) D.H. Lawrence   (d) None of these

7. **Who was Dr. Sadao?**
   (a) An Iranian doctor   (b) An American doctor
   (c) A Japanese doctor   (d) None of these

8. **Where did Dr. Sadao find American soldier?**
   (a) in the park   (b) in the battlefield
   (c) outside his house   (d) None of these

9. **Why did Dr. Sadao treat the soldier when he was from enemy's nationality?**
   (a) He was a doctor
   (b) It was against his professional ethics
   (c) As a doctor he could not let anyone die
   (d) All of the above

10. **What was the name of the American soldier?**
    (a) Tom   (b) Harry
    (c) Sadao   (d) Hamel

11. **How did Hana help Dr. Sadao?**
    (a) by assisting him
    (b) by giving him money
    (c) by giving him tools
    (d) by working as a nurse

12. **Why did Dr. Sadao become irritatable and impatient with his patient?**
    (a) because of his inability to leave the white man to help his distressed wife
    (b) because of many patients
    (c) because of General's pressure
    (d) All of the above

13. **Why did Doctor's wife feel distressed?**
    (a) Seeing many patients
    (b) Seeing General's reaction
    (c) Seeing the orders
    (d) Seeing Whiteman's blood

14. **What was Hana's reaction over her husband's words?**
    (a) she vomited outside the operation room
    (b) she shouted
    (c) she cried
    (d) she stopped helping him

15. **Why did the surgeon speak sharply to his wife?**
    (a) to get things he needed
    (b) to get her help in treating the wounded man
    (c) to stop any disturbance that could lead to harm the wounded man.
    (d) None of the above

16. **What kind of person was Sadao's father?**
    (a) a serious
    (b) a jollygood man
    (c) very strict
    (d) a true patriot and traditional person

17. **Why did Sadao marry a Japanese girl only?**
    (a) because he liked Japanese
    (b) he didn't like any other nationality
    (c) because of his father's fear
    (d) because he didn't want to upset his father

18. **What does the narrator speak about in the beginning of the chapter?**
    (a) the war
    (b) the General
    (c) Dr. Sadao's childhood and his father
    (d) the servants and Dr. Sadao 's wife

19. **Why did Hana wash the wounded man herself?**
    (a) because of her servants
    (b) because her servants ran away
    (c) because her servants refused to help an American enemy soldier
    (d) because she pitied the American enemy soldier

20. **Why did the servants leave Doctor's House?**
    (a) because he was wounded
    (b) because he was dirty
    (c) because there was an American Soldier and they didn't like him
    (d) because he didn't pay them

21. **Why was Dr. Sadao not sent to the battlefield?**
    (a) because he had no interest
    (b) he didn't love his country
    (c) he was supposed to offer his services to the General who was in pain
    (d) All of the above

22. **Why did the messenger come to the doctor?**
    (a) to meet him
    (b) for checkup
    (c) to inform about the General's pain
    (d) All of the above

23. **Seeing the messenger, what was Hana's reaction?**
    (a) She got frightened
    (b) She thought he has come to arrest her husband
    (c) General's man
    (d) All of the above

24. **What kind of person was the General?**
    (a) a kind hearted   (b) a wise man
    (c) a selfish man   (d) None of these

25. Why did the General not pass orders to arrest Dr. Sadao for giving space to a whiteman?
    (a) because he trusted him
    (b) because he needed him
    (c) General was not in good health and needed his services
    (d) None of the above
26. Why did General spare the White American soldier?
    (a) to spare his own life
    (b) he himself was in pain
    (c) needed Dr. Sadao's help
    (d) All of the above
27. What conflicting ideas disturb Dr. Sadao's mind after he brought American soldier?
    (a) duty of a doctor and loyalty towards nation
    (b) his wife's health and general's health
    (c) patient's health and servants behaviour
    (d) servants' behaviour and duty of a doctor
28. What was General's plan for American soldier?
    (a) he wanted him to reach safely
    (b) will inform his country
    (c) will get him assassinated by some private assassins
    (d) None of the above
29. How did Dr. Sadao get rid of the American soldier?
    (a) by giving him instructions
    (b) by giving him flashlight to use in times of distress
    (c) by asking him to row to the island
    (d) All of the above
30. What did Doctor give to the soldier?
    (a) his boat
    (b) food to eat
    (c) flashlight to use in distress
    (d) All of the above
31. How did Doctor ensure that the American Soldier had left safely?
    (a) by escorting him
    (b) by seeing no signal of flashlight
    (c) by giving him a call
    (d) None of the above
32. Why did Doctor feel alone at the beach?
    (a) for not bringing his wife with him
    (b) for not listening to General
    (c) for saving an American soldier's life
    (d) None of the above
33. What does Dr. Sadao remember towards the end of the story?
    (a) five American faces
    (b) the professor at whose house he had met Hana
    (c) his first landlady, who was full of prejudice, yet saved his life when he was suffering from influenza
    (d) All of the above
34. What were the dominant traits of Dr. Sadao's personality?
    (a) expertise in his profession and compassion as a human
    (b) obstinate
    (c) patriot
    (d) rude
35. What idea do you form of Dr. Sadao after reading the lesson?
    (a) an excellent doctor
    (b) a compassionate human being
    (c) Sincere and responsible citizen
    (d) All of the above
36. At the age of _____ Dr. Sadao went to America.
    (a) 22   (b) 32
    (c) 12   (d) 42
37. At the age of _____ Dr. Sadao came back to Japan.
    (a) 20   (b) 40
    (c) 50   (d) 30
38. Dr. Sadao has _____ children.
    (a) 4   (b) 5
    (c) 3   (d) 2
39. Dr. Sadao meet Hana in _____.
    (a) Japan   (b) New York
    (c) Paris   (d) America
40. The young prisoner was asked to flash the light _____ if food ran out.
    (a) twice   (b) thrice
    (c) once   (d) not at all

Find the correct statement in the following:

41. (i)   Dr. Sadao Hoki's clinic was built ---- on a spot of the Japanese coast.
    (ii) Sadao knew that his education---- was his father's chief concern.
    (iii) He was very light, like an ant --- that had been half starved for a long time.
    (iv) The servants will come back as soon as the --- foreigner arrives.
42. (i)   The young French, without a word, ----- shook Sadao's hand warmly.
    (ii) The Americans were full of prejudice ---- and it had been bitter to live in it.
    (iii) There was lot of ---- light in the dusk.
    (iv) Outside the door ----- Hana was waiting for Yumi.

Rearrange the sentences in the correct sequence and choose the correct option :

43. (i)   Thus agreed, together they lifted the man.
    (ii) He ran quickly down the steps and behind him Hana came, her wide sleeves flying.
    (iii) At once Yumi left the room.
    (iv) Clouds were rising from the ocean now.
    Options:
    (a) (ii)-(iv)-(i)-(iii)   (b) (iii)-(i)-(ii)-(iv)
    (c) (iv)-(ii)-(i)-(iii)   (d) (ii)-(iv)-(iii)-(i)
44. (i)   Hana went to the wall cupboards and slid back a door and took out a soft quilt.
    (ii) His father would never have received her unless she had been pure in her race.
    (iii) He was taking out the packing now, and the blood began to flow more quickly.
    (iv) It was at this moment that both of them saw something black come out of the mists.
    Options:
    (a) (ii)-(iv)-(i)-(iii)   (b) (iii)-(i)-(ii)-(iv)
    (c) (iv)-(ii)-(i)-(iii)   (d) (ii)-(i)-(iv)-(iii)

Answers

1. The Third Level
—Jack Finney

1. (a) (ii) two levels
   (b) (iv) all of these
   (c) (iii) because he had been there himself
   (d) (i) fully confident
2. (a) (ii) that he wanted to escape the harsh realities of life
   (b) (i) to get away momentary from all the troubles
   (c) (ii) peaceful
   (d) (iv) all of these
3. (a) (i) that he was a simple man
   (b) (i) symbolism
   (c) (iii) to his home
   (d) (ii) he did not want to escape from anywhere
4. (a) (ii) because it had a lot of corridors and staircase
   (b) (iii) simile
   (c) (iii) it is a kind of magical tunnel
   (d) (iv) he was fascinated
5. (a) (iv) Nobody in particular, it is a figure of speech.
   (b) (iii) orthodox, upper class
   (c) (iii) Re-imagining a Warless Future: Technology for Peace
   (d) (iv) option (2) and (4)
6. (d) Jack Finney
7. (a) human tendency of escapism because of the harsh realities of the present
8. (d) in a serious manner
9. (a) a human tendency to escape from the harsh realities of the present to past happy times
10. (c) an imaginary discovery of the narrator's mind
11. (d) as a result of stress and anxiety in his mind
12. (a) In his fantasy he takes a subway or a corridor faster than a bus
13. (d) All of the above
14. (c) into an arched door
15. (d) None of the above
16. (b) Everything was old styled and bigger in size
17. (d) Representing a peaceful, romantic living time
18. (a) a pleasant wish that makes one forget the present
19. (a) Charley's finding of a Third level at Grand Central Station and realisation of his wish to visit Galesberg Illinois
20. (c) Vanderbilt Avenue
21. (a) Roosevelt Hotel
22. (d) All of these
23. (a) For Charley's tendency to treat harsh realities with his imaginary Third Level
24. (d) All of these
25. (a) green eyeshade and long black sleeve protectors
26. (a) To consult the incident of 'Third Level' at Grand Central Station
27. (a) funny and clerk refused to accept money because it was currency of modern times
28. (b) idealised sentimentality
29. (a) knowing the incident of Third Level
30. (a) to escape from the troublesome world
31. (a) A new stamp gets the Postmark and date
32. (d) Sam in 1894
33. (d) a blend of reality with fantasy
34. (c) Third level do exist and Charley was advised to keep looking at this worth seeing place
35. (d) Charley's tendency of escapism from the realities
36. (a) science fiction
37. (b) Louisa
38. (d) lemonade
39. (c) Sam
40. (d) first day cover
41. (iii) All I could hear was the --- empty sound of my own footsteps and I didn't pass a soul.
42. (iv) The corridor I was in began angling left and slanting downward ---- and I thought that was left, but I kept walking.
43. (b) (iii)-(i)-(ii)-(iv)
44. (b) (iii)-(ii)-(i)-(iv)

4. The Enemy
—Pearl S. Buck

1. (a) (iv) she was shocked to see an injured man
   (b) (iv) irony
   (c) (iv) all of these
   (d) (ii) he fell down lying flat on his face
2. (a) (ii) an American
   (b) (i) 1 and 2
   (c) (iv) both (i) and (ii)
   (d) (ii) as he was unconscious
3. (a) (iii) soldier
   (b) (iv) expert
   (c) (iii) it was a gun shot
   (d) (i) few days old
4. (a) (ii) serious concern
   (b) (ii) there was heavy mist
   (c) (iii) three (Hana, Dr. Sadao and soldier)
   (d) (ii) people who makes a living by searching beaches for articles
5. (a) (ii) The manager complained about the employee's sluggishness.
   (b) (iii) Sadao: prudent Hana: suspicious
   (c) (iv) to be in hot water
   (d) (i) Statement 1 is true but Statement 2 is false.

6. (a) Pearl S. Buck
7. (c) A Japanese doctor
8. (c) outside his house
9. (d) All of the above
10. (a) Tom
11. (d) by working as a nurse
12. (a) because of his inability to leave the white man to help his distressed wife
13. (d) Seeing Whiteman's blood
14. (a) she vomited outside the operation room
15. (c) to stop any disturbance that could lead to harm the wounded man.
16. (d) a true patriot and traditional person
17. (d) because he didn't want to upset his father
18. (c) Dr. Sadao's childhood and his father
19. (c) because her servants refused to help an American enemy soldier
20. (c) because there was an American Soldier and they didn't like him
21. (c) he was supposed to offer his services to the General who was in pain
22. (c) to inform about the General's pain
23. (d) All of the above
24. (c) a selfish man
25. (c) General was not in good health and needed his services
26. (d) All of the above
27. (a) duty of a doctor and loyalty towards nation
28. (c) will get him assassinated by some private assassins
29. (d) All of the above
30. (d) All of the above
31. (b) by seeing no signal of flashlight
32. (c) for saving an American soldier's life
33. (d) All of the above
34. (a) expertise in his profession and compassion as a human
35. (d) All of the above
36. (a) 22
37. (a) 30
38. (d) 2
39. (d) America
40. (a) twice
41. (ii) Sadao knew that his education---- was his father's chief concern.
42. (ii) The Americans were full of prejudice ---- and it had been bitter to live in it.
43. (c) (iv)-(ii)-(i)-(iii)
44. (a) (ii)-(iv)-(i)-(iii)

PHYSICAL EDUCATION

SYLLABUS
Physical Education (Code No. 048)
Term - I (Theory)
MCQ Based - 35 Marks

Units	Name	
1	**Planning in Sports** ○ Meaning & Objectives of Planning ○ Various Committees & its Responsibilities (pre; during & post) ○ Tournament – Knock-Out, League Or Round Robin & Combination ○ Procedure To Draw Fixtures – Knock-Out (Bye & Seeding) & League (Staircase & Cyclic)	
2	**Sports & Nutrition** ○ Balanced Diet & Nutrition: Macro & Micro Nutrients ○ Nutritive & Non-Nutritive Components Of Diet ○ Eating For Weight Control – A Healthy Weight, The Pitfalls of Dieting, Food Intolerance & Food Myths	
5	**Children & Women in Sports** ○ Motor development & factors affecting it ○ Exercise Guidelines at different stages of growth & Development ○ Common Postural Deformities - Knock Knee; Flat Foot; Round Shoulders; Lordosis, Kyphosis, Bow Legs and Scoliosis and their corrective measures ○ Sports participation of women in India	
6	**Test & Measurement in Sports** ○ Motor Fitness Test – 50 M Standing Start, 600 M Run/Walk, Sit & Reach, Partial Curl Up, Push Ups (Boys), Modified Push Ups (Girls), Standing Broad Jump, Agility – 4 × 10 M Shuttle Run ○ Measurement of Cardio Vascular Fitness – Harvard Step Test/Rockport Test - Duration of the Exercise in Seconds x 100 5.5 x Pulse count of 1-1.5 Min after Exercise ○ Rikli & Jones - Senior Citizen Fitness Test	
8	**Biomechanics & Sports** ○ Meaning and Importance of Biomechanics in Sports ○ Types of movements (Flexion, Extension, Abduction & Adduction) ○ Newton's Law of Motion & its application in sports	
	Term - I (Practical)	
	Project File (About one sport/game of choice)	05 Marks
	Demonstration of Fitness Activity	05 Marks
	Viva Voce (From Project File; Fitness)	05 Marks

Chapter 1: Planning in Sports

1. What is Bye?
   (a) It's a method of drawing fixture.
   (b) Point system for team games.
   (c) Advantage given to a team to not play in initial round.
   (d) Placing of teams according to previous performance.

2. A tournament where every team plays with every other team once and the number of matches is determined with the help of N(N-1) is called as:
   (a) Single league tournament
   (b) Double league tournament
   (c) Knock-out tournament
   (d) None of them

3. A team which is defeated automatically gets eliminated from the tournament. It is known as—
   (a) League tournament
   (b) Knock-out tournament
   (c) Combination tournament
   (d) None of them

4. A league tournament is otherwise known as :
   (a) Round Robin tournament
   (b) Knock-out tournament
   (c) Combination tournament
   (d) None of them

5. Seeding method refers to :
   (a) Pairing of all weak teams together
   (b) Pairing of all strong teams together
   (c) Strong teams paired with weak or all strong teams grouped in upper half or lower half.
   (d) None of them

6. In special seeding, the seeded players participate directly in the:
   (a) Finals
   (b) Semi-finals
   (c) Quarter-final or semi-final
   (d) None of them

7. A system in which responsibility for planning lies with the highest level is called:
   (a) Centralised planning
   (b) Decentralised planning
   (c) Strategic planning
   (d) Flexible planning

8. Which of the following is not a benefit of planning?
   (a) Coordination of effort
   (b) Preparation for change
   (c) Development of standards
   (d) None of them

9. The total number of matches in a knock out tournament of 34 teams are:
   (a) 31   (b) 32
   (c) 33   (d) 35

10. The basic function of management is :   [CBSE]
    (a) Controlling   (b) Budgeting
    (c) Planning   (d) Organising

11. A good plan should NOT be :
    (a) specific   (b) logical
    (c) autocratic   (d) flexible

12. In planning, defining procedure means :
    (a) setting goals
    (b) making a policy
    (c) laying down rules and regulations
    (d) defining course of action

13. The Committee responsible for liaison with Print media is: [CBSE]
    (a) Technical   (b) Logistics
    (c) Marketing   (d) Finance

14. Purchase of sports equipment is a work of _____ committee:
    (a) Technical   (b) Logistics
    (c) Marketing   (d) Finance

15. Publication of rules and regulations should be done: [CBSE]
    (a) Pre event
    (b) During event
    (c) Post event
    (d) Any time during the event

Directions: In the context of above two statements, which one of the following is correct?
(a) Both (A) and (R) are true and (R) is the correct explanation of (A).
(b) Both (A) and (R) are true, but (R) is not the correct explanation of (A).
(c) (A) is true, but (R) is false.
(d) (A) is false, but (R) is true.

16. **Assertion (A):** Physical Education is an elective discipline.
    Reason (R): Physical Education borrows principles from other allied fields.

17. **Assertion (A):** League tournaments are the best tournaments.
    Reason (R): Every team gets a full opportunity to show its efficiency or performance.

18. **Assertion (A):** Planning is the foremost function in sports as it gives.
    Reason (R): It is because it gives a view of future course of action.

19. Match List – I with List – II and select the correct answer from the code given below:

S. No.	LIST-I	LIST-II
(i)	Staffing	(i) process of creating a comprehensive action
(ii)	Planning	(ii) distributing resources and organizing personnel
(iii)	Organizing	(iii) identifying key staff positions
(iv)	Controlling	(iv) all the processes that leaders create to monitor success

Choose the correct option from the following:

	(i)	(ii)	(iii)	(iv)
(a)	1	3	2	3
(b)	2	1	3	4
(c)	4	2	1	1
(d)	3	4	4	2

20. Name the following objectives of planning.
    (a)
    (b)
    (c)
    (d)

21. Name the type of tournaments for the following sports.
    (a)
    (b)
    (c)
    (d)

22. Given below is the graphical presentation of an event organization:

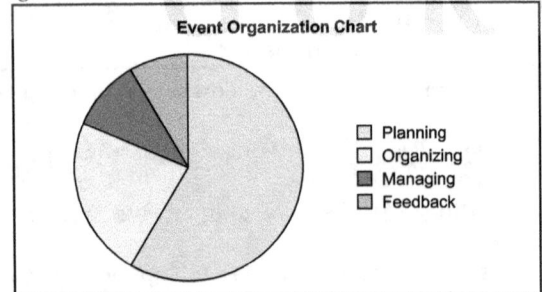

Based on the above given data answer the following questions:
(i) From the above diagram which of the following plays a major role in organizing an event?
    (a) Feedback   (b) Organizing
    (c) Planning   (d) Managing
(ii) Which is the last function during an event organisation?
    (a) Organizing   (b) Planning
    (c) Managing   (d) Feedback
(iii) Which of the following represents the smooth running of the event?
    (a) Managing   (b) Feedback
    (c) Organizing   (d) Planning

23. Given below is the graphical presentation of the types of fixtures:

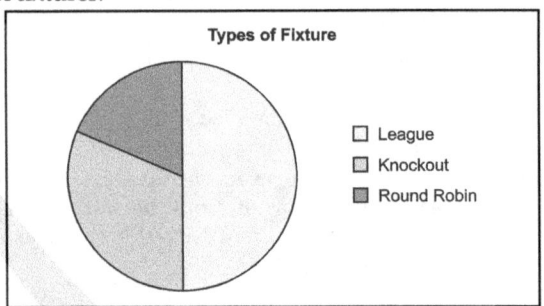

Based on the above given data answer the following questions:
(i) Which of the following is the highest form of fixture?
    (a) League   (b) Knock out
    (c) Round Robin   (d) None of the above
(ii) Which of the following is the next most popular form of fixture?
    (a) League   (b) Knockout
    (c) Round Robin   (d) All of the above
(iii) Which of the following is the least used fixture?
    (a) Knock out   (b) League
    (c) Round Robin   (d) None of the above

24. With the aim of promoting physical fitness and healthy lifestyle amongst students the Physical education Teacher at XYZ School plans to organize intramural competitions at school. For conducting the event he has given this assignment to the students of class XII who have taken up Physical Education subject so that they can get first had experience of organizing events. On the basis of given information answer the following questions: **[CBSE Website]**
(i) The work of committees is divided into _____
    (a) Pre, during and post
    (b) Pre and post
    (c) Pre and during
    (d) During and Post
(ii) Match the following

(a) Technical committee	(i) To provide shifting facility
(b) Finance committee	(ii) To resolve dispute
(c) Transport committee	(iii) To deals with money and expenditure
(d) First aid committee	(iv) To provide medical facility

(a) a–ii, b–iii, c–i, d–iv
(b) a–iii, b–ii, c–i, d–iv
(c) a–ii, b–iii, c–iv, d–i
(d) a–iv, b–iii, c–i, d–ii

(iii) Which is not the objective of Sports Tournament?
(a) To Provide Recreation
(b) To help in overall development
(c) To achieve high performance
(d) To provide opportunity.

25. Below given is the Tournament fixture procedure of a CBSE Football National competition : **[CBSE Website]**

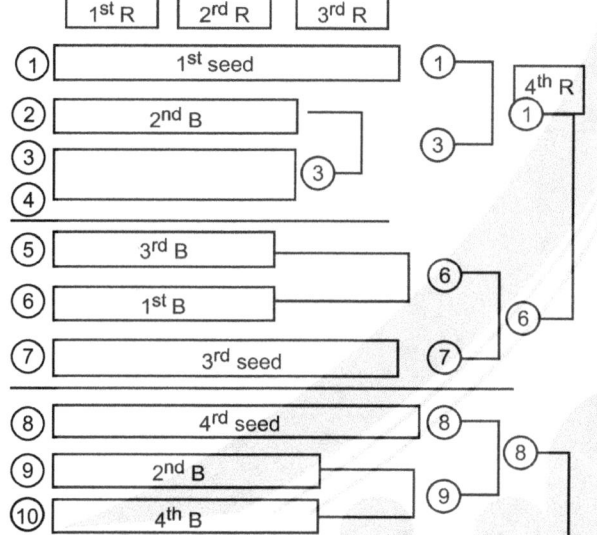

On the basis of the above data, answer the following questions:

(i) What is the number of Non-Seeded Teams in the Tournament?
(a) 04   (b) 09
(c) 12   (d) 07

(ii) The provision which places good teams in separate halves or pools so that they do not play with other good teams at earlier Rounds is known as_____
(a) Bye
(b) League tournament
(c) Seeding method
(d) Knock out tournament

(iii) Which of the following is not a Seeded Team?
(a) Team 10
(b) Team 08
(c) Team 13
(d) Team 07

Answers

1. (c) Advantage given to a team to not play in initial round.
2. (a) Single league tournament
3. (b) Knock-out tournament
4. (a) Round Robin tournament
5. (c) Strong teams paired with weak or all strong teams grouped in upper half or lower half.
6. (c) Quarter-final or semi-final
7. (a) Centralised planning
8. (d) None of them
9. (c) 33
10. (c) Planning
11. (c) autocratic
12. (d) defining course of action
13. (c) Marketing
14. (d) Finance
15. (a) Pre event
16. (a) Both (A) and (R) are true and (R) is the correct explanation of (A).
17. (a) Both (A) and (R) are true and (R) is the correct explanation of (A).
18. (a) Both (A) and (R) are true and (R) is the correct explanation of (A).
19.

List - I	List - II
Planning	process of creating a comprehensive action
Organizing	distributing resources and organizing personnel
Staffing	identifying key staff positions
Controlling	all the processes that leaders create to monitor success

20. (a) Reduced Mistakes
    (b) Decision Making
    (c) Goal Oriented
    (d) Control Over Activities
21. (a) Knock Out Tournament
    (b) League Tournament
    (c) Knock Out Tournament
    (d) League Tournament
22. (i) (c) Planning
    (ii) (d) Feedback
    (iii) (a) Managing

23. (i) (a) League
    (ii) (b) Knockout
    (iii) (c) Round Robin
24. (i) (a) Pre, during and post
    (ii) (a) a–ii, b–iii, c–i, d–iv
    (iii) (c) To achieve high performance
25. (i) (b) 09
    (ii) (c) Seeding method
    (iii) (a) Team 10

Chapter 2

Sports and Nutrition

1. Which of the following food helps in sustaining prolonged routine of exercise?
   - (a) Fats
   - (b) Proteins
   - (c) Vitamins
   - (d) Carbohydrates
2. Vitamin E deficiency causes:
   - (a) Anaemia
   - (b) Weakness in heart and muscle
   - (c) Both (a) and (b)
   - (d) None of them
3. Which of the following is an example of food supplement?
   - (a) Vitamins
   - (b) Fatty acids
   - (c) Both (a) and (b)
   - (d) None of them.
4. Before running a marathon, the trainer asked the athlete to monitor her vitamin and mineral levels to fight against free radicals which :
   - (a) Damages cell
   - (b) Limit conversion of proteins in ATP
   - (c) Reduce effectiveness of electrolytes
   - (d) Destroy stored glucose
5. What is the primary nutrient that contributes to bone health ?
   - (a) Iron
   - (b) Potassium
   - (c) Calcium
   - (d) Phosphorus
6. A weightlifter should include _____ in his/her diet.
   - (a) Carbohydrate
   - (b) Protein
   - (c) Fat
   - (d) Vitamins and minerals
7. The food component present in sugar is:
   - (a) Fats
   - (b) Proteins
   - (c) Vitamins
   - (d) Carbohydrates
8. Potato increases weight it is a _____
   - (a) Myth
   - (b) Fact
   - (c) Situational fact
   - (d) None of them
9. Which of the following is not a trace element?
   - (a) Cu
   - (b) Zn
   - (c) F
   - (d) Na
10. Heavy dose of vitamin A causes-
    - (a) Swelling of feet
    - (b) Digestive problems
    - (c) Liver damage
    - (d) None of them
11. Seeding method refers to:
    - (a) Pairing of all weak teams together
    - (b) Pairing of all strong teams together
    - (c) Strong teams paired with weak or all strong teams grouped in upper half or lower half.
    - (d) None of them
12. The main source of Vitamin C is:
    - (a) Guava
    - (b) Egg
    - (c) Milk
    - (d) Banana
13. Which is NOT a Micronutrient? [CBSE]
    - (a) Minerals
    - (b) Vitamins
    - (c) Water
    - (d) Protein
14. Which of the following is a water-soluble vitamin?
    - (a) Vitamin A
    - (b) Vitamin B
    - (c) Vitamin D
    - (d) Vitamin K
15. Iron is a part of [CBSE]
    - (a) trace minerals
    - (b) macro minerals
    - (c) vitamins
    - (d) carbohydrate

Directions: In the context of above two statements, which one of the following is correct?
- (a) Both (A) and (R) are true and (R) is the correct explanation of (A).
- (b) Both (A) and (R) are true, but (R) is not the correct explanation of (A).
- (c) (A) is true, but (R) is false.
- (d) (A) is false, but (R) is true.

16. **Assertion (A):** The antibodies are created by the proteins in our body.
    Reason (R): Proteins are very important for the maintenance of our health.
17. **Assertion (A):** Potatoes increases the weight.
    Reason (R): It is the fact.
18. **Assertion (A):** Fastening helps to reduce wait.
    Reason (R): It is the myth.
19. Match List – I with List – II and select the correct answer from the code given below:

S. No.	LIST-I Vitamin	LIST-II Disease
(i)	Vitamin A	(i) Pyorrhea
(ii)	Vitamin B	(ii) Rickets
(iii)	Vitamin C	(iii) Beriberi
(iv)	Vitamin D	(iv) Night Blindness

Code	(i)	(ii)	(iii)	(iv)
(a)	2	4	3	1
(b)	1	2	4	3
(c)	4	3	1	2
(d)	3	1	2	4

20. State the nutrients against each of the following food items.

21. List the following as micro or macro nutrients:

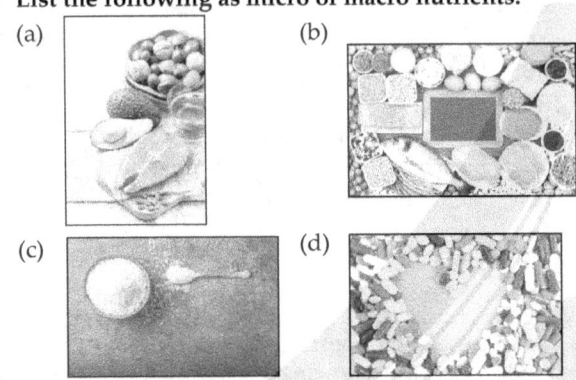

22. Below given is the BMI data of a school's health check-up

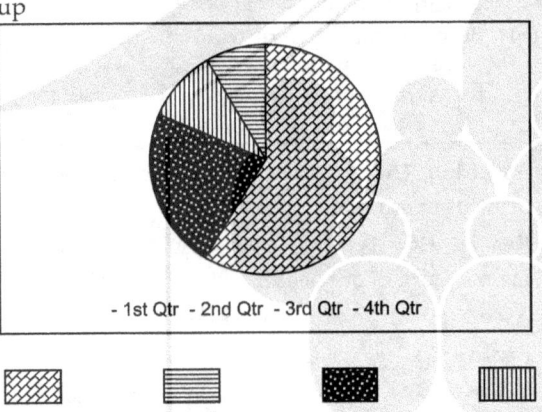

On the basis of the above data; answer the following questions:
(i) In which category does the major student population falls into?
   (a) Obese
   (b) Normal weight
   (c) Under weight
   (d) Over weight
(ii) The school has to develop an activity based program to decrease the number of:

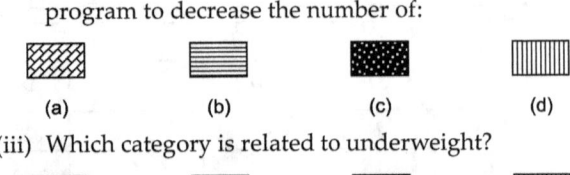

(iii) Which category is related to underweight?

23. Given below is the graphical presentation of the macro and micro nutrients:

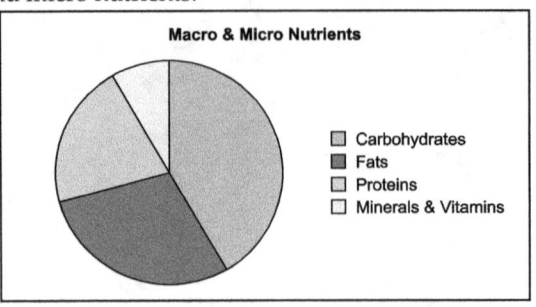

Based on the data given above, answer the following questions:
(i) Which of the following is the most consumed nutrient?
   (a) Carbohydrate
   (b) Protein
   (c) Minerals and Vitamins
   (d) Fats
(ii) Which of the following is a nutrient consumed in small quantities?
   (a) Fats
   (b) Minerals and vitamins
   (c) Proteins
   (d) Carbohydrates
(iii) Which of the following is the second–most consumed nutrient?
   (a) Proteins
   (b) Fats
   (c) Carbohydrates
   (d) Minerals and Vitamins

24. Krishna is a boy of age 10 years. His mother gives him a well-balanced diet everyday. But, he also eats a lot of junk food. He does not like to be in the sun, and has joint pains.

Based on the case study given above, answer the questions given below:
(i) Junk foods consist more of which of the following nutrient?
   (a) Fats   (b) Carbohydrates
   (c) Water   (d) Proteins
(ii) A balanced diet would include
   (a) All nutrients in proportion
   (b) Just a few different nutrients
   (c) Foods with different colour
   (d) Street food
(iii) The sunlight is the rich source of which of the following Vitamins

(a) Vitamin B_{12} (b) Vitamin D
(c) Vitamin E (d) Vitamin K

25. A balanced diet refers to the intake of food constituting all the necessary nutrients. Ram shares his knowledge of 'food and nutrition' with neighbours while visiting his grandparents in a village. Ram notices that few people living in that village are suffering with goiter and severe anaemia.

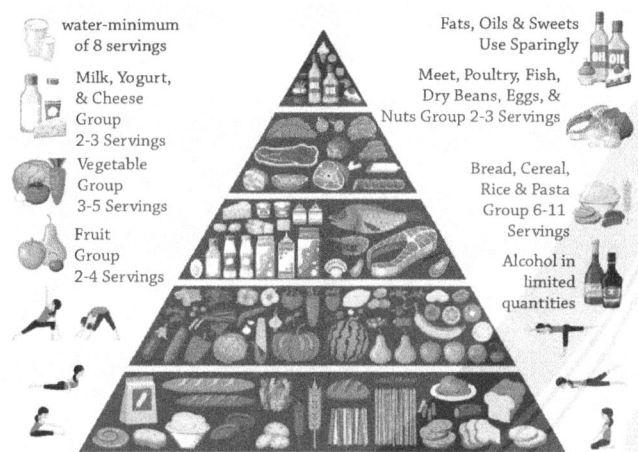

(i) Minerals are placed under _____ nutrient category on basis of required quantity.

(a) Micro (b) macro
(c) roughage (d) Non nutritive

(ii) Goiter is caused due to deficiency of _____.
(a) calcium (b) iodine
(c) selenium (d) iron

(iii) Low levels of this mineral will lead to Anaemia.
(a) Copper (b) Sodium
(c) Iron (d) Calcium

(iv) From the above picture, it can be derived that
(a) Vegetables and fruits are enough to stay healthy
(b) Exercise along with proper nutrition is required
(c) Red and green coloured foods only to be taken
(d) All of the above

(v) Fresh Vegetables and Fruits are rich sources of _____.
(a) Vitamins
(b) Minerals
(c) Both (a) and (b)
(d) Fats

Answers

1. (a) Fats
2. (b) Weakness in heart and muscle
3. (c) Both (a) and (b)
4. (a) Damages cell
5. (c) Calcium
6. (b) Protein
7. (d) Carbohydrates
8. (a) Myth
9. (d) Na
10. (c) Liver damage
11. (c) Strong teams paired with weak or all strong teams grouped in upper half or lower half.
12. (a) Guava
13. (b) Vitamins
14. (a) Vitamin A
15. (b) Macro minerals
16. (a) Both (A) and (R) are true and (R) is the correct explanation of (A).
17. (d) (A) is false, but (R) is true.
18. (a) Both (A) and (R) are true and (R) is the correct explanation of (A).
19. (c)

Vitamin	Disease
Vitamin A	Night Blindness
Vitamin B	Beriberi
Vitamin C	Pyorrhea
Vitamin D	Rickets

20. (a) Carbohydrate
(b) Fats
(c) Vitamins
(d) Proteins
21. (a) Macro Nutrient
(b) Macro Nutrient
(c) Micro Nutrient
(d) Micro Nutrient
22. (i) (b) Normal weight
(ii) (d)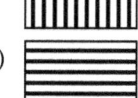
(iii) (b)
23. (i) (a) Carbohydrates
(ii) (a) Minerals and vitamins
(iii) (a) Fats

24. (i) (a) Fats
    (ii) (a) All nutrients in proportion
    (iii) (b) Vitamin D
    (iv) (b) Exercise along with proper nutrition is required
    (v) (c) Both (a) and (b)

25. (i) (a) Micro
    (ii) (b) Iodine
    (iii) (c) Iron

Chapter 5: Children and Women in Sports

1. Which of the following treatments can be used to improve the processes underpinning motor skills?
   (a) Sensory integration therapy
   (b) Mathematic remediation programming
   (c) Exposure and operant conditioning
   (d) None of them

2. Which of these are not gross motor skills?
   (a) Throwing a ball
   (b) Jumping
   (c) Balancing on one foot
   (d) Standing

3. There are how many stages of motor development in children?
   (a) 3 (b) 2
   (c) 4 (d) 5

4. Development of a child's bone, muscles and ability to move around and manipulate their movement is referred to as:
   (a) Motor development (b) Physical activity
   (c) Both (a) and (b) (d) None of them

5. Gross motor development skills, head control, and sitting are the exercise guidelines for children belonging to the age group of:
   (a) 1-2 years (b) 3-7 years
   (c) 8-12 years (d) None of them

6. Writing, Holding, Catching, and Smashing are examples of:
   (a) Gross Motor Development
   (b) Fine Motor Development
   (c) Both (a) and (b)
   (d) None of them

7. There are how many stages of motor development in children?
   (a) 3 (b) 2
   (c) 4 (d) 5

8. Mental development includes:
   (a) External and internal organs
   (b) Reasoning and thinking
   (c) Ethical and moral
   (d) Emotional maturity

9. An activity that is NOT an example of gross motor skills is: [CBSE]
   (a) drawing (b) standing
   (c) throwing a ball (d) jumping

10. An activity that is NOT an example of fine motor skills is:
    (a) using cutlery
    (b) riding a bike
    (c) building a toy tower
    (d) cutting shapes using scissors

11. Rate at which the activity is being performed is known as: [CBSE]
    (a) Volume (b) Intensity
    (c) Type of Activity (d) Frequency

12. Minimum duration of activity should be _ per week at vigorous intensity in adults above 65 years of age.
    (a) 75 minutes (b) 150 minutes
    (c) 300 minutes (d) 450 minutes

13. The term Lordosis comes from the Greek lordos which means ....
    (a) Bent backward (b) Move forward
    (c) Rotate (d) None of these

14. Scoliosis is a position in which the ....is tilted to either side of the body.
    (a) Spine (b) Knee
    (c) Foot (d) Leg

15. Bow Legs, also known as ....is a position of knees in which legs look like a bow when the legs curve outward at the knees while the feet and ankles touch.
    (a) Pranayama (b) Genu varum
    (c) Posture (d) All of these

Directions: In the context of above two statements, which one of the following is correct?
(a) Both (A) and (R) are true and (R) is the correct explanation of (A).
(b) Both (A) and (R) are true, but (R) is not the correct explanation of (A).
(c) (A) is true, but (R) is false.
(d) (A) is false, but (R) is true.

16. **Assertion (A):** During this stage of growth and development such exercise or physical activity should be encouraged which helps in developing competence movement skills (throwing jumping, catching or kicking the ball).
    Reason (R): Early childhood is the age from 3-7 years.

17. **Assertion (A):** Flat foot is a type of physical deformity.
    Reason (R): It occurs in athletes.

18. **Assertion (A):** Knock Knee is the physical deformity.

Reason (R): Yogic exercise which help in treatment of knock knee: Padmasana (Lotus posture), Vatayanasan (Horse face posture), Bhadrasana.

19. Match List – I with List – II and select the correct answer from the code given below:

S. No.	LIST-I		LIST-II
(i)	Bow legs	(i)	Rickets
(ii)	Round shoulders	(ii)	Bent backward.
(iii)	Scoliosis	(iii)	Strengthening and stretching of muscles
(iv)	Lordosis	(iv)	Knee and ankle touch

Choose the correct option from the following:

	(i)	(ii)	(iii)	(iv)
(a)	1	3	2	3
(b)	2	1	3	4
(c)	4	3	1	2
(d)	3	4	4	2

20. Name the following motor development activities:

(a) (b) (c) (d)

21. Name the following postural impairment:

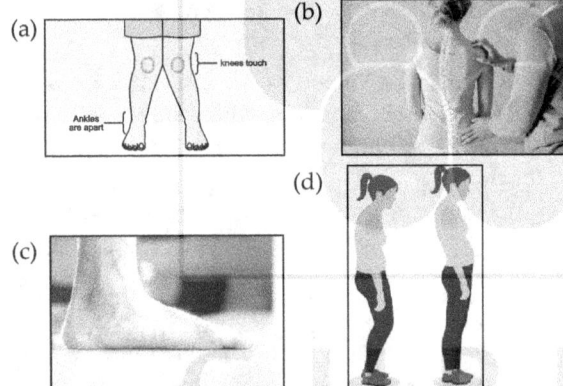

(a) (b) (c) (d)

22. Data of number of students falling in different age groups was collected from ABC School in Agra. The PT teacher wants to design exercises for different age groups. Answer the following questions based on the graph given below:

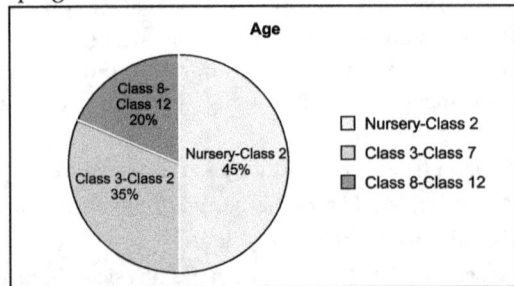

Nursery- Class 2 has children of the Age Group 3-7 years

Class 3-7 has children of age group 8-12 years

Class 8-12 has children of age group 13-18 years

(i) Exercises like running, swimming, etc, which build agility, coordination and balance would be the most suitable for which age group?
 (a) Nursery- Class (b) Class 3- Class 7
 (c) Class 8-Class 12 (d) Both (b) and (c)

(ii) Classes 8-12 should have exercises which help them in muscle training atleast:
 (a) 30 mins, twice a week
 (b) 60 mins, once a week
 (c) 60-120 mins, 3 days a week
 (d) 30 mins, 4 times a week

(iii) For Classes Nursery- Class 2, the PT period should have which of the following activities:
 (a) Endurance building, disciplined exercise
 (b) Running etc along with periodic completions
 (c) Movement based exercises coupled with recreative methods
 (d) None of these.

23. Suresh is extremely fond of Cricket as a sport, and wants to take it up as a profession. However, he always had pain whenever he would run and would sometimes also complain of pain after prolonged standing. With reference to this, answer the following:

(i) Suresh dipped his feet in water and then walked on the floor, he did not obtain an arch, so he most likely has which one of the following problems
 (a) Knock Knee (b) Scoliosis
 (c) Flat foot (d) Bow Legs

(ii) What could be the probable cause of this problem:
 (a) Weak muscles
 (b) Sudden rise in body weight
 (c) Deficiency of Calcium, Vitamin D
 (d) Only (a) and (b)

(iii) To rectify this problem, which Yogasana would prove to be the most fruitful?
 (a) Gomukhasana (b) Chakrasana
 (c) Halasana (d) Vajrasana

24. Posture plays a very significant role in our daily activities. Correct posture means the balancing of body in accurate and proper manner. Various types of postural deformities can be identified in individuals.

[CBSE Website]

(i) From the above given picture, the deformities seen on the left most is caused due to deficiency of _____ .
    (a) Iron   (b) Calcium
    (c) Vit-D   (d) Both (b) and (c)

(ii) Walking on the inner edge of the feet can be a remedy for _____ .
    (a) Bow legs   (b) Flat foot
    (c) Overweight   (d) leg deformity

(iii) The person in the middle is suffering with _____.
    (a) Rickets   (b) Flatfoot
    (c) Knock knees   (d) Elephant foot

(iv) Horse-riding is the best exercise for clearing this deformity
    (a) Knock knees   (b) Bow legs
    (c) Flat foot   (d) All of the above

(v) Performing this asana regularly can be a remedy for Knock-knees
    (a) Padmasana   (b) Tadasana
    (c) Vajrasana   (d) Halasana

25. Sheethal spent her weekend checking the health status of all the security guards of her huge gated community as a part of project work assigned by PE teachers. She found out that more than half of them have shown a significant deformity in the upper part of their vertebral column. **[CBSE Website]**

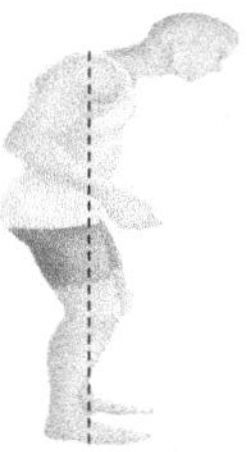

(i) The term used to define this deformity is _____.
    (a) Lordosis   (b) Scoliosis
    (c) Kyphosis   (d) Both (a) and (b)

(ii) This deformity is mainly caused due to _____.
    (a) Carrying heavy loads
    (b) Lack of exercise
    (c) Weak muscles   (d) All of the above

(iii) The asana/s which helps in rectifying such condition/is/are _____.
    (a) Chakrasana   (b) Dhanurasana
    (c) Halasana   (d) Both (a) and (b)

(iv) Bending head backward in standing position helps in getting rid of _____.
    (a) Lordosis   (b) Kyphosis
    (c) Scoliosis   (d) Both (a) and (b)

(v) Due to Covid Pandemic, most of the children attending online classes with bad sitting posture may experience this condition later.
    (a) Kyphosis   (b) Lordosis
    (c) Scoliosis   (d) Flat foot

Answers

1. (a) Sensory integration therapy
2. (d) Standing
3. (c) 4
4. (a) Motor development
5. (a) 1-2 years
6. (b) Fine Motor Development
7. (c) 4
8. (b) Reasoning and thinking
9. (a) drawing
10. (b) riding a bike
11. (b) Intensity
12. (b) 150 minutes
13. (a) Bent backward
14. (a) Spine
15. (b) Genu varum
16. (b) Both (A) and (R) are true, but (R) is not the correct explanation of (A).
17. (b) Both (A) and (R) are true, but (R) is not the correct explanation of (A).
18. (a) Both (A) and (R) are true and (R) is the correct explanation of (A).
19.

LIST-I	LIST-II
Round shoulders	Strengthening and stretching of muscles
Scoliosis	Rickets
Lordosis	Bent backward.
Bow legs	Knee and ankle touch

20. (a) Jump
    (a) Throw
    (a) Kick
    (a) Run
21. (a) Knock knees
    (b) Kyphosis

  (c) Flat Foot
  (d) Round shoulders
22. (i) (d) Both (b) and (c)
 (ii) (c) 60-120 mins, 3 days a week
 (iii) (c) Movement based exercises coupled with recreative methods
23. (i) (c) Flat foot
 (ii) (d) Only (a) and (b)
 (iii) (d) Vajrasana
24. (i) (d) Both (b) and (c)
 (ii) (a) Bow legs
 (iii) (c) Knock knees
 (iv) (a) Knock knees
 (v) (a) Padmasana
25. (i) (c) Kyphosis
 (ii) (d) All of the above
 (iii) (d) Both (a) and (b)
 (iv) (b) Kyphosis
 (v) (a) Kyphosis

Chapter 6

Test and Measurement in Sports

1. On average, how long does the statutory assessment process take?
   (a) Up to 26 weeks
   (b) Up to 12 weeks
   (c) Up to 8 weeks
   (d) Up to 52 weeks
2. Partial curl up is to test. [CBSE]
   (a) agility and speed
   (b) leg strength and endurance
   (c) abdominal strength and endurance
   (d) upper body strength and endurance
3. Sit and reach test measures _ .
   (a) endurance
   (b) flexibility
   (c) strength
   (d) speed
4. Which is not an item of Barrow motor ability test? [CBSE]
   (a) Medicine Ball Put
   (b) Zig Zag Run
   (c) Standing Broad Jump
   (d) Push-ups
5. What is the weight of Medicine ball for boys in medicine ball put?
   (a) 1 kg
   (b) 2 kg
   (c) 3 kg
   (d) 4kg
6. The test duration for the Harvard fitness test is.
   (a) 3minutes
   (b) 4 minutes
   (c) 5 minutes
   (d) 6 minutes
7. To determine VO_2 max which of the following is not required? [CBSE]
   (a) Weight
   (b) Gender
   (c) Age
   (d) Name
8. Which is not an item of Rikli and Jones Test?
   (a) 8 Foot Up and Go
   (b) Sit and Reach test
   (c) 6 Minute Walk Test
   (d) Arms Curl Test
9. What is the weight of dumbbell for men in arm curl of Rikli and Jones Test?
   (a) 5 pounds
   (b) 6 pounds
   (c) 8 pounds
   (d) 10 pounds
10. The tests which we use for cardiovascular fitness are the Harvard Step Test and Rockport Test.
    (a) Harvard step test
    (b) Sit and Reach test
    (c) 6 Minute Walk Test
    (d) Arms Curl Test
11. The injury that is not frequently occurring but also is not the least to occur:
    (a) Head Injury
    (b) Ankle Injury
    (c) Knee Injury
    (d) Muscle Tear
12. In case of Sajid's knee injury which of the following PRICE process will first be administered:
    (a) Icing
    (b) Rest
    (c) Elevation
    (d) Pressure Assessment
13. For the Head injury in Sajid's case which of the following assessments will be considered as most important:
    (a) Cervical Protection
    (b) Consciousness
    (c) Breathing
    (d) Heart Rate
14. While Sajid lay injured what would be the prime steps taken on ground:
    (a) Stop the match for some time
    (b) Continue Playing
    (c) Call for medical assistance
    (d) Let Sajid walk away from the ground on his own
15. ………………..test measures the explosive leg power.
    (a) Standing broad jump
    (b) Harvard step test
    (c) Sit and Reach test
    (d) 6 Minute Walk Test

Directions: In the context of above two statements, which one of the following is correct?
(a) Both (A) and (R) are true and (R) is the correct explanation of (A).
(b) Both (A) and (R) are true, but (R) is not the correct explanation of (A).
(c) (A) is true, but (R) is false.
(d) (A) is false, but (R) is true.

16. **Assertion (A):** Test protocol is the correct procedure for carrying out a test.
    Reason (R): If a test is done incorrectly, it might affect the results.
17. **Assertion (A):** Testing motor fitness consists of measuring of all components of motor fitness.
    Reason (R): Motor fitness test provides to the student a score regarding the level of fitness, effectiveness of any training programme.
18. **Assertion (A):** To determine running speed and acceleration of a student.
    Reason (R): There will be distance of 50 meters between two straight lines.
19. Match List – I with List – II and select the correct answer from the code given below:

S. No.	LIST-I	LIST-II
(i)	Arm curl test	A. lower back flexibility
(ii)	Back scratch test	B. upper body strength
(iii)	Six minute walk test	C. cardio-vascular endurance
(iv)	Chair sit and Reach test	D. upper body flexibility

Choose the correct option from the following:
(a) 1–B, 2–D, 3–C, 4–A (b) 1–C, 2–B, 3–D, 4–A
(c) 1–C, 2–B, 3–A, 4–D (d) 1–D, 2–C, 3–B, 4–A.

20.

(i) Both the tests shown in the picture are conducted to check _____ fitness.
   (a) Muscular
   (b) Skeletal
   (c) Cardiovascular
   (d) Respiratory

(ii) The height of the bench used in the first picture is _____ cm for women.
   (a) 45   (b) 50
   (c) 40   (d) 55

(iii) The test shown in the first picture was developed by :
   (a) Coubertin   (b) Brouha
   (c) Sheldon   (d) James

(iv) The name of the test shown in the second picture is :
   (a) Rikli & Jones test
   (b) Harvard step test
   (c) Rockport test
   (d) Barrow test

(v) How many times pulse rates are taken to estimate the fitness level :
   (a) 3   (b) 2
   (c) 5   (d) 4

21. Rajesh went to an old age home on the occasion of his birthday. At that time all the inmates in the home were assembled in one place. When he enquired, they replied that they have a physical fitness test.

(i) Give any one standard physical fitness test for senior citizen :
   (a) Push ups
   (b) Standing Broad jump
   (c) Zig zag run
   (d) Eight foot up and go test

(ii) Chair stand test is used for measuring the :
   (a) Lower body strength
   (b) Upper body test
   (c) Aerobic fitness
   (d) Anaerobic fitness

(iii) The weight of dumbbells in Arm Curl test for men is :
   (a) 5 pounds   (b) 4 pounds
   (c) 8 pounds   (d) 10 pounds

22. Below given is the BMI data of general population's health check-up for the months of EBC (Economic Backward Class), Youth, Senior Citizens and Athletes:

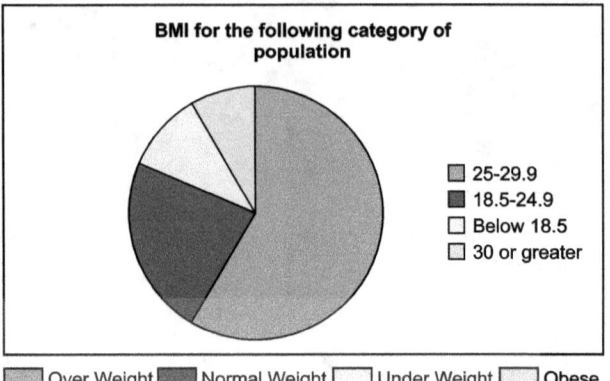

On the bases of the above data, answer the following questions:

(i) Which of the following category does most of the population fall into:
   (a) Obese   (b) Normal weight
   (c) Over weight   (d) Under weight

(ii) Which of the following category of people are likely to live a healthy life style:
   (a) Under weight (b) Normal weight
   (c) Obese   (d) Over Weight

(iii) Which category is related to underweight?
   (a) Obese   (b) Over weight
   (c) Normal weight (d) Under weight

23. Below given is the Injury data of Athletes playing football :

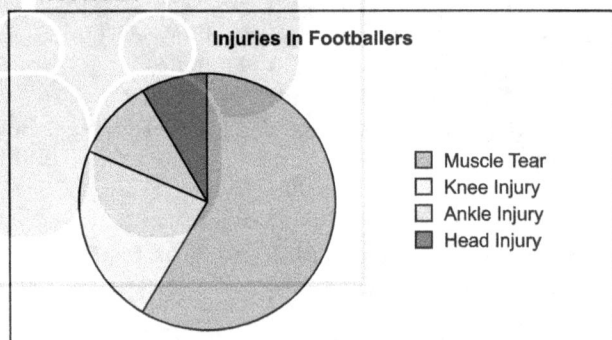

On the bases of the above data, answer the following questions:

(i) A. Most of the footballers suffer from which of the following injury :
   (a) Head Injury   (b) Ankle Injury
   (c) Muscle Injury (d) Knee Injury

(ii) B. The least occurring injury in soccer would be :
   (a) Head Injury   (b) Ankle Injury
   (c) Knee Injury   (d) Muscle Tear

(iii) C. The most frequently occurring injury after muscle tear would be :
   (a) Muscle Tear   (b) Ankle Injury
   (c) Head Injury   (d) Knee Injury

24. Anurag is a 22 year old youth suffering from obesity. During the recent medical check-up at the hospital he was advised to perform physical activity and diet control for curing it.

Based on this case answer the following questions:
   (i) Anurag should indulge in which of the following activity:
      (a) Regular walks
      (b) Sleeping
      (c) Listening to music
      (d) Watching a football match on ground
   (ii) The BMI Index of an obese person is:
      (a) >18.5   (b) 25-29.9
      (c) 30 or more (d) 18.5-24
   (iii) Due to obesity Anurag should avoid which of the following food:
      (a) Rice
      (b) Chicken
      (c) Chocolates
      (d) Junk Food

25. Mr. Lakshman, aged 65 years worked as a civil engineer in a construction company. He had to walk and climb a lot as part of his job. After retirement, he settled with his son spending time with his grandchildren. Now a days he is experiencing difficulty in doing certain chores which involves physical movement. [CBSE Website]

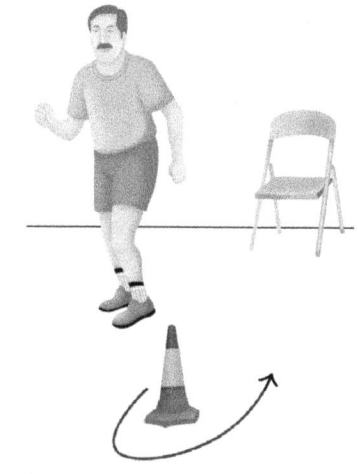

   (i) Which of the following tests would you recommend to check Mr. Lakshman's fitness?
      (a) Harvard step test (b) Rikli & jones test
      (c) AAHPER test   (d) Rock port test
   (ii) How many series of tests are there in the prescribed fitness test for Mr. Lakshman?
      (a) 8   (b) 6
      (c) 5   (d) 4
   (iii) Chair sit & reach test is done to check _____.
      (a) Agility   (b) Speed
      (c) Flexibility (d) Strength
   (iv) Pick the odd man out
      (a) Arm curl test   (b) Chair stand test
      (c) 6 min walk test (d) Partial curl up
   (v) The 8 foot up & go test, as shown in the picture is performed to assess _____.
      (a) Agility (b) Endurance
      (c) Speed   (d) Strength

Answers

1. (a) Up to 26 weeks
2. (c) Abdominal strength and endurance
3. (b) flexibility
4. (b) Zig Zag Run
5. (c) 3 kg
6. (c) 5 minutes
7. (d) Name
8. (b) Sit and Reach test
9. (c) 8 pounds
10. (a) Harvard step test
11. (b) Ankle Injury
12. (d) Pressure Assessment
13. (c) Breathing
14. (a) Stop the match for some time
15. (a) Standing broad jump
16. (b) Both (A) and (R) are true but (R) is not the correct explanation of (A).
17. (a) Both (A) and (R) are true and (R) is the correct explanation of (A).
18. (b) Both (A) and (R) are true but (R) is not the correct explanation of (A).
19. (a) 1–B, 2–D, 3–C, 4–A

List - I	List - II
Arm curl test	Upper body strength
Back scratch test	Upper body flexibility
Six minute walk test	Cardio-vascular endurance
Chair sit and Reach test	Lower back flexibility

20. (i) (c) Cardiovascular
    (ii) (a) 45
    (iii) (b) Brouha

(iv) (c) Rockport test
(v) (a) 3
21. (i) (d) Eight foot up and go test
    (ii) (a) Lower body strength
    (iii) (a) 8 Pounds
22. (i) (c) Over weight
    (ii) (b) Normal weight
    (iii) (a) Obese
23. (i) (c) Muscle Injury
    (ii) (a) Head Injury
    (iii) (d) Knee Injury
24. (i) (a) Regular walks
    (ii) (a) 30 or more
    (iii) (a) Junk Food
25. (i) (b) Rikli & jones test
    (ii) (b) 6
    (iii) (c) Flexibility
    (iv) (d) Partial curl up
    (v) (a) Agility

Chapter 8

Biomechanics and Sports

1. Acceleration of an object will increase as the net force increases depending on its:
   (a) Density   (b) Mass
   (c) Shape   (d) Volume
2. In normal walking at a person's preferred speed, the ratio of the durations of the stance and swing phases is roughly:
   (a) 1-1   (b) 2-3
   (c) 2-1   (d) 3-2
3. In plantar flexion of the foot about the ankle joint:
   (a) The foot moves upwards towards the front of the calf
   (b) The foot moves upwards towards the rear of the calf
   (c) The foot moves sideways
   (d) None the above
4. At touchdown in walking, the knee is normally:
   (a) Fully extended   (b) Slightly flexed
   (c) Fully flexed   (d) Slightly expended
5. Flexion and extension are:
   (a) Movements in the frontal plane about the sagittal axis
   (b) Movements in the sagittal plane about the frontal axis
   (c) Movements in the horizontal plane about the vertical axis
   (d) None of the above.
6. Internal and external rotation are movements in which anatomical plane?
   (a) Sagittal   (b) Frontal
   (c) Horizontal (d) None of these
7. Movements that occur primarily in the sagittal plane are:
   (a) Adduction, lateral flexion, flexion, dorsiflexion
   (b) Flexion, extension, dorsiflexion, plantar flexion
   (c) Flexion, extension, dorsiflexion, internal-external rotation
   (d) Supination and pronation of the forearm.
8. Abduction and adduction take place about which axis?
   (a) Oblique
   (b) Longitudinal or vertical
   (c) Frontal or mediolateral
   (d) Sagittal or anteroposterior
9. Flexion and extension are:
   (a) Movements in the frontal plane about the sagittal axis
   (b) Movements in the sagittal plane about the frontal axis
   (c) Movements in the horizontal plane about the vertical axis
   (d) None of the above
10. How do we define the phases into which we often break fundamental movements to simplify biomechanical analysis?
    (a) Biomechanically distinct functions and easily identified boundaries
    (b) Easily identified functions and clearly defined boundaries
    (c) Anatomically distinct functions and easily identified boundaries
    (d) Medically distinct functions and clearly defined boundaries
11. In plantar flexion of the foot about the ankle joint:
    (a) The foot moves upwards towards the front of the calf
    (b) The foot moves upwards towards the rear of the calf
    (c) The foot moves sideways
    (d) None of the above
12. Movements that occur primarily in the sagittal plane are:
    (a) Adduction, lateral flexion, flexion, dorsiflexion
    (b) Flexion, extension, dorsiflexion, plantar flexion
    (c) Flexion, extension, dorsiflexion, internal-external rotation
    (d) Supination and pronation of the forearm.
13. The plane which divides the body into a left and a right is called: [CBSE]
    (a) coronal plane   (b) sagittal plane
    (c) vertical plane   (d) transverse plane
14. Sports biomechanics cab be described as:
    (a) mechanics of sports   (b) kinesiology
    (c) physics of sports   (d) sports dynamics
15. Newton's Second Law of Motion is also known as: [CBSE]
    (a) Law of Reaction   (b) Law of Inertia
    (c) Resultant Force   (d) Law of Effect

> **Directions:** In the context of above two statements, which one of the following is correct?
> (a) Both (A) and (R) are true and (R) is the correct explanation of (A).
> (b) Both (A) and (R) are true, but (R) is not the correct explanation of (A).
> (c) (A) is true, but (R) is false.
> (d) (A) is false, but (R) is true.

16. **Assertion (A):** Sports biomechanics is a quantitative based study and analysis of professional athletes/sportspersons and sports activities in general.
    Reason (R): In simple terms, it may be described as the physics of sports.

17. **Assertion (A):** Sports biomechanics is limited to the study those individuals who are involved in exercise or sports or any physical activity.
    Reason (R): Performance enhancement is one of the area of the study in sports biomechanics.

18. **Assertion (A):** Sportsperson's performance can be improved by improving her/his technique.
    Reason (R): The application of biomechanical principles can be applied to improve technique.

19. Match List – I with List – II and select the correct answer from the code given below:

S. No.	LIST-I	LIST-II
(i)	Abrasion	A. Joint Injuries
(ii)	Green stick fractures	B. Soft tissue injuries
(iii)	Shoulder Dislocation	C. Cause of sport injuries
(iv)	Lack of fitness	D. Bone injuries

Choose the correct option from the following:
(a) 1–D, 2–A, 3–C, 4–B
(b) 1–B, 2–A, 3–C, 4–D
(c) 1–B, 2–D, 3–A, 4–C
(d) 1–A, 2–D, 3–B, 4–C.

20. Identify the human movement and give their names:

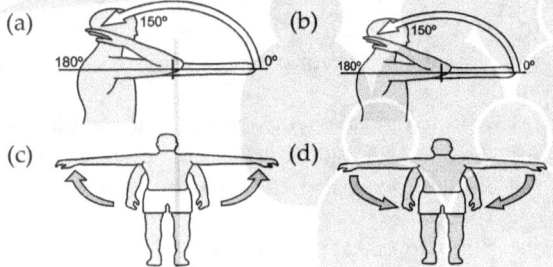

21. Below given are the types of movements in the human body:

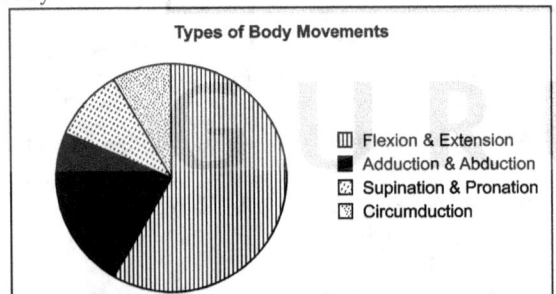

On the bases of the above data, answer the following questions:
(i) Which of the following is the most commonly used movement in the human body:
   (a) Flexion and Extension
   (b) Adduction and Abduction
   (c) Supination and Pronation
   (d) Circumduction

(ii) Which is the least movement in the above mentioned graph:
   (a) Supination and Pronation
   (b) Circumduction
   (c) Adduction and Abduction
   (d) Flexion and Extension

(iii) Which of the following is the second most used movement in the human body:
   (a) Flexion and Extension
   (b) Circumduction
   (c) Adduction and Abduction
   (d) Supination and Pronation

22. Vishal is about to start a race of 100 meter sprinting. He is ready at the start line, and begins running at the sound of the gunshot and wins the race.
Based on this case answer the following questions:
(i) While at the start line which of the following Newton's Law works on the body of Vishal:
   (a) Law of Gravity
   (b) Law of Acceleration
   (c) Law of Action Reaction
   (d) Law of Inertia

(ii) As Vishal sprints on the track which of the following Newton's Law is applicable:
   (a) Law of Acceleration
   (b) Law of Action Reaction
   (c) Law of Hooke
   (d) Law of Ohm

(iii) While sprinting Vishal's leg move back and forth at the hip joint. Which type of movement occurs at the hip joint?
   (a) Flexion and Extension
   (b) Adduction and Abduction
   (c) Dorsi and Planter Flexion
   (d) Supination and Pronation

23. The teachers as well as coaches always make their best efforts to improve the performance of their students in various competitive games and sports. They can help to improve the performance of students if they have adequate knowledge of biomechanics. **[CBSE Website]**

(i) The more force one exerts on the downward bounce, the higher the ball bounces into the air. Which law is this statement being referred to?
   (a) Newton's 1st law
   (b) Newton's 2nd law
   (c) Newton's 3rd law
   (d) Law of gravitation

(ii) Among the above given pictures, Newton's 3rd law is depicted in
 (a) First (b) Second
 (c) Both (d) None of these

(iii) The acceleration of an object depends directly upon the net force acting upon the object and inversely upon the object's
 (a) Weight (b) Mass
 (c) Height (d) Density

(iv) The study of human body and various forces acting on it is
 (a) Biology (b) Biomechanics
 (c) Physiology (d) Anatomy

(v) A high jumper can jump higher off a solid surface because it opposes his or her body with as much force as he or she is able to generate. This example refers to
 (a) Law of conservation
 (b) Law of inertia
 (c) Law of action & reaction
 (d) Law of gravity

24. Sohan, a new student in the school was very much interested in taking part in the school sports events. He was taught the latest rules and regulations of football game. In due course, he learnt biomechanical aspects of the game including various movements.
[CBSE Website]

  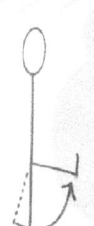 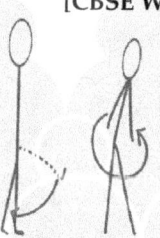

(i) The type of movement in which the angle between joint decreases is called
 (a) Flexion (b) Extension
 (c) Gliding (d) Sliding

(ii) Straightening parts of a joint so that the angle increases
 (a) Flexion (b) Extension
 (c) Abduction (d) Adduction

(iii) Moving a part away from mid line is
 (a) Flexion (b) Extension
 (c) Abduction (d) Adduction

(iv) Moving a part towards the mid line is
 (a) Flexion (b) Extension
 (c) Abduction (d) Adduction

(v) Flexion and extension comes under _____ movement.
 (a) Gliding (b) Angular
 (c) Rotation (d) Circumduction

25. In biomechanics class, Gopi, the teacher, brings the students to the physics lab of his school. The students get confused. After the completion of the class, they realize the fact. **[CBSE Website]**

(i) Why does the teacher bring the students to physics lab for biomechanics class?
 (a) It deals with physics principle
 (b) Sliding friction
 (c) Rolling friction
 (d) Static friction

(ii) Biomechanics is associated with
 (a) Mechanic
 (b) Physics
 (c) Mechanic and Physics
 (d) Mechanic and Anatomy

(iii) Friction can be increased by which of the following?
 (a) Smooth surface
 (b) Dry surface
 (c) Decrease the Weight
 (d) All of this

Answers

1. (b) Mass
2. (d) 3-2
3. (b) The foot moves upwards towards the rear of the calf
4. (b) Slightly flexed
5. (b) Movements in the sagittal plane about the frontal axis
6. (c) Horizontal
7. (b) Flexion, extension, dorsiflexion, plantar flexion
8. (d) Sagittal or anteroposterior
9. (b) Movements in the sagittal plane about the frontal axis
10. (a) Biomechanically distinct functions and easily identified boundaries
11. (b) The foot moves upwards towards the rear of the calf
12. (b) Flexion, extension, dorsiflexion, plantar flexion
13. (b) sagittal plane
14. (c) physics of sports
15. (c) Resultant Force
16. (b) Both (A) and (R) are true but (R) is not the correct explanation of (A).
17. (b) Both (A) and (R) are true but (R) is not the correct explanation of (A).

18. (a) Both (A) and (R) are true and (R) is the correct explanation of (A).

19.

LIST-I	LIST-II
Abrasion	Soft tissue injuries
Green stick fractures	Bone injuries
Shoulder Dislocation	Joint Injuries
Lack of fitness	Cause of sport injuries

20. (a) Flexion
    (b) Extension
    (c) Abduction
    (d) Adduction

21. (i) (a) Flexion and Extension
    (ii) (b) Circumduction
    (iii) (c) Adduction and Abduction

22. (i) (b) Law of Inertia
    (ii) (a) Law of Acceleration
    (iii) (a) Flexion and Extension

23. (i) (c) Newton's 3rd law
    (ii) (c) Both
    (iii) (b) Mass
    (iv) (b) Biomechanics
    (v) (c) Law of action & reaction

24. (i) (a) Flexion
    (ii) (b) Extension
    (iii) (c) Abduction
    (iv) (d) Adduction
    (v) (b) Angular

25. (i) (a) It deals with physics principle
    (ii) (d) Mechanic and Anatomy
    (iii) (b) Dry surface

PHYSICS

SYLLABUS
Physics (Code No. 042)

Time : 90 Minutes   Max. Marks : 35

		No. of Periods	Marks
Unit–I	**Electrostatics**	23	17
	Chapter–1: Electric Charges and Fields		
	Chapter–2: Electrostatic Potential and Capacitance		
Unit-II	**Current Electricity**	15	
	Chapter–3: Current Electricity		
Unit-III	**Magnetic Effects of Current and Magnetism**	16	18
	Chapter–4: Moving Charges and Magnetism		
	Chapter–5: Magnetism and Matter		
Unit-IV	**Electromagnetic Induction and Alternating Currents**	19	
	Chapter–6: Electromagnetic Induction Chapter 7: Alternating currents		
	Total	**73**	**35**

Unit I: Electrostatics   23 Periods

Chapter–1: Electric Charges and Fields

Electric Charges; Conservation of charge, Coulomb's law-force between two-point charges, forces between multiple charges; superposition principle and continuous charge distribution. Electric field, electric field due to a point charge, electric field lines, electric dipole, electric field due to a dipole, torque on a dipole in uniform electric field. Electric flux, statement of Gauss's theorem and its applications to find field due to infinitely long straight wire, uniformly charged infinite plane sheet

Chapter–2: Electrostatic Potential and Capacitance

Electric potential, potential difference, electric potential due to a point charge, a dipole and system of charges; equipotential surfaces, electrical potential energy of a system of two-point charges and of electric dipole in an electrostatic field. Conductors and insulators, free charges and bound charges inside a conductor. Dielectrics and electric polarisation, capacitors and capacitance, combination of capacitors in series and in parallel, capacitance of a parallel plate capacitor with and without dielectric medium between the plates, energy stored in a capacitor.

Unit II: Current Electricity   15 Periods

Chapter–3: Current Electricity

Electric current, flow of electric charges in a metallic conductor, drift velocity, mobility and their relation with electric current; Ohm's law, electrical resistance, V-I characteristics (linear and non-linear), electrical energy and power, electrical resistivity and conductivity; temperature dependence of resistance. Internal resistance of a cell, potential difference and emf of a cell, combination of cells in series and in parallel, Kirchhoff's laws and simple applications, Wheatstone bridge, meter bridge(qualitative ideas only). Potentiometer - principle and its applications to measure potential difference and for comparing EMF of two cells; measurement of internal resistance of a cell (qualitative ideas only)

Unit III: Magnetic Effects of Current and Magnetism   16 Periods

Chapter–4: Moving Charges and Magnetism

Concept of magnetic field, Oersted's experiment. Biot - Savart law and its application to current carrying circular loop. Ampere's law and its applications to infinitely long straight wire. Straight and toroidal solenoids (only qualitative treatment), force on a moving charge in uniform magnetic and electric fields. Force on a current-carrying conductor in a uniform magnetic field, force between two parallel current-carrying conductors-definition of ampere, torque experienced by a current loop in uniform magnetic field; moving coil galvanometer-its current sensitivity and conversion to ammeter and voltmeter.

Chapter–5: Magnetism and Matter

Current loop as a magnetic dipole and its magnetic dipole moment, magnetic dipole moment of a revolving electron, bar magnet as an equivalent solenoid, magnetic field lines; earth's magnetic field and magnetic elements.

Unit IV: Electromagnetic Induction and Alternating Currents — 19 Periods

Chapter–6: Electromagnetic Induction

Electromagnetic induction; Faraday's laws, induced EMF and current; Lenz's Law, Eddy currents. Self and mutual induction.

Chapter–7: Alternating Current

Alternating currents, peak and RMS value of alternating current/voltage; reactance and impedance; LC oscillations (qualitative treatment only), LCR series circuit, resonance; power in AC circuits. AC generator and transformer.

Chapter 1
Electric Charges and Fields

1. Which one of the following is the unit of electric charge?
   (a) Coulomb
   (b) Newton
   (c) Volt
   (d) Coulomb/volt

2. The electric charge always resides:
   (a) at the centre of charged conductor
   (b) at the interior of charged conductor
   (c) on the outer surface of charged conductor
   (d) randomly all over the charged conductor

3. One metallic sphere A is given positive charge whereas another identical metallic sphere B of exactly same mass as of A is given equal amount of negative charge. Then:
   (a) mass of A and mass of B still remain equal
   (b) mass of A increases
   (c) mass of B decreases
   (d) mass of B increases

4. The figure shows a charge $+q$ at point P held in equilibrium in air with the help of four $+q$ charges situated at the vertices of a square. The net electrostatic force on q is given by:

   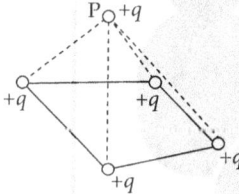

   (a) Newton's law
   (b) Coulomb's law
   (c) Principle of superposition
   (d) Net electric flux out the position of $+q$

5. The force of repulsion between two electrons at a certain distance is F. The force between two protons separated by the same distance is: ($m_p = 1836\, m_e$)
   (a) 2F
   (b) F
   (c) 1836F
   (d) F/1836

6. Two point charges of +3 μC and +4 μC repel each other with a force of 10 N. If each is given an additional charge of –6 μC, the new force is:
   (a) 6 N
   (b) 6.5 N
   (c) 7.5 N
   (d) 7 N

7. The electrostatic attracting force on a small sphere of charge 0.2 μC due to another small sphere of charge –0.3 μC in air is 0.3 N. The distance between the two spheres is:
   (a) 43.2×10^{-6} m
   (b) 4.24×10^{-3} m
   (c) 4.24×10^{-2} m
   (d) 4.24 m

8. If charge q is placed at the centre of the line joining two equal charges Q, the system of these charges will be in equilibrium if q is:
   (a) –4Q
   (b) –Q/4
   (c) –Q/2
   (d) +Q/2

9. Three charges each equal to 1 μC are placed at the corners of an equilateral triangle. If force between any two charges is F, then the net force on either will be:
   (a) $\sqrt{3}F$
   (b) $\sqrt{2}F$
   (c) 3F
   (d) $\dfrac{F}{3}$

10. Three charges are placed at the vertices of an equilateral triangle of side 'a' as shown in the following figure. The force experienced by the charge placed at the vertex A in a direction normal to BC is:

    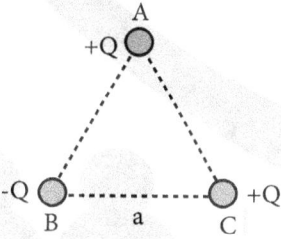

    (a) $Q^2/(4\pi\varepsilon_0 a^2)$
    (b) $-Q^2/(4\pi\varepsilon_0 a^2)$
    (c) Zero
    (d) 20 N

11. Three equal charges are placed on the three corners of a square. If the force between q_1 and q_2 is F_{12} and that between q_1 and q_3 is F_{13}, the ratio of magnitudes $\dfrac{F_{12}}{F_{13}}$ is:
    (a) 0.5
    (b) 1
    (c) 1.5
    (d) 2

12. Two positive point charges are 3 m apart and their combined charge is 20 μC. If the force between them is 0.075 N, then the charges are:
    (a) 10 μC, 10 μC
    (b) 15 μC, 5 μC
    (c) 12 μC, 8 μC
    (d) 14 μC, 6 μC

13. Four point charges are placed at the corners of a square ABCD of side 10 cm, as shown in figure. The force on a charge of 1 μC placed at the centre of square is:

    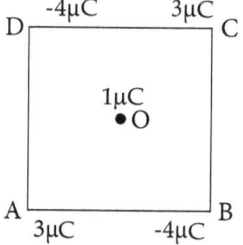

(a) 7 N (b) 12 N
(c) 18 N (d) Zero

14. A charge q_1 exerts some force on a second charge q_2. If third charge q_3 is brought near, the force of q_1 exerted on q_2:
    (a) decreases
    (b) increases
    (c) remains unchanged
    (d) increases if q_3 is of the same sign as q_1 and decreases if q_3 is of opposite sign

15. Two charges, each equal to q, are kept at $x = -a$ and $x = a$ on the x-axis. A particle of mass m and charge $q_0 = q/2$ is placed at the origin. If charge q_0 is given a small displacement ($y \ll a$) along the y-axis, the net force acting on the particle is proportional to:
    (a) y (b) $\dfrac{1}{y}$
    (c) $-y$ (d) $-\dfrac{1}{y}$

16. Two insulated charged metallic spheres P and Q have their centres separated by a distance of 50 cm. The radii of P and Q are negligible compared to the distance of separation. The mutual force of electrostatic repulsion if the charge on each is 3.2×10^{-2} C is:
    (a) 3.69×10^{-3} N (b) 4.69×10^{-3} N
    (c) 2.69×10^{-3} N (d) 3.69×10^{-4} N

17. Among two discs A and B, first have radius 10 cm and charge 10^{-6} C and second have radius 30 cm and charge 10^{-5} C. When they are touched, charge on both q_A and q_B respectively will, be:
    (a) $q_A = 2.75$ μC, $q_B = 3.15$ μC
    (b) $q_A = 1.09$ μC, $q_B = 1.53$ μC
    (c) $q_A = q_B = 5.5$ μC
    (d) None of these

18. The force per unit charge is known as _____.
    (a) electric flux (b) electric field
    (c) electric current (d) electric potential

19. If an electron has an initial velocity in a direction different from that of an electric field, the path of the electron is:
    (a) a straight line (b) a circle
    (c) an ellipse (d) a parabola

20. If one penetrates a uniformly charged spherical cloud, electric field strength:
    (a) decreases directly as the distance from the centre
    (b) increases directly as the distance from the centre
    (c) remains constant
    (d) None of these

21. Electric lines of force about a negative point charge are _____.
    (a) circular anticlockwise (b) circular clockwise
    (c) radial, inwards (d) radial, outwards

22. Electric lines of force:
    (a) exist everywhere
    (b) exist only in the immediate vicinity of electric charges
    (c) exist only when both positive and negative charges are near one another
    (d) are imaginary

23. The electric field at a point on equatorial line of a dipole and direction of the dipole moment:
    (a) will be parallel
    (b) will be in opposite direction
    (c) will be perpendicular
    (d) are not related

24. Which of the following is deflected by electric field?
    (a) X-rays (b) γ-rays
    (c) Neutrons (d) α-particles

25. An electron is moving towards x-axis. An electric field is along −x-axis direction then path of electron is:
    (a) a straight line (b) a circle
    (c) an ellipse (d) a parabola

26. If the charge on an object is halved then electric field becomes:
    (a) half (b) double
    (c) unchanged (d) thrice

27. A force of 2.56 N acts on a charge of 16×10^{-4} C. The intensity of electric field at that point is:
    (a) 1600 NC^{-1} (b) 150 NC^{-1}
    (c) 16 NC^{-1} (d) 1.5 NC^{-1}

28. A conducting sphere of radius 10 cm has unknown charge. If the electric field at a distance 20 cm from the centre of the sphere is 1.2×10^3 NC^{-1} and points radially inwards. The net charge on the sphere is:
    (a) -4.5×10^{-9} C (b) 4.5×10^9 C
    (c) -5.3×10^{-9} C (d) 5.3×10^9 C

29. If a dipole of dipole moment $\vec{p}$ is placed in a uniform electric field $\vec{E}$, then torque acting on it is given by:
    (a) $\vec{\tau} = \vec{p}\vec{E}$ (b) $\vec{\tau} = \vec{p} + \vec{E}$
    (c) $\vec{\tau} = \vec{p} \times \vec{E}$ (d) $\vec{\tau} = \vec{p} - \vec{E}$

30. A metallic sphere is placed in a uniform electric field. The line of force follows the path(s) shown in the figure as:

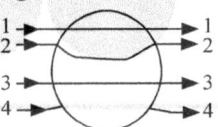

    (a) 1 (b) 2
    (c) 3 (d) 4

31. If E_a be the electric field strength of a short dipole at a point on its axial line and E_e that on the equatorial line at the same distance, then:
    (a) $E_e = 2E_a$ (b) $E_e = E_a$
    (c) $E_a = 2E_e$ (d) $E_e = 4E_a$

32. When an electric dipole $\vec{p}$ is placed in a uniform electric field $\vec{E}$ then at what angle between $\vec{p}$ and $\vec{E}$ the value of torque will be maximum:
    (a) 90° (b) 0°
    (c) 180° (d) 45°

33. An electric dipole is placed at an angle of 30° to a nonuniform electric field. The dipole will experience:

(a) a translational force only in the direction of the field
(b) a translational force only in the direction normal to the direction of the field
(c) a torque as well as a translational force
(d) a torque only

34. Which of the following figure represents the electric field lines due to a single positive charge?

(a) 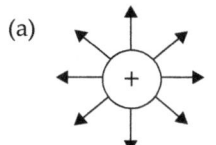 (b)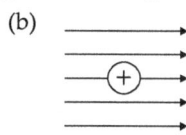

(c) 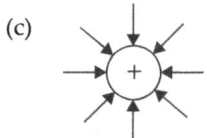 (d)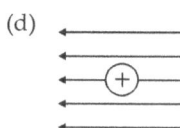

35. The electric field near a conducting surface having a uniform surface charge density is given by:
(a) $\dfrac{\sigma}{\varepsilon_0}$ and is parallel to the surface
(b) $\dfrac{2\sigma}{\varepsilon_0}$ and is parallel to the surface
(c) $\dfrac{\sigma}{\varepsilon_0}$ and is normal to the surface
(d) $\dfrac{2\sigma}{\varepsilon_0}$ and is normal to the surface

36. The electric field at a point on axial line of a dipole and direction of the dipole moment:
(a) will be parallel and in same direction
(b) will be in opposite direction
(c) will be perpendicular
(d) are not related

37. Which of the following statements about dipole moment is not true?
(a) The dimensions of dipole moment are $[L^1 T^0 A^0]$.
(b) The unit of dipole moment is Cm^{-1}.
(c) Dipole moment is vector quantity and directed from negative to positive charge.
(d) Dipole moment is a scalar quantity and has magnitude charge equal to the potential of separation between charges.

38. Match Column I with Column II with appropriate matching.

Column I	Column II
A. $\vec{E}$	(i) electric field lines
B. $\vec{p}$	(ii) $\dfrac{q}{4\pi\varepsilon_0 r^3}\vec{r}$
C. Two lines of force do not intersect each other	(iii) dipole field
D. Field produced by a dipole	(iv) $q \times 2a\hat{p}$

(a) A-(iv), B-(i), C-(ii), D-(iii)
(b) A-(ii), B-(iv), C-(i), D-(iii)
(c) A-(iii), B-(i), C-(iv), D-(ii)
(d) A-(iv), B-(iii), C-(i), D-(ii)

39. The SI unit of electric flux is:
(a) weber
(b) newton per coulomb
(c) volt × meter
(d) joule per coulomb

40. The surface considered for Gauss's law is called:
(a) Closed surface
(b) Spherical surface
(c) Gaussian surface
(d) Plane surface

41. The total flux through the faces of the cube with side of length a if a charge $2q$ is placed at corner A of the cube is:

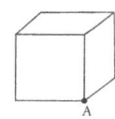

(a) $\dfrac{q}{8\varepsilon_0}$
(b) $\dfrac{q}{2\varepsilon_0}$
(c) $\dfrac{q}{4\varepsilon_0}$
(d) $\dfrac{2q}{\varepsilon_0}$

42. Which of the following statements is not true about Gauss's law?
(a) Gauss's law is not much useful in calculating electrostatic field when the system has some symmetry.
(b) Gauss's law is based on the inverse square dependence on distance contained in the coulomb's law.
(c) Gauss's law is true for any closed surface.
(d) The term q on the right side of Gauss's law includes the sum of all charges enclosed by the surface.

43. In the figure the net electric flux through the area A is $\phi = \vec{E}.\vec{A}$ when the system is in air. On immersing the system in water the net electric flux through the area:

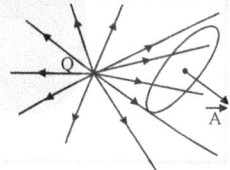

(a) becomes zero
(b) remains same
(c) increases
(d) decreases

44. Two infinite plane parallel sheets, separated by a distance d have equal and opposite uniform charge densities σ. Electric field at a point between the sheets is:
(a) $\dfrac{\sigma}{2\varepsilon_0}$
(b) $\dfrac{\sigma}{\varepsilon_0}$
(c) Zero
(d) depends on the location of the point

45. Two large, thin metal plates are parallel and close to each other. On their inner faces, the plates have surface charge densities of opposite signs and of magnitude 18×10^{-22} Cm^{-2}. The electric field between the plates is:

(a) 2.03×10^{-10} NC^{-1} (b) 3.03×10^{-10} NC^{-1}
(c) 2.03×10^{-12} NC^{-1} (d) 4.03×10^{-10} NC^{-1}

46. The electric flux through a closed Gaussion Surface depend upon: [CBSE, 2020]
    (a) Net charge enclosed and permittivity of the medium
    (b) Net charge enclosed, permittivity of the medium and size of the gaussion surface
    (c) Net charge enclosed only
    (d) Permittivity of the medium only

47. In figure, two positive charges, q_2 and q_3 fixed along the y axis, exert a net electric force in the +x-direction on a charge fixed along the x-axis. If a positive charge Q is added at $(x, 0)$, the force on q_1:
    [NCERT Exemplar]

    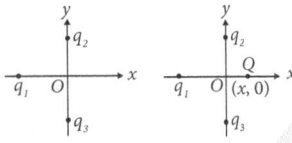

    (a) shall increase along the positive x-axis.
    (b) shall decrease along the positive x-axis.
    (c) shall point along the negative x-axis.
    (d) shall increase but the direction changes because of the intersection of Q with q_2 and q_3.

48. The electric flux through the surface:
    [NCERT Exemplar]

    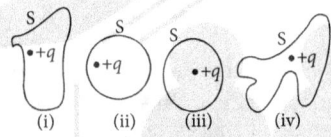

    (a) in figure (iv) is the largest
    (b) in figure (iii) is the least
    (c) in figure (ii) is same as in figure (iii) but is smaller than figure (iv)
    (d) is the same for all the figures

49. Figure shows electric field lines in which an electric dipole $\vec{p}$ is placed as shown. Which of the following statements is correct? [NCERT Exemplar]

    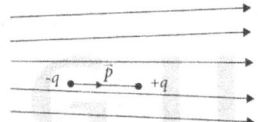

    (a) The dipole will not experience any force.
    (b) The dipole will experience a force towards right.
    (c) The dipole will experience a force towards left.
    (d) The dipole will experience a force upwards.

50. A hemisphere is uniformly charged positively. The electric field at a point on a diameter away from the centre is directed: [NCERT Exemplar]
    (a) perpendicular to the diameter
    (b) parallel to the diameter
    (c) at an angle tilted towards the diameter
    (d) at an angle tilted away from the diameter

51. Five charges q_1, q_2, q_3, q_4, and q_5 are fixed at their positions as shown in figure. S is Gaussian surface. The Gauss's law is given by $\int \vec{E}.\vec{ds} = \dfrac{q}{\varepsilon_0}$. Which of the following statements is correct? [NCERT Exemplar]

    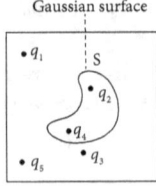

    (a) $\vec{E}$ on the LHS of the above equation will have a contribution from q_1, q_5, and q_3 while q on the RHS will have a contribution from q_2 and q_4 only.
    (b) $\vec{E}$ on the LHS of the above equation will have a contribution from all charges while q on the RHS will have a contribution from q_2 and q_4 only.
    (c) $\vec{E}$ on the LHS of the above equation will have a contribution from all charges while q on the RHS will have a contribution from q_1, q_3, and q_5 only.
    (d) Both $\vec{E}$ on the LHS and q on the RHS will have a contribution from q_2 and q_4 only.

Directions: In the following questions, a statement of assertion is followed by a statement of reason. Mark the correct choice as:
(a) If both assertion and reason are true and reason is the correct explanation of assertion.
(b) If both assertion and reason are true, but reason is not the correct explanation of assertion.
(c) If assertion is true, but reason is false.
(d) If both assertion and reason are false.

52. **Assertion:** The charge on any body can be increased or decreased in terms of e.
    Reason: Quantization of charge means that the charge on a body is the integral multiple of e.

53. **Assertion:** The properties that the force with which two charges attract or repel each other are not affected by the presence of a third charge.
    Reason: Force on any charge due to a number of other charges is the vector sum of all the forces on that charge due to other charges, taken one at a time.

54. **Assertion:** When we rub a glass rod with silk, the rod gets negatively charged and the silk gets positively charged.
    Reason: On rubbing, electrons from silk cloth move to the glass rod.

55. **Assertion:** Consider two identical charges placed distance 2d apart, along x-axis. The equilibrium of a positive test charge placed at the point O midway between them is stable for displacements along the x-axis.
    Reason: Force on test charge is zero.

    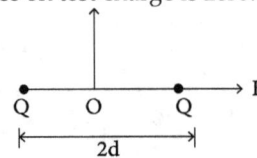

56. **Assertion:** Coulomb force is the dominating force in the universe.
    Reason: Coulomb force is weaker than the gravitational force.
57. **Assertion:** When charges are shared between any two bodies, no charge is really lost, but some loss of energy does occur.
    Reason: Some of the energy is dissipated in the form of heat, sparkling, etc.
58. **Assertion:** If there exists coulomb attraction between two bodies, both of them must be charged.
    Reason: In coulomb attraction, two bodies are positively charged.
59. **Assertion:** The positive charge particle is placed in front of a spherical uncharged conductor. The number of lines of forces terminating on the sphere will be more than those emerging from it.
    Reason: The surface charge density at a point on the sphere nearest to the point charge will be negative and maximum in magnitude compared to other points on the sphere.
60. **Assertion:** A point charge is brought in an electric field, the field at a nearby point will increase or decrease, depending on the nature of charge.
    Reason: The electric field is independent of the nature of charge.
61. **Assertion:** On going away from a point charge or a small electric dipole, electric field decreases at the same rate in both the cases.
    Reason: Electric field is inversely proportional to cube of distance from the charge or an electric dipole.
62. **Assertion:** Electrostatic field lines start at positive charges and end at negative charges.
    Reason: Field lines are continuous curves without any breaks and they form closed loop.
63. **Faraday Cage:**
    A Faraday cage or Faraday shield is an enclosure made of a conducting material. The fields within a conductor cancel out with any external fields so the electric field within the enclosure is zero. These Faraday cages act as a big hollow conductors, you can put things in it to shield them from electrical fields. Any electrical shocks the cage receives, pass harmlessly around the outside of the cage.

(i) Which of the following material can be used to make a Faraday cage?
 (a) Plastic (b) Glass
 (c) Copper (d) Wood
(ii) Example of a real-world Faraday cage is:
 (a) Car (b) Plastic box
 (c) Lighting rod (d) Metal rod
(iii) What is the electrical force inside a Faraday cage when it is struck by lightning?
 (a) The same as the lightning
 (b) Half that of the lightning
 (c) Zero
 (d) A quarter of the lightning
(iv) An isolated point charge +q is placed inside the Faraday cage. Its surface must have charge equal to:
 (a) Zero (b) +q
 (c) –q (d) +2q
(v) A point charge of 2C is placed at centre of Faraday cage in the shape of cube with surface of 9 cm edge. The number of electric field lines passing through the cube normally will be:
 (a) 1.9105 Nm²/C entering the surface
 (b) 1.9105 Nm²/C leaving the surface
 (c) 2.0105 Nm²/C leaving the surface
 (d) 2.0105 Nm²/C entering the surface

64. **Gauss theorem:**
Gauss theorem is mainly used to find out the electric flux linked to a closed surface. It does not depend upon the shape or size of surface. According to this theorem, the electric flux linked to a closed surface is equal to $\left(\dfrac{1}{\varepsilon_0}\right)$ times the charge enclosed by the surface.

Let we have a charge q, now if we want to find out the net flux linked to a closed surface around it them,

$$\text{Electric flux } \phi = \oint_s \vec{E}.\vec{ds} = \dfrac{q}{\varepsilon_0}$$

(i) Gauss theorem is used to find out:
 (a) Electric force (b) Electric flux
 (c) Electric potential (d) None of these.
(ii) This theorem is applied over a........surface:
 (a) Closed surface (b) Open surface
 (c) Both (a) and (b) (d) None of these
(iii) Gauss theorem does not depends upon the.........of surface:
 (a) Shape (b) Size
 (c) Area (d) Both (a) and (b)
(iv) If we increase the charge enclosed by the surface then electric flux will:
 (a) Increases (b) Decreases
 (c) Remain same (d) Both (a) and (b)
(v) Net flux linked to a closed surface around a charge particle is.............times the charge.
 (a) ε_0 (b) $\dfrac{1}{\varepsilon_0}$
 (c) ε_0^2 (d) None of these.

65. A system of closely spaced electric charge form a continuous charge distribution. To find the field of a continuous charge distribution, we divide the charge into infinitesimal charge elements. Each infinitesimal charge element is then considered as a point charge and electric field $d\vec{E}$ is determined due to this charge at given point. The net field at the given point is the summation of fields of all the elements i.e., $\vec{E} = \int d\vec{E}$

(i) How many electrons must be added to an isolated spherical conductor of radius 20 cm to produce an electric field 1000 N/C just outside the surface?

(a) 2.77×10^{20} (b) 2.77×10^{10}
(c) 1.77×10^{10} (d) 5.4×10^{10}

(ii) A circular annulus of inner radius r and outer radius R has a uniform charge density a. What will be the total charge on the annulus?
(a) $a(R^2 - r^2)$ (b) $\pi a(R^2 - r^2)$
(c) $a(R - r)$ (d) $\pi a R^2$

(iii) What is the dimension of linear charge density?
(a) $[ATL^{-1}]$ (b) $[AT^{-1}L]$
(c) $[ATL]$ (d) $[A^{-1}T^{-1}L]$

(iv) A charge is distributed along an infinite curved line in space with linear charge distribution λ. What will be the amount of force on a point charge q kept at a certain distance from the line?
(a) $q\int \dfrac{\lambda}{r^2}\hat{r}\, dl$ (b) $q\int \dfrac{\lambda}{r^2}\hat{r}\, dr$
(c) $q\int \dfrac{\lambda}{r^3}\hat{r}\, dl$ (d) $q\int \dfrac{\lambda}{r^2}\, dl$

(v) Charge leaks from sharp points because
(a) $\sigma \propto R$ (b) $\sigma \propto 1/R$
(c) $\sigma \propto R^2$ (d) $\sigma \propto \dfrac{1}{R^2}$

66. Microwave oven works on the principle of torque acting on an electric dipole. The food we consume has water molecules which are permanent electric dipoles. Oven produces microwaves that are oscillating electromagnetic fields and produce torque on the water molecules. Due to this torque on each water molecules, the molecules rotate very fast and produce thermal energy. Thus, heat generated is used to heat the food.

(i) An electric dipole is placed at an angle of 30° to a uniform electric field.
The dipole will experience
(a) a torque as well as translational force.
(b) a torque only
(c) a translational force only in the direction of the field.
(d) a translational force only in a direction normal to direction of the field.

(ii) An electric dipole is placed in a non-uniform electric field, what acts on it?
(a) only torque (b) only force
(c) both (a) and (b) (d) none of these

(iii) An electric dipole of moment $\vec{p}$ in placed in a uniform electric field $\vec{E}$. The maximum torque experienced by the dipole is
(a) pE (b) p/E
(c) E/p (d) $\vec{p}.\vec{E}$

(iv) Let E_a be the electric field due to a dipole in its axial plane distant l and let E_q be the field in the equatorial plane distant l. The relation between E_a and E_q is
(a) $E_a = E_q$ (b) $E_a = 2E_q$
(c) $E_q = 2 E_a$ (d) $E_a = 3 E_q$

(v) A point P lies on the perpendicular bisector of an electric dipole of dipole moment p. If the distance of P from the dipole is r (much larger than the size of the dipole) then the electric field at P is proportional to:
(a) p^{-1} and e^{-2} (b) p and r^{-2}
(c) p^2 and r^{-3} (d) p and r^{-3}

67. The number of electric field lines crossing a given area kept normal to the electric field lines is called electric flux. It is usually denoted by ϕ, and its unit is Nm^2C^{-1}. For a simpler understanding of electric flux, the following figure is useful.

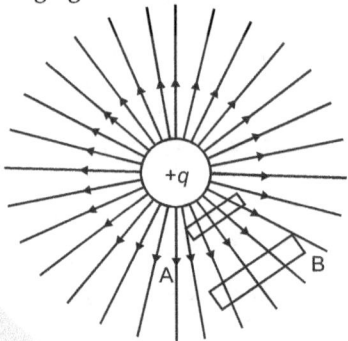

The electric field of a point charge is drawn in the figure. Consider two small rectangular area elements placed normal to the field at regions A and B. Even though these elements have the same area, the number of electric field lines crossing the element in region A is more than that crossing the element in region B. The electric field strength for a point charge decreases as the distance increases, then for a point charge electric flux also decreases as the distance increases.

(i) A sphere encloses an electric dipole within it. The total electric flux across the sphere is :
(a) zero
(b) half that due to a single charge
(c) double that due to a single charge
(d) dependent on the position of the dipole

(ii) Shown below is a distribution of charges.

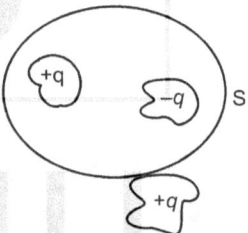

The flux of electric field due to these charges through the surface S is.
(a) $\dfrac{3q}{\varepsilon_0}$ (b) $\dfrac{2q}{\varepsilon_0}$
(c) $\dfrac{q}{\varepsilon_0}$ (d) Zero

(iii) A square surface of side L metres is in the plane of the paper. A uniform electric field $\vec{E}$ (Volt m^{-1}), also in the plane of the paper, is limited only to the lower half of the square surface as shown in the figure. The electric flux (in SI units) associated with the surface is :

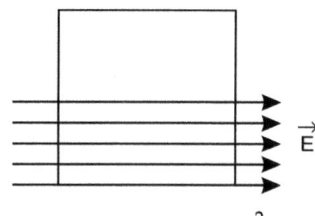

(a) EL^2 (b) $\dfrac{EL^2}{2\varepsilon_0}$

(c) $\dfrac{EL^2}{2}$ (d) Zero

(iv) A cylinder of radius R and length L is placed in a uniform electric field E parallel to the cylinder axis. The total flux for the surface of the cylinder is given by :
(a) $2\pi R^2 E$ (b) $\pi R^2/E$
(c) $\pi^2 R^2/E$ (d) zero

(v) In a region, the intensity of an electric field is given by $\vec{E} = 2\hat{i} + 3\hat{j} + \hat{k}$ in NC^{-1}. The electric flux through a surface $\vec{S} = 10\hat{i}$ m^2 in the region is :
(a) 5 Nm² C^{-1} (b) 10 Nm² C^{-1}
(c) 15 Nm² C^{-1} (d) 20 Nm² C^{-1}

Answers

1. (a) Coulomb
   Explanation: Unit of electric charge is Coulomb (C).

2. (c) on the outer surface of charged conductor
   Explanation: Electric charge always resides on the outer surface of charged conductor.

3. (d) mass of B increases
   Explanation: Negative charge means excess of electrons which increases the mass of sphere B, whereas positive charge on sphere A is given by removal of electrons.

4. (c) Principle of superposition
   Explanation: The weight mg of the charge hold in air is in equilibrium with net electrostatic force exerted by the four charges situated at the corners. The net electrostatic force is given by the vector sum of the individual forces exerted by the charges at the corners. This is principle of superposition.

5. (b) F
   Explanation: Electrostatic force is given by,
   $$F = \dfrac{1}{4\pi\varepsilon_0}\dfrac{q_1 q_2}{r^2}$$
   Here, charge and distance are same. So, force between two protons will be same.

6. (c) 7.5 N
   Explanation: Given that,
   $q_1 = 3\ \mu C,\ q_2 = +4\ \mu C,\ F = 10$ N
   $q_1' = +3 - 6 = -3\ \mu C,\ q_2' = +4 - 6 = -2\ \mu C$
   $\therefore\ \dfrac{F'}{F} = \dfrac{(q_1')(q_2')}{q_1 q_2}$
   $= \dfrac{(-3)\times(-2)}{2\times 4} = \dfrac{3}{4}$
   $\therefore\ F' = \dfrac{3}{4}\times F$
   $= \dfrac{3}{4}\times 10$
   $= 7.5$ N

7. (c) 4.24×10^{-2} m
   Explanation: Given that,
   $q_1 = 0.2\ \mu C = 0.2\times 10^{-6}$ C

$q_2 = -0.3\ \mu C = -0.3\times 10^{-6}$ C, F = 0.3 N
As, $F = \dfrac{q_1 q_2}{4\pi\varepsilon_0 r^2}$
$\therefore\ r^2 = \dfrac{q_1 q_2}{4\pi\varepsilon_0 F}$
$r^2 = \dfrac{0.2\times 10^{-6}\times 0.3\times 10^{-6}\times 9\times 10^9}{0.3}$
$= 1.8\times 10^{-3}$
$\therefore\ r = (1.8\times 10^{-3})^{1/2}$
$= 4.25\times 10^{-2}$ m

8. (b) $-Q/4$
   Explanation: For equilibrium, net force on Q = 0
   Let, the distance between line joining two equal charges Q is x unit.
   $\therefore\ \dfrac{kQQ}{(2x)^2} + \dfrac{kqQ}{x^2} = 0$
   $\therefore\ q = -Q/4$

9. (a) $\sqrt{3}F$
   Explanation: Each charge experiences two forces inclined at 60°. Therefore,
   $R = \sqrt{F^2 + F^2 + 2FF\cos 60°}$
   $= \sqrt{3F^2}$
   $= \sqrt{3}F$

10. (c) Zero
    Explanation: As we know that,

    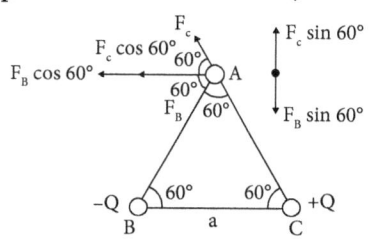

    $\left|\vec{F_B}\right| = \left|\vec{F_C}\right| = k\dfrac{Q^2}{a^2}$

    Hence, force exprienced by the change at A in the direction normal to BC is zero.

11. (d) 2
Explanation: By using Coulomb's law

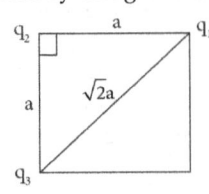

$$F_{12} = \frac{1}{4\pi\varepsilon_0} \times \frac{q^2}{a^2}$$

$$F_{13} = \frac{1}{4\pi\varepsilon_0} \times \frac{q^2}{(a\sqrt{2})^2}$$

$$\therefore \quad \frac{F_{12}}{F_{13}} = 2$$

12. (b) 15 μC, 5 μC
Explanation: By using Coulomb's law,

$$F = \frac{1}{4\pi\varepsilon_0} \times \frac{q_1 q_2}{r^2}$$

$$0.075 = \frac{9 \times 10^9 (q_1 q_2)}{(3)^2}$$

$$q_1 q_2 = \frac{0.075 \times 9}{9 \times 10^9}$$

$$= 75 \times 10^{-12} \qquad \ldots(i)$$

$$\Rightarrow \quad q_1 + q_2 = 20 \times 10^{-6}$$
$$\Rightarrow \quad q_1 = 20 \times 10^{-6}$$
$$\Rightarrow \quad (20 \times 10^{-6} - q_2) q_2 = 75 \times 10^{-12} \ldots[\text{By using (i)}]$$
$$\Rightarrow \quad 20 \times 10^{-6} q_2 - q_2^2 = 75 \times 10^{-12}$$
$$\Rightarrow \quad q_2 = 15 \times 10^{-6} \text{ or } q_2 = 5 \times 10^{-6}$$

∴ Two charge are 15 μC, 5 μC.

13. (d) Zero
Explanation: Forces of repulsion on 1 μC charge at O due to 3 μC charge, at A and C are equal and opposite. So they cancel each other. Similarly, forces of attraction of 1 μC charge at O due to –4 μC charges at B and D are also equal and opposite. So they also cancel each other.
Hence the net force on the charge of 1 μC at O is zero.

14. (c) remains unchanged
Explanation: The force will still remain $\frac{q_1 q_2}{4\pi\varepsilon_0 r^2}$ according to the superposition principle.

15. (a) y
Explanation:

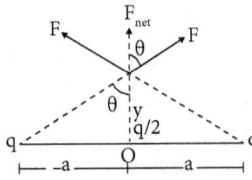

$F_{net} = 2F \cos\theta$

$$= \frac{2 \times kq^2}{2(a^2+y^2)} \times \cos\theta$$

$$= \frac{kq^2}{(a^2+y^2)} \times \frac{y}{\sqrt{(a^2+y^2)}}$$

For $y \ll a$

$$F = \frac{kq^2 y}{a^3}$$

$F \propto y$

16. (a) 3.69×10^{-3} N
Explanation: Given that,
$q_1 = q_2 = 3.2 \times 10^{-7}$ C, $r = 50$ cm $= 0.5$ m

$$\therefore \quad F = \frac{1}{4\pi\varepsilon_0} \frac{q_1 q_2}{r^2}$$

$$\therefore \quad F = \frac{9 \times 10^9 (3.2 \times 10^{-7})^2}{(0.5)^2}$$

$$= 3.69 \times 10^{-3} \text{ N}$$

17. (c) $q_A = q_B = 5.5$ μC
Explanation: The charge on disc A is 10^{-6} C. The charge on disc B is 10×10^{-6} C. The total charge on both $= 11 \times 10^{-6}$ C. When touched, this charge will be distributed equally, i.e., 5.5×10^{-6} C or 5.5 μC on each disc.

18. (b) electric field
Explanation: Force per unit charge is electric field.

19. (d) a parabola
Explanation: Charged particles move in parabolas if projected into an electric field in a direction at right angles to the field.

20. (a) decreases directly as the distance from the centre
Explanation: Electric Field is directly proportional to the magnitude of charge and inversely proportional to the square of the distance from the charge.

21. (c) radial, inwards
Explanation: Electric lines of force about a negative point charge are radial, inwards.

22. (d) are imaginary
Explanation: An electric line of force is an imaginary continuous line or curve drawn in an electric field.

23. (b) will be in opposite direction
Explanation: The direction of electric field at equatorial point A or B will be in opposite direction, as that of direction of dipole moment.

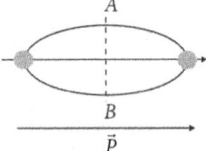

24. (d) α-particles
Explanation: α-particles are charged particles, so they are deflected by electric field.

25. (a) a straight line
Explanation: Charged particles move in straight lines and accelerate (or decelerate) if projected into an electric field along the direction of the field.

26. (a) half

Explanation: As we know that,
$$E = \frac{1}{4\pi\varepsilon_0}\frac{q}{r^2}$$
$$\Rightarrow E \propto q$$
So, when charge is halved electric field becomes half.

27. (a) 1600 NC^{-1}

Explanation: As we know that,
$$E = \frac{F}{q}$$
$$\therefore E = \frac{2.56}{16 \times 10^{-4}}$$
$$= 1600 \text{ NC}^{-1}$$

28. (c) -5.3×10^{-9} C

Explanation: Given that,
$r = 20$ cm $= 0.2$ m, $E = -1.2 \times 10^3$ NC^{-1}
$$\therefore E = \frac{q}{4\pi\varepsilon_0 r^2}$$
$$\therefore q = (4\pi\varepsilon_0 r^2)E$$
$$= \frac{(0.2)^2 \times (-1.2 \times 10^3)}{9 \times 10^9}$$
$$= -5.3 \times 10^{-9} \text{ C}$$

29. (c) $\vec{\tau} = \vec{p} \times \vec{E}$

Explanation: Given that,
Dipole moment of the dipole = $\vec{p}$ and uniform electric field = $\vec{E}$. We know that dipole moment $(\vec{p}) = qa$ (where q is the charge and a is dipole length). And when a dipole of dipole moment $\vec{p}$ is placed in uniform electric field $\vec{E}$, then torque $(\vec{\tau})$ = Electric force × perpendicular distance between the two forces = $qaE \sin\theta$ or $\vec{\tau} = pE \sin\theta$
or $\vec{\tau} = \vec{p} \times \vec{E}$ (vector form).

30. (d) 4

Explanation: Electric field inside the sphere will be zero.

31. (c) $E_a = 2E_e$

Explanation: As we know that,
$$E_a = \frac{2kp}{r^3}$$
$$E_e = \frac{kp}{r^3}$$
$$\therefore E_a = 2E_e$$

32. (a) 90°

Explanation: As we know that,
$$\vec{\tau} = \vec{p} \times \vec{E}$$
$$= pE \sin\theta$$
So, torque will be maximum at 90°.

33. (c) a torque as well as a translational force

Explanation: As we know that,

The electric field will be different at the location of force on the two charges. Therefore, the two charges will be unequal. This will result in a force as well as torque.

34. (a) Electric field line will be radially outwards.

Explanation: The field lines of a single positive charge are radially outward.

35. (c) $\frac{\sigma}{\varepsilon_0}$ and is normal to the surface

Explanation: Electric field near the conductor surface is given by $\frac{\sigma}{\varepsilon_0}$ and it is perpendicular to surface.

36. (a) will be parallel and in same direction

Explanation: Electric dipole moment is directed from negative charge to positive charge. The direction of electric field strength on the axial line is also the same.

37. (d) Dipole moment is a scalar quantity and has magnitude charge equal to the potential of separation between charges.

Explanation: Dipole moment is a vector quantity and has magnitude of $2qa$ and it is in the direction of the dipole axis from $-q$ to q.

38. (b) A-(ii), B-(iv), C-(i), D-(iii)

Explanation: As we know that,
$$\vec{E} = \frac{q}{4\pi\varepsilon_0 r^3}\vec{r}, \vec{p} = q \times 2a\hat{p}$$
Field produced by a dipole is known as dipole field.
Electric field lines do not intersect each other.

39. (c) volt × meter

Explanation: SI unit of electric flux is
$$\frac{N \times m^2}{C} = \frac{J \times m}{C} = \text{volt} \times m.$$

40. (c) Gaussian surface

Explanation: The surface that we choose for the application of Gauss's law is called Gaussian surface.

41. (c) $\frac{q}{4\varepsilon_0}$

Explanation: In the figure, when a charge $2q$ is placed at corner A of the cube, it is being shared equally by eight cubes. So, total flux through the faces of the given cube = $\frac{q}{4\varepsilon_0}$

42. (a) Gauss's law is not much useful in calculating electrostatic field when the system has some symmetry.
    Explanation: Gauss's law is often useful towards a much easier calculation of electrostatic field when the system has some symmetry. This is facilitated by the choice of a suitable Gaussian surface.

43. (d) decreases
    Explanation: Since, electric field $\vec{E}$ decreases inside water, therefore, flux $\phi = \vec{E} \cdot \vec{A}$ also decreases.

44. (b) $\dfrac{\sigma}{\varepsilon_0}$
    Explanation: As we know that,
    $$E = \dfrac{\sigma}{\varepsilon_0}$$

45. (a) 2.03×10^{-10} NC^{-1}
    Explanation: As we know that,
    $$\because \quad E = \dfrac{\sigma}{\varepsilon_0}$$
    $$\therefore \quad E = \dfrac{18 \times 10^{-22}}{8.85 \times 10^{-12}}$$
    $$= 2.03 \times 10^{-10} \text{ NC}^{-1}$$

46. (a) Net charge enclosed and permittivity of the medium.
    Explanation: Electric flux $\phi = \dfrac{q}{\varepsilon}$

47. (a) shall increase along the positive x-axis.
    Explanation: As shown in the figure, since positive charge q_2 and q_3 exert a net force in the +X-direction on the charge q_1 fixed along the x-axis, the charge q_1 is negative. Obviously, due to addition of positive charge Q at $(x, 0)$, the force on $-q$ shall increase along the positive x-axis.

    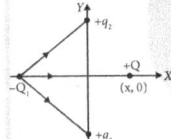

48. (d) is the same for all the figures
    Explanation: As per Gauss's theorem in electrostatics, the electric flux through a surface depends only on the amount of charge enclosed by the surface. It does not depend on size and shape of the surface. Therefore, electric flux through the surface is the same for all figures.

49. (c) The dipole will experience a force towards left.
    Explanation: The spacing between electric lines of force increases from left to right. So, E on left is greater than E on right. Force on $+q$ charge of dipole is smaller and to the right. Force on $-q$ charge of dipole is bigger and to the left. Hence the dipole will experience a force towards the left.

50. (a) perpendicular to the diameter
    Explanation: When the point is on the diameter and away from the centre of hemisphere which is charged uniformly and positively, the component of electric field intensity parallel to the diameter cancel out. So the electric field is perpendicular to the diameter.

51. (b) $\vec{E}$ on the LHS of the above equation will have a contribution from all charges while q on the RHS will have a contribution from q_2 and q_4 only.
    Explanation: By using Gauss's law,
    $\vec{E}$ on the LHS of the above equation will have a contribution from all charges while q on the RHS will have a contribution from q_2 and q_4 only.

52. (a) Protons and electrons are the only basic charges in the universe. All the observable charges have to be integral multiple of e. Thus, if a body contains n_1 electrons and n_2 protons, the total amount of charge on the body is $n_2 e + n_1 (-e) = (n_2 - n_1) e$. Since n_1 and n_2 are integers, their difference is also an integer. Thus, the charge on any body is always an integral multiple of e and can be increased or decreased in terms of e.

53. (b) Force on any charge due to a number of other charges is the vector sum of all the forces on that charge due to the other charges, taken one at a time. The individual force is unaffected due to the presence of other charges. This is the principle of superposition of charges.

54. (d) When we rub a glass rod with silk cloth, electrons from the glass rod are transferred to the silk cloth. Thus the rod gets positively charged and the silk gets negatively charged.

55. (b) If positive charge is displaced along x-axis, then net force will always act in a direction opposite to that of displacement and the test charge will always come back to its original position.

56. (d) Gravitational force is the dominating force in nature and not coulomb's force. Gravitational force is the weakest force. Also, Coulomb's force >> gravitational force.

57. (a) Charges are conserved by the law of conservation of charges. Energy is also conserved, if we take in account of the loss of energy by heat, sparking etc.

58. (d) Coulomb attraction exists even when one body is charged, and the other is uncharged.

59. (d) No. of lines entering the surface = No. of lines leaving the surface.

60. (c) The electric field will increase if positive charge is brought in an electric field.

61. (d) The rate of decrease of electric field is different in the two cases. In case of a point charge, it decreases as $1/r^2$ but in the case of electric dipole, it decreases more rapidly, as $E \propto 1/r^3$.

62. (c) Electrostatic field lines are continuous curves without any breaks. They start at positive charges and end at negative charges. They cannot form closed loops.

63. (i) (c) Copper, as Faraday cage is made from conducting material.
    (ii) (a) Car, as it can save us from lightning.
    (iii) (c) Zero, as electrical field inside the age is zero.
    (iv) (c) $-q$, charge is $+q$ inside it. so, $-q$ will be induced on outer surface

(v) Correct option is not given.

$$\phi = \frac{q}{\varepsilon_0} = \frac{2}{8.85 \times 10^{-12}}$$

$$= 2.25 \times 10^{11} \text{ Nm}^2/\text{C}$$

leaving the surface

64. (i) (b) Electric flux
 (ii) (a) Closed surface
 (iii) (d) both (a) and (b)
 (iv) (a) increase
 (v) (b) $\frac{1}{\varepsilon_0}$

65. (i) (b) The electric field is given by

$$E = k\frac{Q}{r^2}$$

$$\therefore \quad Q = \frac{Er^2}{k} = \frac{1000 \times (0.2)^2}{9 \times 10^9}$$

$$= 4.44 \times 10^{-9}$$

Number of electrons required for this amount of charge is $= \frac{4.44 \times 10^{-9}}{1.602 \times 10^{-19}} = 2.77 \times 10^{10}$

(ii) (b) Total surface area of the annulus = $\pi (R^2 - r^2)$ because it has outer radius R and inner radius r. We know surface charge density is the amount of charge stored on the unit surface area. In this case, surface charge density is a. Therefore, total charge on the annulus = $\pi a (R^2 - r^2)$.

(iii) (a) $\lambda = \frac{\text{Amount of charge}}{\text{Total length}} = \frac{Q}{l}$

$$= \frac{[AT]}{[L]} = [ATL^{-1}]$$

(iv) (a) Let the point charge is situated at a distance, r from small part at dl on the line. The charge stored in stated small part = λdl. The force due to that small part will be directed towards the unit vector $\hat{r}$. Therefore, force on that charge due to the entire linear charge distribution

$$= q\int \frac{\lambda}{r^2} \hat{r}\, dl \, .$$

(v) (b) $\sigma \propto 1/R$

66. (i) (a) In a non-uniform electric field, an electric dipole experiences both a torque and a translational force.
 (ii) (c) In a non-uniform electric field, an electric dipole experiences both a net force and a torque.
 (iii) (a) $\tau_{max} = pE \sin 90° = pE$
 (iv) (b) Electric field at any axial point is twice the electric field at the same distance along the equatorial line.
 $\therefore \quad E_a = 2E_q$
 (v) (d) At any far away equatorial point of an electric dipole,

$$E = \frac{1}{4\pi\varepsilon_0}\frac{p}{r^3} \quad i.e., \, E \propto pr^{-3}$$

67. (i) (a) The net charge enclosed by the sphere is zero.
 (ii) (d) Charges present outside the closed surface do not contribute towards electric flux.
 (iii) (d) As electric field is parallel to the square surface, electric flux crossing this surface will be zero.
 (iv) (d) Flux through surface A,
 $\phi_A = E \times \pi R^2$
 And $\phi_B = -E \times \pi R^2$

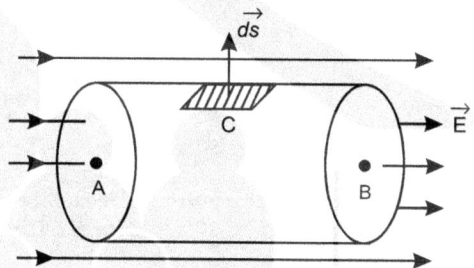

Flux through curved surface

$C = \int \vec{E}.\vec{ds} = \int E ds \cos 90° = 0$

$\therefore$ Total flux through cylinder

$= \phi_A + \phi_B + \phi_C = 0$

(v) (d) $\vec{E} = 2\hat{i}+3\hat{j}+\hat{k}$ NC^{-1}, $\vec{S} = 10\hat{i}$ m^2

Electric flux $\phi_E = \vec{E}.\vec{S}$

$= (2\hat{i}+3\hat{j}+\hat{k}\text{NC}^{-1}),(10\hat{i}\text{ m}^2)$

$= 20$ Nm^2 C^{-1}

Chapter 2

Electrostatic Potential and Capacitance

1. The electric potential inside a conducting sphere:
   (a) increases from centre to surface
   (b) decreases from centre to surface
   (c) remains constant from centre to surface
   (d) is zero at every point inside

2. One volt is equivalent to:
   (a) newton/second   (b) newton/coulomb
   (c) joule/coulomb   (d) joule/second

3. The potential at a point due to a charge of 4×10^{-7} C located 10 cm away is?
   (a) 3.6×10^5 V   (b) 3.6×10^4 V
   (c) 4.5×10^4 V   (d) 4.5×10^5 V

4. The value of electric potential at any point due to any electric dipole is:
   (a) $k.\dfrac{\vec{p} \times \vec{r}}{r^2}$ (b) $k.\dfrac{\vec{p} \times \vec{r}}{r^3}$
   (c) $k.\dfrac{\vec{p} \cdot \vec{r}}{r^2}$ (d) $k.\dfrac{\vec{p} \cdot \vec{r}}{r^3}$

5. The electric potential at a point in free space due to a charge Q coulomb is $Q \times 10^{11}$ V. The electric field at that point is:
   (a) $12\pi\varepsilon_0 Q \times 10^{22}$ Vm^{-1} (b) $4\pi\varepsilon_0 Q \times 10^{20}$ Vm^{-1}
   (c) $12\pi\varepsilon_0 Q \times 10^{20}$ Vm^{-1} (d) $4\pi\varepsilon_0 Q \times 10^{22}$ Vm^{-1}.

6. An electric dipole is placed at the centre of a hollow conducting sphere. Which of the following is correct?:
   (a) Electric field is zero at every point of the sphere
   (b) Electric field is not zero anywhere on the sphere
   (c) The flux of electric field is not zero through the sphere
   (d) None of these

7. Figure shows the field lines of a positive point charge. The work done by the field in moving a small positive charge from Q to P is:

   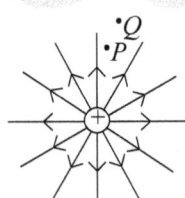

   (a) zero   (b) positive
   (c) negative (d) data insufficient.

8. As shown in the figure, charges +q and −q are placed at the vertices B and C of an isosceles triangle. The potential at the vertex A is:

   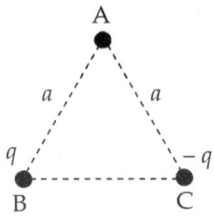

   (a) $\dfrac{1}{4\pi\varepsilon_0} \cdot \dfrac{2q}{\sqrt{a^2}}$ (b) $\dfrac{1}{4\pi\varepsilon_0} \cdot \dfrac{q}{\sqrt{a^2}}$
   (c) $\dfrac{1}{4\pi\varepsilon_0} \cdot \dfrac{(-q)}{\sqrt{a^2}}$ (d) zero

9. Four charges each equal to q are placed at the corners of a square of side l. The electric potential at the centre of the square is :
   (a) $\dfrac{1}{4\pi\varepsilon_0} \dfrac{4q}{l}$ (b) $\dfrac{1}{4\pi\varepsilon_0} \dfrac{4q}{\sqrt{2}l}$
   (c) $\dfrac{1}{\pi\varepsilon_0} \dfrac{\sqrt{2}q}{l}$ (d) $\dfrac{1}{\pi\varepsilon_0} \dfrac{2q}{l}$

10. Can two equipotential surfaces intersect each other?
    (a) Yes
    (b) No
    (c) Sometimes
    (d) Only when surfaces intersect at 90°

11. If a unit positive charge is taken from one point to another over an equipotential surface, then:
    (a) work is done on the charge
    (b) work is done by the charge
    (c) work done is constant
    (d) no work is done

12. A hollow conducting sphere is placed in an electric field produced by a point charge placed at P as shown in figure. Let V_A, V_B, V_C be the potentials at points A, B and C respectively. Then:

    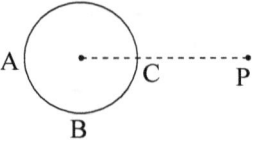

    (a) $V_C > V_B$ (b) $V_B > V_C$
    (c) $V_A > V_B$ (d) $V_A = V_C$.

13. A test charge is moved from lower potential point to a higher potential point. The potential energy of test charge will:
    (a) remains the same   (b) increase
    (c) decrease   (d) becomes zero

14. The potential energy of a system of two charges is negative when:
    (a) both the charges are positive
    (b) both the charges are negative
    (c) one charge is positive and other is negative
    (d) both the charges are separated by infinite distance

15. An electric dipole of moment $\vec{p}$ is placed normal to the lines of force of electric field intensity $\vec{E}$, then the work done in deflecting it through an angle of 180° is:
    (a) pE (b) $2pE$
    (c) $-2pE$ (d) zero

16. When one electron is taken towards the other electron, then the electric potential energy of system :
    (a) decreases   (b) increases
    (c) remains unchanged   (d) becomes zero

17. Q amount of electric charge is present on the surface of a sphere having radius R. Then electrical potential energy of this system is:
    (a) $\dfrac{kQ}{R}$ (b) $\dfrac{kQ^2}{R^2}$
    (c) $\dfrac{kQ^2}{2R}$ (d) $\dfrac{kQ^2}{2R^2}$

18. The electrostatic potential energy of a charge of 5 C at a point in the electrostatic field is 50 J. The potential at that point is:
    (a) 0.1 V   (b) 5 V
    (c) 10 V   (d) 250 V

19. Two charges of equal magnitude 'q' are placed in air at a distance '$2a$' apart and third charge '$-2q$' is placed at midpoint. The potential energy of the system is: (ε_0 = permittivity of free space) :
    (a) $-\dfrac{q^2}{8\pi\varepsilon_0 a}$ (b) $-\dfrac{3q^2}{8\pi\varepsilon_0 a}$
    (c) $-\dfrac{5q^2}{8\pi\varepsilon_0 a}$ (d) $-\dfrac{7q^2}{8\pi\varepsilon_0 a}$

20. A conductor which can be given almost unlimited charge is_____.
    (a) copper   (b) air
    (c) gold   (d) earth

21. If a conductor has a potential zero and there are no charges anywhere else outside, then :
    (a) there must be charges on the surface or inside itself.
    (b) there cannot be any charge in the body of the conductor
    (c) there must be charges only on the surface.
    (d) both (a) and (b) are correct

22. There are two metallic spheres of same radii but one is solid and the other is hollow, then
    (a) solid sphere can be given more charge.
    (b) hollow sphere can be given more charge.
    (c) they can be charged equally (maximum).
    (d) none of the above

23. A conductor with a positive charge:
    (a) is always at positive potential
    (b) is always at zero potential
    (c) is always at negative potential
    (d) may be at positive, zero or negative potential

24. When air is replaced by a dielectric medium of constant K, the maximum force of attraction between two charges separated by a distance:
    (a) increases K times   (b) remains unchanged
    (c) decreases K times   (d) increases K^{-1} times

25. Dielectric constant of a medium is also known as:
    (a) relative permeability   (b) permeability
    (c) permittivity   (d) relative permittivity

26. On decreasing the distance between the plates of a parallel plate capacitor, its capacitance:
    (a) remains unaffected
    (b) decreases
    (c) first increases then decreases
    (d) increases

27. Energy is stored in a capacitor in the form of:
    (a) magnetic energy   (b) light energy
    (c) heat energy   (d) electrostatic energy

28. If in a parallel plate capacitor, which is connected to a battery, we fill dielectrics in whole space of its plates, then which of the following increases?:
    (a) Q and V   (b) V and E
    (c) E and C   (d) Q and C

29. In a parallel plate capacitor, the capacity increases if:
    (a) area of the plate is decreased
    (b) distance between the plates increases
    (c) area of the plate is increased
    (d) dielectric constant decreases

30. The energy stored in a condenser of capacity C which has been raised to a potential V is given by::
    (a) $\dfrac{1}{2}CV$ (b) $\dfrac{1}{2}CV^2$
    (c) CV (d) CV^2

31. The work done in placing a charge of 8×10^{-18} C on a condenser of capacity 100 μF is:
    (a) 3.2×10^{-26} J   (b) 3.2×10^{-31} J
    (c) 3.2×10^{-32} J   (d) 4×10^{-26} J

32. A parallel plate capacitor has two square plates with equal and opposite charges. The surface charge densities on the plates are +σ and −σ respectively. In the region between the plates the magnitude of the electric field is:
    (a) $\dfrac{\sigma}{2\varepsilon_0}$ (b) $\dfrac{\sigma}{\varepsilon_0}$
    (c) 0   (d) None of these

33. In a charged capacitor, the energy resides:
    (a) in the positive charges
    (b) in both the positive and negative charges
    (c) in the field between the plates
    (d) around the edges of the capacitor plates

34. The capacitor, whose capacitance is 6μF, 6μF and 3μF respectively are connected in series with 20 V line. Find the charge on 3 μF:

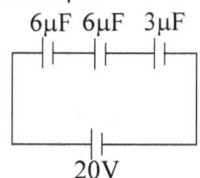

(a) 30 μC (b) 48 μC
(c) 60 μC (d) 120 μC

35. A parallel plate air capacitor has a capacitance of 100 μF. The plates are at a distance d apart. If a slab of thickness t ($t < d$) and dielectric constant 5 is introduced between the parallel plates, then the capacitance will be:
(a) 30 μC (b) 100 μC
(c) 200 μC (d) 500 μC

36. A network of six identical capacitors, each of value C is made as shown in the figure. Equivalent capacitance between points A and B is:

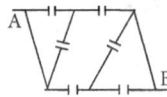

(a) C/4 (b) 3C/4
(c) 4C/3 (d) 3C

37. A parallel plate capacitor is connected across a 2 V battery and charged. The battery is then disconnected and a glass slab is introduced between plates. Which of the following pairs of quantities decreases?:
(a) Charge and potential difference.
(b) Potential difference and energy stored.
(c) Energy stored and capacitance.
(d) Capacitance and charge.

38. For the configuration of media of permittivity's ε_0, ε, and ε_0 between parallel plates each of area A, as shown in figure the equivalent capacitance is:

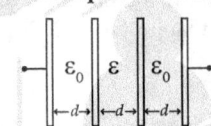

(a) $\varepsilon_0 A/d$ (b) $\varepsilon\varepsilon_0 A/d$
(c) $\dfrac{\varepsilon\varepsilon_0 A}{d(\varepsilon+\varepsilon_0)}$ (d) $\dfrac{\varepsilon\varepsilon_0 A}{(2\varepsilon+\varepsilon_0)d}$

39. The total energy stored in the condenser system shown in the figure will be:

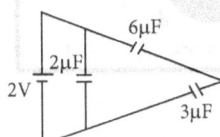

(a) 0.8 μJ (b) 80 μJ
(c) 8 μJ (d) 800 μJ

40. What is the effective capacitance between points X and Y?

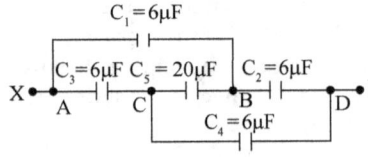

(a) 24 μF (b) 18 μF
(c) 12 μF (d) 6 μF

41. A positively charged particle is released from rest in a uniform electric field. The electric potential energy of the charge: [NCERT Exemplar]

(a) remains a constant because the electric field is uniform.
(b) increases because the charge moves along the electric field.
(c) decreases because the charge moves along the electric field.
(d) decreases because the charge moves opposite to the electric field

42. Figure shows some equipotential lines distributed in space. A charged object is moved from point A to point B. [NCERT Exemplar]

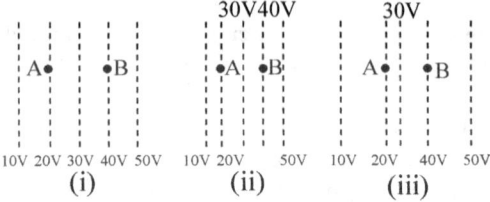

(a) The work done in figure (i) is the greatest
(b) The work done in figure (ii) is the least
(c) The work done is the same in figure (i), (ii) and (iii).
(d) The work done in figure (iii) is greater than figure (ii) but equal to that in figure (i).

43. The electrostatic potential on the surface of a charged conducting sphere is 100 V. Two statements are made in this regard.
S_1: At any point inside the sphere, electric intensity is zero.
S_2: At any point inside the sphere, the electrostatic potential is 100 V.
Which of the following is a correct statement?: [NCERT Exemplar]
(a) S_1 is true but S_2 is false
(b) Both S_1 and S_2 are false
(c) S_1 is true, S_2 is also true and S_1 is the cause of S_2.
(d) S_1 is true, S_2 is also true but the statements are independent

44. Equipotentials at a great distance from a collection of charges whose total sum is not zero are approximately: [NCERT Exemplar]
(a) spheres (b) planes
(c) paraboloids (d) ellipsoids

45. A capacitor of 4 μF is connected as shown in the circuit. The internal resistance of the battery is 0.5 Ω. The amount of charge on the capacitor plates will be: [NCERT Exemplar]

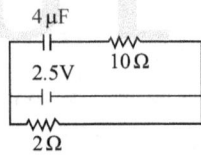

(a) 0 (b) 4 μF
(c) 16 μF (d) 8 μF

46. A parallel plate capacitor is made of two dielectric blocks in series. One of the blocks has thickness d_1 and dielectric constant K_1, and the other has thickness d_2 and dielectric constant K_2 as shown in figure. This arrangement can be thought as a dielectric slab of thickness d ($=d_1 + d_2$) and effective dielectric constant K. The K is: [NCERT Exemplar]

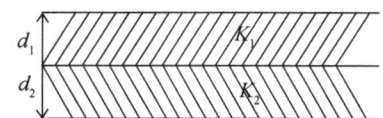

(a) $\dfrac{K_1 d_1 + K_2 d_2}{d_1 + d_2}$ (b) $\dfrac{K_1 d_1 + K_2 d_2}{K_1 + K_2}$

(c) $\dfrac{K_1 K_2 (d_1 + d_2)}{K_2 d_1 + K_1 d_2}$ (d) $\dfrac{2 K_1 K_2}{K_1 + K_2}$

47. A proton released from rest in an electric field, will start moving towards a region of .... potential in the field. **[CBSE 2020]**
    (a) increasing (b) decreasing
    (c) same (d) none of these

48. The physical quantity having SI unit $NC^{-1}m$ is.......... **[CBSE 2020]**
    (a) Electric potential (b) Electric force
    (c) Electric field intensity (d) None of these

Directions: In the following questions, a statement of assertion is followed by a statement of reason. Mark the correct choice as:
(a) If both assertion and reason are true and reason is the correct explanation of assertion.
(b) If both assertion and reason are true, but reason is not the correct explanation of assertion.
(c) If assertion is true, but reason is false.
(d) If both assertion and reason are false.

49. **Assertion:** Work done in moving a charge between any two points in an electric field is dependent of the path followed by the charge, between these points.
    Reason: Electrostatic force is a non-conservative force.

50. **Assertion:** The electric potential at any point on the equatorial plane of a dipole is non-zero.
    Reason: The work done in bringing a unit positive charge from infinity to a point in equatorial plane is not equal for the two charges of the dipole.

51. **Assertion:** For a non-uniformly charged thin circular ring with net charge is zero, the electric field at any point on axis of the ring is zero.
    Reason: For a non-uniformly charged thin circular ring with net charge zero, the electric potential at each point on axis of the ring is non-zero.

52. **Assertion:** For a point charge, concentric spheres centered at a location of the charge are equipotential surfaces.
    Reason: An equipotential surface is a surface over which potential has constant value.

53. **Assertion:** Electric potential and electric potential energy are different quantities.
    Reason: For a system of positive test charge and point charge electric potential energy = electric potential.

54. **Assertion:** Surface of a symmetrical conductor can be treated as equipotential surface.
    Reason: Charge can easily flow in a conductor.

55. **Assertion:** Two adjacent conductors of unequal dimensions, carrying the same positive charge have a potential difference between them.
    Reason: The potential of a conductor depends upon the charge given to it.

56. **Assertion:** When a dielectric slab is gradually inserted between the plates of an isolated parallel plate capacitor, the energy of the system decreases.
    Reason: The force between the plates decreases.

57. **Assertion:** Polar molecules have temporary dipole moment.
    Reason: In polar molecule, the centres of positive and negative charges coincide even when there is no external field.

58. **Assertion:** If three capacitors of capacitance $C_1 < C_2 < C_3$ are connected in parallel then their equivalent capacitance $C_p > C_s$.
    Reason: $\dfrac{1}{C_p} = \dfrac{1}{C_1} + \dfrac{1}{C_2} + \dfrac{1}{C_3}$

59. **Assertion:** If the distance between parallel plates of a capacitor is halved and dielectric constant is made three times, then the capacitor becomes six times.
    Reason: Capacity of the capacitor does not depend upon the nature of the material.

60. **Assertion:** In Van de Graaff generator, the process of spraying the charge is called electron discharge.
    Reason: Van de Graaff generator produces high voltage and high current.

61. The electric field at a point is the force experienced by unit positive charge at that point. It is a vector quantity. The electric field due to a point charge q at a distance r from it is given by:
    $$E = \dfrac{1}{4\pi\varepsilon_0} \dfrac{q}{r^2}$$
    Its direction is towards the charge when it is negative and away from the charge when the charge is positive. If there are a system of charges, then field due to each charge will get added vectorially. Electric potential at a point is the work done in bringing unit positive charge from infinity to that point. The potential due to a point charge at a distance r from it is given by:
    $$V = \dfrac{1}{4\pi\varepsilon_0} \dfrac{q}{r}$$
    If there are a number of charge in the vicinity of the point, then the potential due to each charge gets add up algebraically (one need to specify the sign of the charge in calculation).
    Now consider the following situation.
    Four charges $+q$, $+q$, $-q$ and $-q$ are placed at the four corners A, B, C and D respectively of a square of side a arranged in the same order. Midpoint of BC is E and that of CD is F. O is the centre of the square.
    (i) The direction of the net electric field at O is towards:
        (a) AB (b) BC
        (c) CD (d) AD
    (ii) The magnitude of the electric field at O is:
        (a) $\dfrac{q}{\sqrt{2\pi\varepsilon_0 a^2}}$ (b) $\dfrac{q}{\sqrt{3\pi\varepsilon_0 a^2}}$
        (c) $\dfrac{\sqrt{3}q}{\pi\varepsilon_0 a^2}$ (d) $\dfrac{\sqrt{2}q}{\pi\varepsilon_0 a^2}$
    (iii) The electric potential at O is:

(a) $\dfrac{\sqrt{2}q}{\pi\varepsilon_0 a}$ (b) $\dfrac{\sqrt{3}q}{\pi\varepsilon_0 a}$

(c) $\dfrac{q}{\pi\varepsilon_0 a}$ (d) 0

(iv) The work done in carrying a change from O to E is:

(a) $\dfrac{\sqrt{2}qe}{\pi\varepsilon_0 a}$ (b) $\dfrac{qe}{\pi\varepsilon_0 a}\left(\dfrac{1}{\sqrt{5}}-1\right)$

(c) $\dfrac{qe}{\pi\varepsilon_0 a}\left(\dfrac{1}{\sqrt{5}}+1\right)$ (d) 0

(v) The work done in carrying a charge from O to F is:

(a) $\dfrac{\sqrt{2}qe}{\pi\varepsilon_0 a}$ (b) $\dfrac{qe}{\pi\varepsilon_0 a}\left(\dfrac{1}{\sqrt{5}}-1\right)$

(c) $\dfrac{qe}{\pi\varepsilon_0 a}\left(\dfrac{1}{\sqrt{5}}+1\right)$ (d) 0

62. The potential due to a point charge is spherically symmetric since it depends only on the distance r. But the potential due to a dipole is not spherically symmetric because the potential depend on the angle between $\vec{p}$ and position vector $\vec{r}$ of the point. However, the dipole potential is axially symmetric. If the position vector $\vec{r}$ is rotated about $\vec{p}$ by keeping θ fixed, then all points on the cone at the same distance r will have the same potential as shown in figure. In this figure, all the points located on the circular part will have the same potential.

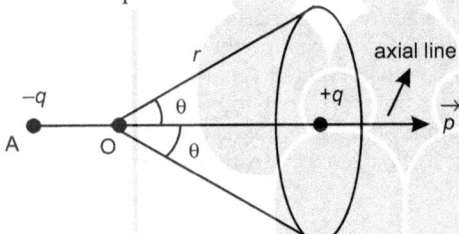

(i) Two equal and opposite charge (+q and –q) are situated at x-distance from each other, the value of potential at very far point will depend upon.

(a) only on q (b) only on x

(c) on qx (d) on $\dfrac{q}{x}$

(ii) The ratio of electric field and potential (E/V) at mid-point of electric dipole for which separation is l.

(a) $1/l$ (b) l
(c) $2/l$ (d) none of these

(iii) An electric dipole has a pair of equal and opposite point charges +q and q separated by a distance 2x. The axis of the dipole is defined as :

(a) Direction from positive charge to negative charge
(b) Direction from negative charge to positive charge
(c) Perpendicular to the line joining the two charge drawn at the centre and pointing upwards direction.
(d) Perpendicular to the line joining the two charges drawn at the centre and pointing downward direction.

(iv) Electric potential at an equatorial point of a small dipole with dipole moment p (r, distance from the dipole) is :

(a) zero (b) $\dfrac{p}{4\pi\varepsilon_0 r^2}$

(c) $\dfrac{p}{4\pi\varepsilon_0 r^3}$ (d) $\dfrac{2p}{4\pi\varepsilon_0 r^3}$

(v) The value of electric potential at any point due to any electric dipole is :

(a) $k\,\dfrac{\vec{p}\times\vec{r}}{r^2}$ (b) $k\,\dfrac{\vec{p}\times\vec{r}}{r^3}$

(c) $k\,\dfrac{\vec{p}\cdot\vec{r}}{r^2}$ (d) $k\,\dfrac{\vec{p}\cdot\vec{r}}{r^3}$

63. An electrical conductor has a large number of mobile charges which are free to move in the material. In a metallic conductor, these mobile charges are free electrons which are not bound to any atom and therefore are free to move on the surface of the conductor. When there is no external electric field, the free electrons are in continuous random motion in all directions. As a result, there is no net motion of electrons along any particular direction which implies that the conductor is in electrostatic equilibrium. Thus, at electrostatic equilibrium, there is no net current in the conductor.

(i) The dielectric between the conductors reduces the electric intensity.
(a) to zero (b) between them
(c) with no change (d) none of the above

(ii) Which group among the following is insulator?
(a) Silver, copper, gold
(b) Paper, glass, cotton
(c) The human body, wood, iron
(d) Glass, copper, paper

(iii) Insulation breakdown may occur at ....
(a) High temperature
(b) Low temperature
(c) At any temperature
(d) Depends on pressure

(iv) Conductors are materials that allow
(a) Allow the flow of heat
(b) Does not allow heat to flow
(c) Allows cold to flow
(d) Stops cold from passing through

(v) Good conductors have many loosely bound
(a) atoms (b) protons
(c) molecules (d) electrons

64. Sometimes we notice that the ceiling fan does not start rotating soon as it is switched on. But when we rotate the blades, it starts to rotate as usual. Why it is so? We know that to rotate any object, there must be a torque applied on the object. For the ceiling fan, the initial torque is given by the capacitor widely known as a condenser, if the condenser is faulty, it will not give sufficient initial torque to rotate the blades when the fan is switched on.

(i) Capacitance (in F) of a spherial capacitor of radius 1 m is :
(a) 1.1×10^{-10} (b) 10^{-6}
(c) 9×10^{-9} (d) 10^{-3}

(ii) A sheet of aluminium foil of negligible thickness is introduced between the plates of a capacitor. The capacitance of the capacitor. The capacitance of the capacitor.
(a) decreases (b) remains unchanged
(c) becomes infinite (d) increases

(iii) When a capacitor is connected to a battery
(a) a current flows in the circuit for some time, then decreases to zero.
(b) no current flows in the circuit at all
(c) an alternating current flows in the circuit
(d) none of the above

(iv) If potential difference across a capacitor is changed from 15V to 30V, work done is W. What will be the work done when potential difference is changed from 30V to 60V?
(a) W (b) 4W
(c) 3W (d) 2W

(v) When 1.0×10^{12} electrons are transferred from one conductor to another of a capacitor, a potential difference of 10 V develops between the two conductors. What is the capacitance of the capacitor?
(a) 1.6×10^{-4} F (b) 1.6×10^{-8} F
(c) 1.6×10^{-9} F (d) 11.6×10^{-8} F

65. Several capacitors can be connected together to be used in a variety of applications. Multiple connections of capacitors behave as a single equivalent capacitor. The total capacitance of this equivalent single capacitor depends both on the individual capacitors and how they are connected. Capacitors can be arranged in two simple and common type of connections, known as series and parallel for which we can easily calculate the total capacitance. These two basic combination, series and parallel, can also be used as part of more complex connections.

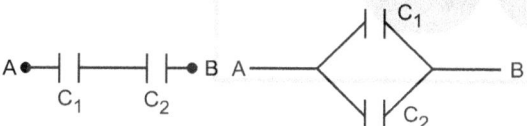

(i) Three capacitors of capacitances 1μF, 2μF and 3μF are connected in series and a potential difference of 11 V is applied across the combination. Then, the p.d. across the plates of 1μF capacitor is :
(a) 2 V (b) 4 V
(c) 1 V (d) 6 V

(ii) The equivalent capacitance is :

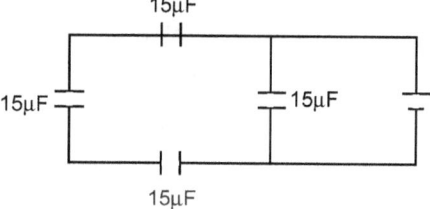

(a) 15μF (b) 20μF
(c) 25μF (d) 30μF

(iii) In the given figure, the capacitors C_1, C_3, C_4, C_5 have a capacitance 4μF each. If the capacitor C_2 has a capacitance 10μF, then effective capacitance between A and B will be :
(a) 2μF (b) 4μF
(c) 6μF (d) 8μF

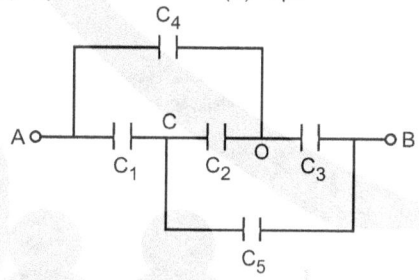

(iv) Given a number of capacitors labelled as 8μF = 250 V. Find the minimum number of capacitors needed to get an arrangement equivalent to 16μF = 1000 V
(a) 4 (b) 16
(c) 32 (d) 64

(v) The equivalent capacity of two capacitors in series is 3μF and in parallel is 16μF. Their individual capacities are
(a) 12, 4 (b) 8, 8
(c) 10, 16 (d) 12, 2

Answers

1. (c) remains constant from centre to surface
   Explanation: Electric potential inside a conductor is constant and it is equal to that on the surface of the conductor

2. (c) joule/coulomb
   Explanation: By using $V = \dfrac{W}{Q}$

3. (b) 3.6×10^4 V
   Explanation: Given that,
   $q = 4 \times 10^{-7}$ C, $r = 10$ cm $= 0.1$ m
   Since potential,
   $V = \dfrac{1}{4\pi\varepsilon_0} \dfrac{q}{r}$
   $= \dfrac{9 \times 10^9 \times 4 \times 10^{-7}}{0.1}$
   $= 3.6 \times 10^4$ V

4. (d) $k \cdot \dfrac{\vec{p} \cdot \vec{r}}{r^3}$
   Explanation: As we know that,
   $V = \dfrac{1}{4\pi\varepsilon_0} \dfrac{p\cos\theta}{r^2}$

5. (d) $4\pi\varepsilon_0 Q \times 10^{22}$ Vm^{-1}
   Explanation: Given that,
   $$V = \frac{Q}{4\pi\varepsilon_0 r} = Q \times 10^{11} V$$
   $\therefore \quad 4\pi\varepsilon_0 r = 10^{-11}$ ...(i)
   Now, $E = \frac{Q \times 4\pi\varepsilon_0}{(4\pi\varepsilon_0 r)^2}$
   $= \frac{Q \times 4\pi\varepsilon_0}{(10^{-11})^2}$ ...[By using (i)]
   $= 4\pi\varepsilon_0 Q \times 10^{22}$ Vm^{-1}

6. (b) Electric field is not zero anywhere on the sphere
   Explanation: When electric dipole is held in the sphere, electric field is not zero anywhere on the sphere. However, net electric flux through the sphere is zero.

7. (c) negative
   Explanation: In moving a small positive charge from Q to P, work has to be done by an external agency against the electric field. Therefore, work done by the field is negative.

8. (d) zero
   Explanation: Potential at A = Potential due to (+q) charge + Potential due to (−q) charge
   $= \frac{1}{4\pi\varepsilon_0} \cdot \frac{q}{\sqrt{a^2}} + \frac{1}{4\pi\varepsilon_0} \cdot \frac{(-q)}{\sqrt{a^2}} = 0$

9. (c) $\frac{1}{\pi\varepsilon_0} \frac{\sqrt{2}q}{l}$
   Explanation: As we know that,
   $$V = \frac{1}{4\pi\varepsilon_0} \frac{q}{r}$$

   Electric potential due to each charge at the centre of the square is $\frac{1}{4\pi\varepsilon_0} \frac{\sqrt{2}q}{l}$
   Hence total potential is,
   $= 4 \times \frac{1}{4\pi\varepsilon_0} \frac{\sqrt{2}q}{l}$
   $= \frac{1}{\pi\varepsilon_0} \frac{\sqrt{2}q}{l}$

10. (b) No
    Explanation: Intersection of two equipotential surfaces at a point will give two directions of electric field intensity at that point, which is not possible.

11. (d) no work is done
    Explanation: On the equipotential surface, electric field is normal to the charged surface (where potential exists) So that no work will be done.

12. (d) $V_A = V_C$
    Explanation: Conducting surface behaves as equipotential surface.

13. (b) increase
    Explanation: By using,
    $U = QV$
    $\because \quad Q = +1, U = V$
    At high potential, potential energy will be high and lower potential, low energy it will have.

14. (c) one charge is positive and other is negative
    Explanation: The potential energy is negative whenever there is attraction. Since a positive and negative charge attract each other, therefore, their energy is negative. When both the charges are separated by infinite distance, they do not attract each other and their energy is zero.

15. (d) zero
    Explanation: As we know that,
    $W = pE(\cos 90° - \cos 270°)$
    $= 0$

16. (b) increases
    Explanation: Potential energy of the system,
    $$U = \frac{1}{4\pi\varepsilon_0} \frac{(-e) \times (-e)}{r}$$

17. (c) $\frac{1}{2} \frac{kQ^2}{R}$
    Explanation: As we know that,
    $U = \int_0^Q V \, dq$
    $= \int_0^Q \frac{kq}{R} dq$
    $= \frac{1}{2} \frac{kQ^2}{R}$

18. (c) 10 V
    Explanation: As we know that, Potential = potential energy/test charge.

19. (d) $-\frac{7q^2}{8\pi\varepsilon_0 a}$
    Explanation: As we know that,
    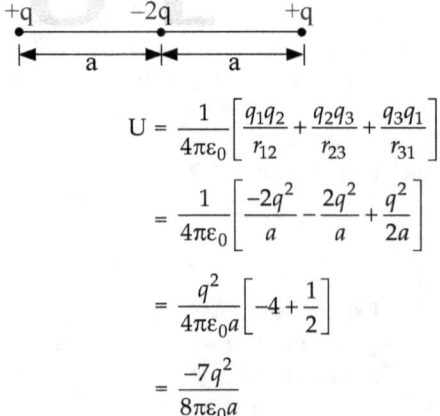
    $U = \frac{1}{4\pi\varepsilon_0}\left[\frac{q_1 q_2}{r_{12}} + \frac{q_2 q_3}{r_{23}} + \frac{q_3 q_1}{r_{31}}\right]$
    $= \frac{1}{4\pi\varepsilon_0}\left[\frac{-2q^2}{a} - \frac{2q^2}{a} + \frac{q^2}{2a}\right]$
    $= \frac{q^2}{4\pi\varepsilon_0 a}\left[-4 + \frac{1}{2}\right]$
    $= \frac{-7q^2}{8\pi\varepsilon_0 a}$

20. (d) earth
    Explanation: Earth is conductor which can be given almost unlimited charge.
21. (c) there must be charges only on the surface.
    Explanation: If a conductor has a non-zero potential and there are no charges anywhere else outside, then there must be charges on the surface of the conductor or inside the conductor. There cannot be any charge in the body of the conductor.
22. (c) they can be charged equally (maximum)
    Explanation: In case of metallic sphere either solid or hollow, the charge will reside on the surface of the sphere. Since both spheres have same surface area, they can hold equal amount of maximum charge.
23. (d) may be at positive, zero or negative potential
    Explanation: The conductor may be at positive, zero or negative potential, it is according to the way one defines the zero potential.
24. (c) decreases K times
    Explanation: As we know that,
    $$F_m = \frac{F_o}{K}$$
    So, the maximum force decreases by K times.
25. (d) relative permittivity
    Explanation: As we know that,
    $$k = \varepsilon_r = \frac{\varepsilon}{\varepsilon_0} = \text{Relative permittivity}$$
26. (d) increases
    Explanation: Since capacitance $C = \frac{\varepsilon_0 A}{d}$ as d decreases capacitance increases.
27. (d) electrostatic energy
    Explanation: Energy stored in a capacitor is electrostatic energy.
28. (d) Q and C
    Explanation: By using,
    $$C = \frac{\varepsilon_0 KA}{d} \text{ and } q = CV$$
29. (c) area of the plate is increased
    Explanation: As we know that,
    $$C = \frac{\varepsilon_0 KA}{d}$$
    $$\Rightarrow \quad C \propto A$$
30. (b) $\frac{1}{2}CV^2$
    Explanation: As we know that,
    $$U = \int_0^V CV dV = \frac{1}{2}CV^2$$
31. (b) 3.2×10^{-31} J
    Explanation: As we know that,
    $$W = \frac{1}{2}\frac{q^2}{C}$$
    $$= \frac{(8 \times 10^{-18})^2}{2 \times 100 \times 10^{-6}}$$
    $$= 3.2 \times 10^{-31} \text{ J}$$
32. (b) $\frac{\sigma}{\varepsilon_0}$
    Explanation: As we know that,
    $$E = \frac{\sigma}{2\varepsilon_0} - \left(-\frac{\sigma}{2\varepsilon_0}\right)$$
    $$= \frac{\sigma}{\varepsilon_0}$$
33. (c) in the field between the plates
    Explanation: Energy resides in the field between the plates in a charged capacitor.
34. (a) 30 µF
    Explanation: In series $\frac{1}{C} = \frac{1}{C_1} + \frac{1}{C_2} + \frac{1}{C_3}$ and charge on each capacitor is same.
    $$\therefore \quad \frac{1}{C} = \frac{1}{6} + \frac{1}{6} + \frac{1}{3}$$
    $$C = \frac{3}{2} \quad \ldots(i)$$
    $$\because \quad q = CV$$
    $$\because \quad q = 20 \times \frac{3}{2} \quad [\text{By using (i)}]$$
    $$= 30 \text{ µC}$$
35. (c) 200 µF
    Explanation: Capacitance will increase but not five times (because dielectric is not filled completely). Hence, new capacitance may be 200 µF.
36. (c) 4C/3
    Explanation: The network is equivalent to

    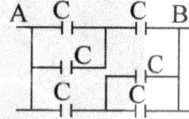

    Therefore equivalent capacitance
    = (2C series C] // [C series 2C)
    $$= 2\left(\frac{2C \times C}{2C + C}\right) = \frac{4C}{3}$$
37. (b) Potential difference and energy stored
    Explanation: When battery is disconnected, charge remains constant. On introducing glass slab, capacity increases. Potential difference and energy stored decreases.
38. (d) $\frac{\varepsilon \varepsilon_0 A}{(2\varepsilon + \varepsilon_0)d}$
    Explanation: As we know that,
    $$C_{eq} = \frac{\varepsilon_0}{\frac{d}{K_1} + \frac{d}{K_2} + \frac{d}{K_3}} A$$
    $$\therefore \quad K_1 = K_3 = 1, K_2 = \varepsilon/\varepsilon_0$$
    $$\therefore \quad C_{eq} = \frac{\varepsilon_0}{d + \frac{d}{\varepsilon/\varepsilon_0} + d} A$$
    $$= \frac{\varepsilon \varepsilon_0}{d(2\varepsilon + \varepsilon_0)} A$$

39. (c) $8\ \mu J$
Explanation: As we know that,
$3\mu F$ and $6\mu F$ are in series
$\therefore \quad \dfrac{3\times 6}{(3+6)} = 2\ \mu F$

This is in parallel with $2\ \mu F$.
So, total capacitance in the circuit is $4\ \mu F$.
$$Q = CV$$
$$\text{Energy} = \dfrac{1}{2}QV = (1/2)V^2 C$$
$$= (1/2) \times 2^2 \times 4 \times 10^{-6}\ J$$
$$= 8\ \mu J$$

40. (d) $6\ \mu F$
Explanation: By using,

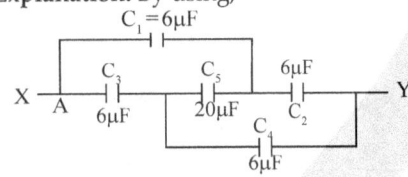

Equivalent circuit

As $\dfrac{C_1}{C_3} = \dfrac{C_2}{C_4}$

Hence no charge will flow through $20\ \mu F$

C_1 and C_2 are in series, also C_3 and C_4 are in series.
Hence,
$$C' = 3\ \mu F,\ C'' = 3\ \mu F$$
C' and C'' are in parallel hence net capacitance
$$= C' + C'' = 3 + 3 = 6\ \mu F$$

41. (c) decreases because the charge moves along the electric field.
Explanation: As the charge move along the electric field its electric potential energy decreases.

42. (c) The work done is the same in figure (i), (ii) and (iii)
Explanation: In all the three figures, $V_A = 20$ V and $V_B = 40$ V. Work done in carrying a charge q from A to B is $W = q\ (V_B - V_A)$

43. (c) S_1 is true, S_2 is also true and S_1 is the cause of S_2.
Explanation: Potential at any point inside a charged conducting sphere = potential on the surface,
$$V = \dfrac{Kq}{R} = 100\ V$$
Now, $\quad E = -\dfrac{dV}{dr} = 0 \quad (\because V\ \text{is constant})$

44. (a) spheres

Explanation: For a collection of charges, whose total sum is not zero, equipotentials at large distances must be spheres only.

45. (d) $8\ \mu C$
Explanation: Current in the lower arm of the circuit
$$I = \dfrac{2.5\ V}{2\Omega + 0.5\Omega} = 1 A$$

Potential difference across the internal resistance of cell
$$= (0.5\ \Omega)(1\ A) = 0.5\ V$$
and potential difference across the $4\mu F$ capacitor
$$= 2.5\ V - 0.5\ V = 2\ V$$
Charge on the capacitor plates,
$$Q = CV = 4 \times 2 = 8\ \mu C$$

46. (c) $\dfrac{K_1 K_2 (d_1 + d_2)}{K_2 d_1 + K_1 d_2}$

Explanation: The capacities of two individual condensers are,
$$C_1 = \dfrac{K_1 \varepsilon_0 A}{d_1}\ \text{and}\ C_2 = \dfrac{K_2 \varepsilon_0 A}{d_2}$$

The arrangement is equivalent to two capacitors joined in series.
So, equivalent capacitance,
$$\dfrac{1}{C_{eq}} = \dfrac{1}{C_1} + \dfrac{1}{C_2} = \dfrac{d_1}{K_1 \varepsilon_0 A} + \dfrac{d_2}{K_2 \varepsilon_0 A}$$
$$= \dfrac{1}{\varepsilon_0 A}\left[\dfrac{d_1}{K_1} + \dfrac{d_2}{K_2}\right] = \dfrac{1}{\varepsilon_0 A}\left[\dfrac{K_2 d_1 + K_1 d_2}{K_1 K_2}\right]$$
or $\quad = \varepsilon_0 A \left(\dfrac{K_1 K_2}{K_2 d_1 + K_1 d_2}\right) \quad \ldots\text{(i)}$

Also $C_{eq} = \dfrac{K \varepsilon_0 A}{d_1 + d_2} \quad \ldots\text{(ii)}$

From (i) and (ii)
$$\varepsilon_0 A \left(\dfrac{K_1 K_2}{d_2 K_1 + d_1 K_2}\right) = \varepsilon_0 A\left(\dfrac{K}{d_1 + d_2}\right)$$
$\therefore \quad K = \dfrac{K_1 K_2 (d_1 + d_2)}{d_2 K_1 + d_1 K_2}$

47. (b) decreasing
Explanation: $V \propto \dfrac{1}{r}$

48. (a) Electric potential
Explanation: $V = E, d = NC^{-1}.\ m$

49. (d) Electrostatic force is conservative force.

50. (d) The electric potential at any point on equatorial plane of a dipole is zero.

51. (d) For a non-uniformly charged thin circular ring with net zero charge, electric potential at each point on its axis is zero. Hence electric field at each point on its axis must be perpendicular to the axis. So assertion is false and reason is false.

52. (b) An equipotential surface is a surface over which potential is constant.

53. (c) Potential and potential energy are different quantities and cannot be equated.

54. (a) Potential is constant on the surface of a sphere so it behaves as an equipotential surface.

55. (b) Let us consider two spherical shells of radii r_1 and r_2 which are possessing the same positive charge Q. Therefore the potential on the surface of each conductor will be,
$V_1 = \dfrac{kQ}{r_1}$ and $V_2 = \dfrac{kQ}{r_2}$ since $r_1 \neq r_2$

$V_1 \neq V_2$ and consequently there will be a potential difference between the two conductors.

56. (c) $C' = KC$, and $U' = \dfrac{q^2}{2C'} = \dfrac{q^2}{2KC}$

57. (d) The molecules of a substance may be polar or non-polar. In a non-polar molecule, the centres of positive and negative charges coincide. This molecule has no permanent dipole moment. On the other hand, a polar molecule is one in which the centres of positive and negative charges are separated, even when there is no external field. Such molecules have a permanent dipole moment.

58. (c) Equivalent capacitance of parallel combination is $C_p = C_1 + C_2 + C_3$.

59. (b) By the formula capacitance of a capacitor,
$C_1 = \varepsilon_0 \times \dfrac{KA}{d}$

$C_1 \propto \dfrac{K}{d}$

$\therefore \dfrac{C_1}{C_2} = \dfrac{K_1}{d_1} \times \dfrac{d_2}{K_2} = \dfrac{K}{d} \times \dfrac{d/2}{3K} = \dfrac{1}{6}$

or $C_2 = 6C_1$

Again for capacity of a capacitor $C = Q/V$. Therefore, capacity of a capacitor does not depend upon the nature of the material of the capacitor.

60. (d) In Van de Graaff generator, the process of spraying the charge is called corona discharge. Van de Graaff generator produces high voltage and low current.

61. (i) (c) CD

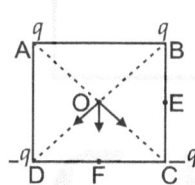

(ii) (d) $\dfrac{\sqrt{2}q}{\pi\varepsilon_0 a^2}$

$E_O = 4 \times \dfrac{1}{4\pi\varepsilon_0} \dfrac{q}{(a/\sqrt{2})^2} \times \dfrac{1}{\sqrt{2}} = \dfrac{\sqrt{2}q}{\pi\varepsilon_0 a^2}$

(iii) (d) 0

Charges at A and C and those at B and D symmetrical with O.

(iv) (d) 0

$V_E = 0$. Therefore, no potential difference between O and E. Work require to shift change from O to E is 0.

(v) (b) $\dfrac{q_e}{\pi\varepsilon_0 a}\left(\dfrac{1}{\sqrt{5}} - 1\right)$. This depend on the potential at F.

$V_F = 2 \times \dfrac{1}{4\pi\varepsilon_0}\left[\dfrac{q}{(a^2 + a^2/4)^{1/2}} - \dfrac{q}{a/2}\right] = \dfrac{q}{\pi\varepsilon_0 a}\left(\dfrac{1}{\sqrt{5}} - 1\right)$

$W_{OF} = e(V_F - V_O) = \dfrac{q e}{\pi\varepsilon_0 a}\left(\dfrac{1}{\sqrt{5}} - 1\right)$

62. (i) (c) on qx

(ii) (d) Electric field at 'O', $E = \dfrac{2kq}{l^2}$

Potential at 'O'
$V = 0$
$\therefore E/V = \infty$

$\overset{-q}{\underset{A}{\bullet}} \quad \overset{}{\underset{O}{\bullet}} \quad \overset{+q}{\underset{B}{\bullet}}$
$\longleftarrow l \longrightarrow$

(iii) (b) Direction from positive charge to negative charge.

(iv) (a) On equatorial point electric potential due to an electric dipole in zero.

(v) (d) Potential due to dipole in general position in given by
$v = \dfrac{k.p\cos\theta}{r^2}$

$\Rightarrow v = \dfrac{kp\cos\theta \, r}{r^3} = k\dfrac{\vec{p}.\vec{r}}{r^3}$

63. (i) (b) Due to polarisation of the dielectric, the electric field between the conductors decreases.

(ii) (b) Glass, paper and cotton are good quality insulators. The rest options contain one or more conducting materials. Silver is the best conductor material available in nature. But it is costly. So it can't is used in the electricity distribution system.

(iii) (a) At high temperature, electrons of insulators get excited and then the electron can overcome the large energy band gaps between valence and conduction bands. So, a large number of electrons travel to the conduction band and they act as conductor i.e., insulation breakdown occurs.

(iv) (a) Allow the flow of heat

(v) (d) electrons.

64. (i) (a) For a spherical conductor
$C = 4\pi\varepsilon_0 r = \dfrac{1}{9 \times 10^9} \times 1 = 1.1 \times 10^{-10}$ F

(ii) (b) As aluminium is a metal and its thickness is negligible, the potential difference between the plates remain unchanged. Thus the capacitance will remain unchanged.

(iii) (a) A current flows in the circuit during the time the capacitor is charged. After the capacitor gets fully charged, the current stops flowing.

(iv) (b) $W = \dfrac{1}{2}CV^2 \Rightarrow W \propto V^2$

$$\therefore \quad \frac{W_2}{W_1} = \left(\frac{\Delta V_2}{\Delta V_1}\right)^2 = \left(\frac{60-30}{30-15}\right)^2 = 4$$

or $W_2 = 4W_1 = 4W$

(v) (b) $q = ne = 1.0 \times 10^{12} \times 1.6 \times 10^{-19}$
$= 1.6 \times 10^{-7}$ C
$V = 10$ V

$$\therefore \quad C = \frac{q}{V} = \frac{1.6 \times 10^{-7}}{10}$$
$= 1.6 \times 10^{-8}$ F

65. (i) (d)

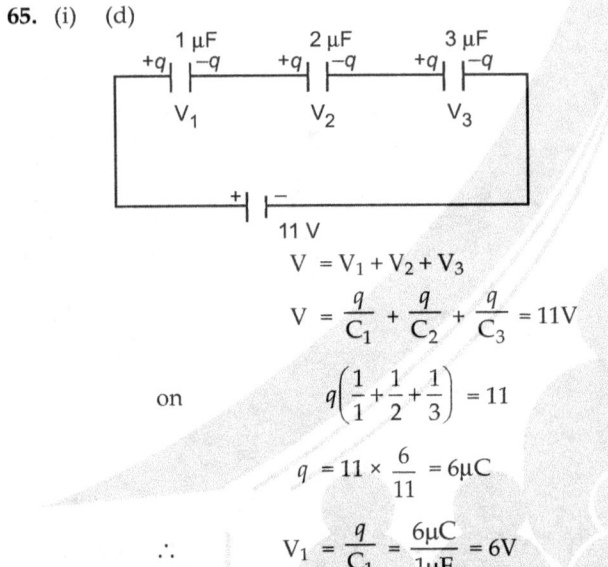

$V = V_1 + V_2 + V_3$

$$V = \frac{q}{C_1} + \frac{q}{C_2} + \frac{q}{C_3} = 11V$$

on $q\left(\frac{1}{1} + \frac{1}{2} + \frac{1}{3}\right) = 11$

$q = 11 \times \frac{6}{11} = 6\mu C$

$$\therefore \quad V_1 = \frac{q}{C_1} = \frac{6\mu C}{1\mu F} = 6V$$

(ii) (b) Three 15μF capacitors on the left are connected in series. Then equivalent capacitances C' is given by,

$$\frac{1}{C'} = \frac{1}{15} + \frac{1}{15} + \frac{1}{15} = \frac{1}{5}$$

or $C' = 5\mu F$

Now C' is in parallel with fourth 15μF capacitor,

$\therefore \quad C_{eq} = C' + 15 = 5 + 15 = 20\mu F$

(iii) (b) $\frac{C_1}{C_5} = \frac{C_4}{C_3} = \frac{4}{4}$

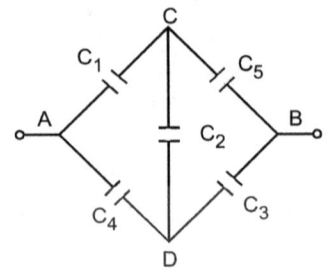

The wheatstone bridge is balanced.
So, C_2 is ineffective

$$C_{ACB} = \frac{C_1 \times C_5}{C_1 + C_5} = \frac{4 \times 4}{4+4} = 2\mu F$$

$$C_{ADB} = \frac{C_3 \times C_4}{C_3 + C_4} = \frac{4 \times 4}{4+4} = 2\mu F$$

$\therefore \quad C_{AB} = C_{ACB} + C_{ADB} = 2 + 2 = 4\mu F$

(iv) (c) We can connect 4 capacitors in series across 1000 V. Its capacitance will be 2μF. And 8 such combinations in parallel will give 16μF capacitance.
∴ Total number of capacitors = 4 × 8 = 32

(v) (a) $C_p = C_1 + C_2 = 16\mu F$

$$C_s = \frac{C_1 C_2}{C_1 + C_2} = 3\mu F$$

or $C_1 C_2 = 3(C_1 + C_2) = 3 \times 16 = 48\mu F$
or $C_1(16 - C_1) = 48$
$\therefore C_1 = 12\mu F, C_2 = 4\mu F$

Chapter 3

Current Electricity

1. The time rate of flow of charge through any cross section of a conductor is _____
   (a) electric potential   (b) electric current
   (c) electric intensity   (d) electric charge

2. When no current is passed through a conductor:
   (a) the free electrons do not move
   (b) the average speed of a free electron over a large period of time is not zero
   (c) the average velocity of a free electron over a large period of time is zero
   (d) the average of the velocities of all the free electrons at an instant is non-zero

3. Drift velocity of electrons is due to:
   (a) motion of conduction electrons due to random collisions.
   (b) motion of conduction electrons due to electric field E.
   (c) repulsion to the conduction electrons due to inner electrons of ions.
   (d) collision of conduction electrons with each other.

4. The I-V characteristics shown in figure represents:

   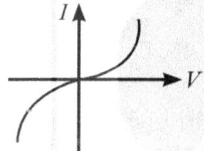

   (a) ohmic conductors   (b) non-ohmic conductors
   (c) insulators   (d) superconductors

5. If a current of 0.5 A flows in a 60 W lamp, then the total charge passing through it in two hours will be:
   (a) 1800 C   (b) 2400 C
   (c) 3000 C   (d) 3600 C

6. The relaxation time in conductors:
   (a) increases with the increases of temperature
   (b) decreases with the increases of temperature
   (c) it does not depend on temperature
   (d) all of sudden changes at 400 K

7. A steady current of 1 A is flowing through the conductor. The number of electrons flowing through the cross-section of the conductor in 1 sec is:
   (a) 6.25×10^{15} (b) 6.25×10^{17}
   (c) 6.25×10^{19} (d) 6.25×10^{18}

8. A metal wire is subjected to a constant potential difference. When the temperature of the metal wire increases, the drift velocity of the electron in it:
   (a) increases, thermal velocity of electron increases
   (b) decreases, thermal velocity of electron increases
   (c) increases, thermal velocity of electron decreases
   (d) decreases, thermal velocity of electron decreases

9. If N, e, τ and m are representing electron density, charge, relaxation time and mass of an electron respectively, then the resistance of wire of length l and cross-sectional area A is given by:
   (a) $\dfrac{ml}{Ne^2 A\tau}$ (b) $\dfrac{2m\tau A}{Ne^2 l}$
   (c) $\dfrac{Ne^2 \tau A}{2ml}$ (d) $\dfrac{Ne^2 A}{2m\tau l}$

10. The electric resistance of a certain wire of iron is R. If its length and radius are both doubled, then:
    (a) the resistance and the specific resistance will both remain unchanged
    (b) the resistance will be doubled, and the specific resistance will be halved
    (c) the resistance will be halved, and the specific resistance will remain unchanged
    (d) the resistance will be halved, and the specific resistance will be doubled

11. The direction of drift velocity in a conductor is:
    (a) opposite to that of applied electric field
    (b) opposite to the flow of positive charge
    (c) in the direction of the flow of electrons
    (d) All of these

12. Two wires A and B of the same material, having radii in the ratio 1:2 and carry currents in the ratio 4:1. The ratio of drift speed of electrons in A and B is:
    (a) 16:1   (b) 1:16
    (c) 1:4   (d) 4:1

13. When a current I is set up in a wire of radius r, the drift velocity is v_d. If the same current is set up through a wire of radius $2r$, the drift velocity will be:
    (a) $4v_d$ (b) $2v_d$
    (c) $v_d/2$ (d) $v_d/4$

14. Drift velocity of a free electron inside a conductor is:
    (a) the thermal speed of the free electron
    (b) the speed with which a free electron emerges out of the conductor
    (c) the average speed acquired by the electron in any direction
    (d) the average speed of the electron between successive collisions in the direction opposite to the applied electric field

15. If the resistance of a conductor is 5Ω at 50° C and 7Ω at 100° C, then mean temperature coefficient of resistance (of material) is:
    (a) 0.013/°C   (b) 0.004/°C
    (c) 0.006/°C   (d) 0.008/°C

16. A potential difference V is applied to a copper wire. If the potential difference is increased to 2V, then the drift velocity of electrons will:

(a) be double the initial velocity
(b) remain same
(c) be $\sqrt{2}$ times the initial velocity
(d) be half the initial velocity

17. A wire has a non-uniform cross-section as shown in the figure. If a steady current is flowing through it, then the drift speed of the electrons:

(a) is constant throughout the wire
(b) decreases from A to B
(c) increases from A to B
(d) varies randomly

18. A potential difference of 10 V is applied across a conductor of length 0.1 m. If the drift velocity of electrons is 2×10^{-4} m/s, the electron mobility is _____ $m^2V^{-1}s^{-1}$.
(a) 1×10^{-6} (b) 2×10^{-6}
(c) 3×10^{-6} (d) 4×10^{-6}

19. Ohm's law deals with the relation between:
(a) current and potential difference
(b) capacity and charge
(c) capacity and potential
(d) charge and potential difference

20. Ohm's law is valid when the temperature of the conductor is _____:
(a) constant (b) very high
(c) very low (d) varying

21. When the length and area of cross-section both are doubled, then its resistance:
(a) will become half (b) will be doubled
(c) will remain the same (d) will become four times

22. For a metallic wire, the ratio V/I (V = the applied potential difference, I = current flowing):
(a) is independent of temperature.
(b) increases as the temperature rises.
(c) decreases as the temperature rises.
(d) increases or decreases as temperature rises, depending upon the metal.

23. The resistivity of a wire:
(a) increases with the length of the wire.
(b) decreases with the area of cross-section.
(c) decreases with the length and increases with the cross-section of wire.
(d) is unaffected by change in its length and area of cross-section.

24. The resistance of a straight conductor does not depend upon its:
(a) temperature (b) length
(c) material (d) shape of cross-section

25. A certain wire has a resistance R. The resistance of another wire identical with the first except having twice its diameter is:
(a) 2 R (b) 0.25 R
(c) 4 R (d) 0.5 R

26. The reciprocal of resistance is:
(a) conductance (b) voltage
(c) resistivity (d) reactance

27. A wire of resistance 4 Ω is stretched to twice its original length. The resistance of stretched wire would be:
(a) 2 Ω (b) 4 Ω
(c) 8 Ω (d) 16 Ω

28. The V-I characteristics of four circuit elements are shown. Which of these is ohmic?

29. In a closed circuit, the vector sum of total emf is equal to the sum of the _____:
(a) currents
(b) resistances
(c) products of currents and the resistances
(d) products of potential differences

30. Kirchhoff's first law i.e., $\Sigma i = 0$ at a junction is based on the law of conservation of:
(a) charge (b) energy
(c) momentum (d) angular momentum

31. According the Kirchhoff's law, in any analytic circuit, if the direction of current is assumed opposite, then the value of current will be:
(a) i (b) $2i$
(c) $-i$ (d) 0

32. In a wheatstone bridge in the battery and galvanometer are interchanged then the deflection in galvanometer will:
(a) change in previous direction
(b) not change
(c) change in opposite direction
(d) None of these

33. A capacitor is connected to a cell of emf E having some internal resistance r. The potential difference across the:
(a) Cell is < E (b) Cell is E
(c) Capacitor is > E (d) Capacitor is < E

34. The figure shows a network of currents. The magnitude of currents is shown here. The current I will be:

(a) 3 A (b) 9 A
(c) 13 A (d) 19 A

35. Kirchhoff's second law is based on the law of conservation of:
    (a) charge
    (b) energy
    (c) momentum
    (d) sum of mass and energy

36. A meter bridge is setup as shown to determine an unknown resistance X using a standard 10 ohm resistor. The galvanometer shows null point when tapping-key is at 52 cm mark. The end-corrections are 1 cm and 2 cm respectively for the ends A and B. The determined value of X is:

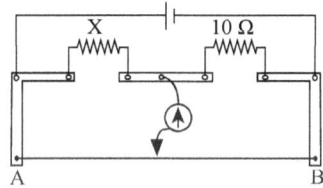

    (a) 10.2 ohm
    (b) 10.6 ohm
    (c) 10.8 ohm
    (d) 11.1 ohm

37. Consider the circuit shown in the figure. The current I_3 is equal to:

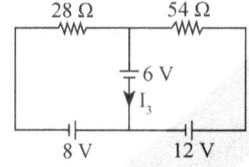

    (a) 5 A
    (b) 3 A
    (c) −3 A
    (d) −5/6 A

38. In meter bridge or Wheatstone bridge for measurement of resistance, the known and the unknown resistance are interchanged. The error so removed is:
    (a) end correction
    (b) index error
    (c) due to temperature effect
    (d) random error

39. The magnitude of I in ampere unit is:

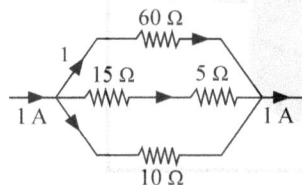

    (a) 0.1
    (b) 0.3
    (c) 0.6
    (d) 0.5

40. A 10 V battery with internal resistance 1 ohm and a 15 V battery with internal resistance 0.6 ohm are connected in parallel to a voltmeter (see figure). The reading in the voltmeter will be close to:

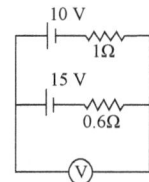

    (a) 12.5 V
    (b) 24.5 V
    (c) 13.1 V
    (d) 11.9 V

41. Shown in the figure below is a meter bridge set up with null deflection in the galvanometer. The value of the unknown resistance R is:

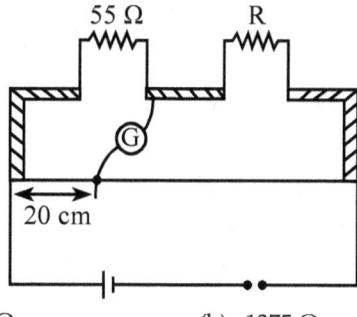

    (a) 55 Ω
    (b) 1375 Ω
    (c) 220 Ω
    (d) 110 Ω

42. The resistances in the two arms of the meter bridge are 5 ohm and R ohm, respectively. When the resistance R is shunted with an equal resistance, the new balance point is at $1.6 l_1$. The resistance R, is:

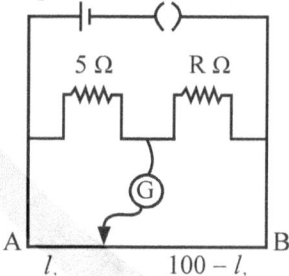

    (a) 10 ohm
    (b) 15 ohm
    (c) 20 ohm
    (d) 25 ohm

43. The instrument among the following which measures the emf of a cell most accurately is:
    (a) a voltmeter
    (b) an ammeter
    (c) potentiometer
    (d) post office box

44. In Wheatstone's bridge, three resistors P, Q, R are connected in three arms in order and 4th arm S is formed by two resistors S_1 and S_2 connected in parallel. The condition for bridge to be balanced is $\dfrac{P}{Q}=$
    (a) $\dfrac{R(S_1+S_2)}{S_1 S_2}$
    (b) $\dfrac{S_1 S_2}{R(S_1+S_2)}$
    (c) $\dfrac{R S_1 S_2}{(S_1+S_2)}$
    (d) $\dfrac{(S_1+S_2)}{R S_1 S_2}$

45. In a potentiometer experiment, when the galvanometer shows no deflection, then no current flows through _____
    (a) potentiometer wire
    (b) galvanometer circuit
    (c) main circuit
    (d) battery

46. A potentiometer is an ideal device for measuring potential difference because:
    (a) it uses a sensitive galvanometer.
    (b) it does not disturb the potential difference it measures.
    (c) it is an elaborate arrangement.
    (d) it has a long wire hence heat developed is quickly radiated.

47. Consider a current carrying wire (current I) in the shape of a circle. Note that as the current progresses along the wire, the direction of j (current density) changes in an exact manner, while the current I remain

unaffected. The agent that is essentially responsible for is: **[NCERT Exemplar]**
(a) source of emf
(b) electric field produced by charges accumulated on the surface of wire.
(c) the charges just behind a given segment of wire which push them just the right way by repulsion.
(d) the charges ahead

48. Which of the following characteristics of electrons determines the current in a conductor? **[NCERT Exemplar]**
(a) Drift velocity alone
(b) Thermal velocity alone
(c) Both drift velocity and thermal velocity
(d) Neither drift nor thermal velocity

49. A resistance R is to be measured using a meter bridge. Student chooses the standard resistance S to be 100 Ω. He finds the null point at l_1 = 2.9 cm. He is told to attempt to improve the accuracy. Which of the following is a useful way? **[NCERT Exemplar]**
(a) He should measure l_1 more accurately.
(b) He should change S to 1000 Ω and repeat the experiment.
(c) He should change S to 3 Ω and repeat the experiment.
(d) He should give up hope of a more accurate measurement with a meter bridge.

50. Two cells of emf's approximately 5V and 10V are to be accurately compared using a potentiometer of length 400 cm: **[NCERT Exemplar]**
(a) The battery that runs the potentiometer should have voltage of 8V
(b) The battery of potentiometer can have a voltage of 15 V and R adjusted so that the potential drop across the wire slightly exceeds 10 V
(c) The first portion of 50 cm of wire itself should have a potential drop of 10 V
(d) Potentiometer is usually used for comparing resistances and not voltages

51. A cell of e.m.f. (E) and internal resistance r is connected acros a variable external resistance R. The graph of terminal potential difference V as function of R is : **[CBSE 2020]**

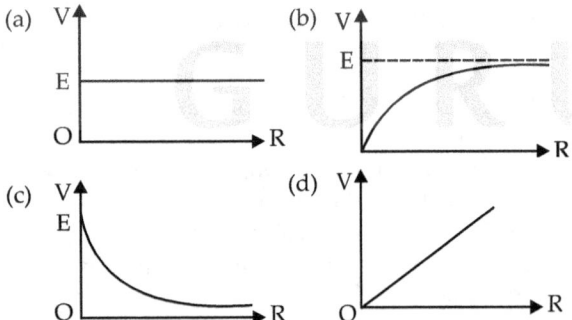

52. A uniform wire of resistance 2R is bent in the form of a circle. The effective resistance between the ends of any diameter of the circle is : **[CBSE 2020]**
(a) 2 R
(b) R
(c) $\frac{R}{2}$
(d) $\frac{R}{4}$

Directions: In the following questions, a statement of assertion is followed by a statement of reason. Mark the correct choice as:
(a) If both assertion and reason are true and reason is the correct explanation of assertion.
(b) If both assertion and reason are true, but reason is not the correct explanation of assertion.
(c) If assertion is true, but reason is false.
(d) If both assertion and reason are false.

53. **Assertion:** The current density $\vec{j}$ at any point in ohmic resistor is in direction of electric field $\vec{E}$ at that point.
Reason: A point charge when released from rest in a region having only electrostatic field always moves along electric lines of force.

54. **Assertion:** The 200 W bulbs glows with more brightness then 100 W bulbs.
Reason: A 100 W bulb has more resistance than a 200 W bulb.

55. **Assertion:** Bending a wire does not effect electrical resistance.
Reason: Resistance of wire is proportional to resistivity of material.

56. **Assertion:** Fuse wire must have high resistance and low melting point.
Reason: Fuse is used for small current flow only.

57. **Assertion:** Drift speed v_d is the average speed between two successive collisions.
Reason: If Δl is the average distance moved between two collision and Δt is the corresponding time, then
$$v_d = \lim_{\Delta t \to 0} \frac{\Delta l}{\Delta t}$$

58. **Assertion:** Two electric bulbs of 50 W and 100 W are given. When connected in series 50 W bulb glows more but when connected parallel 100 W bulb glows more.
Reason: In series combination, power is directly proportional to the resistance of circuit. But in parallel combination, power is inversely proportional to the resistance of the circuit.

59. **Assertion:** When current through a bulb decreases by 0.5%, the glow of bulb decreases by 1%.
Reason: Glow (Power) which is directly proportional to square of current.

60. **Assertion:** For a conductor, resistivity increases with increase in temperature.
Reason: Since $\rho = \frac{m}{ne^2\tau}$ when temperature increases the random motion of free electrons increases and vibration of ions increases which decreases τ.

61. **Assertion:** Two bulbs of same wattage, one having a carbon filament and the other having a metallic filament are connected in series. Metallic bulbs will glow more brightly than carbon filament bulb.
Reason: Carbon is a semiconductor.

62. **Assertion:** Kirchhoff's junction rule can be applied to a junction of several lines or a point in a line.
Reason: When steady current is flowing, there is no accumulation of charges at any junction or at any point in a line.

63. **Assertion:** In meter bridge experiment, a high resistance is always connected in series with a galvanometer.
    Reason: As resistance increase current more accurately then ammeter.

64. **Assertion:** The emf of driver cell in potentiometer experiment should be greater than emf of cell to be determined.
    Reason: The fall of potential across the potentiometer wire should not be less than emf of cell to be determined.

65. The resistance of a conductor depends on its length L and area of cross section A. It also depends on the nature of the material and temperature. If the temperature is kept constant, the resistance of a conductor is directly proportional to its length and inversely to its area of cross section.

    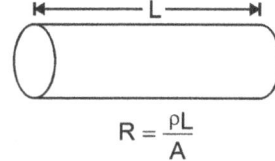

    This can be given : $R = \dfrac{\rho L}{A}$, where ρ is a constant called the resistivity of the material of the conductor. As temperature increases, the resistivity of a conductor will also increase. But it is not a linear relationship. In SI system, resistance is expressed in ohm (Ω) and resistivity in ohm-metre ($\Omega - m$).

    (i) A cylindrical wire has a resistance of 18Ω. The resistance of another wire of the same material with the same cross section, but 1.5 times the length is:
    (a) 18Ω (b) 27Ω
    (c) 12Ω (d) 9Ω

    (ii) If a cuboidal conductor is as follows, then its resistance is the most between which pair of points?

    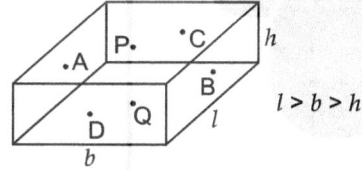

    P and Q are the centres of top and bottom surfaces, A and B are those of longer sides and C and D are centres of shorter sides.
    (a) AB
    (b) CD
    (c) PQ
    (d) All have the same resistance

    (iii) R is the resistance of a cylindrical wire. If it is stretched to twice of its length, keeping the volume constant, the new resistance will be:
    (a) R (b) 2R
    (c) 4R (d) R/2

    (iv) In an experiment, a sample of wire has a resistance 20Ω at $15°C$. If the experiment is conducted keeping the same wire sample at a temperature of $30°C$, then the possible value of its resistance can be:
    (a) 20Ω (b) 10Ω
    (c) 15Ω (d) 22.5Ω

    (v) In an experiment, a particular wire sample (A) has a resistance 10Ω. The person who conducts the experiment has three more sample of wires (B, C and D) of three different materials. All the four samples have the same length and same area of cross section. Resistance of sample B is 15Ω, that of C is 18Ω and that of D is 5Ω.
    Choose the incorrect statement from the following.
    (a) Resistivity of material of A is less than that of C
    (b) Resistivity of material of A twice that of D
    (c) Resistivity of B is thrice the resistivity of D
    (d) Resistivity of material of C is greater than that of B

66. When an inductor is connected to a source of emf and the switch is closed, initially the inductor offers infinite reactance to the current. As a result, first after closing the switch, the current in the circuit will be zero. But as time passes, the reactance reduces and after a long time the current through the inductor will be maximum.
    Now consider the following circuit.

    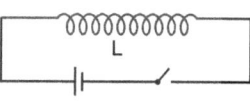
    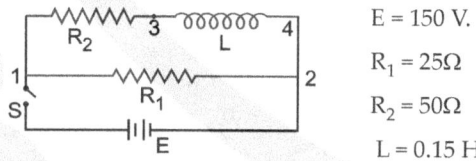

    E = 150 V.
    $R_1 = 25\Omega$
    $R_2 = 50\Omega$
    L = 0.15 H

    Switch S is closed at $t = 0$. Just after switch is closed.
    (i) Which point 1 or 2 is at a higher potential.
    (a) 1
    (b) 2
    (c) Both at same potential
    (d) None of these.

    (ii) The potential difference V_{12} across R_1 is
    (a) 75 V (b) 125 V
    (c) 150 V (d) 112.5 V

    (iii) The potential difference V_{34} across L is:
    (a) 75 V (b) 125 V
    (c) 150 V (d) 112.5 V

    (iv) Now the switch is opened after a long time just after opening the switch, the potential difference across R_1 is
    (a) 37.5 V (b) 75 V
    (c) 64 V (d) 112.5 V

    (v) Which point 3 or 4 is at lights potential?
    (a) 3
    (b) 4
    (c) 3 and 4 at the same potential
    (d) None of these

67. The typical drift velocity of electrons in the wire is 10^{-4} ms^{-1} of an electron drifts with this speed, then the electrons leaving the battery will take hours to reach the light bulb. Then how electric bulb glows as soon as we switch on the battery? When battery is switched on, the electrons begin to move away from the negative terminal of the battery and this electron exerts force on the nearby electrons. This process creates a propogating influence (electric field) that travels through the wire at the speed of light. In other words, the energy is transported from the battery to light bulb at the speed

of light through propagating influence (electric field). Due to this reason, the light bulb glows as soon as the battery is switched on.

(i) Given a current carrying wire of non-uniform cross-section, which of the following is constant throughout the length of the wire?
 (a) current, electric field and drift speed
 (b) drift speed only
 (c) current and drift speed
 (d) current only

(ii) Consider a copper wire of length L, cross-sectional area A. It has n number of free electrons per unit volume. Which of the following is the correct expression of drift velocity of the electrons when the wire carries a steady current I
 (a) $\dfrac{I}{neL}$ (b) $\dfrac{I}{n^2 eL}$
 (c) $\dfrac{I}{neA}$ (d) $\dfrac{I}{ne^2 LA}$

(iii) An electric cell of e.m.f. E is connected across copper wire of diameter d and length l. The drift velocity of electrons in the wire is v_d. If the length of the wire is changed to $2l$, the new drift velocity of electrons in the copper wire will be
 (a) v_d (b) $2v_d$
 (c) $v_d/2$ (d) $v_d/4$

(iv) Drift velocity v_d varies with the intensity of electric field as per the relation.
 (a) $v_d \propto E$ (b) $v_d \propto \dfrac{1}{E}$
 (c) $v_d =$ constant (d) $v_d \propto E^2$

(v) When an electrical appliance is switched on, it responds almost immediately, because
 (a) The electrons in the connecting wires move with the speed of light.
 (b) The electrical signal is carried by electromagnetic waves moving with the speed of light.
 (c) The electrons move with speed which is close to but less than speed of light.
 (d) The electrons are stagnant

68. The human body contains a large amount of water which has low resistance of around 200 Ω and the dry skin has high resistance of around 500 kΩ. But when the skin is wet, the resistance is reduced to around 1000 Ω. This is the reason, repairing the electrical connection with the wet skin is always dangerous.

(i) A wire of radius r has resistance R. If it is stretched to the wire of $\dfrac{r}{2}$ radius, then the resistance becomes
 (a) 2R (b) 4R
 (c) 16R (d) zero

(ii) The electric resistance of a certain wire of iron is R. If its length and radius are both doubled, then
 (a) the resistance will be halved and the specific resistance will remain unchanged.
 (b) the resistance will be doubled and the specific resistance will be halved.
 (c) the resistance will be halved and the specific resistance will be doubled.
 (d) the resistance and the specific resistance will both remain unchanged.

(iii) A wire of resistance 10 Ω is elongated by 10%. The resistance of the elongated wire is
 (a) 10.1 Ω (b) 11.1 Ω
 (c) 12.1 Ω (d) 13.1 Ω

(iv) What length of the wire (specific resistance 48×10^{-8} Ω – m) is needed to make a resistance of 4.2 Ω? (Diameter = 0.4 mm)
 (a) 1.1 m (b) 3.1 m
 (c) 2.1 m (d) 4.1 m

(v) The ratio of masses of three wires is 1 : 2 : 3 and that of their length is 3 : 2 : 1. If the wires are made of same material, the ratio of their resistances will be:
 (a) 1 : 1 : 1 (b) 1 : 2 : 3
 (c) 9 : 4 : 1 (d) 27 : 6 : 1

69. Wheatstone bridge is an arrangement of four resistances which can be used to measure one of them in terms of rest. Here arms AB and BC are called ratio arms and arms AC and BD are called conjugate arms. The bridge is said to be balanced when deflection in galvanometer is zero i.e., no current flows through the galvanometer or in other words, $V_B = V_D$. In the balanced condition $\dfrac{P}{Q} = \dfrac{R}{S}$, on mutually changing the position of cell and galvanometer, this condition will not change.

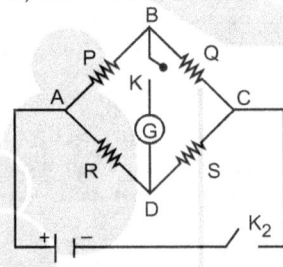

(i) In a wheatstone bridge, three resistances P, Q and R are connected in the three arms and the fourth arm is formed by two resistances S_1 and S_2 connected in parallel. The condition for the bridge to be balanced will be
 (a) $\dfrac{P}{Q} = \dfrac{R(S_1 + S_2)}{2 S_1 S_2}$ (b) $\dfrac{P}{Q} = \dfrac{R}{S_1 + S_2}$
 (c) $\dfrac{P}{Q} = \dfrac{2R}{S_1 + S_2}$ (d) $\dfrac{P}{Q} = \dfrac{R(S_1 + S_2)}{S_1 S_2}$

(ii) In the balanced wheatstone's bridge circuit as shown in the figure, when the key is pressed, what will be the change in the reading of the galvanometer?

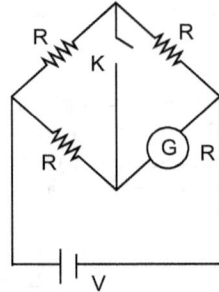

(a) remains same (b) increased
(c) decreased (d) none of these
(iii) What is the current in BD?

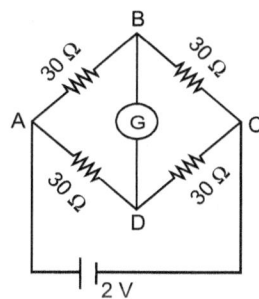

(a) zero (b) 0.033 A
(c) 0.066 A (d) none of these
(iv) The equivalent resistance between A and B of the circuit is

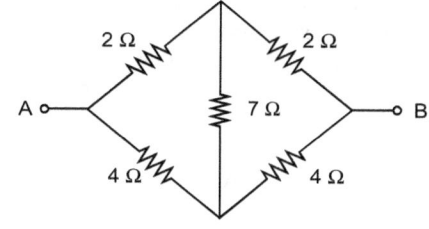

(a) $\frac{13}{12}$ | (b) $\frac{8}{3}$ |
(c) 8 Ω (d) $\frac{4}{3}$ |

(v) Three resistance P, Q, R each of 2 Ω and an unknown resistance S form the four arms of a. Wheatstone bridge circuit, when a resistance of 6 Ω is connected in parallel to S, the bridge gets balanced. What is the value of S?
(a) 2 Ω (b) 3 Ω
(c) 6 Ω (d) 1 Ω

Answers

1. (b) electric current
   Explanation: The time rate of flow of charge through any cross section of a conductor is electric current.

2. (d) the average of the velocities of all the free electrons at an instant is non-zero
   Explanation: Average of the velocities of all free electrons at an instant is non-zero, if not current is passed through a conductor.

3. (b) motion of conduction electrons due to electric field E.
   Explanation: Motion of conduction electrons due to random collisions has no preferred direction and average to zero. Drift velocity is caused due to motion of conduction electrons due to applied electric field.

4. (b) non-ohmic conductors
   Explanation: The figure is showing I-V characteristics of nonohmic or non-linear conductors.

5. (d) 3600 C
   Explanation: As we know that,
   $$I = \frac{q}{t}$$
   $$q = It$$
   $$= 0.5 \times 7200$$
   $$= 3600 \text{ C}.$$

6. (b) decreases with the increases of temperature
   Explanation: Because as temperature increases, the resistivity increases and hence the relaxation time decreases for conductors,
   $$\tau \propto \frac{1}{\rho}$$

7. (d) 6.25×10^{18}
   Explanation: As we know that,
   $$q = It$$
   $$\Rightarrow ne = It$$
   $$\therefore n = \frac{It}{e}$$
   $$= \frac{1 \times 1}{1.6 \times 10^{-19}}$$
   $$= 6.25 \times 10^{18}.$$

8. (b) decreases, thermal velocity of electron increases
   Explanation: When the temperature increases, resistance increases. As the emf applied is the same, the current density decreases the drift velocity decreases. But the rms velocity of the electron due to thermal motion is proportional to $\sqrt{T}$. Therefore, the thermal velocity increases.

9. (a) $\frac{ml}{Ne^2 A\tau}$
   Explanation: If N, e, τ and m are representing electron density, charge, relaxation time and mass of an electron respectively, then the resistance of wire of length l and cross-sectional area A is,
   $$\frac{ml}{Ne^2 A\tau}$$

10. (c) the resistance will be halved, and the specific resistance will remain unchanged
    Explanation: According to the given condition,
    $$R = \frac{\rho l_1}{A_1}$$
    now, $l_2 = 2l_1$
    $A_2 = \pi(r_2)^2$
    $= \pi(2r_1)^2 = 4\pi r_1^2 = 4A_1$
    $$\therefore R_2 = \frac{\rho(2l_1)}{4A_1} = \frac{\rho l}{2A} = \frac{R}{2}$$
    Resistance is halved, but specific resistance remains the same.

11. (d) All of these

Explanation: The direction of drift velocity in a conductor is - opposite to that of applied electric field, opposite to the flow of positive charge, and in the direction of the flow of electrons.

12. (a) 16:1
    Explanation: Current flowing through the conductor, $I = nev_d A$. Hence,
    $$\frac{4}{1} = \frac{nev_{d_1}\pi(1)^2}{nev_{d_2}\pi(2)^2}$$
    $$\Rightarrow \frac{v_{d_1}}{v_{d_2}} = \frac{4 \times 1}{1}$$
    $$= \frac{16}{1}.$$

13. (d) $v_d/4$
    Explanation: As we know that,
    $$I = nAev_d$$
    or, $v_d \propto 1/\pi r^2$
    If $r \to 2r$, then
    $$v_d' = 1/\pi(2r)^2$$
    $$v_d' = \frac{v_d}{4}.$$

14. (d) the average speed of the electron between successive collisions in the direction opposite to the applied electric field
    Explanation: When no emf is applied, the electrons move randomly inside the conductor. When emf is applied, electrons drift opposite to the applied emf and collide with each other. Between the collisions, average speed in the direction of field is V_d.

15. (a) 0.013/°C
    Explanation: According to the given condition,
    $5\,\Omega = R_0(1 + \alpha \times 50)$ ...(i)
    and $7\,\Omega = R_0(1 + \alpha \times 100)$ ...(ii)
    Divide equation (i) by (ii)
    $$\frac{5}{7} = \frac{1 + 50\alpha}{1 + 100\alpha}$$
    $$\alpha = \frac{2}{150}$$
    $= 0.0133$°C.

16. (a) be double the initial velocity
    Explanation: As we know that,
    $I = nev_d$
    ∴ $I \propto v_d$
    From Ohm's law, $V \propto I \propto v_d$
    If the potential difference is doubled, drift velocity of electrons will also double.

17. (b) decreases from A to B
    Explanation: As area increases, v_d decreases.

18. (b) 2×10^{-6}
    Explanation: As we know that,
    $$E = \frac{V}{l} = \frac{10}{0.1}$$
    $= 100$ V/m
    ∴ $\mu = \frac{V_d}{E}$

    $= \frac{2 \times 10^{-4}}{100}$
    $= 2 \times 10^{-6}$ m^{2}v^{-1}s^{-1}.

19. (a) current and potential difference
    Explanation: Ohm's law deals with the relation between current and potential difference.

20. (a) constant
    Explanation: Ohm's law is valid when the temperature of the conductor is constant.

21. (c) will remain the same
    Explanation: As we know that,
    $$R_1 \propto \frac{l}{A}$$
    $$\Rightarrow R_2 \propto \frac{2l}{2A}$$
    i.e., $R_2 \propto \frac{l}{A}$
    ∴ $R_1 = R_2$.

22. (b) increases as the temperature rises
    Explanation: As we know that,
    $\frac{V}{I} = R$ and $R \propto$ temperature.

23. (d) is unaffected by change in its length and area of cross-section.
    Explanation: Resistivity is the property of the material. It does not depend upon size and shape.

24. (d) shape of cross-section
    Explanation: As we know that
    $$R = \frac{\rho l}{A}$$
    So that, R is independent of shape of cross-section.

25. (b) 0.25 R
    Explanation: As we know that,
    $$R \propto \frac{1}{A}$$
    $$\Rightarrow R \propto \frac{1}{r^2}$$
    $$R \propto \frac{1}{d^2} \quad (d = \text{diameter of wire})$$

26. (a) conductance
    Explanation: The reciprocal of resistance is called conductance.

27. (d) 16 Ω
    Explanation: Let R be the resistance and l be the original length. At constant volume, $R \propto l^2$
    Resistance of stretched wire is,
    $R' = 4R$
    $= 4(4)$
    $= 16\,\Omega$.

28. (a)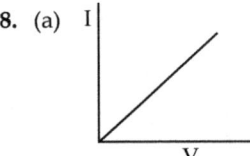

Explanation: For ohmic circuit, V ∝ I
Graph of such is a straight line through origin with positive slope.

29. (c) products of currents and the resistances
Explanation: In a closed circuit, the vector sum of total emf is equal to the sum of the products of currents and the resistances.

30. (a) charge
Explanation: Kirchhoff's first law is based on the law of conservation of charge.

31. (c) $-i$
Explanation: According the Kirchhoff's law, in any analytic circuit, if the direction of current is assumed opposite, then the value of current will be $-i$.

32. (b) not change
Explanation: The deflection in galvanometer will not be changed due to interchange of battery and the galvanometer.

33. (b) Cell is E
Explanation: In the given case, cell is in open circuit mode (I = 0). So voltage across the cell is equal to its emf.

34. (c) 13 A
Explanation: On applying Kirchhoff's current law, I = 13 A.

35. (b) energy
Explanation: Kirchhoff's second law is based on the law of conservation of energy.

36. (b) 10.6 ohm
Explanation: According to the balance condition of meter bridge,
$$\frac{X}{10} = \frac{(52+1)}{(48+2)}$$
∴   X = 10.6 Ω.

37. (d) $-5/6$ A
Explanation: Suppose currents through different paths of the circuit are as follows,

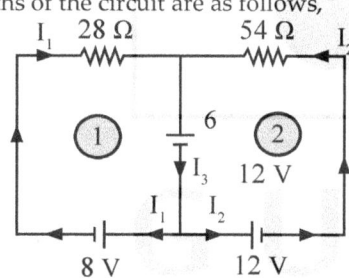

After applying KVL for loop (1) and loop (2),
$28I_1 = -6 - 8$
⇒ $I_1 = -\frac{1}{2}$ A
and $54I_2 = -6 - 12$
⇒ $I_2 = -\frac{1}{3}$ A
Hence, $I_3 = I_1 + I_2$
$= -\frac{5}{6}$ A.

38. (a) end correction

Explanation: In meter bridge experiment, it is assumed that the resistance of the L shaped plate is negligible, but actually it is not so. The error created due to this is called end error. To remove this the resistance box and the unknown resistance must be interchanged and then the mean reading must be taken.

39. (a) 0.1
Explanation: Applying Kirchhoff's law in following figure,

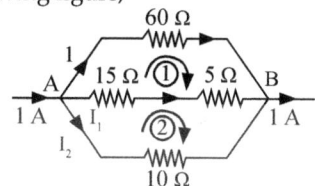

At junction A,
$I + I_1 + I_2 = 1$ …(i)
For Loop (1),
$-60I + (15+5)I_1 = 0$
⇒ $I_1 = 3I$ …(ii)
For Loop (2)
$-(15+5)I_1 + 10I_2 = 0$
⇒ $I_2 = 2I_1$
$= 2(3I)$
$= 6I$ …(iii)
On solving equation (i), (ii) and (iii),
I = 0.1 A.

40. (c) 13.1 V
Explanation: As the two cells oppose each other hence, the effective emf in closed circuit is 15 – 10 = 5 V and net resistance is 1 + 0.6 = 1.6 ohm (because in the closed circuit the internal resistance of two cells are in series.)
Current in the circuit,
$$I = \frac{\text{effective emf}}{\text{total resistance}}$$
$= \frac{5}{1.6}$ A

The potential difference across voltmeter will be same as the terminal voltage of either cell. Since the current is drawn from the cell of 15 V.
∴ $V_1 = E_1 - Ir_1$
$= 15 - \frac{5}{1.6} \times 0.6$
$= 13.1$ V

41. (c) 220 Ω
Explanation: For balanced meter bridge,
$$\frac{55}{R} = \frac{20}{80}$$
⇒   R = 220 Ω.

42. (b) 15 ohm
Explanation: Initially,
$$\frac{5}{l_1} = \frac{R}{100 - l_1}$$ …(i)
Finally,
$$\frac{5}{1.6l_1} = \frac{R/2}{(100 - 1.6l_1)}$$ …(ii)

$$\therefore \quad \frac{R}{1.6(100 - l_1)} = \frac{R}{2(100 - 1.6l_1)}$$

$$\therefore \quad 100 - 1.6l_1 = 200 - 3.2l_1$$

$$\therefore \quad 1.6l_1 = 40$$

$$\therefore \quad l_1 = 25 \text{ cm}$$

From equation (i),

$$\frac{5}{25} = \frac{R}{75}$$

$$\Rightarrow \quad R = 15 \, \Omega.$$

43. (c) potentiometer

    Explanation: The instrument among the following which measures the emf of a cell most accurately is potentiometer.

44. (a) $\dfrac{R(S_1 + S_2)}{S_1 S_2}$

    Explanation: For balancing the bridge,

    $$\frac{P}{Q} = \frac{R}{S}$$

    $$\therefore \quad S = \frac{S_1 S_2}{S_1 + S_2} \quad (\because S_1, S_2 \text{ are in parallel})$$

    $$\therefore \quad \frac{P}{Q} = \frac{R(S_1 + S_2)}{S_1 S_2}$$

45. (b) galvanometer circuit

    Explanation: When the resistance in the main circuit is increased, the current through the wire due to auxiliary battery decreases. This decrease in potential gradient increases the balancing length. Hence balance point can be shifted from 6th to 8th wire.

46. (b) it does not disturb the potential difference it measures.

    Explanation: In balance condition, potentiometer doesn't draw any current from secondary circuit.

47. (b) electric field produced by charges accumulated on the surface of wire.

    Explanation: As we know, electric current per unit area is called current density. The current density is also directed along E and is also a vector.
    Conductivity is given by,

    $$\sigma = \frac{1}{\rho} = \frac{l}{RA}$$

    Electric field is given by,

    $$J = \sigma E$$

    So, current density changes due to electric field produced by charges accumulated on the surface of wire.

48. (a) Drift velocity alone

    Explanation: We know that the relationship between current and drift speed is,

    $$I = Anev_d$$

    That means, $I \propto v_d$
    Hence, only drift velocity determines the current in a conductor.

49. (c) He should change S to 3 Ω and repeat the experiment.

    Explanation: To improve accuracy, balance point should be obtained near the midpoint on the bridge. This means, l is approximately is equal to 50 cm. This need choosing of resistance S suitably. For given value of l_1

    $$\frac{R}{S} = \frac{l_1}{100 - l_1} = \frac{2.9}{97.1}$$

    $$S \approx 33 \, R$$

    To make R/S ratio 1:1, value of S should be reduced by 33 times.
    And $\qquad S = 100$ ohm
    Hence required,

    $$S = \frac{100}{33} \approx 3 \, \Omega$$

50. (b) The battery of potentiometer can have a voltage of 15 V and R adjusted so that the potential drop across the wire slightly exceeds 10 V

    Explanation: The potential drop across wires of potentiometer should be more than emf of primary cells. Here, values of emfs of two cells are given as 5 V and 10 V, so the potential drop along the potentiometer wire must be more than 10 V. So battery should be of 15 V and about 4 V potential is dropped by using variable resistance.

51. (b)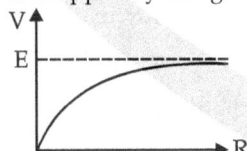

    Explanation: $V = \dfrac{ER}{R+r}$

    $$= \frac{E}{1 + \dfrac{r}{R}}$$

    when $\quad R \to \infty, V = E$
    $\qquad R \to 0, V = 0$

52. (c) $\dfrac{R}{2}$

    Explanation:

    $$\frac{1}{R'} = \frac{1}{R} + \frac{1}{R} = \frac{2}{R}$$

    $$R' = \frac{R}{2}$$

53. (c) From relation $\vec{j} = \sigma \vec{E}$ the current density $\vec{j}$ at any point in ohmic resistor is in direction of electric field $\vec{E}$ at that point. In space having non-uniform electric field, charges released from rest may not move along electric line of force. Hence, assertion is correct while reason is incorrect.

54. (a) As we know that,

    $$P = \frac{V^2}{R}$$

    $$\Rightarrow \quad R = \frac{V^2}{P}$$

    $$\Rightarrow \quad R \propto \frac{1}{P}$$

55. (a) Resistance of wire $R = \rho \dfrac{l}{A}$

    where ρ is resistivity of material which does not depend on the geometry of wire. Since when wire is bent, resistivity, length and area of cross-section do not change, therefore resistance of wire also remains same.

56. (c) Fuse wire must have high resistance because in series, current remains same, therefore according to Joule's law,

    $$H = \dfrac{I^2 Rt}{4.2} \text{ cal}$$

    Heat produced is high if R is high. The melting point must be low so that wire may melt with increase in temperature. As the current equal to maximum safe value, flows through the fuse wire, it heats up, melts and break the circuit.

57. (c) Drift speed is the average speed between two successive collision.

58. (a) Resistance of 50 W bulb is two times the resistance of 100 W bulb. When bulbs are connected in series, 50 W bulb will glow more as $P = i^2 R$ (current remains same in series). In parallel, the 100 W bulb will glow more as $P = \dfrac{V^2}{R}$ (potential difference remains same in parallel).

59. (a) As we know that,
    Glow = Power (P) = $I^2 R$
    $\therefore \quad \dfrac{dP}{P} = 2\left(\dfrac{dI}{I}\right) = 2 \times 0.5 = 1\%$

60. (a) When temperature increases, the random motion of electrons and vibration of ions increases which results in more frequent collisions of electrons with the ions. Due to this the average time between the successive collisions, denoted by τ, decreases which increases ρ.

61. (d) When two bulbs are connected in series, the resistance of the circuit increases and so the voltage in each decreases, hence the brightness and the temperature also decreases. Due to decrease in temperature, the resistance of the carbon filament will slightly increase while that of metal filament will decrease. Hence, carbon filament bulb will glow more brightly $P = i^2 R$. Also carbon is not a semiconductor.

62. (a) **Junction rule or Kirchhoff's first law or Kirchhoff's current law (KCL)** states that the algebraic sum of the currents meeting at a junction (point) in an electrical circuit is always zero. Or, the sum of currents flowing towards the junction is equal to sum of currents leaving the junction.
    $\Sigma I = 0$
    $I_1 + I_3 = I_2 + I_4$

63. (c) The resistance of the galvanometer is fixed. In meter bridge experiments, to protect the galvanometer from a high current, high resistance is connected to the galvanometer in order to protect it from damage.

64. (a) If either emf of the driver cell or potential difference across the whole potentiometer wire is lesser than the emf of then experimental cell, then balance point will not obtained.

65. (i) (b) $R \propto L$

    (ii) (b) $R \propto \dfrac{L}{A}$; L is the most and A is the least between C and D.

    (iii) (c) $R \propto \dfrac{L}{A}$; Length gets doubled and A becomes halved, resistance becomes 4 times.

    (iv) (d) As temperature increases, resistivity increases, thereby increasing the resistance.

    (v) (c) Resistivity of B is thrice the resistivity of D.

66. (i) (a) Just after the switch is closed, the inductor offers infinite resistance. Current occur across R_1 only point 1 is at a higher potential.

    (ii) (c) $V_{12} = E = 150$ V

    (iii) (c) $V_{34} = V_{12} = 150$ V

    (iv) (b) Just before opening the switch, the current through the inductor

    $$i_0 = \dfrac{E}{R_2} = \dfrac{150}{50} = 3A$$

    $i_1 = i - i_0 = 6 - 3 = 3$ Amp
    $V_1 = i_1 R_1 = 3.25 = 75 \Omega$

    (v) (b) Point 3 will be at a higher potential. Point 4 is at lighter potential.

67. (i) (d) In steady state, current at each cross-section will be same. Both drift velocity and electric field density on current density $\vec{J}$, which depends on cross-sectional area A.

    (ii) (c) $\dfrac{I}{neA}$

    (iii) (c) $v_d = \dfrac{I}{neA}$ and $v_d' = \dfrac{E}{\rho \times 2l \times n \times e}$

    $\Rightarrow v_d = \dfrac{E \times A}{\rho \times l \times n \times e \times A} = \dfrac{E}{\rho \times l \times n \times e}$

    $\Rightarrow \dfrac{v_d'}{v_d} = \dfrac{1}{2} \Rightarrow v_d' = \dfrac{v_d}{2}$

    (iv) (a) $v_d = \dfrac{e}{m} \times \dfrac{V}{l} \tau$ or $v_d = \dfrac{e}{m} \dfrac{El}{l} \tau$ [$\because V = El$]
    $\therefore v_d \propto E$

    (v) (b) It is the electric field that is set up which moves with the velocity of light in that medium.

68. (i) (c) The volume of the wire remains unchanged,
    $V = A_1 l_1 = A_2 l_2$

    $\dfrac{r}{2} = \dfrac{A_2}{A_1} = \dfrac{r_2^2}{r_1^2} = \dfrac{(r/2)^2}{r^2} = \dfrac{1}{4}$

$$\frac{R_1}{R_2} = \frac{l_1}{l_2} \times \frac{A_2}{A_1} = \frac{1}{4} \times \frac{1}{4} = \frac{1}{16}$$

or $R_2 = 16 R_1 = 16 R$

(ii) (a) original resistance
$$R = \rho \cdot \frac{l}{A} = \rho \cdot \frac{l}{\pi r^2}$$

when both length and radius are doubled,
$$R' = \rho \cdot \frac{2l}{\pi(2r)^2} = \frac{1}{2} \rho \cdot \frac{l}{\pi r^2} = \frac{1}{2} R$$

(iii) (c) New length,
$l' = l + 10\% \text{ of } l = 1.1\, l$

As, $V = Al = A'l'$

$\therefore \quad \dfrac{A}{A'} = \dfrac{l'}{l} = 1.1$

$$\dfrac{R'}{R} = \dfrac{l'}{l} \times \dfrac{A}{A'} = 1.1 \times 1.1 = 1.21$$

$R' = 1.21\, R = 1.21 \times 10 = 12.1\, \Omega$

(iv) (a) $l = \dfrac{RA}{\rho} = \dfrac{R \times \pi D^2}{4\rho}$

$= \dfrac{4.2 \times 2.2 \times (0.4 \times 10^{-3})^2}{7 \times 4 \times 48 \times 10^{-8}}$

$= 1.1$ m

(v) (d) Mass = volume × density = Ald

or $A = \dfrac{m}{ld}$

$\therefore \quad R = \rho \cdot \dfrac{l}{A} = \rho \cdot \dfrac{l}{m/ld} = \rho \cdot \dfrac{l^2 d}{m}$

i.e. $R \propto \dfrac{l^2}{m}$

Given, $m_1 : m_2 : m_3 = 1 : 2 : 3$
and, $l_1 : l_2 : l_3 = 3 : 2 : 1$

$\therefore R_1 : R_2 : R_3 = \dfrac{3^2}{1} : \dfrac{2^2}{2} : \dfrac{1^2}{3} = 9 : 2 : \dfrac{1}{3}$

$= 27 : 6 : 1$

69. (i) (d) Equivalent resistance of the parallel combination of S_1 and S_2 is
$$S = \dfrac{S_1 S_2}{S_1 + S_2}$$

For the balanced wheatstone bridge,
$$\dfrac{P}{Q} = \dfrac{R}{S} = \dfrac{R(S_1 + S_2)}{S_1 S_2}$$

(ii) (a) As the wheatstone bridge is balanced, the pressing of key K makes no effect. The reading of the galvanometer G remains the same.

(iii) (a) As $\dfrac{30}{30} = \dfrac{30}{30}$

The wheatstone bridge is balanced. No current flows in arms BD.

(iv) (b) The circuit is a balanced wheatstone bridge because $\dfrac{2}{2} = \dfrac{4}{4}$

The 7 Ω resistance is ineffective,
∴ Resistance of the upper arms = 2 + 2 = 4 Ω
Resistance of the lower arms = 4 + 4 = 8 Ω
These two resistance are in parallel,

$\therefore R_{AB} = \dfrac{4 \times 8}{4 + 8} = \dfrac{32}{12} = \dfrac{8}{3}$

(v) (b) The fourth arm has resistance S and 6 Ω in parallel with equivalent resistance $= \dfrac{6S}{6+S} \Omega$.

For the balanced wheatstone bridge,
$$\dfrac{P}{Q} = \dfrac{R}{\left(\dfrac{6S}{6+S}\right)} \text{ or } \dfrac{2}{2} = \dfrac{2(6+S)}{6S}$$

or $3S = 6 + S$ or $S = 3\, \Omega$

Chapter 4

Moving Charges and Magnetism

1. Magnetic field can be produced by:
   (a) a charge at rest.
   (b) a changing electric field.
   (c) a moving charge.
   (d) both (b) and (c)

2. A particle of mass m and charge q enters a magnetic field B perpendicularly with a velocity v. The radius of the circular path described by it will be:
   (a) $\dfrac{mq}{Bv}$
   (b) $\dfrac{Bq}{mv}$
   (c) $\dfrac{mv}{Bq}$
   (d) $\dfrac{mB}{qv}$

3. A charged particle moving in a magnetic field experiences a resultant force:
   (a) in the direction perpendicular to both the field and its velocity.
   (b) in the direction of the field.
   (c) in the direction opposite to that of the field.
   (d) none of the above.

4. A charged particle moves with a velocity v in a uniform magnetic field $\vec{B}$. The magnetic force experienced by the particle is:
   (a) never zero.
   (b) always zero.
   (c) zero, if $\vec{B}$ and $\vec{v}$ are parallel.
   (d) zero, if $\vec{B}$ and $\vec{v}$ are perpendicular.

5. A charged particle of mass m and charge q travels on a circular path of radius r that is perpendicular to a magnetic field B. The time taken by the particle to complete one revolution is:
   (a) $\dfrac{2\pi m}{qB}$
   (b) $\dfrac{2\pi qB}{m}$
   (c) $\dfrac{2\pi mq}{B}$
   (d) $\dfrac{2\pi q^2 B}{m}$

6. If we double the radius of a coil keeping the current through it unchanged, what happens to the magnetic field on its axis at very-very far away points?
   (a) Halved
   (b) Doubled
   (c) Becomes four times
   (d) Remains unchanged

7. An electron and a proton enter a magnetic field with equal velocities. Which one of them experiences more force?
   (a) Proton
   (b) Electron
   (c) Both experience same force
   (d) It cannot be predicted.

8. A charge of 1 C is moving in a magnetic field of 0.5 T with velocity of 10 m/s. Force experienced is:
   (a) 0.5 N
   (b) 5 N
   (c) 10 N
   (d) 0 N

9. Lorentz force is:
   (a) the vector sum of electrostatic and magnetic force acting on a moving charged particle.
   (b) the vector sum of gravitational and magnetic force acting on a moving charged particle.
   (c) electrostatic force acting on a charged particle
   (d) magnetic force acting on a moving charged particle.

10. A charged particle is moving with velocity v in a magnetic field of induction B. The force on the particle will be maximum when:
    (a) v and B are at an angle of 45°.
    (b) v and B are perpendicular.
    (c) v and B are in the same directions.
    (d) v and B are in opposite directions.

11. An α-particle enters a magnetic field of 1 T with a velocity 10^6 m/s in a direction perpendicular to the field. The force on α-particle is:
    (a) 1.6×10^{-3} N
    (b) 3.2×10^{-13} N
    (c) 4.8×10^{-13} N
    (d) 6.4×10^{-13} N

12. A 2 MeV proton is moving perpendicular to a uniform magnetic field of 2.5 T. The force on the proton is:
    (a) 2.5×10^{-10} N
    (b) 2.5×10^{-11} N
    (c) 7.6×10^{-11} N
    (d) 7.6×10^{-12} N

13. Two electrons move parallel to each other with equal speed v. The ratio of magnetic and electrical forces between them is:
    (a) $\dfrac{c}{v}$
    (b) $\dfrac{v}{c}$
    (c) $\dfrac{c^2}{v^2}$
    (d) $\dfrac{v^2}{c^2}$

14. A proton and a deuterium nucleus having certain kinetic energies enter in a uniform magnetic field with same component of velocity in the direction of magnetic field. Which of the following is correct?
    (a) Which particle has greater pitch depends on the fact that which particle has greater component of velocity perpendicular to magnetic field.
    (b) Deuterium nucleus has greater pitch of helical motion.
    (c) Proton has greater pitch of helical motion.
    (d) Both particles have same pitch of helical motion.

15. A proton of mass m and charge q is moving in a plane with kinetic energy E. If there exists a uniform magnetic field B, perpendicular to the plane of the motion, the proton will move in a circular path of radius:

(a) $\dfrac{2Em}{qB}$ (b) $\dfrac{\sqrt{Em}}{2qB}$

(c) $\dfrac{\sqrt{2Em}}{qB}$ (d) $\dfrac{\sqrt{2Eq}}{mB}$

16. Biot-Savart law indicates that the moving electron velocity (v) produce a magnetic field B such that:
    (a) $B \perp v$
    (b) $B \parallel v$
    (c) it is along the line joining electron and point of observation
    (d) it obeys inverse cube law

17. Magnetic field at any point on the axis of a current element is _____.
    (a) maximum
    (b) minimum
    (c) a constant
    (d) zero

18. Magnetic field due to a ring having n turns at a distance x on its axis is proportional to (if r = radius of ring):
    (a) $\dfrac{r}{(x^2 + r^2)}$ (b) $\dfrac{nr^2}{(x^2 + r^2)^{3/2}}$
    (c) $\dfrac{r^2}{(x^2 + r^2)^{3/2}}$ (d) $\dfrac{n^2 r^2}{(x^2 + r^2)^{3/2}}$

19. A current of 10 A is passing through a long wire which has semicircular loop of the radius 20 cm as shown in the figure. Magnetic field produced at the centre of the loop is:

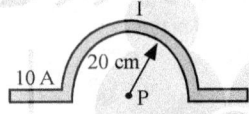

    (a) $4\pi\mu T$ (b) $2\pi\mu T$
    (c) $10\pi\mu T$ (d) $5\pi\mu T$

20. A coil having N turns, carry a current as shown in the figure. The magnetic field intensity at point P is:

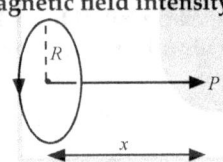

    (a) Zero   (b) $\dfrac{\mu_0 NI}{2R}$
    (c) $\dfrac{\mu_0 NIR^2}{(R+x)^2}$ (d) $\dfrac{\mu_0 NIR^2}{2(R^2+x^2)^{3/2}}$

21. Ampere's circuital law states that:
    (a) the line integral of magnetic field along the boundary of the open surface is equal to μ_0 times the total current passing near the surface.
    (b) the line integral of magnetic field along the boundary of the open surface is equal to μ_0 times the total current passing through the surface.
    (c) the surface integral of magnetic field over the open surface is equal to μ_0 times the total current passing through the surface.
    (d) the surface integral of magnetic field over the open surface is equal to μ_0 times the total current passing near the surface.

22. The magnetic induction at any point due to a long straight wire carrying a current is:
    (a) inversely proportional to the distance from wire.
    (b) inversely proportional to the square of the distance from the wire.
    (c) does not depend on distance.
    (d) proportional to the distance from the wire.

23. The strength of the magnetic field at a point r near a long straight current carrying wire is B. The field at a distance $\dfrac{r}{2}$ will be:
    (a) 2B   (b) 4B
    (c) $\dfrac{B}{2}$ (d) $\dfrac{B}{4}$

24. A toroidal coil has 3000 turns. The inner and outer radii are 10 cm and 14 cm respectively. If current flowing is 5 A, then the magnetic field inside the toroid will be:
    (a) 0.25 T   (b) 25×10^{-3} T
    (c) 25×10^{-4} T   (d) 25×10^{-5} T

25. A current of 1 A is passed through a straight wire of length 2 m. The magnetic field at a point in air at a distance of 3 m from either end of wire and lying on the axis of wire will be:
    (a) Zero   (b) $\dfrac{\mu_0}{2\pi}$ T
    (c) $\dfrac{\mu_0}{4\pi}$ T   (d) $\dfrac{\mu_0}{8\pi}$ T

26. A solenoid of length 0.6 m has a radius of 2 cm and is made up of 600 turns. If it carries a current of 4 A, then the magnitude of the magnetic field inside the solenoid is:
    (a) 5.024×10^{-3} T   (b) 6.024×10^{-3} T
    (c) 7.024×10^{-3} T   (d) 8.024×10^{-3} T

27. 20 A current is flowing in a long straight wire. The intensity of magnetic field at a distance 10 cm from the wire will be:
    (a) 4×10^{-5} Wb/m^2 (b) 6×10^{-5} Wb/m^2
    (c) 8×10^{-5} Wb/m^2 (d) 9×10^{-5} Wb/m^2

28. Two thin, long, parallel wires, separated by a distance d carry a current of i A in the same direction. They will:
    (a) attract each other with a force of $\dfrac{\mu_0 i^2}{(2\pi d)}$
    (b) attract each other with a force of $\dfrac{\mu_0 i^2}{(2\pi d^2)}$
    (c) repel each other with a force of $\dfrac{\mu_0 i^2}{(2\pi d)}$
    (d) repel each other with a force of $\dfrac{\mu_0 i^2}{(2\pi d^2)}$

29. A solenoid 1.5 m long and 0.4 cm in diameter possesses 10 turns per cm length. A current of 5 A flows through it. The magnetic field at the axis inside the solenoid is:
    (a) $4\pi \times 10^{-3}$ T   (b) $4\pi \times 10^{-2}$ T
    (c) $2\pi \times 10^{-5}$ T   (d) $2\pi \times 10^{-3}$ T

30. A current carrying loop is placed in a uniform magnetic field. The torque acting on it does not depend upon the _____.
    (a) area of loop
    (b) number of turns
    (c) shape of loop
    (d) angle between normal of coil and magnetic field

31. Which of the following is experienced by a current carrying loop in a uniform magnetic field?
    (a) Torque only.
    (b) Force only.
    (c) Neither torque nor force.
    (d) Both torque and force.

32. A current loop of area A, number of turns N is placed in a uniform magnetic induction B. The angle between the plane of the loop and B is θ. The torque acting on the loop will be:
    (a) NIABtanθ
    (b) NIABsinθ
    (c) NIABcosθ
    (d) NIAB

33. If the coil, having cross-section area 0.1 m² and carrying a current 2 A is placed in a uniform field of 0.2 T with the normal to the coil making an angle of 45° with the direction of the field, then the torque experienced by the coil will be:
    (a) 0.05 Nm
    (b) 0.028 Nm
    (c) 0.038 Nm
    (d) 0.04 Nm

34. A moving coil sensitive galvanometer gives at once much more deflection. To control its speed of deflection:
    (a) the body of galvanometer should be earthed.
    (b) a high resistance is to be connected across its terminals.
    (c) a magnet should be placed near the coil.
    (d) a small copper wire should be connected across its terminals.

35. If the current is doubled, the deflection is also doubled in:
    (a) a ohmmeter
    (b) a tangent galvanometer
    (c) a moving coil galvanometer
    (d) both (b) and (c)

36. A milli voltmeter of 25 milli volt range is to be converted into an ammeter of 25 A range. The value (in Ω) of necessary shunt will be:
    (a) 0.001
    (b) 0.01
    (c) 0.05
    (d) 1

37. A galvanometer of resistance 25 Ω is shunted by 2.5 Ω resistance. The part (fraction) of the total current that flows through the galvanometer is given as:
    (a) $\frac{I_G}{I_0} = \frac{3}{11}$
    (b) $\frac{I_G}{I_0} = \frac{1}{11}$
    (c) $\frac{I_G}{I_0} = \frac{2}{11}$
    (d) $\frac{I_G}{I_0} = \frac{4}{11}$

38. The galvanometer cannot as such be used as an ammeter to measure the value of current in a given circuit. The following reasons are:
    (i) galvanometer gives full scale deflection for a small current.
    (ii) galvanometer has a large resistance.
    (iii) a galvanometer can give inaccurate values.
    (a) (i) and (iii)
    (b) (i) and (ii)
    (c) (ii) and (iii)
    (d) (i), (ii), and (iii)

39. The coil of a moving coil galvanometer has 1000 turns each of area 3 × 10⁻⁴ m². Its suspension fibre has restoring torque of 2 × 10⁻⁷ Nm per degree and the radial magnetic field of induction 0.08 Wb/m². If a current of 10 μA is passed through it, then the deflection produced is:
    (a) 0.8°
    (b) 0.6°
    (c) 1.2°
    (d) 1.0°

40. A galvanometer having a coil resistance of 60 Ω shows full scale deflection when a current of 1A passes through it. It can be converted into an ammeter to read currents upto 5 A by:
    (a) putting in series a resistance of 15 Ω
    (b) putting in parallel a resistance of 15 Ω
    (c) putting in series a resistance of 240 Ω
    (d) putting in parallel a resistance of 240 Ω

41. Current flows in three long straight parallel long wires as shown in figure. The force on 10 cm length of wire Q is:

    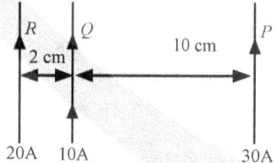

    (a) 1.4 × 10⁻⁴ N towards right
    (b) 1.4 × 10⁻⁴ N towards left
    (c) 2.6 × 10⁻⁴ N towards right
    (d) 2.6 × 10⁻⁴ N towards left

42. Two charged particles traverse identical helical paths in a completely opposite sense in a uniform magnetic field B = B₀k. [NCERT Exemplar]
    (a) They have equal z-components of momenta.
    (b) They must have equal charges.
    (c) They necessarily represent a particle-antiparticle pair.
    (d) The charge to mass ratio satisfy:
    $\left(\frac{e}{m}\right)_1 + \left(\frac{e}{m}\right)_2 = 0$.

43. Biot-Savart law indicates that the moving electrons (velocity v) produce a magnetic field B such that: [NCERT Exemplar]
    (a) $B \perp v$
    (b) $B \parallel v$
    (c) it obeys inverse cube law.
    (d) it is along the line joining the electron and point of observation.

44. An electron is projected with uniform velocity along the axis of a current carrying long solenoid. Which of the following is true? [NCERT Exemplar]
    (a) The electron will be accelerated along the axis.
    (b) The electron path will be circular about the axis.
    (c) The electron will experience a force at 45° to the axis and hence execute a helical path.
    (d) The electron will continue to move with uniform velocity along the axis of the solenoid.

45. A current I flows through a long straight conductor which is bent into a circular loop of radius R in the middle as shown in the figure.

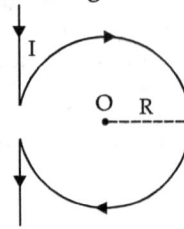

The magnitude of the net magnetic field at point O will be : [CBSE 2020]

(a) Zero
(b) $\dfrac{\mu_0 I}{2R}(1+\pi)$
(c) $\dfrac{\mu_0 I}{2\pi R}$
(d) $\dfrac{\mu_0 I}{2R}\left(1-\dfrac{1}{\pi}\right)$

46. A current of 10A is flowing from east to west in a long straight wire kept on a horizontal table. The magnetic field developed at a distance of 10 cm due north on the table is : [CBSE 2020]
    (a) 2×10^{-5} T, acting downwards
    (b) 2×10^{-5} T, acting upwards
    (c) 4×10^{-5} T, acting downwards
    (d) 4×10^{-5} T, acting upwards

47. An electron and a proton are moving along the same direction with the same kinetic energy. They enter a uniform magnetic field acting perpendicular to their velocities. The dependence of radius of their path on their masses is : [CBSE 2020]
    (a) $r \propto m$
    (b) $r \propto \sqrt{m}$
    (c) $r \propto \dfrac{1}{m}$
    (d) $\dfrac{1}{\sqrt{m}}$

48. A charge particle after being accelerated through a potential difference 'V' enters in a uniform magnetic field and moves in a circle of radius r. If V is doubled, the radius of the circle will become : [CBSE 2020]
    (a) $2r$
    (b) $\sqrt{2}r$
    (c) $4r$
    (d) $\dfrac{r}{\sqrt{2}r}$

Directions: In the following questions, a statement of assertion is followed by a statement of reason. Mark the correct choice as:
(a) If both assertion and reason are true and reason is the correct explanation of assertion.
(b) If both assertion and reason are true, but reason is not the correct explanation of assertion.
(c) If assertion is true, but reason is false.
(d) If both assertion and reason are false.

49. **Assertion:** When a test charge moves through the magnetic field, its momentum changes but kinetic energy remains constant.
    Reason: The magnetic force acts as a centripetal force, which is perpendicular to the instantaneous velocity and so does no work.

50. **Assertion:** Magnetic field interacts with a moving charge and not with a stationary charge.
    Reason: A moving charge produces a magnetic field.

51. **Assertion:** Free electron always keeps on moving in a conductor even then no magnetic force act on them in magnetic field unless a current is passed through it.
    Reason: The average velocity of free electron is zero.

52. **Assertion:** Ampere's law used for the closed loop shown in figure is written as $\oint \vec{B}.\vec{dl} = \mu_0 (i_1 - i_2)$. Right side of it does not include i_3 because it produces no magnetic field at the loop.

    Reason: The line integral of magnetic field produced by i_3 over the closed loop is non zero.

53. **Assertion:** Two beams of electrons travelling in the same direction repel each other.
    Reason: The electrostatic interaction is less than the magnetic interaction.

54. **Assertion:** If the current in a solenoid is reversed in direction while keeping the same magnitude, the magnetic field energy stored in the solenoid decreases.
    Reason: Magnetic field energy density is proportional to square of current.

55. **Assertion:** The magnetic field produced by a current carrying solenoid is independent of its length and cross-sectional area.
    Reason: The magnetic field inside the solenoid is uniform.

56. **Assertion:** If an electron, while coming vertically from outer space, enters the earth's magnetic field, it is deflected towards west.
    Reason: Electron has negative charge.

57. **Assertion:** If two long wires, hanging freely are connected to a battery in series, they come closer to each other.
    Reason: Force of attraction acts between the two wires carrying current.

58. **Assertion:** In a shunted galvanometer only 10% current passes through the galvanometer. The resistance of the galvanometer is G. Then resistance of the shunt is G/9.
    Reason: If S is the resistance of the shunt, then voltage across S and G is same.

59. **Assertion:** To convert a galvanometer into an ammeter a small resistance is connected in parallel with it.
    Reason: The small resistance increases the combined resistance of the combination.

60. **Assertion:** An ammeter is always connected in series whereas a voltmeter is connected in parallel.
    Reason: An ammeter is a low resistance galvanometer while a voltmeter is high resistance galvanometer.

61. **Assertion:** If an electron and proton enter a perpendicular magnetic field with equal momentum, then radius of curve for electron is more than that of proton.
    Reason: Electron has less mass than proton.

62. A charged particle enters into a uniform magnetic field and follows a circular path as shown. This happens when the particle enters perpendicular to the magnetic field. It gets deflected by magnetic Lorentz force Arrows indicate the direction of motion of the charged particle.

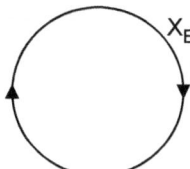

If $\vec{v}$ the velocity of the particle of charge q and B is the magnetic field, then the force acting on the particle is given by: $\vec{F} = q(\vec{v} \times \vec{B})$.

If the particle velocity is perpendicular to the magnetic field, then the magnitude of the force is $F = qvB$. This force provides the necessary centripetal force for the particle and the radius of the circular path is given by: $r = \dfrac{mv}{qB}$, where m is the mass of the particle.

The direction of deflection also depends on the nature of the charge. If the particle enters the fields at an angle other than 90°, then, the path of the particle will be helical (not circular).

(i) Which of the following particles will not get affected if sent into a magnetic field normal to it?
  (a) Alpha   (b) Positron
  (c) Neutron   (d) Electron

(ii) When a proton and an electron enter a magnetic field normal to it, which of the following statements is correct (assume, their speeds are equal)?
  (a) They will get deflected in opposite directions.
  (b) Radius of circular path of electron will be less
  (c) Radius of circular path of proton will be less
  (d) Both (a) and (b)

(iii) A deutron (nucleus of deuterium) enters a magnetic field parallel to it. Its path inside the field will be (consider, no other force can act on it):
  (a) Straight line
  (b) Circle
  (c) Helix
  (d) Parabola

(iv) If a proton, a deuteron and an alpha particle are projected into a magnetic field perpendicular to it with the same speed, which of them will have the path of highest radius?
  (a) Proton   (b) Deuteron
  (c) Alpha particle (d) Both (b) and (c)

(v) An electron enters a magnetic field making an angle of 45° with it. The path of the electron will be:
  (a) Straight line (b) Circle
  (c) Helix   (d) Parabola

63. Biot Savart law was given by Biot and Savart after doing many experiments. This law is related with the magnetic field induced at a point due to a small current carrying element (conductor). According to the law the magnetic field induced at a point near the current carrying element is directly proportional to the current flowing in conductor, length of the element, sin θ and inversely proportional to the square of the distance of point from the element.

$$dB = \dfrac{\mu_0}{4\pi} \dfrac{idl \sin\theta}{r^2}$$

(i) Biot Savart law was given by:
  (a) Oersted   (b) Ampere
  (c) Biot and Savart (d) Maxwell

(ii) Biot Savart law is related with the _____ induced at a point near current carrying element.
  (a) Magnetic field (b) Gravitational field
  (c) Electric field (d) None of these

(iii) Induced magnetic field is directly proportional to:
  (a) i (b) dl
  (c) $\sin\theta$ (d) All of these

(iv) The magnetic field induced at a point is inversely proportional to:
  (a) r^2 (b) r^3
  (c) $\dfrac{1}{r}$ (d) $\dfrac{1}{r^2}$

(v) As the distance between the point and current carrying element decreases, dB:
  (a) Increases   (b) Decreases
  (c) Remains same   (d) Both (a) and (b)

64. In certain polar regions, a splendid display of colours is seen in the sky. The appearance of dancing green pink lights is fascinating, and equally puzzling. Consider a charged particle of mass m and charge q, entering a region of magnetic field B with an initial velocity v. Let this velocity have a component v_p parallel to the magnetic field and a component v_n normal to it. There is no force on a charged particle in the direction of the field. Hence the particle continues to travel with the velocity v_p parallel to the field. The normal component v_n of the particle results in a Lorentz force ($v_n \times $B) which is perpendicular to both v_n and B. The particle thus has a tendency to perform a circular motion in a plane perpendicular to the magnetic field. When this is coupled with the velocity parallel to the field, the resulting trajectory will be a helix along the magnetic field line. Even if the field line bends, the helically moving particle is trapped and guided to move around the field line. Since the Lorentz force is normal to the velocity of each point, the field does no work on the particle and the magnitude of velocity remains the same. During a solar flare, a large number of electrons and protons are ejected from the sun. Some of them get trapped in the earth's magnetic field and move in helical paths along the field lines. The field lines come closer to each other near the magnetic poles. Hence the density of charges increases near the poles. These particles collide with atoms and molecules of the atmosphere. Excited oxygen atoms emit green light and excited nitrogen atoms emits pink light. This phenomenon is called Aurora Borealis in Physical Science.

(i) Which of the following defines the exact meaning of magnetic field ?
  (a) Magnetic field is a scalar field that describes the magnetic influence on moving electric charges, electric currents, and magnetic materials.
  (b) Magnetic field is a vector field that describes the magnetic influence on moving electric charges, electric currents, and magnetic materials.
  (c) Both scalar and vector fields that describe the magnetic influence on moving electric charges, electric currents, and magnetic materials.
  (d) Magnetic field is a vector field that describes the magnetic influence on static electric charges, electric currents, and magnetic materials.

(ii) Which of the following defines the exact meaning of Lorentz force?
  (a) The Lorentz force is the combination of electric and magnetic force on a point charge due to electromagnetic fields
  (b) The Lorentz force is the combination of electric and magnetic force on a point charge due to gravitational fields
  (c) The Lorentz force is the combination of gravitational force and magnetic force on a point charge due to electromagnetic fields
  (d) The Lorentz force is the combination of electric and centripetal force on a point charge due to electromagnetic fields

(iii) Which of the following defines the exact meaning of Circular motion ?
  (a) Circular motion is a apparent outward force on a mass when it is rotated.
  (b) Circular motion vector field that describes the magnetic influence on moving electric charges, electric currents, and magnetic materials.
  (c) Circular motion in an object is the rate of change of its position with respect to a frame of reference, and is a function of time.
  (d) Circular motion is a movement of an object along the circumference of a circle or rotation along a circular path.

(iv) What does Aurora Borealis mean ?
  (a) The Aurora Borealis, otherwise known as the Northern Lights, is a physics phenomenon that can be magical to observe, striking onlookers to wonder about the cause of the whimsical lights that dance overhead.
  (b) The Aurora Borealis, otherwise known as the Southern Lights, is a physics phenomenon that can be magical to observe, striking onlookers to wonder about the cause of the whimsical lights that dance overhead.
  (c) The Aurora Borealis, otherwise known as the Eastern Lights, is a physics phenomenon that can be magical to observe, striking onlookers to wonder about the cause of the whimsical lights that dance overhead.
  (d) The Aurora Borealis is a apparent outward force on a mass when it is rotated.

(v) Consider a tightly wound 100 turn coil of radius 10 cm, carrying a current of 1 A. What is the magnitude of the magnetic field at the centre of the coil?
  (a) 2.28×10^{-4} T (b) 6.28×10^{-4} T
  (c) 3.28×10^{-4} T (d) 5.28×10^{-4} T

65. The solenoid and the toroid are two pieces of equipment which generate magnetic fields. The synchrotron uses a combination of both to generate the high magnetic fields required. In both, solenoid and toroid, we come across a situation of high symmetry where Ampere's law can be conveniently applied. By long solenoid we mean that the solenoid's length is large compared to its radius. It consists of a long wire wound in the form of a helix where the neighbouring turns are closely spaced. So each turn can be regarded as a circular loop. The net magnetic field is the vector sum of the fields due to all the turns. Enamelled wires are used for winding so that turns are insulated from each other. As the solenoid is made longer it appears like a long cylindrical metal sheet. The field outside the solenoid approaches zero. We shall assume that the field outside is zero. The field inside becomes everywhere parallel to the axis. Consider a rectangular Amperian loop abcd. Along cd the field is zero as argued above. Along transverse sections bc and ad, the field component is zero. Thus, these two sections make no contribution. The direction of the field is given by the right-hand rule. The solenoid is commonly used to obtain a uniform magnetic field.

(i) Which of the following generates magnetic field?
  (a) Solenoid
  (b) Toroid
  (c) Both solenoid and toroid
  (d) None of the above

(ii) Which of the following usually uses a combination of solenoid and toroid to generate the high magnetic fields?
  (a) Synchrotron   (b) Aurora Borealis
  (c) Enamelled wires (d) Amperian loop

(iii) The field outside the solenoid approaches the value of :
  (a) Zero   (b) One
  (c) Two   (d) Three

(iv) The solenoid is commonly used to obtain a .... magnetic field.
  (a) Zigzag   (b) Uniform
  (c) Circular (d) Semi-circular

(v) A solenoid of length 0.5 m has a radius of 1 cm and is made up of 500 turns. It carries a current of 5 A. What is the magnitude of the magnetic field inside the solenoid?
  (a) 6.28×10^{-3} T (b) 3.28×10^{-4} T
  (c) 2.28×10^{-4} T (d) 4.28×10^{-4} T

66. We know that orbits of charged particles are helical. If the magnetic field is non-uniform, but does not change much during one circular orbit, then the radius of the helix will decrease as it enters stronger magnetic field and the radius will increase when it enters weaker magnetic fields. We consider two solenoids at a distance from each other, enclosed in an evacuated. Charged particles moving in the region between the two solenoids will start with a small radius. The radius

will increase as field decreases and the radius will decrease again as field due to the second solenoid takes over. The solenoids act as a mirror or reflector. This makes the particles turn back when they approach the solenoid. Such an arrangement will act like magnetic bottle or magnetic container. The particles will never touch the sides of the container. Such magnetic bottles are of great use in confining the high energy plasma in fusion experiments. The plasma will destroy any other form of material container because of its high temperature. Another useful container is a toroid. Toroids are expected to play a key role in the tokamak, an equipment for plasma confinement in fusion power reactors. There is an international collaboration called the International Thermonuclear Experimental Reactor (ITER), being set up in France, for achieving controlled fusion, of which India is a collaborating nation.

(i) What is the full form of ITER ?
(a) Indian Technical Experimental Reactor
(b) Indian Thermonuclear Experimental Reactor
(c) International Thermal Experimental Reactor
(d) International Thermonuclear Experimental Reactor

(ii) What will happen, if the magnetic field is non-uniform, but does not change much during one circular orbit?
(a) Radius of the helix will decrease
(b) Radius of the helix will increase
(c) Will remain constant
(d) All of the above are possible

(iii) The solenoids act as :
(a) Mirror
(b) Reflector
(c) Both mirror and reflector
(d) None of the above

(iv) Which of the following equipment is used for plasma confinement in fusion power reactors?
(a) Toroids   (b) Tokamak
(c) Sakamak   (d) Solenoid

(v) A solenoid of length 0.5 m has a radius of 1 cm and is made up of 500 turns. It carries a current of 5 A. What is the magnitude of the magnetic field inside the solenoid?
(a) 6.28×10^{-5} T   (b) 6.28×10^{-3} T
(c) 6.28×10^{7} T   (d) 6.28×10^{9} T

Answers

1. **(d)** both (b) and (c)
   Explanation: A magnetic field is produced around a changing electric field or a moving charge.

2. **(c)** $\dfrac{mv}{Bq}$
   Explanation: Force,
   $$F = qvB = \dfrac{mv^2}{R}$$
   $\therefore \quad R = \dfrac{mv}{Bq}$

3. **(a)** in the direction perpendicular to both the field and its velocity.
   Explanation: Since,
   $$\vec{F} = q\left(\vec{v} \times \vec{B}\right)$$

4. **(c)** zero, if $\vec{B}$ and $\vec{v}$ are parallel.
   Explanation: Since,
   $$\vec{F} = q\left(\vec{v} \times \vec{B}\right)$$
   if, $\vec{v} \| \vec{B}$
   then, $\vec{F} = 0$

5. **(a)** $\dfrac{2\pi m}{qB}$
   Explanation: Equating magnetic force to centripetal force.
   $$\dfrac{mv^2}{r} = qvB\sin 90°$$
   $$r = \dfrac{mv}{qB} \quad ..(i)$$
   Time to complete one revolution,
   $$T = \dfrac{2\pi r}{v} = \dfrac{2\pi m}{qB} \quad ...(\text{from (i)})$$

6. **(c)** Become four times
   Explanation: At far away point.
   $$B = \dfrac{\mu_0}{4\pi} \dfrac{2\pi I R^2}{x^3}$$
   $\Rightarrow B \propto R^2$
   Hence, when R is doubled. B becomes for times.

7. **(c)** Both experience same force
   Explanation: Force on a charged particle in a magnetic field is independent of mass. It is given by $q_0\left(\vec{v} \times \vec{B}\right)$.
   Both electron and proton carry same amount of charge.

8. **(b)** 5 N
   Explanation: Force on change due to magnetic field.
   $$F = qvB$$
   Therefore,
   $$F = 1 \times 0.5 \times 10$$
   $$= 5 \text{ N}$$

9. **(a)** the vector sum of electrostatic and magnetic force acting on a moving charged particle.
   Explanation: As Lorentz force is given by,
   $$\vec{F} = q\left(\vec{E} + \vec{v} \times \vec{B}\right)$$

$$= q\vec{E} + q\left(\vec{v} \times \vec{B}\right)$$

$$\vec{F} = \vec{F_E} + \vec{F_B}$$

10. (b) v and B are perpendicular.
    Explanation: Since,
    $$F = q(v \times B)$$
    or $$|F| = qvB\sin\theta$$
    F will be maximum when $\theta = 90°$

11. (b) 3.2×10^{-13} M
    Explanation: Force acting on a charge q moving with velocity v in magnetic field of intensity B is given by,
    $$F = qvB\sin\theta$$
    $$= qvB \quad ...(\because \theta = 90°, \therefore \sin\theta = 1)$$
    Given that,
    $$q = 2 \times 1.6 \times 10^{-19} \text{ (α-particle)}$$
    $$v = 10^6 \text{ m/s}$$
    $$B = 1 \text{ T}$$
    Substituting these values, we get
    $$F = 2 \times 1.6 \times 10^{-19} \times 10^6 \times 1$$
    $$= 3.2 \times 10^{-13} \text{ N}$$

12. (d) 7.85×10^{-12} N
    Explanation: We know that,
    $$F = qvB$$
    $$= 1.6 \times 10^{-19} \times \left(\sqrt{\frac{2E}{m}}\right) 2.5$$
    $$= 4 \times 10^{-19} \sqrt{\frac{2 \times 2 \times 1.6 \times 10^{-19} \times 10^6}{1.66 \times 10^{-27}}}$$
    $$= 7.85 \times 10^{-12} \text{ N}$$

13. (d) $\dfrac{v^2}{c^2}$
    Explanation: Electrostatic force,
    $$F_e = \frac{1}{4\pi\varepsilon_0} \times \frac{e^2}{r^2}$$
    Magnetic force,
    $$F_m = \frac{\mu_0}{4\pi}\left(\frac{e^2 v^2}{r^2}\right)$$
    $$\therefore \quad \frac{F_m}{F_e} = \mu_0\varepsilon_0 v^2 = \frac{v^2}{c^2} \quad ...\left(\because \mu_0\varepsilon_0 = \frac{1}{c^2}\right)$$

14. (b) Deuterium nucleus has greater pitch of helical motion.
    Explanation: Due to perpendicular component both will execute circular motion for which $T = \dfrac{2\pi m}{qB}$. Since, q is same, therefore $T \propto m$. Hence, deuterium nucleus will travel more distance.

15. (c) $\dfrac{\sqrt{2Em}}{qB}$
    Explanation: Since,
    $$r = \frac{mv}{qB}$$

    $$= \frac{\sqrt{2Em}}{qB}$$

16. (a) $B \perp v$
    Explanation: We know that,
    $$d\vec{B} = \frac{\mu_0}{4\pi}\frac{q\left(\vec{v} \times \vec{r}\right)}{r^3}$$
    i.e., $\vec{B}$ is perpendicular to $\vec{v}$ and $\vec{r}$ both.

17. (d) zero
    Explanation: We know that,
    $$dB = \frac{\mu_0}{4\pi}\frac{Idl\sin\theta}{r^2}$$
    At any point on axis,
    $$\theta = 0°$$
    $$\Rightarrow \sin\theta = 0$$
    $$\therefore dB = 0$$

18. (b) $\dfrac{nr^2}{(x^2 + r^2)^{3/2}}$
    Explanation: Magnetic field on the axis of circular coil carrying current,
    $$B = \frac{\mu_0}{4\pi}\frac{2\pi nIr^2}{(x^2+r^2)^{3/2}}$$
    $$\Rightarrow B \propto \frac{nr^2}{(x^2+r^2)^{3/2}}$$

19. (d) 5π μT
    Explanation: Since,
    $$B = 10^{-7} \times \frac{\pi \times I}{r}$$
    $$= 10^{-7} \times \frac{\pi \times 10}{20 \times 10^{-2}}$$
    $$\Rightarrow B = 5\pi\mu T$$

20. (d) $\dfrac{\mu_0 NIR^2}{2(R^2+x^2)^{3/2}}$
    Explanation: The magnetic field intensity at point P due to current carrying coil having N turns and radius R is given by,
    $$B = \frac{\mu_0}{4\pi}\frac{2\pi(NI)R^2}{(R^2+x^2)^{3/2}}$$
    or $$B = \frac{\mu_0 NIR^2}{2(R^2+x^2)^{3/2}}$$

21. (b) the line integral of magnetic field along the boundary of the open surface is equal to μ_0 times the total current passing through the surface.
    Explanation: According to Ampere's circuital law,
    $$\oint \vec{B}.\vec{dl} = \mu_0 I$$

22. (a) inversely proportional to the distance from wire.
    Explanation: Since,
    $$B = \frac{\mu_0 I}{2\pi r}$$

Moving Charges and Magnetism | 159

or $B \propto \dfrac{I}{r}$

23. (a) 2B
    Explanation: Since,
    $$B \propto \dfrac{I}{r}$$
    $$\Rightarrow \dfrac{B_1}{B_2} = \dfrac{r_2}{r_1}$$
    $$\Rightarrow \dfrac{B_1}{B_2} = \dfrac{\frac{r}{2}}{r}$$
    $$\Rightarrow B_2 = 2B$$

24. (b) 25×10^{-3} T
    Explanation: Mean radius
    $$= \dfrac{10 + 14}{2}$$
    $$= 12 \text{ cm}$$
    The magnetic field B,
    $$B = \mu_0 n I \quad \ldots \left(\because n = \dfrac{N}{2\pi r} \right)$$
    $$= 4\pi \times 10^{-7} \times \dfrac{3000 \times 100}{2\pi \times 12} \times 5$$
    $$= 25 \times 10^{-3} \text{ T}$$

25. (a) Zero
    Explanation: The magnetic field at any point on the axis of wire will be zero.

26. (a) 5.024×10^{-3} T
    Explanation: Here,
    $$n = \dfrac{600}{0.6}$$
    $$= 1000 \text{ turns/m}$$
    $$I = 4A$$
    $$l = 0.6 \text{ m}$$
    $$r = 0.02 \text{ m}$$
    $$\therefore \dfrac{l}{r} = 30 \text{ i.e. } l \gg r$$
    Hence, we can used long solenoid formula, then,
    $$\therefore B = \mu_0 n I$$
    $$= 4\pi \times 10^{-7} \times 10^3 \times 4$$
    $$= 50.25 \times 10^{-4}$$
    $$= 5.024 \times 10^{-3} \text{ T}$$

27. (a) 4×10^{-5} Wb/m²
    Explanation: We know that,
    $$B = \dfrac{\mu_0}{4\pi} \dfrac{2I}{r}$$
    $$= 10^{-7} \times \dfrac{2 \times 20}{10 \times 10^{-2}}$$
    $$= 4 \times 10^{-5} \text{ Wb/m}^2$$

28. (a) attract each other with a force of $\dfrac{\mu_0 i^2}{(2\pi d)}$
    Explanation: We know that,
    $$\dfrac{F}{l} = \dfrac{\mu_0 I_1 I_2}{2\pi d}$$
    $$= \dfrac{\mu_0 I^2}{2\pi d}$$
    The two wires will attract each other as current is in the same direction.

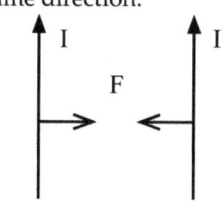

29. (d) $2\pi \times 10^{-3}$ T
    Explanation: We know that,
    $$B = \mu_0 n I$$
    as $n = 10$ turns/cm
    $$= 1000 \text{ turns/m}$$
    $$B = 4\pi \times 10^{-7} \times 10^3 \times 5$$
    $$B = 2\pi \times 10^{-3} \text{ T}$$

30. (c) shape of loop
    Explanation: We know that,
    $$\tau = MB \sin \theta$$
    $$= NIBA \sin \theta$$
    τ does not depend upon shape of the loop.

31. (a) Torque only.
    Explanation: Current carrying coil is a closed loop. Net force acting on the coil due to uniform magnetic field is always zero. But there will be non-zero torque acting on the coil, except when plane of the coil is perpendicular to the field.

32. (c) NIAB cos θ
    Explanation: We know that,
    $$\vec{\tau} = NI\vec{A} \times \vec{B}$$
    $$= NIAB \sin \alpha$$
    but $\alpha = 90 - \theta$
    $$\vec{\tau} = NIAB \sin(90 - \theta)$$
    $$= NIAB \cos \theta$$

33. (b) 0.028 Nm
    Explanation: We know that,
    $$\tau = MB \sin \theta$$
    $$= IAB \sin \theta$$
    $$= 2 \times 0.1 \times 0.2 \sin 45°$$
    $$= 0.028 \text{ Nm}$$

34. (c) a magnet should be placed near the coil.
    Explanation: Magnet provides damping.

35. (c) a moving coil galvanometer
    Explanation: In moving coil galvanometer
    $$I \propto \theta$$
    So deflection increases with increasing current and vice versa.

36. (a) 0.001

   Explanation: Galvanometer is converted into ammeter, by connecting a shunt, in parallel with it.

   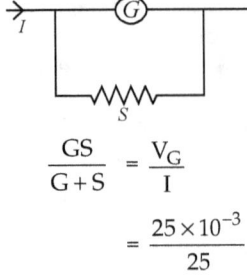

   $$\frac{GS}{G+S} = \frac{V_G}{I}$$

   $$= \frac{25 \times 10^{-3}}{25}$$

   $$\frac{GS}{G+S} = 0.001 \, \Omega$$

   Here $S \ll G$ so $S = 0.001 \, \Omega$

37. (b) $\dfrac{I_G}{I_0} = \dfrac{1}{11}$

   Explanation: We know that,

   $$\frac{I_G}{I_0} = \frac{S}{S+G}$$

   $$= \frac{2.5}{2.5 + 25}$$

   $$\therefore \frac{I_G}{I_0} = \frac{2.5}{27.5}$$

   $$= \frac{25}{275}$$

   $$= \frac{1}{11}$$

38. (b) (i) and (ii)

   Explanation: The galvanometer cannot as such be used as an ammeter to measure the value of the current in a given circuit. This is for two reasons:
   (i) Galvanometer is a very sensitive device, it gives a full-scale deflection for a current of the order of μA.
   (ii) For measuring currents, the galvanometer has to be connected in series and as it has a large resistance, this will change the value of the current in the circuit.

39. (c) 1.2°

   Explanation: We know that,

   $$NIAB = k\alpha$$

   $$\therefore \alpha = \frac{NIAB}{k}$$

   $$\therefore \alpha = \frac{1000 \times 10^{-5} \times 3 \times 10^{-4} \times 8 \times 10^{-2}}{2 \times 10^{-7}}$$

   $$= 1.2°$$

40. (a) putting in series a resistance of 15 Ω

   Explanation: Give,
   $G = 60 \, \Omega$
   $I_g = 1.0 \, A$
   $I = 5A$

   Let S be the shunt resistance connected in parallel to galvanometer.

   $$I_g G = (I - I_g)S$$

   $$S = \frac{I_g G}{I - I_g}$$

   $$= \frac{1}{5-1} \times 60$$

   $$= 15 \, \Omega$$

   Thus by putting 15 Ω in parallel, the galvanometer can be converted into an ammeter.

41. (a) 1.4×10^{-4} N towards right

   Explanation: Force per unit length experienced by a current carrying long conductor due to another current carrying conductor placed parallel at a distance r apart is given by,

   $$\frac{E}{l} = \frac{\mu_0}{4\pi} \cdot \frac{2I_1 I_2}{r}$$

   $$\Rightarrow F = \frac{\mu_0}{4\pi} \cdot \frac{2I_1 I_2}{r} \times l \quad …(i)$$

   Using relation (i), we have,
   Force on 10 cm length of wire Q due to wire P,

   $$F_1 = \frac{\mu_0}{4\pi} \frac{2I_1 I_2}{r} \times l$$

   $$= \frac{10^{-7} \times 2 \times 30 \times 10}{(10 \times 10^{-2})} \times (10 \times 10^{-2})$$

   On solving, we get,

   $$F_1 = 6 \times 10^{-5} \, N$$

   $$= 0.60 \times 10^{-4} \, N$$

   This force is repulsive and acts towards left.
   Similarly, force on 10 cm length of wire Q due to wire R,

   $$F_2 = \frac{\mu_0}{4\pi} \frac{2I_1 I_2}{r'} \times l$$

   $$= \frac{10^{-7} \times 2 \times 10 \times 20}{(2 \times 10^{-2})} \times (10 \times 10^{-2})$$

   On solving, we get,

   $$F_2 = 2 \times 10^{-4} \, N$$

   This force is repulsive and acts towards right.
   Hence, resultant force is given by

   $$F = F_2 - F_1$$

   $$= 2 \times 10^{-4} - 0.6 \times 10^{-4}$$

   $$= 1.4 \times 10^{-4} \, N \quad \text{(towards right)}$$

42. (d) The charge to mass ratio satisfy:

   $$\left(\frac{e}{m}\right)_1 + \left(\frac{e}{m}\right)_2 = 0.$$

   Explanation: Charged particles traverse identical helical paths in a completely opposite sense in a uniform magnetic field B, LHS for two particles should be same and of opposite sign. Therefore,

   $$\left(\frac{e}{m}\right)_1 + \left(\frac{e}{m}\right)_2 = 0$$

Moving Charges and Magnetism | 161

43. (a) $\vec{B} \perp \vec{v}$

   Explanation: According to the Biot-Savart law, the magnitude of $\vec{B}$ is:

   $B \propto |q|$
   $B \propto v$
   $B \propto \sin \phi$
   $B \propto \dfrac{1}{r^2}$

   $B \propto \dfrac{|q| v \sin \phi}{r^2}$

   $B = \dfrac{\mu_0}{4\pi} \dfrac{|q| v \sin \phi}{r^2}$

   where, $\dfrac{\mu_0}{4\pi}$ is a proportionality constant, r is the magnitude of position vector from charge to that point at which we have to find the magnetic field and ϕ is the angle between $\vec{v}$ and $\vec{r}$.

   or, $\vec{B} = \dfrac{\mu_0}{4\pi} \dfrac{|q|(\vec{v} \times \vec{r})}{|r^3|} \hat{n}$

   where, $\hat{n}$ is the direction of $\vec{B}$ which is in the direction of cross product of $\vec{v}$ and $\vec{r}$ we can say that $\vec{B} \perp$ both $\vec{v}$ and $\vec{r}$.

44. (d) The electron will continue to move with uniform velocity along the axis of the solenoid.

   Explanation: Let the electron (e) is projected with a uniform velocity (v) in a uniform magnetic field B. The magnitude of force on it is,

   $|\vec{F}| = -e|\vec{v} \times \vec{B}|$
   $= -evB \sin \theta$

   As $\theta = 0°$,

   $|\vec{F}| = -evB \sin 0°$
   $= 0$

   Hence the electron with continue to move with a uniform velocity along the axis of the solenoid.

45. (d) $\dfrac{\mu_0 I}{2R}\left(1 - \dfrac{1}{\pi}\right)$

46. (a) 2×10^{-5} T, acting downwards.

   Explanation: $\vec{B} = \dfrac{\mu_0 I}{2\pi r}$

   $= \dfrac{\mu_0}{2\pi} \cdot \dfrac{2I}{r}$

   $= 10^{-7} \cdot \dfrac{2 \times 10}{0.10}$

   $\vec{B} = 2 \times 10^{-8}$ T

   By using, right hand rule it should be acting downwards.

47. (a) $r \propto m$

   Explanation: $r = \dfrac{mv}{qB}$

   $\therefore \quad r \propto m$

48. (d) $\sqrt{2} r$

   Explanation: radius of circular path

   $r' = \dfrac{mV'}{qB} = \dfrac{m}{qB}\sqrt{\dfrac{2qV'}{m}}$

   $= \dfrac{1}{B}\sqrt{\dfrac{2mV'}{q}}$

   $= \dfrac{1}{B}\sqrt{\dfrac{2m(2V)}{q}}$

   $= \dfrac{1}{B}\sqrt{\dfrac{2mV}{q}} \cdot \sqrt{2} = \sqrt{2} r$

49. (a) Kinetic energy of the charged particle remains same in the circular path while velocity and momentum of the particle changes because of continuous change in the direction of motion.

50. (a) A moving charge experiences a force in magnetic field. It is because of interaction of two magnetic fields, one which is produced due to the motion of charge and other in which charge is moving.

51. (a) In the absence of the electric current, the free electrons in a conductor are in a state of random motion, like molecules in a gas. Their average velocity is zero i.e., they do not have any net velocity in a direction. As a result, there is no net magnetic force on the free electrons in the magnetic field. On passing the current, the free electrons acquire drift velocity in a definite direction, hence magnetic force acts on them, unless the field has no perpendicular component.

52. (d) The magnetic field at any point on the closed loop is due to all the three currents, but line integral of i_3 over the closed loop will be zero.

53. (c) Two beams of electrons travelling in the same direction repel each other because the electrostatic interaction is more than the magnetic interaction.

54. (d) Reversing the direction of the current reverses the direction of the magnetic field. However, it has no effect on the magnetic-field energy density, which is proportional to the square of the magnitude of the magnetic field.

55. (b) We know that,

   $B = \mu_0 n I$

   which is independent of length and cross-sectional area.

56. (b) We know that the direction of the earth's magnetic field is toward north and the velocity of electron is vertically downward. Applying Fleming's left hand rule, the direction of force is towards west. Therefore, an electron coming from outer space will be deflected toward west.

57. (d) When two long parallel wires, are connected to a battery in series. They carry currents in opposite directions, hence they repel each other.

58. (b) Potential drop across galvanometer = Potential drop across the shunt.

i.e., $I_g G = (I - I_g) S$

$\Rightarrow S = \dfrac{I_g}{I - I_g} G$

For $I_g = \dfrac{I}{10}$

$S = \dfrac{\frac{I}{10}}{\left(I - \frac{I}{10}\right)} G = \dfrac{G}{9}$

59. (c) An ammeter should have a low resistance which we get when we connect low resistance in parallel with galvanometer.

60. (a) An ammeter is a low resistance device and is connected in series so as the whole circuit current flows through it for an accurate measurement. A voltmeter is a device of having high resistance. So, if we connect it in series, it would hinder the current flow in the circuit hence open circuit results.

61. (b) When a charged particle enters in perpendicular magnetic field than radius of curved path is given by,

$r = \dfrac{mv}{qB} = \dfrac{p}{qB}$

As momentum p as constant,

$r \propto \dfrac{1}{q}$

As e^- and proton have same charge,

$\dfrac{r_e^-}{r_p^+} = \dfrac{q_0^-}{q_e^+} = 1$

Assertion is false, but reason is true.

62. (i) (c) Neutron
Neutral particles are not affected by magnetic field.

(ii) (d) Both (a) and (b)
Opposite deflection because of opposite charge. Lighter particle gets deflected more.

(iii) (a) Straight line
$\vec{F} = q(\vec{v} \times \vec{B})$; If velocity is parallel or antiparallel to the field, the particle goes unaffected.

(iv) (d) Both (b) and (c)
$r = \dfrac{mv}{qB} \Rightarrow r \propto \dfrac{m}{q}$

(v) (c) Helix
Angle with the field is $0° < \theta < 90°$. Hence path will be helical.

63. (i) (c) Biot and Savart
(ii) (a) Magnetic field
(iii) (d) All of these; $\therefore dB = \dfrac{\mu_0 i}{4\pi} \dfrac{dl \sin\theta}{r^2}$
(iv) (a) r^2

(v) (a) Increases; $\therefore dB \propto \dfrac{1}{r^2}$

64. (i) (b) The exact meaning of magnetic field is a vector field that describes the magnetic influence on moving electric charges, electric currents, and magnetic materials.

(ii) (a) The Lorentz force is the combination of electric and magnetic force on a point charge due to electromagnetic fields. A particle of charge q moving with a velocity v in an electric field E and a magnetic field B experiences a force of $F = qE + qv \times B$.

(iii) (d) Circular motion is a movement of an object along the circumference of a circle or rotation along a circular path. It can be uniform, with constant angular rate of rotation and constant speed, or non-uniform with a changing rate of rotation. The rotation around a fixed axis of a three-dimensional body involves circular motion of its parts.

(iv) (a) The Aurora Borealis, otherwise known as the Northern Lights, is a physics phenomenon that can be magical to observe, striking onlookers to wonder about the cause of the whimsical lights that dance overhead. This extraordinary display is caused by charged particles being expelled into space from the sun.

(v) (b) Since the coil is tightly wound, we may take each circular element to have the same radius R = 10 cm = 0.1 m. The number of turns N = 100. The magnitude of the magnetic field is,

$B = \dfrac{\mu_0 NI}{2R}$

$\dfrac{4\pi \times 10^{-7} \times 10^2 \times 1}{2 \times 10^{-1}} = 2\pi \times 10^{-4}$

$= 6.28 \times 10^{-4}$ T

65. (i) (c) The solenoid and the toroid are two pieces of equipment which generate magnetic fields.

(ii) (a) The synchrotron uses a combination of both to generate the high magnetic fields required.

(iii) (a) The field outside the solenoid approaches zero. We shall assume that the field outside is zero. The field inside becomes everywhere parallel to the axis.

(iv) (b) The solenoid is commonly used to obtain a uniform magnetic field.

(v) (a) The number of turns per unit length is,

$n = \dfrac{500}{0.5} = 1000$ turns/m

The length $l = 0.5$ m and radius $r = 0.01$ m.

Thus, $\dfrac{l}{a} = 50$ i.e., $l \gg a$.

Hence, we can use the long solenoid formula, namely,

$B = \mu_0 n I$
$= 4\pi \times 10^{-7} \times 10^3 \times 5$
$= 6.28 \times 10^{-3}$ T

66. (i) (d) The full form of ITER is International Thermonuclear Experimental Reactor. It is an international nuclear fusion research and engineering megaproject aimed at replicating the fusion processes of the Sun to create energy on earth.

(ii) (a) If the magnetic field is non-uniform, but does not change much during one circular orbit, then the radius of the helix will decrease as it enters stronger magnetic field.

(iii) (c) The solenoids act as a mirror or reflector. This makes the particles turn back when they approach the solenoid.

(iv) (a) Toroids are expected to play a key role in the tokamak, an equipment for plasma confinement in fusion power reactors.

(v) (b) The number of turns per unit length is
$$n = \frac{500}{0.5}$$
$$= 1000 \text{ turns/m}$$
The length $l = 0.5$ m and radius $r = 0.01$ m.

Thus, $\frac{l}{a} = 50$ i.e., $l \gg a$.

Hence, we can use the long solenoid formula,
$$B = \mu_0 n I$$
$$= 4p \times 10^7 \times 10^3 \times 5$$
$$= 6.28 \times 10^{-3} \text{ T}$$

Chapter 5: Magnetism and Matter

1. If a hole is made at the centre of a bar magnet, then its magnetic moment _____.
   (a) does not change
   (b) decreases
   (c) increases
   (d) vanishes

2. On cutting a solenoid in half, the field lines remain _____, emerging from one face of the solenoid and entering into the other face:
   (a) alternate
   (b) discontinuous
   (c) continuous
   (d) irregular

3. The north pole of a magnet is brought near a stationary negatively charged conductor. Will the pole experience any force?
   (a) Yes
   (b) No
   (c) Depends on the magnitude of pole strength
   (d) Can't say

4. The magnetic moment of a bar magnet is thus _____ to the magnetic moment of an equivalent solenoid that produces the same magnetic field.
   (a) same
   (b) different
   (c) unequal
   (d) equal

5. The incorrect statement regarding the lines of force of the magnetic field B is:
   (a) Magnetic lines of force form a close curve.
   (b) Due to a magnet, magnetic lines of force never cut each other.
   (c) Magnetic intensity is a measure of lines of force passing through unit area held normal to it.
   (d) Inside a magnet, its magnetic lines of force move from north pole of a magnet toward is south pole.

6. The magnetic dipole moment of a solenoid having N turns is given as::
   (a) NIA
   (b) NIA^2
   (c) NI^2A
   (d) NI^2A^2

7. In the case of bar magnet, lines of magnetic induction:
   (a) run continuously through the bar and outside
   (b) emerge in circular paths from the middle of the bar
   (c) are produced only at the north pole like rays of light from a bulb
   (d) start from the north pole and end at the south pole

8. The magnetic induction B and the force F on a pole m are related by:
   (a) $F = mB$
   (b) $F = \dfrac{m}{B}$
   (c) $B = mF$
   (d) $F = \dfrac{B}{m}$

9. A north pole of strength 50 Am and south pole of strength 100 Am are separated by a distance of 10 cm in air. Find the force between them.
   (a) 20×10^{-6} N
   (b) 25×10^{-3} N
   (c) 30×10^{-18} N
   (d) 50×10^{-3} N

10. The strength of the earth's magnetic field is:
    (a) zero everywhere
    (b) constant everywhere
    (c) vary from place to place on the earth's surface
    (d) having very high value

11. Horizontal component of earth's magnetic field remains zero at:
    (a) magnetic poles
    (b) equator
    (c) an altitude of 60°
    (d) a latitude of 60°

12. Which of the following is responsible for the earth's magnetic field?
    (a) Rotational motion of earth.
    (b) Translational motion of earth.
    (c) Convective currents in earth's core.
    (d) Diversive current in earth's core

13. The vertical component of earth's magnetic field is zero at:
    (a) magnetic equator
    (b) magnetic poles
    (c) geographical poles
    (d) north pole

14. At neutral point, the horizontal component of the magnetic field due to a magnet is:
    (a) in the opposite direction of the earth's horizontal magnetic field
    (b) equal to earth's horizontal magnetic field
    (c) in the same direction of the earth's horizontal magnetic field
    (d) both (a) and (b)

15. A dip circle is placed in a plane perpendicular to the magnetic meridian. The apparent angle of dip is:
    (a) 0°
    (b) 45°
    (c) 60°
    (d) 90°

16. At a certain place, the horizontal component of earth's magnetic field is $\sqrt{3}$ times the vertical component. The angle of dip at that place is:
    (a) 30°
    (b) 45°
    (c) 60°
    (d) 90°

17. The horizontal component of the earth's magnetic field is 3.6×10^{-5} T where the dip angle is 60°. The magnitude of the earth's magnetic field is:
    (a) 2.1×10^{-4} T
    (b) 2.8×10^{-4} T
    (c) 3.6×10^{-5} T
    (d) 7.2×10^{-5} T

18. The angle of dip at a place is 40.6° and the intensity of the vertical component of the earth's magnetic field $V = 6 \times 10^{-5}$ T. The total intensity of the earth's magnetic field (B) at this place is:
    (a) 51×10^{-5} T
    (b) 6×10^{-4} T
    (c) 7×10^{-5} T
    (d) 9.2×10^{-5} T

19. A torque of 10^{-5} Nm is required to hold a magnet at 90° with the horizontal component H of the earth's magnetic field. The torque to hold it at 30° will be:
    (a) $\frac{1}{3} \times 10^{-5}$ Nm
    (b) 5×10^{-6} Nm
    (c) $3\sqrt{3} \times 10^{-6}$ Nm
    (d) Insufficient data

20. The earth's magnetic field at some place on magnetic equator of earth is 0.5×10^{-4} T. Consider the radius of earth at that place as 6400 km. Then, magnetic dipole moment of the earth is Am^2:
    ($\mu_0 = 4\pi \times 10^{-7}$ TmA^{-1})
    (a) 1.05×10^{23}
    (b) 1.15×10^{23}
    (c) 1.31×10^{23}
    (d) 1.62×10^{23}

21. At a certain place, horizontal component is $\sqrt{3}$ times the vertical component. The angle of dip at this place is:
    (a) $\frac{\pi}{8}$
    (b) $\frac{\pi}{6}$
    (c) $\frac{\pi}{3}$
    (d) 0

22. At a certain place, the angle of dip is 30° and the horizontal component of earth's magnetic field is 0.50 oersted. The earth's total magnetic field (in oersted) is:
    (a) $\frac{1}{2}$
    (b) $\sqrt{3}$
    (c) $\frac{1}{\sqrt{3}}$
    (d) 1

23. A toroid of n turns, mean radius R and cross-sectional radius a carries current I. It is placed on a horizontal table taken as x-y plane. Its magnetic moment m: [NCERT Exemplar]
    (a) is non zero and points in the z-direction by symmetry.
    (b) points along the axis of the toroid ($m = m\phi$).
    (c) is zero, otherwise there would be a field falling as $\frac{1}{r^3}$ at large distances outside the toroid.
    (d) is pointing radially outwards.

24. The magnetic field of earth can be modelled by that of a point dipole placed at the centre of the earth. The dipole axis makes an angle of 11.3° with the axis of earth. At Mumbai, declination is nearly zero. Then,: [NCERT Exemplar]
    (a) the declination varies between 11.3° W to 11.3° E.
    (b) the least declination is 0°.
    (c) the plane defined by dipole axis and earth axis passes through Greenwich.
    (d) declination averaged over earth must be always negative

25. In a permanent magnet at room temperature: [NCERT Exemplar]
    (a) magnetic moment of each molecule is zero.
    (b) the individual molecules have non zero magnetic moment which are all perfectly aligned.
    (c) domains are partially aligned.
    (d) domains are all perfectly aligned.

26. Consider the two idealised systems: (i) a parallel plate capacitor with large plates and small separation and (ii) a long solenoid of length L >> R, radius of cross-section. In (i) E is ideally treated as a constant between plates and zero outside. In (ii) magnetic field is constant inside the solenoid and zero outside. These idealised assumptions, however, contradict fundamental laws as below: [NCERT Exemplar]
    (a) case (i) contradicts Gauss's law for electrostatic fields.
    (b) case (ii) contradicts Gauss's law for magnetic fields.
    (c) case (i) agrees with $\oint E.dl = 0$.
    (d) case (ii) contradicts $\oint H.dl = I_{en}$.

27. The magnetic dipole moment of a current loop is independent of:
    (a) area of the loop
    (b) current in the loop
    (c) magnetic field in which it is lying
    (d) number of turns

28. A circular loop carrying current of radius 100 mm has a magnetic induction of 3.6×10^{-5} T at its centre. Calculate the dipole moment.
    (a) 15 mAm^2
    (b) 45 mAm^2
    (c) 60 mAm^2
    (d) 180 mAm^2

29. The magnetic moment of a circular coil carrying current is:
    (a) directly proportional to the square of the length of the wire in the coil.
    (b) directly proportional to the length of the wire in the coil.
    (c) inversely proportional to the square of the length of the wire in the coil
    (d) inversely proportional to the length of the wire in the coil

30. The orbital speed of electron orbiting around a nucleus in a circular orbit of radius 50 pm is 2.2×10^6 ms^{-1}. Then the magnetic dipole moment of an electron is:
    (a) 8.8×10^{-25} Am^2
    (b) 8.8×10^{-26} Nm
    (c) 1.6×10^{-19} Am^2
    (d) 5.3×10^{-21} Am^2

31. A circular current loop of magnetic moment M is in an arbitrary orientation in an external magnetic field B. The work done to rotate the loop by 30° about an axis perpendicular to its plane is: [NCERT Exemplar]
    (a) MB q
    (b) $\sqrt{3}\frac{MB}{2}$
    (c) $\frac{MB}{2}$
    (d) Zero

32. A current carrying circular loop of radius R is placed in the x-y plane with centre at the origin. Half of the loop with $x > 0$ is now bent so that it now lies in the y-z plane. [NCERT Exemplar]
    (a) The magnitude of magnetic moment now diminishes.
    (b) The magnetic moment does not change.
    (c) The magnitude of B at (0, 0, z), z >> R increases.
    (d) The magnitude of B at (0, 0, z), z >> R is unchanged.

33. The lines of force due to horizontal component of earth's magnetic field are :

(a) straight and parallel (b) concentric circles
(c) parabolic (d) elliptical

34. In a plane perpendicular to magnetic meridian the dip needle will be :
    (a) vertical
    (b) horizontal
    (c) inclined equal to the angle of dip at that place
    (d) pointing in any direction

35. Earth's magnetic field inside a closed iron box, as compared to outside is :
    (a) more (b) less
    (c) same (d) zero

36. If the current (I) flowing through a circular coil, its radius (R) and number of turns (N) in it are each doubled, magnetic flux density at its centre becomes :
    (a) two times (b) four times
    (c) eight times (d) sixteen times

Directions: In the following questions, a statement of assertion is followed by a statement of reason. Mark the correct choice as:
(a) If both assertion and reason are true and reason is the correct explanation of assertion.
(b) If both assertion and reason are true, but reason is not the correct explanation of assertion.
(c) If assertion is true, but reason is false.
(d) If both assertion and reason are false.

---

37. **Assertion:** Two short magnets are placed on a cork which floats on water. The magnets are placed such that the axis of one produced bisects the axis of other at right angles. Then the cork has neither translational nor rotational motion.

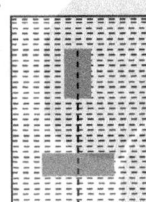

    Reason: Net force on the cork is zero.

38. **Assertion:** When a magnetic dipole is placed in a non uniform magnetic field, only a torque acts on the dipole.
    Reason: Force would not act on dipole if magnetic field were uniform.

39. **Assertion:** Magnetic moment of helium atom is zero.
    Reason: All the electron are paired in helium atom orbitals.

40. **Assertion:** Gauss theorem is not applicable in magnetism.
    Reason: Mono magnetic pole does not exist.

41. **Assertion:** The true geographic north direction is found by using a compass needle.
    Reason: The magnetic meridian of the earth is along the axis of rotation of the earth.

42. **Assertion:** In the northern hemisphere the north pole of the dip needle dips downwards.
    Reason: The north pole of earth as a bar magnet lies in the northern hemisphere.

43. **Assertion:** If a compass needle be kept at magnetic north pole of the earth, the compass needle may stay in any direction.
    Reason: Dip needle will stay vertical at the north pole of earth.

44. **Assertion:** To protect any instrument from external magnetic field, it is put inside an iron box.
    Reason: Iron is a magnetic substance.

45. A suspended magnet gets aligned with the earth's magnetic field at that place. Along the equator, a suspended magnet will align horizontally. The orientation of the magnet depends on the dip angle at that place. Angle of dip is the angle between the net magnetic field of earth and the horizontal. At equator, angle of dip is 0 (zero) and at poles its value is 90°. This means, at equator, the earth's magnetic field is completely horizontal and at poles. The Earth's magnetic field is vertical.

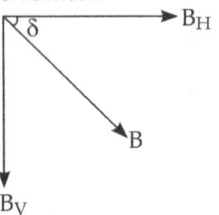

If δ is the angle of dip at a place and B is the Earth's magnetic field, then the horizontal component of Earth's magnetic field $B_H = B \cos \delta$ the vertical component $B_V = B \sin \delta$

$$\Rightarrow B = \sqrt{B_H^2 + B_V^2}$$

Also $\tan \delta = \dfrac{B_V}{B_H}$

(i) A magnet stands vertical at a place when suspended that place will be:
    (a) At equator (b) At poles
    (c) At 30° latitude (d) At 60° latitude

(ii) The angle of dip of a face where the magnet gets aligned completely horizontal is:
    (a) 0° (b) 90°
    (c) 30° (d) 45°

(iii) The horizontal and vertical components of the magnetic field at a place are $\dfrac{\sqrt{3}}{2}B$ and $\dfrac{B}{2}$ respectively.
When a magnet is left free at that place, the angle made by its magnetic axis with the horizontal is:
    (a) 45° (b) 30°
    (c) 60° (d) 15°

(iv) Earth's magnetic field always has a vertical component except at:
    (a) Poles (b) Equator
    (c) 30° latitude (d) 75° latitude

(v) The magnetic field due to earth has a horizontal component of 26μT at a place where the dip is 60°. Vertical component of the field at that point is:
    (a) 25 μT (b) 30 μT
    (c) 45 μT (d) 54 μT

46. Magnets: no doubt, its behaviour will attract everyone. The world enjoys its benefits, to lead a modern luxurious life. The study of magnets fascinated scientists around our globe for many centuries and even now, door for research on magnets is still open. The needle in a magnetic compass or freely suspended magnet comes

to rest in a position which is approximately along the geographical north-south direction of the Earth. William Gilbert in 1600 proposed that Earth itself behaves like a gigantic powerful bar magnet. Goven suggested that the Earth's magnetic field is due to hot rays coming out from the Sun. These rays will heat up the air near equatorial region- once air becomes hotter, it rises above and will move towards northern and southern hemispheres and get electrified. This may be responsible to magnetize the ferromagnetic materials near the Earth's the surface. Till date so many theories completely explains the cause for the Earth's magnetism.

(i) The ultimate individual unit of magnetism in any magnet is called
   (a) North pole   (b) South pole
   (c) Dipole   (d) Quadrupole

(ii) Magnetic meridian is a
   (a) point   (b) horizontal plane
   (c) vertical plane   (d) line along N–S

(iii) At the magnetic poles of the earth, a compass needle will be
   (a) vertical   (b) bent slightly
   (c) horizontal
   (d) inclined at 45° to the horizontal

(iv) Due to earth's magnetic field, the charged cosmic ray particles
   (a) require greater kinetic energy to reach the equator than pole
   (b) require less kinetic energy to reach the equator than pole
   (c) can never reach the pole
   (d) can never reach the equator.

(v) Great circle on the earth perpendicular to the magnetic axis is
   (a) Magnetic meridian
   (b) Magnetic equator
   (c) Geographic meridian
   (d) Magnetic axis

47. A bar magnet consists of two equal and opposite magnetic poles separated by a small distance. Poles are not exactly at the ends. The shortest distance between two poles is called effective length (l_e) and is less than its geometric length (l_g). For bar magnet $l_e = 2l$ and $l_e = \frac{5}{6} l_g$. For semi-circular magnet $l_g = \pi R$ and $l_e = 2R$.

Magnetic moment or magnetic dipole moment $\vec{m}$ represents the strength of magnet. Mathematically it is defined as the product of the strength of either pole and effective length. Magnetic field of a bar magnet at an axial point is given by

$$B_{axial} = \frac{\mu_0}{4\pi} \cdot \frac{2mr}{(r^2 - l^2)^2}$$

Where r is the distance of the point from the centre of the magnet.
while on equatorial line it is given by

$$B_{equal} = \frac{\mu_0}{4\pi} \cdot \frac{m}{(r^2 + l^2)^{3/2}}$$

(i) A bar magnet is placed inside a non-uniform magnetic field. It experiences
   (a) a force and a torque
   (b) a force but not a torque
   (c) a torque but not a force
   (d) neither a force nor a torque

(ii) A bar magnet of magnetic moment M is cut into parts of equal lengths. The magnetic moment and pole strength of either part is
   (a) M/2, m/2   (b) M, m/2
   (c) M/2, m (d) M, m

(iii) A bar magnet is hold perpendicular to a uniform field. If the couple acting on the magnet is to be halved, by rotating it, the angle by which it is to be rotated is
   (a) 30°   (b) 60°
   (c) 45°   (d) 90°

(iv) The couple acting on a magnet of length 10 cm and pole strength 15 Am, kept in field of B = 2×10^{-5} T, at an angle of 30°, is
   (a) 1.5×10^{-5} Nm   (b) 1.5×10^{-3} Nm
   (c) 1.5×10^{-2} Nm   (d) 1.5×10^{-6} Nm

(v) At a point on the right bisector of a magnetic dipole, the magnetic
   (a) potential varies as $\frac{1}{r^2}$
   (b) potential is zero at all point on the right bisector
   (c) field varies as r^3
   (d) field is perpendicular to the axis of dipole

48. The magnitude and direction of the magnetic field of the earth at a place are completely given by certain quantities known as magnetic elements. They are magnetic declination (θ) angle of inclination or dip (φ) and horizontal component of earth's magnetic field. Magnetic declination is the angle between geographic and the magnetic meridian planes. Dip is the angle between the direction of intensity of total magnetic field of earth and a horizontal line in the magnetic meridian. Earth's magnetic field is horizontal only at the magnetic equator. At any other place, the total intensity can be resolved into horizontal and vertical component.

(i) Horizontal and vertical components of earth's magnetic field are equal, then angle of dip is
   (a) 60°   (b) 45°
   (c) 30°   (d) 90°

(ii) Angle of dip is 90° at
   (a) poles   (b) equator
   (c) both (a) and (b)   (d) none of these

(iii) Lines of force, due to earth's horizontal magnetic field, are
   (a) elliptical   (b) curved lines
   (c) concentric circles   (d) parallel and straight

(iv) At a certain place on earth's $B_H = \frac{1}{\sqrt{3}} B_V$, dip angle is :
   (a) 60°   (b) 30°
   (c) 45°   (d) 90°

(v) Which of the following relation is correct in magnetism ?
   (a) $I^2 = V^2 + H^2$ (b) $V = I^2 + H^2$
   (c) $I = V + H$ (d) $V^2 = I + H$

Answers

1. (a) does not change
Explanation: As its pole strength and length remains same.

2. (c) continuous
Explanation: The field lines remain continuous, emerging from one face of the solenoid and entering into the other face.

3. (b) No
Explanation: No, a stationary charge does not produce magnetic field.

4. (d) equal
Explanation: The magnetic moment of a bar magnet is thus equal to the magnetic moment of an equivalent solenoid that produces the same magnetic field.

5. (d) Inside a magnet, its magnetic lines of force move from north pole of a magnet towards its south pole.
Explanation: Inside a magnet, magnetic lines of force move from south pole to north pole.

6. (a) NIA
Explanation: Each turn of the solenoid behaves as a small dipole having dipole moment IA.

7. (a) run continuously through the bar and outside
Explanation: In the bar magnet, lines of magnetic induction run continuously through the bar and outside.

8. (a) $F = mB$
Explanation: Magnetic induction is defined as the force exerted on a fictitious dipole of unit pole strength.
$$\therefore \quad B = \frac{F}{m}$$
$$\Rightarrow \quad F = mB$$

9. (d) 50×10^{-3} N
Explanation: Force between magnetic poles in air is given by,
Given that,
$$F = \frac{\mu_0}{4\pi} \times \frac{m_1 m_2}{r^2}$$
Given that,
$m_1 = 50$ Am
$m_2 = 100$ Am
$r = 10$ cm $= 0.1$ m
$\mu_0 =$ permeability of air
$= 4\pi \times 10^{-7}$ Hm^{-1}
$$\therefore \quad F = \frac{4\pi \times 10^{-7}}{4\pi} \cdot \frac{50 \times 100}{0.1 \times 0.1}$$
$$= 50 \times 10^{-3} \text{ N}$$

10. (c) vary from place to place on the earth's surface
Explanation: The strength of the earth's magnetic field is not constant. It varies from one place to other place on the surface of earth. Its value being of the order of 10^{-5} T.

11. (a) magnetic poles
Explanation: At magnetic poles, the angle of dip is 90°. Hence the horizontal component,
$$B_H = B \cos\theta$$
$$= 0$$

12. (c) Convective currents in earth's core.
Explanation: The earth's core is hot and molten. Hence, convective current in earth's core is responsible for its magnetic field.

13. (a) magnetic equator
Explanation: At magnetic equator, the angle of dip is 0°. Hence the vertical component,
$$B_v = B \sin\delta$$
$$= 0$$

14. (d) both (a) and (b)
Explanation: At neutral point,
$$B_{eq} = -B_H$$
$$B_a = -B_H$$

15. (d) 90°
Explanation: We know that,
$$\tan\delta = \frac{V}{H}$$
Here, $H = 0$
$\Rightarrow \quad \tan\delta = \infty$
$\Rightarrow \quad \delta = 90°$

16. (a) 30°
Explanation: Since,
$$B_H = \sqrt{3} B_V$$
Also, $\tan\delta = \frac{B_V}{B_H}$
$$= \frac{1}{\sqrt{3}}$$
$\therefore \quad \delta = 30°$

17. (d) 7.2×10^{-5} T
Explanation: Horizontal component of earth's field.

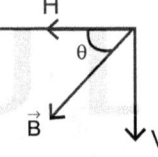

$H = B \cos\theta$
since, $\theta = 60°$
$3.6 \times 10^{-5} = B \times \frac{1}{2}$
$\Rightarrow \quad B = 7.2 \times 10^{-5}$ T

18. (d) 9.2×10^{-5} T
Explanation: From the relation,
$$B_V = B \sin\delta$$
$$B = \frac{B_V}{\sin\delta}$$

$$= \frac{6 \times 10^{-5}}{\sin 40.6°}$$

$$= \frac{6 \times 10^{-5}}{0.65}$$

∴ $B = 9.2 \times 10^{-5}$ T

19. (b) 5×10^{-6} Nm

Explanation: The torque acting on the magnet of magnetic moment M, when held at angle θ to magnetic field B,

$$\tau = MB \sin \theta$$
$$= MB \sin 30°$$
$$= 0.5 \times 10^{-5}$$
$$= 5 \times 10^{-6} \text{ Nm}$$

20. (c) 1.31×10^{23}

Explanation: We know that,

$$B_H = \frac{\mu_0 M}{4d^3}$$

$$\Rightarrow \quad M = \frac{4\pi d^3 B_H}{\mu_0}$$

$$M = \frac{0.5 \times 10^{-4} \times (6.4 \times 10^6)^3}{10^{-7}}$$

$$= 1.31 \times 10^{23} \text{ Am}^2$$

21. (b) $\frac{\pi}{6}$

Explanation: Since,

$$\tan \delta = \frac{V}{H} = \frac{V}{\sqrt{3}V} = \frac{1}{\sqrt{3}}$$

∴ $d = 30°$

$$= \frac{\pi}{6} \text{ radian}$$

22. (c) $\frac{1}{\sqrt{3}}$

Explanation: Since,

$$B = \frac{H}{\cos \theta} = \frac{0.50}{\cos 30°}$$

$$= \frac{0.50 \times 2}{\sqrt{3}} = \frac{1}{\sqrt{3}}$$

23. (c) is zero, otherwise there would be a field falling as $\frac{1}{r^3}$ at large distances outside the toroid.

Explanation: The magnetic field is only confined inside the body of a toroid in the form of concentric magnetic lines of force. For any point inside the empty space surrounded by toroid and outside the toroid, the magnetic field B is zero because the net current enclosed in these spaces is zero. Thus, the magnetic moment of toroid is zero.

24. (a) the declination varies between 11.3° W to 11.3°E.

Explanation: The magnetic field lines of the earth resemble that of a hypothetical magnetic dipole located at the centre of the earth.

The axis of the dipole does not coincide with the axis of rotation of the earth and it is tilted at some angle (angle of declination). Here in this situation the angle of declination is approximately 11.3° with respect to the later. Here two possibilities arises as shown in the figure below.

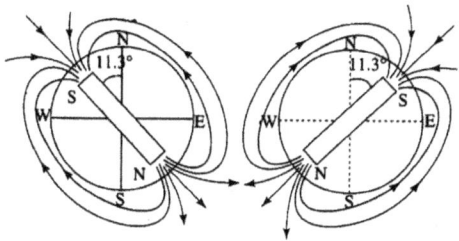

Hence, the declination varies between 11.3° W to 11.3°E.

25. (d) domains are all perfectly aligned

Explanation: At room temperature, the permanent magnet retains ferromagnetic property for a long period of time. The individual atoms in a ferromagnetic material possess a dipole moment as in a paramagnetic material. However, they interact with one another in such a way that they spontaneously align themselves in a common direction over a macroscopic volume called domain. Thus, we can say that in a permanent magnet at room temperature, domains are all perfectly aligned.

26. (b) case (ii) contradicts Gauss's law for magnetic fields

Explanation: According to Gauss's law in magnetism, $\oint B.ds = 0$ which implies that number of magnetic field lines entering the Gaussian surface is equal to the number of magnetic field lines leaving it. Therefore, case (ii) is not possible.

27. (c) magnetic field in which it is lying

Explanation: Current loop acts as a magnetic dipole. Its magnetic moment is given by,

$$M = NIA$$

where,   N = number of turns,
         I = current in a loop,
         A = area of the loop

From the above relation, we can conclude that magnetic dipole moment of a current loop is independent of magnetic field in which it is lying.

28. (d) 180 mAm^2

Explanation: Here,

$$B = 3.6 \times 10^{-5} \text{ T}$$
$$r = 100 \text{ mm}$$
$$= 0.1 \text{ m}$$

$$B = \frac{\mu_0}{4\pi} \frac{2\pi I}{r}$$

or, $$I = \frac{Br}{\left(\frac{\mu_0}{4\pi}\right) 2\pi}$$

$$= \frac{3.6 \times 10^{-5} \times 0.1}{10^{-7} \times 2 \times 3.14}$$

$$M = IA$$

$$= \frac{3.6 \times 10^{-5} \times 0.1}{10^{-7} \times 2 \times 3.14} \times 3.14 \times (0.1)^2$$

$$= 180 \text{ mAm}^2$$

29. (a) directly proportional to the square of the length of the wire in the coil.
    Explanation: We know that,
    $$M = NIA$$
    $$\Rightarrow M \propto A$$
    $$\Rightarrow M \propto r^2$$
    As, $l = 2\pi r$
    $$\Rightarrow l \propto r$$
    $$\Rightarrow M \propto l^2$$

30. (a) 8.8×10^{-25} Am^2
    Explanation: Magnetic dipole moment,
    $$M = IA$$
    $$= \frac{e}{T} \times \pi r^2$$
    $$= \frac{e}{\left(\frac{2\pi r}{v}\right)} \times \pi r^2$$
    $$= \frac{erv}{2}$$
    $$= \frac{1.6 \times 10^{-19} \times 50 \times 10^{-12} \times 2.2 \times 10^6}{2}$$
    $$= 8.8 \times 10^{-25} \text{ Am}^2$$

31. (d) Zero
    Explanation: The rotation of loop by 30° about an axis perpendicular to its plane make no change in the angle made by axis of the loop with the direction of magnetic field, therefore, the work done to rotate the loop is zero.

32. (a) The magnitude of magnetic moment now diminishes.
    Explanation: The magnitudes of magnetic moment of each semicircular loop of radius R lie in the x-y plane and the y-z plane is $M_1 = M_2 = I\dfrac{\pi R^2}{2}$
    and the direction of magnetic moments are along z-direction and x-direction respectively.
    Their resultant,
    $$M_{net} = \sqrt{M_1^2 + M_2^2}$$
    $$= \sqrt{2}I\frac{\pi R^2}{2}$$
    $$= \frac{M}{\sqrt{2}}$$
    So, $M_{net} < M$ or M diminishes.

33. (a) straight and parallel
34. (a) vertical
35. (b) less
36. (a) two times
37. (a) Since both the magnets exert equal and opposite force/torque on each other. Hence, net force/torque on cork will be zero.
38. (d) In a non uniform magnetic field, both a torque and a net force acts on the dipole. If magnetic field were uniform, net force on dipole would be zero.

39. (a) Helium atom has paired electrons so their electron spin are opposite to each other and hence its net magnetic moment is zero.

40. (a) The magnetic flux though any closed surface is zero.

41. (d) The compass needle enables us to locate magnetic north pole. If magnetic declination at that particular place is known, then true geographic north-south direction can be located. Therefore, the assertion is false. Similarly, reason is also false. This is because magnetic meridian is the vertical plane passing through magnetic axis. Magnetic axis is inclined at a certain angle θ to geographical axis and earth rotates about geographic axis.

42. (c) In the northern hemisphere, magnetic needle comes to rest along north-south direction. So that a greater dip angle is expected in northern hemisphere.

43. (b) At magnetic poles of the earth, the only vertical component of the earth's field acts, horizontal component is zero. A compass needle is free to rotate in horizontal plane and is affected by horizontal component only. Thus there will be no effect on the magnetic field on the compass needle. So the needle may stop in any direction. The angle of dip at the magnetic north pole is 90° and hence the dip needle will become vertical.

44. (b) Iron is ferromagnetic in nature. Lines of force due to external magnetic field prefer to pass through iron.

45. (i) (b) At poles.
    Net magnetic field is vertical at poles.
    (ii) (a) 0°
    Earth's magnetic field is completely horizontal at equator. Angle of dip is 0° at equator.
    (iii) (b) 30°
    $B \cos \delta = \dfrac{\sqrt{3}}{2} B \Rightarrow \cos \delta = \dfrac{\sqrt{3}}{2}, \delta = 30°$
    (iv) (b) Equator
    At equator, the magnetic field line are parallel with the surface of the earth.
    (v) (c) 45 μT
    $B_v = B_H \tan \delta$
    $= 26$ μT $\times \tan 60°$
    $= 45$ μT.

46. (i) (c) Monopole does not exist
    (ii) (c) vertical plane
    (iii) (b) bent slightly
    (iv) (a) At the equator, the earth's magnetic field is perpendicular to the direction of motion of the charged cosmic ray particles. As these particles gets deflected due to earth's magnetic field, so they require greater kinetic energy to reach the equator than the poles.
    (v) (b) Magnetic equator

47. (i) (a) In a non-uniform magnetic field, a magnetic needle experiences both a net force and a torque.

(ii) (c) When a bar magnet is cut into parts of equal length, pole strength of each part is same as that of original magnet but magnetic moment is halved because length is halved.

(iii) (b) $\tau_1 = mB \sin 90° = mB$

$\tau_2 = mB \sin \theta = \dfrac{1}{2} \tau_1 = \dfrac{1}{2} mB$

$\therefore \sin \theta = \dfrac{1}{2}$ or $\theta = 30°$

Angle of rotation = $90° - 30° = 60°$

(iv) (a) $\tau = 15 \times 0.10 \times 2 \times 10^{-5} \sin 30°$

$(\because \tau = mB \sin \theta)$

$= 1.5 \times 10^{-5}$ Nm

(v) (b) Magnetic potential at any point is the amount of work done in bringing a unit north pole from infinity to that point. At any point on the right bisector, the potentials due to two poles are equal and opposite.

48. (i) (b) $\tan \delta = \dfrac{B_V}{B_H} = 1$ or $\delta = 45°$

(ii) (a) Angle of dip is 90° at poles

(iii) (d) Due to earth's horizontal magnetic field, the lines of force are straight and parallel.

(iv) (a) $\tan \delta = \dfrac{B_V}{B_H} = \sqrt{3}, \delta = 60°$

(v) (a) If vertical and horizontal components of earth's magnetic field intensity I are V and H respectively, then

$I = \sqrt{(V^2 + H^2)}$

❏❏

Chapter 6: Electromagnetic Induction

1. A moving conductor coil in a magnetic field produces an induced emf. This is in accordance with :
   (a) Lenz's Law
   (b) Coulomb's Law
   (c) Faraday's Law
   (d) Ampere's Law

2. An induced emf is produced when a magnet is plunge into a coil. The strength of the induced emf is independent of:
   (a) number of turns of coil
   (b) speed with which the magnet is moved
   (c) the strength of the magnet
   (d) the resistivity of the wire of the coil

3. The magnetic flux through a coil is inversely proportional to:
   (a) magnetic field
   (b) number of turns
   (c) area
   (d) none of these

4. Faraday's laws are consequences of conservation of :
   (a) energy and magnetic field
   (b) energy
   (c) magnetic field
   (d) charge

5. Lenz's law gives:
   (a) the direction of the induced current
   (b) the magnitude of the induced emf
   (c) the magnitude of the induced current
   (d) both the magnitude and direction of the induced current

6. Which of the following phenomena makes use of electromagnetic induction?
   (a) Magnetising an iron piece with a bar magnet
   (b) Generation of hydroelectricity
   (c) Magnetising a soft iron piece by placing inside a current carrying solenoid
   (d) Charging a storage battery

7. The magnetic flux (ϕ) linked with a coil due to its own magnetic field is related to the number (N) of turns of the coil as:
   (a) $\phi \propto N^2$
   (b) $\phi \propto N^{-1}$
   (c) $\phi \propto N$
   (d) $\phi \propto N^{-2}$

8. In electromagnetic induction, the induced charge is independent of:
   (a) resistance of the coil
   (b) change of flux
   (c) time
   (d) None of these

9. To induce an emf in a coil, the linking magnetic flux:
   (a) must remain constant
   (b) can either increase or decrease
   (c) must increase
   (d) must decrease

10. The magnetic flux through a circuit of resistance R changes by an amount $\Delta\phi$ in a time Δt. Then the total quantity of electric charge Q that passes through any point in the circuit during the time Δt is represented by:
    (a) $Q = \dfrac{\Delta\phi}{R}$
    (b) $Q = R\dfrac{\Delta\phi}{\Delta t}$
    (c) $Q = \dfrac{1}{R} \cdot \dfrac{\Delta\phi}{\Delta t}$
    (d) $Q = \dfrac{\Delta\phi}{\Delta t}$

11. A coil has 200 turns and area of 70 cm². The magnetic field perpendicular to the plane of the coil is 0.3 Wb/m² and take 0.1 s to rotate through 180°. The value of the induced emf will be:
    (a) 84 V
    (b) 42 V
    (c) 8.4 V
    (d) 4.2 V

12. The expression for the induced emf contains a negative sign $\left(e = \dfrac{d\phi}{dt}\right)$. What is the significance of the negative sign?
    (a) The induced emf is opposite to the direction of the flux.
    (b) The induced emf is produced only, when the magnetic flux decreases.
    (c) The induced emf opposes the changes in the magnetic flux
    (d) None of the above

13. Lenz's and Faraday's law is expressed by the following formula (here e = induced emf, ϕ = magnetic flux in one turn and N = number of turns):
    (a) $e = -N\dfrac{d\phi}{dt}$
    (b) $e = N\dfrac{d\phi}{dt}$
    (c) $e = -\phi\dfrac{dN}{dt}$
    (d) $e = -\dfrac{d}{dt}\left(\dfrac{\phi}{N}\right)$

14. A rectangular coil of 100 turns and size 0.1 m × 0.05 m is placed perpendicular to a magnetic field of 0.1 T. If the field drops to 0.05 T in 0.05 s, the magnitude of the emf induced in the coil is:
    (a) 0.5
    (b) 3
    (c) 2
    (d) 6

15. An electron moves along the line AB, which lies in the same plane as a circular loop of conducting wires as shown in the diagram. What will be the direction of current induced if any, in the loop?

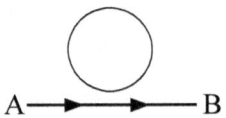

    (a) The current will change direction as the electron passes by

(b) The current will be anticlockwise
(c) The current will be clockwise
(d) No current will be induced

16. **Eddy currents may be reduced by using:**
    (a) thick piece of cobalt
    (b) thick piece of nickel
    (c) laminated core of steel
    (d) laminated core of soft iron

17. **When current changes from 13 A to 7 A in 0.5 s through a coil, the emf induced is 3×10^{-4} V. The coefficient of self induction is::**
    (a) 25×10^{-6} H
    (b) 25×10^{-5} H
    (c) 25×10^{-4} H
    (d) 25×10^{-3} H

18. **If a current of 3 A flowing in the primary coil is reduced to zero in 0.01 s then the induced emf in the secondary coil is 1500 V, the mutual inductance between the two coils is:**
    (a) 0.5 H
    (b) 1.5 H
    (c) 5 H
    (d) 10 H

19. **Magnetic flux of 10 µWb is linked with a coil, when a current of 2 mA flows through it. What is the self inductance of the coil?**
    (a) 20 mH
    (b) 10 mH
    (c) 15 mH
    (d) 5 mH

20. **For two coils with number of turns 500 and 200 each of length 1 m and cross-sectional area 4×10^{-4} m², the mutual inductance is**
    (a) 0.5 µH
    (b) 0.5 H
    (c) 5 µH
    (d) 0.05 mH

21. **When current I passes through an inductor of self inductance L, energy stored in it is $\frac{1}{2}LI^2$. This is stored in the _____.**
    (a) electric field
    (b) magnetic field
    (c) voltage
    (d) current

22. **A small coil of N_1 turns, l_1 length is tightly wound over the centre of a long solenoid of length l_2, area of cross-section A and number of turns N_2. If a current I flows in the small coil, then the flux through the long solenoid is:**
    (a) Zero
    (b) $\dfrac{\mu_0 N_1 N_2 A I}{l_1}$
    (c) $\dfrac{\mu_0 N_1^2 A I}{l_1}$
    (d) Infinite

23. **Which of the following is not a factor to determine the mutual inductance of the two coils:**
    (a) Current through each coil
    (b) The number of turns of each coil
    (c) Separation between the coils
    (d) The shape of each coil

24. **Mutual inductance of two coils can be increased by:**
    (a) winding the coils on wooden cores
    (b) decreasing the number of turns in the coils
    (c) increasing the number of turns in the coils
    (d) none of these

25. **The mutual inductance between two coils depends upon _____.**
    (a) medium between the coils
    (b) separation between coils
    (c) neither A nor B
    (d) both A and B

26. **Self-inductance _____ when the number of turns of a coil is doubled.**
    (a) is halved
    (b) is doubled
    (c) becomes four times
    (d) becomes one quarter

27. **Self induction of a solenoid is:**
    (a) inversely proportional to area of cross section
    (b) directly proportional to area of cross section
    (c) directly proportional to its length
    (d) directly proportional to current flowing through the coil

28. **Two solenoids of same cross sectional area have their lengths and number of turns in ratio of 1:2 both. The ratio of self-inductance of two solenoids is:**
    (a) 1:2
    (b) 2:1
    (c) 1:4
    (d) 1:1

29. **For perfect coupling of two coils of inductance L_1 and L_2 their mutual inductance M should be given by:**
    (a) $M = \sqrt{L_1 L_2}$
    (b) $M = \dfrac{L_1}{L_2}$
    (c) $M = \left(\dfrac{L_1}{L_2}\right)^{1/2}$
    (d) $M = L_1 L_2$

30. **In an inductor of inductance L = 100 mH, a current of I = 10 A is flowing. The energy stored in the inductor is:**
    (a) 1000 J
    (b) 100 J
    (c) 10 J
    (d) 5 J

31. **What will be the self-inductance of a coil of 100 turns if a current of 5 A produces a magnetic flux of 5×10^{-5} Wb?**
    (a) 1 µH
    (b) 10 µH
    (c) 1 mH
    (d) 10 mH

32. **If the current 30 A flowing in the primary coil is made zero in 0.1 s. The emf induced in the secondary coil is 1.5 V. The mutual inductance between the coil is::**
    (a) 0.1 H
    (b) 0.2 H
    (c) 0.005 H
    (d) 1.05 H

33. **The physical quantity which is measured in the unit of WbA^{-1} is:**
    (a) magnetic flux
    (b) self-inductance
    (c) mutual inductance
    (d) both (b) and (c)

34. **The coefficient of mutual inductance of two coils is 6 mH. If the current flowing in one is 2 A, then the induced emf in the second coil will be:**
    (a) Zero
    (b) 2 mV
    (c) 3 mV
    (d) 3 V

35. **An emf of 12 V is induced in a given coil when the current in it changes at the rate of 48 A/min. The inductance of the coil is::**
    (a) 9.6 H
    (b) 15 H
    (c) 0.25 H
    (d) 1.5 H

36. **The mutual inductance of a pair of coils is 0.75 H. If current in the primary coil changes from 0.5 A to zero in 0.01 s, find average induced emf in secondary coil:**

(a) 22.5 V (b) 12.5 V
(c) 25.5 V (d) 37.5 V

37. In an inductor, having a self-inductance of 10 H, the current changes from 10 A to 5 A in 0.2 s. The induced emf in a inductor is::
    (a) 2·5 V (b) 10 V
    (c) 25 V (d) 250 V

38. Energy stored in a coil of self-inductance 40 mH carrying a steady current of 2 A is:
    (a) 8 J (b) 0.08 J
    (c) 0.8 J (d) 80 J

39. The mutual inductance of an induction coil is 5 H. In the primary coil, the current reduces from 5 A to zero in 10^{-3} s. What is the induced emf in the secondary coil?:
    (a) Zero (b) 2500 V
    (c) 2510 V (d) 25000 V

40. An air core solenoid has 1000 turns and is one meter long. It cross-sectional area is 10 cm². Its self-inductance is:
    (a) 0.1256 mH (b) 1.256 mH
    (c) 12.56 mH (d) 125.6 mH

41. A square of side L m lies in the x-y plane in a region, where the magnetic field is given by, $B = B_0 (2\hat{i} + 3\hat{j} + 4\hat{k})$ T, where B_0 is constant. The magnitude of flux passing through the square is: [NCERT Exemplar]
    (a) $2B_0 L^2$ Wb (b) $3B_0 L^2$ Wb
    (c) $4B_0 L^2$ Wb (d) $\sqrt{29} B_0 L^2$ Wb

42. A loop, made of straight edges has six corners at A(0,0,0), B(L,0,0), C(L,L,0), D(0,L,0), E(0,L,L), and F(0,0,L). A magnetic field $B = B_0 (\hat{i} + \hat{k})$ T is present in the region. The flux passing through the loop ABCDEFA (in that order) is: [NCERT Exemplar]
    (a) $B_0 L^2$ Wb (b) $2B_0 L^2$ Wb
    (c) $\sqrt{2} B_0 L^2$ Wb (d) $4B_0 L^2$ Wb

43. There are two coils A and B as shown in the figure. A current starts flowing in B as shown, when A is moved towards B and stops when A stops moving. The current in A is counter clockwise. B is kept stationary when A moves. We can infer that:

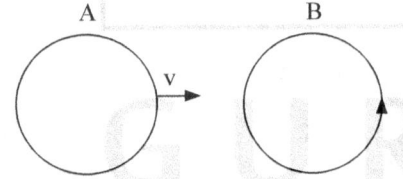

[NCERT Exemplar]
    (a) there is a constant current in the clockwise direction in A
    (b) there is a varying current in A
    (c) there is no current in A
    (d) there is a constant current in the counter clockwise direction in A

44. Same as problem 43 except the coil A is made to rotate about a vertical axis as shown in the figure. No current flows in B if A is at rest. The current in coil A, when the current in B (at t = 0) is counter clockwise and the coil A is as shown at this instant, t = 0, is:
[NCERT Exemplar]

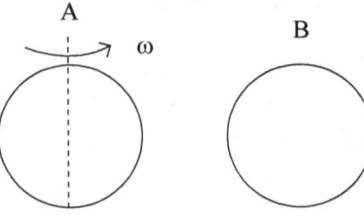

    (a) constant current clockwise
    (b) varying current clockwise
    (c) varying current counter clockwise
    (d) constant current counter clockwise

45. The self-inductance L of a solenoid of length l and area of cross section A, with a fixed number of turns N increases as: [NCERT Exemplar]
    (a) l and A increase.
    (b) l decreases and A increases.
    (c) l increases and A decreases.
    (d) both l and A decrease

46. A circular loop of radius r, carrying a current I lies in y-z plane with its centre at the origin. The net magnetic flux through the loop is : [CBSE 2020]
    (a) directly proportional to r
    (b) zero
    (c) inversely proportional to r
    (d) directly proportional to I

Directions: In the following questions, a statement of assertion is followed by a statement of reason. Mark the correct choice as:
(a) If both assertion and reason are true and reason is the correct explanation of assertion.
(b) If both assertion and reason are true, but reason is not the correct explanation of assertion.
(c) If assertion is true, but reason is false.
(d) If both assertion and reason are false.

47. **Assertion:** Faraday's laws are consequence of conservation of energy.
    Reason: In a purely resistive AC circuit, the current lags behind the emf in phase.

48. **Assertion:** Lenz's law is based on the principle of conservation of energy.
    Reason: Induced emf always opposes the change in magnetic flux responsible for its production.

49. **Assertion:** Two identical loops, one of copper and another of aluminium are rotated with the same speed in the same magnetic field. The emf induced in both the loop will be same.
    Reason: The magnitude of induced emf is directly proportional to the rate of change of magnetic flux linked with the circuit.

50. **Assertion:** An aircraft flies along the meridian, the potential at the ends of its wings will be the same.
    Reason: Whenever there is change in the magnetic flux emf induces.

51. **Assertion:** An induced current will be developed in a conductor, if it is moved in a direction parallel to magnetic field.
    Reason: Whenever there is relative motion between loop and magnet an induced current is produced in the loop.

52. **Assertion:** Eddy currents are produced in any metallic conductor when magnetic flux is changed around it.
    Reason: Electric potential determines the flow of charge.
53. **Assertion:** An artificial satellite with a metal surface is moving above the earth in a circular orbit. A current will be induced in satellite if the plane of the orbit is inclined to the plane of the equator.
    Reason: The current will be induced only when the speed of satellite is more than 8 km/sec.
54. **Assertion:** An induced emf is generated when magnet is withdrawn from the solenoid.
    Reason: The relative motion between magnet and solenoid induces emf.
55. **Assertion:** Only a change in magnetic flux will maintain an induced current in the coil.
    Reason: The presence of large magnetic flux through a coil maintains a current in the coil if the circuit is continuous.
56. **Assertion:** Mutual inductance of a pair of coils depends on their separation as well as their relative orientation.
    Reason: Mutual inductance depends upon the length of the coil only.
57. **Assertion:** In the phenomenon of mutual induction, self induction of each of the coil persists.
    Reason: Self induction arises due to change in current in the coil itself. In mutual induction current changes in both the individual coil.
58. **Assertion:** The self-inductance of a long solenoid is proportional to the area of cross-section and length of the solenoid.
    Reason: Self-inductance of a solenoid is independent of the number of turns per unit length.
59. **Assertion:** When two coils are wound on each other, the mutual induction between the coils is maximum.
    Reason: Mutual induction does not depend on the orientation of the coils.
60. **Assertion:** Inductance coil are made of copper.
    Reason: Induced current is more in wire having less resistance.
61. **Lenz's Law**
    This law is mostly used to find the direction current induced in a circuit. According to this law the polarity of e.m.f. induced in the circuit is such that it opposes or checks the variation in magnetic flux responsible for it. It we move north pole of a bar magnet towards coil, then magnetic flux linked with the coil changes (i.e., increases). Due to this current is induced in the coil in anticlockwise direction. The magnetic moment related with the induced current has north polarity towards the north pole. If we move away the bar magnet then magnetic moment has south polarity.

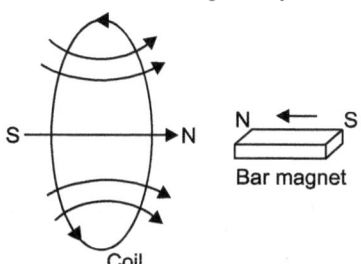

Lenz's law obeys the law of conservation of energy.
(i) Lenz's law is used to find the direction of:
  (a) Electric field   (b) Force
  (c) Induced current   (d) Electrostatic force
(ii) Lenz law follows the law of:
  (a) Conservation of force
  (b) Conservation of mass
  (c) Conservation of momentum
  (d) Conservation of energy
(iii) What will be the polarity of magnetic moment towards has magnet if we move the north of magnet towards coil ?
  (a) North   (b) South
  (c) Both (a) and (b) (d) None of these
(iv) If we move away the bar magnet from coil then what will be the direction of induced current in coil.
  (a) Clockwise   (b) Anticlockwise
  (c) Both (a) and (b) (d) None of these
(v) As we move the north pole of magnet towards coil, the magnetic flux linked with the coil.
  (a) Increases   (b) Decreases
  (c) Remain same   (d) None of these

62. From the experimental observations, Faraday arrived at a conclusion that an emf is induced in a coil when magnetic flux through the coil changes with time. The change in magnetic flux induces emf in coil C_1. It was this induced emf which caused electric current to flow in coil C_1 and through the galvanometer. When the tapping key K is pressed, the current in coil C_2 (and the resulting magnetic field) rises from zero to a maximum value in a short time. Consequently, the magnetic flux through the neighbouring coil C_1 also increases. It is the change in magnetic flux through coil C_1 that produces an induced emf in coil C_1. The SI Unit of magnetic flux is weber (Wb). When the key is held pressed, current in coil C_2 is constant. Therefore, there is no change in the magnetic flux through coil C_1 and the current in coil C_1 drops to zero. When the key is released, the current in C_2 and the resulting magnetic field decreases from the maximum value to zero in a short time. This results in a decrease in magnetic flux through coil C_1 and hence again induces an electric current in coil C_1. The common point in all these observations is that the time rate of change of magnetic flux through a circuit induces emf in it. Faraday stated experimental observations in the form of a law called Faraday's law of electromagnetic induction. The law is stated below.

The magnitude of the induced emf in a circuit is equal to the time rate of change of magnetic flux through the circuit.
(i) What is the full form of *emf* ?
  (a) Electron movement force
  (b) Electromotive force
  (c) Electron monitoring force
  (d) Electromagnetic field
(ii) Which of the following scientist arrived at a conclusion that an emf is induced in a coil when magnetic flux through the coil changes with time :
  (a) Michael Faraday
  (b) Joseph Henry

(c) Both Faraday and Henry
(d) Blaise Pascal

(iii) What is the SI unit of Magnetic flux ?
    (a) Pascal   (b) Coulumb
    (c) Weber   (d) Tesla

(iv) Who among the following scientist gave this statement "The magnitude of the induced emf in a circuit is equal to the time rate of change of magnetic flux through the circuit."
    (a) John Dalton   (b) Joseph Henry
    (c) Blaise Pascal   (d) Michael Faraday

(v) A rod of length 0.4 metre moves in a direction perpendicular to a magnetic field of magnitude 1.2 Tesla. The e.m.f. induced in the moving rod is found to be 2.40 V. What is the speed of the rod ?
    (a) 0.48 m/s   (b) 2.88 m/s
    (c) 7.2 m/s   (d) 5.0 m/s

63. So far we have studied the electric currents induced in well defined paths in conductors like circular loops. Even when bulk pieces of conductors are subjected to changing magnetic flux, induced currents are produced in them. However, their flow patterns resemble swirling eddies in water. This effect was discovered by physicist Foucault (1819-1868) and these currents are called eddy currents. A copper plate is allowed to swing like a simple pendulum between the pole pieces of a strong magnet. It is found that the motion is damped and in a little while, the plate comes to a halt in the magnetic field. We can explain this phenomenon on the basis of electromagnetic induction. Magnetic flux associated with the plate keeps on changing as the plate moves in and out of the region between magnetic poles. The flux change induces eddy currents in the plate. Directions of eddy currents are opposite when the plate swings into the region between the poles and when it swings out of the region.

(i) In which year Foucault was born ?
    (a) 1819   (b) 1825
    (c) 1838   (d) 1868

(ii) Even when bulk pieces of conductors are subjected to changing magnetic flux, induced currents are produced in them. This effect was discovered by which of the following scientist?
    (a) John Dalton
    (b) Jean Bernard Leon Foucault
    (c) Heinrich Friedrich Lenz
    (d) Michael Faraday

(iii) What is called Magnetic flux?
    (a) Magnetic flux is a vector field that describes the magnetic influence on moving electric charges, electric currents, and magnetic materials.
    (b) Magnetic flux is the production of an electromotive force across an electrical conductor in a changing magnetic field.
    (c) Magnetic flux is a measurement of the total magnetic field which passes through a given area.
    (d) Magnetic flux is a rectangular piece of an object that shows permanent magnetic properties and are made from the ferromagnetic substance.

(iv) Eddy current can be defined as
    (a) Eddy currents are loops of electrical current induced within conductors by a changing magnetic field in the conductor according to Faraday's law of induction.
    (b) Eddy currents are the magnitude of the induced emf in a circuit is equal to the time rate of change of magnetic flux through the circuit.
    (c) Eddy currents are the polarity of induced emf is such that it tends to produce a current which opposes the change in magnetic flux that produced it.
    (d) None of the above.

(v) If a current of 2 amperes gives rise a magnetic flux of 5×10^{-5} Weber through a coil having 100 turns, then the magnetic energy stored in the medium surrounding the coil is :
    (a) 5 Joules   (b) 50 Joules
    (c) 5×10^{-3} Joules   (d) 0.5 Joules

64. An electric current can be induced in a coil by flux change produced by another coil in its vicinity or flux change produced by the same coil. These two situations are described separately in the next two sub-sections. However, in both the cases, the flux through a coil is proportional to the current. That is, $\phi_B \propto I$. Further, if the geometry of the coil does not vary with time then,

$$\frac{d\phi_B}{dt} \propto \frac{dI}{dt}$$

For a closely wound coil of N turns, the same magnetic flux is linked with all the turns. When the flux ϕ_B through the coil changes, each turn contributes to the induced emf. Therefore, a term called *flux linkage* is used which is equal to $N\phi_B$ for a closely wound coil and in such a case $N\phi_B \propto I$ The constant of proportionality, in this relation, is called *inductance*. We shall see that inductance depends only on the geometry of the coil and intrinsic material properties. This aspect is akin to capacitance for which a parallel plate capacitor depends on the plate area and plate separation (geometry) and the dielectric constant K of the intervening medium (intrinsic material property). Inductance is a scalar quantity. It has the dimensions of $[M L^2 T^{-2} A^{-2}]$ given by the dimensions of flux divided by the dimensions of current. The SI unit of inductance is henry and is denoted by H. It is named in honour of Joseph Henry who discovered electromagnetic induction in USA, independently of Faraday in England.

(i) Who among the following discovered electromagnetic induction in USA?
    (a) Joseph Henry
    (b) Jean Bernard Leon Foucault
    (c) Heinrich Friedrich Lenz
    (d) Michael Faraday

(ii) What is the SI unit of inductance?
    (a) Coulomb   (b) Henry
    (c) Tesla   (d) Newton

(iii) Flux Linkage can be defined as :
    (a) Flux linkage is the loops of electrical current induced within conductors by a changing magnetic field in the conductor according to Faraday's law of induction.

(b) Flux linkage is the magnitude of the induced emf in a circuit is equal to the rate of change of magnetic flux through the circuit.
(c) Flux linkage is the polarity of induced emf is such that it tends to produce a current which opposes the change in magnetic flux that produced it.
(d) Flux linkage is the Flux through a coil multiplied by the number of turns the flux passes through. Flux linkage can also be expressed as the time integral of the voltage over the winding and measured in volt seconds.

(iv) Which of the following is dimension of inductance?
(a) $[M L T^{-2} A^{-2}]$ (b) $[M L^2 T^{-2} A^{-2}]$
(c) $[M L^1 T^{-2} A^{-2}]$ (d) $[M L^0 T^{-2} A^{-2}]$

(v) What will be the self inductance of a coil of 100 turns, if current of 2 ampere gives rise to a magnetic flux of 5×10^{-5} Weber through the coil :
(a) 2.5 Henry (b) 2.5 milli Henry
(c) 2.5×10^{-4} Henry (d) 0.25 Henry

65. The phenomenon of electromagnetic induction has been technologically exploited in many ways. An exceptionally important application is the generation of alternating currents (ac). The modern ac generator with a typical output capacity of 100 MW is a highly evolved machine. The Yugoslav inventor Nicola Tesla is credited with the development of the machine. One method to induce an emf or current in a loop is through a change in the loop's orientation or a change in its effective area. As the coil rotates in a magnetic field B, the effective area of the loop (the face perpendicular to the field) is A cos θ, where θ is the angle between A and B. This method of producing a flux change is the principle of operation of a simple ac generator. An ac generator converts mechanical energy into electrical energy.

AC Generator consists of a coil mounted on a rotor shaft. The axis of rotation of the coil is perpendicular to the direction of the magnetic field. The coil (called armature) is mechanically rotated in the uniform magnetic field by some external means. The rotation of the coil causes the magnetic flux through it to change, so an emf is induced in the coil. The ends of the coil are connected to an external circuit by means of slip rings and brushes.

(i) Which of the following electrical appliances converts mechanical energy into electrical energy?
(a) Dynamo (b) Capacitor
(c) Galvanometer (d) AC Generator

(ii) Who among the following is credited with the development of the machine?
(a) Charles Newton
(b) John Dalton
(c) Nicola Tesla
(d) John Dalton

(iii) Which of the following statement is correct regarding formation of ac generator?
(a) The axis of rotation of the coil is parallel to the direction of the magnetic field.
(b) The axis of rotation of the coil is inversely proportional to the direction of the magnetic field.
(c) The axis of rotation of the coil is perpendicular to the direction of the magnetic field.
(d) The axis of rotation of the coil is directly proportional to the direction of the magnetic field.

(iv) Which of the following part in AC Generator is mechanically rotated in the uniform magnetic field by some external means?
(a) Rotor (b) Armature
(c) Shaft (d) None of these

(v) Babita peddles a stationary bicycle. The pedals of the bicycle are attached to a 100 turn coil of area 0.10 m². The coil rotates at half a revolution per second and it is placed in a uniform magnetic field of 0.01 T perpendicular to the axis of rotation of the coil. What is the maximum voltage generated in the coil?
(a) 0.614 V. (b) 0.114 V.
(c) 0.214 V. (d) 0.314 V.

Answers

1. (c) Faraday's Law
   Explanation: Faraday's law of induction is a basic law of electromagnetism predicting how a magnetic field will interact with an electric circuit to produce an electromotive force.

2. (d) the resistivity of the wire of the coil
   Explanation: When the conductor is moved in a stationary magnetic field to procure a change in the flux linkage, the emf is statically induced.

3. (d) None of these
   Explanation: The magnetic flux through some surface is proportional to the number of field lines passing through that surface.

4. (b) energy
   Explanation: Faraday's laws involve conversion of mechanical energy into electric energy. This is in accordance with the law of conservation of energy.

5. (a) the direction of the induced current
   Explanation: Lenz's law states that an induced electric current flows in a direction such that the current opposes the change that induced it.

6. (b) Generation of hydroelectricity.
   Explanation: Hydroelectric plant uses mechanical energy of water to move a magnetic field passes coils of wire to generate voltage.

7. (a) $\phi \propto N^2$
   Explanation: Since,
   $$\phi = N\vec{B}.\vec{A} \text{ and } B \propto N.$$

8. (c) time
   Explanation: We know that,
   $$e = \frac{d\phi}{dt}$$
   where $\phi = NBA$

$$q = \frac{e}{R} dt$$
$$= \frac{\Delta\phi}{R}$$

9. (b) can either increase or decrease
   Explanation: Emf is induced when there is change in magnetic flux in the coil.

10. (a) $Q = \frac{\Delta\phi}{R}$
    Explanation: Since,
    $$\frac{\Delta\phi}{\Delta t} = \varepsilon$$
    $$= IR$$
    $$\Rightarrow \Delta\phi = (I\Delta t)R$$
    $$= QR$$
    $$\Rightarrow Q = \frac{\Delta\phi}{R}$$

11. (c) 8, 4V
    Explanation: As we know that,
    Change in flux = 2BAN
    $\therefore$ Induced emf $= \frac{2 \times 0.3 \times 200 \times 70 \times 10^{-4}}{0.1}$
    V = 8.4V

12. (c) The induced emf opposes the changes in the magnetic flux.
    Explanation: The negative sign gives the direction of the induced emf.

13. (a) $e = -N\frac{d\phi}{dt}$
    Explanation: Induced emf $e = -N\frac{d\phi}{dt}$, where N is the number of turns of the coil.

14. (a) 0.5
    Explanation: Hence, area of coil
    $A = 0.1 \text{ m} \times 0.05 \text{ m}$
    $= 5 \times 10^{-3} \text{ m}^2$
    $N = 100$
    Initial flux linked with the coil,
    $\phi_1 = BA \cos\theta$
    $= 0.1 \times 5 \times 10^{-3} \cos 0°$
    $= 5 \times 10^{-4} \text{ Wb}$
    Final flux linked with the coil,
    $\phi_2 = 0.05 \times 5 \times 10^{-3} \cos 0°$
    $= 25 \times 10^{-5} \text{ Wb}$
    $= 2.5 \times 10^{-4} \text{ Wb}$
    The magnitude of induced emf in the coil is,
    $e = \frac{N|\Delta\phi|}{\Delta t}$
    $= \frac{N|\phi_2 - \phi_1|}{t}$
    $= \frac{100|2.5 \times 10^{-4} - 5 \times 10^{-4}|}{0.05}$
    $= \frac{100 \times 2.5 \times 10^{-4}}{0.05}$ V
    $= 0.05$ V

15. (a) The current will change direction as the electron passes by
    Explanation: If electron is moving from left to right, the flux linked with the loop (which is into the page) will first increase and then decrease as the electron passes by. So, the induced current in the loop will be first anticlockwise and will change direction as the electron passes by.

16. (d) laminated core of soft iron
    Explanation: To reduce eddy current, the resistance of the core should be increased.

17. (a) 25×10^{-6} H
    Explanation: Coefficient of self induction is given by,
    $$e = -L\frac{dI}{dt}$$
    $\therefore$
    $$L = -\frac{e}{\frac{dI}{dt}}$$
    $$= -\frac{300 \times 10^{-6} \times 0.5}{(7-13)}$$
    $$= 25 \times 10^{-6} \text{ H}$$

18. (c) 5 H
    Explanation: Since,
    $$e = -M\frac{dI}{dt}$$
    $$1500 = -M\left(\frac{0-3}{0.01}\right)$$
    $$M = \frac{1500 \times 0.01}{3}$$
    $$= 5 \text{ H}$$

19. (d) 5 mH
    Explanation: We know that,
    $\phi = LI$
    $\Rightarrow L = \frac{\phi}{I}$
    $= \frac{10 \times 10^{-6}}{2 \times 10^{-3}}$
    $= 5$ mH

20. (d) 0.05 mH
    Explanation: From the formula,
    $M = \frac{\mu_0 n_2 n_1 A}{l}$
    $= \frac{4\pi \times 10^{-7} \times 500 \times 200 \times \frac{4}{10^4}}{1}$
    $= 150\pi \times 10^{-7}$
    $= 0.05 \times 10^{-3}$ H

21. (b) magnetic field
    Explanation: Inductor is used to store magnetic field.

22. (b) $\dfrac{\mu_0 N_1 N_2 A I}{l_1}$

 Explanation: If we try to find field of the small coil and then calculate flux through long solenoid, the problem becomes very difficult. So, we use the following fact about mutual inductance.
$$\phi = N_2 B A$$
$$= \dfrac{N_2 \mu_0 N_1 I A}{l_1}$$

23. (a) Current through each coil

 Explanation: Mutual inductance of two coils is
$$M = \dfrac{\mu_0 N_1 N_2 A}{l}$$
 Thus, M is independent of current passing through each coil.

24. (c) increasing the number of turns in the coils

 Explanation: As we know that,
$$M = \dfrac{\mu_0 N_1 N_2 A}{l}$$
 i.e., M can be increased by increasing the number of turns in the coils.

25. (d) both A and B

 Explanation: Mutual inductance of two coils is,
$$M = \dfrac{\mu_0 N_1 N_2 A}{l}$$

26. (c) becomes four times

 Explanation: We know that,
$$L \propto \dfrac{N^2}{l}$$

27. (b) directly proportional to area of cross section

 Explanation: We know that,
$$L = \dfrac{\mu_0 N^2 A}{l}$$

28. (a) 1:2

 Explanation: We know that,
$$\dfrac{l_1}{l_2} = \dfrac{1}{2} \text{ and } \dfrac{N_1}{N_2} = \dfrac{1}{2}$$
 From,
$$L = \dfrac{\mu_0 N^2 A}{l} \propto \dfrac{N^2}{l}$$
 We get,
$$\dfrac{L_1}{L_2} = \dfrac{\left(\dfrac{N_1}{N_2}\right)^2}{\left(\dfrac{l_1}{l_2}\right)}$$
$$= \dfrac{\left(\dfrac{1}{2}\right)^2}{\dfrac{1}{2}}$$
$$= \dfrac{1}{2}$$

29. (a) $M = \sqrt{L_1 L_2}$

 Explanation: Since coefficient of coupling is given by,
$$K = \dfrac{M}{\sqrt{L_1 L_2}}$$

30. (d) 5 J

 Explanation: Energy stored,
$$U = \dfrac{1}{2} L i^2$$
$$= \dfrac{1}{2} \times 100 \times 10^{-3} \times (10)^2$$
$$= 5 \text{ J}$$

31. (c) 1 mH

 Explanation: Self-inductance,
$$L = \dfrac{N \phi}{I}$$
$$= \dfrac{100 \times 5 \times 10^{-5}}{5}$$
$$= 10^{-3} \text{ H}$$

32. (c) 0.05 H

 Explanation: We know that,
$$e = M \dfrac{dI}{dt}$$
$$\Rightarrow \quad 1.5 = M \times \dfrac{30}{0.1}$$
$$\therefore \quad M = 0.005 \text{ H}$$

33. (d) both (b) and (c)

 Explanation: Inductance is measured in WbA^{-1}.

34. (a) Zero

 Explanation: In secondary, emf induces only when current through primary changes.

35. (b) 15 H

 Explanation: Since,
$$E = L \dfrac{dI}{dt}$$
 Hence, $L = E \dfrac{dt}{dI}$
$$= 12 \times \dfrac{60}{48}$$
$$= 12 \text{ H}$$

36. (d) 37.5 V

 Explanation: Given,
$$M = 0.75 \text{ H}$$
$$\dfrac{dI}{dt} = \dfrac{0.5 - 0}{0.01}$$
$$= 50 \text{ A/s}$$
 Therefore, average induced emf in secondary coil.
$$e = M \dfrac{dI}{dt}$$
$$= 0.75 \times 50$$
$$= 37.5 \text{ V}$$

37. (d) 250 V
    Explanation: Here,
    $$L = 10 \text{ H}$$
    $$dI = 10 - 5 = 5 \text{ A}$$
    $$dt = 0.2 \text{ s}$$
    $$\therefore \quad e = \frac{L dI}{dt}$$
    $$= \frac{10 \times 5}{0.2}$$
    $$= 250 \text{ V}$$

38. (b) 0.08 J
    Explanation: Energy stored in a self-inductance coil is given by,
    $$E = \frac{1}{2} L I^2$$
    $$= \frac{1}{2} \times 40 \times 10^{-3} \times 4 = 0.08 \text{ J}$$

39. (d) 25000 V
    Explanation: Since,
    $$e = -M \frac{dI}{dt} = -5 \times \frac{(-5)}{10^{-3}} = 25000 \text{ V}$$

40. (b) 1.256 mH
    Explanation: Self-inductance of solenoid coil having N number of turns, length l and area of cross-section A is given by,
    $$L = \mu_0 \frac{N^2}{l} A$$
    Here, $N = 1000$,
    $A = 10 \text{ cm}^2$
    or, $A = 10 \times 10^{-4} \text{ m}^2$
    and, $l = 1 \text{ m}$
    Substituting these values in the above equation, we get,
    $$L = 4\pi \times 10^{-7} \times \frac{(1000)^2}{1} \times 10 \times 10^{-4}$$
    $\Rightarrow \quad L = 1.256 \text{ mH}$

41. (c) $4 B_0 L^2$ Wb
    Explanation: Given,
    $$\vec{B} = B_0 (2\hat{i} + 3\hat{j} + 4\hat{k}) \text{ T}$$
    Area of square,
    $$\vec{A} = L^2 \hat{k} \text{ m}^2$$
    $\therefore \quad \phi = \vec{B} \cdot \vec{A}$
    $$= B_0 (2\hat{i} + 3\hat{j} + 4\hat{k}) \cdot L^2 \hat{k} = 4 B_0 L^2 \text{ Wb}$$

42. (b) $2 B_0 L^2$ Wb
    Explanation: In this problem first we have to analyse area vector, loop ABCDA lies in x-y plane whose area vector $\vec{A} = L^2 \hat{k}$ whereas loop ADEFA lies in y-z plane whose area vector $\vec{A} = L^2 \hat{i}$.
    And the magnetic flux is,
    $$\phi_m = \vec{B} \cdot \vec{A}$$
    $$\vec{A} = \vec{A_1} + \vec{A_2} = (L^2 \hat{k} + L^2 \hat{i})$$
    and, $\vec{B} = B_0 = (\hat{i} + \hat{k})$
    Now,
    $$\phi_m = \vec{B} \cdot \vec{A}$$
    $$= B_0 (\hat{i} + \hat{k}) \cdot (L^2 \hat{k} + L^2 \hat{i})$$
    $$= 2 B_0 L^2 \text{ Wb}$$

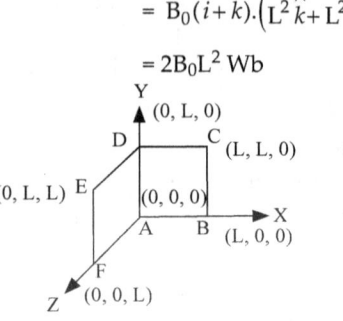

43. (d) there is a constant current in the counter clockwise direction in A
    Explanation: Due to variation in the flux linked with coil B an emf will be induced in coil B. Current in coil B becomes zero when coil A stops moving, it is possible only if the current in coil A is constant. If the current in coil A would be variable, there must be some changing flux and then there must be an induced emf. Hence an induced current will be in coil B even when coil A is not moving.

44. (a) constant current clockwise
    Explanation: When the current in coil B (at $t = 0$) is counter clockwise and the coil A is considered above it. The counter clockwise flow of the current in coil B is equivalent to north pole of magnet and magnetic field lines are eliminating upward to coil A. When coil A starts rotating at $t = 0$, the current in A is constant along clockwise direction by Lenz's rule.

45. (b) l decreases and A increases
    Explanation: For a solenoid of length l and area of cross section A with fixed number of turns N, the self-inductance L is given by,
    $$L = \frac{\mu_0 N^2 A}{l}$$
    So, L increases when l decreases and A increases

46. (b) zero.
    Explanation: Circular loop behaves as a magnetic dipole, whose one surface will be N-pole and another will be S-pole. Therefore, magnetic lines of force emerge from north will meet as south. Hence, total magnetic flux through y-z plane is zero.

47. (c) According to Faraday's laws, the conversion of mechanical energy into electrical energy. This is in accordance with the law of conservation of energy. It is also clearly known that in pure resistance, the emf is in phase with the current.

48. (a) Lenz's Law is based on conservation of energy and induced emf opposes the cause of it i.e., change in magnetic flux.

49. (a) Since both the loops are identical (same area and number of turns) and moving with a same speed in same magnetic field. Therefore, same emf is induced in both the coils. But the induced current

will be more in the copper loop as its resistance will be lesser as compared to that of the aluminium loop.

50. (*) As the aircraft flies, magnetic flux changes through its wings due to the vertical component of the earth's magnetic field. Due to this, induced emf is produced across the wings of the aircraft. Therefore, the wings of the aircraft will not be at the same potential. Hence the given assertion is false and reason is true.

   * The answer is not given in the options.

51. (d) Induced current will not be developed in a conductor, if it is moved in direction parallel to magnetic field. It is because, in this case, the Lorentz force on free electrons in the conductor is zero. The induced emf is produced only when the magnetic flux linked with the loop changes.

52. (b) When a metallic conductor is moved in a magnetic field; magnetic flux is varied. It disturbs the free electrons of the metal and set up an induced emf in it. As there are no free ends of the metal i.e., it will be closed in itself so there will be induced current.

53. (c) When the satellite moves in inclined plane with equatorial plane (including orbit around the poles), the value of magnetic field will change both in magnitude and direction. Due to this, the magnetic flux through the satellite will change and hence induced currents will be produced in the metal of the satellite. But no current will induced if satellite orbits in the equatorial plane because the magnetic flux does not change through the metal of the satellite in this plane.

54. (a) Emf is induced when there is change in magnetic flux.

55. (c) Presence of magnetic flux cannot produce current.

56. (c) The mutual inductance in case of a medium of relative permeability present is,
$$M = \frac{\mu_0 \mu_r \pi N_1 N_2 r_2^2}{l}$$

57. (c) Mutual inductance is the phenomenon according to which an opposing emf produces flux in a coil as a result of change in current on magnetic flux linked with a neighbouring coil. But When 2 coils are inductively coupled in additions to induced emf produced due to mutual induction, also induced emf is produced in each of two coils due to self induction.

58. (c) The self-inductance of a solenoid is given by,
$L = \mu_r \mu_0 n^2 Al$.

59. (c) The manner in which the two coils are oriented, determines the coefficient of coupling between them.
$$M = K \cdot \sqrt{L_1 L_2}$$
When the two coils are wound on each other, the coefficient of coupling is maximum and hence mutual inductance between the coil is maximum.

60. (a) The inductance coils made of copper will have very small ohmic resistance. Due to change in magnetic flux a large induced current will be produced in such an inductance, which will offer appreciable opposition to the flow of current.

61. (i) (c) Induced current
    (ii) (d) Conservation of energy
    (iii) (a) North
    (iv) (a) Clockwise
    (v) (a) Increases

62. (i) (b) The full form of *emf* is Electromotive force.
    (ii) (a) From the experimental observations, Faraday arrived at a conclusion that an emf is induced in a coil when magnetic flux through the coil changes with time.
    (iii) (c) Magnetic flux is a measurement of the total magnetic field which passes through a given area. The SI Unit of magnetic flux is weber (Wb).
    (iv) (d) Michael Faraday stated experimental observations in the form of a law called Faraday's law of electromagnetic induction. The law is stated that "The magnitude of the induced emf in a circuit is equal to the rate of change of magnetic flux through the circuit".
    (v) (d) Speed of the rod = $\frac{V}{Bl} = \frac{2.40}{1.2 \times 0.4}$
    = 5.0 m/sec

63. (i) (a) Jean Bernard Leon Foucault was born on 18 September, 1819. He was French Physicist.
    (ii) (b) Even when bulk pieces of conductors are subjected to changing magnetic flux, induced currents are produced in them. This effect was discovered by Jean Bernard Leon Foucault.
    (iii) (c) Magnetic flux is a measurement of the total magnetic field which passes through a given area. It is a useful tool for helping describe the effects of the magnetic force on something occupying a given area. The measurement of magnetic flux is tied to the particular area chosen.
    (iv) (a) Eddy currents are loops of electrical current induced within conductors by a changing magnetic field in the conductor according to Faraday's law of induction. Eddy currents flow in closed loops within conductors, in planes perpendicular to the magnetic field.
    (v) (c) Magnetic energy stored
    $$E = \frac{1}{2} Li^2$$
    But $N\varphi = Li$
    $$L = \frac{N\phi}{i}$$
    $$E = \frac{1}{2} \cdot \frac{N\phi}{i} i^2$$
    $$= \frac{1}{2} N\varphi i$$
    or, $E = \frac{1}{2} \times 100 \times 5 \times 10^{-5} \times 2$
    $= 5 \times 10^{-3}$ Joules

64. (i) (a) Joseph Henry who discovered electromagnetic induction in USA. He was an American scientist.

(ii) (b) The SI unit of inductance is henry and is denoted by H.

(iii) (d) Flux linkage is the Flux through a coil multiplied by the number of turns the flux passes through.

(iv) (b) Inductance has the dimensions of $[ML^2T^{-2}A^{-2}]$ given by the dimensions of flux divided by the dimensions of current.

(v) (b) $N\phi = Li$

or, $L = \dfrac{N\phi}{i} = \dfrac{100 \times 5 \times 10^{-5}}{2}$

$= 2.5 \times 10^{-3} = 2.5$ milli Henry

65. (i) (d) An AC generator converts mechanical energy into electrical energy. AC generator, also known as alternators.

(ii) (c) The Yugoslav inventor Nicola Tesla and futurist best known for his contributions to the design of the modern alternating current (AC) electricity supply system.

(iii) (c) AC Generator consists of a coil mounted on a rotor shaft. The axis of rotation of the coil is perpendicular to the direction of the magnetic field.

(iv) (b) The coil (called armature) is mechanically rotated in the uniform magnetic field by some external means. The rotation of the coil causes the magnetic flux through it to change, so an emf is induced in the coil.

(v) (d) Here $\nu = 0.5$ Hz;

$N = 100$,

$A = 0.1$ m^2

and $B = 0.01$ T.

$\epsilon_0 = NBA(2\pi\nu)$

$= 100 \times 0.01 \times 0.1 \times 2 \times 3.14 \times 0.5$

$= 0.314$ V

Hence, the maximum voltage is 0.314 V.

Chapter 7: Alternating Current

1. Alternating current cannot be measured by DC ammeter because:
   (a) AC is virtual
   (b) AC changes its direction
   (c) AC cannot pass through DC ammeter
   (d) Average value of complete cycle is zero

2. The alternating current of equivalent value of $\frac{I_0}{\sqrt{2}}$ is:
   (a) rms current
   (b) DC current
   (c) Peak current
   (d) all of these

3. In an AC circuit $I = 100 \sin 200\pi t$. The time required for the current to achieve its peak value will be:
   (a) $\frac{1}{200}$ s
   (b) $\frac{1}{400}$ s
   (c) $\frac{1}{100}$ s
   (d) $\frac{1}{300}$ s

4. The ratio of mean value over half cycle to rms value of AC is:
   (a) $\sqrt{2} : 1$
   (b) $2 : \pi$
   (c) $2\sqrt{2} : \pi$
   (d) $\sqrt{2} : \pi$

5. The peak value of an alternating emf E given by $E = E_0 \cos \omega t$ is 10 V and its frequency is 50 Hz. At time $t = \frac{1}{600}$ s, the instantaneous emf is:
   (a) $5\sqrt{3}$ V
   (b) 5 V
   (c) 10 V
   (d) 1 V

6. The frequency of an alternating voltage is 50 cps and its amplitude is 120 V. Then the rms value of voltage is:
   (a) 56.5 V
   (b) 70.7 V
   (c) 101.3 V
   (d) 84.8 V

7. A 40 Ω electric heater is connected to a 200 V, 50 Hz mains supply. The peak value of electric current flowing in the circuit is approximately:
   (a) 10 A
   (b) 5 A
   (c) 7 A
   (d) 2.5 A

8. In the case of an inductor:
   (a) Voltage leads the current by $\frac{\pi}{4}$
   (b) Voltage leads the current by $\frac{\pi}{3}$
   (c) Voltage leads the current by $\frac{\pi}{2}$
   (d) Voltage lags the current by $\frac{\pi}{2}$

9. A resistance of 20 Ω is connected to a source of an alternating potential $V = 220 \sin (100\pi t)$. The time taken by the current to change from its peak value to rms value is:
   (a) 2.5×10^{-3} s
   (b) 25×10^{-3} s
   (c) 0.25 s
   (d) 0.2 s

10. The rms value of an AC of 50 Hz is 10 A. The time taken by the alternating current in reaching from zero to maximum value and the peak value of current will be:
    (a) 1×10^{-2} s and 7.07 A
    (b) 2×10^{-2} s and 14.14 A
    (c) 5×10^{-3} s and 14.14 A
    (d) 5×10^{-3} s and 7.07 A

11. Determine the rms value of the emf given by,
    $E \text{ (in V)} = 8 \sin (\omega t) + 6 \sin (2\omega t)$
    (a) $10\sqrt{2}$ V
    (b) 10 V
    (c) $5\sqrt{2}$ V
    (d) $7\sqrt{2}$ V

12. An alternating current of frequency f is flowing in a circuit containing a resistor of resistance R and a choke of inductance L in series. The impedance of this circuit is:
    (a) $R + 2\pi f\pi L$
    (b) $\sqrt{R^2 + L^2}$
    (c) $\sqrt{R^2 + 2\pi f L}$
    (d) $\sqrt{R^2 + 4\pi^2 f^2 L^2}$

13. A generator produces a voltage that is given by $V = 240 \sin 120t$ V, where t is in seconds. The frequency and rms voltage are nearly:
    (a) 19 Hz and 120 V
    (b) 19 Hz and 170 V
    (c) 60 Hz and 240 V
    (d) 754 Hz and 170 V

14. The instantaneous voltage through a device of impedance 20 Ω is $e = 80 \sin 100\pi t$. The effective value of the current is:
    (a) 1.732 A
    (b) 2.828 A
    (c) 3 A
    (d) 4 A

15. A 15 μF capacitor is connected to 220 V, 50 Hz source. Find the capacitive reactance and the rms current.
    (a) 212.1 Ω; 1.037 A
    (b) 212.1 Ω; 2.037 A
    (c) 412.1 Ω; 1.037 A
    (d) 412.1 Ω; 2.037 A

16. In an AC circuit an alternating voltage $V = 200\sqrt{2} \sin 100t$ is connected to a capacitor of capacity 1 μF. The rms value of the current in the circuit is:
    (a) 10 mA
    (b) 20 mA
    (c) 100 mA
    (d) 200 mA

17. In an LR circuit, the value of L is $\left(\frac{0.4}{\pi}\right)$ and the value of R is 30 Ω. If in the circuit, an alternating emf of 200 V at 50 cps is connected, the impedance of the circuit and current will be:

(a) 50 Ω, 4 A (b) 40.4 Ω, 5 A
(c) 30.7 Ω, 6.5 A (d) 11.4 Ω, 17.5 A

18. In an AC circuit the voltage applied is $E = E_0 \sin \omega t$. The resulting current in the circuit is $I = I_0 \sin\left(\omega t - \dfrac{\pi}{2}\right)$. The power consumption in the circuit is given by:
(a) $P = \dfrac{E_0 I_0}{2}$
(b) $P = \dfrac{E_0 I_0}{\sqrt{2}}$
(c) $P = \sqrt{2} E_0 I_0$
(d) $P = 0$

19. In an LCR series AC circuit, the voltage across each of the components, L, C and R is 50 V. The voltage across the LC combination will be:
(a) 0 V
(b) 50 V
(c) $50\sqrt{2}$ V
(d) 100 V

20. Find the capacitive reactance of 10 μF capacitor, when it is part of a circuit, whose frequency is 100 Hz.
(a) 159.2 Ω
(b) 412.1 Ω
(c) 612.1 Ω
(d) 812.1 Ω

21. The resonant frequency of a circuit is f. If the capacitance is made 4 times the initial values, then the resonant frequency will become:
(a) $\dfrac{f}{2}$
(b) f
(c) $2f$
(d) $\dfrac{f}{4}$

22. A coil of 10 Ω and 10 mH is connected in parallel to a capacitor of 0.1 μF. The impedance of the circuit at resonance is:
(a) 10^3 Ω
(b) 10^6 Ω
(c) 10^2 Ω
(d) 10^4 Ω

23. Which of the following curves correctly represent the variation of capacitive reactance (X_C) with frequency (v)?

(a)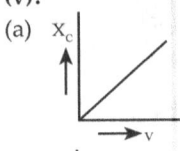
(b)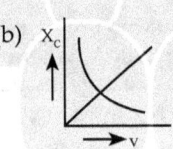
(c)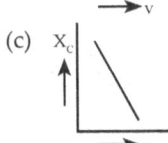
(d)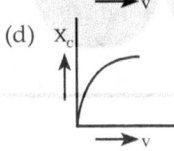

24. How does the current in an RC circuit vary when the charge on the capacitor builds up?
(a) It decreases linearly
(b) It increases linearly
(c) It decreases exponentially
(d) It increases exponentially

25. The impedance in a circuit containing a resistance of 1 Ω and an inductance of 0.1 H in series for AC of 50 Hz is:
(a) $\sqrt{10}$ Ω
(b) $10\sqrt{10}$ Ω
(c) 100 Ω
(d) $100\sqrt{10}$ Ω

26. An ac circuit contains a resistance R, capacitance C and inductance L in series with a source of emf $e = e_0 \sin(\omega t + f)$. The current through the circuit is maximum when:
(a) $\omega^2 = LC$
(b) $\omega L = \dfrac{1}{\omega C}$
(c) $R = L = C$
(d) $\omega = LCR$

27. A charged 30 μF capacitor is connected to a 27 mH inductor. The angular frequency of free oscillations of the circuit is:
(a) 1.1×10^3 rad s^{-1}
(b) 2.1×10^3 rad s^{-1}
(c) 3.1×10^3 rad s^{-1}
(d) 4.1×10^3 rad s^{-1}

28. The frequency of the output signal becomes _____ times by doubling the value of the capacitance in the LC oscillator circuit.
(a) $\dfrac{1}{2}$
(b) 2
(c) $\sqrt{2}$
(d) $\dfrac{1}{\sqrt{2}}$

29. In an LCR circuit, the sharpness of resonance depends on:
(a) Resistance (R)
(b) Capacitance (C)
(c) Inductance (L)
(d) All of these

30. The average power dissipation in a pure capacitor in AC circuit is:
(a) CV^2
(b) $2CV^2$
(c) $\dfrac{CV^2}{2}$
(d) Zero

31. In a series resonant circuit, having L, C, and R as its elements, the resonant current is i. The power dissipated in circuit at resonance is:
(a) Zero
(b) $i^2 R$
(c) $i^2 \omega L$
(d) $\dfrac{i^2 R}{\left(\omega L - \dfrac{1}{\omega C}\right)}$

32. An AC supply gives 30 V$_{rms}$ which passes through 10Ω resistance. The power dissipated in it is:
(a) $45\sqrt{2}$ W
(b) $90\sqrt{2}$ W
(c) 45 W
(d) 90 W

33. In a series LCR circuit alternating emf (e) and current (i) are given by the equation $v = v_0 \sin \omega t$, $i = i_0 \sin\left(\omega t + \dfrac{\pi}{3}\right)$. The average power dissipated in the circuit over a cycle of AC is:
(a) Zero
(b) $\dfrac{v_0 i_0}{2}$
(c) $\dfrac{v_0 i_0}{4}$
(d) $\dfrac{\sqrt{3}}{2} v_0 i_0$

34. In an AC circuit, the current flowing in inductance is $I = 5 \sin(100t - \pi/2)$ A and the potential difference is $V = 200 \sin(100t)$ V. The power consumption is equal to:
(a) Zero
(b) 20 V
(c) 40 W
(d) 1000 W

35. The power factor in an AC series LR circuit is:
(a) $\dfrac{L}{R}$
(b) $\sqrt{R^2 + L^2\omega^2}$
(c) $R\sqrt{R^2 + L^2\omega^2}$
(d) $\dfrac{R}{\sqrt{R^2 + L^2\omega^2}}$

36. A transformer is employed to:
    (a) Convert DC into AC
    (b) Convert AC into DC
    (c) Obtain a suitable DC voltage
    (d) Obtain a suitable AC voltage
37. The loss of energy in the form of heat in the iron core of a transformer is:
    (a) Copper loss   (b) Iron loss
    (c) Mechanical loss   (d) None of these
38. The core of any transformer is laminated so as to:
    (a) Make it light weight
    (b) Make it robust and strong
    (c) Increase the secondary voltage
    (d) Reduce the energy loss due to eddy currents
39. A step up transformer has transformation ratio 5:3. What is voltage in secondary if voltage in primary is 60 V?
    (a) 60 V   (b) 180 V
    (c) 20 V   (d) 100 V
40. A transformer has 50 turns in the primary and 100 in the secondary. If the primary is connected to a 220 V DC supply, what will be the voltage across the secondary?
    (a) 19 V   (b) 30 V
    (c) 62 V   (d) 0 V
41. The primary of a transformer has 400 turns while the secondary has 2000 turns. If the power output from the secondary at 1000 V is 12 kW, what is the primary voltage?
    (a) 200 V   (b) 400 V
    (c) 300 V   (d) 500 V
42. A step-down transformer is used on a 1000 V line to deliver 20 A at 120 V at the secondary coil. If the efficiency of the transformer is 80% the current drawn from the line is:
    (a) 0.3 A   (b) 3 A
    (c) 30 A   (d) 24 A
43. If the rms current in a 50 Hz AC circuit is 5 A, the value of the current $\frac{1}{300}$ s after its value becomes zero is:
    [NCERT Exemplar]
    (a) $5\sqrt{2}$ A   (b) $5\sqrt{\frac{3}{2}}$ A
    (c) $\frac{5}{6}$ A   (d) $\frac{5}{\sqrt{2}}$ A
44. An alternating current generator has an internal resistance R_g and an internal reactance X_g. It is used to supply power to a passive load consisting of a resistance R_g and a reactance X_L. For maximum power to be delivered from the generator to the load, the value of X_L is equal to: [NCERT Exemplar]
    (a) zero   (b) X_g
    (c) $-X_g$ (d) R_g
45. When a voltage measuring device is connected to AC mains, the meter shows the steady input voltage of 220 V. This means: [NCERT Exemplar]
    (a) Input voltage cannot be AC voltage, but a DC voltage.
    (b) maximum input voltage is 220 V.
    (c) the meter reads not v but $<v^2>$ and is calibrated to read $\sqrt{<v^2>}$
    (d) the pointer of the meter is stuck by some mechanical defect.
46. To reduce the resonant frequency in an LCR series circuit with a generator: [NCERT Exemplar]
    (a) the generator frequency should be reduced.
    (b) another capacitor should be added in parallel to the first.
    (c) the iron core of the inductor should be removed.
    (d) dielectric in the capacitor should be removed.
47. Which of the following combinations should be selected for better tuning of an LCR circuit used for communication? [NCERT Exemplar]
    (a) R = 20 Ω, L = 1.5 H, C = 35 μF.
    (b) R = 25 Ω, L = 2.5 H, C = 45 μF.
    (c) R = 15 Ω, L = 3.5 H, C = 30 μF.
    (d) R = 25 Ω, L = 1.5 H, C = 45 μF.
48. An inductor of reactance 1 Ω and a resistor of 2 Ω are connected in series to the terminals of a 6 V (rms) AC source. The power dissipated in the circuit is:
    [NCERT Exemplar]
    (a) 8 W   (b) 12 W
    (c) 14.4 W   (d) 18 W
49. The output of a step-down transformer is measured to be 24 V when connected to a 12 W light bulb. The value of the peak current is: [NCERT Exemplar]
    (a) $\frac{1}{\sqrt{2}}$ A   (b) $\sqrt{2}$ A
    (c) 2 A   (d) $2\sqrt{2}$ A
50. The selectivity of a series LCR a.c. circuit in large, when [CBSE 2020]
    (a) L is large, R is large
    (b) L is small and R is small
    (c) L is large and R is small
    (d) L = R
51. The phase difference between the current and the voltage in series LCR circuit at resonance is: [CBSE 2020]
    (a) π   (b) π/2
    (c) π/3   (d) zero

Directions: In the following questions, a statement of assertion is followed by a statement of reason. Mark the correct choice as:
(a) If both assertion and reason are true and reason is the correct explanation of assertion.
(b) If both assertion and reason are true, but reason is not the correct explanation of assertion.
(c) If assertion is true but reason is false.
(d) If both assertion and reason are false.

52. **Assertion:** AC is more dangerous in use than DC.
    Reason: It is because the peak value of AC is greater than indicated value.
53. **Assertion:** Average value of AC over a complete cycle is always zero.

Reason: Average value of AC is always defined over half cycle.

54. **Assertion:** The alternating current lags behind the emf by a phase angle of $\frac{\pi}{2}$, when AC flows through an inductor.
    Reason: The inductive reactance increases as the frequency of AC source decreases.

55. **Assertion:** Capacitor serves as a block for DC and offers an easy path to AC.
    Reason: Capacitive reactance is inversely proportional to frequency.

56. **Assertion:** In series LCR resonance circuit, the impedance is equal to the ohmic resistance.
    Reason: At resonance, the inductive reactance exceeds the capacitive reactance.

57. **Assertion:** An alternating current shows magnetic effect.
    Reason: Alternating current varies with time.

58. **Assertion:** In series LCR circuit resonance can take place.
    Reason: Resonance takes place if inductance and capacitive reactance are equal and opposite.

59. **Assertion:** Power factor correction is must in heavy machinery.
    Reason: A low power factor implies larger power loss in transmission.

60. **Assertion:** Choke coil is preferred over a resistor to adjust current in an AC circuit.
    Reason: Power factor for inductance is zero.

61. **Assertion:** When AC circuit contain resistor only, its power is minimum.
    Reason: Power of a circuit is independent of phase angle.

62. **Assertion:** A transformer cannot work on DC supply.
    Reason: DC changes neither in magnitude nor in direction.

63. **Assertion:** A laminated core is used in transformers to increase eddy currents.
    Reason: The efficiency of a transformer increases with increase in eddy currents.

64. **Assertion:** Soft iron is used as a core of transformer.
    Reason: Area of hysteresis loop for soft iron is small.

65. **Assertion:** An ac generator is based on the phenomenon of electromagnetic induction.
    Reason: In single coil, we consider self-induction only.

66. The figure shows a series LCR circuit:

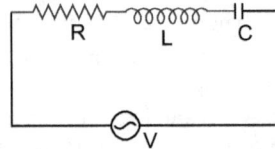

For such a circuit, the impedance Z is given by.
$Z = \sqrt{R^2 + (X_L - X_C)^2}$ where X_L and X_C are inductive and capacitive resistances respectively. As the frequency of a.c. is increased, at a particular frequency. X_L become, equal to X_C. For that frequency maximum current occurs. This is because impedance becomes equal to its least value R. Current through the circuit I = V/R. The circuit behaves like a pure resistive circuit and current and voltage will be in phase. This is called resonance. Frequency of a.c. at which resonance occurs is called resonant frequency. If frequency is less than the resonant frequency, then the capacitive reactance will be more. The circuit will be capacitive in nature and current leads voltage. On the other hand, if frequency is more than the resonant frequency inductive reactance will be more. Circuit is inductive in nature and current lags the voltage.

An LCR circuit with a resistance 50 Ω has a resonant angular frequency 2×10^3 rad/s. At resonance, the voltage across the resistance and inductance are 25 V and 20 V respectively. Then

(i) The value of inductance is:
  (a) 20 mH (b) 10 mH
  (c) 40 mH (d) 25 mH

(ii) The value of capacitance is:
  (a) 25 µF (b) 1 µF
  (c) 2 µF   (d) 12.5 µF

(iii) The impedance at resonance is:
  (a) 50 Ω   (b) 16 Ω
  (c) 64 Ω   (d) 25 Ω

(iv) Which of the following angular frequency of a.c. will see the circuit as inductive in nature?
  (a) 1.5×10^3 rad/s (b) 10^3 rad/s
  (c) 2×10^3 rad/s   (d) 5×10^3 rad/s

(v) At angular frequency 10^3 rad/s, the nature of circuit:
  (a) Inductive   (b) Capacitive
  (c) Resistive   (d) None of these

67. A series LCR circuit consist of series combination of a resistance, a inductor and a capacitance. A similar series LCR circuit is shown in figure. The given series LCR circuit is connected across a 200 V 60 Hz line consisting of capacitive reactance 30 Ω a non-inductive resistor of 44 Ω and a coil of inductive reactance 90 Ω and resistance 36 Ω.

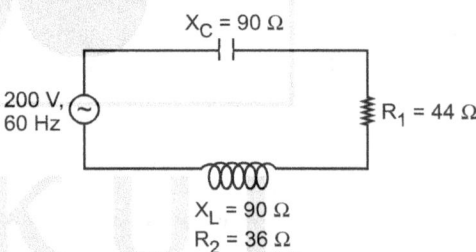

(i) Calculate the total impedance of the circuit.
  (a) 1000 Ω (b) 100 Ω
  (c) 3600 Ω (d) 4900 Ω

(ii) Calculate the current flowing in the circuit.
  (a) 1 A (b) 5 A
  (c) 2 A (d) 10 A

(iii) What is the impedance of the coil?
  (a) 97 Ω   (b) 87 Ω
  (c) 100 Ω (d) 110 Ω

(iv) What is the potential difference across the coil?
  (a) 194 V (b) 186 V
  (c) 180 V (d) 190 V

(v) Calculate the power dissipiated in the coil.
(a) 100 W (b) 122 W
(c) 130 W (d) 144 W

68. A transformer is an electrical device which is used for changing the a.c. voltage. It is based on the phenomenon of mutual induction i.e. whenever the amount of magnetic flux linked with a coil changes, an e.m.f. is induced in the neighbouring coil. For an ideal transformer, the resistance of the primary and secondary winding are negligible.

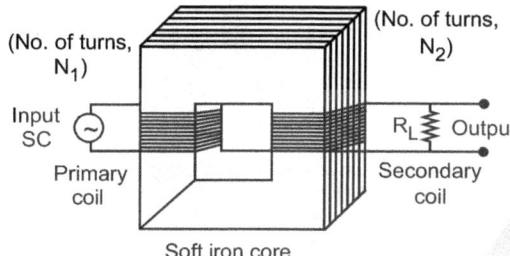

It can be shown that $\dfrac{E_s}{E_p} = \dfrac{I_p}{I_s} = \dfrac{n_s}{n_p} = k$

where the symbols have their standard meanings.
For a step up transformer, $n_s > n_p$; $E_s > E_p$; $k > 1$;
$\therefore I_s < I_p$
For a step down transformer, $n_s < n_p$; $E_s < E_p$; $k < 1$
The above relations are on the assumptions that efficiency of transformer is 100%

Infact, efficiency $\eta = \dfrac{\text{output power}}{\text{input power}} = \dfrac{E_s I_s}{E_p I_p}$

(i) Which of the following quantity remains constant in an ideal transformer?
(a) Current (b) Voltage
(c) Power (d) All of these

(ii) Transformer is used to:
(a) convert ac to dc voltage
(b) convert dc to ac voltage
(c) obtain desired dc power
(d) obtain desired ac voltage and current

(iii) The number of turns in primary coil a transformer is 20 and the number of turns in a secondary is 10. If the voltage across the primary is 220 ac V. What is the voltage across secondary?
(a) 100 ac V (b) 120 ac V
(c) 110 ac V (d) 220 ac V

(iv) In a transformer the number of primary turns is four times that of the secondary turns. Its primary is connected to an a.c. source of voltage V. Then
(a) current through its secondary is about four times that of the current through its primary.
(b) voltage across its secondary is about four times that of voltage across its primary.
(c) voltage across its secondary is about two times that of voltage across its primary.
(d) voltage across its secondary is about $\dfrac{1}{2\sqrt{2}}$ times that of the voltage across its primary.

(v) A transformer is used to light 100 W–110 V lamp from 220 V mains. If the main current is 0.5 A, the efficiency of the transformer is:

(a) 95% (b) 99%
(c) 90% (d) 96%

69. A series LCR circuit is connected to an a.c. source of variable frequency. A suitable phasor diagram for the amplitude of the current and phase angle has been mentioned below. Answer the following questions based on the concept of LCR circuit

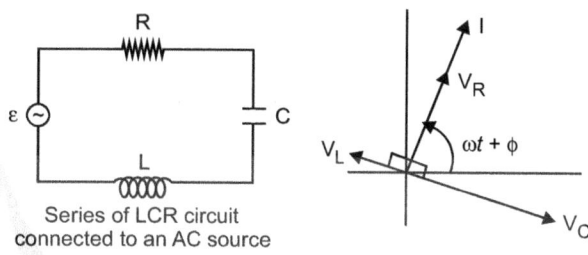

Series of LCR circuit connected to an AC source

(i) If $X_C > X_L$ and ϕ is positive, the circuit is predominantly
(a) Inductive (b) Capacitive
(c) Neutral (d) None of these

(ii) If $X_C < X_L$ and ϕ is negative, the circuit is predominantly
(a) Inductive (b) Capacitive
(c) Neutral (d) None of these

(iii) At resonant frequency
(a) $\omega - \sqrt{\dfrac{L}{C}}$ (b) $\omega - \dfrac{1}{\sqrt{LC}}$
(c) $\omega - \sqrt{LC}$ (d) None of these

(iv) At resonant frequency the impedance of the LCR circuit is:
(a) Maximum
(b) Minimum
(c) $z = \sqrt{R^2 + (X_C - X_L)^2}$
(d) None of these

(v) The ratio $\dfrac{\omega_0 L}{R}$ is also called the quality factor, Q of the circuit. The larger the value of Q
(a) The sharper the resonance
(b) The less sharp the resonance
(c) Resonance is independent of the value of Q
(d) None of these

70. **Step-down Transformer in the Transmission of Electric Power**

Step-down transformers are used to decrease or step-down voltage. These are used when voltage need to be lowered for use in homes and factories.

A small town with a demand of 800 kW of electric power at 220 V is situated 15 km away from an electric plant generating power at 440 V. The resistance of the two wire line carrying is 0.5 Ω per km. The town gets power from the line through a 4000–220 V step-down transformer at a sub-station in the town.

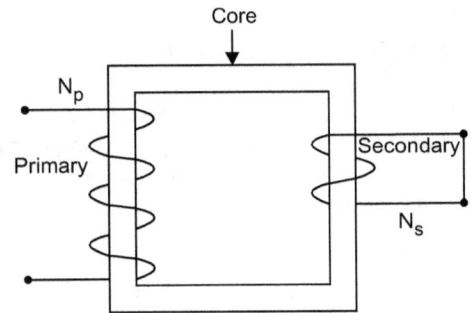

(i) The value of total resistance of the wires is :
(a) 25 Ω (b) 30 Ω
(c) 35 Ω (d) 15 Ω

(ii) The line power loss in the form of heat is :
(a) 550 kW (b) 650 kW
(c) 600 kW (d) 700 kW

(iii) How much power must be plant supply, assuming there is negligible power loss due to leakage ?
(a) 600 kW (b) 1600 kW
(c) 500 W   (d) 1400 kW

(iv) The voltage drop in the power line is :
(a) 1700 V (b) 3000 V
(c) 2000 V (d) 2800 V

(v) The total value of voltage transmitted from the plant is :
(a) 500 V   (b) 4000 V
(c) 3000 V (d) 7000 V

Answers

1. (d) Average value of complete cycle is zero
Explanation: In DC ammeter, a coil is free to rotate in the magnetic field of a fixed magnet. If an alternating current is passed through such a coil, the torque will reverse its direction each time the current changes direction and the average value of the torque will be zero.

2. (a) rms current
Explanation: We know that,
$$\text{rms current} = \frac{I_0}{\sqrt{2}}$$

3. (b) $\frac{1}{400}$ s
Explanation: The current takes $\frac{T}{4}$ s to reach the peak value.
In the given question,
$$\frac{2\pi}{T} = 200\pi$$
$$\Rightarrow T = \frac{1}{100} \text{ s}$$
∴ Time to reach the peak value = $\frac{1}{400}$ s.

4. (c) $2\sqrt{2} : \pi$
Explanation: We know that,
$$I_{rms} = \frac{I_0}{\sqrt{2}}$$
and $I_m = \frac{2I_0}{\pi}$
∴ $\frac{I_m}{I_{rms}} = \frac{2\sqrt{2}}{\pi}$

5. (a) $5\sqrt{3}$ V
Explanation: We know that,
$$E = E_0 \cos \omega t$$
$$= E_0 \cos \frac{2\pi t}{T}$$
$$= 10 \cos \frac{2\pi \times 50 \times 1}{600}$$
$$= 10 \cos \frac{\pi}{6}$$
$$= 5\sqrt{3} \text{ V.}$$

6. (d) 84.8 V
Explanation: We know that,
$$V_{rms} = \frac{V_0}{\sqrt{2}}$$
$$= \frac{120}{1.414}$$
$$= 84.8 \text{ V.}$$

7. (c) 7 A
Explanation: Since,
$$I_{rms} = \frac{E_{rms}}{R}$$
$$= \frac{200}{40}$$
$$= 5 \text{ A}$$
∴ $I_a = I_{rms} \sqrt{2}$
$$= 7.07 \text{ A.}$$

8. (c) Voltage leads the current by $\frac{\pi}{2}$
Explanation: In an inductor voltage leads the current by $\frac{\pi}{2}$ or current lags the voltage by $\frac{\pi}{2}$.

9. (a) 2.5×10^{-3} s
Explanation: Peak value to rms value means, current becomes $\frac{1}{\sqrt{2}}$ times.
If peak is at $t = 0$, current is of the form.
$$I = I_0 \cos 100\pi t$$
$$\Rightarrow \frac{1}{\sqrt{2}} \times I_0 = I_0 \cos 100\pi t$$
$$\Rightarrow \cos \frac{\pi}{4} = \cos 100\pi t$$

$\Rightarrow \qquad t = \dfrac{1}{400}$ s

$= 2.5 \times 10^{-3}$ s.

10. (c) 5×10^{-3} s and 14.14 A

Explanation: Time taken by the current to reach the maximum value.

$t = \dfrac{T}{4}$

$= \dfrac{1}{4v}$

$= \dfrac{1}{4 \times 50}$

$= 5 \times 10^{-3}$ s

$I_0 = I_{rms}\sqrt{2}$

$= 10\sqrt{2}$

$= 14.14$ A.

11. (c) $5\sqrt{2}$ V

Explanation: According to questions,

$E = 8 \sin \omega t + 6 \sin 2\omega t$

$\Rightarrow \qquad E_0 = \sqrt{8^2 + 6^2}$

$= 10$ V

$E_{rms} = \dfrac{10}{\sqrt{2}}$

$= 5\sqrt{2}$ V.

12. (d) $\sqrt{R^2 + 4\pi^2 f^2 L^2}$

Explanation: We know that

$Z = \sqrt{R^2 + X_L^2}$

and $\qquad X_L = \omega L$

$\omega = 2\pi f$

$\therefore \qquad Z = \sqrt{R^2 + 4\pi^2 f^2 L^2}$

13. (b) 19 Hz and 170 V

Explanation: Given,

$V = 240 \sin 120t$ V

Comparing with $V = V_0 \sin \omega t$

$V_0 = 240$ V

$\omega = 120$ rad/s

$V_{rms} = \dfrac{V_0}{\sqrt{2}}$

$= \dfrac{240}{\sqrt{2}} = 169.7$

≈ 170 V

$\omega = 2\pi f$

$f = \dfrac{\omega}{2\pi}$

$= \dfrac{120}{2\pi}$

$= 19$ Hz.

14. (b) 2.828 A

Explanation: Given,

$e = 80 \sin 100\pi t$ ...(i)

Standard equation of instantaneous voltage is given by

$e = e_m \sin \omega t$ ...(ii)

Compare (i) and (ii), we get

$e_m = 80$ V where e_m is the voltage amplitude.

Current amplitude,

$I_m = \dfrac{e_m}{Z}$

$= \dfrac{80}{20} = 4$ A

where Z = impendence.

$I_{rms} = \dfrac{4}{\sqrt{2}}$

$= \dfrac{4\sqrt{2}}{2}$

$= 2\sqrt{2}$

$= 2.828$ A.

15. (a) 212.1 Ω; 1.037 A

Explanation: We know that,

$X_C = \dfrac{1}{\omega C}$

$= \dfrac{1}{2\pi v C}$

$= \dfrac{1}{2 \times \dfrac{22}{7} \times 50 \times 15 \times 10^{-6}}$

$= 212.1$ Ω

$I_{rms} = \dfrac{E_{rms}}{X_C}$

$= \dfrac{220}{212.1}$

$= 1.037$ A.

16. (b) 20 mA

Explanation: We know that,

$V_{rms} = \dfrac{200\sqrt{2}}{\sqrt{2}}$

$= 200$ V

$I_{rms} = \dfrac{V_{rms}}{X_C} = \dfrac{V_{rms}}{1/WC}$

$= \dfrac{200}{\dfrac{1}{100 \times 10^{-6}}}$

$= 2 \times 10^{-2}$

$= 20$ mA.

17. (a) 50 Ω, 4 A

Explanation: We know that

$Z = \sqrt{R^2 + X_L^2}$

$= \sqrt{R^2 + (2\pi f L)^2}$

$= \sqrt{(30)^2 + \left(2\pi \times 50 \times \dfrac{0.4}{\pi}\right)^2}$

$$= \sqrt{900 + 1600}$$
$$= 50 \, \Omega$$
$$i = \frac{V}{Z}$$
$$= \frac{200}{50}$$
$$= 4 \, A.$$

18. (d) P = 0

    Explanation: We know that power consumed in AC circuit is given by
    $$P = E_{rms} I_{rms} \cos \phi$$
    Here, $E = E_a \sin \omega t$
    $$I = I_0 \sin \left(\omega t - \frac{\pi}{2} \right)$$
    which implies that the phase difference,
    $$\phi = \frac{\pi}{2}$$
    $\therefore$
    $$P = E_{rms} I_{rms} \cos \frac{\pi}{2}$$
    $$= 0 \qquad \ldots \left(\because \cos \frac{\pi}{2} = 0 \right)$$

19. (a) 0 V

    Explanation: Since the phase difference between L & C is π.
    $\therefore$ Now voltage difference across LC
    $$= 50 - 50$$
    $$= 0.$$

20. (a) 159.2 Ω

    Explanation: We know that
    $$X_C = \frac{1}{\omega C}$$
    $$= \frac{1}{2\pi f C}$$
    $$= \frac{1}{2 \times 3.14 \times 100 \times 10^{-5}}$$
    $$= 159.2 \, \Omega.$$

21. (a) $\frac{f}{2}$

    Explanation: Since,
    $$f = \frac{1}{2\pi \sqrt{LC}}$$
    $\Rightarrow$ $f \propto \frac{1}{\sqrt{C}}$

22. (d) 10^4

    Explanation: At parallel resonance,
    $$Z_{max} = \frac{L}{RC}$$
    $$= \frac{10 \times 10^{-3}}{10 \times 0.1 \times 10^{-6}}$$
    $$= 10^4 \, \Omega.$$

23. (b)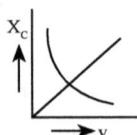

    Explanation: We know that,
    $$X_C = \frac{1}{\omega C}$$
    $$= \frac{1}{2\pi v C}$$
    $$X_C \propto \frac{1}{v}.$$

24. (c) It decreases exponentially.

    Explanation: The current in RC circuit decreases both during charging as well as discharging.

25. (b) $10\sqrt{10} \, \Omega$

    Explanation: We know that,
    $$Z = \sqrt{R^2 + \omega^2 L^2}$$
    $$= \sqrt{R^2 + 4\pi^2 f^2 L^2}$$
    $$= \sqrt{1^2 + 4 \times (10)(50)^2 (0.1)^2}$$
    $\therefore$
    $$Z = \sqrt{1 + 1000}$$
    $$= \sqrt{1001}$$
    $$\approx 10\sqrt{10}.$$

26. (b) $\omega L = \frac{1}{\omega C}$

    Explanation: When $\omega L = \frac{1}{\omega C}$, the circuit is in resonance. Impedance is equal to resistance alone.

27. (a) 1.1×10^3 rad s^{-1}

    Explanation: Here,
    $$C = 30 \, \mu F$$
    $$= 30 \times 10^{-6} \, F$$
    $$L = 27 \, mH$$
    $$= 27 \times 10^{-3} \, H$$
    $\therefore$
    $$\omega = \frac{1}{\sqrt{LC}}$$
    $$= \frac{1}{\sqrt{27 \times 10^{-3} \times 30 \times 10^{-6}}}$$
    $$= \frac{1}{\sqrt{81 \times 10^{-8}}}$$
    $$= \frac{10^4}{9}$$
    $$= 1.1 \times 10^3 \, rad \, s^{-1}.$$

28. (d) $\frac{1}{\sqrt{2}}$

    Explanation: Since
    $$v = \frac{1}{2\pi} \sqrt{\frac{1}{LC}}$$
    $\Rightarrow$
    $$v \propto \frac{1}{\sqrt{C}}$$

29. (d) All of these

    Explanation: Since quality factor,
    $$Q = \frac{1}{R}\sqrt{\frac{L}{C}}$$

30. (d) Zero

    Explanation: Average power in AC circuit is given by
    $$P = V_{rms} I_{rms} \cos\phi$$
    For pure capacitive circuit,
    $$\phi = 90°, \cos 90° = 0$$
    So, $P = 0$.

31. (b) $i^2 R$

    Explanation: At resonance,
    $$\omega L = \frac{1}{\omega C}$$
    and $I = \frac{E}{R}$

    So power dissipated in circuit is,
    $$P = I^2 R.$$

32. (d) 90 W

    Explanation: We know that,
    $$P = \frac{V_{rms}^2}{R}$$
    $$= \frac{(30)^2}{10} = 90 \text{ W}$$

33. (c) $\frac{v_0 i_0}{4}$

    Explanation: We know that,
    $$P_{avg} = V_{rms} I_{rms} \cos\phi$$
    $$= \left(\frac{v_0}{\sqrt{2}}\right)\left(\frac{I_0}{\sqrt{2}}\right)\left(\cos\frac{\pi}{3}\right)$$
    $$= \frac{v_0 I_0}{4}.$$

34. (a) Zero

    Explanation: Power,
    $$P = I_{rms} \times V_{rms} \times \cos\phi$$
    In the given problem, the phase difference between voltage and current is $\frac{\pi}{2}$. Hence
    $$P = I_{rms} \times V_{rms} \times \cos\left(\frac{\pi}{2}\right)$$
    $$= 0.$$

35. (d) $\frac{R}{\sqrt{R^2 + L^2\omega^2}}$

    Explanation: Power factor is given by,
    $$\cos\theta = \frac{R}{Z}$$
    $$= \frac{R}{\sqrt{R^2 + L^2\omega^2}}$$

36. (d) Obtain a suitable AC voltage

    Explanation: A transformer is a device to convert alternating current at high voltage into low voltage and vice versa.

37. (b) Iron loss

    Explanation: Iron loss is the energy loss in the form of heat due to the formation of eddy currents in the iron core of the transformer.

38. (d) Reduce the energy loss due to eddy currents

    Explanation: The lamination on the core of the transformer increases its resistance which reduces eddy current.

39. (d) 100 V

    Explanation: Transformation ratio
    $$k = \frac{V_S}{V_P}$$
    $$\Rightarrow \frac{5}{3} = \frac{V_S}{60}$$
    $$\Rightarrow V_S = 100 \text{ V}$$

40. (d) 0 V

    Explanation: A transformer does not work on DC. Therefore, voltage across the secondary will be zero.

41. (a) 200 V

    Explanation: According to the question,
    $$N_P = 400$$
    $$N_S = 2000$$
    and $V_S = 1000 \text{ V}$

    We know, $\frac{V_P}{V_S} = \frac{N_P}{N_S}$
    $$V_P = \frac{V_S \times N_P}{N_S}$$
    $$= \frac{1000 \times 400}{2000}$$
    $$= 200 \text{ V}.$$

42. (b) 3 A

    Explanation: We know that,
    $$\eta = \frac{E_S I_S}{E_P I_P}$$
    Here, $\eta = 80\%$
    $$= \frac{80}{100}$$
    $$E_S = 120 \text{ V}$$
    $$I_S = 20 \text{ A}$$
    $$E_P = 1000 \text{ V}$$
    $$\therefore \frac{80}{100} = \frac{120 \times 20}{1000 \times I_P}$$
    or $I_P = 3$ A.

43. (b) $5\sqrt{\frac{3}{2}}$ A

    Explanation: According to the question,
    $$f = 50 \text{ Hz}$$
    $$I_{rms} = 5 \text{ A}$$
    $$t = \frac{1}{300} \text{ s}$$
    $$I_0 = \sqrt{2}(I_{rms})$$

From
$$= 5\sqrt{2}$$
$$= 5\sqrt{2} \text{ A}$$
$$I = I_0 \sin \omega t$$
$$= 5\sqrt{2} \sin 2\pi f t$$
$$= 5\sqrt{2} \sin 2\pi \times 50 \times \frac{1}{300}$$
$$= 5\sqrt{2} \sin \frac{\pi}{3}$$
$$= 5\sqrt{2} \times \frac{\sqrt{3}}{2}$$
$$= 5\sqrt{\frac{3}{2}} \text{ A}.$$

44. (c) $-X_g$
    Explanation: For maximum power to be delivered from the generator (or internal reactance X_g) to the load (of reactance, X_L).
    $\Rightarrow X_L + X_g = 0$ (The total reactance must vanish)
    $\Rightarrow X_L = -X_g$.

45. (c) the meter reads not v but $<v^2>$ and is calibrated to read $\sqrt{<v^2>}$
    Explanation: The voltmeter connected to AC mains calibrated to read *rms* value $\sqrt{<v^2>}$.

46. (b) another capacitor should be added in parallel to the first.
    Explanation: Resonant frequency in an LCR circuit is given by,
    $$\nu_0 = \frac{1}{2\pi\sqrt{LC}}$$
    If L or C increases, the resonant frequency, will reduce.
    To increase capacitance, we must connected another capacitor parallel to it.

47. (c) R = 15 Ω, L = 3.5 H, C = 30 μF.
    Explanation: We know quality factor should be high for better turning.
    Quality factor (Q) for an LCR circuit is
    $$Q = \frac{1}{R}\sqrt{\frac{L}{C}}$$
    where R is the resistance, L is the inductance and C is the capacitance of the circuit.
    For high Q factor R should be low, L should be high and C should be low. These conditions are best satisfied by the values given in option (c).

48. (c) 14.4 W
    Explanation: According to the questions,
    $$X_L = 1 \text{ Ω}, R = 2 \text{ Ω}$$
    $$E_{rms} = 6 \text{ V}$$
    Average power dissipated in the circuit,
    $$P_{av} = E_{rms} I_{rms} \cos\phi \quad ...(i)$$
    $$I_{rms} = \frac{E_{rms}}{Z}$$
    $$Z = \sqrt{R^2 + X_L^2}$$

$$I_{rms} = \frac{6}{\sqrt{5}} \text{ A}$$
$$\cos\phi = \frac{R}{Z}$$
$$= \frac{2}{\sqrt{5}}$$
$$P_{av} = 6 \times \frac{6}{\sqrt{5}} \times \frac{2}{\sqrt{5}} \quad \text{[from (i)]}$$
$$= \frac{72}{\sqrt{5}\sqrt{5}}$$
$$= \frac{72}{5}$$
$$= 14.4 \text{ W}.$$

49. (a) $\frac{1}{\sqrt{2}}$ A
    Explanation: According to the problem output/secondary voltage $V_S = 24$ V
    Power associated with secondary $P_S = 12$ W
    $$I_S = \frac{P_S}{V_S}$$
    $$= \frac{12}{24}$$
    $$= 0.5 \text{ A}$$
    Amplitude of the current in the secondary winding
    $$I_0 = I_S\sqrt{2}$$
    $$= (0.5)(1.414)$$
    $$= 0.707$$
    $$= \frac{1}{\sqrt{2}} \text{ A}.$$

50. (c) L is Large and R is Small.
    Explanation: Since, selectivity depends on the quality of resonance. The quality factor is given by $Q = \omega_0 L/R$. High value of quality factor make sure that the resonance curve is sharp, sharper the resonance curve, more selective is the LCR circuit.

51. (d) zero
    Explanation: At resonance, the circuit is purely resistive and there is no phase difference between current and voltage.

52. (a) AC is more dangerous in use than DC. It is because the peak value of AC is greater than indicated value.

53. (b) The mean or average value of alternating current or emf during a half cycle is given by,
    $$I_m = 0.636 I_0$$
    or
    $$E_m = 0.636 E_0$$
    During the next half cycle, the mean value of AC will be equal in magnitude but opposite in direction. For this reason the average value of AC over a complete cycle is always zero. So the average value is always defined over a half cycle of AC.

54. (c) When AC flows through an inductor current lags behind the emf, by phase of $\frac{\pi}{2}$ inductive reactance,

$X_L = \omega L$
$= 2\pi f L$

So, when frequency increases correspondingly inductive reactance also increases.

55. (a) The capacitive reactance of capacitor is given by,

$$X_C = \frac{1}{\omega C}$$

$$= \frac{1}{2\pi f C}$$

So this is infinite for DC ($f = 0$) and has a very small value for AC. Therefore, a capacitor blocks DC.

56. (c) In series resonance circuit, inductive reactance is equal to capacitive reactance.

i.e., $\omega L = \dfrac{1}{\omega C}$

$\therefore$ $Z = \sqrt{R^2 + \left(\omega L - \dfrac{1}{\omega C}\right)^2}$

$= R$

57. (b) Like direct current, an alternating current also produces magnetic field. But the magnitude and direction of the field goes on changing continuously with time.

58. (a) At resonant frequency,

$X_L = X_C$
$Z = R$ (minimum)

Therefore, current in the circuit is maximum.

59. (b) A heavy machinery requires a large power.
The average power is given by,

$$P_{av} = E_{rms} I_{rms} \cos\phi$$

The required power can be supplied to the heavy machinery either by supplying larger current or by improving power factor. The first method is costly therefore second one is used.

60. (a) We can use a capacitor of suitable capacitance as a choke coil, because average power consumed per cycle in an ideal capacitor is zero. Therefore, like a choke coil, a condenser can reduce AC without power dissipation.

61. (d) The power of an AC circuit is given by,

$$P = EI \cos\phi$$

where, $\cos\phi$ is power factor and ϕ is phase angle. In case of circuit containing resistance only, phase angle is zero and power factor is equal to one. Therefore, power is maximum in case of circuit containing resistor only.

62. (a) Transformer works on AC only, AC changes in magnitude as well as in direction and induces emf.

63. (d) Large eddy currents are produced in non-laminated iron core of the transformer by the induced emf, as the resistance of bulk iron core is very small. By using thin iron sheets as core the resistance is increased. Laminating the core substantially reduces the eddy currents. Eddy current heats up the core of the transformer. More the eddy currents greater is the loss of energy and the efficiency goes down.

64. (a) Hysteresis loss in the core of transformer is directly proportional to the hysteresis loop area of the core material. Since, soft iron has narrow hysteresis loop area, that is why soft iron core is used in the transformer.

65. (b) According to electromagnetic induction, whenever the magnetic flux changes an emf will be induced in the coil.

66. (i) (a) $X_L = \dfrac{V_L}{I}$

$I = \dfrac{V_R}{R} = \dfrac{25}{50} = \dfrac{1}{2}$

$X_L = \dfrac{20}{1/2} = 40\,\Omega$

But $X_L = \omega L \Rightarrow L = \dfrac{X_L}{\omega} = \dfrac{40}{2\times 10^3}$

$= 20 \times 10^{-3} = 20$ mH

(ii) (d) $\omega^2 = \dfrac{1}{LC} \Rightarrow C = \dfrac{1}{\omega^2 L}$

$= \dfrac{1}{(2\times 10^3)^2 \times 20 \times 10^{-3}} = 12.5\,\mu F$

(iii) (a) At resonance, the impedance equal just resistance.

(iv) (d) For inductive nature $\omega > \omega_r$.

(v) (b) If $\omega < \omega_r$, the circuit will be capacitive in nature.

67. (i) (b) $Z = \sqrt{(R_1 + R_2)^2 + (X_L - X_C)^2}$

$= \sqrt{(44 + 36)^2 + (90 - 30)^2} = 100\,\Omega$

(ii) (c) Current, $I = \dfrac{V}{Z} = \dfrac{200}{100} = 2$ A

(iii) (a) Impedance of the coil. $Z_L = \sqrt{R_2^2 + X_L^2}$

$= \sqrt{(36)^2 + (90)^2} = 97\,\Omega$

(iv) (a) Potential difference aross the coil, $V_L = IZ_L$
$= 2 \times 97 = 194$ V

(v) (d) Power dissipated in the inductive coil.
$P = I^2 R_2$
$= (2)^2 \times 36 = 144$ W

68. (i) (c) In an ideal transformer, there is no power loss. The efficiency of an ideal transformer is $\eta = 1$ (i.e. 100%) i.e. input power = output power.

(ii) (d) Transformer is used to obtain desired ac voltage and current.

(iii) (c) For a transformer, $\dfrac{V_s}{V_p} = \dfrac{N_s}{N_p}$

where N denotes number of turns and V = voltage.

$\therefore \dfrac{V_s}{220} = \dfrac{10}{20}$

$\therefore V_s = 110$ ac V

(iv) (a) In a transformer the primary and secondary currents are related by

$$I_s = \left(\frac{N_p}{N_s}\right) I_p$$

and the voltages are related by

$$V_s = \left(\frac{N_s}{N_p}\right) V_p$$

where subscripts p and s refer to the primary and secondary of the transformer.

Here, $\quad V_p = V_s \dfrac{N_p}{N_s} = 4$

$\therefore \quad I_s = 4 I_p$

and $\quad V_s = \left(\dfrac{1}{4}\right) V = \dfrac{V}{4}$

(v) (c) The efficiency of the transformer is

$$\eta = \frac{\text{Output power }(P_{out})}{\text{Input power }(P_{in})} \times 100$$

Here, $P_{out} = 100$ W, $P_{in} = (220$ V$)(0.5$ A$) = 110$ W

$\therefore \quad \eta = \dfrac{100 \text{ W}}{110 \text{ W}} \times 100 = 90\%$

69. (i) (b) Capacitive
    (ii) (a) Inductive
    (iii) (b) $\omega = \dfrac{1}{\sqrt{LC}}$
    (iv) (b) Minimum
    (v) (a) The sharper the resonance

70. (i) (d) Resistance of the two wire lines carrying power = 0.5 Ω/km
    Total resistance = (15 + 15) 0.5 = 15 Ω
    (ii) (c) Line power loss = $I^2 R$
    RMS current in the coil,
    $$I = \frac{P}{V_1} = \frac{800 \times 10^3}{4000} = 200 \text{ A}$$
    ∴ Power loss = $(200)^2 \times 15 = 600$ kW
    (iii) (d) Assuming that the power loss is negligible due to the leakage of the current.
    The total power supplied by the plant
    = 800 kW + 600 kW = 1400 kW
    (iv) (b) Voltage drop in the power line = IR
    = 200 × 15 = 3000 V
    (v) (d) Total voltage transmitted from the plant
    = 3000 V + 4000 V = 7000 V

CHEMISTRY

SYLLABUS
Biology (Code No. 043)
Course Structure

S. No.	Units	Periods	Marks
1.	Solid State	8	10
2.	Solutions	8	
3.	p-Block Elements	7	10
4.	Haloalkanes and Haloarenes	9	15
5.	Alcohols, Phenols and Ethers	9	
6.	Biomolecules	8	
Total		49	35

Chapter-1: Solid State

Classification of solids based on different binding forces: molecular, ionic, covalent and metallic solids, amorphous and crystalline solids (elementary idea). Unit cell in two dimensional and three dimensional lattices, calculation of density of unit cell, packing in solids, packing efficiency, voids, number of atoms per unit cell in a cubic unit cell, point defects.

Chapter-2: Solutions

Types of solutions, expression of concentration of solutions of solids in liquids, solubility of gases in liquids, solid solutions, Raoult's law, colligative properties - relative lowering of vapour pressure, elevation of boiling point, depression of freezing point, osmotic pressure, determination of molecular masses using colligative properties.

Chapter-7: p-Block Elements

Group -15 Elements: General introduction, electronic configuration, occurrence, oxidation states, trends in physical and chemical properties; Nitrogen preparation properties and uses; compounds of Nitrogen: preparation and properties of Ammonia and Nitric Acid.

Group 16 Elements: General introduction, electronic configuration, oxidation states, occurrence, trends in physical and chemical properties, dioxygen: preparation, properties and uses, classification of Oxides, Ozone, Sulphur -allotropic forms; compounds of Sulphur: preparation properties and uses of Sulphur dioxide, Sulphuric Acid: properties and uses; Oxoacids of Sulphur (Structures only).

Group 17 Elements: General introduction, electronic configuration, oxidation states, occurrence, trends in physical and chemical properties; compounds of halogens, Preparation, properties and uses of Chlorine and Hydrochloric acid, interhalogen compounds, Oxoacids of halogens (structures only).

Group 18 Elements: General introduction, electronic configuration, occurrence, trends in physical and chemical properties, uses.

Chapter-10: Haloalkanes and Haloarenes

Haloalkanes: Nomenclature, nature of C–X bond, physical and chemical properties, optical rotation mechanism of substitution reactions.

Haloarenes: Nature of C–X bond, substitution reactions (Directive influence of halogen in monosubstituted compounds only).

Chapter-11: Alcohols, Phenols and Ethers

Alcohols: Nomenclature, methods of preparation, physical and chemical properties (of primary alcohols only), identification of primary, secondary and tertiary alcohols, mechanism of dehydration.

Phenols: Nomenclature, methods of preparation, physical and chemical properties, acidic nature of phenol, electrophillic substitution reactions, uses of phenols.

Ethers: Nomenclature, methods of preparation, physical and chemical properties, uses.

Chapter-14: Biomolecules

Carbohydrates - Classification (aldoses and ketoses), monosaccaharides (glucose and fructose), D-L configuration Proteins-Elementary idea of - amino acids, peptide bond, polypeptides, proteins, structure of proteins - primary, secondary, tertiary structure and quaternary structures (qualitative idea only), denaturation of proteins. Nucleic Acids: DNA and RNA

Chapter 1

Solid State

1. Copper has the face centered cubic structure. The coordination number of each ion is:
   (a) 4   (b) 12
   (c) 14   (d) 8

2. Which of the following arrangements shows schematic alignment of magnetic moments of antiferromagnetic substances? [NCERT Exemplar]
   (a) ↑↑↑↑↑↑
   (b) ↓↓↓↓↓↓
   (c) ↑↑↓↑↑↓
   (d) ↑↓↑↓↑↓

3. Designation of the patten as AB, AB, AB .... etc., of successive vertical layers of identical atoms gives the arrangement called as:
   (a) Hexagonal close packing (hcp)
   (b) Cubic close packing (ccp)
   (c) Face centered cubic (fcc)
   (d) Body centered cubic (bcc)

4. Cubic close packing arrangement is also known as:
   (a) Hexagonal close packing
   (b) Face centered cubic
   (c) Body centered cubic
   (d) None of these

5. In a rock salt structure each Cl^- ion is surrounded by:
   (a) 4 Na^+ ion   (b) 6 Na^+ ions
   (c) 8 Na^+ ions   (d) 12 Na^+ ions

6. CsCl has which type of lattice?
   (a) sc   (b) fcc
   (c) cubic structure   (d) hcp

7. Which of the following is an example of covalent crystal solid?
   (a) Si   (b) Al
   (c) Ar   (d) NaF

8. The solid NaCl is a bad conductor of electricity since:
   (a) In solid NaCl there are no ions
   (b) Solid NaCl is covalent
   (c) In solid NaCl there is no movement of ions
   (d) In solid NaCl these are no electrons

9. In a solid lattice the cation has left a lattice site and is located at an interstitial position, the lattice defect is:
   (a) Interstitial defect   (b) Valency defect
   (c) Frenkel defect   (d) Schottky defect

10. Which of the following is not a characteristic of a crystalline solid? [NCERT Exemplar]
    (a) Definite and characteristic heat of fusion
    (b) Isotropic nature.
    (c) A regular periodically repeated pattern of arrangement of constituent particles in the entire crystal.
    (d) A true solid

11. Schottky defect in crystal is observed when:
    (a) An ion leaves in normal site and occupies the interstitial site
    (b) Equal number of cations and anions are missing from the lattice
    (c) Unequal number of cations and anions are missing from the lattice
    (d) Density of the crystal is increased

12. How many kinds of space lattice are possible in a cubic crystal?
    (a) 23   (b) 7
    (c) 30   (d) 14

13. A solid has a structure in which 'W' atoms are located at the corners of a cubic lattice, 'O' atoms at the centre of edges and 'Na' atoms at the centre of the cube. The formula for the compound is:
    (a) $NaWO_2$ (b) $NaWO_3$
    (c) Na_2WO_3 (d) $NaWO_4$

14. In a compound, atoms of element Y forms ccp lattice and those of element X occupy $\frac{2}{3}$rd of tetrahedral voids, the formula of the compound will be:
    (a) X_4Y_3 (b) X_2Y_3
    (c) X_2Y (d) X_3X_4

15. Which of the following is an example of paramagnetic solid?
    (a) NaCl   (b) KF
    (c) TiO_2 (d) CuO

16. A substance A_xB_y crystallizes in a face centered cubic (fcc) lattice in which atoms 'A' occupy each corner of the cube, atoms 'B' occupy the centres of each of the cube. Identify the correct composition of the substance A_xB_y:
    (a) AB_3
    (b) A_4B_3
    (c) A_3B
    (d) Composition cannot be specified

17. The crystal showing Frenkel defect is:
    (a)

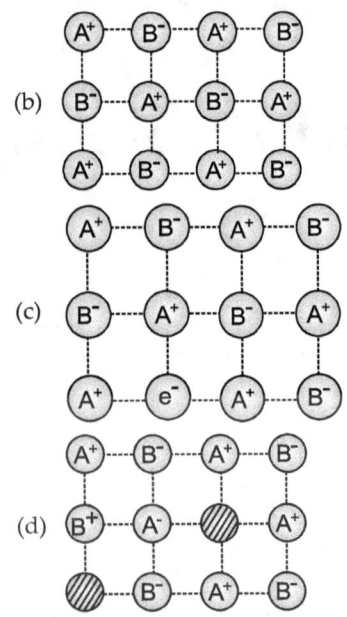

18. Which of the following is a network solid?
    [NCERT Exemplar]
    (a) SO₂ (Solid) (b) I₂
    (c) Diamond (d) H₂O (Ice)

19. Relationship between atomic radius (r) and the edge length 'a' of a body centred cubic unit cell is.
    (a) $r = \dfrac{a}{2}$ (b) $r = \sqrt{\dfrac{a}{2}}$
    (c) $r = \dfrac{\sqrt{3}}{4}a$ (d) $r = \dfrac{3a}{2}$

20. Which among the following will show anisotropy?
    (a) Rubber (b) NaBr
    (c) Plastic (d) Glass

21. Iodine molecules are held in the crystals lattice by _____.
    (a) London forces
    (b) Dipole-dipole interactions
    (c) Covalent bonds
    (d) Coulombic forces

22. The number of atoms present in FCC unit cells.
    (a) 1 (b) 2
    (c) 3 (d) 4

23. The crystal system of a compound with unit cell dimensions $a = 0.920$ nm, $b = 0.920$ nm and $c = 0.304$ nm and $\alpha = \beta = 90°$ and $\gamma = 120°$ is:
    (a) Hexagonal (b) Rhombohedral
    (c) Cubic (d) Orthorhombic

24. In an orthorhombic crystal system axial angles $\alpha = \beta = \gamma$ are:
    (a) Equal to 90° (b) Less than 90°
    (c) Greater than 90° (d) None of these

25. Close packing is maximum in the crystal, which is:
    (a) bcc (b) fcc
    (c) Simple cubic (d) all.

26. Which of the solids show the following properties?
    (i) Electrical conductivity
    (ii) Malleability
    (iii) Ductility
    (iv) Fairly high melting point
    (a) Molecular solids (b) Metallic solids
    (c) Covalent solids (d) Ionic solids

27. Which of the following is a molecular crystal?
    (a) Rock salt (b) Quartz
    (c) Dry ice (d) Diamond

28. The appearance of colour in solid alkali metal halides is generally due to:
    (a) Schottky defect (b) Frenkel defect
    (c) Interstitial position (d) F-centres

29. The percentage of empty space in a body centred cubic arrangement is _____. [NCERT Exemplar]
    (a) 74 (b) 68
    (c) 32 (d) 26

30. Piezoelectric crystals are used in:
    (a) Radio (b) T.V.
    (c) Record player (d) Refrigerator

31. In a crystal, the atoms are located at the position of:
    (a) Maximum potential energy
    (b) Minimum potential energy
    (c) Zero potential energy
    (d) Infinite potential energy

32. The sharp melting point of crystalline solids is due to _____. [NCERT Exemplar]
    (a) a regular arrangement of constituent particles observed over a short distance in the crystal lattice.
    (b) a regular arrangement of constituent particles observed over a long distance in the crystal lattice.
    (c) same arrangement of constituent particles in different directions.
    (d) different arrangement of constituent particles in different directions.

33. The packing fraction for a body centred cube is:
    (a) 0.42 (b) 0.54
    (c) 0.68 (d) 0.74

34. The unit cell of aluminium is a cube with an edge length of 405 pm. The density of aluminium is 2.70 gcm⁻³. What is the structure of unit cell of aluminium?
    (a) Simple cubic cell
    (b) End centred cubic cell
    (c) Face centred cubic cell
    (d) Body centred cubic cell

35. Which of the following statements are correct?
    [NCERT Exemplar]
    (a) Ferrimagnetic substances lose ferrimagnetism on heating and become paramagnetic.
    (b) Ferrimagnetic substances do not lose ferrimagnetism on heating and remain ferrimagnetic.
    (c) Antiferromagnetic substances have domain structures similar to ferromagnetic substances and their magnetic moments are not cancelled by each other.
    (d) In ferromagnetic substances all the domains get oriented in the direction of magnetic field and remain as such even after removing magnetic field.

36. Crystalline solids are anisotropic in nature. What is the meaning of anisotropic in the given statement?
    (a) A regular pattern of arrangement of particles which repeats itself periodically over the entire crystal.
    (b) Different values of some of physical properties are shown when measured along different directions in the same crystals.
    (c) An irregular arrangement of particles over the entire crystal.
    (d) Same values of some of physical properties are shown when measured along different directions in the same crystals.

37. Study the figure of a solid given below depicting the arrangement of particles. Which is the most appropriate term used for the figure?

    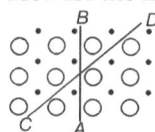

    (a) Amorphous nature   (b) Anisotropy
    (c) Irregular shape   (d) Isotropy

38. Tetragonal crystal system has the following unit cell dimensions:
    (a) $a = b \neq c, \alpha = \beta = 90°, \gamma = 120°$
    (b) $a \neq b \neq c, \alpha = \beta = \gamma = 90°$
    (c) $a = b \neq c, \alpha = \beta = \gamma = 90°$
    (d) $a = b = c, \alpha = \beta = \gamma = 90°$

39. Which of the following statements(s) is/are incorrect?
    (i) Only 1/8th portion of an atom located at corner of a cubic unit cell is in its neighboring unit cell
    (ii) Total number of atoms per unit cell for a face centred cubic unit cell is 3
    (iii) Atom located at the body centre is shared twenty two adjacent unit cells
    (a) (ii) and (iii)   (b) (ii) only
    (c) (i) and (ii)   (d) (iii) only

40. The lattice site in a pure crystal cannot be occupied by _____. [NCERT Exemplar]
    (a) molecule   (b) ion
    (c) electron   (d) atom

41. What is the effect of Frenkel defect on the density of ionic solids?
    (a) There is no relationship between density of a crystal and defect present in it.
    (b) The density of the crystal remains unchanged.
    (c) The density of the crystal decreases.
    (d) The density of the crystal increases.

42. Graphite is a good conductor of electricity due to the presence of _____.
    (a) lone pair of electrons
    (b) free valence electrons
    (c) cations
    (d) anions

43. Which of the following statements is not true about amorphous solids?
    (a) On heating they may become crystalline at certain temperature.
    (b) They may become crystalline on keeping for long time.
    (c) Amorphous solids can be moulded by heating.
    (d) They are anisotropic in nature.

44. Which of the following defects is also known as dislocation defect?
    (a) Frenkel defect
    (b) Schottky defect
    (c) Non-stoichiometric defect
    (d) Simple interstitial defect

45. Which kind of defects are introduced by doping?
    (a) Dislocation defects   (b) Schottky defects
    (c) Frenkel defects   (d) Electronic defects

Directions: In the following questions, a statement of assertion is followed by a statement of reason. Mark the correct choice as:
(a) If both assertion and reason are true and reason is the correct explanation of assertion.
(b) If both assertion and reason are true, but reason is not the correct explanation of assertion.
(c) If assertion is true, but reason is false.
(d) If assertion is false but reason is true.

46. **Assertion:** Quartz glass is crystalline solid and quartz is an amorphous solid.
    Reason: Quartz glass has no long range order.

47. **Assertion:** Graphite is a good conductor of electricity however diamond belongs to the category of insulators.
    Reason: Graphite is soft in nature on the other hand diamond is very hard and brittle.

48. **Assertion:** In crystalline solids, the value of resistance is different in different directions.
    Reason: Crystalline solids are isotropic in nature.

49. **Assertion:** Glass panes fixed to windows or panes of old buildings are found to be slightly thicker at the bottom.
    Reason: Amorphous solids have a tendency to flow.

50. **Assertion:** Face-centred cubic cell has four atoms per unit cell.
    Reason: In fcc unit, there are eight atoms at the corner and six atoms at face centers.

51. **Assertion:** CsCl has body centred cubic arrangement.
    Reason: CsCl has one Cs^+ ion and eight Cl^- ions in its unit cell.

52. **Assertion:** In crystal lattice, the size of the tetrahedral hole is large than an octahedral hole.
    Reason: The cations occupy less space than anions in crystal packing.

53. **Assertion:** On heating ferromagnetic or ferrimagnetic substances, they become paramagnetic.
    Reason: The electrons change their spin on heating.

54. **Assertion:** The total number of atoms present in a simple cubic unit cell is one.
    Reason: Simple cubic unit cell has atoms at its corners, each of which is shared between eight adjacent unit cells.

55. **Assertion:** The packing efficiency is maximum for the fcc structure.
    Reason: The coordination number is 12 in fcc structures.

56. Read the passage given below and answer the following questions:
    Point defects play an important part in determining the physical properties of most crystalline substances,

most notably those controlling the transport of matter and the properties that stem from it. Even a crystal of high purity under conditions of no irradiation contains point defects in thermal equilibrium. Some lattice sites are vacant, and some atoms are displaced from their normal lattice sites into interstitial positions or onto "wrong" lattice sites. For stoichiometric compounds of high purity, the concentrations of these point defects are very low, even at temperatures up to the melting point. A meaningful model, then, is to consider the crystal as a solvent containing a very dilute solution of simple, individual vacancies and interstitials. Long-range interactions among the defects and with impurity atoms, and short-range interactions that produce pairs or other clusters can be introduced in a first order approximation.

The following questions are multiple choice questions. Choose the most appropriate answer:

(i) Which one of the given below statements is wrong about Frenkel defect:
  (a) It is a combination of vacancy and interstitial defects.
  (b) Cations leave their actual lattice sites and occupy the interstitial space in the solid.
  (c) Density remains the same.
  (d) Density of the crystal increases.

(ii) Which one of the following is an 'interstitial void'?
  (a) Octahedral void
  (b) Tetrahedral void
  (c) None of the above
  (d) Both (a) and (b)

(iii) This type of defect arises due to absence of equal number of cations and anions from lattice sites in the crystalline solid of the type A^+B^- and it lowers the density of the crystal.
  (a) Vacancy defect (b) Schottky defect
  (c) Interstitial defect (d) Frenkel defect

(iv) Which one of the following cannot be called as a 'non-stoichiometric defect'?
  (a) Metal excess defect due to anion vacancies.
  (b) Metal excess defect due to presence of extra cations.
  (c) Metal deficiency due to absence of cations.
  (d) Combination of vacancy and interstitial defects.

57. Read the passage given below and answer the following questions:

Ionic solids and melts are compounds in which the interactions are dominated by electrostatic effects. However, the polarization of the ions also plays an important role in many respects as has been clarified in recent years thanks to the development of realistic polarizable interaction potentials. After detailing these models, we illustrate the importance of polarization effects on a series of examples concerning the structural properties, such as the stabilization of particular crystal structures or the formation of highly-coordinated multivalent ions in the melts, as well as the dynamic properties such as the diffusion of ionic species. The effects on the structure of molten salt interfaces (with vacuum and electrified metal) is also described.

Although most of the results described here concern inorganic compounds (molten fluorides and chlorides, ionic oxides...), the particular case of the room-temperature ionic liquids, a special class of molten salts in which at least one species is organic, will also be briefly discussed to indicate how the ideas gained from the study of 'simple' molten salts are being transferred to these more complex systems.

The following questions are multiple choice questions. Choose the most appropriate answer:

(i) Which statement is incorrect about crystalline solids?
  (a) They have long range order.
  (b) They have definite melting point
  (c) They are rigid and incompressible
  (d) They break into two pieces with irregular surface

(ii) Which one of the following is an ionic solid?
  (a) SiO_2 (b) SiC
  (c) ZnS   (d) CCl_4

(iii) Boiling point range of metallic solids can be best given as:
  (a) 450 – 800 K   (b) 300 – 600 K
  (c) 1500 – 2000 K (d) 800 – 1000 K

(iv) "Atoms are arranged at the corners and at the centre of each faces of the unit cell'. Which one of the following best describes the statement?
  (a) Body centered cubic
  (b) Face centered cubic
  (c) Simple cubic
  (d) Side centered cubic

58. Read the passage given below and answer the following questions:

Co-ordination is the number of nearest equidistant neighbouring atoms surrounding a particular atom under considertion. As the co-ordination number decreases, the packing factor decreases. For ionic solids, the bonds are non-directional and promotes for close packing. In this case, ligancy is the number of anious surrounding a central cation. The ligancy is a function of ion sizes and depends on radius ratio $\left(\dfrac{r_e}{r_a}\right)$.

$$\dfrac{\text{Radius of the cation}(r_e)}{\text{Radius of the anion}(r_a)}$$

The following questions are multiple choice questions. Choose the most appropriate answer:

(i) The ionic radius of an anion is 2·11 Å. The radius of the smallest cation with ligancy 8 will be:
  (a) 2·11 Å   (b) 1·545 Å
  (c) 2·455 Å   (d) 4·211 Å

(ii) The co-ordination number of cation in zinc blende is :
  (a) 4   (b) 6
  (c) 8   (d) 12

(iii) For an octahedral arrangement the lowest radius ratio is:
  (a) 0.155   (b) 0.732
  (c) 0.144   (d) 0.225

(iv) The ratio of cation radius to anion radius in an ionic crystal is greater than 0.732. Its co-ordination number is:
(a) 1 (b) 4
(c) 6 (d) 8

59. Read the passage given below and answer the following questions:

Unit calls are comprised of empty spaces existing between spheres. This is called void space or hole. Two types of interstitial voids are present in three dimensional close packing system.

Tetrahedral voids and octahedral voids. All the atoms in a crystal lattice passes vibrational energy and at temperatures above absolute zero, a finite number of atoms acquire sufficient energy to break their bonds & get free from their positions. Thus point defects are created. There are mainly two types of stoichiometric point defects present—Schottky defects & Frenkel defects.

In three questions, a statement of assertion followed by a statement of reason is given. Choose the correct answer out of the following choices.

(a) Assertion & reason both are correct statements and reason is correct explanation for assertion.
(b) Assertion & reason both are correct statements and reason is not correct explanation for assertion.
(c) Assertion is correct statement but reason is wrong statement.
(d) Assertion is wrong statement but reason is correct statement.

(i) **Assertion :** The number of tetrahedral void in double the number of octahedral void.
Reason: The size of the tetrahedral void is half of that of the octahedral void.

(ii) **Assertion :** In bcc arrangement co-ordination number is eight.
Reason: In bcc arrangement atoms occupy cubic voids.

OR

Assertion : Due to frenkel defect there is no effect on density of a solid.
Reason: Ions shift from lattice sites to interstitial sites in frenkel defects.

(iii) **Assertion :** Schottky defect is generally shown by the compounds with high co-ordination number.
Reason: In schottky defect equal number of cation and anions are missing from their lattice sites.

(iv) **Assertion :** In NaCl crystal, the Na$^+$ ion occupies the octahedral void while Cl$^-$ ions occupy the vertices of octahedron.
Reason: The radius ratio of Na$^+$: Cl$^-$ ions lies between 0.4 to 0.7.

60. Read the passage given below and answer the following questions:

The hexagonal close packed structure shows that each sphere is surrounded by twelve neighbouring spheres—six in the same layer and three each in the above & below layers. In cubic close packing structure mode of packing has cubic symmetry & the lattice points are parellel to the diagonal of the unit cell. The mode of packing of body centred cubic arrangement each sphere is in contact with eight spheres—four spheres each in upper and lower layer.

The following questions are multiple choice questions. Choose the most appropriate answer:

(i) In a cubic cell, the contribution of an atom at the face of a unit cell is_____.
(a) 3 (b) $\frac{1}{2}$
(c) 1 (d) 2

(ii) The percentage of empty space in a body centred cubic arrangement is_____.
(a) 74 (b) 68
(c) 32 (d) 26

OR

The correct order of the packing efficiency of different type of unit cells is_____
(a) fcc ⟨ bcc ⟩ simple cubic
(b) bcc ⟨ fcc ⟩ simple cubic
(c) fcc ⟩ bcc ⟩ simple cubic
(d) fcc ⟨ bcc ⟨ simple cubic

(iii) In which of the following arrangements octahedral voids are formed?
(a) fcc (b) bcc
(c) simple cubic (d) all of these

(iv) A metallic crystal crystalises into a lattice containing a sequence of layers AB AB AB...... any packing of spheres leaves out voids in the lattice. What percentage by volume of this lattice is empty space?
(a) 74% (b) 26%
(c) 50% (d) None of these

Answers

1. (b) 12

    Explanation: The number of spheres which are touching a given sphere is said to be coordination number. As copper has face-centered cubic structure, any atom present in this lattice touches 12 other atoms. Hence the co-ordination number of each ion is 12.

2. (d) ↑↓↑↓↑↓

    Explanation: In anti-ferromagnetic substances, their domains are oppositely oriented and cancel out each other's magnetic moment.

3. (a) Hexagonal close packing (hcp)

    Explanation: Each type of packing structure has a unique arrangement of atoms. Here all options belong to spatial three dimensional arrangement. In Hexagonal close packing (hcp) observed packing arrangement is AB, AB, AB......etc.

4. (b) Face centered cubic

    Explanation: Face centred cubic unit cell is a cubic close packed unit cell where it has points at all the corners as well as at the centre of each of the six faces.

5. (b) 6 Na⁺ ions
   Explanation: In rock salt crystal structure the larger chloride ions are arranged in a cubic array while the smaller sodium ions fill all the tetrahedral voids between them. In solid NaCl, each ion is surrounded by 6 ions of the opposite charge due to electrostatic interactions. Hence, here each Cl⁻ ion is surrounded by 6 Na⊕ ions.

6. (c) cubic structure
   Explanation: CsCl has a cubic structure where the Cs(or Cl) ions sit at the eight corners of the cube and the Cl or Cs sit at the centre of the cube.

7. (a) Si
   Explanation: Covalent crystals are formed by sharing of valence electrons between two atoms leading to the formation of covalent bonds. NaF is ionic compound, Al is a metal & Ar is a noble gas. As in 'Si' crystal constituent 'Si' atoms attached by covalent bonds. 'Si' is a covalent crystal.

8. (c) In solid NaCl there is no movement of ions
   Explanation: In solid NaCl, ions are bound by strong electrostatic forces. We know ions can carry current. In solid NaCl there is no free ions to move, so it is a bad conductor of electricity.

9. (c) Frenkel defect
   Explanation: Frenkel defect is observed a solid lattice where the cation has left a lattice site and is located at interstitial position.

10. (b) Isotropic nature.
    Explanation: Covalent solids are anisotropic in nature.

11. (b) Equal number of cations and anions are missing from the lattice.
    Explanation: Schottky defect changes the density as equal number of cations & anions are missing from the lattice.

12. (b) 7
    Explanation: 7 types of space lattice possible in a cubic crystal are as follows cubic, Tetragonal, Hexagonal, Trigonal, orthorhombic, Homoclinic and Triclinic.

13. (b) NaWO₃
    Explanation: The contribution of the 'W' atoms to the unit cell = $\frac{1}{8} \times 8 = 1$.
    The contribution of 'O' atoms to the unit cell = $\frac{1}{4} \times 12 = 3$
    The contribution of 'Na' atoms to the unit cell = 1.
    The ratio of number of atoms in the cube
    W : O : Na = 1 : 3 : 1
    ∴ formula = Na W O₃.

14. (a) X₄Y₃
    Explanation: As 'Y' occupies ccp lattice hence the effective number of Y = 4. 'X' occupies $\frac{2}{3}$rd of tetrahedral voids. Number of tetrahedral voids generated in any unit cell is = 2Z = 2× 4 = 8.
    As 'X' occupies $\frac{2}{3}$rd of tetrahedral voids, effective number of 'X' = $\frac{2}{3} \times 8 = \frac{16}{3}$.
    ∴ X = $\frac{16}{3}$ & Y = 4.
    The formula of the compound will be X₄Y₃.

15. (d) CuO
    Explanation: NaCl cannot be paramagnetic as in Na⁺ & Cl⁻ all the electrons are paired. In TiO₂, Ti⁺⁴ is in d^0 configuration. KF cannot be paramagnetic as in K⊕ & F⊖ all the electrons are paired.
    In CuO, Cu⁺² is in d^9 electronic configuration & hence CuO has unpaired electron & it is paramagnetic.

16. (a) AB₃
    Explanation: A_XB_Y crystallises in a fcc lattices. As 'A' atoms occupy each corner of the cube, the number of atoms of 'A' is $8 \times \frac{1}{8} = 1$. As 'B' atoms occupy the centre of each face of the cube, the number of atoms of 'B' = $6 \times \frac{1}{2} = 3$.
    Hence the formula is AB₃.

17. (a)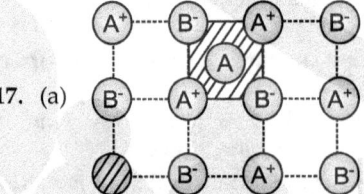
    Explanation: As in Frenkel defect, the cation has moved to a new place between cations and anions.

18. (c) Diamond
    Explanation: Covalent Network Solids are giant covalent substances like diamond, graphite and silicon dioxide (silicon (IV) oxide).

19. (c) $r = \frac{\sqrt{3}}{4}a$
    Explanation: $4r = \sqrt{3}a$
    ∴ $r = \frac{\sqrt{3}}{4}a$.

20. (b) NaBr
    Explanation: Only crystalline solids show anisotropy.

21. (a) London forces
    Explanation: Iodine molecules are a class of non-polar molecular solid in which constituent's molecules are held together by London or dispersion forces. These solids are soft and non-conductor of electricity.

22. (d) 4
    Explanation: In a FCC lattice there are 6 points in 6 faces each of which is shared by two cubes. So, share of a unit cube is $\frac{1}{2} \times 6 = 3$, bisects one point, of four corners. So, the number of atoms present in

unit cell is (3 + 1) = 4.
23. (a) Hexagonal
Explanation: Here the dimensions are :
$a = b \neq c$ and $\alpha = \beta = 90°$ & $\gamma = 120°$
∴ Hence the cubic system in hexagonal.
24. (a) Equal to 90°
Explanation: In orthorhombic, crystal system, all the three edge length are unequal but all the angles are equal to 90°.
25. (b) fcc
Explanation: The close packing in the crystal in 0.52, 0.68 and 0.74 for simple cubic, body centered cubic and face-centered cubic respectively. So, close packing is maximum in fcc.
26. (b) Metallic solids
Explanation: Metallic solids conduct electricity in solid state as well as in molten state and are malleable, ductile and have fairly high melting point.
27. (c) Dry ice
Explanation: Dry ice is a molecular crystal as it consists of molecules of carbon dioxide rather than individual carbon or oxygen atoms.
28. (d) F-centres
Explanation: As colourless ionic crystal converts into coloured ionic crystal due to F-centre defect.
29. (c) 32
Explanation: Packing efficiency (i.e., space occupied) for bcc is 68% of empty space = 100 − 68 = 32%.
30. (c) Record player
Explanation: In record player piezoelectric crystals can generate very high frequency ultrasound.
31. (b) Minimum potential energy
Explanation: In order to attain greater stability, there is an equilibrium between attractive and repulsive forces exist between the atoms. It happens only when the potential energy is minimum.
32. (b) a regular arrangement of constituent particles observed over a long distance in the crystal lattice.
Explanation: Crystals tend to have relatively sharp, well defined melting points because all the component atoms, molecules, or ions are at the same distance from the same number and type of neighbours; that is, the regularity of the crystalline lattice creates local environments that are the same.
33. (c) 0.68
Explanation: As in body centered cubic structure volume occupied per unit cell by particles is 68%.
34. (c) Face centred cubic cell
Explanation: As we know,
$$\rho = \frac{Z \times M}{N_A \times V}$$
$$\Rightarrow 2.70 = \frac{Z \times 27}{6.023 \times 10^{23} \times (405 \times 10^{-10})^3}$$
$$Z = 4$$
Hence, structure of aluminium unit cell is fcc or face-centred.

35. (a,d) Ferrimagnetic substances lose ferrimagnetism on heating and become paramagnetic.
Explanation : In ferromagnetic substances all the domains get oriented in the direction of magnetic field and remain as such even after removing magnetic field.
36. (b) Different values of some of physical properties are shown when measured along different directions in the same crystals.
Explanation: Crystalline solids are anisotropic in nature that is some of their physical properties like electrical resistance or refractive index show different values when measured along different directions in the same crystals.
37. (b) Anisotropy
Explanation: The different constituent particles of a crystalline solid fall in different ways due to the regular arrangement of constituent particles. Anisotropy occurs when the values of attributes such as electrical conductivity and thermal expansion do not remain constant in all directions.
38. (c) $a = b \neq c, \alpha = \beta = \gamma = 90°$
Explanation: Tetragonal system has the unit cell dimension $a = b \neq c, \alpha = \beta = \gamma = 90°$.
39. (a) (ii) and (iii)
Explanation: Total number of atoms per unit cell for a face centred cubic unit is 4. The atom at the body centre completely belongs to the unit cell in which it is present
40. (c) electron
Explanation: Lattice sites in a pure crystal are occupied by the constituent units like atoms, molecules, ions but not occupied by electrons.
41. (b) The density of the crystal remains unchanged.
Explanation: In Frenkel defect, ions get displaced from their original position and move to interstitial sites. Hence, there is no change in the density of the crystal.
42. (b) free valence electrons
Explanation: Metallic solids conduct electricity in solid state as well as in molten state and are malleable, ductile and have fairly high melting point.
43. (c) Amorphous solids can be moulded by heating
Explanation: Molecular crystals are bad conductors of electricity as the electrons are localised in the bonds.
44. (a) Frenkel defect
Explanation: Frenkel defect is also known as dislocation defect as in this the smaller ion (usually cations) is dislocated from its normal site to an interstitial site.
45. (d) Electronic defects
Explanation: Doping can be done with an impurity which is electron rich or electron deficient as compared to the intrinsic semiconductor silicon or germanium. Such impurities introduce electronic defects.

46. (d) The structure of quartz is crystalline and that of quartz glass is amorphous. The two structures are almost identical yet in case of amorphous quartz glass, there is no long range order.

47. (b) Diamond is bad conductor of electricity because cell valence electrons of carbon are involved in bonding. In graphite however three out of four valence electrons are involved in bonding and the fourth electron remain free between adjacent layers which makes it a good conductor. Graphite is soft because parallel layers are held together by weak Vander Waal's force. However, diamond is hard due to compact three-dimensional network of bonding.

48. (c) Crystalline solids are anisotropic in nature that is, some of their physical properties like electrical resistance show different values along different directions due to different arrangement of particles in different directions.

49. (a) Solids have a tendency to flow, though very slowly. Glass is sometimes called a supercooled liquid because it does not form a crystalline structure, but instead forms an amorphous solid that allows molecules in the material to continue to move.

50. (a) The face-centred cubic structure has atoms located at each of the corners and the centres of all the cubic faces. Each of the corner atoms is the corner of another cube so the corner atoms are shared among eight-unit cells.

51. (c) CsCl has one Cs^+ ion and one Cl^- ion in its unit cell.

52. (d) Tetrahedral holes are smaller in size than octahedral holes. Cations usually occupy less space than anions.

53. (a) All magnetically ordered solids (ferromagnetic, ferrimagnetic and anti frerromagnetic solids) transform to the paramagnetic state at high temperature due to the randomisation of spins.

54. (a) In a simple cubic unit cell, the total number of atoms is $8 \times \dfrac{1}{8} = 1$.

55. (b) In fcc unit cell, CCP arrangement is present with packing efficiency of 74.01% (maximum).

56. (i) (d) Density of the crystal increases.
    (ii) (d) Both (a) and (b)
    (iii) (b) Schottky defect
    (iv) (d) Combination of vacancy and interstitial defects.

57. (i) (d) They break into two pieces with irregular surface
    (ii) (c) ZnS
    (iii) (c) 1500 – 2000 K
    (iv) (c) face centered cubic
    (v) (d) both (a) and (b)

58. (i) (b) 1·545 Å
    (ii) (c) 8
    (iii) (c) 0·414
    (iv) (d) 8

59. (i) (d) Assertion is wrong statement but reason is correct statement.
    (ii) (c) Assertion is correct statement but reason is wrong statement.
    (iii) (c) Assertion is correct statement but reason is wrong statement.
    (iv) (c) Assertion is correct statement but reason is wrong statement.
    (v) (d) Assertion is wrong statement but reason is correct statement.

60. (i) (b) $\dfrac{1}{2}$
    (ii) (c) 32
    OR
    (c) fcc ⟩ bcc ⟩ simple cubic
    (iii) (a) fcc
    (iv) (b) 26%

Chapter 2

Solutions

1. The molal freezing point constant of water is 1.86 K kg mol^{-1}. Therefore, the freezing point of 0·1M NaCl solution in water is expected to be:
   (a) −1.86°C (b) −0.372°C
   (c) −0.186°C (d) +0.372°C

2. Of the following terms used for denoting concentration of a solution, the one which does not gets affected by temperature is:
   (a) Molarity (b) Molality
   (c) Normality (d) Formality

3. The term homogenous mixtures signify that:
   (a) Both composition and properties are uniform throughout the mixture.
   (b) Its properties are uniform throughout the mixture.
   (c) Its composition is uniform throughout the mixture.
   (d) Neither composition nor properties are uniform throughout the mixture.

4. For a dissociated solute in solution the value of van't Hoff factor is:
   (a) Zero (b) One
   (c) Greater than one (d) Less than one

5. A beaker contains a solution of substance 'A'. Precipitation of substance 'A' takes place when small amount of 'A' is added to the solution. The solution is _____. [NCERT Exemplar]
   (a) saturated (b) supersaturated
   (c) unsaturated (d) concentrated

6. The solubility of a gas varies directly with pressure of the gas, is based upon:
   (a) Raoult's law
   (b) Henry's law
   (c) Nernst's distribution law
   (d) None of these

7. The relative lowering of vapour pressure of a solvent by the addition of a solute is:
   (a) Proportional to the molarity of the solution
   (b) Proportional to the molality of the solution
   (c) Equal to the mole fraction of the solute
   (d) Equal to the mole fraction of the solvent

8. Which solution is isotonic to the blood?
   (a) 0·75% by weight of NaCl approximately
   (b) 0·99% by weight of NaCl approximately
   (c) 0·90% by weight of NaCl approximately
   (d) None of these

9. The osmotic pressure of equimolar solution of NaCl, $BaCl_2$ and glucose will be in the order of:
   (a) NaCl > $BaCl_2$ > Glucose
   (b) $BaCl_2$ > NaCl > Glucose
   (c) Glucose > NaCl > $BaCl_2$
   (d) NaCl > Glucose > $BaCl_2$

10. Which of the following is not a colligative property?
    (a) Depression in freezing point
    (b) Elevation in boiling point
    (c) Osmotic pressure
    (d) Modification of refractive index

11. Which of the following statements is false? [NCERT Exemplar]
    (a) Two different solutions of sucrose of same molality prepared in different solvents will have the same depression in freezing point.
    (b) The osmotic pressure of a solution is given by the equation P = CRT (where C is the molarity of the solution).
    (c) Decreasing order of osmotic pressure for 0.01 M aqueous solutions of barium chloride, potassium chloride, acetic acid and sucrose is $BaCl_2$ > KCl > CH_3COOH > sucrose.
    (d) According to Raoult's law, the vapour pressure exerted by a volatile component of a solution is directly proportional to its mole fraction in the solution.

12. Determination of correct molecular mass from Raoult's law is applicable to:
    (a) An electrolyte in solution
    (b) A non-electrolyte in dilute solution
    (c) A non-electrolyte in conc. solution
    (d) An electrolyte in a liquid solvent

13. The number of moles of solute present in 1000 gm of the solvent is known as:
    (a) Molarity (b) Molality
    (c) Normality (d) Mole fraction

14. Which of the following 0·1 M aqueous solution will have the lowest freezing point?
    (a) Potassium sulphate (b) Sodium chloride
    (c) Urea (d) Glucose

15. Colligative properties of the solution depends on:
    (a) Nature of solute
    (b) Nature of solvent
    (c) Number of particles present in the solution
    (d) Number of moles of solvent only

16. Solution that obeys Raoult's law:
    (a) Normal (b) Molar
    (c) Ideal (d) Saturated

17. A liquid pair of benzene-toluene shows:
    (a) Positive deviation from Raoult's law

(b) Negative deviation from Raoult's law
(c) Practically no deviation from Raoult's law
(d) Irregular deviation from Raoult's law

18. If 0.1 M solution of glucose and 0.1 M solution of urea are placed on two sides of the semipermeable membrane to equal heights, then it will be correct to say that,
    (a) Water will flow from urea solution to glucose.
    (b) Urea will flow towards glucose solution.
    (c) Glucose will flow towards urea solution.
    (d) There will be no net movement across the membrane

19. 12g of urea is dissolved in 1 litre of water and 68·4 g of sucrose is dissolved in 1 litre of water. The lowering of vapour pressure in the first case is:
    (a) Equal to second   (b) Greater than second
    (c) Less than second   (d) Double that of second

20. Consider the Fig. and mark the correct option. [NCERT Exemplar]

    (a) water will move from side (A) to side (B) if a pressure lower than osmotic pressure is applied on piston (B).
    (b) water will move from side (B) to side (A) if a pressure greater than osmotic pressure is applied on piston (B).
    (c) water will move from side (B) to side (A) if a pressure equal to osmotic pressure is applied on piston (B).
    (d) water will move from side (A) to side (B) if pressure equal to osmotic pressure is applied on piston (A).

21. Which one of the following statements is correct?
    (a) Lowering in vapour pressure is a colligative property.
    (b) The depression in freezing point is directly proportional to molality of the solution.
    (c) A plant cell swells when placed in hypertonic solution.
    (d) A saturated solution will remain saturated at all temperatures.

22. When 0.1 mole urea is dissolved in 9.9 mole water, then the vapour pressure is :
    (a) Increased by 1%   (b) Increased by 10%
    (c) Decreased by 1%   (d) Decreased by 10%

23. The solubility of a gas varies directly with pressure of the gas is based upon:
    (a) Raoult's law
    (b) Henry's law
    (c) Nernst's distribution law
    (d) None of these

24. The molal elevation constant is the ratio of the elevation in boiling point to :
    (a) Molarity
    (b) Molality
    (c) Mole fraction of solute
    (d) Mole fraction of solvent

25. Which of the following is an example of aldohexose?
    (a) Ribose   (b) Fructose
    (c) Sucrose   (d) Glucose

26. Osmotic pressure of a dilute solution is given by :
    (a) $P = P_0 x$ (b) $pV = nRT$
    (c) $p = VRT$ (d) None of these

27. Which of the following is not a colligative property?
    (a) Osmotic pressure
    (b) Boiling point
    (c) Vapour pressure
    (d) Electrical conductivity

28. Addition of common salt in water causes:
    (a) Increase in M.P of solution.
    (b) Increase in B.P of solution.
    (c) Decrease in B.P of solution.
    (d) Decrease in both M.P & B.P.

29. Which solution is isotonic to the blood?
    (a) 0.75% by weight of NaCl approximately
    (b) 0.99% by weight of NaCl approximately
    (c) 0.90% by weight of NaCl approximately
    (d) None of these

30. A liquid pair of benzene-toluene shows:
    (a) Positive deviation from Raoult's law.
    (b) Negative deviation from Raoult's law.
    (c) Practically no deviation from Raoult's law.
    (d) Irregular deviation from Raoult's law.

31. On dissolving sugar in water at room temperature solution feels cool to touch. Under which of the following cases dissolution of sugar will be most rapid? [NCERT Exemplar]
    (a) Sugar crystals in cold water.
    (b) Sugar crystals in hot water.
    (c) Powdered sugar in cold water.
    (d) Powdered sugar in hot water.

32. An example of intensive property is:
    (a) Number of moles   (b) Mass
    (c) Volume   (d) Density

33. The molecular weight of sodium chloride determined by measuring the osmotic pressure of its aqueous solution is:
    (a) Double the theoretical value
    (b) Same as the theoretical value
    (c) Half the theoretical value
    (d) Three times the theoretical value

34. Molecular weight of non-volatile solute can be determined by:
    (a) Victor-Mayer's method
    (b) Graham's law of diffusion
    (c) Gay Lussac's law
    (d) Raoult's law

35. On the basis of information given below, mark the correct option. Information: On adding acetone to methanol some of the hydrogen bonds between methanol molecules break. [NCERT Exemplar]

Information:
(a) At specific composition methanol-acetone mixture will form minimum boiling azeotrope and will show positive deviation from Raoult's law.
(b) At specific composition methanol-acetone mixture forms maximum boiling azeotrope and will show positive deviation from Raoult's law.
(c) At specific composition methanol-acetone mixture will form minimum boiling azeotrope and will show-negative deviation from Raoult's law.
(d) At specific composition methanol-acetone mixture will form maximum boiling azeotrope and will show negative deviation from Raoult's law.

36. Which of the following statement is false? [NCERT Exemplar]
(a) Two different solutions of sucrose of same molality-prepared in different solvents will have the same depression in freezing point.
(b) The osmotic pressure of a solution is given by the equation π = CRT (where C is the molarity of the solution).
(c) Decreasing order of osmotic pressure for 0.01 M aqueous solutions of barium chloride, potassium chloride, acetic acid and sucrose is $BaCl_2$ > KCl > CH_2COOH > sucrose
(d) According to Raoult's law, the vapour pressure exerted by a volatile component of a solution is directly proportional to its mole fraction in the solution.

37. What is the molarity of a solution containing 10 g of NaOH in 500 mL of solution?
(a) 0.25 mol L^{-1}
(b) 0.75 mol L^{-1}
(c) 0.5 mol L^{-1}
(d) 1.25 mol L^{-1}

38. For mixture containing "four" components which of the following is correct in term of mole fraction?
(a) $n_1 + n_2 + n_3 + n_4 = 1$
(b) $x_1 = \dfrac{n_1}{n_1 + n_2 + n_3 + n_4} = \dfrac{n_1}{\sum n}$
(c) $\dfrac{n_3}{n_1 + n_2 + n_3} = x_3$
(d) $x_1 + x_2 + x_3 + x_4 \uparrow 1$

39. Match the columns:

	Column I		Column II
A	Mass percentage	(p)	Medicine and pharmacy
B	Mass by volume	(q)	Concentration of pollutants in water
C	ppm	(r)	Industrial chemical application
D	Volume percentage	(s)	Liquid solutions

(a) A-(q), B-(p), C-(s), D-(r)
(b) A-(r), B-(p), C-(q), D-(s)
(c) A-(r), B-(q), C-(s), D-(p)
(d) A-(s), B-(r), C-(p), D-(q)

40. Consider the two figures given below.

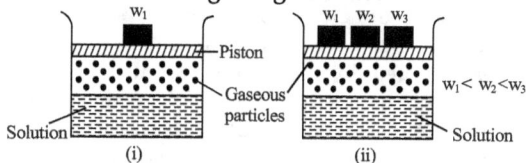

Which one of the following statements regarding the experiment is true?
(a) The solubility of a gas remains unaffected by change in weights.
(b) The solubility of a gas is equal in both beakers.
(c) The solubility of a gas in beaker (i) is less than that in beaker (ii).
(d) The solubility of a gas in liquid in beaker (i) is greater than that in beaker (ii).

41. On the basis of the figure given below which one of the following is not true?

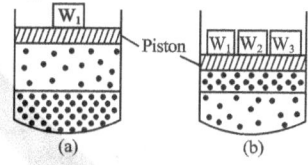

(a) Rate at which gaseous particles are striking the solution to enter it, increases.
(b) Rate at which gaseous particles are striking the solution to enter it, decreases.
(c) In figure (b) on compressing the gas number of gaseous particles per unit volume over the solution increases.
(d) In figure (a) assuming the state of dynamic equilibrium rate of gaseous particles entering and leaving the solution phase is same.

42. At high altitudes the partial pressure of oxygen is less than that at the ground level. This leads to the,
(a) Low concentrations of oxygen in the blood and tissues.
(b) High concentrations of oxygen in the blood and tissues.
(c) Release of dissolved gases and formation of bubbles of nitrogen in the blood.
(d) Thickening of blood and tissues.

43. The given graph shows the vapour pressure-temperature curves for some liquids.

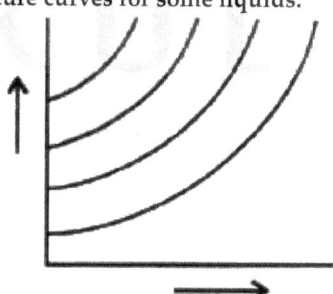

Liquids A, B, C and D respectively are,
(a) Ethyl alcohol, acetone, diethyl ether, water
(b) Water, ethyl alcohol, acetone, diethyl ether
(c) Acetone, ethyl alcohol, diethyl ether, water
(d) Diethyl ether, acetone, ethyl alcohol, water

44. Relative lowering of vapour pressure, osmotic Pressure of a solution and elevation in boiling points are _____ properties. Osmosis is the passage of _____ through a semipermeable membrane from a solution of _____ towards a solution of _____ Osmotic pressure is equivalent to mechanical pressure which must be applied on _____ to prevent osmosis. In the above paragraph p, q, r, s and t respectively:
    (a) Colligative, solvent, lower concentration, higher concentration, solution.
    (b) Colligative, solution, lower concentration, higher concentration, solvent.
    (c) Colligative, solvent, higher concentration, lower concentration, solution.
    (d) Colligative, solution, higher concentration, lower concentration, solution.

45. The molecular weight of benzoic acid in benzene as determined by depression in freezing point method corresponds to the,
    (a) Solvation of benzoic acid.
    (b) Trimerization of benzoic acid.
    (c) Dimerization of benzoic acid.
    (d) Ionization of benzoic acid.

Directions: In the following questions, a statement of assertion is followed by a statement of reason. Mark the correct choice as:
(a) If both assertion and reason are true and reason is the correct explanation of assertion.
(b) If both assertion and reason are true, but reason is not the correct explanation of assertion.
(c) If assertion is true, but reason is false.
(d) If assertion is false but reason is true.

46. **Assertion:** The concentration of pollutants in water or atmosphere is often expressed in terms of ppm.
    Reason: Concentration in parts per million can be expressed as mass to mass, volume to volume and mass to volume

47. **Assertion:** 0.1 M solution of KCl has greater osmotic pressure than 0.1 M solution of glucose at same temperature.
    Reason: In solution, KCl dissociates to produce more number of particles. [CBSE, 2020]

48. **Assertion:** When a solution is separated from the pure solvent by a semi-permeable membrane, the solvent molecules pass through it from pure solvent side to the solution side.
    Reason: Diffusion of solvent occurs from a region of high concentration solution to a region of low concentration solution.

49. **Assertion:** In solution, amalgam of mercury with sodium is an example of solid solutions.
    Reason: Mercury is solvent and sodium is solute in the solution.

50. **Assertion:** Molarity of a solution in liquid state changes with temperature.
    Reason: The volume of a solution changes with change in temperature.

51. **Assertion:** Pressure have any effect on solubility of solids in liquids.
    Reason: Solids and liquids are not incompressible.

52. **Assertion:** Elevation in boiling point is a colligative property.
    Reason: Elevation in boiling point is directly proportional to molarity. [CBSE, 2020]

53. **Assertion:** Azeotropic mixtures are not formed only by non-ideal solutions and they may have boiling points either greater than both the components or less than both the components.
    Reason: The composition of the vapour phase is not same as that of the liquid phase of an azeotropic mixture.

54. **Assertion:** At equilibrium, vapour phase will not be always rich in component which is more volatile.
    Reason: The composition of vapour phase in equilibrium with the solution is not determined by the partial pressures of the components.

55. **Assertion:** An ideal solution obeys Henry's law.
    Reason: In an ideal solution, solute-solute as well as solvent solvent interactions are similar to solute-solvent interaction. [CBSE, 2020]

56. Read the passage given below and answer the following questions: [CBSE Website]
Boiling point or freezing point of liquid solution would be affected by the dissolved solids in the liquid phase. A soluble solid in solution has the effect of raising its boiling point and depressing its freezing point. The addition of non-volatile substances to a solvent decreases the vapor pressure and the added solute particles affect the formation of pure solvent crystals. According to many researches the decrease in freezing point directly correlated to the concentration of solutes dissolved in the solvent. This phenomenon is expressed as freezing point depression and it is useful for several applications such as freeze concentration of liquid food and to find the molar mass of an unknown solute in the solution. Freeze concentration is a high quality liquid food concentration method where water is removed by forming ice crystals. This is done by cooling the liquid food below the freezing point of the solution. The freezing point depression is referred as a colligative property and it is proportional to the molar concentration of the solution (m), along with vapor pressure lowering, boiling point elevation, and osmotic pressure. These are physical characteristics of solutions that depend only on the identity of the solvent and the concentration of the solute. The characters are not depending on the solute's identity.

(i) When a non volatile solid is added to pure water it will:
   (a) boil above 100°C and freeze above 0°C
   (b) boil below 100°C and freeze above 0°C
   (c) boil above 100°C and freeze below 0°C
   (d) boil below 100°C and freeze below 0°C

(ii) Colligative properties are:
   (a) dependent only on the concentration of the solute and independent of the solvent's and solute's identity.
   (b) dependent only on the identity of the solute and the concentration of the solute and independent of the solvent's identity.
   (c) dependent on the identity of the solvent and solute and thus on the concentration of the solute.
   (d) dependent only on the identity of the solvent and the concentration of the solute and independent of the solute's identity.

(iii) Assume three samples of juices A, B and C have glucose as the only sugar present in them. The concentration of sample A, B and C are 0.1M, .5M and 0.2 M respectively. Freezing point will be highest for the fruit juice:
   (a) A
   (b) B
   (c) C
   (d) All have same freezing point

(iv) Identify which of the following is a colligative property :
   (a) freezing point
   (b) boiling point
   (c) osmotic pressure
   (d) all of the above

57. Read the passage given below and answer the following questions:

The vapor pressure of a solvent decrease when a nonvolatile component is dissolved in the liquid phase. The depression of the vapor pressure of the solution (at constant temperature) results in a rise of the boiling point of the solution (at constant pressure). The elevation in boiling point, being a colligative property, depends on the concentration of the dissolved particles and on the nature of the solvent. In dilute solutions it is observed to be relatively independent of the nature of the solute.

In these questions, a statement of assertion followed by a statement of reason is given. Choose the correct answer out of the following choices.

(i) Assertion and reason both are correct statements and reason is correct explanation for assertion.
(ii) Assertion and reason both are correct statements but reason is not correct explanation for assertion.
(iii) Assertion is correct statement but reason is wrong statement.
(iv) Assertion is wrong statement but reason is correct statement.

(a) **Assertion:** At boiling point, vapour pressure of a liquid is equal to the atmospheric pressure.
   Reason: Vapour pressure of a liquid decreases with a liquid.

(b) **Assertion:** Blood cells collapse when suspended in saline water, having more concentration compared to fluid inside the blood cells.
   Reason: Solvent molecules always flow from higher concentration to lower concentration.

(c) **Assertion:** When NaCl is added to water a depression in freezing point is observed.
   Reason: The lowering of the vapour pressure of a solution causes depression in the freezing point compared to the pure solvent.

(d) **Assertion:** Colligative property is used to determine the molecular mass of particle.
   Reason: Colligative properties depend upon number of solute particles in solution irrespective of their nature.

OR

Assertion: Colloidal solution show colligative properties.

Reason: Colloidal particles are large in size.

58. Read the passage given below and answer the following questions:

At the freezing point of solvent, the solid and the liquid are in equilibrium. Therefore, a solution will freeze when its vapour pressure becomes equal to the vapour pressure of the pure solid solvent.

It has been observed that when a non-volatile solute is added to a solvent, the freezing point of the solution is always lower than of the pure solvent. Depression in freezing point can be given as, $\Delta T_f = K_f m$

Where, K_f = Molal freezing point depression constant

or we can write, $\Delta T_f = \dfrac{K_f \times W_g \times 1000}{W_A \times M_B}$

In these questions, (Q. No. i-iv), a statement of assertion followed by a statement of reason is given. Choose the correct answer out of the following choices.

(i) Assertion and reason both are correct statements and reason is correct explanation for assertion.
(ii) Assertion and reason both are correct statements but reason is not correct explanation for assertion.
(iii) Assertion is correct statement but reason is wrong statement.
(iv) Assertion is wrong statement but reason is correct statement.

(a) **Assertion:** 0.1 M solution of glucose has same depression in the freezing point as 0.1 M solution of urea.
   Reason: K_f for both has same value.

OR

Assertion: Increasing pressure on pure water decreases its freezing point.
Reason: Density of water is maximum at 273 K.

(b) **Assertion:** Larger the value of cryoscopic constant of the solvent, lesser will be the freezing point of the solution.
   Reason: Extent of depression in the freezing point depends on the nature of the solvent.

(c) **Assertion:** The water pouch of instant cold pack for treating injuries breaks when squeezed and NH_4NO_3 dissolves thus lowering the temperature.
   Reason: Addition of non-volatile solute into solvent results into depression of freezing point of solvent.

(d) **Assertion:** If a non-volatile solute is mixed in solution then elevation in boiling point and depression in freezing point both will be same.
   Reason: Elevation in boiling point and depression in freezing point both depend on number of particles of solute.

59. Read the passage given below and answer the following questions:

In general, the vapor-pressure change due to the addition of a solute to a solvent mixture does not follow Raoult's law. We have demonstrated thermodynamically that if one adds to a binary solvent mixture solute and solvents in such a way that the vapor-phase composition remains constant, then the decrease of total pressure follows Raoult's law; a supplementary term which vanishes for very dilute solute concentration is introduced as a consequence of the non-ideality of the ternary solution. Precise vapor-pressure measurements of dilute solutions of electrolytes and non-electrolytes in a 40.000 wt. % water-tetrahydrofuran mixture is used in order to illustrate the applicability of Raoult's law under the above conditions. These may be regarded as a particular case of what has been called endostatic conditions, i.e., addition of a solute under constant solvent activity ratio.

The following questions are multiple choice questions. Choose the most appropriate answer:

(i) In comparison to a 0.01 M solution of glucose, the depression in freezing point of a 0.01 M $MgCl_2$ solution is _____.
 (a) The same (b) About twice
 (c) About three times (d) About six times

(ii) According to Raoult's law,
 (a) The vapour pressure exerted by a volatile component of a solution is directly proportional to its mole fraction in the solution.
 (b) The vapour pressure exerted by a non-volatile component of a solution is directly proportional to its mole fraction in the solution.
 (c) The vapour pressure exerted by a volatile component of a solution is inversely proportional to its mole fraction in the solution.
 (d) The vapour pressure exerted by a volatile component of a solution is directly proportional to its volume in the solution.

(iii) Which of the following is incorrect for an ideal solution?
 (a) $\Delta H_{mix} = 0$
 (b) $\Delta V_{mix} = 0$
 (c) $\Delta P = P_{obs} - P_{calculated} = 0$
 (d) $\Delta G_{mix} = 0$

(iv) Which of the following condition is not satisfied by an ideal solution?
 (a) $\Delta H_{mix} = 0$
 (b) $\Delta V_{mix} = 0$
 (c) Raoult's Law is obeyed
 (d) Formation of an azeotropic mixture

OR

The boiling point of an azeotropic mixture of water and ethanol is less than that of water and ethanol. The mixture shows:
 (a) No deviation from Raoult's Law.
 (b) Positive deviation from Raoult's Law.
 (c) Negative deviation from Raoult's Law.
 (d) That the solution is unsaturated.

60. Read the passage given below and answer the following questions:

At 298K, the vapour pressure of pure benzene. C_6H_6 is 0.256 bar and the vapour pressure of pure toluene $C_6H_5CH_3$ is 0.0925 bar. Two mixtures were prepared as follows:
(I) 7.8g of C_6H_6 + 9.2g of toluene
(II) 3.9g of C_6H_6 + 13.8 g of toluene

The following questions are multiple choice questions. Choose the most appropriate answer:

(i) The total vapour pressure (bar) of solution 1 is:
 (a) 0.128 (b) 0.174
 (c) 0.198 (d) 0.258

(ii) Which of the given solutions have higher vapour pressure?
 (a) I
 (b) II
 (c) Both have equal vapour pressure
 (d) Cannot be predicted

(iii) Mole fraction of benzene is vapour phase in solution I is:
 (a) 0.128 (b) 0.174
 (c) 0.734 (d) 0.266

(iv) Which of the following statements is/are correct?
 (I) Mole fraction of toluene in vapour phase is more in solution I.
 (II) Mole fraction of toleuene in vapour phase is less in solutioon I.
 (III) Mole fraction of benzene in vapour phase is less in solution I.
 (a) Only II (b) Only I
 (c) I Only III (d) II and III

OR

Solution I is an example of a/an:
 (a) Ideal solution
 (b) non-ideal solution with positive deviation
 (c) non-ideal solution with negative deviation
 (d) can't be predicted

Answers

1. (b) $-0.372°C$

 Explanation: $\Delta T_f = K_f \times m \times i$
 $i = 2$ (for NaCl → $Na^+ + Cl^-$)
 M = 0.1 molal
 $K_f = 1.86°C$/molal
 where i is van't hoff constant/factor
 $\Delta T_f = 2 \times 1.86 \times 0.1 = 0.372°C$

 Therefore, now freezing point = $0 - 0.372°C = -0.372°C$.

2. (b) Molality

 Explanation: Molality is not affected by temperature as volume is not involved in molality which changes with temperature. Molality = Moles of solute/Weight of solvent (kg).

3. (a) Both composition and properties are uniform throughout the mixture.
   Explanation: In homogeneous mixtures composition and properties both are uniform throughout the mixture.

4. (c) Greater than one
   Explanation: The Van't Hoff factor (i) expresses how many ions and particles are formed (on an average) in a solution from one formula unit of solute. When solute particles dissociate in solution, i is greater than 1 and when solute particles associate in solution, i is less than 1.

5. (b) supersaturated
   Explanation: A supersaturated solution is one in which a small amount of solute is given to a solution and it does not dissolve and precipitates.

6. (d) None of these
   Explanation: Henry's law is one of the gas laws formulated by William Henry in 1803 and states: "At a constant temperature, the amount of a given gas that dissolves in a given type and volume of liquid is directly proportional to the partial pressure of that gas in equilibrium with that liquid." An equivalent way of stating the law is that the solubility of a gas in a liquid is directly proportional to the partial pressure of the gas above the liquid.

7. (c) Equal to the mole fraction of the solute
   Explanation: Relative lowering of vapour pressure : The vapour pressure of a liquid is the pressure of the vapour which is in equilibrium with that liquid. The vapour pressure of a solvent is lowered when a non-volatile solute is dissolved in it to form a solution. The reduction of vapour pressure of solvent is given as
   $p^1 = X.p^0$
   p^1 is vapour pressure of the solution.
   p^0 is the vapour pressure of pure solvent
   x is the mole fraction of solute
   Relative lowering of vapour pressure is $p^1/p^0 = X$

8. (c) 0·90% by weight of NaCl approximately
   Explanation: The intracellular fluid of erythrocytes is a solution of salts, glucose, protein and hemoglobin. A 0.9% NaCl solution is said to be isotonic: when blood cells reside in such a medium, the intracellular and extracellular fluids are in osmotic equilibrium across the cell membrane, and there is no net influx or efflux of water.

9. (b) $BaCl_2$ > NaCl > Glucose
   Explanation: Osmotic pressure is a colligative property, and more the number of particles more the osmotic pressure.
   $\pi = iCRT$
   Hence, the order is $BaCl_2$ > NaCl > Glucose since the concentration is same and i for $BaCl_2$ is 3, NaCl is 2 and glucose is 1.

10. (d) Modification of refractive index
    Explanation: Followings are the colligative properties :
    • Relative Lowering of Vapour Pressure
    • Elevation of Boiling Point
    • Depression of Freezing Point
    • Osmotic Pressure

11. (a) Two different solutions of sucrose of same molality prepared in different solvents will have the same depression in freezing point.
    Explanation: Depression in freezing point depends on the concentration (molarity) of solution and also on solvent taken.

12. (b) A non-electrolyte in dilute solution
    Explanation: As Raoult's law is applicable for a dilute solution having non-electrolyte solute. Thus, the determination of correct molecular mass from Raoult's law is applicable to a non-electrolyte in a dilute solution.

13. (b) Molality
    Explanation: The number of moles of solute present in 1000 gm (or 1 kg) of solvent is known as molality.

14. (a) Potassium sulphate
    Explanation: Urea and glucose do not dissociate in solution. Sodium chloride gives two ions and potassium sulphate gives three ions per formula unit. Therefore, the effective number of particles is maximum in potassium sulphate, and it shows the maximum depression in freezing point.

15. (d) Number of moles of solvent only
    Explanation: Colligative properties: Those physical properties of a solution which depend upon the number of particles in a given volume of the solution or the mole fraction of the solute are called colligative properties. The following four properties are colligative properties :
    (i) Lowering of vapour pressure of the solvent
    (ii) Elevation in boiling point of the solvent
    (iii) Depression in freezing point of solvent
    (iv) Osmotic pressure

16. (c) Ideal
    Explanation: A solution that obeys Raoult's law is known as ideal solution. Since Raoult's law only works for ideal solutions. An ideal solution is defined as one which obeys Raoult's law.

17. (c) Practically no deviation from Raoult's law
    Explanation: A liquid pair of benzene-toluene shows practically no deviation from Raoult's law. Raoult's law is a law of physical chemistry, with implications in thermodynamics.

18. (d) There will be no net movement across the membrane
    Explanation: As both the solutions are isotonic hence there is no net movement of the solvent occurs through the semipermeable membrane between two solutions.

19. (a) Equal to second
    Explanation: Moles of Urea = $\dfrac{12}{60} = 0.2$
    Moles of Sucrose = $\dfrac{68.4}{342} = 0.2$
    Both are non-electrolyte hence lowering of vapour pressure will be same.

20. (b) water will move from side (B) to side (A) if a pressure greater than osmotic pressure is applied on piston (B).
    Explanation: Water will move from side B (concentrated sodium chloride solution) to side A (fresh water) if a pressure greater than osmotic pressure is applied on piston B.
21. (b) The depression in freezing point is directly proportional to molality of the solution.
    Explanation: Solubility changes with temperature. A plant cell shrinks in hypertonic solution. Relative lowering of vapour pressure is a colligative property.
22. (c) Decreased by 1%
    Explanation: When 0.1 mole urea is dissolved in 9.9 mole water, then the vapour pressure is Decreased by 1%.
23. (b) Henry's law
    Explanation: Henry's law states that at a constant temperature, the solubility of a gas is directly proportional to the pressure of the gas.
    In other words, the partial pressure of the gas in vapour phase (p) is proportional to the mole fraction of the gas (X) in the solution.
    $p = K_H X$
    Here, K_H is the Henry's law constant
24. (b) Molality
    Explanation: Due to presence of solute in the solution, the boiling point of the solution is greater than the boiling point of pure solvent. This is known as elevation in boiling point and it can be represented as:
    $\Delta T_b = K_b \times$ molality
25. (d) Glucose
    Explanation: Glucose contains an aldehyde group, i.e. an aldose and six carbons, i.e. a hexose. Therefore, we can say that glucose is an example of aldohexose.
26. (b) $PV = nRT$
    Explanation: Osmotic pressure is the pressure that must be applied to a solution to halt the flow of solvent molecules through a semipermeable membrane (osmosis). Osmotic pressure of a dilute solution is given by $PV = nRT$
27. (d) Electrical conductivity
    Explanation: Those properties of ideal solutions which depend only on the number of particles of the solute (molecules or ions) dissolved in a definite amount of the solvent and do not depend on the nature of solute are called colligative properties. The important colligative properties are:
    (i) Relative lowering of vapour pressure
    (ii) Osmotic pressure
    (iii) Elevation in boiling point
    (iv) Depression in freezing point
28. (b) Increase in B.P of solution.
    Explanation: Addition of common salt in water causes increase in B.P of solution.
29. (c) 0.90% by weight of NaCl approximately
    Explanation: 0.5 - 0.9% NaCl - an isotonic solution wont damage blood cells or tissues, and a slightly hypotonic solution will drive water into tissues, which is where you want it to go in a dehydrated patient.
30. (c) Practically no deviation from Raoult's law
    Explanation: Liquid pair benzene-toluene shows practically no deviation from Raoult's Law. Raoult's law states that a solvent's partial vapour pressure in a solution (or mixture) is equal or identical to the vapour pressure of the pure solvent multiplied by its mole fraction in the solution.
31. (d) Powdered sugar in hot water.
    Explanation: Powdered sugar has large surface area and thus, dissolves faster in hot water. As solution feels cool to touch, dissolution is endothermic so, dissolution will be favoured at high temperature.
32. (d) Density
    Explanation: The ratio of two extensive properties of the same object or system is an intensive property. For example, the ratio of an object's mass and volume, which are two extensive properties, is density, which is an intensive property.
33. (a) Double the theoretical value
    Explanation: Molecular mass of NaCl determined by osmotic pressure measurement is found to be half of the actual value.
34. (d) Raoult's law
    Explanation: Raoult's law states that the vapour pressure of a solvent above a solution is equal to the vapour pressure of the pure solvent at the same temperature scaled by the mole fraction of the solvent present.
    $P_{solution} = \chi_{solvent} P^0_{solvent}$
    The molar mass of a non-volatile solute be determined by using following equation.
    $$\frac{P^\circ - P}{P^\circ} = \frac{W_2 W_1}{W_1 W_2}$$
    P^0 = vapour pressure of pure solvent
    P = vapour pressure of solution
    W_2 = Mass of solute.
    M_2 = Molar mass of solute.
    W_1 = Mass of solvent.
    M_1 = Molar mass of solvent.
35. (a) At specific composition methanol-acetone mixture will form minimum boiling azeotrope and will show positive deviation from Raoult's law.
    Explanation: At specific composition methanol-acetone mixture will show positive deviation from Raoult's law as it has lesser interactions than methanol-methanol and acetone-acetone interactions. Hence it forms minimum boiling azeotrope.
36. (b) The osmotic pressure of a solution is given by the equation π = CRT (where C is the molarity of the solution).

Solutions | 215

Explanation: Value of A is different for different solvents. Thus, according to relation, even for same molal solutions depression in freezing point will be different.

37. (c) 0.5 mol L^{-1}
Explanation: According to equation, No. of moles of NaOH = $\frac{10}{40}$ = 0.25 mole Molarity = $\frac{(0.25 \times 1000)}{500}$
= 0.5 mol L^{-1}

38. (b) $x_1 = \frac{n_1}{n_1 + n_2 + n_3 + n_4} = \frac{n_1}{\sum n}$
Explanation: In a given solution sum of all the mole fraction is unity i.e. $n_1/(n_1 + n_2 + n_3) = x_1$ and $x_1 + x_2 + x_3 + x_4 = 1$

39. (b) A-(r), B-(p), C-(q), D-(s)
Explanation: Mass percentage is Industrial chemical application, Mass by volume is Medicine and pharmacy, ppm is Concentration of pollutants in water, and Volume percentage is Liquid solutions.

40. (c) The solubility of a gas in beaker (i) is less than that in beaker (ii).
Explanation: The solubility of gas in a liquid increases with increase in pressure and is directly proportional to the pressure of the gas.

41. (b) Rate at which gaseous particles are striking the solution to enter it, decreases.
Explanation: On increasing the pressure over the solution phase by compressing the gas to a smaller volume (in fig. b) increase the number of gaseous particles per unit volume over the solution and also the rate at which the gaseous particles are striking the surface of solution to enter it. The solubility of the gas will increase until a new equilibrium is reached resulting in an increase in the pressure of a gas above the solution and thus its solubility increases. On increasing the pressure over the solution phase by compressing the gas to a smaller volume (in fig. b) increase the number of gaseous particles per unit volume over the solution and also the rate at which the gaseous particles are striking the surface of solution to enter it. The solubility of the gas will increase until a new equilibrium is reached resulting in an increase in the pressure of a gas above the solution and thus its solubility increases.

42. (a) Low concentrations of oxygen in blood and tissues.
Explanation: At high altitudes the partial pressure of oxygen is less than that at the ground level. This leads to low concentrations of oxygen in the blood and tissues of people living at high altitudes or climbers.

43. (d) Diethyl ether, acetone, ethyl alcohol, water
Explanation: The vapour pressure increases with decrease in intermolecular forces. When the forces are weak, the liquid has high volatility and maximum vapour pressure. Diethyl ether has highest vapour pressure while water has lowest vapour pressure.

44. (a) Colligative, solvent, lower concentration, higher concentration, solution.
Explanation: Relative lowering of vapour pressure, osmotic pressure of a solution and elevation in boiling points are colligative properties. Osmosis is the passage of, solvent through a semipermeable membrane from a solution of lower concentration towards a solution of higher concentration. Osmotic pressure is equivalent to mechanical pressure which must be applied on solution to prevent osmosis.

45. (c) Dimerization of benzoic acid.
Explanation: Benzoic acid exists as dimer in benzene.

46. (d) When a solute is present in trace quantities it is convenient to express concentration in ppm.

47. (a) KCl can dissociate in water but glucose does not. Due to dissociation of ions, solution exhibit higher colligative property.

48. (c) With the semipermeable membrane in place, and if one compartment contains the pure solvent, this can never happen; no matter how much liquid flows through the membrane, the solvent in the right side will always be more concentrated than that in the left side.

49. (c) Amalgam of mercury with sodium is an example of liquid in solid type solid solution. Here mercury (liquid metal) acts as solute and sodium as solvent.

50. (a) Molarity is the number of moles of solute dissolved per litre of solution. Molarity changes as temperature changes.

51. (a) Liquids and solids exhibit practically no change of solubility with changes in pressure. Gases as might be expected, increase in solubility with an increase in pressure.

52. (c) Elevation in boiling point is directly proportional to molality.

53. (b) Non-ideal solutions with positive deviation or more vapour pressure than expected, boil at a lower temperature than the Components, while those with negative departure boil at a higher temperature.

54. (d) At equilibrium, the vapour phase will always be rich in volatile components. The higher liquid's vapour pressure is at a given temperature the higher its volatility and the lower the liquid's typical boiling point. The partial pressure of components determines the composition of the vapour phase in equilibrium with the solution.

55. (d) An ideal solution obeys Raoult's law.

56. (i) (b) boil below 100°C and freeze above 0°C
(ii) (d) dependent only on the identity of the solvent and the concentration of the solute and independent of the solute's identity.
(iii) (a) A
(iv) (d) all of the above

57. (i) (c) Assertion is correct statement but reason is wrong statement.
(ii) (c) Assertion is correct statement but reason is wrong statement.
(iii) (a) Assertion and reason both are correct statements and reason is correct explanation for assertion.

(iv) (b) Assertion and reason both are correct statements but reason is not correct explanation for assertion.

OR

(b) Assertion and reason both are correct statements but reason is not correct explanation for assertion.

58. (i) (b) Assertion and reason both are correct statements but reason is not correct explanation for assertion.
(ii) (a) Assertion and reason both are correct statements and reason is correct explanation for assertion.
(iii) (a) Assertion and reason both are correct statements and reason is correct explanation for assertion.
(iv) (d) Assertion is wrong statement but reason is correct statement.

59. (i) (c) about three times
(ii) (a) The vapour pressure exerted by a volatile component of a solution is directly proportional to its mole fraction in the solution.
(iii) (d) $\Delta G_{mix} = 0$
(iv) (d) Formation of an azeotropic mixture.

OR

(b) Positive deviation from Raoult's Law.

60. (i) (b) 0.174
(ii) (a) I
(iii) (c) 0.174
(iv) (a) only II

OR

(a) ideal solution

❏❏

Chapter 7

p-Block Elements

1. The geometry of XeF$_6$ molecule and the hybridization of Xe atom in the molecule is:
   (a) Distorted octahedral and sp^3d^3
   (b) Square planar and sp^3d^2
   (c) Pyramidal and sp^3
   (d) Octahedral and sp^3d^3

2. If chlorine gas is passed through hot NaOH solution, two changes are observed in the oxidation number of chlorine during the reaction. These are _____ and _____. [NCERT Exemplar]
   (a) 0 to +5
   (b) 0 to +3
   (c) 0 to –1
   (d) 0 to +1

3. The tendency of group 16 elements to form catenated compounds is greatest in case of:
   (a) Oxygen
   (b) Sulphur
   (c) Selenium
   (d) Tellurium

4. The minimum bond angle in hydrides of group 16 elements is in:
   (a) H$_2$O
   (b) H$_2$Te
   (c) H$_2$Se
   (d) H$_2$S

5. Which of the following has lowest reducing character?
   (a) H$_2$O
   (b) H$_2$S
   (c) H$_2$Te
   (d) H$_2$Se

6. Which of the following mainly exhibits (– 2) oxidation state?
   (a) S
   (b) O
   (c) Se
   (d) Te

7. Oxygen molecule is:
   (a) Paramagnetic
   (b) Diamagnetic
   (c) Ferromagnetic
   (d) Ferrimagnetic

8. The halogen with highest electron affinity:
   (a) F
   (b) Cl
   (c) Br
   (d) I

9. The halide ion easiest to oxidise is:
   (a) F$^-$
   (b) Cl$^-$
   (c) Br$^-$
   (d) I$^-$

10. Which of the following options are not in accordance with the property mentioned against them? [NCERT Exemplar]
    (a) F$_2$ > Cl$_2$ > Br$_2$ > I$_2$ Oxidising power.
    (b) MI > MBr > MCl > MF Ionic character of metal halide.
    (c) F$_2$ > Cl$_2$ > Br$_2$ > I$_2$ Bond dissociation enthalpy.
    (d) HI < HBr < HCl < HF Hydrogen-halogen bond strength.

11. The low bond energy is best explained by:
    (a) The attainment of noble gas configuration
    (b) The low electron affinity of F
    (c) Repulsion by electron pairs on F
    (d) The small size of F

12. The oxo-acid of halogen with maximum acidic character is:
    (a) HClO$_4$
    (b) HClO$_3$
    (c) HClO$_2$
    (d) HClO

13. Which of the following reaction will not occur spontaneously?
    (a) F$_2$ + 2Cl$^-$ $\longrightarrow$ 2F$^-$ + Cl$_2$
    (b) I$_2$ + 2Br$^-$ $\longrightarrow$ 2I$^-$ + Br$_2$
    (c) Br$_2$ + 2I$^-$ $\longrightarrow$ 2Br$^-$ + I$_2$
    (d) 2I$^-$ + Cl$_2^-$ $\longrightarrow$ 2Cl$^-$ + I$_2$

14. The high viscosity and high boiling point of HF is due to:
    (a) Low dissociation energy of F$_2$ molecule
    (b) Associated nature due to hydrogen bonding
    (c) Ionic character of HF
    (d) High electronegativity of fluorine

15. The most powerful oxidising agent is:
    (a) Fluorine
    (b) Chlorine
    (c) Bromine
    (d) Iodine

16. Shape of ClF$_3$ is:
    (a) Trigonal planar
    (b) Tetrahedral
    (c) T-Shaped
    (d) Distorted octahedral

17. Which of the following statements are correct? [NCERT Exemplar]
    (a) Among halogens, radius ratio between iodine and fluorine is maximum.
    (b) Leaving F—F bond, all halogens have weaker X—X bond than X—X' bond in interhalogens.
    (c) Among interhalogen compounds maximum number of atoms are present in iodine fluoride.
    (d) Interhalogen compounds are more reactive than halogen compounds.

18. Which noble gas was discovered in chromosphere?
    (a) He
    (b) Ar
    (c) Xe
    (d) Rn

19. XeF$_2$ molecule is:
    (a) Trigonal planar
    (b) Square planar
    (c) Linear
    (d) Pyramidal

20. The noble gas used in the treatment of Cancer is:
    (a) Argon
    (b) Xenon
    (c) Radon
    (d) Helium

21. In XeF$_2$, Xenon involves the hybridisation:
    (a) sp
    (b) sp^2
    (c) sp^3d
    (d) sp^3

22. Which one of the following displaces bromine form an aqueous solution of bromine?
    (a) Cl_2
    (b) Cl^-
    (c) I_2
    (d) I_3^-
23. When SO_2 gas is passed through acidified $K_2Cr_2O_7$ solution, the colour of the solution changes to:
    (a) Red
    (b) Black
    (c) Orange
    (d) Green
24. Which of the following reagent does not give O_2 gas on reaction with Ozone?
    (a) $KMnO_4$
    (b) $SnCl_2/HCl$
    (c) $FeSO_4/H_2SO_4$
    (d) PbS
25. Aqua regia is a mixture of:
    (a) Conc. HNO_3 and conc. H_2SO_4
    (b) Conc. HCl and conc. H_2SO_4 in the ratio of 3 : 1
    (c) Conc. HCl and conc. HNO_3 in the ratio of 3 : 1
    (d) None of these
26. Tailing of mercury is due to the formation of:
    (a) Hg_2O
    (b) HgO
    (c) $Hg(OH)_2$
    (d) $HgCl_2$
27. Which one is called oleum?
    (a) Liq. NH_3
    (b) $H_2SO_4 + SO_3$
    (c) Conc. HNO_3
    (d) Dilute solution of H_2O_2
28. Which one absorbs U.V. radiation in stratosphere?
    (a) CO_2
    (b) N_2
    (c) O_3
    (d) H_2
29. Which of the following has lowest reducing character?
    (a) H_2O
    (b) H_2S
    (c) H_2Te
    (d) H_2Se
30. Among the following halogens, the one which does not forms an oxyacid is:
    (a) Fluorine
    (b) Chlorine
    (c) Bromine
    (d) Iodine
31. Oxygen molecule is :
    (a) Paramagnetic
    (b) Diamagnetic
    (c) Ferromagnetic
    (d) Ferrimagnetic
32. Which of the following has lowest reducing character?
    (a) H_2O
    (b) H_2S
    (c) H_2Te
    (d) H_2Se
33. Among the following halogens, the one which does not forms an oxyacid is:
    (a) Fluorine
    (b) Chlorine
    (c) Bromine
    (d) Iodine
34. Reduction potentials of some ions are given below. Arrange them in decreasing order of oxidising power.

Ion	ClO_4^-	IO_4^-	BrO_4^-
Reduction potential E^-/V	$E^- = 1.19V$	$E^- = 1.65V$	$E^- = 1.74V$

    [NCERT Exemplar]
    (a) $ClO_4^- > IO_4^- > BrO_4^-$
    (b) $IO_4^- > BrO_4^- > ClO_4^-$
    (c) $BrO_4^- > IO_4^- > ClO_4^-$
    (d) $BrO_4^- > ClO_4^- > IO_4^-$
35. Among the following halogens, the one which does not forms an oxyacid is:
    (a) Fluorine
    (b) Chlorine
    (c) Bromine
    (d) Iodine
36. The reaction, $3ClO^- (aq) \longrightarrow ClO_3^- (aq) + 2Cl^- (aq)$, is an example of:
    (a) Oxidation reaction
    (b) Reduction reaction
    (c) Disproportionation reaction
    (d) Decomposition reaction
37. Which of the following is not an interhalogen compound?
    (a) ICl_4^-
    (b) ClF_5
    (c) IPO_4
    (d) ClF_3
38. Ozone turns trimethyl paper:
    (a) Green
    (b) Violet
    (c) Red
    (d) Black
39. What is the valence shell electronic configuration of p-block elements?
    (a) ns^2
    (b) $ns^2 np^{1-5}$
    (c) $ns^2 np^{1-6}$
    (d) None of these
40. The incorrect trend regarding group 16 hydrides (H_2E) is:
    (a) down the group, the H-E-H bond angle increases
    (b) the acidic character of hydrides increases down the group
    (c) except water, all hydrides possess reducing properties
    (d) thermal stability of hydrides decreases down the group
41. Group 16 elements have lower value of first ionisation enthalpy as compared to group 15 elements because:
    (a) half-filled p-orbitals in group 15 elements are more stable
    (b) group 16 elements have smaller size than group 15 elements
    (c) group 16 elements contain double bond while group 15 elements have triple bond
    (d) group 16 elements have more number of electrons in p-orbitals
42. Solid oxygen has a pale blue colour which is attributed to:
    (a) electronic transitions from the singlet ground state to the triplet excited state
    (b) electronic transitions from antibonding π-molecular orbitals to bonding $\sigma 2p_2$ M.O.s
    (c) electronic transitions from the triplet ground state to anti bonding $\sigma 2p_2$ molecular orbital
    (d) electronic transitions from the triplet ground state to the excited singlet state
43. Which of the following is the balanced equation describing the combustion of elemental sulphur?
    (a) $2H_2S + 3O_2 \rightarrow 2SO_2 + 2H_2O$
    (b) $H_2S + 2O_2 \rightarrow SO_3 + H_2O$
    (c) $2SO_3 \rightarrow 2S + 3O_2$
    (d) $S + O_2 \rightarrow SO_2$
44. In which of the following reactions conc. H_2SO_4 is used as an oxidising reagent? [NCERT Exemplar]
    (a) $CaF_2 + H_2SO_4 \rightarrow CaSO_4 + 2HF$
    (b) $2HI + H_2SO_4 \rightarrow I_2 + SO_2 + 2H_2O$

(c) Cu + 2H$_2$SO$_4$ → CuSO$_4$ + SO$_2$ + 2H$_2$O
(d) NaCl + H$_2$SO$_4$ → NaHSO$_4$ + HCl

45. **Dry SO$_2$ does not bleach dry flowers because:**
    (a) nascent hydrogen responsible for bleaching is produced only in presence of moisture
    (b) water is the actual reducing agent responsible for bleaching
    (c) water is stronger acid than SO$_2$
    (d) the OH$^-$ ions produced by water cause bleaching

Directions: In the following questions, a statement of assertion is followed by a statement of reason. Mark the correct choice as:
(a) If both assertion and reason are true and reason is the correct explanation of assertion.
(b) If both assertion and reason are true, but reason is not the correct explanation of assertion.
(c) If assertion is true, but reason is false.
(d) If assertion is false but reason is true.

46. **Assertion:** Valency of noble gas is 0.
    Reason: Noble gases possess complete octet.

47. **Assertion:** F$_2$ has lower bond dissociation enthalpy than Cl$_2$. [CBSE, 2020]
    Reason: Fluorine is more electronegative than chlorine.

48. **Assertion:** Acidic character of group 16 hydrides increases from H$_2$O to H$_2$Te.
    Reason: Thermal stability of hydrides decreases down the group.

49. **Assertion:** Interhalogen compounds are more reactive than halogens (except fluorine).
    Reason: They all undergo hydrolysis giving halide ion derived from the smaller halogen and anion derived from larger halogen.

50. **Assertion:** Halogens are not found in free state in nature.
    Reason: Halogens are highly reactive compounds.

51. **Assertion:** F$_2$ has low reactivity.
    Reason: F-F bond has low Δ_{bond} H [CBSE, 2020]

52. **Assertion:** Ozone layer in the upper region of atmosphere protects earth from UV radiations of sun.
    Reason: Ozone is a powerful oxidising agent as compared to oxygen.

53. **Assertion:** S shows paramagnetic nature, when present in vapour state.
    Reason: S exists as S$_2$ in vapour state.

54. **Assertion:** F$_2$ is a strong oxidising agent. [CBSE, 2020]
    Reason: Electron gain enthalpy of fluorine is less negative.

55. **Assertion:** PbI$_4$ is not a stable compound.
    Reason: Iodide stabilizes higher oxidation state.

56. **Assertion:** Solubility of noble gases in water decreases with increasing size of the noble gas.
    Reason: Solubility of noble gases in water is due to dipole-induced dipole interaction.

57. **Read the passage given below and answer the following questions:** [CBSE Website]
    In spite of the predictions of stable noble gas compounds since at least 1902, unsuccessful attempts at their synthesis gave rise to the widely held opinion that noble gases are not only noble but also inert. It was not until 1962 that this dogma was shattered when Bartlett in Canada published the first stable noble gas compound XePtF$_6$. This discovery triggered a worldwide frenzy in this area, and within a short time span many new xenon, radon, and krypton compounds were prepared and characterized. The recent discoveries show the ability of xenon to act as a ligand. The discovery by Seppelt's group that more than one xenon atom can attach itself to a metal center which in the case of gold leads to surprisingly stable Au- Xe bonds. The bonding in [AuXe$_4$]$^{2+}$ involves 4 Xe ligands attached by relatively strong bonds to a single Au(II) center in a square planar arrangement with a Xe-Au bond length of about 274 pm. This discovery provides not only the first example of multiple xenon ligands but also represents the first strong metal - xenon bond.

    (i) In the complex ion [AuXe$_4$]$^{2+}$, Xe acts as :
        (a) central atom   (b) ligand
        (c) chelating agent   (d) electrophile
    (ii) Hybridisation shown by Au in [AuXe$_4$]$^{2+}$ is :
        (a) sp^3 (b) sp^3d
        (c) sp^3d^2 (d) sp^2
    (iii) Compounds of noble gases except___are known.
        (a) Krypton   (b) Radon
        (c) Helium   (d) Xenon
    (iv) Xe is a_____ligand:
        (a) ambidentate   (b) bidentate
        (c) unidentate   (d) hexadentate

58. **Read the passage given below and answer the following questions:** [CBSE Website]
    In the last 10 years much has been learned about the molecular structure of elemental sulfur. It is now known that many different types of rings are sufficiently metastable to exist at room temperature for several days. It is known that at high temperature, the equilibrium composition allows for a variety of rings and chains to exist in comparable concentration, and it is known that at the boiling point and above, the vapor as well as the liquid contains small species with three, four and five atoms.

    The sulfur atom has the same number of valence electrons as oxygen. Thus, sulfur atoms S$_2$ and S$_3$ have physical and chemical properties analogous to those of oxygen and ozone. S$_2$ has a ground state of $3\text{S}\sigma 3s^2\sigma^* 3s^2\sigma 3pz^2\pi 3px^2 =\pi 3py 2\pi^* 3px1 =\pi^* 3py^1$. S$_3$, thiozone has a well- known uv spectrum, and has a bent structure, analogous to its isovalent molecules O3, SO$_2$, and S$_2$O. The chemistry of the two elements, sulphur and oxygen, differs because sulfur has a pronounced tendency for catenation. The most frequently quoted explanation is based on the electron structure of the atom. Sulfur has low-lying unoccupied 3d orbitals, and it is widely believed that the 4s and 3d orbitals of sulfur participate in bonding in a manner similar to the participation of 2s and 2p orbitals in carbon.

    In the following questions, a statement of assertion followed by a statement of reason is given. Choose the correct answer out of the following choices on the basis of the above passage.
    (a) Assertion and reason both are correct statements and reason is correct explanation for assertion.

(b) Assertion and reason both are correct statements but reason is not correct explanation for assertion.
(c) Assertion is correct statement but reason is wrong statement.
(d) Assertion is wrong statement but reason is correct statement.

(i) **Assertion:** Sulphur belongs to same group in the periodic table as oxygen.
Reason: S_2 has properties analogous to O_2.

(ii) **Assertion:** Thiozone has bent structure like ozone.
Reason: Ozone has a lone pair which makes the molecule bent.

(iii) **Assertion:** S_2 is paramagnetic in nature.
Reason: The electrons in π^*3px and π^*3py orbitals in S_2 are unpaired.

(iv) **Assertion:** Sulphur has a greater tendency for catenation than oxygen.
Reason: $3d$ and $4s$ orbitals of Sulphur have same energy.

59. **Read the passage given below and answer the following questions:**

Current investigations, for example, on antimony(III) and arsenic(III) halogen compounds, have indicated quite similar structural principles as in Te(IV) analogues. In the series of the binary halides of selenium and tellurium, the crystal structure determinations of tellurium tetrafluoride and of tellurium tetrachloride on twinned crystals were the key to understanding the various and partly contradictory spectroscopic and other macroscopic properties, as well as the synthetic potential of the compounds. The chapter discusses the characteristic structural and bonding features of the halogen compounds of the chalcogen(IV systems, in which the role of the inert pair determines much of the stereochemistry and reactive properties of the whole class of compounds. SCl_4, as the only stable tetrahalide of sulfur besides SF_4, is known to be easily prepared at temperatures below –34°C from the elements or from the reversible reaction of equimolar amounts of SC_{12} and chlorine.

The following questions are multiple choice questions. Choose the most appropriate answer:

(i) Bond enthalpy terms in group 16 follow which one of the following trends?
(a) S–S > O–O
(b) Se–Se > S–S
(c) S = S > O = O
(d) S–F < O–F

(ii) Which statement is incorrect about sulphuric acid?
(a) Crystalline H_2SO_4 possesses a hydrogen-bonded 3-dimensional network.
(b) Pure liquid H_2SO_4 is viscous because of intramolecular hydrogen bonding.
(c) H_2SO_4 is dibasic. In the first and second acid dissociation steps, it behaves as a strong and as a fairly weak acid, respectively.
(d) None of the above

(iii) The boiling points of hydrides of group 16 are in the order:
(a) $H_2O > H_2Te > H_2S > H_2Se$
(b) $H_2O > H_2S > H_2Se > H_2Te$
(c) $H_2O > H_2Te > H_2Se > H_2S$
(d) None of these

OR

H_2S is more acidic than H_2O because:
(a) Oxygen is more electronegative than sulphur.
(b) Atomic number of sulphur is higher than oxygen.
(c) H — S bond dissociation energy is less as compared to H — O bond.
(d) H — O bond dissociation energy is less also compared to H — S bond.

(iv) Which one of the group 16 elements given below hardly show -2 oxidation state?
(a) Selenium
(b) Tellurium
(c) Polonium
(d) Oxygen

60. **Read the passage given below and answer the following questions:**

The atmosphere is the principal nitrogen reservoir, with over 99% of the total in the form of N_2. Nitrogen in terrestrial system occurs mainly as a constituent in soil organic matter, with litter and soil inorganic nitrogen accounting for the majority (97%). Biomass accounts for just fewer than 3% of this, 95% occurs in plant tissue. Dinitrogen, in dissolved form (N_2, aq), is the most abundant nitrogen form in the world's oceans. Nitrogen also occurs in both inorganic forms (e.g., nitrate, nitrite, ammonia, hydrazine, nitrous oxide, and nitrogen dioxide) and organic forms (e.g., amino acids, amines, and amides). Amino acids are minor but important constituents of dissolved organic content.

(i) The valence shell electronic configuration of group 15 elements is ns^2np^3. Electronic configuration of Bismuth is:
(a) $[He]2s^2\,2p^5$
(b) $[Xe]f^{14}\,5d^{10}\,6s^2\,6p^3$
(c) $[Kr]4d^{10}\,5s^2\,5p^5$
(d) $[Ar]3d^{10}\,4s^2\,4p^3$

(ii) Ionisation enthalpy decreases down the group 15 because:
(a) atomic size increases gradually
(b) atomic size decreases gradually
(c) atomic size does not change going down the group
(d) atomic size decreases slightly

(iii) Which one of the following elements have a unique property to form $p\pi$-$p\pi$ multiple bonds with itself?
(a) Bi
(b) As
(c) P
(d) N

(iv) Which one of the following best describes the types of oxides formed by nitrogen family elements?
(a) EO_3 and EO_5
(b) E_2O_3 and E_2O_5
(c) E_3O and E_2O
(d) EO_5 and E_2O_5

(v) A thermal decomposition method that yields very pure nitrogen uses the following as reactant(s)
(a) barium azide
(b) sodium nitride
(c) ammonium chloride
(d) magnesium nitride

61. **Read the passage given below and answer the following questions:**

Phosphorus signifies an essential element in molecular biology, yet given the limited solubility of phosphates on early Earth, alternative sources like meteoritic phosphides have been proposed to incorporate phosphorus into biomolecules under prebiotic terrestrial conditions. Here, we report on a previously overlooked source of prebiotic phosphorus from interstellar phosphine (PH_3) that produces key phosphorus oxoacids—phosphoric acid (H_3PO_4), phosphonic acid (H_3PO_3), and pyrophosphoric acid ($H_4P_2O_7$)—in interstellar analog ices exposed to ionizing radiation at temperatures as low as 5 K.

(i) Which one of the following is not an oxoacid of phosphorus
 (a) polymetaphosphoric acid
 (b) hypophosphorus acid
 (c) metapyro phosphoric acid
 (d) orthophosphoric acid

(ii) What is the three-dimensional structure of PCl_3
 (a) tetrahedral
 (b) trigonal bipyramidal
 (c) planar bipyramidal
 (d) square planar

(iii) Hypophosphorus acid is a good:
 (a) oxidising agent (b) drying agent
 (c) reducing agent (d) fumigating agent

(iv) Passing dry chlorine over heated white phosphorus yeilds:
 (a) phosphorus chloride
 (b) phosphorus oxide
 (c) phosphorus tetrachloride
 (d) phosphorus trichloride

(v) Phosphine reacts with hydrobromic acid to give:
 (a) phosphonium hydroxide
 (b) phosphonium bromide
 (c) phosphonic acid
 (d) phosphorus

Answers

1. (a) Distorted octahedral and sp^3d^3
 Explanation: The geometry of XeF_6 molecule and the hybridization of Xe atom in the molecule are distorted octahedral and sp^3d^3 respectively. Xe has 6 bond pairs of electrons and one lone pair of electrons. Xe atom possess sp^3d^3 hybridization which results in the electronic geometry of pentagonal bipyramidal and molecular geometry of distorted octahedral.

2. (a,c) 0 to +5, 0 to –1
 Explanation: $6NaOH$ (Hot) + $3Cl_2$ → $5NaCl$ + $NaClO_3$
 Therefore, oxidation no. of Chlorine changes from 0 to +5 and 0 to –1.

3. (b) Sulphur
 Explanation: Catenation is the property of forming bond with a maximum number of atoms. In group sixteen elements, sulphur has maximum catenation property because of high bonding energy of sulphur atoms. Its electronegativity is close to that of carbon, which helps easy bonding with many atoms.

4. (b) H_2Te
 Explanation: All these are the hydrides of 16th group elements in which the central atom undergo sp^3 hybridization and should possess the bond angle 109° but the bond angle distorts due to the repulsion between lone pair and lone pair. But this repulsion is minimum in H_2Te as the tellurium has large size which makes the repulsion minimum.

5. (a) H_2O
 Explanation: H_2O has the least reducing character among the given options. The reducing nature of an atom or compound depends on how easily it donates or release electrons. The reducing nature of hydrides increases so the order is $H_2O < H_2S < H_2Se < H_2Te$

6. (b) O
 Explanation: Oxygen generally exhibits an oxidation state of -2. The oxidation state, sometimes referred to as oxidation number, describes the degree of oxidation (loss of electrons) of an atom in a chemical compound.

7. (a) Paramagnetic
 Explanation: Oxygen is paramagnetic due to the presence of two unpaired electrons in $\pi*^2\pi x\pi^2 px*$ and $\pi*^2 py\pi^2 py*$ molecular orbital. The paramagnetic property of the oxygen molecule is due to the presence of unpaired electrons.

8. (b) Cl
 Explanation: As moving down the group electron affinity of elements decreases. But in case of fluorine, it is a small atom with a small amount of space available in its $2p$ orbital. Because of this, any new electron trying to attach to fluorine experiences lower electron affinity from the electrons already living in the element's $2p$ orbital. Since chlorine's outermost orbital is a $3p$ orbital, there is more space, and the electrons in this orbital are inclined to share this space with an extra electron. Therefore, chlorine has a higher electron affinity than fluorine, and this orbital structure causes it to have the highest electron affinity of all of the elements. Hence electron affinity of chlorine is higher in halogens.

9. (d) I^-
 Explanation: The order of atomic size or ionic size of the elements in group 17 is as follows: $I^- > Br^- > Cl^- > F^-$. As the size of the atoms increase the distance of the electrons from the nucleus increases and so the attraction of the nucleus over the valence shell electrons decrease and the electrons are easily lost and the atoms are easily oxidized.
 Hence, the most easily oxidizable ion in the above anions is I^-.

10. (b,c) MI > MBr > MCl > MF Ionic character of metal halide.
    $F_2 > Cl_2 > Br_2 > I_2$ Bond dissociation enthalpy.
    Explanation: Halogens reacts with metals to form metal halides. The ionic character of the halides decreases in the order of MF > MCl > MBr > MI. Bond dissociation enthalpy of halogens decreases to the order of $Cl_2 > F_2 > Br_2 > I_2$. Bond dissociation enthalpy of Cl_2 is greater than F_2 because of large electron-electron repulsion among lone pairs of F_2 molecule.

11. (c) Repulsion by electron pairs on F
    Explanation: Due to smaller bond length of fluorine, the lone pairs are nearer and so inter electronic repulsions between the lone pairs is more so it has low bond energy.

12. (a) $HClO_4$
    Explanation: The acidic strength of oxyacids of chlorine will be in the order $HClO < HClO_2 < HClO_3 < HClO_4$.

13. (b) $I_2 + 2Br^- \longrightarrow 2I^- + Br_2$ reaction will not occur spontaneously.
    Explanation: A spontaneous reaction is a reaction that favours the formation of products at the conditions under which the reaction is occurring. A roaring bonfire is an example of a spontaneous reaction. Whereas a non spontaneous reaction is a reaction that does not favour the formation of products at the given set of conditions.

14. (b) Associated nature due to hydrogen bonding
    Explanation: Hydrogen fluoride does not boil until 20°C in contrast to the heavier hydrogen halides, which boil between −85°C (−120°F) and −35°C (−30°F). This hydrogen bonding between HF molecules gives rise to high viscosity in the liquid phase and lowers than expected pressure in the gas phase.

15. (a) Fluorine
    Explanation: If a halogen has a high electron affinity, low dissociation energy, and high hydration energy of its ion. It will have high oxidizing power. Although fluorine has a lower electron affinity than chlorine but has low dissociation energy and high hydration energy. Therefore fluorine is the strongest oxidizing agent.

16. (c) T-Shaped
    Explanation: Chlorine trifluoride has 10 electrons around the central chlorine atom. This means there are five electron pairs arranged in a trigonal bipyramidal shape with a 175° F−Cl−F bond angle. There are two equatorial lone pairs making the final structure T−shaped.

17. (a,c,d)
    Explanation: (i) Among group 17 elements radius ratio of iodine and fluorine is maximum because size of iodine is largest and fluorine is smallest in the group. (ii) The correct statement is inter halogen compounds are more reactive than halogens (except Fluorine). This is because X−X′ bond in interhalogen is weaker than X−X bond in halogens except F−F. (iii) As the ratio between radii of X and X′ increase, the number of atoms per molecule also increases. Thus, iodine (VII) fluoride should have maximum number of atoms as the ratio of radii between I and F will be maximum.
    (iv) Interhalogen compounds are more reactive than halogens (except fluorine). This is because X−X′ bond in interhalogen is weaker than X−X′ bond in halogens.

18. (a) He
    Explanation: Pierre Janssen and Joseph Norman Lockyer had discovered a new element on 18 August, 1868 while looking at the chromosphere of the Sun, and named it helium (He) after the Greek word for the Sun. No chemical analysis was possible at the time, but helium was later found to be a noble gas.

19. (c) Linear
    Explanation: XeF_2 is a linear molecule due to the arrangement of fluorine atoms and the lone pairs of electrons in the symmetric arrangement

20. (c) Radon
    Explanation: Radon due to its radioactive nature is used in treatment of cancer (radiotherapy). Radon is a chemical element with the symbol Rn and atomic number 86. It is a radioactive, colourless, odourless, tasteless noble gas. It occurs naturally in minute quantities as an intermediate step in the normal radioactive decay chains through which thorium and uranium slowly decay into lead and various other short-lived radioactive elements

21. (c) sp^3d
    Explanation: The hybridization of XeF_2 (Xenon Difluoride) is a sp^3d type. Hybridization is a concept in which the atomic orbitals of different atoms contribute to form newly hybridized orbitals. The participating atoms in the molecule share their electrons to form new hybrid orbitals. Valence electrons are the maximum number of electrons in which an atom can contribute to the hybridization of a molecule

22. (a) Cl_2
    Explanation: Chlorine (Cl_2) displaces bromine from an aqueous solution containing bromide. Reactivity of chlorine is more than that of bromine. So chlorine replaces bromine

23. (d) Green
    Explanation: When SO_2 is passed through acidified $K_2Cr_2O_7$ solution, the orange colour of the solution changes to green due to formation of chromic sulphate.
    $K_2Cr_2O_7 + 3SO_2 + H_2SO_4 \rightarrow K_2SO_4 + Cr_2(SO_4)_2$
    $+ 7H_2O + 3S$

24. (d) PbS
    Explanation: PbS reagent does not give O_2 gas on reaction with Ozone.
    $SnCl_2 + HCl + O_3 \rightarrow SnCl_4 + H_2O$
    $FeSO_4 + H_2SO_4 + O_3 \rightarrow Fe_2(SO_4)_3 + H_2O + O_2$
    $SO_2 + O_3 \rightarrow SO_3 + O_2$
    $Hg + O_3 \rightarrow HgO_2$

25. (c) Conc. HCl and conc. HNO_3 in the ratio of 3:1
    Explanation: qua regia is a mixture of nitric acid and hydrochloric acid, optimally in a molar ratio of 1:3. Aqua regia is a yellow-orange (sometimes red) fuming liquid, so named by all chemists

because it can dissolve the noble metals gold and platinum, though not all metals.

26. (a) Hg_2O
    Explanation: The tailing of mercury is the reaction of mercury with ozone due to which mercury loses its meniscus and it starts sticking to the walls of the thermometer due to the formation of the mercurous oxide. The meniscus can be restored by shaking with water. The tailing of mercury on exposure to air shows a change in oxidation number by one. The reaction is as follows: $2Hg + O_3 \rightarrow Hg_2O + O_2$

27. (b) $H_2SO_4 + SO_3$
    Explanation: Oleum is produced in the contact process, where sulfur is oxidized to sulfur trioxide which is subsequently dissolved in concentrated sulfuric acid. Sulfuric acid itself is regenerated by dilution of part of the oleum. Sulfur trioxide produced by the contact process is absorbed in concentrated sulfuric acid.

28. (c) O_3
    Explanation: The ozone layer or ozone shield is a region of Earth's stratosphere that absorbs most of the Sun's ultraviolet radiation. It contains a high concentration of ozone (O_3) in relation to other parts of the atmosphere, although still small in relation to other gases in the stratosphere.

29. (a) H_2O
    Explanation: H_2S is the effective reducing agent. Reducing agent is the one which reduce the oxidizing agent. It becomes H_2SO_4 after receiving oxygen atoms.

30. (a) Fluorine
    Explanation: Fluorine does not form any oxy-acid. An oxyacid, oxoacid, or ternary acid is an acid that contains oxygen. Specifically, it is a compound that contains hydrogen, oxygen, and at least one other element, with at least one hydrogen atom bonded to oxygen that can dissociate to produce the H^+ cation and the anion of the acid.

31. (a) Paramagnetic
    Explanation: According to molecular orbital Theory (MOT), there is 1 unpaired electron in the $\pi^2 px$ anti-bonding orbital and another unpaired electron in $\pi^2 py$ anti-bonding orbital. As molecules containing unpaired electrons are strongly attracted by magnetic field, hence oxygen has paramagnetic nature. Unpaired electrons spin in the same direction as each other which increases magnetic field effect.

32. (a) H_2O
    Explanation: H_2O has lowest reducing character. Water is an inorganic, transparent, tasteless, odorless, and nearly colourless chemical substance, which is the main constituent of Earth's hydrosphere and the fluids of all known living organisms (in which it acts as a solvent. It is vital for all known forms of life, even though it provides no calories or organic nutrients. It's chemical formula H_2O.

33. (a) Fluorine
    Explanation: Fluorine, being the most electronegative, never shows positive oxidation states, hence F does not form oxy-acids. Other halogens have the tendency to show positive oxidation states and hence form oxy-acids.

34. (c) $BrO_4^- > IO_4^- > ClO_4^-$
    Explanation: The reduction potential of the substance is the ability of the substance to be reduced. So as the reduction potential increases reducing ability of the substance increases. It means oxidizing power of the substance (The ability of the substance to make the other substance to lose the electrons increases which noting but oxidizing power) increases. So the decreasing order of oxidizing power is $BrO_4^- > IO_4^- > ClO_4^-$

35. (a) Fluorine
    Explanation: Among the halogens, fluorine does not form an oxyacid due to high electronegativity and small size. Fluorine forms only one oxyacid, i.e. HOF, Hypofluorous acid or fluoric acid.

36. (c) Disproportionation reaction
    Explanation: The reaction $3ClO^-$ (aq) $\rightarrow ClO_3^-$ (aq) $+ 2Cl^-$ (aq.) is an example of disproportionation reaction. In this reaction, chlorine is oxidized as well as reduced. The oxidation states of chlorine in ClO^- (aq), ClO_3^- (aq) and Cl^- (aq.) are +1, +5 and −1 respectively.

37. (c) IPO_4
    Explanation: Interhalogen compounds are formed when halogen group elements react with each other. In other words, it is a molecule which consists of two or more different elements of group 17. There are four types of interhalogen compounds: Diatomic interhalogens (AX), Tetratomic interhalogens (AX_3), Hexatomic interhalogens (AX_5) and Octatomic interhalogens (AX_7). ICl_4^-, ClF_5, ClF_3 are the examples of Interhalogen compounds.

38. (b) Violet
    Explanation: Ozone turns trimethyl paper to violet colour.

39. (c) The valence shell electronic configuration of p-block element is ns^2np^{1-6}.
    Explanation: The valence shell electronic configuration of p-block element is ns^2np^{1-6}. The general electronic outer configuration for p block components is $ns^2np^{(1-6)}$. The general electronic outer f block element configuration is $(n-2)f^{(0-14)}(n-1)d^{(0-1)}ns^2$.

40. (a) down the group, the H-E-H bond angle increases
    Explanation: The acidic character of hydrides increases down the group. Except water, all hydrides possess reducing properties and thermal stability of hydrides decreases down the group.

41. (a) half-filled p-orbitals in group 15 elements are more stable
    Explanation: Group 16 elements have a lower value of first ionization enthalpy as compared to group 15 elements. As group 15 elements have half filled p-orbital due to which group 15 has got extra stability.

42. (d) electronic transitions from the triplet ground state to the excited singlet state
    Explanation: Solid oxygen has a pale blue colour which is attributed to electronic transition from

the singlet ground state to the triplet ground state electronic transitions from antibonding r* molecular orbitals (triplet state) to bonding (doublet) molecular orbitals electronic transitions from the antibonding it molecular orbitals (triplet state) to excited anti bonding O_2 molecular orbital (singlet state) electronic transitions from the triplet ground state to the singlet ground state.

43. (d) $S + O_2 \rightarrow SO_2$
    Explanation: In the given combination reaction $S + O_2 \rightarrow SO_2$, we have S and O_2 combining to form SO_2. Carefully count the atoms up on each side of the equation and then make sure are equal. The number of S atoms on each side of the equation is equal. The number of O atoms on each side of the equation is equal.

44. (b,c)
    Explanation: Among the given four options (b) and (c) represent the oxidizing behaviour of H_2SO_4. In (b) reaction it oxidizes HI and itself reduces to SO_2 oxidation state of central atom Sulphur decreases from +6 to +4. In option (c) it oxidizes copper and itself gets reduced to SO_2.

45. (a) nascent hydrogen responsible for bleaching is produced only in presence of moisture.
    Explanation: Dry SO_2 does not bleach dry flowers because nascent hydrogen responsible for bleaching is produced only in presence of moisture. In bleaching by SO_2, H_2O is important in order to produce nascent hydrogen which is responsible for the bleaching action.
    $SO_2 + 2H_2O \rightarrow H_2SO_4 + 2 [H]$

46. (a) Noble gases possess the electronic configuration ns^2np^6 and has 8 electrons in their outer shell, hence there valency is 0.

47. (b) Flourine has low bond dissociation enthalpy due to small atomic size number of electrons create large repulsion in bonded electron.

48. (b) The acidic character increases down the group and thermal stability of hydrides decreases down the group due to decrease in bond (H—E) dissociation enthalpy down the group.

49. (b) Interhalogen compounds are more reactive than halogens because X—X' bond in interhalogens is weaker than X—X bond in halogen (except F—F bond).

50. (a) It is fact that halogens are highly reactive as they have seven electrons in their outermost orbit and they want to stabilize by acquiring an electron. Therefore, they do not occur in free state.

51. (d) F_2 is more reactive than other halogens because its valence electrons are more closer to nucleus and its more electronegative so, bonded electrons repel each other causing low bond dissociation enthalpy.

52. (b) Ozone layer filters the radiation coming from sun, hence serves as the protective layer.

53. (a) In vapour state S exists as S_2 and it behaves like O_2. It has 2 unpaired electrons in antibonding pi orbitals. Presence of these unpaired electrons make S paramagnetic.

54. (b) As F_2 has low bond dissociation energy and high hydration energy than Cl_2 but less electron gain enthalpy due to its smaller size. Due to these factors F_2 wins in getting reduced fastly.

55. (c) Small highly electronegative atoms such as F^- can stabilise higher oxidation state.

56. (d) PbI_4 is not a stable compound because Pb shows (II) oxidation state more frequently than Pb (IV) due to inert pair effect. Iodide cannot stabilize higher oxidation states.

57. (i) (a) central atom
    (ii) (b) sp^3d
    (iii) (c) Helium
    (iv) (c) unidentate

58. (i) (b) Assertion and reason both are correct statements but reason is not correct explanation for assertion.
    (ii) (b) Assertion and reason both are correct statements but reason is not correct explanation for assertion.
    (iii) (a) Assertion and reason both are correct statements and reason is correct explanation for assertion.
    (iv) (c) Assertion is correct statement but reason is wrong statement.

59. (i) (a) S–S > O–O
    (ii) (b) Pure liquid H_2SO_4 is viscous because of intramolecular hydrogen bonding
    (iii) (b) $H_2O > H_2S > H_2Se > H_2Te$
    OR
    (b) atomic number of sulphur is higher than oxygen.
    (iv) (c) Polonium

60. (i) (b) $[Xe]^4f^{14} 5d^{10} 6s^2 6p^5$
    (ii) (a) atomic size increases gradually
    (iii) (d) N
    (iv) (b) E_2O_3 and E_2O_5
    (v) (a) barium azide

61. (i) (c) metapyrophosphoric acid
    (ii) (b) trigonal bipyramidal
    (iii) (c) reducing agent
    (iv) (d) phosphorus trichloride
    (v) (b) phosphonium bromide

❏❏

Chapter 10

Haloalkanes & Haloarenes

1. The conversion of an alkyl halide into an alcohol by aqueous NaOH is classified as: [CBSE, 2020]
   (a) a dehydrohalogenation reaction
   (b) a substitution reaction
   (c) an addition reaction
   (d) a dehydration reaction

2. Ethylene chloride and ethylidene chloride are isomers. Identify the correct statements. [NCERT Exemplar]
   (a) Both the compounds form same product on treatment with alcoholic KOH.
   (b) Both the compounds form same product on treatment with aq.NaOH.
   (c) Both the compounds form same product on reduction.
   (d) Both the compounds are optically active.

3. What is the IUPAC name of $CH_3-\underset{\underset{CH_3}{|}}{\overset{\overset{CH_3}{|}}{C}}-CH_2Cl$?
   (a) 2-dimethylchloropropane
   (b) 1-chloro-2-dimethyl-pentane
   (c) 2, 2-dimethyl-chlorobutane
   (d) 1-chloro-2, 2-dimethyl propane

4. Halogenation of alkane gives:
   (a) Only required alkyl halide
   (b) Alkyl halide and unreacted halogen
   (c) A mixture of mono-, di-, tri- and tetra-halogen derivatives
   (d) Alkyl halide and unreacted alkane

5. Which of the following compound has been suggested as causing depletion of the ozone layer in the upper stratosphere?
   (a) CH_4
   (b) CCl_2F_2
   (c) CF_4
   (d) CH_2Cl_2

6. Which of the following reagent cannot be used to prepare an alkyl chloride from an alcohol?
   (a) $HCl + ZnCl_2$
   (b) $SOCl_2$
   (c) NaCl
   (d) PCl_5

7. Chloromethane on treatment with excess of ammonia yields mainly: [NCERT Exemplar]
   (a) N, N-Dimethylmethanamine $\left(CH_3-N\begin{matrix}CH_3\\CH_3\end{matrix}\right)$
   (b) N–methylmethanamine ($CH_3-NH-CH_3$)
   (c) Methanamine (CH_3NH_2)
   (d) Mixture containing all these in equal proportion

8. Carbylamine test involves heating a mixture of:
   (a) Alcoholic KOH, methyl iodide, and sodium metal
   (b) Alcoholic KOH, methyl iodide, and primary amine
   (c) Alcoholic KOH, chloroform, and primary amine
   (d) Alcoholic KOH, methyl alcohol, and primary amine

9. When chloroform is heated with aqueous NaOH, it gives:
   (a) Formic acid
   (b) Sodium formate
   (c) Acetic acid
   (d) Sodium acetate

10. Which alkyl halides react most readily by nucleophilic substitution?
    (a) CH_3CH_2Cl
    (b) CH_3CH_2I
    (c) CH_3CH_2Br
    (d) CH_3CH_2F

11. What should be the correct IUPAC name for diethylbromomethane? [NCERT Exemplar]
    (a) 1-Bromo-1,1-diethylmethane
    (b) 3-Bromopentane
    (c) 1-Bromo-1-ethylpropane
    (d) 1-Bromopentane

12. Conversion of ethyl bromide to ethylene is an example of:
    (a) Hydrohalogenation
    (b) Intramolecular dehydrohalogenation
    (c) Dehydration
    (d) Hydration

13. Which of the following compound is an organometallic compound?
    (a) CH_3COOAg
    (b) CH_3MgI
    (c) $MgCl_2$
    (d) CH_3-O-Na

14. The reaction,
    $2C_2H_5Br + 2Na \xrightarrow{dry\ ether} C_2H_5-C_2H_5 + 2NaBr$ is an example of:
    (a) The Wurtz reaction
    (b) Sandmeyer's reaction
    (c) Aldol condensation
    (d) Williamson's reaction

15. Grignard's reagent is prepared by the action of magnesium metal on:
    (a) Alcohol
    (b) Phenol
    (c) Alkyl halide
    (d) Benzene

16. Which of the following is halogen exchange reaction? [NCERT Exemplar]
    (a) $RX + NaI \rightarrow RI + NaX$
    (b) $\underset{}{>}C=C\underset{}{<} + HX \rightarrow \underset{H}{>}C-\underset{H}{C}\underset{}{<}$
    (c) $R-OH + HX \xrightarrow{ZnCl_2} R-X + H_2O$
    (d) $C_6H_5CH_3 + X_2 \xrightarrow[dark]{Fe} o\text{-}XC_6H_4CH_3 + p\text{-}XC_6H_4CH_3$

17. 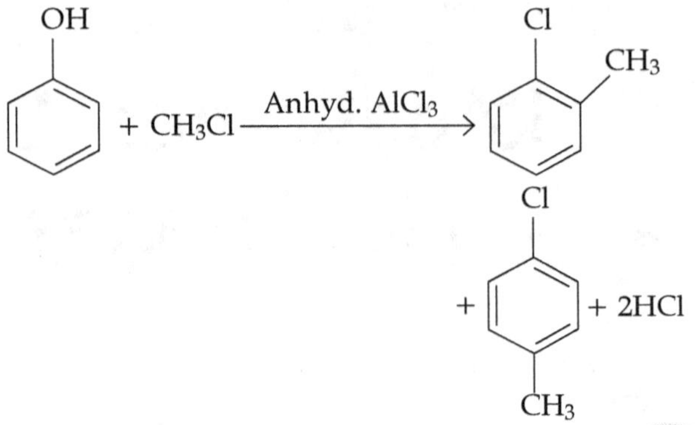 [Reaction: Phenol + CH₃Cl → (with Anhyd. AlCl₃) → o-chlorotoluene + p-chlorotoluene + 2HCl]

The above reaction is known as:
(a) Wurtz-Fittig reaction
(b) Friedel Craft's reaction
(c) Sandmeyer's reaction
(d) Swarts reaction

18. Which reagent will you use for the following reaction? [NCERT Exemplar]
$CH_3CH_2CH_2CH_3 \rightarrow CH_3CH_2CH_2CH_2Cl + CH_3CH_2CHClCH_3$
(a) Cl_2/UV light
(b) $NaCl + H_2SO_4$
(c) Cl_2 gas in dark
(d) Cl_2 gas in the presence of iron in dark

19. The following compound is called:

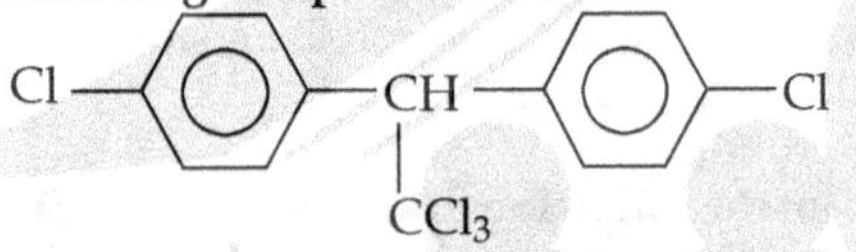

Cl—C₆H₄—CH(CCl₃)—C₆H₄—Cl

(a) Chloral
(b) DDT
(c) Lindane
(d) BHC

20. DDT is prepared by the reaction of chlorobenzene with (in the presence of conc. H_2SO_4):
(a) Chloral
(b) Chlorine
(c) Chloroform
(d) Carbon tetrachloride

21. Preparation of alkyl halides in laboratory is least preferred by:
(a) Treatment of alcohols
(b) Addition of hydrogen halides to alkenes
(c) Halide exchange
(d) Direct halogenation of alkanes

22. Identify A, B, C and D:

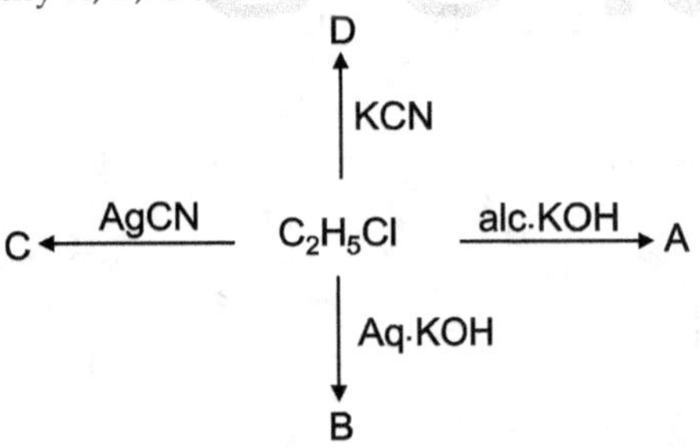

C ←(AgCN)— C_2H_5Cl —(alc.KOH)→ A
          ↑KCN (→D)
          ↓Aq.KOH
          B

(a) A = C_2H_4, B = C_2H_5OH, C = C_2H_5NC, D = C_2H_5CN
(b) A = C_2H_5OH, B = C_2H_4, C = C_2H_5CN, D = C_2H_5NC
(c) A = C_2H_4, B = C_2H_5OH, C = C_2H_5CN, D = C_2H_5NC
(d) A = C_2H_5OH, B = C_2H_4, C = C_2H_5NC, D = C_2H_5CN

23. When chloroform is heated with aqueous NaOH, it gives:
(a) Formic acid
(b) Sodium formate
(c) Acetic acid
(d) Sodium acetate

24. Alkyl halides undergo:
(a) Electrophilic substitution reactions
(b) Electrophilic addition reactions
(c) Nucleophilic substitution reactions
(d) Nucleophilic addition reactions

25. A primary alkyl halide would prefer to undergo ....
(a) SN_1 reaction
(b) SN_2 reaction
(c) α-Elimination
(d) Racemisation

26. The action of sodium on alkyl halide to form an alkane is called:
(a) Grignard reaction
(b) Wurtz coupling reaction
(c) Isocyanide reaction
(d) Halogenation reaction

27. Identify the true statement for chloroform:
(a) Its exposure causes cardiac damage
(b) If immersed in chloroform, the skin gets sored.
(c) Central nervous system remains unaffected of chloroform.
(d) 700 ppm of chloroform causes dizziness

28. A sample of chloroform being used as anaesthetic is tested by:
(a) Fehling solution
(b) Ammonical Cu_2Cl_2
(c) $AgNO_3$ solution after boiling with alcoholic KOH solution
(d) None of the above

29. In mid-1960, it is used as cleaning fluid, degreasing agent, spot remover, and fire extinguisher. Which of the solvent is used in mid-1960?
(a) Carbon tetrachloride
(b) Chloroform
(c) Iodoform
(d) Dichloromethane

30. p–p'-dichlorodiphenyl trichloroethane is used as:
(a) Insecticide
(b) Anaesthetic
(c) Antiseptic
(d) Refrigerant

31. Ethylidene chloride is a/an _____ [NCERT Exemplar]
(a) vic-dihalide
(b) Gem-dihalide
(c) Allylic halide
(d) Vinylic halide

32. p - p'-dichlorodiphenyl trichloroethane is used as:
(a) Insecticide
(b) Anaesthetic
(c) Antiseptic
(d) Refrigerant

33. The major product of the following reaction is:

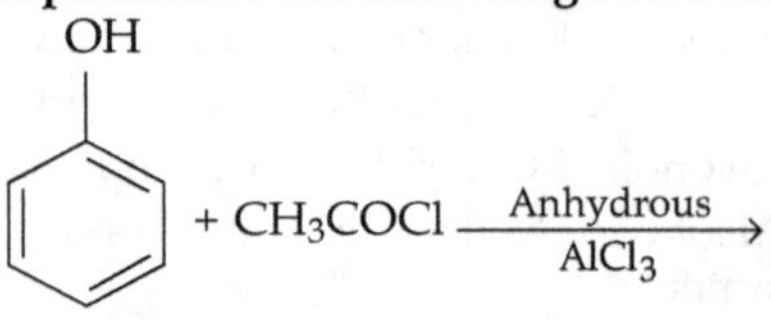

Phenol + CH_3COCl —(Anhydrous $AlCl_3$)→

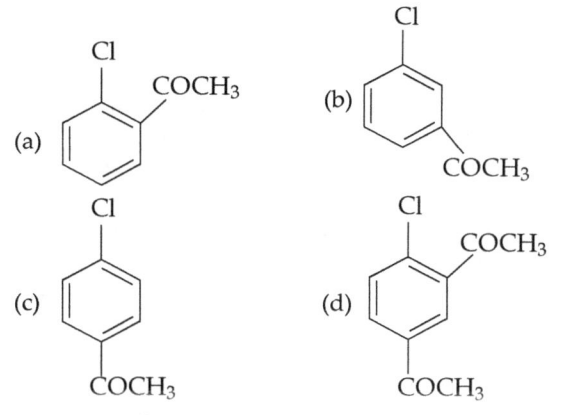

34. The action of sodium on alkyl halide to form an alkane is called:
    (a) Grignard reaction
    (b) Wurtz coupling reaction
    (c) Isocyanide reaction
    (d) Halogenation reaction

35. Alkyl halides undergo:
    (a) Electrophilic substitution reactions
    (b) Electrophilic addition reactions
    (c) Nucleophilic substitution reactions
    (d) Nucleophilic addition reactions

36. The position of –Br in the compound in $CH_3CH=CHC(Br)(CH_3)_2$ can be classified as _____.
    [NCERT Exemplar]
    (a) Allyl   (b) Aryl
    (c) Vinyl   (d) Secondary

37. Which of the following poisonous gas is formed when chloroform is exposed to light and air?
    (a) Mustard gas   (b) Carbon monoxide
    (c) Phosgene   (d) Chlorine

38. $R - X + AgF \rightarrow RF + AgX$ belongs to which type of reaction.
    (a) Exchange of halogen, Swarts reaction
    (b) Dehalogenation, Swarts reaction
    (c) Exchange of halogen, Finkelstein reaction
    (d) none of the above

39. An organic compound A forms B with sodium metal and again A forms C with PCl_5 but B and C form diethyl ether. Therefore A, B and C are:
    (a) C_2H_5OH, C_2H_5ONa, C_2H_5Cl
    (b) C_2H_5Cl, C_2H_5ONa, C_2H_5OH
    (c) C_2H_5OH, C_2H_6, C_2H_5Cl
    (d) C_2H_5OH, C_2H_5Cl, C_2H_5ONa

40. Consider the following reaction:
    $$H_3C-\underset{D}{CH}-\underset{CH_3}{CH}-CH_3 + Br^\bullet \rightarrow X + HBr$$
    Identify the structure of the major product X.
    (a) $H_3C-\overset{\bullet}{CH}-\underset{D}{CH}-\underset{CH_3}{CH}-CH_2$

(b) $H_3C-\underset{D}{CH}-\overset{\bullet}{\underset{CH_3}{C}}-CH_3$

(c) $H_3C-\overset{\bullet}{\underset{D}{C}}-\underset{CH_3}{CH}-CH_3$

(d) $H_3C-\overset{\bullet}{CH}-\underset{CH_3}{CH}-CH_3$

41. Halogenation of alkanes is:
    (a) A reductive process
    (b) An oxidative process
    (c) An isothermal process
    (d) An endothermal process

42. Identify A, B and C in the given sequence of reactions,
    $$H_2C=CH_2 + Br_2 \xrightarrow[B]{A} \underset{C}{BrCH_2CH_2Br}$$

	A	B	C
(a)	CCl_4	Colourless	Reddish brown
(b)	CCl_4	Reddish brown	Colourless
(c)	CBr_4	Colourless	Reddish brown
(d)	CBr_4	Reddish brown	Colourless

43. $\underset{H}{\overset{Me}{Ph}}\!\!\!>\!\!\text{OH} \xrightarrow[\text{in } C_5H_5N]{SOCl_2}$

    Which statement is true for the above reaction?
    (a) Retention of configuration
    (b) Inversion of configuration
    (c) Inversion and retention both
    (d) None of the above

44. Chlorobenzene is:
    (a) Less reactive than benzyl chloride
    (b) More reactive than ethyl bromide
    (c) Nearly as reactive as methyl chloride
    (d) More reactive than isopropyl chloride

45. Chlorobenzene on treatment with sodium in dry ether gives diphenyl. The name of the reaction is:
    (a) Fittig reaction   (b) Wurtz-Fittig reaction
    (c) Sandmeyer reaction   (d) Gattermann reaction

Directions: In the following questions, a statement of assertion is followed by a statement of reason. Mark the correct choice as:
(a) If both assertion and reason are true and reason is the correct explanation of assertion.
(b) If both assertion and reason are true, but reason is not the correct explanation of assertion.
(c) If assertion is true, but reason is false.
(d) If assertion is false but reason is true.

46. **Assertion:** $(CH_3)_3C-O-CH_3$ give $(CH_3)_3C-I$ and CH_3OH on treatment with HI.
    Reason: The reaction occurs by SN_1 mechanism.
    [CBSE, 2020]

47. **Assertion:** Hydrogen iodide readily reacts with alkenes to form alkyl halides.
    Reason: Aqueous hydrohalogen acids are used to prepare alkyl halides from alkenes.

48. **Assertion:** CHCl₃ is stored in dark bottles.
    Reason: CHCl₃ is oxidised in dark.
49. **Assertion:** CCl₄ is a fire extinguisher.
    Reason: CCl₄ is insoluble in water.
50. **Assertion:** CH₂=CH—CH₂—X is an example of allyl halides.
    Reason: These are the compounds in which the halogen atom is bonded to an sp^2 hybridised carbon atom.
51. **Assertion:** Alkylbenzene is not prepared by Friedel-Crafts alkylation of benzene.
    Reason: Alkyl halides are less reactive than aryl halides.
52. **Assertion:** Aryl halides cannot be prepared by replacement of hydroxyl group of phenol by halogen atom.
    Reason: Phenols react with halogen acids violently.
53. **Assertion:** Exposure of ultraviolet rays to human causes the skin cancer, disorder and disrupt the immune system.
    Reason: Carbon tetrachloride is released into air it rises to atmosphere and deplets the ozone layer.
54. **Assertion:** The boiling points of alkyl halides decrease in the order : RI > RBr > RCl > RF
    Reason: The boiling points of alkyl chlorides, bromides and iodides are considerably higher than that of the hydrocarbon of comparable molecular mass.
55. **Assertion:** Electron withdrawing groups in aryl halides increase the reactivity towards nucleophilic substitution.
    Reason: 2, 4-Dinitrochlorobenzene is less reactive than chlorobenzene.
56. **Read the passage given below and answer the following questions:**

    Experimental kinetic data on reactions of the chlorine atom with halogenated derivatives of methane and ethane (37 reactions) have been analyzed by the intersecting-parabolas method. The following five factors have an effect on the activation energy of these reactions: the enthalpy of reaction, triplet repulsion, the electronegativities of the reaction center atoms, the dipole–dipole and multidipole interactions between the reaction center and polar groups, and the effect of π electrons in the vicinity of the reaction center. The increments characterizing the contribution from each factor to the activation energy of the reaction have been calculated. The contribution from the polar interaction, ΔEμ, to the activation energy depends on the dipole moment of the polar group and obeys the following empirical equation: ln (ΔEμ/Σμ) = – 0.74 + 0.87 (ΔE μ/Σμ) – 0.084 (ΔEμ/Σμ)².

    The following questions are multiple choice questions. Choose the most appropriate answer:
    (i) Nucleophilic reactions are the most useful classes of organic reactions of alkyl halides in which halogens are bonded to _____ hybridized carbon.
    (a) sp_2
    (b) sp_3
    (c) sp
    (d) none of the above
    (ii) The spatial arrangement of four groups (valences) around a central carbon atom is tetrahedral and if all the substituents attached to that carbon are different, and then such a carbon is called ____
    (a) Achiral
    (b) Chiral
    (c) Asymmetric
    (d) Symmetric
    (iii) In alkyl halides, due to greater polarity as well as higher molecular mass, as compared to the parent hydrocarbon, the intermolecular _____ and _____ of attraction are stronger in the halogen derivatives.
    (a) dipole-dipole and van der Waals forces
    (b) Hydrogen bond and dipole-dipole forces
    (c) van der Waals and hydrogen bond forces
    (d) dipole-dipole and London forces.
    (iv) Alkyl halides are prepared from alcohols, which are easily accessible. The hydroxyl group of an alcohol is replaced by halogen on reactions with certain compounds. Which one of the below compounds is inappropriate as a reagent?
    (a) Concentrated halogen acid
    (b) Sodium dihalide
    (c) Thionyl chloride
    (d) Phosphorus halides

    OR

    Which of the following is not an Electrophilic substitution reaction of haloarenes?
    (a) Sulphonation
    (b) Nitration
    (c) Halogenation
    (d) Wurtz-Fittig reaction

57. **Read the passage given below and answer the following questions:** [CBSE Website]

    Nucleophilic substitution reaction of haloalkane can be conducted according to both S_N^1 and S_N^2 mechanisms. However, which mechanism it is based on is related to such factors as the structure of haloalkane, and properties of leaving group, nucleophilic reagent and solvent.

    Influences of halogen: No matter which mechanism the nucleophilic substitution reaction is based on, the leaving group always leave the central carbon atom with electron pair. This is just the opposite of the situation that nucleophilic reagent attacks the central carbon atom with electron pair. Therefore, the weaker the alkalinity of leaving group is, the more stable the anion formed is and it will be more easier for the leaving group to leave the central carbon atom; that is to say, the reactant is more easier to be substituted. The alkalinity order of halogen ion is I⁻ < Br⁻ < Cl⁻ < F⁻ and the order of their leaving tendency should be I⁻ > Br⁻ > Cl⁻ > F⁻. Therefore, in four halides with the same alkyl and different halogens, the order of substitution reaction rate is RI > RBr > RCl > RF . In addition, if the leaving group is very easy to leave, many carbocation intermediates are generated in the reaction and the reaction is 1 based on S_N^2 mechanism. If the leaving group is not easy to leave, the reaction is based on S_N mechanism. Influences of solvent polarity: In S_1 reaction, the polarity of the system increases from the reactant to the transition state, because polar solvent has a greater stabilizing effect on the transition state than the reactant, thereby reduce activation energy and accelerate the reaction.

    Influences of solvent polarity: In S_N reaction, the polarity of the system generally does not change from the reactant to the transition state and only charge dispersion occurs. At this time, polar solvent has a great stabilizing effect on Nu than the transition state, thereby increasing activation energy and slow down the reaction rate. For example, the decomposition rate (S_N^1) of tertiary chlorobutane in 25°C water (dielectric constant 79) is 300000 times faster than in ethanol (dielectric constant 24). The reaction rate (S_N^2) of 2-bromopropane and NaOH in ethanol containing 40% water is twice slower than in absolute ethanol. In a word, the level of solvent polarity has influence on both S_N^1 and S_N^2 reactions, but with different results. Generally 2 speaking, weak polar solvent is favorable for S_N^2 reaction, while strong polar solvent is favorable for S_N^1 reaction, because only under the action of polar solvent can halogenated hydrocarbon dissociate into carbocation and halogen ion and solvents with a strong polarity is favorable for solvation of carbocation, increasing its stability. Generally speaking, the substitution reaction of tertiary haloalkane is based on S_N strong polarity (for example, ethanol containing water). mechanism in solvents with a strong polarity (for example, ethanol containing water).

(i) S_N^1 mechanism is favoured in which of the following solvents:
   (a) benzene
   (b) carbon tetrachloride
   (c) acetic acid
   (d) carbon disulphide

(ii) S_N^1 reaction will be fastest in which of the following solvents?
   (a) Acetone (dielectric constant 21)
   (b) Ethanol (dielectric constant 24)
   (c) Methanol (dielectric constant 32)
   (d) Chloroform (dielectric constant 5)

(iii) Polar solvents make the reaction faster as they:
   (a) destabilize transition state and decrease the activation energy
   (b) destabilize transition state and increase the activation energy
   (c) stabilize transition state and increase the activation energy
   (d) stabilize transition state and decrease the activation energy

(iv) S_N^1 reaction will be fastest in case of:
   (a) 1-Chloro-2-methyl propane
   (b) 1-Iodo-2-methyl propane
   (c) 1-Chlorobutane
   (d) 1-Iodobutane

58. Read the passage given below and answer the following questions:

Haloalkanes and alcohols are important starting materials in the synthesis of compounds having other functional groups. Primary haloalkanes react with hydroxide ion to give alcohols, although we will see that elimination reactions compete with substitution for secondary and tertiary halides.

When comparing alkanes and haloalkanes, we will see that haloalkanes have higher boiling points than alkanes containing the same number of carbons. London dispersion forces are the first of two types of forces that contribute to this physical property. London dispersion forces increase with molecular surface area. In comparing haloalkanes with alkanes, haloalkanes exhibit an increase in surface area due to the substitution of a halogen for hydrogen. The increase in surface area leads to an increase in London dispersion forces, which then results in a higher boiling point.

$$\text{furan-CH}_2\text{Br} \xrightarrow{\text{OH}^-} \text{furan-CH}_2\text{OH} + \text{Br}^-$$

(i) Which of the following undergoes nucleophilic substitution exclusively by S_N^1 mechanism?
   (a) Benzyl Chloride (b) Ethyl chloride
   (c) Chlorobenzene   (d) Isopropyl chloride

(ii) Which of the following is most reactive towards S_N^1 reaction?
   (a) $C_6H_5CH(CH_3)Br$ (b) $C_8H_5CH_2Br$
   (c) $C_6H_5CH(C_6H_5)Br$ (d) $C_6H_5C(CH_3)C_6H_5Br$

(iii) The addition of HBr is easiest in which one of the following substrates:
   (a) $CH_2=CHCl$ (b) $ClCH=CHCl$
   (c) $CH_3-CH=CH_2$ (d) $(CH_3)_2C=CH_2$

(iv) Which among MeX, R-CH$_2$X, R$_2$CHX, R$_3$CX is most reactive towards S_N^2 reaction:
   (a) CH_3X (b) RCH_2X
   (c) R_3CHX (d) R_3CX

(v) $(CH_3)_3$C MgBr on reaction with D_2O produces:
   (a) $(CH_3)_3CD$ (b) $(CH_3)_3COD$
   (c) $(CH_3)_3CD$ (d) $(CD_3)_3OD$

59. Read the passage given below and answer the following questions:

A catalytic protocol for the conversion of haloarenes into the corresponding nitroarenes is presented using copper salts under ligand free conditions. Several structurally divergent haloarenes including iodoarenes, bromoarenes, and heterocyclic haloarenes were converted into respective nitroarenes in moderate to good yields with complete regioselectivity.

$$\text{Ar}^-\text{X} + \text{KNO}_2 \xrightarrow[\text{DMSO}_2\ 120\text{-}130°C,\ 48h]{\text{Cu(OSO}_2\text{CF}_3)_2\ (25\ \text{mol\%})} \text{Ar}^-\text{NO}_2$$

X = I, Br
Ar = ary, heteroaryl
up to 84% yield
24 examples

If a hydrogen atom is replaced from an aromatic hydrocarbon by a halogen atom the resulting compound formed is known as haloarene. It is also known as aryl halide or halogenoarene. In a haloalkene (R – X), X represents halogen group. It is attached to an sp^3 hybridized atom of an alkyl group whereas in haloarene (Ar – X) the halogen is attached to an sp^2 hybridized atom of an aryl group.

(i) n Friedel-Crafts synthesis of toluene, reactants in addition to anhydrous AlCl$_3$ are:
   (a) $C_6H_6 + CH_4$ (b) $C_6H_6 + CH_3Br$
   (c) $C_5H_5Cl + CH_3Cl$ (d) $C_6H_5 + CH_4$

(ii) In haloarene compounds, halogen combines with carbon having which hybridisation?
   (a) sp^2 (b) sp^3
   (c) sp (d) dsp^2

(iii) Haloarenes do not react through SN_1 mechanism because:
   (a) phenyl cation formed as a result of self ionisation is not resonance stabilised
   (b) phenyl cation is not formed
   (c) C-X bond in haloarenes is large
   (d) both (b) and (c)

(iv) During electrophilic substitution reaction in haloarenes, halogen atom behaves as:
   (a) deactivating substituent
   (b) activating substituent
   (c) deactivating and meta directing substituent
   (d) deactivating and ortho/para directing substituent

(v) Chlorobenzene when heated with aqueous sodium hydroxide at 623K and 300 atm yields:
   (a) phenol
   (b) dichlorobenzene
   (c) benzene
   (d) 2-hydroxy chlorobenzene

60. Read the passage given below and answer the following questions:

Classical molecular dynamics simulations with a polarizable force field were used to study adsorption of gas-phase alkyl halides to the surface of liquid water and their hydration properties in the interfacial environment. A systematic investigation has been performed for a set of monosubstituted alkyl chlorides, bromides and iodides of the alkyl chain length from one to five carbon atoms ($C_nH_{2n+1}X$, $n = 1-5$, $X = Cl$, Br, or I). All alkyl halides readily adsorb to the water surface and exhibit a strong preference for interfacial (partial) hydration. When adsorbed, the alkyl halide molecules reside primarily in the outermost region of the water–vapor interface. The (incomplete) hydration shell of the surface-adsorbed methyl halide species is centered on the methyl end of the molecule, with the halogen atom largely exposed and facing away from water into the gas phase.

(i) Assertion and reason both are correct statements and reason is correct explanation for assertion.
(ii) Assertion and reason both are correct statements but reason is not correct explanation for assertion.
(iii) Assertion is correct statement but reason is wrong statement.
(iv) Assertion is wrong statement but reason is correct statement.

(a) **Assertion:** There is a retention of configuration in 1-Chloro-2-methylbutane obtained from 2-methylbutan 1-ol.
Reason: The reactions where retention of configuration is observed do not preserve the integrity of the spatial arrangement of reactant.

(b) **Assertion:** A mixture containing two enantiomeres in equal proportions will have zero optical rotation.
Reason: Rotation due to one isomer is cancelled by the rotation due to the other isomer.

(c) **Assertion:** Carbon-halogen bond in alkyl halide is a non-polar bond.
Reason: Halogen atoms are more electronegative than carbon.

(d) **Assertion:** Reaction of aryl chlorides with iodine need an oxidising agent to be added in order to get a smooth reaction.
Reason: Reactions with iodine are irreversible in nature.

(e) **Assertion:** To obtain pure alkyl halides from alcohols thionyl chlorides are the reagents of choice.
Reason: Thionyl chloride reacts with alcohols to give alkyl halide.

Answers

1. (b) a substitution reaction
   Explanation: Alkyl halide converted into an alcohol by alkaline hydrolysis. This process occurs due to a substitution reaction where the –X atom is substituted by a –OH group.
   Chemical Reaction: R–X + NaOH → R–OH + NaX
   Hence, it is an example of a substitution reaction.

2. (a) Both the compounds form same product on treatment with alcoholic KOH.
   Explanation: Ethylene chloride and ethylidene chloride on treatment with alc. KOH show elimination reaction and form ethyne as the product and both these compounds form same products (ethane) on reduction

3. (d) 1-chloro-2, 2-dimethyl propane
   Explanation: As per the IUPAC nomenclature, the numbering of the compound should begin with functional group and then lowest "Locant Rule" should be followed. Hence, the IUPAC name of the compound is 1-Chloro-2,2-dimethyl propane.

4. (c) A mixture of mono-, di-, tri- and tetra-halogen derivatives
   Explanation: When halogen reacts with an alkane in the presence of sunlight or heat leads to the formation of a haloalkane (alkyl halide). Depending on the proportion of the two reactants that are used, various products of different amount are produced. For example, in the case of methane (CH_4), a large excess of the hydrocarbon favours formation of methyl chloride as the primary

product; whereas, an excess of chlorine favours formation of chloroform ($CHCl_3$) and carbon tetrachloride (CCl_4). Similarly, in general a mixture of mono-, di-, tri- and tetra-halogen derivatives is formed.

5. (b) CCl_2F_2

   Explanation: Chlorofluorocarbons (CFCs) have significant potential to deplete ozone layer in the Earth's atmosphere, which blocks the inflow of the harmful UV rays. CFCs causes depletion of stratospheric ozone layer and as a consequence it contributes to the global warming.

6. (c) NaCl

   Explanation: Alkyl Chloride is an ionic compound which cannot displace -OH group by Cl. Rest all other reagents (HCl + $ZnCl_2$, $SOCl_2$, PCl_5) displaces -OH from alcohol and provide Cl.

7. (c) Methanamine (CH_3NH_2)

   Explanation: Primary amine is obtained as a major product by taking large excess of ammonia. $CH_3Cl + NH_3 \rightarrow CH_3NH_2 + HCl$

8. (c) Alcoholic KOH, chloroform, and primary amine

   Explanation: Aliphatic and aromatic primary amines on heating with CCl_4 and alcoholic potassium hydroxide (alc. KOH) gives smelling alkyl isocyanides or carbylamines. So, Carbylamine test is performed in alcoholic KOH by heating a mixture of chloroform, and primary amine.

9. (b) Sodium formate

   Explanation: Chloroform when heated with aqueous solution of caustic soda, first it produces formic acid which reacts further and form sodium formate.

   $CHCl_3 + 3NaOH \rightarrow CH(OH)_3 \xrightarrow{-H_2O} HCOOH \xrightarrow{NaOH} HCOONa$

10. (b) CH_3CH_2I

    Explanation: The melting and boiling points of molecular compounds are generally quite low compared to those of ionic compounds. Ionic solids typically melt at high temperatures and boil at even higher temperatures. For example, sodium chloride melts at 801°C and boils at 1413°C. So in this case CH_3CH_2I will react most readily by nucleophilic substitution

11. (b) 3-Bromopentane

    Explanation: $\overset{5}{H_3}\overset{4}{CH_2}\overset{3}{C}-\overset{|}{\underset{Br}{CH}}-\overset{2}{CH_2}\overset{1}{CH_3}$

12. (b) Intramolecular dehydrohalogenation

    Explanation: In ethyl alcohol, the attacking species is the ethoxide anion, which is a much stronger base than the hydroxide anion, so it directly extracts the beta hydrogen from ethyl bromide, followed by elimination of the bromide anion from the adjacent carbon atom to form ethene. So, it is an example of Intramolecular dehydrohalogenation.

13. (b) CH_3MgI

    Explanation: An organometallic compounds containing at least one chemical bond between a carbon atom of an organic molecule and a metal are called organometallic coordination compounds. Here CH_3MgI is an organometallic compound.

14. (a) The Wurtz reaction

    Explanation: The reaction, $C_2H_5Br + 2Na + C_2H_5Br \rightarrow C_4H_{10} + 2NaBr$ is known as Wurtz reaction.

15. (c) Alkyl halide

    Explanation: Grignard reagents is prepared by the reaction of an alkyl or aryl halide with magnesium metal.

16. (a) $RX + NaI \rightarrow RI + NaX$

    Explanation: Exchange of halogen between RX and NaI.

17. (d) Swarts reaction

    Explanation: Swarts' reaction generally produces alkyl fluorides from alkyl chlorides or alkyl bromides. This reaction is conducted by heating of the alkyl chloride/bromide in the presence of the fluoride of some heavy metals such as silver fluoride.

18. (a) Cl_2/UV light

    Explanation: Direct chlorination of alkanes takes place in presence of sunlight (UV light).

19. (b) DDT

    Explanation: Common name of the given compound is DDT (Dichloro-Diphenyl Trichloroethane).

20. (a) Chloral

    Explanation: DDT, prepared by the reaction of chloral with chlorobenzene in the presence of sulphuric acid.

21. (a) Treatment of alcohols

    Explanation: By a nucleophilic substitution reaction, Alkyl halides on alkaline hydrolysis get transformed into alcohols, where the –X atom is substituted by –OH group. The primary alkyl halides undergo nucleophilic substitution reaction.

22. (a) A = C_2H_4, B = C_2H_5OH, C = C_2H_5NC, D = C_2H_5CN

    Explanation: For the formation of compound A and B, elimination reaction and substitution of -OH will take place, respectively. As an exception case, for the compound C '-NC' will attack to the C_2H_5. For the formation of D simply -CN will add to C_2H_5.

23. (b) Sodium formate

    Explanation: Heating chloroform with aqueous sodium hydroxide solution forms sodium formate. $CHCl_3 + 4NaOH(aq) = 3NaCl + HCOONa + 2H_2O$

24. (c) Nucleophilic substitution reactions

    Explanation: Alkyl halides can undergo two major types of reactions - substitution and/or elimination. It is called substitution reaction because the electrophilic alkyl halide forms a new bond with the nucleophile which replaces the halogen at the alpha-carbon. Hence the correct answer would be Nucleophilic substitution reactions.

25. (b) SN2 reaction.
    Explanation: As primary alkyl halide is least sterically hindered among primary, secondary and tertiary alkyl halides, therefore primary alkyl halides undergo S_N^2 reaction.

26. (b) Wurtz coupling reaction
    Explanation: Wurtz-reaction
    $CH_3Br + 2Na + BrCH_2CH_3 \rightarrow CH_3CH_2CH_3 + 2NaBr$
    Methyl bromide   Ethyl bromide   Propane
    $CH_3CH_2Br + 2Na + BrCH_2CH_3 \rightarrow CH_3CH_2CH_2CH_3 + 2NaBr$
    Ethyl bromide   Ethyl bromide   Butane
    $CH_3Br + 2Na + BrCH_3 \rightarrow CH_3CH_3 + 2NaBr$
    Methyl bromide   Methyl bromide   Ethane

27. (a) Its exposure causes cardiac damage
    Explanation: Chloroform is harmful for the health. It can cause damages to the heart.

28. (c) AgNO3 solution after boiling with alcoholic KOH solution
    Explanation: A pure sample does not give ppt with aq. $AgNO_3$.

29. (a) Carbon tetrachloride
    In mid 1960s, tetrachloromethane (or carbon tetrachloride) was also widely used as a cleaning fluid. It is used both in industry, as a degreasing agent and in the home, as a spot remover as fire extinguisher.

30. (c) Antiseptic
    Explanation: Common name of the compound Dichloro-Diphenyl Trichloroethane is DDT, which is a colourless, tasteless and odourless organic compound used as an insecticides or pesticide.

31. (b) Gem-dihalide
    Explanation: Gem-dihalides are named as alkylidene halides having halogen atoms on the same carbon atom.

32. (a) Insecticide
    Explanation: Wurtz-reaction. This is a coupling reaction in organic chemistry and recently inorganic main-group polymers, where two alkyl halides are reacted with sodium metal in dry ether solution to form a higher alkane.

33. (c) [Phenol + CH3COCl → (Anhydrous AlCl3) → 4-hydroxyacetophenone (OH, COCH3)]

34. (b) Wurtz coupling reaction
    Explanation: Wurtz-reaction is a coupling reaction in organic chemistry, where two alkyl halides react with sodium metal in dry ether solution to form a higher alkane.

35. (c) Nucleophilic substitution reactions
    Explanation: Alkyl halides can undergo two major types of reactions - substitution and/or elimination. It is called substitution reaction because the electrophilic alkyl halide forms a new bond with the nucleophile which replaces the halogen at the alpha-carbon. Hence the correct answer would be Nucleophilic substitution reactions.

36. (d) Secondary
    Explanation: Aryl halides are less reactive towards nucleophilic substitution reactions as C—X bond acquires a partial double bond character due to resonance.

37. (c) Phosgene
    Explanation: When Chloroform is exposed to air and sunlight, it undergoes oxidation and releases a poisonous gas called Phosgene gas ($COCl_2$) and Hydrochloric acid (HCl).

    $Cl_3C-H + [O] \xrightarrow[\text{air}]{\text{light}} Cl_3C-OH \longrightarrow$
    $Cl_2C=O + HCl$
    (Phosgene gas)

38. (a) Exchange of halogen, Swarts reaction
    Explanation: Exchange of halogen is taking place between alkyl halides and AgF.

39. (a) $C_2H_5OH, C_2H_5ONa, C_2H_5Cl$
    Explanation:
    $C_2H_5OH (A) + Na \rightarrow C_2H_5ONa$
    (B)
    $C_2H_5OH (A) + PCl_5 \rightarrow C_2H_5Cl$ (C)
    $C_2H_5ONa + C_2H_5Cl \rightarrow C_2H_5OC_2H_5 + NaCl$
    (B)   (C)

40. (b) $H_3C-CH-\overset{\bullet}{C}-CH_3$
            | |
            D CH_3
    Explanation: Tertiary free radicals are most stable.

41. (b) An oxidative process
    Explanation: Oxidation of the alkanes takes place during halogenation.

42. (b) CCl_4 Reddish brown Colourless
    Explanation: Addition of bromine in CCl_4 to an alkene results in discharge of reddish-brown colour of bromine constitutes. It is an important method for detection of double bond in a molecule. The electrophilic addition results in the synthesis of vic-dibromides, which are colourless

43. (b) Inversion of configuration
    Explanation: Stronger nucleophilic Cl^- attacks from back and causes inversion of configuration.

44. (a) Less reactive than benzyl chloride
    Explanation: In chlorobenzene, the lone pairs present on Cl atom get involved in resonance with π electrons of benzene due to which C—Cl bond acquires double bond character, i.e. it becomes shorter and hence strong. Hence, reactivity decreases.

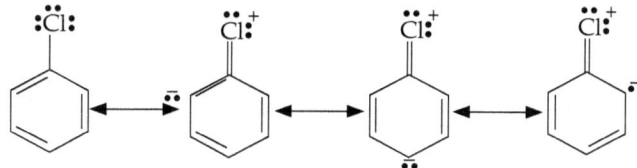

45. (a) Fittig reaction
    Explanation: If only aryl halide reacts with sodium in presence of other, the reaction is called "Fitting" reaction.

46. (a) SN_1 reaction occurs in compound that has steric hindrance and $(CH_3)_3-C-OCH_3$ has very much hindrance to attack by reagent.
47. (c) Dry gaseous hydrohalogen acids are better electrophiles. In aqueous solution, H_2O. acting as nucleophile may produce alcohol.
48. (c) $CHCl_3$ is stored in dark bottles to avoid reaction in the presence of light. $CHCl_3$ in the presence of light gets oxidised by air.
49. (b) CCl_4 is carbon tetrachloride and is used in fire extinguisher because it is a heavy non-combustible liquid. CCl_4 is insoluble in water due to absence of hydrogen atom that can form hydrogen bonding with water.
50. (c) Allyl halides are the compounds in which the halogen atom is bonded to an sp^3 hybridised carbon atom next to carbon-carbon double bond.
51. (c) Aryl halides are more stable and less reactive due to resonance where the lone pair of electrons are in conjugation with a *pi* bond.
52. (c) Aryl halides cannot be prepared by replacing hydroxyl group of phenols because the carbon oxygen bond in phenols has a partial double bond character and is difficult to break being stronger than a single bond.
53. (b) The ozone layer is depleted as carbon tetrachloride rises into the atmosphere. As the ozone layer depletes, human beings are exposed to more UV radiation, which leads to an increase in skin cancer, eye disease, and disorder, as well as immune system disruption.
54. (b) The boiling point of the identical hydrocarbon component is determined by the atomic mass of the halogen atom. The boiling point of a halogen atom increases as its mass increases. As a result, the boiling point of halogen atoms lowers as the atomic mass of the halogen atom decreases.
55. (c) When electron withdrawing groups (nitro, cyano) are present at the ortho/para position, halobenzenes become reactive to nucleophile substitution reaction. This is evident by the fact that 2. 4-dinitrochlorobenzene requires milder hydrolysis condition than chlorobenzene.
56. (i) (b) sp_3
    (ii) (b) chiral
    (iii) (a) dipole-dipole and van der Waals forces
    (iv) (b) sodium dihalide
    OR
    (d) Wurtz-Fittig reaction
57. (i) (c) acetic acid
    (ii) (c) Methanol (dielectric constant 32)
    (iii) (c) stabilize transition state and increase the activation energy
    (iv) (b) 1-Iodo-2-methyl propane
58. (i) (a) Benzyl Chloride
    (ii) (d) $C_6H_5C(CH_3)C_6H_5Br$
    (iii) (d) $(CH_3)_2C = CH_2$
    (iv) (a) CH_3X
    (v) (a) $(CH_3)_3CD$
59. (i) (b) $C_6H_6 + CH_3Br$
    (ii) (a) sp^2
    (iii) (a) phenyl cation formed as a result of self ionisation is not resonance stabilised
    (iv) (d) deactivating and ortho/para directing substituent
    (v) (a) phenol
60. (i) (c) Assertion is correct statement but reason is wrong statement.
    (ii) (a) Assertion and reason both are correct statements and reason is correct explanation for assertion.
    (iii) (d) Carbon-halogen bond in alkyl halide is a polar bond because halogen atoms are more electronegative than carbon.
    (iv) (c) Assertion is correct statement but reason is wrong statement.
    (v) (b) Assertion and reason both are correct statements but reason is not correct explanation for assertion.

Chapter 11: Alcohols, Phenols & Ethers

1. When acetaldehyde is treated with Grignard reagent, followed by hydrolysis the product formed is:
   (a) Primary alcohol
   (b) Secondary alcohol
   (c) Carboxylic acid
   (d) Tertiary alcohol

2. When oxalic acid is heated with glycerol we get:
   (a) Formic acid
   (b) Acetic acid
   (c) Lactic acid
   (d) Tartaric acid

3. Ethanol on heating with conc. H_2SO_4 at 445 K gives:
   (a) Diethyl sulphate
   (b) Ethylene, C_2H_4
   (c) Diethyl ether, $(C_2H_5)_2O$
   (d) Ethyl hydrogensulphate, $C_2H_5HSO_4$

4. Which of the following is most acidic?
   (a) H_2O
   (b) CH_3OH
   (c) C_2H_5OH
   (d) $CH_3CH_2CH_2OH$

5. Which of the following has highest boiling point?
   (a) $CH_3CH_2CH_2OH$
   (c) $(CH_3)_2CH-CH_2OH$
   (b) $CH_3CH_2CH_2CH_2OH$
   (d) $(CH_3)_3C-OH$

6. $C_6H_5Cl \xrightarrow[624K, 300atm]{NaOH(aq)}$ A. Here, A is:
   (a) Phenol
   (b) Sodium phenoxide
   (c) Benzene
   (d) Cyclohexyl chloride

7. Which one of the following will produce a primary alcohol by reacting with CH_3MgI?
   (a) Acetone
   (b) Methyl cyanide
   (c) Ethylene oxide
   (d) Ethyl acetate

8. In the sequence HO—C$_6$H$_4$—SO$_3$H $\xrightarrow[H_2O]{Br_2}$ X, is:
   (a) 2-Bromo-4-hydroxybenzene sulphonic acid
   (b) 3, 5-Dibromo-4-hydroxybenzene sulphonic acid
   (c) 2-Bromophenol
   (d) 2, 4, 6-Tribromophenol

9. Phenol can be distinguished from ethyl alcohol by all reagents except:
   (a) NaOH
   (b) $FeCl_3$
   (c) Br_2/H_2O
   (d) Na

10. Which of the following species can act as the strongest base? [NCERT Exemplar]
    (a) ⁻OH
    (b) ⁻OR
    (c) ⁻O C$_6$H$_5$
    (d)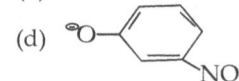

11. Chlorine reacts with ethanol to give:
    (a) Diethyl chloride
    (b) Chloroform
    (c) Acetaldehyde
    (d) Chloral

12. Which of the following alcohol is least soluble in water?
    (a) N-Butyl alcohol
    (b) Iso-Butyl alcohol
    (c) Tert-Butyl alcohol
    (d) Sec-Butyl alcohol

13. Glycerol on heating with potassium bisulphate yields:
    (a) Acetone
    (b) Glyceraldehyde
    (c) Acrolein
    (d) Propanol

14. The reaction of Lucas reagent is fastest with:
    (a) $(CH_3)_3COH$
    (b) $(CH_3)_2CHOH$
    (c) $CH_3(CH_2)_2OH$
    (d) CH_3CH_2OH

15. The ionization constant of phenol is higher than that of ethanol because:
    (a) Phenoxide ion is a stronger base than ethoxide ion
    (b) Phenoxide ion is stabilized through delocalization
    (c) Phenoxide ion is less stable than ethoxide ion
    (d) Phenoxide ion is bulkier than ethoxide ion

16. The correct order of boiling points for primary (1°), secondary (2°) and tertiary alcohol (3°) is:
    (a) 1° > 2° > 3°
    (b) 3° > 2° > 1°
    (c) 2° > 1° > 3°
    (d) 2° > 3° > 1°

17. Which of the following is the most suitable method for removing the traces of water from ethanol?
    (a) Heating with Na metal
    (b) Passing dry HCl gas through it
    (c) Distilling Cl⁻
    (d) Reacting with Mg

18. Phenol is heated with $CHCl_3$ and alcoholic KOH when salicylaldehyde is produced. This reaction is known as:
    (a) Rosenmund's reaction
    (b) Reimer-Tiemann reaction
    (c) Friedel-Crafts reaction
    (d) Sommelet reaction

19. Lucas test is used for distinction of:
    (a) Alcohols
    (b) Phenols
    (c) Alkyl halides
    (d) Aldehydes

20.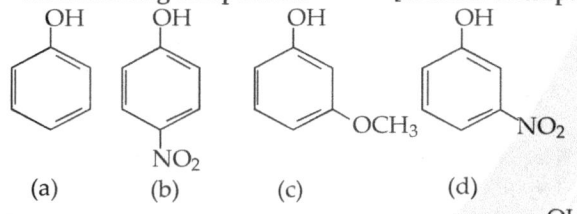

The electrophile involved in the above reaction is:
(a) Dichloromethyl cation (⁺CHCl₂)
(b) Dichlorocarbene (: CCl₂)
(c) Trichloromethyl anion (⁻CCl₃)
(d) Formyl cation (⁺CHO)

21. Mark the correct order of decreasing acid strength of the following compounds. [NCERT Exemplar]

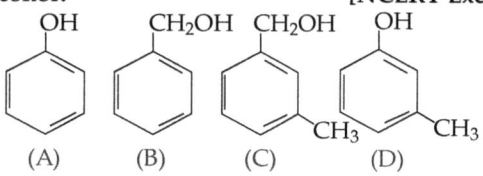

(a) e > d > b > a > c
(b) b > d > a > c > e
(c) d > e > c > b > a
(d) e > d > c > b > a

22. Which of the following is simple ether?
(a) C₂H₅OCH₃
(b) CH₃OCH₃
(c) C₆H₅OCH₃
(d) All are simple ethers.

23. Alcohols of low molecular weight are:
(a) insoluble in water
(b) soluble in water
(c) insoluble in all solvents
(d) soluble in water on heating

24. The boiling point of methanol is greater than that of methyl thiol because:
(a) There is intermolecular hydrogen bonding in methanol and no hydrogen bonding in methyl thiol.
(b) There is intramolecular hydrogen bonding in methanol and no hydrogen bonding in methyl thiol.
(c) There is intramolecular hydrogen bonding in methanol and intermolecular hydrogen bonding in methyl thiol.
(d) There is no hydrogen bonding in methanol and intermolecular hydrogen bonding in methyl thiol.

25. In the reaction of phenol with CHCl₃ and aqueous NaOH at 70°C, the electrophile attacking the ring is:
(a) CHCl₃
(b) CHCl₂
(c) CCl₂
(d) COCl₂

26. Which of the following statements about phenol are incorrect?
(i) It is insoluble in water.
(ii) It has lower melting point as compared to aromatic hydrocarbons of comparable molecular weight.
(iii) It does not show acidic property.
(iv) It has higher boiling point than toluene.
(a) (i) and (ii) are correct
(b) (i) and (iii) are correct
(c) (ii) and (iv) are correct
(d) (i), (ii) and (iii) are correct

27. Which of the following compounds is aromatic alcohol? [NCERT Exemplar]

(a) A, B, C, D
(b) A, D
(c) B, C
(d) A

28. Alcohols can be obtained from all methods except:
(a) Hydroboration-oxidation
(b) Oxymercuration-demercuration
(c) Reduction of aldehyde/ketones with Zn-Hg/HCl
(d) By fermentation of starch

29. When phenol is treated with excess of bromine water, it gives:
(a) m-bromophenol
(b) o- and p-bromophenol
(c) 2, 4-dibromophenol
(d) 2, 4, 6-tribromophenol

30. Which of the following reactions will yield phenol? [NCERT Exemplar]

31. Match column I and column II and choose the correct combination from the given options.

	Column I		Column II
A	Antifreeze used in car engine	(i)	Methanol
B	Solvent used in perfumes	(ii)	Phenol
C	Starting material for picric acid	(iii)	Ethylene glycol
D	Wood spirit	(iv)	Ethanol

(a) A-(iv), B-(ii), C-(iii), D-(i)
(b) A-(iv), B-(ii), C-(i), D-(iii)
(c) A-(i), B-(iii), C-(ii), D-(iv)
(d) A-(iii), B-(iv), C-(ii), D-(i)

32. In the following reaction, reactant A is:

$$A \xrightarrow[\text{dil. H}_2\text{SO}_4]{K_2Cr_2O_7} B \xrightarrow[H_2O]{CH_3MgI} CH_3-\underset{\underset{OH}{|}}{\overset{\overset{CH_3}{|}}{C}}-CH_3$$

(a) C_2H_5OH
(b) CH_3COOH
(c) CH_3COCH_3
(d) $CH_3CHOHCH_3$

33. Which of the following statements are correct?
    (i) A secondary alcohol on oxidation gives a ketone.
    (ii) Ethanol reacts with conc. H_2SO_4 at 180°C to yield ethylene.
    (iii) Hydrogen gas is liberated when sodium is added to alcohol.
    (iv) Methanol reacts with iodine and sodium hydroxide to give a yellow precipitate of iodoform.
    (a) (i) and (ii) are correct
    (b) (i) and (iii) are correct
    (c) (ii) and (iv) are correct
    (d) (i), (ii), and (iii) are correct

34. Which of the following is not true in case of reaction with heated copper at 300°C?
    (a) Primary alcohol → Aldehyde
    (b) Secondary alcohol → Ketone
    (c) Tertiary alcohol → Olefin
    (d) Phenol → Benzyl alcohol

35. In cold countries, ethylene glycol is added to water in the radiators to:
    (a) Lower the viscosity
    (b) Reduce the viscosity
    (c) Make water a better lubricant
    (d) Bring down the specific heat of water

Directions: In the following questions, a statement of assertion is followed by a statement of reason. Mark the correct choice as:
(a) If both assertion and reason are true and reason is the correct explanation of assertion.
(b) If both assertion and reason are true, but reason is not the correct explanation of assertion.
(c) If assertion is true, but reason is false.
(d) If assertion is false but reason is true.

---

36. **Assertion:** $(CH_3)_3$–CONa and CH_3CH_2Br react to form $(CH_3)_3C-O-CH_2CH_3$
    Reason: Good yields of ethers are obtained when tert-alkyl halides are treated with alkoxides.

37. **Assertion:** Ortho and para-nitro phenols can be separated by steam distillation.
    Reason: Ortho isomer associates through intermolecular hydrogen bonding while Para isomer associates through intramolecular hydrogen bonding. **[CBSE 2020]**

38. **Assertion:** In Lucas test, 3° alcohols react immediately.
    Reason: An equimolar mixture of anhyd. $ZnCl_2$ and conc. HCl is called Lucas reagent.

39. **Assertion:** The water solubility of the alcohols follow the order: tert-butyl alcohol > sec-butyl alcohol > n-butyl alcohol.
    Reason: Alcohols form H-bonding with water to show soluble nature.

40. **Assertion:** Tert-butyl alcohol undergoes acid catalysed dehydration readily than propanol.
    Reason: 3° Alcohols do not give Victor-Meyer's test.

41. **Assertion:** Phenol is less acidic than p-nitrophenol.
    Reason: Phenolate ion is more stable than p-nitrophenolate ion.

42. **Assertion:** Reimer-Tiemann reaction of phenol with CCl_4 in NaOH at 340 K gives salicylic acid as the major product.
    Reason: The reaction occurs through intermediate formation of dichlorocarbene.

43. **Assertion:** The C—O—C bond angle in ethers is slightly less than tetrahedral angle.
    Reason: Due to the repulsive interaction between the two alkyl groups in ethers. **[CBSE 2020]**

44. **Assertion:** Phenol undergo Kolbe reaction, ethanol does not.
    Reason: Phenoxide ion is more basic than ethoxide ion.

45. **Assertion:** Etherates are coordination complexes of ethers with Lewis acids.
    Reason: Ethers are easily cleaved by mineral acids such as HCl and H_2SO_4 at 373 K.

46. **Assertion:** Boiling points of alcohols are higher than that of ethers of comparable molecular mass.
    Reason: Alcohols can form intermolecular hydrogen bonding while ethers can not.

47. Read the passage given below and answer the following questions:
    An efficient, aerobic catalytic system for the transformation of alcohols into carbonyl compounds under mild conditions, copper-based catalyst has been discovered. This copper-based catalytic system utilises oxygen or air as the ultimate, stoichiometric oxidant, producing water as the only by-product.

    $$R_2\underset{H}{\overset{R_1}{>}}OH \xrightarrow[\substack{2 \text{ equiv. } K_2CO_3; \\ 5\% DBADH_2:O_2 \\ \text{Toluene: } 70° \text{ to } 90°C}]{5\% CuCl:5\% \text{ Phen}} R_2\overset{R_1}{>}{=}O$$

    A wide range of primary, secondary, allylic, and benzylic alcohols can be smoothly oxidised to the corresponding aldehydes or ketones in good to excellent yields. Air can be conveniently used instead of oxygen without affecting the efficiency of the process. However, the use air requires slightly longer reaction times.
    This process is not only economically viable and applicable to large-scale reactions, but it is also environmentally friendly.

    The following questions are multiple choice questions. Choose the most appropriate answer:
    (i) The copper based catalyst mentioned in the study above can be used to convert:
      (a) propanol to propanonic acid
      (b) propanone to propanoic acid
      (c) propanone to propan-2-ol
      (d) propan-2-ol to propanone

(ii) The carbonyl compound formed when ethanol gets oxidised using this copper-based catalyst can also be obtained by ozonolysis of:
   (a) But-1-ene   (b) But-2-ene
   (c) Ethene   (d) Pent-1-ene

   OR

   Which of the following is a secondary allylic alcohol?
   (a) But-3-en-2-ol (b) But-2-en-2-ol
   (c) Prop-2-enol   (d) Butan-2-ol

(iii) Benzyl alcohol on treatment with this copper-based catalyst gives a compound 'A' which on reaction with KOH gives compounds 'B' and 'C'. Compound 'B' on oxidation with $KMnO_4$-KOH gives compound 'C'. Compounds 'A', 'B' and 'C' respectively are:
   (a) Benzaldehyde, Benzyl alcohol, potassium salt of Benzoic acid
   (b) Benzaldehyde, potassium salt of Benzoic acid, Benzyl alcohol
   (c) Benzaldehyde, Benzoic acid, Benzyl alcohol
   (d) Benzoic acid, Benzyl alcohol, Benzaldehyde

(iv) An organic compound 'X' with molecular formula C_3H_8O on reaction with this copper based catalyst gives compound 'Y' which reduces Tollen's reagent. 'X' on reaction with sodium metal gives 'Z'. What is the product of reaction of 'Z' with 2-chloro-2-methylpropane?
   (a) $CH_3CH_2CH_2OC(CH_3)_3$
   (b) $CH_3CH_2OC(CH_3)_3$
   (c) $CH_2 = C(CH_3)_2$
   (d) $CH_3CH_2CH = C(CH_3)_2$

48. **Read the passage given below and answer the following questions:**

   In 2005, the ACS Green Chemistry Institute (GCI) and the global pharmaceutical corporations developed the ACS GCI Pharmaceutical Roundtable to encourage the development of green chemistry and green engineering in the pharmaceutical industry. The Roundtable has established a list of key research areas including the direct nucleophilic reactions of alcohols. The substitution of activated alcohols is a frequently used approach for the preparation of active pharmaceutical ingredients. Alcohols are transformed into the reactive halides or sulfonate esters, thereby allowing their reaction with nucleophiles. Although the direct nucleophilic substitution of an alcohol should be an attractive process, as one of the byproducts from the reaction yields water, hydroxide is a poor leaving group that hinders the reaction. Recently, the direct substitution of allylic, benzylic, and tertiary alcohols has been achieved through an S_N^1 reaction with catalytic amounts of Brönsted or Lewis acids. In this review, the approaches leading to a greener process are examined in detail, and the advances achieved to date in this important transformation are presented.

   In these questions, a statement of assertion followed by a statement of reason is given. Choose the correct answer out of the following choices.

   In these questions, a statement of assertion followed by a statement of reason is given. Choose the correct answer out of the following choices.

   (a) Assertion and reason both are correct statements and reason is correct explanation for assertion.
   (b) Assertion and reason both are correct statements but reason is not correct explanation for assertion.
   (c) Assertion is correct statement but reason is wrong statement.
   (d) Assertion is wrong statement but reason is correct statement.

   (i) **Assertion:** Alcohols are soluble in water.
   Reason: Alcohol molecules can form hydrogen bonds with water molecules.

   (ii) **Assertion:** Presence of –OH group deactivates the aromatic ring towards electrophilic aromatic substitution.
   Reason: The –OH group creates a resonance effect in aromatic ring.

   (iii) **Assertion:** Aliphatic alcohols can be converted into alkyl bromides using phosphorus tribromide.
   Reason: The –OH group of an aliphatic alcohol can undergo direct S_N1 reaction under acidic conditions.

   (iv) **Assertion:** Alkenes can be obtained by treating aliphatic alcohols with conc. H_2SO_4.
   Reason: Alcohols undergo dehydration upon treatment with basic reagents.

   OR

   Assertion: The C–O–H bond angle in aliphatic alcohols is slightly less than the tetrahedral angle.
   Reason: The unshared pair of electrons on oxygen atom repel each other.

49. **Read the passage given below and answer the following questions:**

   The acylation of alcohols, phenols, and amines is one of the most frequently used processes in organic chemistry. It provides an economical and efficient method for protecting hydroxyl groups during oxidation, peptide coupling, and glycosidation reactions. Acylation is usually carried out by treatment of an alcohol or amine with carboxylic acid chlorides or anhydrides in the presence of an acid or a base catalyst in a suitable organic solvent. Basic catalysts such as 4-(dimethylamino) pyridine (DMAP), tributylphosphines, 4-pyrrolidinopyridine, and acidic catalysts like $Sc(OTf)_3$, $Gd(OTf)_3$, lanthanide(III) tosylates, $RuCl_3$, $Al(HSO_4)_3$, $Bi(OTf)_3$, and $LiClO_4$ catalyze acylation reactions with acid chloride or anhydride as the acylating agent under homogenous conditions.

   (a) Assertion and reason both are correct statements and reason is correct explanation for assertion.
   (b) Assertion and reason both are correct statements but reason is not correct explanation for assertion.
   (c) Assertion is correct statement but reason is wrong statement.
   (d) Assertion is wrong statement but reason is correct statement.

   (i) **Assertion:** Reaction of an alcohol with acid chloride is done in presence of pyridine.

Reason: Pyridine is basic in nature.

(ii) **Assertion:** Alcohols can be oxidised to give aldehydes and ketones.

Reason: Oxidation of alcohols result in removal of the -OH group and introduction of =O group on the carbon atom.

(iii) **Assertion:** Ortho nitrophenol is steam volatile while para nitrophenol is not.

Reason: Ortho nitrophenol shows intermolecular hydrogen bonding.

(iv) **Assertion:** The boiling point of an alcohol decreases with increase of branching in the carbon chain.

Reason: With increase in the branching, surface area decreases causing a decrease in the van der Waals forces between molecules.

50. **Read the passage given below and answer the following questions:**

Ether protecting groups are in many respects complimentary to the acetals. Like the acetals they are stable to basic condition and most ethers are also much more acid stable. The most commonly used ethers for protecting purposes, the benzyl ethers, are in addition removable by catalytic hydrogenolysis under very mild, pH neutral, conditions. However, the strongly basic conditions most commonly used for the introduction of an ether protecting group and the lack of regioselectivity put certain restrictions on their use. The triphenylmethyl (trityl) ether group has also found use, especially in carbohydrate chemistry. The bulk of this group gives it a strong preference for the primary hydroxyl group.

(a) Assertion and reason both are correct statements and reason is correct explanation for assertion.

(b) Assertion and reason both are correct statements but reason is not correct explanation for assertion.

(c) Assertion is correct statement but reason is wrong statement.

(d) Assertion is wrong statement but reason is correct statement.

(i) **Assertion:** The formation of ether from alcohol in acidic medium is a bimolecular reaction.

Reason: A protonated alcohol molecule is attacked by another alcohol molecule while ether formation in acidic medium.

(ii) **Assertion:** Dehydration of secondary and tertiary alcohols to give corresponding ethers is not a productive reaction.

Reason: Elimination does not compete with ether formation reaction.

(iii) **Assertion:** Alkyl aryl ethers are cleaved at the alkyl-oxygen bond when reacted with hydrogen halides.

Reason: Aryl oxygen bond are more stable.

(iv) **Assertion:** Anisole undergoes bromination with bromine in absence of iron (III) bromide.

Reason: Iron (III) bromide is used to catalyse halogenation reaction of phenylalkyl ethers.

Answers

1. (b) Secondary alcohol

   Explanation: 1.The product formed is secondary alcohol (R-OH) and magnesium hydroxy halide (R-Mg-X). In this reaction in the presence of ether, Grignard reagent and acetaldehyde reacts with each other and produced compound is further proceeded in the presence of H_3O^+ and as a result 2-butanol (secondary alcohol) and magnesium hydroxyl halide is formed.

2. (a) Formic acid

   Explanation: When oxalic acid is heated with glycerol we get Formic acid.

   $$\begin{array}{c} CH_2-OH \\ | \\ CH-OH \\ | \\ CH_2-OH \end{array} + \begin{array}{c} COOH \\ | \\ COOH \end{array} \xrightarrow[-H_2O]{110°C} \begin{array}{c} CH_2-O-CO-COOH \\ | \\ CH-OH \\ | \\ CH_2-OH \end{array} \xrightarrow{-CO_2}$$

   $$\begin{array}{c} CH_2-O-CO-H \\ | \\ CH-OH \\ | \\ CH_2-OH \end{array} \xrightarrow{Hydrolysis} \begin{array}{c} CH_2-OH \\ | \\ CH-OH \\ | \\ CH_2-OH \end{array} + \begin{array}{c} HCOOH \\ Formic\ acid \end{array}$$

3. (b) Ethylene, C_2H_4

   Explanation: When Ehanol is heated with conc. H_2SO_4 at 445K, by the process of dehydration Ethylene is formed. In this reaction conc. H_2SO_4 acts as a dehydrating agent.

4. (a) H_2O

   Explanation: pKa values of the given compounds are as follows:

   H—OH = 14
   CH_3—OH = 15.5
   CH_3CH_2—OH = 16.0
   CH_3-CH_2-CH_2—OH = 16.85

   One can observe that pKa value increases as the alkyl chain length attached to the –OH group increases. This is due to the electron donating properties of alkyl groups which, in turn, destabilizes the -ve charge on oxygen when the H on the OH ionizes: R—OH = RO$^-$ + H$^+$.

5. (d) $\begin{array}{c} CH_3 \\ | \\ CH_3-C-OH \\ | \\ CH_3 \end{array}$

   Explanation: Among the given compound 4th one has highest intermolecular force, thus it has highest boiling point.

6. (b) Sodium phenoxide

   Explanation: When C_6H_5Cl is put into aqueous solution of NaOH, under the condition of 624K and 300 atm it produces Sodium Phenoxide.

7. (c) Ethylene oxide

    Explanation: The product will be Ethylene oxide.

    $$CH_2-CH_2 + CH_3MgI \rightarrow \underset{Ethylene\ oxide}{\begin{array}{c}CH_2-CH_2\\ |\\ CH_3-OMgI\end{array}} \rightarrow CH_3-CH_2-CH_2-OH + Mg\begin{array}{c}I\\OH\end{array}$$

8. (b) 3, 5-Dibromo-4-hydroxybenzene sulphonic acid

    Explanation: The compound 'X' will be 3, 5-Dibromo-4-hydroxybenzene sulphonic acid.

9. (d) Na

    Explanation: As Sodium (Na) reacts with both phenol and ethyl alcohol, thus it can't be used to distinguish phenol from ethyl alcohol. Rest all can be used to distinguish phenol from ethyl alcohol.

10. (b) $\overset{\ominus}{O}R$

    Explanation: Weakest acid forms the strongest conjugate base. Since, ROH is the weakest acid, so RO^- is the strongest base.

11. (d) Chloral

    Explanation: When chlorine reacts with ethanol, Chloral is formed.

    $$C_2H_5OH \xrightarrow[-2HCl]{Cl_2} CH_3CHO \xrightarrow[-3HCl]{3Cl_2} \underset{Chloral}{CCl_3CHO}$$

12. (a) N-Butyl alcohol

    Explanation: Amongst isomeric alcohols, as branching increases, the surface area of the non-polar hydrocarbon increases, consequently the solubility increases. So, the solubility of Tertiary alcohol will be more compared to other available options.

13. (c) Acrolein

    Explanation: When Glycerol is heated with potassium bisulphate, due to dehydration unsaturated aldehyde i.e. acrylic aldehyde is formed. Hence the product formed is acrylic aldehyde, also called acrolein.

14. (a) $(CH_3)_3COH$

    Explanation: Lucas reagent is a mixture of conc. HCl and anhydrous zinc chloride. We know that the order of reactivity of alcohols towards Lucas reagent is: tertiary > secondary > primary. So among the given options, $(CH_3)_3COH$, a tertiary alcohol, will react most readily with Lucas reagent.

15. (b) Phenoxide ion is stabilized through delocalization

    Explanation: As phenoxide ion is stabilized through delocalization, thus the ionization constant of phenol is higher than that of ethanol.

16. (a) 1° > 2° > 3°

    Explanation: For alcohols boiling points depends upon 3 factors, viz. molecular weight, number of available H-bonds and the surface area of the molecule. If the molecular weight of all the alcohols are more or less same, then the boiling point will also be nearly same. Now, both the number of available H-bonds and the surface area of the molecule are least In 3° alcohols and maximum in 1° alcohols. Hence, 3° alcohols have a least boiling point while 1° alcohols have a maximum boiling point. Hence the correct sequence will be, 1° > 2° > 3°

17. (d) Reacting with Mg

    Explanation: Traces of water can be removed from ethanol by reacting with Mg.

    $Mg + 2CH_3CH_2OH \rightarrow (CH_3CH_2O)_2Mg + H_2$
    $(CH_3CH_2O)_2Mg + H_2O \rightarrow MgO + 2CH_3CH_2OH$

18. (b) Riemer - Tiemann reaction

    Explanation: When Phenol reacts with chloroform and alcoholic KOH to give salicylaldehyde, the reaction is called Reimer-Tiemann reaction.

19. (a) Alcohols

    Explanation: Lucas test in alcohols is conducted to distinguish between primary, secondary, and tertiary alcohols. It is based on the difference in reactivity of the three classes of alcohols with hydrogen halides through a substitution reaction: $ROH + HCl \rightarrow RCl + H_2O$.

20. (b) Dichlorocarbene (: CCl_2)

    Explanation: $NaOH + CCl_3^- \rightarrow :CCl_2 + NaCl + H_2O$
    Here, the electrophile is dichlorocarbene (:CCl_2).

21. (b) b > d > a > c > e

    Explanation: The most acidic is p-nitrophenol, whereas the least acidic is p-methoxyphenol. The acidity is greatest when an electron withdrawing group is parallel to the OH group. The acidity is lowest when an electron releasing group is opposite the OH group.

22. (b) CH_3OCH_3

    Explanation: In general, simple Ether is R–O–R where R is an alkyl group. Hence, here CH_3OCH_3 is the simple ether.

23. (b) soluble in water

    Explanation: The lower alcohols are readily soluble in water and the solubility decreases with the increase in molecular weight. The solubility of alcohols in water can be explained due to the formation of hydrogen bond between the highly polarised —OH groups present both in alcohol and water.

24. (a) There is intermolecular hydrogen bonding in methanol and no hydrogen bonding in methyl thiol.

    Explanation: Methanol has high boiling point than methyl thiol because there is intermolecular hydrogen bonding in methanol and no hydrogen bonding in methyl thiol.

25. (b) $CHCl_2$

    Explanation: When phenol is reacted with $CHCl_3$ and aqueous NaOH at 70°C, the electrophile attacking the ring is CCl_2 (Reimer Tiemann Reaction and Carbene formation).

26. **(d)** (i), (ii) and (iii) are correct
    Explanation: Phenol has higher boiling point than toluene because of hydrogen bonding.
27. **(c)** B, C
    Explanation: Compound (A) i.e., phenol and compound (D) i.e., a derivative of phenol cannot be considered as aromatic alcohol. As phenol is also known as, carbolic acid cannot be considered as aromatic alcohol.
28. **(c)** Reduction of aldehyde/ketones with Zn-Hg/HCl
    Explanation: As per the Clemmensen reduction, reduction of aldehydes and ketones with Zn(Hg)/HCl yields alkanes.
29. **(d)** 2, 4, 6-tribromophenol
    Explanation: When phenol is treated with excess bromine water, it gives 2, 4, 6-tribromophenol.
30. **(a,b,c)**
    Explanation:

    Cl—C$_6$H$_5$ + NaOH $\xrightarrow[300\text{ atm}]{623\text{ K}}$ O$^-$Na$^+$—C$_6$H$_5$ $\xrightarrow{HCl}$ OH—C$_6$H$_5$

    NH$_2$—C$_6$H$_5$ (Aniline) $\xrightarrow[+\text{HCl}]{\text{NaNO}_2}$ N$_2^+$Cl$^-$—C$_6$H$_5$ (Benzene diazonium chloride) $\xrightarrow[\text{Warm}]{\text{H}_2\text{O}}$ OH—C$_6$H$_5$ + N$_2$ + HCl

    C$_6$H$_6$ $\xrightarrow{\text{Oleum}}$ SO$_3$H—C$_6$H$_5$ $\xrightarrow[\text{H}^+]{\text{NaOH}}$ OH—C$_6$H$_5$

31. **(d)** A-(iii), B-(iv), C-(ii), D-(i)
    Explanation: A-(iii) - Ethylene glycol is used as Antifreeze in car engines. B-(iv) – Ethanol is used as solvent in perfumes. C-(ii) – Phenol is used as starting material for picric acid. D-(i) – Methanol is also known as wood spirit.
32. **(d)** CH$_3$CHOHCH$_3$
    Explanation: Complete reaction,
    CH$_3$CHOHCH$_3$ (A) $\xrightarrow[\text{dil. H}_2\text{SO}_4]{\text{K}_2\text{Cr}_2\text{O}_7}$ CH$_3$COCH$_3$ (B) $\xrightarrow[\text{H}_2\text{O}]{\text{CH}_2\text{MgI}}$ (CH$_3$)$_3$COH
33. **(d)** (i), (ii), and (iii) are correct
    Explanation:
    (i) CH$_3$—CH(OH)—CH$_3$ $\xrightarrow{\text{Oxidation}}$ CH$_3$—C(=O)—CH$_3$
    (ii) CH$_3$—CH$_2$—OH $\xrightarrow[180°]{\text{Conc. H}_2\text{SO}_4}$ CH$_2$=CH$_2$ + H$_2$O
    (iii) 2CH$_3$CH$_2$OH + 2Na → 2CH$_3$—CH$_2$—ONa + H$_2$
    (iv) Methanol does not undergo iodoform reaction.
34. **(d)** Phenol → Benzyl alcohol
    Explanation: When primary (1°) alcohols are treated with copper at 300°C, then aldehydes are obtained by dehydrogenation of alcohols. Similarly secondary (2°) alcohols form ketone and alkene is obtained by dehydration of tertiary (3°)-alcohols. But phenol does not respond to this test.
35. **(d)** Bring down the specific heat of water
    Explanation: Ethylene glycol is added to lowering down the freezing point of water so that it does not freeze.
36. **(c)** (CH$_3$)$_3$CONa and CH$_3$CH$_2$Br react to form (CH$_3$)$_3$C—O—CH$_2$CH$_3$. Good yields of ether are obtained when primary alkyl halides are treated with alkoxides derived from any alcohol, 1°, 2°, or 3°.
37. **(c)** Ortho and para isomers of nitro phenol can be separated by steam distillation because of nearby same boiling point of both and Ortho isomers associate by intramolecular hydrogen bonding and Para isomers associate by hydrogen bonding.
38. **(b)** In Lucas test, tertiary alcohols react immediately because of the formation of the more stable tertiary carbocations.
39. **(b)** The tendency to show H-bonding decreases with increasing hydrophobic character of carbon chain. The hydrophobic character of carbon chain increases with the length of carbon chain.
40. **(b)** Alcohols which form the more stable carbocations undergo dehydration more readily. Since tert-butyl alcohol forms more stable tert-butyl cation, therefore, it undergoes dehydration more readily than propanol.
41. **(c)** p-Nitrophenolate ion is more stable than phenolate ion.
42. **(c)** Nucleophilic attack of phenolate ion through the ortho-carbon atom occurs on CCl$_4$ (a neutral electrophile) to form an intermediate which on hydrolysis gives salicylic acid (ArSE reaction).
43. **(d)** In ethers, bond angle around oxygen is not exactly 109° 28'. There is deviation in angle caused due to repulsive interactions between bulkier alkyl groups.
44. **(b)** On using tert-butyl bromide and sodium ethoxide as reactants, the major product would be 2-methylpropene and ethanol (elimination reaction).
45. **(c)** Ethers being Lewis bases form etherates with Lewis acids. Ethers are not easily cleaved by H$_2$SO$_4$.
46. **(a)** Alcohols have high boiling point than ethers because intermolecular H-bonding is found in alcohols.
47. (i) **(d)** Propan-2-ol to propanone
    (ii) **(b)** But-2-ene
    OR
    (a) But-3-en-2-ol
    (iii) **(a)** Benzaldehyde, Benzyl alcohol, potassium Salt of Benzoic acid.
    (iv) **(c)** CH$_2$=C(CH$_3$)$_2$

Alcohols, Phenols & Ethers | 239

7. (c) Ethylene oxide
   Explanation: The product will be Ethylene oxide.

   $$CH_2-CH_2 \text{ (epoxide)} + CH_3MgI \rightarrow \begin{array}{c} CH_2-CH_2 \\ | \\ CH_3-OMgI \end{array} \rightarrow$$

   $$CH_3-CH_2-CH_2-OH + Mg\begin{array}{c} I \\ OH \end{array}$$

   Ethylene oxide

8. (b) 3, 5-Dibromo-4-hydroxybenzene sulphonic acid
   Explanation: The compound 'X' will be 3, 5-Dibromo-4-hydroxybenzene sulphonic acid.

9. (d) Na
   Explanation: As Sodium (Na) reacts with both phenol and ethyl alcohol, thus it can't be used to distinguish phenol from ethyl alcohol. Rest all can be used to distinguish phenol from ethyl alcohol.

10. (b) ⊖OR
    Explanation: Weakest acid forms the strongest conjugate base. Since, ROH is the weakest acid, so RO⁻ is the strongest base.

11. (d) Chloral
    Explanation: When chlorine reacts with ethanol, Chloral is formed.
    $$C_2H_5OH \xrightarrow[-2HCl]{Cl_2} CH_3CHO \xrightarrow[-3HCl]{3Cl_2} CCl_3CHO \text{ (Chloral)}$$

12. (a) N-Butyl alcohol
    Explanation: Amongst isomeric alcohols, as branching increases, the surface area of the non-polar hydrocarbon increases, consequently the solubility increases. So, the solubility of Tertiary alcohol will be more compared to other available options.

13. (c) Acrolein
    Explanation: When Glycerol is heated with potassium bisulphate, due to dehydration unsaturated aldehyde i.e. acrylic aldehyde is formed. Hence the product formed is acrylic aldehyde, also called acrolein.

14. (a) $(CH_3)_3COH$
    Explanation: Lucas reagent is a mixture of conc. HCl and anhydrous zinc chloride. We know that the order of reactivity of alcohols towards Lucas reagent is: tertiary > secondary > primary. So among the given options, $(CH_3)_3COH$, a tertiary alcohol, will react most readily with Lucas reagent.

15. (b) Phenoxide ion is stabilized through delocalization
    Explanation: As phenoxide ion is stabilized through delocalization, thus the ionization constant of phenol is higher than that of ethanol.

16. (a) 1° > 2° > 3°
    Explanation: For alcohols boiling points depends upon 3 factors, viz. molecular weight, number of available H-bonds and the surface area of the molecule. If the molecular weight of all the alcohols are more or less same, then the boiling point will also be nearly same. Now, both the number of available H-bonds and the surface area of the molecule are least In 3° alcohols and maximum in 1° alcohols. Hence, 3° alcohols have a least boiling point while 1° alcohols have a maximum boiling point. Hence the correct sequence will be, 1° > 2° > 3°

17. (d) Reacting with Mg
    Explanation: Traces of water can be removed from ethanol by reacting with Mg.
    $Mg + 2CH_3CH_2OH \rightarrow (CH_3CH_2O)_2Mg + H_2$
    $(CH_3CH_2O)_2Mg + H_2O \rightarrow MgO + 2CH_3CH_2OH$

18. (b) Riemer - Tiemann reaction
    Explanation: When Phenol reacts with chloroform and alcoholic KOH to give salicylaldehyde, the reaction is called Reimer-Tiemann reaction.

19. (a) Alcohols
    Explanation: Lucas test in alcohols is conducted to distinguish between primary, secondary, and tertiary alcohols. It is based on the difference in reactivity of the three classes of alcohols with hydrogen halides through a substitution reaction: $ROH + HCl \rightarrow RCl + H_2O$.

20. (b) Dichlorocarbene (:CCl_2)
    Explanation: $NaOH + CCl_3^- \rightarrow :CCl_2 + NaCl + H_2O$
    Here, the electrophile is dichlorocarbene (:CCl_2).

21. (b) b > d > a > c > e
    Explanation: The most acidic is p-nitrophenol, whereas the least acidic is p-methoxyphenol. The acidity is greatest when an electron withdrawing group is parallel to the OH group. The acidity is lowest when an electron releasing group is opposite the OH group.

22. (b) CH_3OCH_3
    Explanation: In general, simple Ether is R–O–R where R is an alkyl group. Hence, here CH_3OCH_3 is the simple ether.

23. (b) soluble in water
    Explanation: The lower alcohols are readily soluble in water and the solubility decreases with the increase in molecular weight. The solubility of alcohols in water can be explained due to the formation of hydrogen bond between the highly polarised —OH groups present both in alcohol and water.

24. (a) There is intermolecular hydrogen bonding in methanol and no hydrogen bonding in methyl thiol.
    Explanation: Methanol has high boiling point than methyl thiol because there is intermolecular hydrogen bonding in methanol and no hydrogen bonding in methyl thiol.

25. (b) $CHCl_2$
    Explanation: When phenol is reacted with $CHCl_3$ and aqueous NaOH at 70°C, the electrophile attacking the ring is CCl_2 (Reimer Tiemann Reaction and Carbene formation).

26. (d) (i), (ii) and (iii) are correct

Explanation: Phenol has higher boiling point than toluene because of hydrogen bonding.

27. (c) B, C

Explanation: Compound (A) *i.e.*, phenol and compound (D) *i.e.*, a derivative of phenol cannot be considered as aromatic alcohol. As phenol is also known as, carbolic acid cannot be considered as aromatic alcohol.

28. (c) Reduction of aldehyde/ketones with Zn-Hg/HCl

Explanation: As per the Clemmensen reduction, reduction of aldehydes and ketones with Zn(Hg)/HCl yields alkanes.

29. (d) 2, 4, 6-tribromophenol

Explanation: When phenol is treated with excess bromine water, it gives 2, 4, 6-tribromophenol.

30. (a,b,c)

Explanation:

$$C_6H_5Cl + NaOH \xrightarrow[300 \text{ atm}]{623 \text{ K}} C_6H_5O^-Na^+ \xrightarrow{HCl} C_6H_5OH$$

$$C_6H_5NH_2 \xrightarrow[+HCl]{NaNO_2} C_6H_5N_2^+Cl^- \xrightarrow[\text{Warm}]{H_2O} C_6H_5OH + N_2 + HCl$$

Aniline → Benzene diazonium chloride

$$C_6H_6 \xrightarrow{\text{Oleum}} C_6H_5SO_3H \xrightarrow[H^+]{NaOH} C_6H_5OH$$

31. (d) A-(iii), B-(iv), C-(ii), D-(i)

Explanation: A-(iii) - Ethylene glycol is used as Antifreeze in car engines. B-(iv) – Ethanol is used as solvent in perfumes. C-(ii) – Phenol is used as starting material for picric acid. D-(i) – Methanol is also known as wood spirit.

32. (d) $CH_3CHOHCH_3$

Explanation: Complete reaction,

$$\underset{A}{CH_3CHOHCH_3} \xrightarrow[\text{dil. }H_2SO_4]{K_2Cr_2O_7} \underset{B}{CH_3COCH_3} \xrightarrow[H_2O]{CH_3MgI} (CH_3)_3COH$$

33. (d) (i), (ii), and (iii) are correct

Explanation:

(i) $CH_3-\underset{OH}{\underset{|}{CH}}-CH_3 \xrightarrow{\text{Oxidation}} CH_3-\underset{O}{\underset{||}{C}}-CH_3$

(ii) $CH_3-CH_2-OH \xrightarrow[180°]{\text{Conc. }H_2SO_4} CH_2=CH_2 + H_2O$

(iii) $2CH_3CH_2OH + 2Na \rightarrow 2CH_3-CH_2-ONa + H_2$

(iv) Methanol does not undergo iodoform reaction.

34. (d) Phenol → Benzyl alcohol

Explanation: When primary (1°) alcohols are treated with copper at 300°C, then aldehydes are obtained by dehydrogenation of alcohols. Similarly secondary (2°) alcohols form ketone and alkene is obtained by dehydration of tertiary (3°)-alcohols. But phenol does not respond to this test.

35. (d) Bring down the specific heat of water

Explanation: Ethylene glycol is added to lowering down the freezing point of water so that it does not freeze.

36. (c) $(CH_3)_3CONa$ and CH_3CH_2Br react to form $(CH_3)_3C-O-CH_2CH_3$. Good yields of ether are obtained when primary alkyl halides are treated with alkoxides derived from any alcohol, 1°, 2°, or 3°.

37. (c) Ortho and para isomers of nitro phenol can be separated by steam distillation because of nearby same boiling point of both and Ortho isomers associate by intramolecular hydrogen bonding and Para isomers associate by hydrogen bonding.

38. (b) In Lucas test, tertiary alcohols react immediately because of the formation of the more stable tertiary carbocations.

39. (b) The tendency to show H-bonding decreases with increasing hydrophobic character of carbon chain. The hydrophobic character of carbon chain increases with the length of carbon chain.

40. (b) Alcohols which form the more stable carbocations undergo dehydration more readily. Since *tert*-butyl alcohol forms more stable *tert*-butyl cation, therefore, it undergoes dehydration more readily than propanol.

41. (c) *p*-Nitrophenolate ion is more stable than phenolate ion.

42. (c) Nucleophilic attack of phenolate ion through the *ortho*-carbon atom occurs on CCl_4 (a neutral electrophile) to form an intermediate which on hydrolysis gives salicylic acid (ArSE reaction).

43. (d) In ethers, bond angle around oxygen is not exactly 109° 28'. There is deviation in angle caused due to repulsive interactions between bulkier alkyl groups.

44. (b) On using *tert*-butyl bromide and sodium ethoxide as reactants, the major product would be 2-methylpropene and ethanol (elimination reaction).

45. (c) Ethers being Lewis bases form etherates with Lewis acids. Ethers are not easily cleaved by H_2SO_4.

46. (a) Alcohols have high boiling point than ethers because intermolecular H-bonding is found in alcohols.

47. (i) (d) Propan-2-ol to propanone

(ii) (b) But-2-ene

OR

(a) But-3-en-2-ol

(iii) (a) Benzaldehyde, Benzyl alcohol, potassium Salt of Benzoic acid.

(iv) (c) $CH_2=C(CH_3)_2$

48. (i) (a) Assertion and reason both are correct statements and reason is correct explanation for assertion.
   (ii) (d) Assertion is wrong statement but reason is correct statement.
   (iii) (a) Assertion and reason both are correct statements and reason is correct explanation for assertion.
   (iv) (c) Assertion is correct statement but reason is wrong statement.

   OR

   (a) Assertion and reason both are correct statements and reason is correct explanation for assertion.

49. (i) (a) Assertion and reason both are correct statements and reason is correct explanation for assertion.
   (ii) (c) Assertion is correct statement but reason is wrong statement.
   (iii) (c) Assertion is correct statement but reason is wrong statement.
   (iv) (a) Assertion and reason both are correct statements and reason is correct explanation for assertion.

50. (i) (a) Assertion and reason both are correct statements and reason is correct explanation for assertion.
   (ii) (c) Assertion is correct statement but reason is wrong statement.
   (iii) (a) Assertion and reason both are correct statements and reason is correct explanation for assertion.
   (iv) (b) Assertion and reason both are correct statements but reason is not correct explanation for assertion.

❏❏

Chapter 14

Biomolecules

1. Which of the following is an example of fibrous protein?
   (a) Insulin
   (b) Haemoglobin
   (c) Fibroin
   (d) Glycogen

2. α–D(+) glucose and β–D(+) glucose are: [CBSE, 2020]
   (a) Geometrical isomers
   (b) Enantiomers
   (c) Anomers
   (d) Optical isomers

3. The disease albinism is caused by the deficiency of enzyme:
   (a) Trypsin
   (b) Tyrosinase
   (c) Phenylalanine hydroxylase
   (d) None of these

4. Amino acids are: [CBSE, 2020]
   (a) acidic
   (b) basic
   (c) amphoteric
   (d) neutral

5. The deficiency of vitamin D causes:
   (a) Rickets
   (b) Gout
   (c) Scurvy
   (d) Night blindness

6. Which of the following is an example of aldohexose?
   (a) Ribose
   (b) Fructose
   (c) Sucrose
   (d) Glucose

7. The linkage which holds various amino acid units in primary structures of proteins is:
   (a) Glycoside linkage
   (b) Peptide linkage
   (c) Ionic linkage
   (d) Hydrogen bond

8. Maltose on hydrolysis gives:
   (a) α-D-glucose
   (b) α and β-D-glucose
   (c) Glucose and fructose
   (d) Fructose only

9. The amino acids are the end products of the digestion of:
   (a) Lipids
   (b) Fats
   (c) Proteins
   (d) Enzymes

10. α-helix refers to:
    (a) Primary structure of proteins
    (b) Secondary structure of proteins
    (c) Tertiary structure of proteins
    (d) Quaternary structure of proteins

11. Amino acids are classified as acidic, basic or neutral depending upon the relative number of amino and carboxyl groups in their molecule. Which of the following are acidic? [NCERT Exemplar]
    (a) $(CH_3)_2CH-CH-COOH$
            $|$
            NH_2
    (b) $HOOC-CH_2-CH_2-CH-COOH$
                            $|$
                            NH_2
    (c) $H_2N-CH_2-CH_2-CH_2-COOH$
    (d) $HOOC-CH_2-CH-COOH$
                      $|$
                      NH_2

12. The relation between nucleotide triplets and the amino acids is called:
    (a) Transcription
    (b) Duplication
    (c) Genetic code
    (d) Gene

13. Nucleic acids are polymers of:
    (a) Nucleotides
    (b) Nucleosides
    (c) Nuclei of heavy metals
    (d) Proteins

14. The non-proteinous substances which certain enzymes require for their activity are called:
    (a) Catalysts
    (b) Inhibitors
    (c) Co-enzymes
    (d) Epimers

15. Which of the following statements is not true about glucose? [NCERT Exemplar]
    (a) It is an aldohexose.
    (b) On heating with HI it forms n-hexane.
    (c) It is present in furanose form.
    (d) It does not give 2,4-DNP test.

16. Glucose on treatment with NH_2OH undergoes:
    (a) Condensation
    (b) Reduction
    (c) Hydrolysis
    (d) Oxidation

17. Niacin is vitamin:
    (a) B_1
    (b) B_2
    (c) B_{12}
    (d) B_3

18. Which of the following is a ketohexose?
    (a) Fructose
    (b) Maltose
    (c) Glucose
    (d) Ribose

19. The linkage that holds monosaccharide units together in a polysaccharide is called:
    (a) Peptide linkage
    (b) Glycoside linkage
    (c) Ester linkage
    (d) Ionic linkage

20. A nucleoside is made up of:
    (a) A base and sugar
    (b) A base and phosphoric acid
    (c) A sugar and phosphoric acid
    (d) A sugar, a base and phosphoric acid

21. Which one is the complementary base of cytosine in one strand to that in other strand of DNA? [CBSE, 2020]
    (a) Adenine
    (b) Guanine
    (c) Thymine
    (d) Uracil

22. Which of the following base is a purine?
    (a) Thymine (b) Uracil
    (c) Cytosine (d) Adenine
23. Which of the following is a pyrimidine base?
    (a) Adenine (b) Gyanine
    (c) Uracil (d) None of these
24. Which of the following is an example of globular protein?
    (a) Myosin (b) Collagen
    (c) Keratin (d) Haemoglobin
25. An α-helix is a structural feature of:
    [CBSE, 2020]
    (a) Sucrose (b) Polypeptides
    (c) Nucleotides (d) Starch
26. Structure of a disaccharide formed by glucose and fructose is given below. Identify anomeric carbon atoms in monosaccharide units. [NCERT Exemplar]

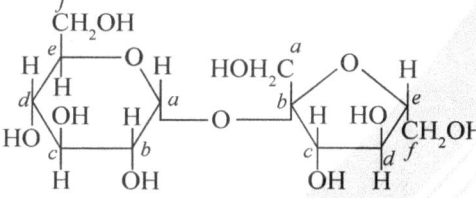

    (a) 'a' carbon of glucose and 'a' carbon of fructose.
    (b) 'a' carbon of glucose and 'e' carbon of fructose.
    (c) 'a' carbon of glucose and 'b' carbon of fructose.
    (d) 'f' carbon of glucose and 'f' carbon of fructose.
27. The main structural feature of proteins is:
    (a) Ether linkage (b) Ester linkage
    (c) Peptide linkage (d) All the three
28. Enzymes are:
    (a) Fatty acids (b) Vitamins
    (c) Proteins (d) None of these
29. Enzymes belong to which class of compounds?
    (a) Polysaccharides
    (b) Polypeptides
    (c) Polynitro heterocyclic compounds
    (d) Hydrocarbons
30. The nucleic acid base having two possible binding sites is:
    (a) Thymine (b) Cytosine
    (c) Guanine (d) Adenine
31. Curdling of milk is an example of:
    (a) breaking of peptide linkage
    (b) hydrolysis of lactose
    (c) breaking of protein into amino acids
    (d) denaturation of protein
32. Proteins are denatured in the:
    (a) Mouth (b) Stomach
    (c) Small intestine (d) Large intestine
33. Globular proteins are present in:
    (a) blood (b) insulin
    (c) milk (d) All of these
34. In which of the following classes does the glucose and mannose are placed?
    (a) Epimers (b) Anomers
    (c) Ketohexose (d) Disaccharide
35. Which of the following pairs represents anomers?
    [NCERT Exemplar]

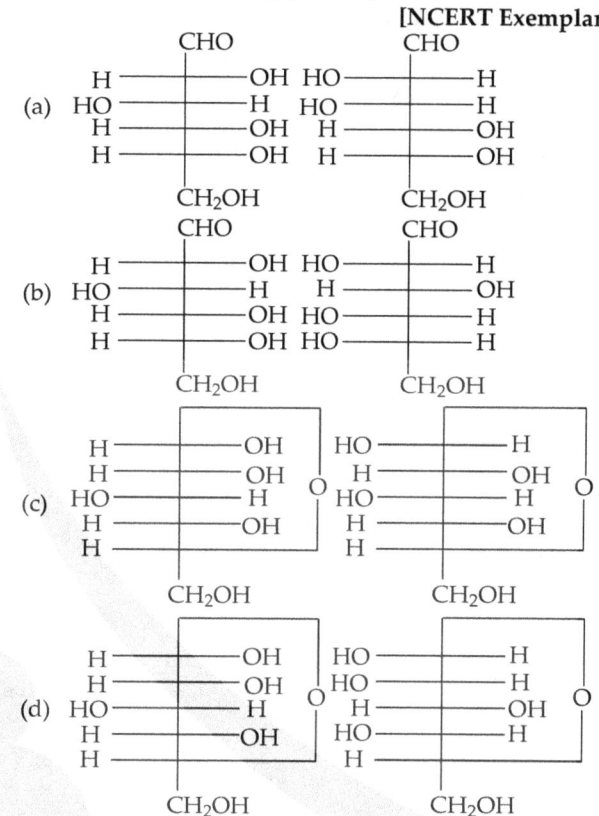

36. Which of the following α-amino acid is not optically active?
    (a) Alanine (b) Glycine
    (c) Phenylalanine (d) All are optically active
37. Select the false statement about the cyclic glucose.
    (a) If the —OH group is added to —CHO group it will form cyclic hemiacetal structure
    (b) Glucose form six membered ring in which —OH is at C-5 position
    (c) Melting point of α-glucose is 423 K and of β-glucose is 419 K

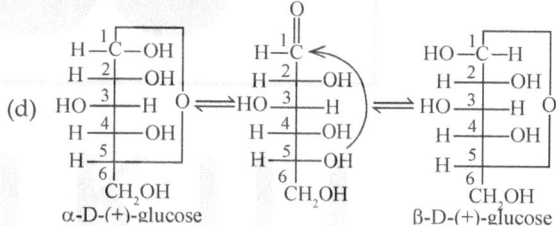

38. α-Amino acids behave as crystalline ionic solids and have high melting point due to the presence of:
    (a) —NH_2 group
    (b) —COOH group
    (c) Both —NH_2 and —COOH group
    (d) None of these
39. Which of the following bases is not present in DNA?
    (a) Adenine (b) Guanine
    (c) Uracil (d) Cytosine
40. Lysine, $H_2N—(CH_2)_4—CH—COOH$ is _____
                                    |
                                   NH_2
    [NCERT Exemplar]

(a) α-Amino acid
(b) Basic amino acid
(c) Amino acid synthesised in body
(d) β-Amino acid

41. Which of the statements about "Denaturation" given below are correct?
    (i) Denaturation of proteins causes loss of secondary and tertiary structures of the proteins
    (ii) Denaturation leads to the conversion of double strand of DNA into single strand
    (iii) Denaturation affects primary structure which gets distorted
    (a) (ii) and (iii)   (b) (i) and (iii)
    (c) (i) and (ii)   (d) (i), (ii) and (iii)

42. Which one of the following pairs is the essential constituent of our food?
    (a) Nucleic acids and lipids
    (b) Proteins and carbohydrates
    (c) Proteins and nucleic acids
    (d) Proteins and lipids

43. Optical rotations of some compounds along with their structures are given below which of them have D configuration. [NCERT Exemplar]

    (a) I, II, III   (b) II, III
    (c) I, II   (d) III

44. Which of the following is β-pyranose among the given options?

Directions: In the following questions, a statement of assertion is followed by a statement of reason. Mark the correct choice as:
(a) If both assertion and reason are true and reason is the correct explanation of assertion.
(b) If both assertion and reason are true, but reason is not the correct explanation of assertion.
(c) If assertion is true, but reason is false.
(d) If assertion is false but reason is true.

45. **Assertion:** When the native protein is subjected to physical changes such as change in temperature or chemical changes such as change in pH, its H-bonds are disturbed. This disturbance unfolds the globules and uncoils the helix. As a result, the protein loses its biological activity. This loss of biological activity by the protein is called denaturation.
Reason: One of the examples of denaturation of proteins is the coagulation of egg white when an egg is boiled.

46. **Assertion:** D (+) – glucose is dextrorotatory in nature.
Reason: 'D' represents its dextrorotatory nature.

47. **Assertion:** The polypeptide chain in globular protein is folded around itself, giving rise to a spherical structure.
Reason: Some enzymes are globular proteins.

48. **Assertion:** There are two common types of secondary structure of proteins:
α-helix structure
β-pleated sheet structure
Reason: In α- Helix structure, the –NH group of an amino acid residue forms H-bond with the $>C=O$ group of the adjacent turn of the right handed screw (α-helix).

49. **Assertion:** DNA is responsible for the transmission of inherent characters from one generation to the next. This process of transmission is called heredity.
Reason: Nucleic acids (both DNA and RNA) are responsible for protein synthesis in a cell.

50. **Assertion:** The helical structure of DNA is double-stranded.
Reason: The helical structure of RNA is single-stranded.

51. **Assertion:** All naturally occurring a-aminoacids except glycine are optically active.
Reason: Most naturally occurring amino acids have L-configuration. [NCERT Exemplar]

52. **Assertion:** In presence of enzyme, substrate molecule can be attacked by the reagent effectively.
Reason: Active sites of enzymes hold the substrate molecule in a suitable position. [NCERT Exemplar]

53. **Assertion:** Glycine must be taken through diet.
Reason: It is an essential amino acid.

54. **Assertion:** β-glycosidic linkage is present in maltose

Reason: Maltose is composed of two glucose units in which C–2 of one glucose unit is linked to C–4 of another glucose unit.

55. **Assertion:** Fibrous protein is a fibre-liked structure formed by the polypeptide chain. These proteins are held together by strong hydrogen and disulphide bonds.
Reason: It is usually soluble in water.

56. Read the passage given below and answer the following questions:
The interactions between DNA/RNA strands are controlled by orthogonal base pairing of adenine (A) to thymine (T) and cytosine (C) to guanine (G) and are essential for fundamental cellular activities and practical molecular therapeutic and diagnostic purposes, such as gene replication, gene regulation and diagnostics as well as anti-sense oligonucleotide drugs. Furthermore, recent years have also witnessed the emerging field of DNA nanotechnology, which uses DNA to

build complex designed molecular nanostructures and molecular machines by taking advantage of its programmability and predictable interactions, allowing for unprecedented precise control of structure and dynamic behaviour at the nanoscale. The properties of DNA strand interactions, such as the thermodynamics and kinetics of duplex formation, determine the assembly efficiency and stability of the DNA structures that affect cellular functions, anti-sense drug efficiency, and the performance of designed molecular machines.

The following questions are multiple choice questions. Choose the most appropriate answer:

(i) Which one of the following is not a pyrimidine derivative?
    (a) Uracil   (b) Thymine
    (c) Cytosine   (d) Guanine

OR

Which one of the following statements is **incorrect** about RNA?
    (a) RNA has a single helix structure
    (b) Sugar unit is ribose
    (c) It is not responsible for protein synthesis
    (d) It contains Uracil

(ii) A chemical or physical change that alters the sequence of bases in DNA molecule is also known as:
    (a) Mutation   (b) Replication
    (c) Translation   (d) Denaturation

(iii) Thymine combines with:
    (a) Only ribose sugar
    (b) Both deoxyribose and ribose sugars
    (c) Only deoxyribose sugar
    (d) None of these

(iv) Double helix completes a spiral at every _____ nucleotides in DNA:
    (a) Five   (b) Twenty
    (c) Ten   (d) Fifteen

57. Read the passage given below and answer the following questions:

Although carbohydrates represent one of the most important families of biomolecules, they remain understudied in comparison to the other biomolecular families (peptides, nucleobases). Beyond their best-known function of energy source in living systems, they act as mediator of molecular recognition processes, carrying molecular information in the so-called "sugar code," just to name one of their countless functions. Owing to their high conformational flexibility, they encode extremely rich information conveyed via the non-covalent hydrogen bonds within the carbohydrate and with other biomolecular assemblies, such as peptide subunits of proteins. Over the last decade there has been tremendous progress in the study of the conformational preferences of neutral oligosaccharides, and of the interactions between carbohydrates and various molecular partners (water, aromatic models, and peptide models), using vibrational spectroscopy as a sensitive probe.

In these questions, a statement of assertion followed by a statement of reason is given. Choose the correct answer out of the following choices.

(a) Assertion and reason both are correct statements and reason is correct explanation for assertion.
(b) Assertion and reason both are correct statements but reason is not correct explanation for assertion.
(c) Assertion is correct statement but reason is wrong statement.
(d) Assertion is wrong statement but reason is correct statement.

(i) **Assertion:** Polysaccharides are also carbohydrates.
Reason: Polysaccharides yield a large number of monosaccharide units on hydrolysis.

(ii) **Assertion:** Glucose is an aldohexose.
Reason: Glucose contains -CHO as functional group and contains six carbon atoms in total.

(iii) **Assertion:** Glycylalanine is a dipeptide.
Reason: A peptide linkage is found between two carbohydrate molecules.

(iv) **Assertion:** Polypeptides with fewer amino acids cannot be called proteins.
Reason: A polypeptide with more than 100 amino acid residues is usually called protein.

OR

Assertion: Glucose is correctly named as D(+)-glucose.
Reason: The letters 'D' and 'L' before the name of any compound indicate the relative configuration of a particular stereoisomer of glyceraldehyde.

58. Read the passage given below and answer the following questions: **[CBSE Website]**

Adenosine triphosphate (ATP) is the energy-carrying molecule found in the cells of all living things. ATP captures chemical energy obtained from the breakdown of food molecules and releases it to fuel other cellular processes. ATP is a nucleotide that consists of three main structures: the nitrogenous base, adenine; the sugar, ribose; and a chain of three phosphate groups bound to ribose. The phosphate tail of ATP is the actual power source which the cell taps. Available energy is contained in the bonds between the phosphates and is released when they are broken, which occurs through the addition of a water molecule (a process called hydrolysis). Usually only the outer phosphate is removed from ATP to yield energy; when this occurs ATP is converted to adenosine diphosphate (ADP), the form of the nucleotide having only two phosphates.

The importance of ATP (adenosine triphosphate) as the main source of chemical energy in living matter and its involvement in cellular processes has long been recognized. The primary mechanism whereby higher organisms, including humans, generate ATP is through mitochondrial oxidative phosphorylation. For the majority of organs, the main metabolic fuel is glucose, which in the presence of oxygen undergoes complete combustion to CO_2 and H_2O:

$$C_6H_{12}O_6 + 6O_2 \rightarrow 6O_2 + 6H_2O + \text{energy}$$

The free energy (ΔG) liberated in this exergonic (ΔG is negative) reaction is partially trapped as ATP in two consecutive processes: glycolysis (cytosol) and oxidative phosphorylation (mitochondria). The first produces 2 mol of ATP per mol of glucose, and the second 36 mol of ATP per mol of glucose. Thus, oxidative phosphorylation yields 17-18 times as much useful energy in the form of ATP as can be obtained from the same amount of glucose by glycolysis alone.

The efficiency of glucose metabolism is the ratio of amount of energy produced when 1 mol of glucose oxidised in cell to the enthalpy of combustion of glucose. The energy lost in the process is in the form of heat. This heat is responsible for keeping us warm.

(i) Cellular oxidation of glucose is a:
   (a) spontaneous and endothermic process
   (b) non spontaneous and exothermic process
   (c) non spontaneous and endothermic process
   (d) spontaneous and exothermic process

(ii) What is the efficiency of glucose metabolism if 1 mole of glucose gives 38ATP energy?(Given: The enthalpy of combustion of glucose is 686 kcal, 1ATP= 7.3kcal)
   (a) 100%   (b) 38%
   (c) 62%   (d) 80%

(iii) Which of the following statement is true?
   (a) ATP is a nucleoside made up of nitrogenous base adenine and ribose sugar.
   (b) ATP consists the nitrogenous base, adenine and the sugar, deoxyribose.
   (c) ATP is a nucleotide which contains a chain of three phosphate groups bound to ribose sugar.
   (d) The nitrogenous base of ATP is the actual power source.

(iv) Nearly 95% of the energy released during cellular respiration is due to:
   (a) glycolysis occurring in cytosol
   (b) oxidative phosphorylation occurring in cytosol
   (c) glycolysis in occurring mitochondria
   (d) oxidative phosphorylation occurring in mitochondria

(v) Which of the following statements is correct:
   (a) ATP is a nucleotide which has three phosphate groups while ADP is a nucleoside which three phosphate groups.
   (b) ADP contains a nitrogenous bases adenine, ribose sugar and two phosphate groups bound to ribose.
   (c) ADP is the main source of chemical energy in living matter.
   (d) ATP and ADP are nucleosides which differ in number of phosphate groups.

59. Read the passage given below and answer the following questions: [CBSE Website]

EVIDENCE FOR THE FIBROUS NATURE OF DNA

The basic chemical formula of DNA is now well established. As shown in Figure 1 it consists of a very long chain, the backbone of which is made up of alternate sugar and phosphate groups, joined together in regular 3' 5' phosphate di-ester linkages. To each sugar is attached a nitrogenous base, only four different kinds of which are commonly found in DNA. Two of these---adenine and guanine--- are purines, and the other two thymine and cytosine-are pyrimidines. A fifth base, 5-methyl cytosine, occurs in smaller amounts in certain organisms, and a sixth, 5-hydroxy-methyl-cytosine, is found instead of cytosine in the T even phages. It should be noted that the chain is unbranched, a consequence of the regular internucleotide linkage. On the other hand the sequence of the different nucleotides is, as far as can be ascertained, completely irregular. Thus, DNA has some features which are regular, and some which are irregular. A similar conception of the DNA molecule as a long thin fiber is obtained from physicochemical analysis involving sedimentation, diffusion, light scattering, and viscosity measurements. These techniques indicate that DNA is a very asymmetrical structure approximately 20 A wide and many thousands of angstroms long. Estimates of its molecular weight currently center between 5×10^6 and 10^7 (approximately 3×10^4 nucleotides). Surprisingly each of these measurements tend to suggest that the DNA is relatively rigid, a puzzling finding in view of the large number of single bonds (5 per nucleotide) in the phosphate-sugar back bone. Recently these indirect inferences have been confirmed by electron microscopy.

(i) Purines present in DNA are:
   (a) adenine and thymine
   (b) guanine and thymine
   (c) cytosine and thymine
   (d) adenine and guanine

(ii) DNA molecule has internucleotide linkage and sequence of the different nucleotides:
   (a) regular, regular   (b) regular, irregular
   (c) irregular, regular (d) irregular, irregular

(iii) DNA has a_____backbone:
   (a) phosphate -purine
   (b) pyrimidines- sugar
   (c) phosphate- sugar
   (d) D.purine- pyrimidine

(iv) Out of the four different kinds of nitrogenous bases which are commonly found in DNA, has been replaced in some organisms.
   (a) adenine   (b) guanine
   (c) cytosine   (d) thymine

60. Read the passage given below and answer the following questions

Carbohydrates are the main source of energy that is ingested by the human body (Caffall et al., 2009) Brain mainly utilizes the glucose. Red blood cells also use glucose only. Fiber in the diet is not digested by human body due to lack of cellulase enzyme. Glucose is the major energy source in the body. Glycogen is the storage form of glucose and glycogen is stored in skeletal muscles and liver. If glucose intake exceeds than it is utilised in the body it is converted into fat.

Riboses are utilised in formation of deoxyribonucleic acid. Carbohydrates are polyhydroxy alcohol with potentially active carbonyl group which may be aldehyde or keto group. Carbohydrates can be classified on the basis of carbon atom present in the carbohydrates. Carbohydrates are classified into four types monosaccharides, disaccharides, oligosaccharides, polysaccharides. Monosaccharides cannot be hydrolyzed further into simpler form. Disaccharides give two monosaccharides on hydrolysis. Polysaccharides may be homopolysaccharides and heteropolysaccharides.

In these questions, a statement of assertion followed by a statement of reason is given. Choose the correct answer out of the following choices.

(a) Assertion and reason both are correct statements and reason is correct explanation for assertion.
(b) Assertion and reason both are correct statements but reason is not correct explanation for assertion.
(c) Assertion is correct statement but reason is wrong statement.
(d) Assertion is wrong statement but reason is correct statement.

(i) **Assertion:** Carbohydrates are more suitable for the production of energy in the body than proteins and fats.
Reason: Carbohydrates can be stored in the tissues as glycogen for use in the production of energy, whenever necessary.

(ii) **Assertion:** Sucrose (cane sugar) is a disaccharide.
Reason: One molecule of sucrose on hydrolysis gives one molecule of glucose and one molecule of fructose.

(iii) **Assertion:** Glucose gives a bright orange precipitate with 2,4-dinitrophenydlhylrazine (2,4-DNP) test.
Reason: Glucose does not contain any free aldehydic group in its cyclic form.

(iv) **Assertion:** Sucrose is a disaccharide and it is also a reducing sugar.
Reason: Carbohydrates are classified on the basis of their behaviour on hydrolysis and also as reducing or non-reducing sugar.

OR

Assertion: Deoxyribose, $C_5H_{10}O_5$ is not a carbohydrate molecule.
Reason: Carbohydrates are hydrates of carbon compounds that may or may not follow $C_x(H_2O)_y$ formula.

Answers

1. **(c)** Fibroin
   Explanation: Silk fibroin is a fibrous protein derived from the Bombyx mori silk worm. It is an amphiphilic block copolymer with a heavy chain composed of 12 repetitive domains predominated by the sequence G-X-G-X-G-X (G = glycine; X = alanine or serine).

2. **(c)** Anomers
   Explanation: α–D–(+)-glucose and β–D–(+)-glucose are those diastereomers that differ in configuration at C-1 atom. Such isomers are referred as anomers. In this case, C-1 carbon atom is the anomeric carbon atom.

   α-D-glucopyranose   β-D-glucopyranose

3. **(b)** Tyrosinase
   Explanation: The disease albinism is caused by the deficiency of tyrosinase enzyme. Albinism is an inherited disorder that is characterized by little or no production of the pigment melanin, due to lack of tyrosine enzyme. This enzyme helps the body to change the amino acid tyrosine into melanin pigment. In albinism suffering person, the enzyme is inactive and no melanin is produced, leading to white hair and very light skin colour.

4. **(c)** amphoteric
   Explanation: Amino acids are amphoteric, which means they have acidic and basic tendencies. The carboxyl group is able to lose a proton and the amine group is able to accept a proton.

5. **(a)** Rickets
   Explanation: Vitamin D is essential for strong bones, because it helps the body use calcium from the diet. Traditionally, vitamin D deficiency has been associated with rickets, a disease in which the bone tissue doesn't properly mineralize, leading to soft bones and skeletal deformities.

6. **(d)** Glucose
   Explanation: Aldohexoses have four chiral centers. Because of that there are 16 possible stereoisomers. Examples of aldohexoses are glucose, mannose, galactose, etc. Glucose is a one of the products of photosynthesis in plants and other photosynthetic organisms. It also serves as an important metabolic intermediate of cellular respiration.

7. **(b)** Peptide linkage
   Explanation: Peptide linkage is the peptide bond formed between the amino acids. It is a covalent bond formed between amino group of one molecule and carboxylic acid group of another molecule. The primary structure of a peptide or protein is the linear sequence of its amino acid structural units. The primary structure of a protein is reported starting from the amino-terminal (N) end to the carboxyl-terminal (C) end.

8. **(a)** α-D-glucose
   Explanation: Maltose is also known as malt sugar. It is a disaccharide, made up of two D - glucose units. The two units of glucose are linked with an alpha 1,4 glycosidic bond. Maltose dissociates it into its monosaccharide after hydrolysis. Using the

hydrolysis reaction of maltose we can determine the products.

9. (c) Proteins
   Explanation: The amino acids are the end products of the digestion of proteins. The hydrolysis of proteins to amino acids is carried out in presence of base or proteolytic enzymes. The amino acids obtained can be separated by various physical techniques such as electrophoresis, paper chromatography and ion exchange chromatography.

10. (b) Secondary structure of proteins
    Explanation: α-helices, β-sheets and random coils are the most common elements of secondary structure in proteins. α-helices are formed and maintained by backbone interactions parallel to the primary axis of the helix.

11. (b,d)
    Explanation:
    (b) $HOOC-CH_2-CH_2-CH-COOH$
    $\qquad\qquad\qquad\qquad\qquad |$
    $\qquad\qquad\qquad\qquad\ NH_2$
    Number of COOH group = 2
    Number of NH_2 group = 1
    Since number of COOH groups (2) > number of NH_2 group (1). Therefore this amino acid a acidic amine acid.
    (d) $HOOC-CH_2-CH_2-CH-COOH$
    $\qquad\qquad\qquad\qquad\qquad |$
    $\qquad\qquad\qquad\qquad\ NH_2$
    Number of COOH group = 2
    Number of NH_3 groups = 1
    Since, Number of COOH group (2) > Number of NH_2 group (1). Therefore amino acid is acidic. Write other two are neutral amino acid as number of NH_2 group is equal to number of COOH group in then.

12. (c) Genetic code
    Explanation: The relationship between the nucleotide triplets and the amino acids is called a genetic code. This determines the sequence of amino acids in the proteins that are synthesized.

13. (a) Nucleotides
    Explanation: DNA and RNA are termed as nucleic acids. They are polymers of nucleotides. A nucleotide consists of a base, a sugar molecule and a phosphate molecule.

14. (c) Co-enzymes
    Explanation: The non-proteinaceous substance, which certain enzymes require for their activity are called coenzymes. Coenzymes are organic molecules that are required by certain enzymes to carry out catalysis. They bind to the active site of the enzyme and participate in catalysis but are not considered substrates of the reaction. They function as intermediate carriers of electrons, specific atoms or functional groups that are transferred in the overall reaction. Example: FAD, NAD^+.

15. (c) It is present in furanose form.
    Explanation: Glucose represents pyranose structure.

16. (a) Condensation
    Explanation: D-glucose reacts with hydroxylamine (NH_2OH) to form an oxime because of the presence of aldehydic (–CHO) group or carbonyl carbon. This happens as the cyclic structure of glucose forms an open chain structure in an aqueous medium, which then reacts with NH_2OH to give an oxime.

17. (d) B_3
    Explanation: Niacin is a form of vitamin B_3. It is found in foods such as yeast, meat, fish, milk, eggs, green vegetables, and cereal grains. Niacin is also produced in the body from tryptophan, which is found in protein-containing food. When taken as a supplement, niacin is often found in combination with other B vitamins.

18. (a) Fructose
    Explanation: Fructose is a ketohexose found in honey and a wide variety of fruits and vegetables. Combined with glucose in an α(1→2)β linkage, it forms sucrose. It makes up one sixth to one third of the total carbohydrate intake of most individuals in industrialized nations.

19. (b) Glycosidic linkage
    Explanation: A glycosidic bond or glycosidic linkage is a type of covalent bond that joins a carbohydrate (sugar) molecule to another group, which may or may not be another carbohydrate.

20. (a) A base and sugar
    Explanation: The sugars which are present in the nucleotide are ribose or deoxyribose. The nitrogenous bases are purines and pyrimidines. The phosphate is present as phosphoric acid. The nucleotide is formed by the union of a phosphate group with a nucleoside. A nucleoside, in fact, contains a sugar molecule along with an organic nitrogenous base.

21. (b) Guanine
    Explanation: Each nucleotide base can hydrogen-bond with a specific partner base in a process known as complementary base pairing: Cytosine forms three hydrogen bonds with guanine, and adenine forms two hydrogen bonds with thymine. These hydrogen-bonded nitrogenous bases are often referred to as base pairs.

22. (d) Adenine
    Explanation: Adenine is an organic base of purine. It has many roles in biochemistry, especially cellular respiration. It is used a chemical component of RNA and DNA.

23. (c) Uracil
    Explanation: Uracil is a common and naturally occurring pyrimidine derivative.

24. (d) Hemoglobin
    Explanation: Hemoglobin is an example of a globular protein. Each hemoglobin molecule is made up of four heme groups surrounding a globin group, forming a tetrahedral structure.

25. (b) Polypeptides
    Explanation: An a-helix is a structural feature of Polypeptides. The amino acids in an α-helix are arranged in a right-handed helical structure where

each amino acid residue corresponds to a 100° turn in the helix and a translation of 1.5 Å (0.15 nm) along the helical axis. Short pieces of left-handed helix sometimes occur with a large content of achiral glycine amino acids, but are unfavorable for the other normal, biological L-amino acids.

26. (c) 'a' carbon of glucose and 'b' carbon of fructose.

    Explanation: In a cyclic structure of glucose or fructose, C atom which is adjacent to oxygen atom is known as anomeric carbon. In the given structures a and b on C which are present adjacent to O atom are anomeric. Both anomeric carbons differ in the configuration of -OH group.

27. (c) Peptide linkage

    Explanation: Peptide bonds are formed by a biochemical reaction that extracts a water molecule as it joins the amino group of one amino acid to the carboxyl group of a neighboring amino acid. The linear sequence of amino acids within a protein is considered the primary structure of the protein.

28. (c) Proteins

    Explanation: Enzymes are proteins, and they make a biochemical reaction more likely to proceed by lowering the activation energy of the reaction, thereby making these reactions proceed thousands or even millions of times faster than they would without a catalyst. Enzymes are highly specific to their substrates.

29. (b) Polypeptides

    Explanation: Enzymes are polypeptides. They are composed primarily of proteins, which are polymers of amino acids. Enzymes can bind prosthetic groups that can participate in enzyme reactions. They bind their substrates at active sites where the catalysed reactions take place.

30. (c) Guanine

    Explanation: Guanine is a purine derivative. It is reported to assemble into square-planar groups that resemble macrocycles, in which the bases interact via hydrogen bonds. Guanine has two possible binding sites.

31. (d) denaturation of protein

    Explanation: Denaturation involves the breaking of many of the weak linkages, or bonds (e.g., hydrogen bonds), within a protein molecule that are responsible for the highly ordered structure of the protein in its natural (native) state. Denatured proteins have a looser, more random structure; most are insoluble.

32. (b) Stomach

    Explanation: A large part of protein digestion takes place in the stomach. The enzyme pepsin plays an important role in the digestion of proteins by breaking down the intact protein to peptides, which are short chains of four to nine amino acids. In the duodenum, other enzymes— trypsin, elastase, and chymotrypsin—act on the peptides reducing them to smaller peptides.

33. (d) All of these

    Explanation: All these are the examples of globular proteins. These are soluble in water.

34. (b) Anomers

    Explanation: Glucose and mannose are classified as anomers.

35. (c)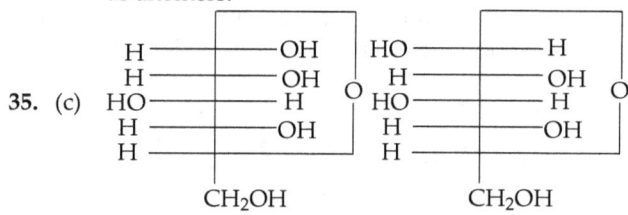

    Explanation: Anomers differ from each other in the configuration of hydroxyl group at C_1 positions.

36. (d) All are optically active

    Explanation: Alanine, Glycine and Phenylalanine all are optically active.

37. (c) Melting point of α-glucose is 423 K and of β-glucose is 419 K

    Explanation: Melting point of α-glucose is 419 K and of β-glucose is 423 K.

38. (b) —COOH group

    Explanation: Amino acids exist as zwitter ions resulting in strong dipole-dipole attraction Amino acids have two functional groups $-NH_2$ and -COOH. Hence the amino acids exist as a dipolar ion (or) zwitter ion. As a result, strong electrostatic forces exist between zwitter ions.

39. (c) Uracil

    Explanation: Uracil is not found in DNA as it uracil has more base pair affinity to adenine, guanine and cytosine. Instead thymine is present in DNA.

40. (a,b)

    Explanation: Lysine and arginine are basic amino acids because it's side chain group contains a full positive charge at the physiological pH

41. (c) (i) and (ii)

    Explanation: When the proteins are subjected to the action of heat, mineral acids or alkali, the water soluble form of globular protein changes to water insoluble fibrous protein. This is called denaturation of proteins. During denaturation secondary and tertiary structures of protein destroyed but primary structures remains intact.

42. (b) Proteins and carbohydrates

    Explanation: Protein and carbohydrates are the essential constituents of our foods.

43. (a) I, II, III

    Explanation: D-configuration of the compounds is always compared to the structure of (+) glycerides. Among the given options I, II, and III shows D-configuration with -OH group on the right side of asymmetric carbon.

44. (b) β-pyranose ring is

45. (a) In a biological system, a protein is found to have a unique three-dimensional structure and a unique biological activity. In such a situation, the proteinm is called native protein. However, when the native protein is subjected to physical changes such as

change in temperature or chemical changes such as change in pH, its H-bonds are disturbed. This disturbance unfolds the globules and uncoils the helix. As a result, the protein loses its biological activity. This loss of biological activity by the protein is called denaturation. During denaturation, the secondary and the tertiary structures of the protein get destroyed, but the primary structure remains unaltered. One of the examples of denaturation of proteins is the coagulation of egg white when an egg is boiled.

46. (c) D corresponds to the position of –OH group on the right side on the farthest asymmetric C-atom.
47. (c) All enzymes are globular proteins.
48. (a) Both assertion and reason are true and reason is correct explanation of assertion.
49. (b) Nucleic acids (both DNA and RNA) are responsible for protein synthesis in a cell. Even though the proteins are synthesised by the various RNA molecules in a cell, the message for the synthesis of a particular protein is present in DNA.
50. (b) Double helix is the description of the structure of a DNA molecule. A DNA molecule consists of two strands that wind around each other like a twisted ladder. RNA is a single-stranded molecule in many of its biological roles and consists of a much shorter chain of nucleotides.
51. (b) All other naturally occurring amino acids, with the exception of glycine, are optically active due to the asymmetric carbon atom. These are available in both D and L configuration. The L configuration is found in the majority of naturally occurring amino acids. The NH_2 group on the left-hand side is used to indicate L amino acids.
52. (a) Because active sites of enzymes retain the substrate molecule in a favourable place, it can be attacked by a reagent effectively when there is an enzyme present. As a result, enzyme-catalyzed reactions are stereospecific.
53. (d) Non-essential amino acids are those that can be produced in the body. Non-essential amino acids, such as glycine, are an example.
54. (d) Because maltose is made up of two glucose units, the C-1 of one of which is linked to the C-4 of the other.
55. (c) Proteins that are fibrous A fibre-like structure is generated when polypeptide chains run parallel and are kept together by hydrogen and disulphide bonds. In most cases, these proteins are water insoluble.
56. (i) (d) Guanine

    OR

    (c) It is not responsible for protein synthesis
    (ii) (a) Mutation

(iii) (c) Only deoxyribose sugar
(iv) (c) Ten

57. (i) (b) Assertion and reason both are correct statements but reason is not correct explanation for assertion.
(ii) (a) Assertion and reason both are correct statements and reason is correct explanation for assertion.
(iii) (c) Assertion is correct statement but reason is wrong statement.
(iv) (d) Assertion is wrong statement but reason is correct statement.

OR

(a) Assertion and reason both are correct statements and reason is correct explanation for assertion.

58. (i) (d) spontaneous and exothermic process
(ii) (b) 38%

(Glucose catabolism yields a TOTAL of 38 ATP. 38 ATP x 7.3 kcal/mol ATP = 262 kcal. Glucose has 686 kcal. Thus the efficiency of glucose metabolism is 262/686 x 100 = 38%.)

(iii) (c) ATP is a nucleotide which contains a chain of three phosphate groups bound to ribose sugar.
(iv) (d) oxidative phosphorylation occurring in mitochondria
(v) (b) ADP contains a nitrogenous bases adenine, ribose sugar and two phosphate groups bound to ribose.

59. (i) (d) adenine and guanine
(ii) (b) regular , irregular
(iii) (c) phosphate- sugar
(iv) (c) cytosine

60. (i) (b) Assertion and reason both are correct statements but reason is not correct explanation for assertion.
(ii) (a) Assertion and reason both are correct statements and reason is correct explanation for assertion.
(iii) (d) Assertion is wrong statement but reason is correct statement.
(iv) (a) Assertion and reason both are correct statements and reason is correct explanation for assertion.

OR

(d) Assertion is wrong statement but reason is correct statement.

MATHEMATICS

SYLLABUS
Mathematics
One Paper

90 minutes   **Max. Marks : 40**

S. No.	Units	Marks
I	Relations and Functions	8
II	Algebra	10
III	Calculus	17
IV	Linear Programming	05
	Total	40
	Internal Assessment	10
Total		50

Unit-I: Relations and Functions

1. Relations and Functions
Types of relations: reflexive, symmetric, transitive and equivalence relations. One to one and onto functions.

2. Inverse Trigonometric Functions
Definition, range, domain, principal value branch.

Unit-II: Algebra

1. Matrices
Concept, notation, order, equality, types of matrices, zero and identity matrix, transpose of a matrix, symmetric and skew symmetric matrices. Operation on matrices: Addition and multiplication and multiplication with a scalar. Simple properties of addition, multiplication and scalar multiplication. Non- commutativity of multiplication of matrices, Invertible matrices; (Here all matrices will have real entries).

2. Determinants
Determinant of a square matrix (up to 3 × 3 matrices), minors, co-factors and applications of determinants in finding the area of a triangle. Adjoint and inverse of a square matrix. Solving system of linear equations in two or three variables (having unique solution) using inverse of a matrix.

Unit-III: Calculus

1. Continuity and Differentiability
Continuity and differentiability, derivative of composite functions, chain rule, derivative of inverse trigonometric functions, derivative of implicit functions. Concept of exponential and logarithmic functions.
Derivatives of logarithmic and exponential functions. Logarithmic differentiation, derivative of functions expressed in parametric forms. Second order derivatives.

2. Applications of Derivatives
Applications of derivatives: increasing/decreasing functions, tangents and normals, maxima and minima (first derivative test motivated geometrically and second derivative test given as a provable tool). Simple problems (that illustrate basic principles and understanding of the subject as well as real-life situations).

Unit-V: Linear Programming

1. Linear Programming

Introduction, related terminology such as constraints, objective function, optimization, different types of linear programming (L.P.) problems. Graphical method of solution for problems in two variables, feasible and infeasible regions (bounded), feasible and infeasible solutions, optimal feasible solutions (up to three non-trivial constraints).

INTERNAL ASSESSMENT	**10 MARKS**
Periodic Test	5 Marks
Mathematics Activities: Activity file record +Term end assessment of one activity & Viva	5 Marks

Note: For activities NCERT Lab Manual may be referred

Chapter 1

Relations and Functions

1. Let R be a relation on the set N of natural numbers defined by nRm if n divides m. Then R is:
   (a) Reflexive and symmetric
   (b) Transitive and symmetric
   (c) Equivalence
   (d) Reflexive, transitive but not symmetric.

2. If the set A contains 7 elements and set B contains 10 elements, then the number of one-one functions from A to B is :
   (a) $^{10}C_7$
   (b) $^{10}C_7 \times 7!$
   (c) 7^{10}
   (d) 10^7

3. Let N be the set of natural numbers and the function $f: N \to N$ be defined by $f(n) = 2n + 3 \; \forall \in N$. Then f is
   (a) surjective
   (b) injective
   (c) bijective
   (d) none of these

4. Set A has 3 elements and the set B has 4 elements. Then the number of injective mappings that can be defined from A to B is:
   (a) 144
   (b) 12
   (c) 24
   (d) 64

5. If $A = \{a, b, c\}$ and $B = \{4, 5, 6\}$, then number of functions from A to B is :
   (a) 9
   (b) 27
   (c) 18
   (d) 81

6. Let $f: R \to R$ be defined by $f(x) = x^2 + 1$. Then, pre-images of 17 and -3, respectively, are:
   (a) $\phi, \{4, -4\}$
   (b) $\{3, -3\}, \phi$
   (c) $\{4, -4\}, \phi$
   (d) $\{4, -4\}, \{2, -2\}$

7. For real numbers x and y, define xRy if and only if $x - y + \sqrt{2}$ is an irrational number. Then the relation R is:
   (a) reflexive
   (b) symmetric
   (c) transitive
   (d) none of these

8. Let $A = \{2, 3, 6\}$. Which of the following relations on A are reflexive?
   (a) $R = \{(2, 2), (3, 3), (6, 6)\}$
   (b) $R = \{(2, 2), (3, 3), (3, 6), (6, 3)\}$
   (c) $R = \{(2, 2), (3, 6), (2, 6)\}$
   (d) None of these

9. Let R be the relation on N defined by $R = \{(x, y): x + 2y = 8\}$. Then, the domain of R is:
   (a) $\{2, 4, 6, 8\}$
   (b) $\{2, 4, 8\}$
   (c) $\{2, 4, 6\}$
   (d) $\{1, 2, 3, 4\}$

10. Let $f: R \to R$ be defined as $f(x) = \begin{cases} 2x, \text{ if } x > 3 \\ x^2, \text{ if } 1 < x \leq 3 \\ 3x, \text{ if } x \leq 1 \end{cases}$.
    Then $f(-1) + f(2) + f(4) =$
    (a) 9
    (b) 14
    (c) 5
    (d) None of these

11. The relation R in the set of natural numbers N defined as $R = \{(x, y) : y = x + 5 \text{ and } x < 4\}$ is :
    (a) reflexive
    (b) symmetric
    (c) transitive
    (d) None of these

12. For the set $A = \{1, 2, 3\}$, define a relation R in the set A as follows
    $R = \{(1, 1), (2, 2), (3, 3), (1, 3)\}$
    Then, the ordered pair to be added to R to make it the smallest equivalence relation is :
    [NCERT Exemplar]
    (a) (1, 3)
    (b) (3, 1)
    (c) (2, 1)
    (d) (1, 2)

13. If $A = \{x \in Z : 0 \leq x \leq 12\}$ and R is the relation in A given by $R = \{(a, b) : a = b\}$. Then, the set of all elements related to 1 is :
    (a) $\{1, 2\}$
    (b) $\{2, 3\}$
    (c) $\{1\}$
    (d) $\{2\}$

14. $f: X \to Y$ is onto, if and only if :
    (a) range of $f = Y$
    (b) range of $f \neq Y$
    (c) range of $f < Y$
    (d) range of $f \geq Y$

15. The number of all one-one functions from set $A = \{1, 2, 3\}$ to itself is :
    (a) 2
    (b) 6
    (c) 3
    (d) 1

16. Let $A = \{1, 2, 3, ..., n\}$ and $B = \{a, b\}$. Then the number of surjections from A into B is :
    (a) $^nP_2$
    (b) $2^n - 2$
    (c) $2^n - 1$
    (d) None of these

17. If the set A contains 5 elements and the set B contains 6 elements, then the number of one-one and onto mappings from A to B is :
    (a) 720
    (b) 120
    (c) 0
    (d) None of these

18. The greatest integer function $f: R \to R$, given by $f(x) = [x]$ is :
    (a) one-one
    (b) onto
    (c) both one-one and onto
    (d) neither one-one nor onto

19. Set A has 3 elements and the set B has 4 element then the total number of injective mapping :
    (a) 144
    (b) 12
    (c) 24
    (d) 64

20. The relation of the relation R = {(x, x²) : x is a prime number less than 13} :
    (a) {2, 3, 5, 7}
    (b) {4, 9, 25, 49, 121}
    (c) {2, 3, 5, 7, 11}
    (d) {1, 4, 9, 25, 49, 121}

21. Let $f : R \to R$ be defined by $f(x) = \dfrac{x^2 - 8}{x^2 + 2}$, then f is :
    (a) One-one but not onto
    (b) One-one and onto
    (c) Onto but not one-one
    (d) Neither one-one nor onto

22. Let R be the relation on the set A = {1, 2, 3, 4} given by R = {(1, 2), (2, 2), (1, 1), (4, 4), (3, 3), (2, 3), (1, 3)}. then :
    (a) R is reflexive and symmetric but not transitive
    (b) R is reflexive and transitive but not symmetric
    (c) R is symmetric and transitive but not reflexive
    (d) R is an equivalance relation

23. R is a relation from {11, 12, 13} to {8, 10, 12} defined by $y = x - 3$ then R^{-1} is :
    (a) {(8, 11), (10, 13)}
    (b) {(11, 8), (13, 10)}
    (c) {(10, 13), (8, 11), (8, 10)}
    (d) None of these

24. Which one of the following is an identity relation?
    (a) (1, 2), (2, 3), (1, 3)
    (b) (5, 5), (4, 4), (2, 2)
    (c) (1, 3), (3, 1), (2, 3)
    (d) None of these

25. Let T be the set of all triangles in the Euclidean plane and let a relation R on T be defined as aRb if a is congruent to b for all $a, b \in T$, then R is :
    (a) Reflexive but not symmetric
    (b) Transitive but not symmetric
    (c) Equivalence
    (d) Neither symmetric nor transitive

26. One-one, onto function is also called :
    (a) Injective function
    (b) Surjective function
    (c) Bijective function
    (d) All of these

27. The relation R on R defined by R = {(a, b) : $a \leq b^3$} is :
    (a) Reflexive
    (b) Symmetric
    (c) Transitive
    (d) None of these

28. The maxium number of equivalence relations on the set A = {1, 2, 3} are: [NCERT Exemplar]
    (a) 1
    (b) 2
    (c) 3
    (d) 5

29. If a relation R on the set {1, 2, 3} be defined by R = {(1, 2)} then R is : [NCERT Exemplar]
    (a) reflexive
    (b) transitive
    (c) symmetric
    (d) none of these

30. Let us define a relation R in R as a aRb if $a \geq b$. Then R is : [NCERT Exemplar]
    (a) an equivalence relation
    (b) reflexive, transitive but not symmetric
    (c) symmetric, transitive but not reflexive
    (d) neither transitive nor reflexive but symmetric

31. Let A = {1, 2, 3} and consider the relation R = {(1, 1), (2, 2), (3, 3), (1, 2), (2, 3)}. Then R is : [NCERT Exemplar]
    (a) reflexive but not symmetric
    (b) reflexive but not transitive
    (c) symmetric and transitive
    (d) niether symmetric nor transitive

32. Let R be the relation in the set {1, 2, 3, 4} given by R = {(1, 2), (2, 2), (1, 1), (4, 4), (1, 3), (3, 3), (3, 2)}. Choose the correct answer. [NCERT]
    (a) R is reflexive and symmetric but not transitive
    (b) R is reflexive and transitive but not symmetric
    (c) R is symmetric and transitive but not reflexive
    (d) R is an equivalence relation

33. Let $f : R \to R$ be defined as $f(x) = x^4$. Choose the correct answer : [NCERT]
    (a) f is one-one onto
    (b) f is many-one onto
    (c) f is one-one but not onto
    (d) f is neither one-one nor onto

Choose the correct option :
(a) Both (A) and (B) are true and R is the correct explanation A.
(b) Both (A) and (R) are true but R is not correct explanation of A.
(c) A is true but R is false.
(d) A is false but R is true.

34. Assertion (R) : The function $f(x) = |x|$ is not one-one.
    Reason (R) : The negative real number are not the images of any real numbers.

35. Assertion (A) : A function $y = f(x)$ is defined by $x^2 - \cos^{-1} y = \pi$, then domain of $f(x)$ is R.
    Reason (R) : $\cos^{-1} y \in [0, \pi]$.

36. Assertion (A) : If $f(x)$ is odd function and $g(x)$ is even function, then $f(x) + g(x)$ is neither even nor odd.
    Reason (R) : Odd function is symmetrical in opposite quadrants and even function is symmetrical about the y-axis.

37. Assertion (A) : Every even function $y = f(x)$ is not one-one, $\forall x \in D_f$.
    Reason (R) : Even function is symmetrical about the y-axis.

38. **Assertion (A)** : The function $f(x) = x^2 - x + 1$, $x \geq \frac{1}{2}$ and $g(x) = \frac{1}{2} + \sqrt{\left(x - \frac{3}{4}\right)}$ then the number of solutions of the equation $f(x) = g(x)$ is two.

    Reason (R) : $f(x)$ and $g(x)$ are mutually inversion.

39. **Assertion (A)** : $f(x) = \sin x + \cos ax$ is a periodic function.

    Reason (R) : a is rational number.

40. **Assertion (A)** : The least period of the function, $f(x) = \cos(\cos x) + \cos(\sin x) + \sin 4x$ is π.

    Reason (R) : $\because f(x + \pi) = f(x)$.

41. **Assertion (A)** : If $f(x + y) + f(x - y) = 2f(x) \cdot f(y)$ $\forall\ x, y \in R$ and $f(0) \neq 0$, then $f(x)$ is an even function.

    Reason (R) : If $f(-x) = f(x)$, then $f(x)$ is an even function.

42. **Assertion (A)** : The equation $x^4 = (\lambda x - 1)^2$ has atmost two real solutions (is $\lambda > 0$).

    Reason (R) : Curves $f(x) = x^4$ and $g(x) = (\lambda x - 1)^2$ has atmost two points.

43. **Assertion (A)** : The domains of $f(x) = \sqrt{\cos(\sin x)}$ and $g(x) = \sqrt{\sin(\cos x)}$ are same.

    Reason (R) : $-1 \leq \cos(\sin x) \leq 1$ and $-1 \leq \sin(\cos x) \leq 1$

44. **Assertion (A)** : If $f(x) = x^5 - 16x + 2$, then $f(x) = 0$ has only one root in the interval $[-1, 1]$.

    Reason (R) : $f(-1)$ and $f(1)$ are of opposite sign.

45. **Assertion (A)** : The domain of the function $f(x) = \sin^{-1} x + \cos^{-1} x + \tan^{-1} x$ is $[-1, 1]$.

    Reason (R) : $\sin^{-1} x$ and $\cos^{-1} x$ is defined in $|x| \leq 1$ and $\tan^{-1} x$ defined for all x.

46. **Assertion (A)** : The period of $f(x) = \sin 3x \cos [3x] - \cos 3x \sin [3x]$ is $\frac{1}{3}$ where [ ] denotes the greatest integer function $\leq x$.

    Reason (R) : The period of $\{x\}$ is 1, where $\{x\}$ denotes the fractional part function of x.

47. **Assertion (A)** : The relation R given by $R = \{(1, 3), (4, 2), (2, 4), (2, 3), (3, 1)\}$ on a set $A = \{1, 2, 3\}$ is not symmetric.

    Reason : For symmetric relation $R = R^{-1}$.

48. **The price of the oranges in the market is dependent on the amount of oranges (in kgs) which can be represented as $y = 3x + 5$. Reema went to buy the oranges for a family function in her house. The total number of oranges she wants to buys is $5 \leq x \leq 10$ according to her assumption of people coming to the party. Answer the following questions on the basis of the given information.**

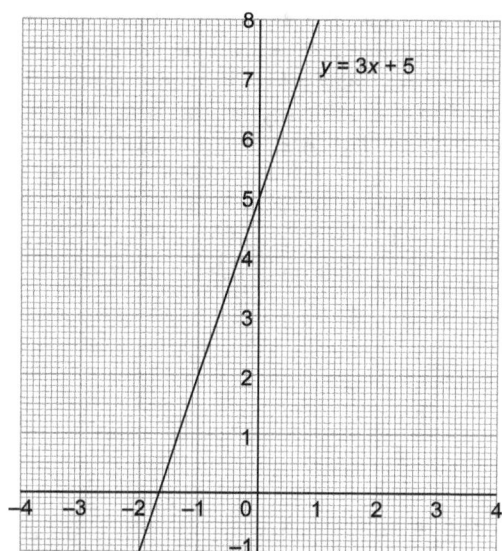

(i) How many ordered pairs can be represented for the equation $y = 3x + 5$ for $5 \leq x \leq 10$?
   (a) 4   (b) 5
   (c) 6   (d) 7

(ii) What is the domain of the given relation $R = \{(5, 20), (6, 23), (7, 26), (8, 29), (9, 32), (10, 35)\}$?
   (a) $\{-5, -4, 0, 1, 2\}$ (b) $\{0, 1, 2, 3, 4, 5\}$
   (c) $\{4, 5, 6, 7, 8\}$ (d) $\{5, 6, 7, 8, 9, 10\}$

(iii) How can range of the relation be represented for the relation $R = \{(5, 20), (6, 23), (7, 26), (8, 29), (9, 32), (10, 35)\}$?
   (a) $\{(x, y) \mid y = x + 3; 3 : 17 \leq x \leq 32\}$
   (b) $\{(x, y) \mid y = x + 3 : 20 \leq x \leq 35\}$
   (c) $\{(x, y) \mid y = x + 3 : 17 < x < 32\}$
   (d) $\{(x, y) \mid y = x + 3 : 20 < x < 35\}$

(iv) What is co-domain for the given relation ?
   (a) $\{(x, y) \mid y = x + 3 : 17 \leq x \leq 32\}$
   (b) $\{(x, y) \mid y = x + 3 : 20 \leq x \leq 35\}$
   (c) $\{(x, y) \mid y = x + 3 : 17 < x < 32\}$
   (d) $\{(x, y) \mid y = x + 3 : 20 < x < 35\}$

(v) How many subsets are there for the given relation $R = \{(5, 20), (6, 23), (7, 26), (9, 29), (9, 32), (10, 35)\}$?
   (a) 16   (b) 32
   (c) 64   (d) 128

49. There is a circular track in a playground where little kids come to play. Mohan whose son is in the 11th standard had taken him to the park. His son is having the difficulty in grasping the concept of the relations. Mohan saw the track and realised that he can teach his son the concept using the real world example. He asked his son to imagine the playground as the mathematical figure of circle and imagine the equation of the circle to be $x^2 + y^2 = 8$.

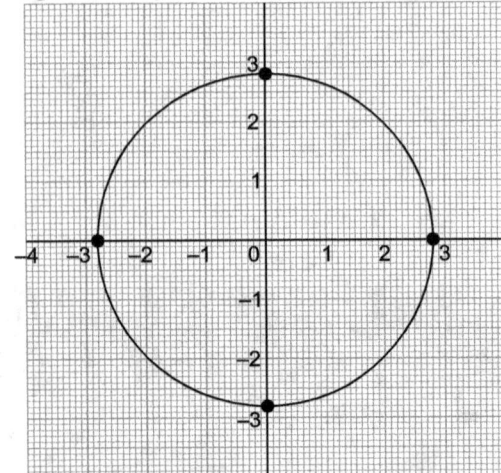

(i) What is the relation called ?
   (a) Set of ordered pair
   (b) Function
   (c) x-value
   (d) y-value

(ii) Which of the following sets will certainly represent the given relation accurately ?
   (a) $\{(0, 8), (1, 7), (2, 2)\}$
   (b) $\{(0, 2\sqrt{2}), (1, \sqrt{7}), (2, 2)\}$
   (c) $\{(0, 0), (1, \sqrt{7}), (2, -2)\}$
   (d) $\{(0, 2\sqrt{3}), (1, 7), (2, 2)\}$

(iii) From the given graph, what values of the x can be in the given relation ?
   (a) Inside the circle
   (b) Outside the circle
   (c) above half of the circle only
   (d) Lower half of the circle only

(iv) What is the maximum value of the range of the given relation ?
   (a) 0
   (b) -2
   (c) $-2\sqrt{2}$
   (d) $2\sqrt{2}$

(v) Waht is the co-domain of the given circle ?

   (a) $(-2, 2)$
   (b) $(-2\sqrt{2}, 2\sqrt{2})$
   (c) $[-2, 2]$
   (d) $[-2\sqrt{2}, 2\sqrt{2}]$

50. Sherlin and Danju are playing Ludo at home during Covid-19. While rolling the dice, Sherlin's sister Raji observed and noted the possible outcomes of the throw every time belongs to set $\{1, 2, 3, 4, 5, 6\}$. Let A be the set of players while B be the set of all possible outcomes.

(i) Let $R : B \to B$ be defined by $R = \{(x, y) : y$ is disivible by $x\}$ is :
   (a) Reflexive and transitive but not symmetric
   (b) Reflexive and symmetric and not transitive
   (c) Not reflexive but symmetric and transitive
   (d) Equivalence

(ii) Raji wants to know the number of functions from A to B. How many number of functions are possible ?
   (a) 6^2 (b) 2^6 (c) $6!$ (d) 2^{12}

(iii) Let R be a relation on B defined by $R = \{(1, 2), (2, 2), (1,3), (3, 4), (3, 1), (4, 3), (5, 5)\}$. Then R is :
   (a) Symmetric
   (b) Reflexive
   (c) Transitive
   (d) None of these three

(iv) Raji wants to know the number of relations possible from A to B. How many numbers of relations are possible ?
   (a) 6^2
   (b) 2^6
   (c) $6!$
   (d) 2^{12}

(v) Let $R : B \to$ be defined by $R = \{(1, 1), (1, 2), (2, 2), (3, 3), (4, 4), (5, 5), (6, 6)\}$, then R is :
   (a) Symmetric
   (b) Reflexive and Transitive
   (c) Transitive and symmetric
   (d) Equivalence

51. Students of Grade 9, planned to plant saplings along straight lines, parallel to each other to one side of the playground ensuring that they had enough play area. Let us assume that they planted

one of the rows of the saplings along the line $y = x - 4$. Let L be the set of all lines which are parallel on the ground and R be a relation on L.

(i) Let relation R be defined by R = {$(L_1, L_2) : L_1 \parallel L_2$ where $L_1, L_2 \in L$} then R is ....
 (a) Equivalence
 (b) Only reflexive
 (c) Not reflexive
 (d) Symmetric but not transitive

(ii) Let R = {$(L_1, L_2) : L_1 + L_2$ where $L_1, L_2 \in L$} which of the following is true ?
 (a) R is symmetric but neither reflexive nor transitive
 (b) R is reflexive and transitive but not symmetric
 (c) R is reflexive but neither symmetric nor transitive
 (d) R is an equivalence relation

(iii) The function $f : R \to R$ defined by $f(x) = x - 4$ is :
 (a) Bijective
 (b) Surjective but not injective
 (c) Injective but not surjective
 (d) Neither surjective nor injective

(iv) Let $f : R \to R$ be defined by $f(x) = x - 4$. Then the range of $f(x)$ is :
 (a) R (b) Z
 (c) W (d) Q

(v) Let R = {$(L_1, L_2) : L_1$ is parallel to L_2 and $L_1 : y = x - 4$} then which of the following can be taken as L_2 ?
 (a) $2x - 2y + 5 = 0$ (b) $2x + y = 5$
 (c) $2x + 2y + 7 = 0$ (d) $x + y = 7$

Solutions

1. (d) Reflexive, transitive but not symmetric
 Explanation :
 Since n divides n, $\forall n \in N$, R is reflexive. R is not symmetric since for $3, 6 \in N$, $3 R 6 \neq 6 R 3$.
 R is transitive since for n, m, r whenever $\dfrac{n}{m}$ and $\dfrac{m}{r}$
 $\Rightarrow \dfrac{n}{r}$, i.e., n divides m and m divides r, then n will divide r.

2. (b) $^{10}C_7 \times 7!$
 Explanation :
 Number of elements in set A = 7
 Number of elements in set B = 10
 Selection of 7 elements from set B is $^{10}C_7$
 and these elements related to one-one to set A is $7!$.
 ∴ Total relations one-one from set A to set B = $^{10}C_7 \times 7!$.

3. (b) injective
 Explanation :
 For one-one $f(x_1) = f(x_2)$
 $2n_1 + 3 = 2n_2 + 3$
 $2n_1 = 2n_2$
 $n_1 = n_2$
 $\Rightarrow f$ is one-one.
 Let $y = f(x) = 2n + 3$
 $y - 3 = 2n$
 $n = \dfrac{y-3}{2} \notin N$
 so, $f(n)$ is not onto.

4. (c) 24
 Explanation :
 The total number of injective mappings from the set containing 3 elements into the set containing 4 elements is $^4P_3 = 4! = 24$.

5. (b) 27
 Explanation :
 Here, A = {a, b, c} and B = {4, 5, 6}
 ∴ $n(A) = 3$ and $n(B) = 3$
 So, number of functions from A to B
 $= 3^3 = 3 \times 3 \times 3 = 27$.

6. (c) {4, – 4}, φ
 Explanation :
 Since for $f^{-1}(17) = x$
 $\Rightarrow f(x) = 17$ or $x^2 + 1 = 17$
 $\Rightarrow x = \pm 4$
 or $f^{-1}(17) = \{4, -4\}$
 and for $f^{-1}(-3) = x$
 $\Rightarrow f(x) = -3$
 $\Rightarrow x^2 + 1 = -3$
 $\Rightarrow x^2 = -4$

Hence $f^{-1}(-3) = \phi$.
So the correct option is (c).

7. **(a)** Reflexive
   The correct option is (a).
8. **(a)** R = {(2, 2), (3, 3), (6, 6)}.
9. **(c)** {2, 4, 6}
   Explanation :
   Since R is defined as $x + 2y = 8$.
   Now, x and y are natural numbers.
   $\therefore \quad x = 2, y = 3$
   Because if we put $x = 3$, y will not be a natural number.
   $$x = 4, y = 2$$
   $$x = 6, y = 1$$
   $\therefore$ Domain of given function is {2, 4, 6}.
10. **(a)** 9
    Explanation :
    $$f(-1) = 3(-1) = -3$$
    $$f(2) = (2)^2 = 4$$
    $$f(4) = 2 \times 4 = 8$$
    $\Rightarrow f(-1) + f(2) + f(3) = -3 + 4 + 8 = 9.$
11. **(d)** None of these
    Explanation :
    $$R = \{(1, 6), (2, 7), (3, 8)\}$$
    $\because \quad (6, 6) \notin R$
    $\Rightarrow$ R is not Reflexive.
    For $\quad (2, 7) \in R$
    $\Rightarrow \quad (2, 7) \in R$ but $(7, 2) \notin R$
    $\Rightarrow$ R is not symmetric.
    Clearly R is not transitive.
    (Since, there is no pair in R such that [(x, y)] and $(y, z) \in R$ then $x \in Z$)
    $\Rightarrow$ R is not equivalence.
12. **(b)** (3, 1)
    Explanation :
    $(1, 1,) \in R$
    $\Rightarrow$ R is Reflexive.
    $(1, 3) \in R$
    $(1, 3) \in R$ but $(3, 1) \notin R$
    $\Rightarrow$ R is not symmetric.
    To make R an equivalence we can add (3, 1).
    Clearly R is reflexive and transitive. For R to be symmetric we should add (3, 1) in R.
13. **(c)** {1}
    Explanation :
    The set of all elemenetss related to one is {$a \in A : a = 1$}.
14. **(a)** range of $f = Y$
    Explanation :
    A function $f: A \to B$ is said to be onto, if for every $b \in B$, there exists an element a in A such that $f(a) = b$.
15. **(b)** 6
    Explanation :
    No. of one-one function $= 3 \times 2 \times 1 = 6$.
16. **(b)** $2^n - 2$
    Explanation :
    Each element in A can mapped on any one of two elements of B.
    Total possible functions $= 2^n$
    Total no. of surjection $= 2^n - 2$.
17. **(c)** 0
    Explanation :
    Total no. of element in set A = 5
    Total no. of element in set B = 6
    As, the no. of bijection from A < n to B can only possible when $n(A) \geq n(B)$.
    But here $n(A) < n(B)$
    Hence, total no. of subjection from A to B is 0.
18. **(b)** onto
    Explanation :
    We know
    $$[2 \cdot 2] = 2$$
    $$1[2 \cdot 5] = 2$$
    $\because \quad [2 \cdot 2] = [2 \cdot 5]$
    but $\quad 2 \cdot 2 \neq 3 \cdot 5$
    $\Rightarrow f$ is not one-one function.
    We know that
    $f(x) = [x]$ is on integers.
    $\Rightarrow f$ is onto.
    $\Rightarrow f$ is not one-one but onto.
19. **(c)** 24
    Explanation :
    Total number of injective $= \dfrac{\lfloor n}{\lfloor n - m}$
    $$= \dfrac{\lfloor 4}{\lfloor 4 - 3}$$
    $$= \dfrac{4 \times 3 \times 2}{1}$$
    $$= 24$$
20. **(b)** {4, 9, 25, 49, 121}
    Explanation :
    R = {(2, 4), (3, 9), (5, 25), (7, 49), (11, 121)}
    Range = {4, 9, 25, 49, 121}.
21. **(d)** Neither one-one nor onto
    Explanation :
    $$f(x) = \dfrac{x^2 - 8}{x^2 + 2}$$
    $$f(3) = \dfrac{9 - 8}{9 + 2} = \dfrac{1}{11}$$
    $$f(-3) = \dfrac{9 - 8}{9 + 2} = \dfrac{1}{11}$$

⇒ f is not one-one.
$$f(x) = \frac{x^2 - 8}{x^2 + 2} = 1 - \frac{10}{x^2 + 2}$$
So minimum value of $f(x) = 1 - 5 = -4$
∴ It is not onto.
Hence it is neither one-one nor onto.

22. (b) R is reflexive and transitive but not symmetric
    Explanation :
    ∵ $(1, 2) \in R$
    But $(2, 1) \notin R$
    ∴ R is not symmetric.

23. (a) {(8, 11), (10, 13)}
    Explanation :
    A = {11, 12, 13},
    B = {8, 10, 12}
    A R B, $y = x - 3$
    R = {(11, 8), (13, 10)}
    ∴ R^{-1} = {(8, 11), (10, 13)}.

24. (b) (5, 5), (4, 4), (2, 2)
    Explanation :
    A relation is called an identity relation if A = {(a, a) : a ∈ A}
    So, (5, 5), (4, 4), (2, 2) is an identity relation.

25. (c) Equivalence
    Explanation :
    Each triangle is congruent to itself.
    ∴ Relation is reflexive.
    Suppose $\triangle ABC \cong \triangle PQR$
    then $\triangle PQR \cong \triangle ABC$
    ∴ Relation is symmetric.
    Suppose $\triangle ABC \cong \triangle PQR$,
    and $\triangle PQR \cong \triangle XYZ$
    then $\triangle ABC \cong \triangle XYZ$
    ∴ Relation is transitive.
    ∴ Relation is an equivalence.

26. (c) Bijective function

27. (d) None of these
    Explanation :
    $a \leq b^3$ if $a = -2$ then $b = -8$
    ∵ $-2 \nleq 8$
    ∴ It is not reflexive.
    Also, less than or equal to relation is not symmetric and transitive.

28. (d) 5
    Explanation :
    Given that, A = {1, 2, 3}
    Now, number of equivalence relations as follows:
    R_1 = {(1, 1), (2, 2), (3, 3)}
    R_2 = {(1, 1), (2, 2), (3, 3), (1, 2), (2, 1)}
    R_3 = {(1, 1), (2, 2), (3, 3), (1, 3), (3, 1)}
    R_4 = {(1, 1), (2, 2), (3, 3), (2, 3), (3, 2)}
    R_5 = {(1, 2, 3) ⇔ A × A = A^2}
    ∴ Maximum number of equivalence relation is '5'.

29. (d) None of these
    Explanation :
    R on the set {1, 2, 3} be defined by R = {(1, 2)}
    It is clear that R is not reflexive, transitive and symmetric.

30. (b) reflexive, transitive but not symmetric
    Explanation :
    Given that, aRb if $a \geq b$
    ⇒ $aRa \Rightarrow a \geq a$ which is true.
    Let aRb, $a \geq b$, then $b \geq a$ which is not true, so R is not symmetric.
    But aRb and bRc
    ⇒ $a \geq b$ and $b \geq c$
    ⇒ $a \geq c$
    Hence, R is transitive.

31. (a) reflexive but not symmetric
    Explanation :
    Given that,
    A = {1, 2, 3}
    and R = {(1, 1), (2, 2), (3, 3), (1, 2), (2, 3), (1, 3)}
    ∵ (1, 1), (2, 2), (3, 3) ∈ R
    Hence, R is reflexive.
    (1, 2) ∈ R but (2, 1) ∉ R
    Hence, R is not symmetric.
    (1, 2) ∈ R and (2, 3) ∈ R
    ⇒ (1, 3) ∈ R
    Hence, R is transitive.

32. (b) R is reflexive and transitive but not symmetric
    Explanation :
    R = {(1, 2), (2, 2), (1, 1), (4, 4), (1, 3), (3, 3), (3, 2)}
    It is seen that $(a, a) \in R$, for every $a \in \{1, 2, 3, 4\}$.
    ∴ R is reflexive.
    It is seen that $(1, 2) \in R$, but $(2, 1) \notin R$.
    ∴ R is not symmetric.
    Also, it is observed that $(a, b), (b, c) \in R \Rightarrow (a, c) \in R$ for all $a, b, c \in \{1, 2, 3, 4\}$.
    ∴ R is transitive.
    Hence, R is reflexive and transitive but not symmetric.

33. (d) f is neither one-one nor onto
    Explanation :
    $f : R \to R$ is defined as $f(x) = x^4$
    Let $x, y \in R$ such that
    $f(x) = f(y)$
    ⇒ $x^4 = y^4$
    $x^4 - y^4 = 0$
    $(x^2 + y^2)$
    $(x^2 - y^2) = 0$
    $x^2 = y^2$
    ⇒ $x = \pm y$

∴ $f(x_1) = f(x_2)$ does not imply that $x_1 = x_2$
For instance,
$f(1) = f(-1) = 1$.

34. (c) A is true but R is false.
    Explanation:
    The function $f(x) = |x|$ is many one
    ∴ $f(-x) = f(x)$.
    i.e., not one-one and the image of $-x$ is x.

35. (d) A is false but R is true.
    Explanation:
    ∵ $x^2 - \cos y = \pi$
    ⇒ $\cos^{-1} y = (x^2 - \pi)$
    ∵ $0 \le \cos^{-1} y \le \pi$
    ⇒ $0 \le x^2 - \pi \le \pi$
    ⇒ $\pi \le x^2 \le 2\pi$
    ∴ $x \in [-\sqrt{2\pi}, -\sqrt{\pi}] \cup [\sqrt{\pi}, -\sqrt{2\pi}]$

36. (b) Both (A) and (R) are true but R is not correct explanation of A.
    Explanation:
    ∵ $f(x)$ is odd
    ⇒ $f(-x) = -f(x)$
    and $g(x)$ is even ⇒ $g(-x) = g(x)$
    Let $F(x) = f(x) + g(x)$
    ∴ $F(-x) = f(-x) + g(-x) = -f(x) + g(x)$
    $\ne \pm F(x)$
    ∴ $F(x)$ is neither even nor odd.

37. (a) Both (A) and (B) are true and R is the correct explanation A.
    Explanation:
    Since every even function is symmetrical about the y-axis.
    ∴ Any line parallel to x-axis cuts the graph at more than one point, then $f(x)$ is not one-one $\forall$ $x \in D_f$.

38. (d) A is false but R is true.
    Explanation:
    Let $y = x^2 - x + 1$
    ⇒ $x^2 - x + 1 - y = 0$
    ∴ $x = \dfrac{1 \pm \sqrt{1 - 4 \cdot 1 \cdot (1-y)}}{2}$
    $= \dfrac{1}{2} \pm \sqrt{y - \dfrac{3}{4}}$
    $= \dfrac{1}{2} + \sqrt{y - \dfrac{3}{4}}, \left(\because x \ge \dfrac{1}{2}\right)$
    $= g(y)$
    ∴ $y = g^{-1}(x) \Rightarrow f(x) = g^{-1}(x)$
    Hence, $f(x)$ and $g(x)$ are mutually inversion.
    ⇒ The graph of the original and inversion functions can intersect only on the straight line $y = x$
    ∴ $x = f(x)$
    ⇒ $x = x^2 - x + 1$
    ⇒ $x^2 - 2x + 1 = 0$
    ⇒ $(x-1)^2 = 0$
    ∴ $x = 1$.

39. (a) Both (A) and (B) are true and R is the correct explanation A.
    Explanation:
    ∵ Period of $\sin x$ is $\dfrac{2\pi}{l}$ and period of $\cos ax = \dfrac{2\pi}{a}$
    Hence, period of $f(x)$ = LCM of $\left\{\dfrac{2\pi}{1}, \dfrac{2\pi}{a}\right\}$
    $= \dfrac{\text{LCM of } \{2\pi, 2\pi\}}{\text{HCF of } \{l, a\}} = \dfrac{2\pi}{k}$
    when k is HCF of l and a.
    ⇒ $\dfrac{1}{k} = $ integer $= q$ (say) ($\ne 0$)
    and $\dfrac{a}{k} = $ integer $= p$ (say)
    ∴ $\dfrac{a/k}{1/k} = \dfrac{p}{q}$
    ⇒ $a = \dfrac{p}{q}$
    ⇒ a is rational.

40. (d) A is false but R is true.
    Explanation:
    Let $f(x)$ be periodic with period λ, $\lambda \ne 0$, $\lambda > 0$
    ∴ $f(x + \lambda) = f(x)$
    ⇒ $\cos(\cos(x+\lambda)) + \cos(\sin(x+\lambda)) + \sin(4(x+\lambda))$
    $= \cos(\cos x) + \cos(\sin x) + \sin 4x$
    Put $x = 0$,
    $\cos(\cos \lambda) + \cos(\sin \lambda) + \sin(4\lambda)$
    $= \cos(1) + \cos(0) + \sin(0)$
    $= \cos(\sin \pi/2) + \cos(\cos \pi/2) + \sin(2\pi)$
    ⇒ $\lambda = \pi/2$

41. (b) Both (A) and (R) are true but R is not correct explanation of A.
    Explanation:
    Given $f(x+y) + f(x-y) = 2f(x)f(y)$ ...(i)
    Replacing x by y and y by x in equation (i), then
    $f(y+x) + f(y-x) = 2f(y)f(x)$ ...(ii)
    ∴ From equations (i) and (ii), we get
    $f(y-x) = f(x-y)$
    Putting $y = 2x$, then $f(x) = f(-x)$
    Hence, $f(x)$ is an even function.

42. (d) A is false but R is true.
    Explanation:
    ∵ $x^4 = (\lambda x - 1)^2$
    $x^2 = \pm(\lambda x - 1)$
    ⇒ $x^2 = \lambda x - 1$
    ∴ $x^2 - \lambda x + 1 = 0$
    ⇒ $x = \dfrac{\lambda \pm \sqrt{(\lambda^2 - 4)}}{2}$
    ∴ $\lambda^2 - 4 \ge 0$

$\Rightarrow \lambda \in (-\infty, -2] \cup [2, \infty)$
but $\lambda > 0 \therefore \lambda \in [2, \infty)$
and $x^2 = -(\lambda x - 1)$
$x^2 + \lambda x - 1 = 0$
$$x = \frac{-\lambda \pm \sqrt{(\lambda^2 + 4)}}{2}$$
$\lambda > 0$
$\Rightarrow$ Infinite solutions.
cut at two points.

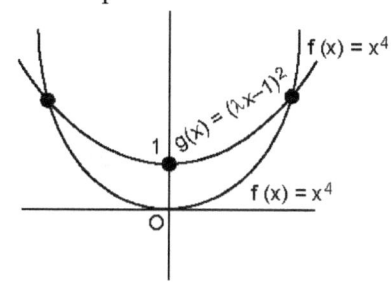

43. (d) A is false but R is true.
    Explanation :
    $\cos(\sin x) \geq 0$
    $\Rightarrow 2n\pi - \frac{\pi}{2} \leq \sin(x) \leq 2n\pi + \frac{\pi}{2}, n \in I$
    but $\quad -1 \leq \sin x \leq 1$
    $\Rightarrow \quad -1 \leq \sin x \leq 1$
    $\Rightarrow \quad x \in R$
    $\therefore \quad D_f = R$
    Also, $\sin(\cos x) \geq 0$
    $\Rightarrow \quad 2n\pi \leq \cos x \leq 2n\pi + \pi, n \in I$
    but $\quad -1 \leq \cos x \leq 1$
    $\Rightarrow \quad 0 \leq \cos x \leq 1$
    $\Rightarrow \quad x \in \left[2p\pi - \frac{\pi}{2}, 2p\pi + \frac{\pi}{2}\right], p \in I$
    $\therefore \quad D_g = \left[2p\pi - \frac{\pi}{2}, 2p\pi + \frac{\pi}{2}\right], p \in I$
    $\Rightarrow \quad D_f \neq D_g$

44. (b) Both (A) and (R) are true but R is not correct explanation of A.
    Explanation :
    $\because \quad f(-1) = -1 + 16 + 2 = 17$
    and $\quad f(1) = 1 - 16 + 2 = -13$

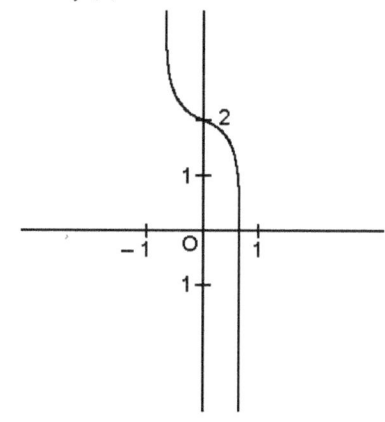

45. (a) Both (A) and (B) are true and R is the correct explanation A.
    Explanation :
    $\because \sin^{-1} x$ is defined in $[-1, 1]$
    $\cos^{-1} x$ is defined in $[-1, 1]$
    and $\tan^{-1} x$ is defined in R.
    Hence, $f(x)$ is defined in $[-1, 1]$.

46. (a) Both (A) and (B) are true and R is the correct explanation A.
    Explanation :
    $\because \quad f(x) = \sin 3x \cos[3x] - \cos 3x \sin[3x]$
    $= \sin(3x - [3x])$
    $= \sin[\{3x\}]$
    $\because \quad \{x\} = x - \{x\}$ is periodic with period 1
    $\therefore$ Period of $\{3x\}$ is $\frac{1}{3}$.

47. (a) Both (A) and (B) are true and R is the correct explanation A.
    Explanation :
    R = {(1, 3), (4, 2), (2, 4), (2, 3), (3, 1)} as (2, 3) ∈ R but (3, 2) ∉ R
    $\Rightarrow$ is not symmetric.

48. (i) (c) The relation will be given by (x, y).
    So, R = {(5, 20), (6, 23), (7, 26), (8, 29), (9, 32), (10, 35)} Hence, there are 6 relations.
    (ii) (d) The domain is the first element of the relation R = {(5, 20), (6, 23), (7, 26), (8, 29), (9, 32), (10, 35)}
    So, domain is {5, 6, 7, 8, 9, 10}.
    (iii) (a) Given the relation R = {(5, 20), (6, 23), (7, 26), (8, 29), (9, 32), (10, 35)}, the range is the second value of the ordered pair.
    As it can be seen that any value is three more than the previous value. So, the range can be represented as $\{(x, y) \mid y = x + 3 : 17 \leq x \leq 32\}$.
    (iv) (a) It is known that co-domain is the set of all possible outputs. So, the co-domain is
    $\{(x, y) \mid y = x + 3 : 17 \leq x \leq 32\}$.
    (v) (c) The relation is R = {(5, 20), (6, 23), (7, 26), (8, 29), (9, 32), (10, 35). The number of subsets is 2^n. As there are 6 elements in the relation, the number of subsets is $2^6 = 64$.

49. (i) (a) The relation is the set of ordered pairs.
    (ii) (b) The relation is $x^2 + y^2 = 8$. So, $y = \sqrt{8 - x^2}$.
    Only the ordered pairs $\{(0, 2\sqrt{2}), (1, \sqrt{7}), (2, 2)\}$ can give the relation accurately.
    (iii) (a) All the value taken inside and on the circle will satisfy the given equation.
    (iv) (d) The maximum value that y can have is $2\sqrt{2}$, which can be the maximum value of the range.

(v) (d) It is known that co-domain is the set of all possible outputs. So, the co-domain is $[-2\sqrt{2}, 2\sqrt{2}]$.

50. (i) (a) $\quad B = \{1, 2, 3, 4, 5, 6\}$
Since x is divisible by x.
So x is reflexive.
If $(x, y) \in R$ then $(y \notin x) R$
$(2, 4) \in R$, as 4 is divisible by 2
$(4, 2) \notin R$
R is not symmetric.
If $(x, y) \in R$ and $(y, z) \in R$, then
$(x, z) \in R$
$\Rightarrow$ If y is divisible by x and z divisible by y then z divisible by x
$\Rightarrow$ R is transitive.

(ii) (a) A has 2 elements, B has 6 elements.
Number of functions from A to B = 6^2.

(iii) (d) $\quad (1, 1) \notin R$
R is not reflexive.
$(1, 2) \in R$ but $(2, 1) \notin R$
R is not symmetric.
$(1, 3) \in R$
$(3, 4) \in R$
$\Rightarrow (1, 4) \notin R$
R is not transitive.

(iv) (d) Total no of relation
$= 2^{mn}$
$= 2^{\text{Number of element A} \times \text{no. of element in B}}$
$= 2^{2 \times 6}$
$= 2^{12} = 2^{12}$

(v) (b) Here $\quad (1, 1) \in R$
So R is reflexive.
$(1, 2) \in R$ but $(2, 1) \in R$
R is not symmetric of $(x, y) \in R$ and $(y, z) \in R$ then $(x, z) \in R$.
$\therefore$ R is transitive.
Thus, R is reflexive and transitive.

51. (i) (a) $\because$ A line is parallel to itself, so $(L_1, L_2) \in R$ $\forall L_1$
$\Rightarrow$ R is reflexive.
For $(L_1, L_2) \in R$, $(L_1, L_2) \in R$
$\quad L_1 \parallel L_2 \quad$ (L_1 parallel to L_2)
$\quad L_2 \parallel L_1 \quad$ (L_2 parallel to L_1)
$\Rightarrow$ R is symmetric.
For $(L_1, L_2) \in R_1 (L_2, L_3) \in R$

$\quad L_1 \parallel L_2 \quad$ (L_1 parallel to L_2)
$\quad L_2 \parallel L_3 \quad$ (L_2 parallel to L_3)
$\Rightarrow \quad L_1 \parallel L_3 \quad$ (L_1 parallel to L_3)
$\Rightarrow (L_1, L_3) \in R$
$\Rightarrow L_1$ is transitive.
$\Rightarrow$ R is an equivalence relation.
$\Rightarrow$ So option is (a).

(ii) (a) A line is not perpendicular to itself.
$\Rightarrow$ R is not reflexive.
$\Rightarrow (L_1, L_1) \notin R$ for all L_1.
$\Rightarrow$ R is not reflexive.
For $\quad (L_1, L_2) \in R (L_2, L_1) \in R$
$\quad L_1 \perp L_2 \quad$ (L_1 perpendicular to L_2)
$\quad L_2 \perp L_1 \quad$ (L_2 perpendicular to L_1)
$\Rightarrow$ R is symmetric.
If $\quad (x, y) \in R, (y \in z) \in R$
$\Rightarrow \quad x \perp y, y \perp z$
$\Rightarrow x$ does not perpendicular to z.
$\Rightarrow$ R is not transitive.

(iii) (a) For one-one
$f(x_1) = f(x_2)$
$x_1 - 4 = x_2 - 4$
$x_2 = x_2$
$\Rightarrow f(x)$ is one-one.
Let $\quad f(x) = y$
$\quad x - y = y$
$\quad x = y + 4$
$\quad f(x) = x - 4$
$\quad f(y + 4) = y + 4 - 4$
$\quad \quad = y$
$\Rightarrow y$ is onto.
$\Rightarrow y$ is bijective.
$\Rightarrow$ Option is (a).

(iv) (a) For all real value of x, we find a real number $f(x)$.
$\Rightarrow$ Range of $f(x) = R$
$\Rightarrow$ So option is (a).

(v) (a) $\quad L_1 \parallel L_2$
$\Rightarrow$ Slope must be equal.
Slope of $L_1 = 1$
$2x - 2y + 5 = 0$
$\quad \text{slope} = -\dfrac{\text{Coeff. of } x}{\text{Coeff. of } y}$
$\quad = -\dfrac{2}{(-2)} = 1.$

Chapter 2
Inverse Trigonometric Functions

1. If $\cos\left(\sin^{-1}\dfrac{2}{5}+\cos^{-1}x\right)=0$, then x is equal to:

   [NCERT Exemplar]

   (a) $\dfrac{1}{5}$ (b) $\dfrac{2}{5}$

   (c) 0   (d) 1

2. Which of the following corresponds to the principal value branch of $\tan^{-1}x$?

   (a) $\left(-\dfrac{\pi}{2},\dfrac{\pi}{2}\right)$ (b) $\left[-\dfrac{\pi}{2},\dfrac{\pi}{2}\right]$

   (c) $\left(-\dfrac{\pi}{2},\dfrac{\pi}{2}\right)-\{0\}$ (d) $(0,\pi)$

3. The principal value branch of $\sec^{-1}x$ is:

   (a) $\left[-\dfrac{\pi}{2},\dfrac{\pi}{2}\right]-\{0\}$ (b) $[0,-\pi]-\left\{\dfrac{\pi}{2}\right\}$

   (c) $(0,\pi)$ (d) $\left(-\dfrac{\pi}{2},\dfrac{\pi}{2}\right)$

4. The principal value of the expression $\cos^{-1}[\cos(-680°)]$ is:

   (a) $\dfrac{2\pi}{9}$ (b) $\dfrac{-2\pi}{9}$

   (c) $\dfrac{34\pi}{9}$ (d) $\dfrac{\pi}{9}$

5. The value of $\cot(\sin^{-1}x)$ is:

   (a) $\dfrac{\sqrt{1+x^2}}{x}$ (b) $\dfrac{x}{\sqrt{1+x^2}}$

   (c) $\dfrac{1}{x}$ (d) $\dfrac{\sqrt{1-x^2}}{x}$

6. The domain of $\sin^{-1}2x$ is:

   (a) $[0,1]$ (b) $[-1,1]$

   (c) $\left[-\dfrac{1}{2},\dfrac{1}{2}\right]$ (d) $[-2,2]$

7. The principal value of $\sin^{-1}\left(\dfrac{-\sqrt{3}}{2}\right)$ is:

   (a) $-\dfrac{2\pi}{3}$ (b) $-\dfrac{\pi}{3}$

   (c) $\dfrac{4\pi}{3}$ (d) $\dfrac{5\pi}{3}$

8. The domain of $y=\cos^{-1}(x^2-4)$ is:

   (a) $[3,5]$
   (b) $[0,\pi]$
   (c) $[-\sqrt{5},-\sqrt{3}]\cap[-\sqrt{5},\sqrt{3}]$
   (d) $[-\sqrt{5},-\sqrt{3}]\cup[\sqrt{3},\sqrt{5}]$

9. The domain of the function defined by $f(x)=\sin^{-1}x+\cos x$ is:

   (a) $[-1,1]$ (b) $[-1,\pi+1]$
   (c) $(-\infty,\infty)$ (d) ϕ

10. The value of $\sin[2\sin^{-1}(0.6)]$ is:

    (a) .48   (b) .96
    (c) 1.2   (d) $\sin 1.2$

11. The value of $\tan\left\{\cos^{-1}\dfrac{1}{5\sqrt{2}}-\sin^{-1}\dfrac{4}{\sqrt{17}}\right\}$ is:

    (a) $\dfrac{\sqrt{29}}{3}$ (b) $\dfrac{29}{3}$

    (c) $\dfrac{\sqrt{3}}{29}$ (d) $\dfrac{3}{29}$

12. If $\cot^{-1}\left(-\dfrac{1}{5}\right)=\theta$, the value of $\sin\theta$ is:

    (a) $\dfrac{\sqrt{26}}{5}$ (b) $\dfrac{-5}{\sqrt{26}}$

    (c) $\dfrac{\sqrt{5}}{\sqrt{26}}$ (d) $\dfrac{5}{\sqrt{26}}$

13. If $\alpha\le 2\sin^{-1}x+\cos^{-1}x\le\beta$, then:

    (a) $\alpha=\dfrac{-\pi}{2},\beta=\dfrac{\pi}{2}$
    (b) $\alpha=0,\beta=\pi$
    (c) $\alpha=\dfrac{-\pi}{2},\beta=\dfrac{3\pi}{2}$
    (d) $\alpha=0,\beta=2\pi$

14. The value of $\tan^2(\sec^{-1}2)+\cot^2(\csc^{-1}3)$ is:

    (a) 5   (b) 11
    (c) 13   (d) 15

15. The value of $\tan\left[\dfrac{1}{2}\cos^{-1}\left(\dfrac{\sqrt{5}}{3}\right)\right]$ is:

    [CBSE OD, Set-3, 2020]

(a) $\dfrac{3+\sqrt{5}}{2}$ (b) $\dfrac{3-\sqrt{5}}{2}$

(c) $\dfrac{-3+\sqrt{5}}{2}$ (d) $\dfrac{-3-\sqrt{5}}{2}$

16. The principal value of $\tan^{-1}\left(\dfrac{1}{\sqrt{3}}\right)$ is:

(a) $\dfrac{\pi}{2}$ (b) $\dfrac{\pi}{6}$

(c) $\dfrac{\pi}{3}$ (d) π

17. The principal value of $\sec^{-1}\left(\dfrac{-2}{\sqrt{3}}\right)$ is:

(a) $\dfrac{5\pi}{6}$ (b) $\dfrac{2\pi}{3}$

(c) $\dfrac{\pi}{3}$ (d) None of these

18. The inverse of cosine function is defined in the intervals:

(a) $[-\pi, 0]$ (b) $\left[\dfrac{-\pi}{2}, 0\right]$

(c) $\left[0, \dfrac{\pi}{2}\right]$ (d) $\left[\dfrac{\pi}{2}, \pi\right]$

19. If $\sin^{-1} x = y$, then:

(a) $0 \le y \le x$ (b) $\dfrac{-\pi}{2} \le y \le \dfrac{\pi}{2}$

(c) $0 < y < \pi$ (d) $\dfrac{-\pi}{2} < y < \dfrac{\pi}{2}$

20. $\sin\left(\dfrac{\pi}{3} - \sin^{-1}\left(-\dfrac{1}{2}\right)\right)$ is equal to:

(a) 1/2 (b) 1/3
(c) 1/4 (d) 1

21. The value of

$\tan^{-1}\left(\dfrac{-1}{\sqrt{3}}\right) + \cot^{-1}\left(\dfrac{1}{\sqrt{3}}\right) + \tan^{-1}\left(\sin\left(-\dfrac{\pi}{2}\right)\right)$ is:

(a) $\dfrac{\pi}{6}$ (b) $\dfrac{\pi}{12}$

(c) $-\dfrac{\pi}{12}$ (d) $\dfrac{-}{1}$

22. The value of $\tan^{-1}\left[2\sin\left(2\cos^{-1}\dfrac{\sqrt{3}}{2}\right)\right]$ is:

(a) $\dfrac{\pi}{3}$ (b) $\dfrac{2\pi}{3}$

(c) $\dfrac{-\pi}{3}$ (d) $\dfrac{\pi}{6}$

23. The value of $\tan^{-1}\left(\tan\dfrac{5\pi}{6}\right) + \cos^{-1}\left(\cos\dfrac{13\pi}{6}\right)$ is:

(a) 0 (b) $\dfrac{\pi}{3}$

(c) $\dfrac{\pi}{6}$ (d) $\dfrac{2\pi}{3}$

27. The domain of the function $\cos^{-1}(2x-1)$ is: [NCERT Exemplar]

(a) $[0, 1]$ (b) $[-1, 1]$
(c) $(-1, 1)$ (d) $[0, \pi]$

28. The domain of the function defined by $f(x) = \sin^{-1}\sqrt{x-1}$ is: [NCERT Exemplar]

(a) $[1, 2]$ (b) $[-1, 1]$
(c) $[0, 1]$ (d) none of these

29. The value of $\cos^{-1}\left(\cos\dfrac{3\pi}{2}\right)$ is equal to: [NCERT Exemplar]

(a) $\dfrac{\pi}{2}$ (b) $\dfrac{3\pi}{2}$

(c) $\dfrac{5\pi}{2}$ (d) $\dfrac{7\pi}{2}$

30. Solve $\sin(\tan^{-1} x)$, $|x| < 1$ is equal to: [NCERT]

(a) $\dfrac{x}{\sqrt{1-x^2}}$ (b) $\dfrac{1}{\sqrt{1-x^2}}$

(c) $\dfrac{1}{\sqrt{1+x^2}}$ (d) $\dfrac{x}{\sqrt{1+x^2}}$

Choose the correct option:
(a) Both (A) and (R) are true and R is the correct explanation A.
(b) Both (A) and (R) are true but R is not correct explanation of A.
(c) A is true but R is false.
(d) A is false but R is true.

31. **Assertion (A):** $\sin^{-1}(\sin 3) = 3$
    Reason (R): For principal values $\sin^{-1}(\sin x) = +x$

32. **Assertion (A):** The solution of system of equations

$\cos^{-1} x + (\sin^{-1} y)^2 = \dfrac{p\pi^2}{4}$

and $(\cos^{-1} x)(\sin^{-1} y)^2 = \dfrac{\pi^4}{16}$ is $x = \cos\dfrac{\pi^2}{4}$ and $y = \pm 1$,

$\forall p \in I$.

Reason (R): $AM \ge GM$

33. **Assertion (A):** If $\sum\limits_{i=1}^{2n} \sin^{-1} x_i = n\pi$, $n \in N$

Then, $\sum\limits_{i=1}^{n} x_i = \sum\limits_{i=1}^{n} x_i^2 = \sum\limits_{i=1}^{n} x_i^3$

Reason (R): $-\dfrac{\pi}{2} \le \sin^{-1} x \le \dfrac{\pi}{2}$ $\forall x \in [-1, 1]$

34. Assertion : The equation $2(\sin^{-1} x)^2 - 5(\sin^{-1} x + 2) = 0$.
Reason : $\sin^{-1}(\sin x) = x$ if $x \in [-1.57, 1.57]$.

35. Two men on either side of temple of 30m height observe its top at the angle of elevation α and β respectively. The distance between the two men is $40\sqrt{3}\, m$ and distance between men A and the temple is $30\sqrt{3}\, m$.

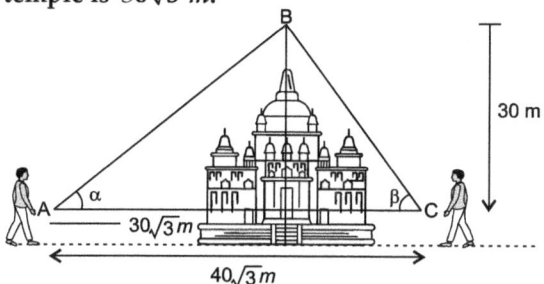

Based on above information answer the following questions:

(i) Find $\angle CAB = \alpha =$

(a) $\sin^{-1} \dfrac{1}{2}$ (b) $\sin^{-1} \dfrac{2}{\sqrt{3}}$

(c) $\sin^{-1} \dfrac{\sqrt{3}}{2}$ (d) $\sin^{-1} 2$

(ii) $\angle CAB = \alpha = ?$

(a) $\cos^{-1} \dfrac{1}{5}$ (b) $\cos^{-1} \dfrac{2}{5}$

(c) $\cos^{-1} \dfrac{\sqrt{3}}{2}$ (d) $\cos^{-1} \dfrac{4}{5}$

(iii) $\angle BCA = \beta = ?$

(a) $\tan^{-1} \dfrac{1}{2}$ (b) $\tan^{-1} 2$

(c) $\tan^{-1} \dfrac{1}{\sqrt{3}}$ (d) $\tan^{-1} \sqrt{3}$

(iv) $\angle ABC = ?$

(a) $\dfrac{\pi}{4}$ (b) $\dfrac{\pi}{6}$

(c) $\dfrac{\pi}{2}$ (d) $\dfrac{\pi}{3}$

(v) Domain and range of $\cos^{-1} x$?

(a) $(-1, 1), (0\, \pi)$ (b) $[-1, 1], (0, \pi)$

(c) $[0, \pi], [-1, 1]$ (d) $(-1, 1), \left[-\dfrac{\pi}{2}, \dfrac{\pi}{2}\right]$

Solutions

1. (b) $\dfrac{2}{5}$

Explanation :
We have,
$$\cos\left(\sin^{-1} \dfrac{2}{5} + \cos^{-1} x\right) = 0$$
$$\Rightarrow \sin^{-1} \dfrac{2}{5} + \cos^{-1} x = \cos^{-1} 0$$
$$\Rightarrow \sin^{-1} \dfrac{2}{5} + \cos^{-1} x = \dfrac{\pi}{2}$$
$$\Rightarrow \sin^{-1} \dfrac{2}{5} + \cos^{-1} x = \dfrac{\pi}{2}$$
$$\Rightarrow \cos^{-1} x = \dfrac{\pi}{2} - \sin^{-1} \dfrac{2}{5}$$
$$\Rightarrow \cos^{-1} x = \cos^{-1} \dfrac{2}{5}$$
$$\left(\because \cos^{-1} x + \sin^{-1} x = \dfrac{\pi}{2}\right)$$
$$\therefore x = \dfrac{2}{5}$$

2. (a) $\left(-\dfrac{\pi}{2}, \dfrac{\pi}{2}\right)$

3. (b) $[0, -\pi] - \left\{\dfrac{\pi}{2}\right\}$

4. (a) $\dfrac{2\pi}{9}$

Explanation :
$\cos^{-1} [\cos(-680°)] - \cos^{-1}[\cos(720° - 40°)]$
$= \cos^{-1}[\cos(-40°)]$
$= \cos^{-1}[\cos(40°)]$
$= 40° = \dfrac{2\pi}{9}$.

5. (d) $\dfrac{\sqrt{1-x^2}}{x}$

Explanation :
Let $\sin^{-1} x = \theta$,
then $\sin\theta = x$
$\Rightarrow \csc\theta = \dfrac{1}{x}$
$\Rightarrow \csc^2\theta = \dfrac{1}{x^2}$
$\Rightarrow 1 + \cot^2\theta = \dfrac{1}{x^2}$
$\Rightarrow \cot\theta = \dfrac{\sqrt{1-x^2}}{x}$
$\Rightarrow \cot(\sin^{-1} x) = \dfrac{\sqrt{1-x^2}}{x}$

6. (c) $\left[-\dfrac{1}{2}, \dfrac{1}{2}\right]$

   Explanation :
   Let $\sin^{-1} 2x = \theta$
   So that $2x = \sin\theta$.
   Now, $-1 \le \sin\theta \le 1$, i.e., $-1 \le 2x \le 1$ which gives
   $-\dfrac{1}{2} \le x \le \dfrac{1}{2}$.

7. (b) $-\dfrac{\pi}{3}$

   Explanation :
   $$\sin^{-1}\left(\dfrac{-\sqrt{3}}{2}\right) = \sin^{-1}\left(-\sin\dfrac{\pi}{3}\right)$$
   $$= -\sin^{-1}\left(\sin\dfrac{\pi}{3}\right)$$
   $$= -\dfrac{\pi}{3}.$$

8. (d) $[-\sqrt{5}, -\sqrt{3}] \cup [\sqrt{3}, \sqrt{5}]$

   Explanation :
   $y = \cos^{-1}(x^2 - 4)$
   $\Rightarrow \cos y = x^2 - 4$
   i.e., $-1 \le x^2 - 4 \le 1$ (since $-1 \le \cos y \le 1$)
   $\Rightarrow 3 \le x^2 \le 5$
   $\Rightarrow \sqrt{3} \le |x| \le \sqrt{5}$
   $\Rightarrow x \in [-\sqrt{5}, -\sqrt{3}] \cup [\sqrt{3}, \sqrt{5}]$

9. (a) $[-1, 1]$

   Explanation :
   The domain of $\cos$ is R and the domain of $\sin^{-1}$ is $[-1, 1]$.
   $\therefore$ The domain of $\cos x + \sin^{-1} x$ is $R \cap [-1, 1]$, i.e., $[-1, 1]$.

10. (b) $\cdot 96$

    Explanation :
    Let $\sin^{-1}(\cdot 6) = \theta$, i.e., $\sin\theta = \cdot 6$.
    Now, $\sin(2\theta) = 2\sin\theta\cos\theta = 2(\cdot 6)(\cdot 8) = \cdot 96$.

11. (d) $\dfrac{3}{29}$

    Explanation :
    $\tan\left\{\cos^{-1}\dfrac{1}{5\sqrt{2}} - \sin^{-1}\dfrac{4}{\sqrt{17}}\right\}$
    Let $A = \cos^{-1}\dfrac{1}{5\sqrt{2}}$
    $\therefore \cos A = \dfrac{1}{5\sqrt{2}}$
    $\Rightarrow \cos^2 A = \dfrac{1}{50}$
    $\Rightarrow \sec^2 A = 50$
    $\Rightarrow \tan^2 A = 50 - 1 = 49$

    and $B = \sin^{-1}\dfrac{4}{\sqrt{17}}$
    $\sin B = \dfrac{4}{\sqrt{17}}$
    $\sin^2 B = \dfrac{16}{17}$
    $\text{cosec}^2 B = \dfrac{17}{16}$
    $\cot^2 B = \dfrac{17}{16} - 1 = \dfrac{1}{16}$
    $\therefore \tan A = 7$ and $\tan B = 4$
    Now, $\tan\left\{\cos^{-1}\dfrac{1}{5\sqrt{2}} - \sin^{-1}\dfrac{4}{\sqrt{17}}\right\}$
    $= \tan(A - B)$
    $= \dfrac{\tan A - \tan B}{1 + \tan A \tan B}$
    $= \dfrac{7 - 4}{1 + 7 \times 4} = \dfrac{3}{29}.$

12. (d) $\dfrac{5}{\sqrt{26}}$

    Explanation :
    Given : $\cot^{-1}\left(\dfrac{-1}{5}\right) = \theta$, where $\theta \in (0, \pi)$
    $\therefore \cot\theta = \dfrac{-1}{5}$
    $\because \sin\theta = \dfrac{1}{\text{cosec}\,\theta} = \dfrac{1}{\sqrt{1 + \cot^2\theta}}$
    $= \dfrac{1}{\sqrt{1 + \left(-\dfrac{1}{5}\right)^2}} = \dfrac{1}{\sqrt{1 + \dfrac{1}{25}}} = \dfrac{1}{\sqrt{\dfrac{26}{25}}}$
    $= \dfrac{5}{\sqrt{26}}$

13. (d) $\alpha = 0, \beta = \pi$

    Explanation :
    We have $\dfrac{-\pi}{2} \le \sin^{-1} x \le \dfrac{\pi}{2}$
    $\Rightarrow \dfrac{-\pi}{2} + \dfrac{\pi}{2} \le \sin^{-1} x + \dfrac{\pi}{2} \le \dfrac{\pi}{2} + \dfrac{\pi}{2}$
    $\Rightarrow 0 \le \sin^{-1} x + (\sin^{-1} x + \cos^{-1} x) \le \pi$
    $\Rightarrow 0 \le 2\sin^{-1} x + \cos^{-1} x \le \pi.$

14. (b) 11

    Explanation :
    $\tan^2(\sec^{-1} 2) + \cot^2(\text{cosec}^{-1} 3)$
    $= \sec^2(\sec^{-1} 2) - 1 + \text{cosec}^2(\text{cosec}^{-1} 3) - 1$
    $= 2^2 \times 1 + 3^2 - 2 = 11.$

Inverse Trigonometric Functions | 269

15. (b) $\dfrac{3-\sqrt{5}}{2}$

Explanation :

Let $y = \tan\left[\dfrac{1}{2}\cos^{-1}\left(\dfrac{\sqrt{5}}{3}\right)\right]$

Putting, $x = \cos^{-1}\left(\dfrac{\sqrt{5}}{3}\right)$

$\Rightarrow \cos x = \dfrac{\sqrt{5}}{3}$ ...(i)

Now, $y = \tan\left(\dfrac{1}{2} \times x\right)$

$y = \tan\left(\dfrac{x}{2}\right)$

$\therefore y = \sqrt{\dfrac{1-\cos(x)}{1+\cos(x)}}$

$\therefore y = \sqrt{\dfrac{1-\sqrt{5}/3}{1+\sqrt{5}/3}}$ [From (i)]

$\therefore y = \sqrt{\dfrac{3-\sqrt{5}}{3+\sqrt{5}}} = \sqrt{\dfrac{(3-\sqrt{5})(3-\sqrt{5})}{(3+\sqrt{5})(3-\sqrt{5})}}$

$\therefore y = \sqrt{\dfrac{(3-\sqrt{5})^2}{9-5}} = \dfrac{3-\sqrt{5}}{\sqrt{4}} = \dfrac{3-\sqrt{5}}{2}$

$\therefore y = \dfrac{3-\sqrt{5}}{2}$

i.e., $\tan\left[\dfrac{1}{2}\cos^{-1}\left(\dfrac{\sqrt{5}}{3}\right)\right] = \dfrac{3-\sqrt{5}}{2}$.

16. (b) $\dfrac{\pi}{6}$

17. (a) $\dfrac{5\pi}{6}$

Explanation :

$\sec^{-1}\left(\dfrac{-2}{\sqrt{3}}\right) = \pi - \sec^{-1}\left(\dfrac{2}{\sqrt{3}}\right)$

$= \pi - \dfrac{\pi}{6} = \dfrac{5\pi}{6}$

18. (a) $[-\pi, 0]$

Explanation :

Cosine functions respected to any interval $[-\pi, 0]$, $[0, \pi]$, $[\pi, 2\pi]$ etc., is bijective with range $[-1, 1]$.

19. (b) $\dfrac{-\pi}{2} \leq y \leq \dfrac{\pi}{2}$

Explanation :

Range of $\sin^{-1} x$ is $\left[\dfrac{-\pi}{2}, \dfrac{\pi}{2}\right]$

$\therefore \dfrac{-\pi}{2} \leq y \leq \dfrac{\pi}{2}$

20. (d) 1

Explanation :

$\sin\left[\dfrac{\pi}{3} - \sin^{-1}\left(-\dfrac{1}{2}\right)\right]$

$= \sin\left[\dfrac{\pi}{3} + \dfrac{\pi}{6}\right]$ $\left[\because \sin^{-1}\left(\dfrac{-1}{2}\right) = \dfrac{-\pi}{6}\right]$

$= \sin\dfrac{\pi}{2} = 1$.

21. (c) $\dfrac{-\pi}{12}$

Explanation :

$\tan^{-1}\left(\dfrac{-1}{\sqrt{3}}\right) + \cot^{-1}\left(\dfrac{1}{\sqrt{3}}\right) + \tan^{-1}\left(\sin\left(-\dfrac{\pi}{2}\right)\right)$

$= \dfrac{-\pi}{6} + \dfrac{\pi}{3} - \dfrac{\pi}{4}$

$= \dfrac{-2\pi + 4\pi - 3\pi}{12} = \dfrac{-\pi}{12}$

$\left[\because \tan^{-1}\left(\dfrac{-1}{\sqrt{3}}\right) = \dfrac{-\pi}{6}, \cot^{-1}\left(\dfrac{1}{\sqrt{3}}\right) = \dfrac{\pi}{3}, \sin\left(\dfrac{-\pi}{2}\right) = -1\right]$

22. (a) $\dfrac{\pi}{3}$

Explanation :

Given, $\tan^{-1}\left[2\sin\left(2\cos^{-1}\dfrac{\sqrt{3}}{2}\right)\right]$

$= \tan^{-1}\left[2\sin\left(2 \times \dfrac{\pi}{6}\right)\right] = \tan^{-1}\left[2\sin\dfrac{\pi}{3}\right]$

$= \tan^{-1}\left(2 \times \dfrac{\sqrt{3}}{2}\right) = \tan^{-1}\sqrt{3} = \dfrac{\pi}{3}$.

23. (a) 0

Explanation :

$\tan^{-1}\left(\tan\dfrac{5\pi}{6}\right) = \tan^{-1}\tan\left(\pi - \dfrac{\pi}{6}\right)$

$= \tan^{-1}\left(-\tan\dfrac{\pi}{6}\right) = \dfrac{-\pi}{6}$

and $\cos^{-1}\left(\cos\dfrac{13\pi}{6}\right)$

$= \cos^{-1}\cos\left(2\pi + \dfrac{\pi}{6}\right) = \cos^{-1}\left(\cos\dfrac{\pi}{6}\right) = \dfrac{\pi}{6}$

$\dfrac{-\pi}{6} + \dfrac{\pi}{6} = 0$.

27. (a) $[0, 1]$

Explanation :

We know that $\cos^{-1} x$ is defined for $x \in [-1, 1]$

$\therefore f(x) = \cos^{-1}(2x - 1)$ is defined if

$-1 \leq 2x - 1 \leq 1$

$\Rightarrow 0 \leq 2x \leq 2$

$\Rightarrow 0 \leq x \leq 1$.

28. (a) $[1, 2]$

Explanation:

We know that $\sin^{-1} x$ is defined for
$$x \in [-1, 1]$$
$\therefore f(x) = \sin^{-1} \sqrt{x-1}$ is defined if
$$\Rightarrow \quad 0 \leq \sqrt{x-1} \leq 1$$
$$\Rightarrow \quad 0 \leq x - 1 \leq 1$$
$$[\because \sqrt{x-1} \geq 0 \text{ and } -1 \leq \sqrt{x-1} \leq 1]$$
$$\Rightarrow \quad 1 \leq x \leq 2$$
$$\therefore \quad x \in [1, 2]$$

29. (a) $\dfrac{\pi}{2}$

Explanation:

$\cos^{-1}\left(\cos \dfrac{3\pi}{2}\right) \neq \dfrac{3\pi}{2}$ as $\dfrac{3\pi}{2} \notin [0, \pi]$

$\therefore \cos^{-1}\left(\cos \dfrac{3\pi}{2}\right) = \cos^{-1} 0 = \dfrac{\pi}{2}$

30. (d) $\dfrac{x}{\sqrt{1+x^2}}$

Explanation:

$$\tan y = x$$
$$\Rightarrow \quad \sin y = \dfrac{x}{\sqrt{1+x^2}}$$

Let $\tan^{-1} x = y$. Then,
$$\therefore \quad y = \sin^{-1}\left(\dfrac{x}{\sqrt{1+x^2}}\right)$$
$$\Rightarrow \quad \tan^{-1} x = \sin^{-1}\left(\dfrac{x}{\sqrt{1+x^2}}\right)$$
$$\therefore \quad \sin(\tan^{-1} x) = \sin\left(\sin^{-1} \dfrac{x}{\sqrt{1+x^2}}\right) = \dfrac{x}{\sqrt{1+x^2}}$$

31. (d) A is false but R is true.

Explanation:

$\because 3 \approx 171°$ (lies in II quadrant)

$\therefore \sin^{-1} \sin 3 = 3 - \pi \neq 3$

But $\sin^{-1} \sin x = x$ for principal values.

32. (a) Both (A) and (R) are true and R is the correct explanation A.

Explanation:

$\because \quad AM \geq GM$

$\therefore \quad \dfrac{\cos^{-1} x + (\sin^{-1} y)^2}{2} \geq \sqrt{(\cos^{-1} x)(\sin^{-1} y)^2}$

$$\Rightarrow \quad \dfrac{p\pi^2}{8} \geq \dfrac{p\pi^2}{8}$$
$$\Rightarrow \quad p \geq 2$$

Thus, we conclude that the only value of p that satisfies all conditions is $p = 2$.

Then, $\cos^{-1} x = (\sin^{-1} y)^2$

$$\Rightarrow \quad (\cos^{-1} x)^2 = \dfrac{\pi^4}{16}$$
$$\Rightarrow \quad \cos^{-1} x = \pm \dfrac{\pi^2}{4}$$
$$\Rightarrow \quad x = \cos\left(\pm \dfrac{\pi^2}{4}\right)$$
$$\therefore \quad x = \cos\left(\dfrac{\pi^2}{4}\right)$$

Also, $(\sin^{-1} y)^4 = \dfrac{\pi^4}{16}$
$$\Rightarrow \quad \sin^{-1} y = \pm \dfrac{\pi}{2}$$
$$\therefore \quad y = \sin\left(\pm \dfrac{\pi}{2}\right)$$
$$= \pm 1$$

33. (a) Both (A) and (R) are true and R is the correct explanation A.

Explanation:

Since, maximum value of $\sin^{-1} x_i$ is $\dfrac{\pi}{2}$

$\therefore \sum_{i=1}^{2n} \sin^{-1} x_i = n\pi$ is possible, if
$$x_1 = x_2 = x_3 = ... = x_{2n} = 1$$

$\therefore \sum_{i=1}^{n} x_i = 1 + 1 + 1 + ...$ upto n times $= n$

$\therefore \sum_{i=1}^{n} x_i^2 = 1^2 + 1^2 + 1^2 + 1^2 + ...$ upto n times $= n$

and $\sum_{i=1}^{n} x_i^3 = 1^3 + 1^3 + 1^3 + ...$ upto n times $= n$

Hence, $\sum_{i=1}^{n} x_i = \sum_{i=1}^{n} x_i^2 = \sum_{i=1}^{n} x_i^3 = n$

34. (d) A is false but R is true.

Explanation:

$2(\sin^{-1} x)^2 - 5(\sin^{-1} x) + 2 = 0$

$$\Rightarrow \quad \sin^{-1} x = \dfrac{5 \pm \sqrt{25-16}}{4} = 2, \dfrac{1}{2}$$

$$\Rightarrow \quad \sin^{-1} x = \dfrac{1}{2}, \sin^{-1} x = 2$$

$\therefore x = \sin\left(\dfrac{1}{2}\right)$ and $x = \sin^{-1} 2$ is not possible

$\therefore x = \sin\left(\dfrac{1}{2}\right)$ is only solution

$\therefore$ Assertion (A) is false.

35. (i) (a)

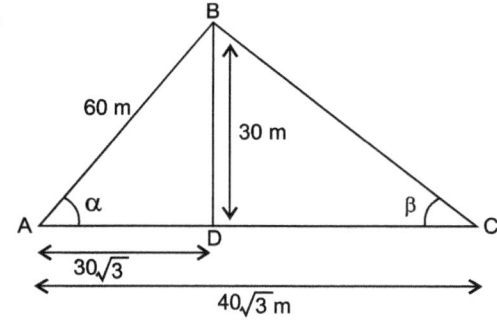

$$\sin \alpha = \frac{BD}{AB}$$
$$AB = \sqrt{(30\sqrt{3})^2 + 30^2}$$
$$= \sqrt{2700 + 900}$$
$$= \sqrt{3600} = 60.$$
$$\sin \alpha = \frac{30}{60} = \frac{1}{2}$$
$$\boxed{\alpha = \sin^{-1} \frac{1}{2}}$$

(ii) (c) $\cos \alpha = \dfrac{AD}{AB} = \dfrac{30\sqrt{3}}{60} = \dfrac{\sqrt{3}}{2}$

$\alpha = \cos^{-1}\left(\dfrac{\sqrt{3}}{2}\right)$

(iii) (d) $\tan \beta = \dfrac{BD}{DC} = \dfrac{30}{10\sqrt{3}} = \dfrac{3}{\sqrt{3}} = \sqrt{3}$

$\boxed{\beta = \tan^{-1} \sqrt{3}}$

(iv) (c) $BC = \sqrt{30^2 + (10\sqrt{3})^2}$
$= \sqrt{900 + 300} = \sqrt{1200} = 20\sqrt{3}\ m$

∵ $AB^2 + BC^2 = AC^2$
$\sqrt{(60)^2 + 1200} = \sqrt{3600 + 1200}$
$AC = \sqrt{4800} = 40\sqrt{3}$

∴ By convex of pythagoras theory
$\angle ABC = \dfrac{\pi}{2}$

(v) (c) $[0, \pi], [-1, 1]$

Chapter 3

Matrices

1. If A and B are square matrices of the same order, then (A + B) (A – B) is equal to:
   (a) $A^2 - B^2$
   (b) $A^2 - BA - AB - B^2$
   (c) $A^2 - B^2 + BA - AB$
   (d) $A^2 - BA + B^2 + AB$

2. If $A = \begin{bmatrix} 2 & -1 & 3 \\ -4 & 5 & 1 \end{bmatrix}$ and $B = \begin{bmatrix} 2 & 3 \\ 4 & -2 \\ 1 & 5 \end{bmatrix}$, then
   (a) only AB is defined
   (b) only BA is defined
   (c) AB and BA both are defined
   (d) AB and BA both are not defined

3. The matrix $A = \begin{bmatrix} 0 & 0 & 5 \\ 0 & 5 & 0 \\ 5 & 0 & 0 \end{bmatrix}$ is a:
   (a) scalar matrix
   (b) diagonal matrix
   (c) unit matrix
   (d) square matrix

4. If A and B are symmetric matrices of the same order, then (AB' – BA') is a
   (a) Skew symmetric matrix
   (b) Null matrix
   (c) Symmetric matrix
   (d) None of these

5. If $A = [2 - 3\ 4]$, $B = \begin{bmatrix} 3 \\ 2 \\ 2 \end{bmatrix}$, $X = [1\ 2\ 3]$ and $Y = \begin{bmatrix} 2 \\ 3 \\ 4 \end{bmatrix}$, then
   AB + XY equals: [CBSE OD, Set-1, 2020]
   (a) [28]
   (b) [24]
   (c) 28
   (d) 24

6. If $[x - 1]\begin{bmatrix} 1 & 0 \\ -2 & 0 \end{bmatrix} = 0$, then x equals:
   [CBSE Delhi Set-2, 2020]
   (a) 0
   (b) – 2
   (c) – 1
   (d) 2

7. Which of the following is a I_2 matrix?
   (a) $\begin{bmatrix} 1 & 1 \\ 1 & 1 \end{bmatrix}$
   (b) $\begin{bmatrix} 1 & 1 \\ 0 & 1 \end{bmatrix}$
   (c) $\begin{bmatrix} 0 & 1 \\ 1 & 0 \end{bmatrix}$
   (d) $\begin{bmatrix} 1 & 0 \\ 0 & 1 \end{bmatrix}$

8. Two matrices A and B are multiplied to get AB if,
   (a) both are rectangular
   (b) both have same order
   (c) no. of columns of A is equal to no. of rows of B
   (d) no. of rows of A is equal to no. of columns of B

9. If A is a matrix of order 3 × 4, then each row of A has:
   (a) 3 elements
   (b) 12 elements
   (c) 7 elements
   (d) 4 elements

10. The matrix $A = \begin{bmatrix} 5 & 0 & 0 \\ 0 & 5 & 0 \\ 0 & 0 & 5 \end{bmatrix}$ is a:
    (a) Scalar matrix
    (b) Diagonal matrix
    (c) Unit matrix
    (d) Square matrix

11. If A is a square matrix of order 3, such that A (adj A) = 10 I, then |adj A| is equal to:
    (a) 1
    (b) 10
    (c) 100
    (d) 101

12. The number of all possible matrices of order 2 × 3 with each entry 0 or 1 is:
    (a) 64
    (b) 12
    (c) 36
    (d) None of these

13. The matrix $A = \begin{bmatrix} 1 & 0 & 0 \\ 0 & 2 & 0 \\ 0 & 0 & 4 \end{bmatrix}$ is a :
    (a) Identity matrix
    (b) Scalar matrix
    (c) Skew-symmetric matrix
    (d) Diagonal matrix

14. For any 2 × 2 matrix, if $A(\text{adj. }A) = \begin{bmatrix} 10 & 0 \\ 0 & 10 \end{bmatrix}$, then |A| is equal to :
    (a) 20
    (b) 100
    (c) 10
    (d) 0

15. A is a scalar matrix with scalar $k \neq 0$ of order 3. Then A^{-1} is:

(a) $\begin{bmatrix} \frac{1}{k} & 0 & 0 \\ 0 & \frac{1}{k} & 0 \\ 0 & 0 & \frac{1}{k} \end{bmatrix}$ (b) $\begin{bmatrix} 0 & 0 & k \\ 0 & k & 0 \\ k & 0 & 0 \end{bmatrix}$

(c) $\begin{bmatrix} \frac{1}{k^2} & 0 & 0 \\ 0 & \frac{1}{k^2} & 0 \\ 0 & 0 & 1/k^2 \end{bmatrix}$ (d) $\begin{bmatrix} k & 0 & 0 \\ 0 & k & 0 \\ 0 & 0 & k \end{bmatrix}$

16. If A is a 3 × 2 matrix, B is a 3 × 3 matrix and C is a 2 × 3 matrix, then the elements in A, B and C are respectively:
    (a) 6, 9, 8
    (b) 6, 9, 6
    (c) 9, 6, 6
    (d) 6, 6, 9

17. If a matrix has 8 elements, then which of the following will not be a possible order of the matrix?
    (a) 1 × 8
    (b) 2 × 4
    (c) 4 × 2
    (d) 4 × 4

18. Total number of possible matrices of order 3 × 3 with each entry 2 or 0 is: [NCERT Exemplar]
    (a) 9
    (b) 27
    (c) 81
    (d) 512

19. The matrix $P = \begin{bmatrix} 0 & 0 & 4 \\ 0 & 4 & 0 \\ 4 & 0 & 0 \end{bmatrix}$ is not a:

    [NCERT Exemplar]
    (a) square matrix
    (b) diagonal matrix
    (c) unit matrix
    (d) None of these

20. Which of the given values of x and y make the following pair of matrices equal:
    $\begin{bmatrix} 3x+7 & 5 \\ y+1 & 2-3x \end{bmatrix} = \begin{bmatrix} 0 & y-2 \\ 8 & 4 \end{bmatrix}$ [NCERT]
    (a) $x = \frac{-1}{3}, y = 7$
    (b) not possible to find
    (c) $y = 7, x = \frac{-2}{3}$
    (d) $x = \frac{-1}{3}, y = \frac{-2}{3}$

21. If $A = \begin{bmatrix} 2 & 3 \\ 1 & 2 \end{bmatrix}, B = \begin{bmatrix} 1 & 3 & 2 \\ 4 & 3 & 1 \end{bmatrix}, C = \begin{bmatrix} 1 \\ 2 \end{bmatrix}$ and

    $D = \begin{bmatrix} 4 & 6 & 8 \\ 5 & 7 & 9 \end{bmatrix}$, then which of the following is defined? [NCERT Exemplar]
    (a) A + B
    (b) B + C
    (c) C + D
    (d) B + D

22. If $\begin{bmatrix} 1 & 2 \\ -2 & -b \end{bmatrix} + \begin{bmatrix} a & 4 \\ 3 & 2 \end{bmatrix} = \begin{bmatrix} 5 & 6 \\ 1 & 0 \end{bmatrix}$, then $a^2 + b^2$ is equal to:

    (a) 20
    (b) 22
    (c) 12
    (d) 10

23. If $A = \begin{bmatrix} 0 & 2 \\ 3 & -4 \end{bmatrix}$ and $kA = \begin{bmatrix} 0 & 3a \\ 2b & 24 \end{bmatrix}$ then the values of k, a, b are respectively:
    (a) −6, −12, −18
    (b) −6, 4, 9
    (c) −6, −4, −9
    (d) −6, 12, 18

24. The product $\begin{bmatrix} a & b \\ -b & a \end{bmatrix}\begin{bmatrix} a & -b \\ b & a \end{bmatrix}$ is equal to:
    (a) $\begin{bmatrix} a^2+b^2 & 0 \\ 0 & a^2+b^2 \end{bmatrix}$
    (b) $\begin{bmatrix} (a+b)^2 & 0 \\ (a+b)^2 & 0 \end{bmatrix}$
    (c) $\begin{bmatrix} a^2+b^2 & 0 \\ a^2+b^2 & 0 \end{bmatrix}$
    (d) $\begin{bmatrix} a & 0 \\ 0 & b \end{bmatrix}$

25. If the product of two matrices is a zero matrix, then :
    (a) atleast one of the matrix is a zero matrix
    (b) both the matrices are zero matrices
    (c) it is not necessary that one of the matrices is a zero matrix
    (d) None of these

26. If $A = \begin{bmatrix} 2 & -1 & 3 \\ -4 & 5 & 1 \end{bmatrix}_{2 \times 3}$ and $B = \begin{bmatrix} 2 & 3 \\ 4 & -2 \\ 1 & 5 \end{bmatrix}_{3 \times 7}$, then :
    (a) only AB is defined
    (b) only BA is defined
    (c) AB and BA both are defined
    (d) AB and BA both are not defined

27. The set of all 2 × 2 matrices which is commutative with the matrix $\begin{bmatrix} 1 & 1 \\ 1 & 0 \end{bmatrix}$ with respect to matrix multiplication is:
    (a) $\begin{bmatrix} p & q \\ r & r \end{bmatrix}$
    (b) $\begin{bmatrix} p & q \\ q & r \end{bmatrix}$
    (c) $\begin{bmatrix} p-q & q \\ q & r \end{bmatrix}$
    (d) $\begin{bmatrix} p & q \\ q & p-q \end{bmatrix}$

28. If A is matrix of order m × n and B is matrix such that AB' and B'A are both defined, then order of matrix B is: [NCERT Exemplar]
    (a) m × n
    (b) n × n
    (c) n × m
    (d) m × n

29. If A and B are square matrices of the same order and AB = 3I, then A^{-1} is equal to:
    (a) 3B
    (b) $\frac{1}{3}B$
    (c) $3B^{-1}$
    (d) $\frac{1}{3}B^{-1}$

30. If $A = \frac{1}{\pi}\begin{bmatrix} \sin^{-1}(x\pi) & \tan^{-1}\left(\frac{x}{\pi}\right) \\ \sin^{-1}\left(\frac{x}{\pi}\right) & \cot^{-1}(\pi x) \end{bmatrix}$,

$B = \dfrac{1}{\pi}\begin{bmatrix} -\cos^{-1}(x\pi) & \tan^{-1}\left(\dfrac{x}{\pi}\right) \\ \sin^{-1}\left(\dfrac{x}{\pi}\right) & -\tan^{-1}(\pi x) \end{bmatrix}$, then A − B is equal to: [NCERT Exemplar]

(a) I
(b) O
(c) 2I
(d) $\dfrac{1}{2}I$

31. If A and B are two matrices of the order 3 × m and 3 × n, respectively, and m = n, then the order of matrix (5A − 2B) is: [NCERT Exemplar]
    (a) m × 3
    (b) 3 × 3
    (c) m × n
    (d) 3 × n

32. If $A = \begin{bmatrix} 0 & 1 \\ 1 & 0 \end{bmatrix}$, then A^2 is equal to: [NCERT Exemplar]

    (a) $\begin{bmatrix} 0 & 1 \\ 1 & 0 \end{bmatrix}$
    (b) $\begin{bmatrix} 1 & 0 \\ 1 & 0 \end{bmatrix}$
    (c) $\begin{bmatrix} 0 & 1 \\ 0 & 1 \end{bmatrix}$
    (d) $\begin{bmatrix} 1 & 0 \\ 0 & 1 \end{bmatrix}$

33. If matrix $A = [a_{ij}]_{2 \times 2}$, where $a_{ij} = \begin{cases} 1 \text{ if } i \ne j \\ 0 \text{ if } i = j \end{cases}$ then A^2 is equal to: [NCERT Exemplar]
    (a) I
    (b) A
    (c) 0
    (d) None of these

34. The matrix $\begin{bmatrix} 1 & 2 & 4 \\ 2 & 5 & 6 \\ 4 & 6 & 7 \end{bmatrix}$ is a [NCERT Exemplar]
    (a) identity matrix
    (b) symmetric matrix
    (c) skew symmetric matrix
    (d) none of these

35. $A = [a_{ij}]_{m \times n}$ is a square matrix, if
    (a) m < n
    (b) m > n
    (c) m = n
    (d) None of these

Choose the correct option :
(a) Both (A) and (R) are true and R is the correct explanation A.
(b) Both (A) and (R) are true but R is not correct explanation of A.
(c) A is true but R is false.
(d) A is false but R is true.

36. **Assertion (A)** : If $A = \begin{pmatrix} 3 & -3 & 4 \\ 2 & -3 & 4 \\ 0 & -1 & 1 \end{pmatrix}$, then adj (adj A) = A.
    Reason (R) : | adj (adj A) | = | A |$^{(n-1)^2}$, A be n rowed non-singular matrix

37. **Assertion (A)** : If $A = \begin{pmatrix} a & 0 & 0 \\ 0 & b & 0 \\ 0 & 0 & c \end{pmatrix}$, then $A^{-1} = \begin{pmatrix} \dfrac{1}{a} & 0 & 0 \\ 0 & \dfrac{1}{b} & 0 \\ 0 & 0 & \dfrac{1}{c} \end{pmatrix}$
    Reason (R) : The inverse of a diagonal matrix is a diagonal matrix.

38. **Assertion (A)** : The rank of a unit matrix of order n × n is n.
    Reason (R) : The rank of a non-singular matrix of order n × n is not n.

39. **Assertion (A)** : The matrix $\begin{bmatrix} a & 0 & 0 & 0 \\ 0 & b & 0 & 0 \\ 0 & 0 & c & 0 \end{bmatrix}$ is a diagonal matrix.
    Reason (R) : $A = [a_{ij}]$ is a square matrix such that $a_{ij} = 0 \; \forall \; i \ne j$, then A is called diagonal matrix.

40. **Assertion (A)** : The inverse of the matrix $A = \begin{pmatrix} 1 & 1 & 1 \\ 1 & 2 & 3 \\ 1 & 4 & 7 \end{pmatrix}$ does not exist.
    Reason (R) : The matrix A is singular.

41. **Assertion (A)** : If A is a matrix of order n × n, then det (kA) = k^n det (A) or | kA | = k^n | A |.
    Reason (R) : If B is a matrix obtained from A by multiplying any row or column by a scalar k, then det B = k det A or | B | = k | A |.

42. **Assertion (A)** : The matrix $A = \dfrac{1}{3}\begin{pmatrix} 1 & -2 & 2 \\ -2 & 1 & 2 \\ -2 & -2 & -1 \end{pmatrix}$ is an orthogonal matrix.
    Reason (R) : If A and B are orthogonal, then AB is also orthogonal.

43. **Assertion (A)** : If A is a skew-symmetric matrix of order 3 × 3, then det (A) = 0 or | A | = 0.
    Reason (R) : If A is a square matrix, then det (A) = det (A′) = det (− A′).

44. **Assertion (A)** : The inverse of $A = \begin{pmatrix} 3 & 4 \\ 3 & 5 \end{pmatrix}$ does not exist.
    Reason (R) : The matrix A is non-singular.

45. **Assertion (A)** : If a matrix of order 2 × 2, commutes with every matrix of order 2 × 2, then it is scalar matrix.
    Reason (R) : A scalar matrix of order 2 × 2 commutes with every 2 × 2 matrix.

46. **Assertion (A)** : The determinant of a matrix A = $[a_{ij}]_{5\times 5}$ where $a_{ij} + a_{ij} = 0$ for all i and j is zero.
    Reason (R) : The determinant of a skew symmetric matrix of odd order is zero.

47. A firm produces three products P_1, P_2 and P_3 requiring the mix-up of three materials M_1, M_2 and M_3 per unit requirement of each product for each material (in units) is represented by matrix A as follows :

$$A = \begin{array}{c} \\ P_1 \\ P_2 \\ P_3 \end{array} \begin{array}{c} M_1 \; M_2 \; M_3 \\ \begin{bmatrix} 2 & 3 & 1 \\ 4 & 2 & 5 \\ 2 & 4 & 2 \end{bmatrix} \end{array}$$

The per unit cost of material M_1, M_2 and M_3 is ₹ 5, ₹ 10 and ₹ 5 respectively.

Attempt the following questions:

(i) If C represents the matrix showing cost of material, the matrix C will be expressed as :

(a) $C = \begin{bmatrix} 10 \\ 5 \\ 5 \end{bmatrix}$ (b) $C = [5 \; 10 \; 15]$

(c) $C = \begin{bmatrix} 5 \\ 10 \\ 5 \end{bmatrix}$ (d) $C = \begin{bmatrix} 15 \\ 10 \\ 20 \end{bmatrix}$

(ii) Expressed matrix B in the order of 3 × 1 if the firm produces 100 units of each product :

(a) $\begin{bmatrix} 100 \\ 100 \\ 100 \end{bmatrix}$ (b) $[100 \; 100 \; 100]$

(c) $\begin{bmatrix} 100 \\ 200 \\ 300 \end{bmatrix}$ (d) $\begin{bmatrix} 10 \\ 20 \\ 30 \end{bmatrix}$

(iii) Find the total requirement of each material for 100 units of each product :

(a) $\begin{bmatrix} 900 \\ 800 \\ 800 \end{bmatrix}$ (b) $\begin{bmatrix} 90 \\ 80 \\ 80 \end{bmatrix}$

(c) $\begin{bmatrix} 190 \\ 200 \\ 80 \end{bmatrix}$ (d) $\begin{bmatrix} 800 \\ 900 \\ 800 \end{bmatrix}$

(iv) Find per unit cost of production of each product as per the unit cost of material given above :

(a) $\begin{bmatrix} 45 \\ 65 \\ 60 \end{bmatrix}$ (b) $\begin{bmatrix} 65 \\ 60 \\ 45 \end{bmatrix}$

(c) $\begin{bmatrix} 60 \\ 65 \\ 40 \end{bmatrix}$ (d) $\begin{bmatrix} 50 \\ 60 \\ 70 \end{bmatrix}$

(v) Find the total cost of production if the firm produces 200 units of each product :

(a) 28,000 (b) 30,000
(c) 34,000 (d) 32,000

48. A concert is organised to earn the revenue of ₹ 1,80,000 which can be distributed among the needy people during the period of Covid-19. The concert hall has 4,000 seats which are divided into two sections A and B. The cost of a ticket in Section A is ₹ 50 and that of Section B is ₹ 40. All the seats are occupied.

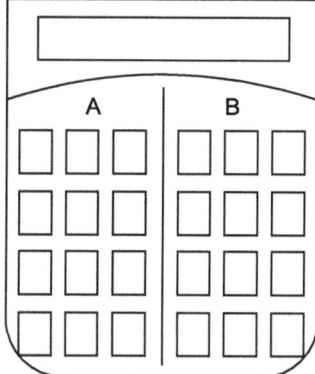

Attempt the following questions :

(i) If x and y are number of seats of Section A and B respectively, then write the equation related to number of seats :

(a) $x - y = 4000$ (b) $x + y = 400$
(c) $x + y = 4000$ (d) $2x + y = 4000$

(ii) What will be relation between x and y for the total revenue ?

(a) $5x + 4y = 18000$ (b) $50x + 40y = 18000$
(c) $5x + 4y = 1800$ (d) $x + y = 180$

(iii) If equations are to be solved through the matrix method in the form of AX = B, then what will be matrix A and matrix B :

(a) $A = \begin{bmatrix} 1 & 1 \\ 5 & 4 \end{bmatrix}, B = \begin{bmatrix} 4000 \\ 18000 \end{bmatrix}$

(b) $A = \begin{bmatrix} 5 & 4 \\ 1 & 1 \end{bmatrix}, B = \begin{bmatrix} 4000 \\ 18000 \end{bmatrix}$

(c) $A = \begin{bmatrix} 1 & 5 \\ 1 & 4 \end{bmatrix}, B = \begin{bmatrix} 18000 \\ 4000 \end{bmatrix}$

(d) $A = \begin{bmatrix} 1 & 4 \\ 1 & 5 \end{bmatrix}, B = \begin{bmatrix} 4000 \\ 18000 \end{bmatrix}$

(iv) The value of X will be equal to $A^{-1}B$, then A^{-1} :

(a) $\begin{bmatrix} -4 & 1 \\ -5 & 1 \end{bmatrix}$ (b) $\begin{bmatrix} -4 & 1 \\ 5 & -1 \end{bmatrix}$

(c) $\begin{bmatrix} 4 & -5 \\ -1 & 1 \end{bmatrix}$ (d) $\begin{bmatrix} -4 & 5 \\ -1 & -1 \end{bmatrix}$

(v) How many seats are there in Section A and Section B of Concert Hall ?

(a) 2000, 4000 (b) 4000, 2000
(c) 2000, 2000 (d) 6000, 4000

49. A mobile shop purchases three types of mobiles namely LG, I-phone and samsung and sells them in two malls of Gurugram. The annual sales in units are given below :

	LG	I-phone	Samsung
Mall I	20	15	35
Mall II	10	20	30

If the sale prices of per unit of LG phone is ₹ 20,000, I-phone ₹ 50,000 and Samsung is ₹ 15,000 respectively and costs per unit for LG ₹ 15,000, I-phone ₹ 40,000 and Samsung ₹ 12,000 respectively. From the above case study give the answers of the following questions :

(i) Represent the matrix Q as quantity sold :

(a) $Q = \begin{bmatrix} 20 & 15 & 35 \\ 10 & 20 & 30 \end{bmatrix}$

(b) $Q = \begin{bmatrix} 200 & 150 & 350 \\ 100 & 200 & 300 \end{bmatrix}$

(c) $Q = \begin{bmatrix} 20 & 10 \\ 15 & 20 \\ 35 & 30 \end{bmatrix}$

(d) $Q = \begin{bmatrix} 200 & 100 \\ 150 & 200 \\ 350 & 300 \end{bmatrix}$

(ii) Express the matrix S as total sales price of the item:

(a) $S = \begin{bmatrix} 20,000 \\ 50,000 \\ 15,000 \end{bmatrix}$

(b) $S = [20,000 \ 50,000 \ 15,000]$

(c) $S = \begin{bmatrix} 50,000 \\ 20,000 \\ 15,000 \end{bmatrix}$

(d) $S = [2,000 \ 5,000 \ 1,500]$

(iii) Express the matrix C as the total cost price of each item :

(a) $C = [15,000 \ 40,000 \ 12,000]$

(b) $C = \begin{bmatrix} 15,000 \\ 40,000 \\ 12,000 \end{bmatrix}$

(c) $C = [1,500 \ 4,000 \ 1,200]$

(d) $C = \begin{bmatrix} 12,000 \\ 15,000 \\ 40,000 \end{bmatrix}$

(iv) Express the matrix P as profit earned on each item :

(a) $P = [3,000 \ 10,000 \ 5,000]$

(b) $P = [5,000 \ 10,000 \ 3,000]$

(c) $P = \begin{bmatrix} 5,000 \\ 10,000 \\ 3,000 \end{bmatrix}$

(d) $P = \begin{bmatrix} 3,000 \\ 5,000 \\ 10,000 \end{bmatrix}$

(v) What is the total amount of profit in Mall I and Mall II if all goods are sold ?

(a) $\begin{bmatrix} 35,500 \\ 34,000 \end{bmatrix}$

(b) $\begin{bmatrix} 3,40,000 \\ 3,55,000 \end{bmatrix}$

(c) $[34,000 \ 35,500]$

(d) $\begin{bmatrix} 3,55,000 \\ 3,40,000 \end{bmatrix}$

50. Two trust A and B receive ₹ 70,000 and ₹ 55,000 respectively from central government to award prize to persons of a district in three fields defence, health services and education. Trust A awarded 10, 5 and 15 persons in the field of defence, health services and education respectively, while B awarded 15, 10 and 5 persons respectively. All three prizes amount of ₹ 6000.

Solve the questions on the above information :

(i) If x, y, z represents the amount of individual prize then write the linear equations :

(a) $x + y + z = 6,000$
$10x + 5y + 15z = 70,000$
$15x + 10y + 5z = 55,000$

(b) $x + 10y + 15z = 6,000$
$x + 5y + 10z = 70,000$
$x + 15y + 5z = 55,000$

(c) $x - y + z = 6,000$
$5y + 15z = 70,000$
$15x + 5z = 55,000$

(d) $x - y - z = 6,000$
$x - 5y + 10z = 70,000$
$15x + 10y + 5z = 55,000$

(ii) If all the equations are written in the form of AX = B then find |A| :

(a) 100   (b) 175
(c) 75   (d) 200

(iii) Find adj A :

(a) $\begin{bmatrix} -125 & 5 & 10 \\ 175 & -10 & -5 \\ 25 & 5 & -5 \end{bmatrix}$

(b) $\begin{bmatrix} -125 & 175 & 25 \\ 5 & -10 & 5 \\ 10 & -5 & -5 \end{bmatrix}$

(c) $\begin{bmatrix} 175 & -10 & -5 \\ 25 & 5 & -5 \\ -125 & 5 & 10 \end{bmatrix}$

(d) $\begin{bmatrix} -125 & 5 & 10 \\ 175 & -10 & -5 \\ 25 & 5 & 5 \end{bmatrix}$

Matrices | 277

(iv) Find A^{-1} :

(a) $\dfrac{1}{75}\begin{bmatrix} -125 & 5 & 10 \\ 175 & -10 & -5 \\ 25 & 5 & -5 \end{bmatrix}$

(b) $\dfrac{1}{75}\begin{bmatrix} -125 & 175 & 25 \\ 5 & -10 & 5 \\ 10 & -5 & -5 \end{bmatrix}$

(c) $\dfrac{1}{75}\begin{bmatrix} 175 & -10 & -5 \\ 25 & 5 & -5 \\ -125 & 5 & 10 \end{bmatrix}$

(d) $\dfrac{1}{75}\begin{bmatrix} -125 & 5 & 10 \\ 175 & -10 & -5 \\ 25 & 5 & 5 \end{bmatrix}$

(v) Find the value of each prize :
 (a) ₹ 2000, ₹ 3000, ₹ 1000
 (b) ₹ 2000, ₹ 1000, ₹ 3000
 (c) ₹ 1000, ₹ 2000, ₹ 3000
 (d) ₹ 3000, ₹ 2000, ₹ 1000

51. Three shopkeepers Ram Lal, Shyam Lal and Ghansham are using polythene bags handmade bags (prepared by prisoners), and newspaper's envelope as carry bags. It is found that the shopkeepers Ram Lal Shyam Lal and Ghansham are using (20, 30, 40), (30, 40, 20) and (40, 20, 30) polythene bags handmade bags and newspapers envelopes respectively. The shopkeepers Ram Lal, Shyam Lal and Ghansham spent ₹ 250, ₹ 270 and ₹ 200 on these carry bags respectively.

(i) What is the cost of one polythene bag?
 (a) ₹ 1 (b) ₹ 2
 (c) ₹ 3 (d) ₹ 5

(ii) What is the cost of one handmade bag?
 (a) ₹ 1 (b) ₹ 2
 (c) ₹ 3 (d) ₹ 5

(iii) What is the cost of one newspaper bag?
 (a) ₹ 1 (b) ₹ 2
 (c) ₹ 3 (d) ₹ 5

(iv) Keeping in mind the social conditions, which shopkeeper is better?
 (a) Ram Lal (b) Shyam Lal
 (c) Ghansham (d) None of these

(v) Keeping in mind the environmental conditions, which shopkeeper is better?
 (a) Ram Lal (b) Shyam Lal
 (c) Ghansham (d) None of these

Solutions

1. (c) $A^2 - B^2 + BA - AB$
 Explanation :
 $(A + B)(A - B) = A(A - B) + B(A - B)$
 $= A^2 - AB + BA - B^2.$

2. (c) AB and BA both are defined
 Explanation :
 Let $A = [a_{ij}]_{2\times 3}$ and $B = [b_{ij}]_{3\times 2}$
 Both AB and BA are defined.
 So the correct option is (c).

3. (d) square matrix
 Explanation :
 As number of rows and columns are equal.

4. (a) Skew symmetric matrix
 Explanation :
 Since $(AB' - BA')' = (AB')' - (BA')'$
 $= (BA' - AB')$
 $= -(AB' - BA').$

5. (a) [28]
 Explanation :
 $AB + XY = [2 -3\ 4]\begin{bmatrix} 3 \\ 2 \\ 2 \end{bmatrix} + [1\ 2\ 3]\begin{bmatrix} 2 \\ 3 \\ 4 \end{bmatrix}$
 $= [8] + [20] = [28]$
 So the correct option is (a).

6. (b) -2
 Explanation : Given :
 $[x-1]\begin{bmatrix} 1 & 0 \\ -2 & 0 \end{bmatrix} = 0$
 $\Rightarrow [x+2\ \ 0] = [0\ 0]$
 $\Rightarrow x + 2 = 0$
 $\Rightarrow x = -2$
 So the correct option is (b).

7. (d) $\begin{bmatrix} 1 & 0 \\ 0 & 1 \end{bmatrix}$

8. (c) no. of columns of A is equal to no. of rows of B.

9. (d) 4 elements
 Explanation :
 Since, 3×4 signifies that there are 3 rows and 4 columns. Then each row has 4 elements.

10. (a) Scalar matrix
 Explanation :
 All elements except diagonal are zero and equal.

11. (c) 100
 Explanation :
 Given: $A(\text{adj } A) = 10\ I$
 We know, $A . \text{adj } A = |A| . I$
 $\therefore$ $|A| = 10$
 $\because$ $|\text{adj } A| = |A|^{n-1}$
 $\therefore$ $|\text{adj } A| = |A|^{3-1} = 10^2 = 100$

12. (a) 64
 Explanation :
 In 2×3 matrix, number of elements are 6.

Each place could have 2 elements

∴ Total possible matrices = 2 × 2 × 2 × 2 × 2 × 2
= 8 × 8 = 64

13. (d) Diagonal matrix
14. (c) 10
    Explanation :

    ∵ $A(\text{adj. } A) = 10\begin{bmatrix} 1 & 0 \\ 0 & 1 \end{bmatrix}$

    $= 10I = 10\, AA^{-1}$

    ∴ $(\text{adj. } A) = 10\, A^{-1}$

    ⇒ $\text{adj. } A = \dfrac{10\, \text{adj. } A}{|A|}$

    ⇒ $|A| = 10$

15. (a) $\begin{bmatrix} \frac{1}{k} & 0 & 0 \\ 0 & \frac{1}{k} & 0 \\ 0 & 0 & \frac{1}{k} \end{bmatrix}$

    Explanation :

    ∵ $A = \begin{bmatrix} k & 0 & 0 \\ 0 & k & 0 \\ 0 & 0 & k \end{bmatrix}$

    ∴ $|A| = k^3$

    and $\text{adj. } A = \begin{bmatrix} k^2 & 0 & 0 \\ 0 & k^2 & 0 \\ 0 & 0 & k^2 \end{bmatrix}$

    ∴ $A^{-1} = \dfrac{1}{|A|}\text{adj. } A = \begin{bmatrix} \frac{1}{k} & 0 & 0 \\ 0 & \frac{1}{k} & 0 \\ 0 & 0 & \frac{1}{k} \end{bmatrix}$

16. (b) 6, 9, 6
    Explanation :
    The number of elements in $m \times n$ matrix is equal to mn.

17. (d) 4 × 4
    Explanation :
    We know that if a matrix is of order $m \times n$, then it has mn elements. Thus, to find all possible orders of a matrix with 8 elements, we will find all ordered pairs of natural numbers, whose product is 8. Thus, all possible ordered pair are (1, 8), (2, 4), (4, 2).

18. (d) 512
    Explanation :
    Number of entries in 3 × 3 matrix is 9. Since, each entry has 2 choices, namely 2 or 0. Therefore, number of possible matrices = $\underbrace{2 \times 2 \times 2 \ldots \times 2}_{9 \text{ times}} = 2^9 = 512$

19. (c) unit matrix
    Explanation :
    If square matrix in which all diagonals elements are 1 and rest are 0, is called unit matrix.

20. (b) not possible to find
    Explanation :
    Consider, $\begin{bmatrix} 3x+7 & 5 \\ y+1 & 2-3x \end{bmatrix} = \begin{bmatrix} 0 & y-2 \\ 8 & 4 \end{bmatrix}$

    ⇒ $3x + 7 = 0; 5 = y - 2; y + 1 = 8; 2 - 3x = 4$

    ⇒ $x = \dfrac{-7}{3}, y = 7; y = 7; x = \dfrac{-2}{3}$

21. (d) B + D
    Explanation :
    Only B + D is defined because matrices of the same order can only be added.

22. (a) 20
    Explanation :
    We have,

    $\begin{bmatrix} 1 & 2 \\ -2 & -b \end{bmatrix} + \begin{bmatrix} a & 4 \\ 3 & 2 \end{bmatrix} = \begin{bmatrix} 5 & 6 \\ 1 & 0 \end{bmatrix}$

    ⇒ $\begin{bmatrix} a+1 & 6 \\ 1 & 2-b \end{bmatrix} = \begin{bmatrix} 5 & 6 \\ 1 & 0 \end{bmatrix}$

    ⇒ $a + 1 = 5, 2 - b = 0$

    ⇒ $a = 4, b = 2$

    ⇒ $a^2 + b^2 = 20$.

23. (c) – 6, – 4, – 9
    Explanation :

    $kA = \begin{bmatrix} 0 & 3a \\ 2b & 24 \end{bmatrix}$

    ⇒ $k\begin{bmatrix} 0 & 2 \\ 3 & -4 \end{bmatrix} = \begin{bmatrix} 0 & 3a \\ 2b & 24 \end{bmatrix}$

    $\begin{bmatrix} 0 & 2k \\ 3k & -4k \end{bmatrix} = \begin{bmatrix} 0 & 3a \\ 2b & 24 \end{bmatrix}$

    $-4k = 24$

    $k = -6$

    ⇒ $3a = 2 \times -6$

    ⇒ $3a = -12$

    ⇒ $a = -4$

    and $3k = 2b$

    $3 \times -6 = 2b$

    $b = -9$.

24. (a) $\begin{bmatrix} a^2+b^2 & 0 \\ 0 & a^2+b^2 \end{bmatrix}$

    Explanation :

    $\begin{bmatrix} a & b \\ -b & a \end{bmatrix}\begin{bmatrix} a & -b \\ b & a \end{bmatrix} = \begin{bmatrix} a^2+b^2 & -ab+ba \\ -ba+ab & b^2+a^2 \end{bmatrix}$

    $= \begin{bmatrix} a^2+b^2 & 0 \\ 0 & a^2+b^2 \end{bmatrix}$

25. (c) it is not necessary that one of the matrices is a zero matrix

    Explanation :

    Let $A = \begin{bmatrix} 0 & -1 \\ 0 & 2 \end{bmatrix}$ and $B = \begin{bmatrix} 3 & 5 \\ 0 & 0 \end{bmatrix}$. Then,

    $AB = O$ but A and B are non-zero.

26. (c) AB and BA both are defined

    Explanation :

    Let $A = [a_{ij}]_{2 \times 3}$ and $B = [b_{ij}]_{3 \times 2}$.

    Since, number of columns of A = number of rows of B

    ∴ AB is defined

    Also, as number of columns of B = number of rows of A.

    ∴ BA is defined.

    Hence, both AB and BA are defined.

27. (d) $\begin{bmatrix} p & q \\ q & p-q \end{bmatrix}$

    Explanation :

    Let $A = \begin{bmatrix} p & q \\ r & s \end{bmatrix}$ be a matrix which commute with

    matrix $B = \begin{bmatrix} 1 & 1 \\ 1 & 0 \end{bmatrix}$.

    Then, $AB = BA$

    $\Rightarrow \begin{bmatrix} p & q \\ r & s \end{bmatrix}\begin{bmatrix} 1 & 1 \\ 1 & 0 \end{bmatrix} = \begin{bmatrix} 1 & 1 \\ 1 & 0 \end{bmatrix}\begin{bmatrix} p & q \\ r & s \end{bmatrix}$

    $\Rightarrow \begin{bmatrix} p+q & p \\ r+s & r \end{bmatrix} = \begin{bmatrix} p+r & q+s \\ p & q \end{bmatrix}$

    Here, both matrices are equal, so we equate the corresponding elements.

    ∴ $p + q = p + r$, $p = q + s$, $r + s = p$ and $r = q$

    $\Rightarrow r = q$ and $s = p - q$

    ∴ $A = \begin{bmatrix} p & q \\ q & p-q \end{bmatrix}$

    Hence, the required set is $\begin{bmatrix} p & q \\ q & p-q \end{bmatrix}$.

28. (d) $m \times n$

    Explanation :

    Let $A = [a_{ij}]_{m \times n}$

    and $B = [b_{ij}]_{p \times q}$

    ∴ $B' = [b_{ji}]_{q \times p}$

    Now, AB' is defined, so $n = q$

    and BA is also defined, so $p = m$

    ∴ Order of B is $m \times n$.

29. (b) $\dfrac{1}{3}B$

    Explanation :

    $AB = 3I$

    $\Rightarrow \dfrac{1}{3}(AB) = I$

    $\Rightarrow A\left(\dfrac{1}{3}B\right) = I$

    $\Rightarrow A^{-1} = \dfrac{1}{3}B$

30. (d) $\dfrac{1}{2}I$

    Explanation :

    We have,

    $B = \begin{bmatrix} -\dfrac{1}{\pi}\cos^{-1} x\pi & \dfrac{1}{\pi}\tan^{-1}\dfrac{x}{\pi} \\ \dfrac{1}{\pi}\sin^{-1}\dfrac{x}{\pi} & -\dfrac{1}{\pi}\tan^{-1}\pi x \end{bmatrix}$ and

    $A = \begin{bmatrix} \dfrac{1}{\pi}\sin^{-1} x\pi & \dfrac{1}{\pi}\tan^{-1}\dfrac{x}{\pi} \\ \dfrac{1}{\pi}\sin^{-1}\dfrac{x}{\pi} & \dfrac{1}{\pi}\cot^{-1}\pi x \end{bmatrix}$

    ∴ $A - B$

    $= \begin{bmatrix} \dfrac{1}{\pi}(\sin^{-1} x\pi + \cos^{-1} x\pi) & 0 \\ 0 & \dfrac{1}{\pi}(\cot^{-1}\pi x + \tan^{-1}\pi x) \end{bmatrix}$

    $= \begin{bmatrix} \dfrac{1}{\pi}\cdot\dfrac{\pi}{2} & 0 \\ 0 & \dfrac{1}{\pi}\cdot\dfrac{\pi}{2} \end{bmatrix} = \dfrac{1}{2}\begin{bmatrix} 1 & 0 \\ 0 & 1 \end{bmatrix} = \dfrac{1}{2}I$

31. (d) $3 \times n$

    Explanation :

    $A_{3 \times m}$ and $B_{3 \times n}$ are two matrices. If $m = n$, then A and B have same orders as $3 \times n$ each, so the order of $(5A - 2B)$ should be same as $3 \times n$.

32. (d) $\begin{bmatrix} 1 & 0 \\ 0 & 1 \end{bmatrix}$

    Explanation :

    $A^2 = A \cdot A$

    $= \begin{bmatrix} 0 & 1 \\ 1 & 0 \end{bmatrix}\begin{bmatrix} 0 & 1 \\ 1 & 0 \end{bmatrix} = \begin{bmatrix} 1 & 0 \\ 0 & 1 \end{bmatrix}$

33. (a) I

    Explanation :

    We have, $A = [a_{ij}]_{2 \times 2}$,

    where $a_{ij} = \begin{cases} 1, & i \neq j \\ 0, & i = j \end{cases}$

    ∴ $A = \begin{bmatrix} 0 & 1 \\ 1 & 0 \end{bmatrix}$

    and $A^2 = \begin{bmatrix} 0 & 1 \\ 1 & 0 \end{bmatrix}\begin{bmatrix} 0 & 1 \\ 1 & 0 \end{bmatrix} = \begin{bmatrix} 1 & 0 \\ 0 & 1 \end{bmatrix} = I$

34. (b) symmetric matrix

Explanation :
We have
$$A = \begin{bmatrix} 1 & 2 & 4 \\ 2 & 5 & 6 \\ 4 & 6 & 7 \end{bmatrix}$$
$\therefore \quad A' = A$
So, the given matrix is a symmetric matrix.

35. (c) $m = n$
Explanation :
It is known that a given matrix is said to be a square matrix if the number of rows is equal to the number of columns.

36. (b) Both (A) and (R) are true but R is not correct explanation of A.
$\quad\quad$ adj (adj A) = $|A|^{n-2} A$
Here, $\quad n = 3$
$\therefore \quad$ (adj) (adj A) = $|A| A$ ...(i)
Now, $\quad |A| = \begin{vmatrix} 3 & -3 & 4 \\ 2 & -3 & 4 \\ 0 & -1 & 1 \end{vmatrix}$
$\quad\quad\quad = 3(-3 + 4) + 3(2) + 4(-2)$
$\quad\quad\quad = 1$
From equation (i),
$\quad\quad$ adj (adj) A = A

37. (b) Both (A) and (R) are true but R is not correct explanation of A.
$$A = \begin{pmatrix} a & 0 & 0 \\ 0 & b & 0 \\ 0 & 0 & c \end{pmatrix}$$
$\therefore \quad |A| = abc$
and $\quad$ adj A = $\begin{pmatrix} bc & 0 & 0 \\ 0 & ca & 0 \\ 0 & 0 & ab \end{pmatrix}$
$\therefore \quad A^{-1} = \dfrac{\text{adj A}}{|A|} = \begin{pmatrix} \frac{1}{a} & 0 & 0 \\ 0 & \frac{1}{b} & 0 \\ 0 & 0 & \frac{1}{c} \end{pmatrix}$

38. (c) A is true but R is false.
In a unit matrix of order $n \times n$,
Number of non-zero rows = n.
$\therefore$ Rank is n.
The rank of non-singular matrix of order $n \times n$ is n.
$\because$ For non-singular, $|A| \neq 0$.

39. (d) A is false but R is true.
$A = \begin{bmatrix} a & 0 & 0 & 0 \\ 0 & b & 0 & 0 \\ 0 & 0 & c & 0 \end{bmatrix}$ is not a diagonal matrix.
Since, A is not a square matrix.

40. (a) Both (A) and (R) are true and R is the correct explanation A.
Explanation :
$$|A| = \begin{vmatrix} 1 & 1 & 1 \\ 1 & 2 & 3 \\ 1 & 4 & 7 \end{vmatrix} = 0$$
$1(14 - 12) - 1(7 - 3) + 1(4 - 2)\; 2 - 4 + 2 = 0$
[$\because$ A is singular]
$\therefore$ A^{-1} does not exist.

41. (a) Both (A) and (R) are true and R is the correct explanation A.
Explanation :
If $\quad A = \begin{pmatrix} a_{11} & a_{12} & a_{13} & \cdots & a_{1n} \\ a_{21} & a_{22} & a_{23} & \cdots & a_{2n} \\ \vdots & \vdots & \vdots & & \vdots \\ a_{m1} & a_{m2} & a_{m3} & \cdots & a_{mn} \end{pmatrix}$
$\therefore \quad kA = \begin{pmatrix} k_{11} & k_{12} & k_{13} & \cdots & k_{1n} \\ k_{21} & k_{22} & k_{23} & \cdots & k_{2n} \\ \vdots & \vdots & \vdots & \vdots & \vdots \\ ka_{m1} & ka_{m2} & ka_{m3} & \cdots & ka_{mn} \end{pmatrix}$
$\therefore \quad |kA| = k^n |A|$

42. (b) Both (A) and (R) are true but R is not correct explanation of A.
Explanation :
$AA' = \dfrac{1}{3}\begin{pmatrix} 1 & -2 & 2 \\ -2 & 1 & 2 \\ -2 & -2 & -1 \end{pmatrix} \cdot \dfrac{1}{3}\begin{pmatrix} 1 & -2 & -2 \\ -2 & 1 & -2 \\ 2 & 2 & -1 \end{pmatrix}$
$= \dfrac{1}{9}\begin{pmatrix} 9 & 0 & 0 \\ 0 & 9 & 0 \\ 0 & 0 & 9 \end{pmatrix} = \begin{pmatrix} 1 & 0 & 0 \\ 0 & 1 & 0 \\ 0 & 0 & 1 \end{pmatrix} = I$
$\therefore$ A is orthogonal.
Also, if A and B are orthogonal, then AB is orthogonal.

43. (c) A is true but R is false.
Explanation :
$A = \begin{pmatrix} 0 & -c & b \\ c & 0 & a \\ -b & -a & 0 \end{pmatrix}$
$A = -A'$ [$\because$ A is skew-symmetric]
$\therefore \quad$ det (A) = det (− A')
$\quad\quad\quad\quad = -$ det (A')
$\quad\quad\quad\quad = -$ det A
$\therefore \quad$ det A = 0
$\because \quad$ det A' = det (− A') is not true.
$\therefore \quad$ det (− A') = (− 1)³ det (A') = − det A'.

44. (d) A is false but R is true.
Explanation :
$\because |A| = \begin{vmatrix} 3 & 4 \\ 3 & 5 \end{vmatrix} = 15 - 12 = 3 \neq 0$

∴ A is non-singular matrix.
∴ A^{-1} is exist.

45. (b) A is false but R is true.
    Explanation:
    Let $A = \begin{pmatrix} a & b \\ c & d \end{pmatrix}$, $B = \begin{pmatrix} x & y \\ z & u \end{pmatrix}$
    $\Rightarrow \quad AB = BA$
    $\Rightarrow \begin{pmatrix} ax+bz & ay+bu \\ cx+dz & cy+du \end{pmatrix} = \begin{pmatrix} ax+cy & bx+dy \\ az+cu & bz+du \end{pmatrix}$

    On comparing, then
    $$ax + bz = ax + cy$$
    $\Rightarrow \quad bz = cy$
    $\Rightarrow \quad \dfrac{z}{c} = \dfrac{y}{b} = \lambda$ (say)
    ∴ $\quad y = b\lambda, z = c\lambda$ ...(i)
    $ay + bu = bx + dy$
    $\Rightarrow \quad ab\lambda + bu = bx + bd\lambda$ [From (i)]
    $\Rightarrow \quad a\lambda + u = x + d\lambda = k$ (let)
    For $\lambda = 0, y = 0, z = 0, u = k, x = k$,
    Then, $B = \begin{pmatrix} k & 0 \\ 0 & k \end{pmatrix}$ = scalar matrix.

    Also, if $A = \begin{pmatrix} a & b \\ c & d \end{pmatrix}$ and $B = \begin{pmatrix} k & 0 \\ 0 & k \end{pmatrix}$,
    Then, $AB = BA = \begin{pmatrix} ak & bk \\ ck & dk \end{pmatrix} = kA$.

46. (a) Both (A) and (B) are true and R is the correct explanation A.
    $A = \begin{pmatrix} a_{11} & a_{12} & a_{13} & a_{14} & a_{15} \\ -a_{12} & a_{22} & a_{23} & a_{24} & a_{25} \\ -a_{13} & -a_{23} & a_{33} & a_{34} & a_{35} \\ -a_{14} & -a_{24} & -a_{34} & a_{44} & a_{45} \\ -a_{15} & -a_{25} & -a_{35} & -a_{45} & a_{55} \end{pmatrix}$

    $A^T = \begin{pmatrix} a_{11} & a_{12} & a_{13} & a_{14} & a_{15} \\ -a_{12} & a_{22} & a_{23} & a_{24} & a_{25} \\ -a_{13} & -a_{23} & a_{33} & a_{34} & a_{35} \\ -a_{14} & -a_{24} & -a_{34} & a_{44} & a_{45} \\ -a_{15} & -a_{25} & -a_{35} & -a_{45} & a_{55} \end{pmatrix} = -A$

    The determinant of skew-symmetric matrix of odd order is 0. Hence, both assertion and reason are correct and reason is the correct explanation for assertion.

47. (i) (c) $C = \begin{matrix} M_1 \\ M_2 \\ M_3 \end{matrix} \begin{bmatrix} 5 \\ 10 \\ 5 \end{bmatrix}$

    (ii) (a) $B = \begin{matrix} P_1 \\ P_2 \\ P_3 \end{matrix} \begin{bmatrix} 100 \\ 100 \\ 100 \end{bmatrix}$

    (iii) (d) The total requirement of each material is given by A'B.
    $A' = \begin{bmatrix} 2 & 4 & 2 \\ 3 & 2 & 4 \\ 1 & 5 & 2 \end{bmatrix}$
    $A'B = \begin{bmatrix} 2 & 4 & 2 \\ 3 & 2 & 4 \\ 1 & 5 & 2 \end{bmatrix} \begin{bmatrix} 100 \\ 100 \\ 100 \end{bmatrix} = \begin{bmatrix} 800 \\ 900 \\ 800 \end{bmatrix}$

    (iv) (a) The per unit cost production of each product is given by
    $AC = \begin{bmatrix} 2 & 3 & 1 \\ 4 & 2 & 5 \\ 2 & 4 & 2 \end{bmatrix} \begin{bmatrix} 5 \\ 10 \\ 5 \end{bmatrix} = \begin{bmatrix} 45 \\ 65 \\ 60 \end{bmatrix}$

    (v) (c) Total cost of production of 200 units
    $= [200 \; 200 \; 200] \begin{bmatrix} 45 \\ 65 \\ 60 \end{bmatrix}$
    $= 9{,}000 + 13{,}000 + 12{,}000$
    $= ₹ 34{,}000$.

48. (i) (b) Let x and y be the no. of seats in section A and section B respectively.
    ∴ $\quad x + y = 4000$

    (ii) (a) $50x + 40y = 1{,}80{,}000$
    $5x + 4y = 18{,}000$

    (iii) (a) Writing these equation in matrix form $AX = B$
    where $\begin{bmatrix} 1 & 1 \\ 5 & 4 \end{bmatrix} \begin{bmatrix} x \\ y \end{bmatrix} = \begin{bmatrix} 4000 \\ 18000 \end{bmatrix}$
    So, $A = \begin{bmatrix} 1 & 1 \\ 5 & 4 \end{bmatrix}, X = \begin{bmatrix} x \\ y \end{bmatrix}, B = \begin{bmatrix} 4000 \\ 18000 \end{bmatrix}$

    (iv) (b) $X = A^{-1}B$
    ∵ $A^{-1} = \dfrac{\text{adj } A}{|A|}$
    $|A| = \begin{bmatrix} 1 & 1 \\ 5 & 4 \end{bmatrix} = 4 - 5 = -1$
    ∴ adj $A = \begin{bmatrix} 4 & -1 \\ -5 & 1 \end{bmatrix}$
    So, $A^{-1} = \dfrac{1}{-1} \begin{bmatrix} 4 & -1 \\ -5 & 1 \end{bmatrix} = \begin{bmatrix} -4 & 1 \\ 5 & -1 \end{bmatrix}$.

    (v) (c) $X = -1 \begin{bmatrix} 4 & -1 \\ -5 & 1 \end{bmatrix} \begin{bmatrix} 4000 \\ 18000 \end{bmatrix}$
    $= \begin{bmatrix} -4 & 1 \\ 5 & -1 \end{bmatrix} \begin{bmatrix} 4000 \\ 18000 \end{bmatrix}$
    $= \begin{bmatrix} 16000 + 18000 \\ 20000 - 18000 \end{bmatrix} = \begin{bmatrix} 2000 \\ 2000 \end{bmatrix}$
    ∴ $x = 2000$ seats in Sec. A
    $y = 2000$ seats in Sec. B.

49. (i) (a) $Q = \begin{bmatrix} 20 & 15 & 35 \\ 10 & 20 & 30 \end{bmatrix}$

(ii) (a) $S = \begin{matrix} \text{LG} \\ \text{IP} \\ \text{Samsung} \end{matrix} \begin{bmatrix} 20{,}000 \\ 50{,}000 \\ 15{,}000 \end{bmatrix}$

(iii) (b) $C = \text{Total Cost} = \begin{matrix} \text{LG} \\ \text{IP} \\ \text{Samsung} \end{matrix} \begin{bmatrix} 15{,}000 \\ 40{,}000 \\ 12{,}000 \end{bmatrix}$

(iv) (c) $P = \text{Profit Matrix} = S - C$

$P = \begin{bmatrix} 20{,}000 \\ 50{,}000 \\ 15{,}000 \end{bmatrix} - \begin{bmatrix} 15{,}000 \\ 40{,}000 \\ 12{,}000 \end{bmatrix} = \begin{bmatrix} 5{,}000 \\ 10{,}000 \\ 3{,}000 \end{bmatrix}$

(v) (d) Total profit in each mall = QP

$= \begin{bmatrix} 20 & 15 & 35 \\ 10 & 20 & 30 \end{bmatrix} \begin{bmatrix} 5{,}000 \\ 10{,}000 \\ 3{,}000 \end{bmatrix}$

$= \begin{bmatrix} 1{,}00{,}000 + 1{,}50{,}000 + 1{,}05{,}000 \\ 50{,}000 + 2{,}00{,}000 + 90{,}000 \end{bmatrix}$

$= \begin{bmatrix} 3{,}55{,}000 \\ 3{,}40{,}000 \end{bmatrix}.$

50. (i) (a) x, y, z represents the amount of individual prize awarded then

$x + y + z = 6000$
$10x + 5y + 15z = 70{,}000$
$15x + 10y + 5z = 55000$

(ii) (c) From Ans. (i), we have

$\begin{bmatrix} 1 & 1 & 1 \\ 10 & 5 & 15 \\ 15 & 10 & 5 \end{bmatrix} \begin{bmatrix} x \\ y \\ z \end{bmatrix} = \begin{bmatrix} 6000 \\ 70000 \\ 55000 \end{bmatrix}$

$AX = B$

On comparing, we get

$A = \begin{bmatrix} 1 & 1 & 1 \\ 10 & 5 & 15 \\ 15 & 10 & 5 \end{bmatrix}$

$\therefore |A| = \begin{vmatrix} 1 & 1 & 1 \\ 10 & 5 & 15 \\ 15 & 10 & 5 \end{vmatrix}$

$= 1(25 - 150) - 1(50 - 225) + (100 - 75)$
$= 75$

(iii) (a) $\text{adj } A = \begin{bmatrix} -125 & 5 & 10 \\ 175 & -10 & -5 \\ 25 & 5 & -5 \end{bmatrix}$

(iv) (a) Since $|A| \neq 0$
So, A^{-1} exists.

$\therefore A^{-1} = \frac{1}{|A|} \text{Adj } A$

$A^{-1} = \frac{1}{75} \begin{bmatrix} -125 & 5 & 10 \\ 175 & -10 & -5 \\ 25 & 5 & -5 \end{bmatrix}$

(v) (b) $X = \frac{1}{75} \begin{bmatrix} -125 & 5 & 10 \\ 175 & -10 & -5 \\ 25 & 5 & -5 \end{bmatrix} \begin{bmatrix} 6000 \\ 70{,}000 \\ 55{,}000 \end{bmatrix}$

$= \frac{1}{75} \begin{bmatrix} 1{,}50{,}000 \\ 75{,}000 \\ 2{,}25{,}000 \end{bmatrix}$

$\begin{bmatrix} x \\ y \\ z \end{bmatrix} = \begin{bmatrix} 2000 \\ 1000 \\ 3000 \end{bmatrix}$

$\therefore x = ₹\ 2000, y = ₹\ 1000, z = ₹\ 3000.$

51. Let the cost of polythene bag, handmade bag and newspaper bag envelops be x, y and z respectively.

$20x + 30y + 40z = 250$

or $2x + 3y + 4z = 25$

Similarly

$3x + 4y + 2z = 27$
$4x + 2y + 32 = 20$

$A = \begin{bmatrix} 2 & 3 & 4 \\ 3 & 4 & 2 \\ 4 & 2 & 3 \end{bmatrix} \quad B = \begin{bmatrix} 25 \\ 27 \\ 20 \end{bmatrix} \quad X = \begin{bmatrix} x \\ y \\ z \end{bmatrix}$

$|A| = 2(18) - 3(1) + 4(-10)$
$= 16 - 3 - 40$
$= -27$

$\text{Adj } A = \begin{bmatrix} 8 & -1 & -10 \\ -1 & -10 & 8 \\ -10 & 8 & -1 \end{bmatrix}$

$A^{-1} = \frac{\text{Adj } A}{|A|}$

$= \frac{-1}{27} \begin{bmatrix} 8 & -1 & -10 \\ -1 & -10 & 8 \\ -10 & 8 & -1 \end{bmatrix}$

$X = A^{-1} B$

$= \frac{-1}{27} \begin{bmatrix} 8 & -1 & -10 \\ -1 & -10 & 8 \\ -10 & 8 & -1 \end{bmatrix} \begin{bmatrix} 25 \\ 27 \\ 20 \end{bmatrix}$

$= \frac{-1}{27} \begin{bmatrix} 200 - 27 - 200 \\ -25 - 270 + 160 \\ 250 + 216 - 20 \end{bmatrix} = \frac{-1}{27} \begin{bmatrix} -27 \\ -135 \\ -54 \end{bmatrix}$

$x = 1, y = 5$ and $z = 2$.

(i) (a) 1
(ii) (d) 5
(iii) (b) 2
(iv) (b) Shyam Lal
(v) (a) Ram Lal

Chapter 4

Determinants

1. If $\begin{vmatrix} 2 & 3 & 2 \\ x & x & x \\ 4 & 9 & 1 \end{vmatrix} + 3 = 0$, then the value of x is:

   [CBSE 2020]
   (a) 3   (b) 0
   (c) -1 (d) 1

2. Let $A = \begin{bmatrix} 200 & 50 \\ 10 & 2 \end{bmatrix}$ and $B = \begin{bmatrix} 50 & 40 \\ 2 & 3 \end{bmatrix}$, then $|AB|$ is equal to: [CBSE 2020]
   (a) 460   (b) 2000
   (c) 3000   (d) -7000

3. If $A = \begin{bmatrix} a & 0 & 0 \\ 0 & a & 0 \\ 0 & 0 & a \end{bmatrix}$, then det (adj A) equals:

   [CBSE 2020]
   (a) a^{27} (b) a^9
   (c) a^6 (d) a^2

4. If A is a square matrix of order 3, such that A (adj A) = 10 I, then |adj A| is equal to: [CBSE 2020]
   (a) 1   (b) 10
   (c) 100   (d) 101

5. If A is a 3×3 matrix such that $|A| = 8$, then $|3A|$ equals: [CBSE 2020]
   (a) 8   (b) 24
   (c) 72   (d) 216

6. If A is a skew symmetric matrix of order 3, then the value of $|A|$ is: [CBSE 2020]
   (a) 3   (b) 0
   (c) 9   (d) 27

7. If $\begin{vmatrix} x & 2 \\ 18 & x \end{vmatrix} = \begin{vmatrix} 6 & 2 \\ 18 & 6 \end{vmatrix}$, then the value of x is:
   (a) ± 2 (b) 0
   (c) ± 3 (d) ± 6

8. The determinant $\begin{vmatrix} x & \sin\theta & \cos\theta \\ -\sin\theta & -x & 1 \\ \cos\theta & 1 & x \end{vmatrix}$ is:
   (a) Independent of θ only
   (b) Independent of x only
   (c) Independent of both θ and x
   (d) None of the above

9. The area of triangle with vertices $(x_1, y_1), (x_2, y_2)$ and (x_3, y_3) is:
   (a) $\Delta = \dfrac{1}{2}\begin{vmatrix} x_1 & y_1 & 1 \\ x_2 & y_2 & 1 \\ x_3 & y_3 & 1 \end{vmatrix}$ (b) $\Delta = \dfrac{1}{2}\begin{vmatrix} x_1 & y_1 & 1 \\ y_1 & y_2 & 1 \\ x_3 & y_3 & 1 \end{vmatrix}$
   (c) $\Delta = \begin{vmatrix} x_1 & y_1 & 1 \\ x_2 & y_2 & 1 \\ x_3 & y_3 & 1 \end{vmatrix}$ (d) None of these

10. The area of the triangle formed by 3 collinear points is:
    (a) one   (b) two
    (c) zero   (d) four

11. Minor of an element of a determinant of order $n(n \geq 2)$ is a determinant of order:
    (a) n (b) $n-1$
    (c) $n-2$ (d) $n+1$

12. If $\Delta = \begin{vmatrix} 1 & a & bc \\ 1 & b & ca \\ 1 & c & ab \end{vmatrix}$, then the minor M_{31} is:
    (a) $-c(a^2 - b^2)$ (b) $c(b^2 - a^2)$
    (c) $c(a^2 + b^2)$ (d) $c(a^2 - b^2)$

13. If $\Delta = \begin{vmatrix} a & h & g \\ h & b & f \\ g & f & c \end{vmatrix}$, then the cofactor A_{21} is:
    (a) $-(hc + fg)$ (b) $fg - hc$
    (c) $fg + hc$ (d) $hc - fg$

14. If $M_{11} = -40$, $M_{12} = -10$ and $M_{13} = 35$ of the determinant $\Delta = \begin{vmatrix} 1 & 3 & -2 \\ 4 & -5 & 6 \\ 3 & 5 & 2 \end{vmatrix}$, then the value of Δ is:
    (a) -80 (b) 60   (c) 70   (d) 100

15. If $\Delta = \begin{vmatrix} a_{11} & a_{12} & a_{13} \\ a_{21} & a_{22} & a_{23} \\ a_{31} & a_{32} & a_{33} \end{vmatrix}$ and A_{ij} is cofactor of a_{ij}, then value of Δ is given by:
    (a) $a_{11}A_{31} + a_{12}A_{32} + a_{13}A_{33}$
    (b) $a_{11}A_{11} + a_{12}A_{21} + a_{13}A_{31}$
    (c) $a_{21}A_{11} + a_{22}A_{12} + a_{23}A_{13}$
    (d) $a_{11}A_{11} + a_{21}A_{21} + a_{31}A_{31}$

16. If $A = \begin{bmatrix} 2 & 3 \\ -4 & -6 \end{bmatrix}$, then which of the following is true?
    (a) $A(\text{adj } A) \neq |A|I$
    (b) $A(\text{adj } A) \neq (\text{Adj } A)A$
    (c) $A(\text{adj } A) = (\text{adj } A)A = |A|I = \begin{bmatrix} 0 & 0 \\ 0 & 0 \end{bmatrix}$
    (d) None of the above

17. If A and B are invertible matrices, then which of the following is not correct?
    (a) $\text{adj } A = |A| \cdot A^{-1}$
    (b) $\det(A)^{-1} = [\det(A)]^{-1}$
    (c) $(AB)^{-1} = B^{-1}A^{-1}$
    (d) $(A+B)^{-1} = B^{-1} + A^{-1}$

18. If $f(x) = \begin{vmatrix} 0 & x-a & x-b \\ x+a & 0 & x-c \\ x+b & x+c & 0 \end{vmatrix}$, then:

    [NCERT Exemplar]
    (a) $f(a) = 0$ (b) $f(b) = 0$
    (c) $f(0) = 0$ (d) $f(1) = 0$

19. If $A = \begin{bmatrix} 2 & \lambda & -3 \\ 0 & 2 & 5 \\ 1 & 1 & 3 \end{bmatrix}$, then A^{-1} exist if:

    [NCERT Exemplar]
    (a) $\lambda = 2$ (b) $\lambda \neq 2$
    (c) $\lambda = -2$ (d) None of these

20. Let A be a square matrix of order 3 × 3, then $|kA|$ is equal to:
    (a) $k|A|$ (b) $k^2|A|$
    (c) $k^3|A|$ (d) $3k|A|$

21. Which of the following is correct?
    (a) Determinant is a square matrix
    (b) Determinant is a number associated to a matrix
    (c) Determinant is a number associated to a square matrix
    (d) None of these

22. If area of a triangle is 35 sq. units with vertices (2, −6), (5, 4) and (k, 4), then k is:
    (a) 12 (b) −2
    (c) −12, 2 (d) 12, −2

23. If $A = \begin{bmatrix} -3 & 5 \\ 2 & 4 \end{bmatrix}$, then which of the following is true?
    (a) $A(\text{adj} \cdot A) = (A)I$
    (b) $A(\text{adj} \cdot A) \neq (\text{adj } A)A$
    (c) $A(\text{adj} \cdot A) = (\text{adj } A)A = |A|I = \begin{bmatrix} 0 & 0 \\ 0 & 0 \end{bmatrix}$
    (d) None of the above

24. If A is an invertible matrix of order 2, then $\det(A^{-1})$ is equal to:
    (a) $\det(A)$ (b) $\frac{1}{\det(A)}$
    (c) 1 (d) 0

25. Find the adjoint of the matrix $A = \begin{bmatrix} 1 & 2 \\ 3 & 4 \end{bmatrix}$:
    (a) $\begin{bmatrix} 4 & 2 \\ 3 & 1 \end{bmatrix}$ (b) $\begin{bmatrix} 4 & -2 \\ -3 & 1 \end{bmatrix}$
    (c) $\begin{bmatrix} 1 & 2 \\ 3 & 4 \end{bmatrix}$ (d) $\begin{bmatrix} 1 & -2 \\ -3 & 4 \end{bmatrix}$

26. Find x, if $\begin{bmatrix} 1 & 2 & x \\ 1 & 1 & 1 \\ 2 & 1 & -1 \end{bmatrix}$ is singular:
    (a) 1 (b) 2
    (c) 3 (d) 4

27. If $A = \begin{bmatrix} 0 & 1 & 1 \\ 1 & 0 & 1 \\ 1 & 1 & 0 \end{bmatrix}$, then $\frac{A^2 - 3I}{2} = $
    (a) A^{-1} (b) $2A$
    (c) $2A^{-1}$ (d) $\frac{3}{2}A^{-1}$

28. Value of $\begin{vmatrix} \cos 15° & \sin 15° \\ \sin 15° & \cos 15° \end{vmatrix}$ is:
    (a) 1 (b) $\frac{1}{2}$
    (c) $\frac{\sqrt{3}}{2}$ (d) None of these

29. The value of $\begin{vmatrix} a & b & c \\ b & c & a \\ c & a & b \end{vmatrix}$ is:
    (a) $abc(a+b+c)$ (b) $a^3 + b^3 + c^3 - 3abc$
    (c) $-a^3 - b^3 - c^3 + 3abc$ (d) None of these

30. Find the value of $\begin{vmatrix} a+ib & c+id \\ c+id & a-ib \end{vmatrix}$:
    (a) $a^2 + b^2 - c^2 - d^2$ (b) $a^2 - b^2 + c^2 - d^2$
    (c) $a^2 + b^2 + c^2 + d^2$ (d) None of these

31. If A is square matrix x, such that $A^2 = I$, then A^{-1} is equal to:
    (a) $2A$ (b) 0
    (c) A (d) $A + 1$

32. If $A(3, 4), B(-7, 2), C(x, y)$ are collinear, then:
    (a) $x + 5y + 17 = 0$ (b) $x + 5y + 13 = 0$
    (c) $x - 5y + 17 = 0$ (d) None of these

33. If the point A(3, –2), B(k, 2) and C(8, 8) are collinear, then the value of k is :
    (a) 2
    (b) –3
    (c) 5
    (d) –4

34. Find the minor of the element of second row and third column in the following determinant :
$$\begin{bmatrix} 2 & -3 & 5 \\ 6 & 0 & 4 \\ 1 & 5 & -7 \end{bmatrix}$$
    (a) 13
    (b) 4
    (c) 5
    (d) 0

Choose the correct option :
(a) Both (A) and (B) are true and R is the correct explanation A.
(b) Both (A) and (R) are true but R is not correct explanation of A.
(c) A is true but R is false.
(d) A is false but R is true.

35. **Assertion (A) :**
$$\begin{vmatrix} a^2+x^2 & ab-cx & ac+bx \\ ab+cx & b^2+x^2 & bc-ax \\ ac-bx & bc+ax & c^2+x^2 \end{vmatrix} = \begin{vmatrix} x & c & -b \\ -c & x & a \\ b & -a & x \end{vmatrix}^2$$

Reason (R) : $\Delta^c = \Delta^{n-1}$ where n is order of determinant, and Δ^c is the determinant of cofactors of Δ.

36. **Assertion (A) :**
$$\begin{vmatrix} \cos(\theta+\alpha) & \cos(\theta+\beta) & \cos(\theta+\gamma) \\ \sin(\theta+\alpha) & \sin(\theta+\beta) & \sin(\theta+\gamma) \\ \sin(\beta-\gamma) & \sin(\gamma-\alpha) & \sin(\alpha-\beta) \end{vmatrix}$$
is independent of θ.

Reason (R) : If $f(\theta) = c$, then $f(\theta)$ is independent of θ.

37. **Assertion (A) :** If $\Delta(x) = \begin{vmatrix} f_1(x) & f_2(x) \\ g_1(x) & g_2(x) \end{vmatrix}$,

then $\Delta'(x) \neq \begin{vmatrix} f_1'(x) & f_2'(x) \\ g_1'(x) & g_2'(x) \end{vmatrix}$

Reason (R) : $\frac{d}{dx}\{f(x) g(x)\} \neq \frac{d}{dx} f(x) \frac{d}{dx} g(x)$.

38. **Assertion (A) :** If $\Delta(x) = \begin{vmatrix} f(x) & g(x) \\ a & b \end{vmatrix}$, then

$$\int \Delta(x)\, dx = \begin{vmatrix} \int f(x)\, dx & \int g(x)\, dx \\ a & b \end{vmatrix}$$

Reason (R) : $\int \lambda f(x)\, dx = \lambda \int f(x)\, dx$

39. **Assertion :** If a, b, c are even natural numbers then
$$\Delta = \begin{vmatrix} a-1 & a & a+1 \\ b-1 & b & b+1 \\ c-1 & c & c+1 \end{vmatrix}$$ is an even natural number.

Reason : Sum and product of two even natural number is also an even natural number.

40. **Assertion :** The matrix $A = \begin{bmatrix} 2 & 3 & -1/2 \\ 7 & 3 & 2 \\ 3 & 1 & 1 \end{bmatrix}$ is singular.

Reason : The value of determinant of matrix A is zero.

41. **Assertion :** For a matrix $A = [a_{ij}]_3$, if det (adj A) = 49, then det (A) = ± 7.

Reason : For a square matrix A of order n. $|\text{adj } A| = |A|^{n-1}$.

42. **Assertion :** Value of x for which the matrix
$$\begin{bmatrix} 2 & 1 & 0 \\ 0 & 1 & 2 \\ 1 & -2 & x \end{bmatrix}$$ is singular is –5.

Reason : A matrix A is singular if $|A| \neq 0$.

43. **Assertion :** Minor of the element 6 in the matrix
$$\begin{bmatrix} 0 & 2 & 6 \\ 1 & 2 & -1 \\ 2 & 1 & 3 \end{bmatrix}$$ is 3.

Reason : Minor of an element a_{ij} of a matix is the determinant obtained by deleting it i^{th} row.

44. **Assertion :** For two matrices A & B of order 3, |A| = 3, |B| = – 4, then |2AB| is – 96.

Reason : For a matrix A of order n & a scalar k, $|kA| = k^n |A|$.

45. **Assertion :** For a matrix $A = A\,(\text{adj } A) = \begin{bmatrix} 5 & 0 \\ 0 & 5 \end{bmatrix}$.

Reason : For a square matrix A, A (adj A) = (adj A)A = |A|I.

46. **Assertion :** Values of k for which area of the triangle with vertices (1, 1), (0, 2), (k, 0) is 3 sq. units are 4 and 8.

Reason : Area of the triangle with vertices (x_1, y_1), (x_2, y_2), (x_3, y_3) is $\frac{1}{2} \begin{vmatrix} x_1 & y_1 & 1 \\ x_2 & y_2 & 1 \\ x_3 & y_3 & 1 \end{vmatrix}$.

47. Manjit wants to donate a rectangular plot of land for a school in his village. When he was asked to give dimensions of the plot, he told that if its length is decreased by 50 m and breadth is increased by 50 m, then its area will remain same but if length is decreased by 10 m and breadth is decreased by 20 m, then its area will decrease by 5300 m².

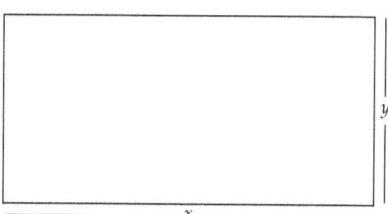

Based on the information given above, answer the following questions :

(i) The equations in terms of x and y are :
   (a) $x - y = 50, 2x - y = 550$
   (b) $x - y = 50, 2x + y = 550$
   (c) $x + y = 50, 2x + y = 550$
   (d) $x + y = 50, 2x + y = 550$

(ii) Which of the following matrix equation represents the given information :
   (a) $\begin{bmatrix} 1 & -1 \\ 2 & 1 \end{bmatrix} \begin{bmatrix} x \\ y \end{bmatrix} = \begin{bmatrix} 50 \\ 550 \end{bmatrix}$
   (b) $\begin{bmatrix} 1 & 1 \\ 2 & 1 \end{bmatrix} \begin{bmatrix} x \\ y \end{bmatrix} = \begin{bmatrix} 50 \\ 550 \end{bmatrix}$
   (c) $\begin{bmatrix} 1 & 1 \\ 2 & -1 \end{bmatrix} \begin{bmatrix} x \\ y \end{bmatrix} = \begin{bmatrix} 50 \\ 550 \end{bmatrix}$
   (d) $\begin{bmatrix} 1 & 1 \\ 2 & 1 \end{bmatrix} \begin{bmatrix} x \\ y \end{bmatrix} = \begin{bmatrix} -50 \\ -550 \end{bmatrix}$

(iii) The value of x (length of rectangular field) is :
   (a) 150 m   (b) 400 m
   (c) 200 m   (d) 320 m

(iv) The value of y (breadth of rectangular field) is :
   (a) 150 m   (b) 200 m
   (c) 430 m   (d) 350 m

(v) How much is the area of rectangular field ?
   (a) 60000 sq. m.   (b) 30000 sq. m.
   (c) 30000 m.   (d) 3000 m.

48. The sum of three numbers x, y, z is 6. If we multiply third number by 3 and add second number to it, we get 11. By adding first and third numbers, we get double fo the second number.

On the basis of above information, answer the following questions :

(i) If we represent the above information in matrix form, we can write it as :
   (a) $\begin{bmatrix} 1 & 1 & 1 \\ 0 & 1 & 3 \\ 1 & 2 & -1 \end{bmatrix} \begin{bmatrix} x \\ y \\ z \end{bmatrix} = \begin{bmatrix} 6 \\ 11 \\ 0 \end{bmatrix}$
   (b) $\begin{bmatrix} 1 & 1 & 1 \\ 0 & 1 & 3 \\ 1 & -2 & 1 \end{bmatrix} \begin{bmatrix} x \\ y \\ z \end{bmatrix} = \begin{bmatrix} 6 \\ 11 \\ 0 \end{bmatrix}$
   (c) $\begin{bmatrix} 1 & 1 & 1 \\ 0 & -1 & 3 \\ 1 & -2 & 1 \end{bmatrix} \begin{bmatrix} x \\ y \\ z \end{bmatrix} = \begin{bmatrix} 6 \\ 11 \\ 0 \end{bmatrix}$
   (d) $\begin{bmatrix} 1 & 1 & 1 \\ 0 & 1 & -3 \\ 1 & -2 & 1 \end{bmatrix} \begin{bmatrix} x \\ y \\ z \end{bmatrix} = \begin{bmatrix} 6 \\ 11 \\ 0 \end{bmatrix}$

(ii) In inverse of matrix $\begin{bmatrix} 1 & 1 & 1 \\ 0 & 1 & 3 \\ 1 & -2 & 1 \end{bmatrix}$ is :

   (a) $\dfrac{1}{9}\begin{bmatrix} 7 & -3 & 2 \\ 3 & 0 & -3 \\ -1 & 3 & 1 \end{bmatrix}$
   (b) $\dfrac{1}{9}\begin{bmatrix} 7 & 3 & -2 \\ 3 & 0 & 3 \\ 1 & 3 & -1 \end{bmatrix}$
   (c) $\dfrac{1}{9}\begin{bmatrix} 7 & -3 & 2 \\ 3 & 0 & -3 \\ 1 & -3 & 1 \end{bmatrix}$
   (d) $\dfrac{1}{9}\begin{bmatrix} 7 & -3 & 2 \\ -3 & 0 & 3 \\ 1 & 3 & -1 \end{bmatrix}$

(iii) The value of x is :
   (a) 1   (b) 2
   (c) 3   (d) 4

(iv) The value of y is :
   (a) 1   (b) 2
   (c) 3   (d) 4

(v) The value of z is :
   (a) 1   (b) 2
   (c) 3   (d) 4

49. A school wants to award their students for the values of honesty, regularity and hardwork with a total cash award of ₹ 6000. Three times the award money for hardwork added to that given for Honesty amounts to ₹ 11,000. The ward money given for honestry and hardwork together is double for regularity. The amount of award for honesty, regularity and hardwork be ₹ x, ₹ y, ₹ z respectively.

On the basis of above information, answer the following questions :

(i) If we represent the above situation in matric form as AX = X, then A =
   (a) $\begin{bmatrix} 6000 \\ 11000 \\ 0 \end{bmatrix}$
   (b) $\begin{bmatrix} 1 & 1 & 1 \\ 1 & 0 & 3 \\ 1 & -2 & 1 \end{bmatrix}$
   (c) $\begin{bmatrix} x \\ y \\ z \end{bmatrix}$
   (d) None of these

(ii) $\begin{bmatrix} 1 & 1 & 1 \\ 1 & 0 & 3 \\ 1 & -2 & 1 \end{bmatrix}^{-1} =$

   (a) $\dfrac{1}{6}\begin{bmatrix} 6 & -3 & 3 \\ 2 & 0 & -2 \\ -2 & 3 & -1 \end{bmatrix}$
   (b) $\dfrac{1}{6}\begin{bmatrix} 6 & 2 & -2 \\ -3 & 0 & 3 \\ 3 & -2 & -1 \end{bmatrix}$

(c) $\dfrac{1}{10}\begin{bmatrix} 6 & -3 & 3 \\ 2 & 0 & -2 \\ -2 & 3 & -1 \end{bmatrix}$

(d) $\dfrac{1}{10}\begin{bmatrix} 6 & 2 & -2 \\ -3 & 0 & 3 \\ 3 & -2 & 1 \end{bmatrix}$

(iii) The value of x is :

(a) 3500 (b) 2000
(c) 1000 (d) 500

(iv) The value of y is :
(a) 3500 (b) 2000
(c) 1000 (d) 500

(v) The value of z is :
(a) 3500 (b) 2000
(c) 1000 (d) 500

Solutions

1. (c) -1

   Explanation :

   Given : $\begin{vmatrix} 2 & 3 & 2 \\ x & x & x \\ 4 & 9 & 1 \end{vmatrix} + 3 = 0$

   $\Rightarrow 2(x - 9x) - 3(x - 4x) + 2(9x - 4x) + 3 = 0$
   $\Rightarrow -16x + 9x + 10x + 3 = 0$
   $\Rightarrow 3x = -3$
   $\Rightarrow x = -1$.

2. (d) -7000

   Explanation :
   $|AB| = |A||B| = (400 - 500)(150 - 80)$
   $= (-100)(70) = -7000$.

3. (c) a^6

   Explanation : $|A| = a^3$
   $\therefore\ |\text{adj } A| = |A|^2 = (a^3)^2 = a^6$.

4. (c) 100

   Explanation : Given : $A(\text{adj } A) = 10I$
   We know, $A \cdot \text{adj } A = |A| \cdot I$
   $\therefore\ |A| = 10$
   $\because\ |\text{adj } A| = |A|^{n-1}$
   $\therefore\ |\text{adj } A| = |A|^{3-1} = 10^2 = 100$.

5. (d) 216

   Explanation :
   Given : $|A| = 8$
   We know, $|kA| = k^3 |A|$, where k is constant
   $\therefore\ |3A| = 3^3 |A| = 27 \times 8 = 216$.

6. (b) 0

   Explanation : Since, A is a skew symmetric matrix.
   $\therefore\ A^T = -A$
   $\Rightarrow |A^T| = |-A|$
   $\Rightarrow |A| = |-1|^3 |A|$
   $\Rightarrow |A| = -|A|$
   $\Rightarrow 2|A| = 0$
   $\Rightarrow |A| = 0$.

7. (d) ± 6

   Explanation :
   $\because\ \begin{vmatrix} x & 2 \\ 18 & x \end{vmatrix} = \begin{vmatrix} 6 & 2 \\ 18 & 6 \end{vmatrix}$

   $\Rightarrow x^2 - 36 = 36 - 36$
   $\Rightarrow x^2 - 36 = 0 \Rightarrow x = \pm 6$

8. (a) Independent of θ only

   Explanation :

   Let $\Delta = \begin{vmatrix} x & \sin\theta & \cos\theta \\ -\sin\theta & -x & 1 \\ \cos\theta & 1 & x \end{vmatrix}$

   $= x(-x^2 - 1) - \sin\theta(-x\sin\theta - \cos\theta)$
   $\qquad\qquad + \cos\theta(-\sin\theta + x\cos\theta)$
   $= -x^3 - x + x\sin^2\theta + \sin\theta\cos\theta - \sin\theta\cos\theta$
   $\qquad\qquad + x\cos^2\theta$
   $= -x^3 - x + x(\sin^2\theta + \cos^2\theta) = -x^3 - x + x$
   $\qquad\qquad [\because \sin^2\theta + \cos^2\theta = 1]$
   $= -x^3$ which is independent of θ.

9. (a) By formula of area of triangle.

10. (c) Zero

    Explanation : The area of triangle formed by three collinear points is zero.

11. (b) $n - 1$

    Explanation : By definition of minor.

12. (d) $c(a^2 - b^2)$

    Explanation :

    $M_{31} = \begin{vmatrix} a & bc \\ b & ca \end{vmatrix} = ca^2 - b^2c = c(a^2 - b^2)$.

13. (b) $fg - hc$

    Explanation :

    $A_{21} = (-1)^{2+1} M_{21} = -M_{21} = -\begin{vmatrix} h & g \\ f & c \end{vmatrix}$

    $= -(hc - fg) = fg - hc$.

14. (a) -80

    Explanation :
    $\Delta = a_{11}A_{11} + a_{12}A_{12} + a_{13}A_{13}$
    $= a_{11}M_{11} - a_{12}M_{12} + a_{13}M_{13}$
    $= 1 \cdot (-40) - 3(-10) + (-2)(35)$
    $= -40 + 30 - 70 = -80$.

15. (d) $a_{11}A_{11} + a_{21}A_{21} + a_{31}A_{31}$

    Explanation :
    $\Delta =$ Sum of product of elements of any row (or column) with their correspoding cofactors.

16. (c) $A(\text{adj } A) = (\text{adj } A)A = |A|I = \begin{bmatrix} 0 & 0 \\ 0 & 0 \end{bmatrix}$

    Explanation : We know, if A is any square matrix of order n, then $A(\text{adj } A) = (\text{adj } A) \cdot A = |A| \cdot I$.

17. (d) $(A + B)^{-1} = B^{-1} + A^{-1}$

    Explanation : Since A and B are invertible matrices. So we can say that
    $$(AB)^{-1} = B^{-1}A^{-1} \quad \ldots(i)$$
    We know that,
    $$A^{-1} = \frac{1}{|A|} (\text{adj } A)$$
    $\Rightarrow \quad \text{adj } A = |A| \cdot A^{-1}$
    Also, $\det (A)^{-1} = [\det (A)]^{-1}$
    $\Rightarrow \quad \det (A)^{-1} = \frac{1}{[\det (A)]}$
    $\Rightarrow \quad \det (A) \cdot \det (A)^{-1} = 1$
    which is true.

18. (c) $f(0) = 0$

    Explanation :
    $$f(x) = \begin{vmatrix} 0 & x-a & x-b \\ x+a & 0 & x-c \\ x+b & x+c & 0 \end{vmatrix}$$
    $$\Rightarrow \quad f(0) = \begin{vmatrix} 0 & -a & -b \\ a & 0 & -c \\ b & c & 0 \end{vmatrix},$$
    which is skew-symmetric determinant of order 3
    Hence $f(0) = 0$.

19. (d) None of these

    Explanation : We have,
    $$A = \begin{bmatrix} 2 & \lambda & -3 \\ 0 & 2 & 5 \\ 1 & 1 & 3 \end{bmatrix}$$
    A^{-1} exists if $|A| \neq 0$
    Now $|A| = 2(6-5) - \lambda(-5) - 3(-2)$
    $= 8 + 5\lambda$
    But $|A| \neq 0$
    $5\lambda + 8 \neq 0 \Rightarrow 5\lambda \neq -8$
    $\Rightarrow \quad \lambda \neq \frac{-8}{5}$
    So, A^{-1} exists if and only if $\neq \frac{-8}{5}$.

20. (c) $k^3|A|$

    Explanation : We know that for $n \times n$ matrix.
    $|(\lambda A)| = \lambda^n (A)$
    Hence, $|kA| = k^3 |A|$.

21. (c) Determinant is a number associated to a square matrix

    Explanation : We know that to every square matrix, $A = [a_{ij}]$ of order n. We can associate a number called the determinant square matrix A, where $a_{ij} = (i, j)^{\text{th}}$ element of A. Thus, the determinant is a number associated to a square matrix.

22. (d) $12, -2$

    Explanation : Area of triangle
    $$\frac{1}{2} \begin{vmatrix} 2 & -6 & 1 \\ 5 & 4 & 1 \\ k & 4 & 1 \end{vmatrix} = \pm 35$$
    $\Rightarrow 2(4-4) + 6(5-k) + 1(120 - 4k) = \pm 70$
    $\Rightarrow \quad 30 - 6k + 20 - 4k = \pm 70$
    $\Rightarrow \quad 50 - 10k = \pm 70$
    $\Rightarrow \quad 5 - k = \pm 7$
    then $5 - k = 7$ and $5 - k = -7$
    $k = -2$
    and $k = 12$.

23. (c) $A (\text{adj} \cdot A) = (A)I$

    Explanation :
    $$A = \begin{bmatrix} -3 & 5 \\ 2 & 4 \end{bmatrix},$$
    $$\text{adj } A = \begin{bmatrix} 4 & -5 \\ -2 & -3 \end{bmatrix}$$
    $$A (\text{adj } A) = \begin{bmatrix} -3 & 5 \\ 2 & 4 \end{bmatrix} \begin{bmatrix} 4 & -5 \\ -2 & -3 \end{bmatrix}$$
    $$= \begin{bmatrix} -12 - 10 & +15 - 15 \\ 8 - 8 & -10 - 12 \end{bmatrix}$$
    $$= \begin{bmatrix} -22 & 0 \\ 0 & -22 \end{bmatrix}$$
    $$= -22 \begin{bmatrix} 1 & 0 \\ 0 & 1 \end{bmatrix}$$
    $\because \quad |A| = -22$
    so $A (\text{adj} \cdot A) = (A)I$.

24. (b) $\frac{1}{\det (A)}$

    Explanation : We know
    $AA^{-1} = I$
    $\therefore \quad |AA^{-1}| = |I|$
    $\Rightarrow \quad |A||A^{-1}| = 1$
    $\Rightarrow \quad |A^{-1}| = \frac{1}{|A|}$

25. (b) $\begin{bmatrix} 4 & -2 \\ -3 & 1 \end{bmatrix}$

    Explanation : Here,
    $$\text{matrix} = \begin{bmatrix} 1 & 2 \\ 3 & 4 \end{bmatrix}$$
    $A_{11} = (-1)^{1+1} (4) = 4$
    $A_{12} = (-1)^{1+2} (3) = -3$

$A_{21} = (-1)^{2+1} (2) = -2$
$A_{22} = (-1)^{2+2} (1) = 1$

adj. A $= \begin{bmatrix} 4 & -3 \\ -2 & 1 \end{bmatrix}^T$

$= \begin{bmatrix} 4 & -2 \\ -3 & 1 \end{bmatrix}$

26. (d) 4

Explanation : If matrix A is singular, then
$$|A| = 0$$
$$\begin{vmatrix} 1 & 2 & x \\ 1 & 1 & 1 \\ 2 & 1 & -1 \end{vmatrix} = 0$$
$\Rightarrow 1(-1-1) - 2(-1-2) + x(1-2) = 0$
$\Rightarrow \quad -2 + 6 + x - 2x = 0$
$\Rightarrow \quad -x = -4$
$\Rightarrow \quad x = 4.$

27. (a) A^{-1}

Explanation :

$A^2 = \begin{bmatrix} 0 & 1 & 1 \\ 1 & 0 & 1 \\ 1 & 1 & 0 \end{bmatrix} \begin{bmatrix} 0 & 1 & 1 \\ 1 & 0 & 1 \\ 1 & 1 & 0 \end{bmatrix}$

$= \begin{bmatrix} 2 & 1 & 1 \\ 1 & 2 & 1 \\ 1 & 1 & 2 \end{bmatrix}$

$\therefore \frac{1}{2}[A^2 - 3I] = \frac{1}{2}\left\{\begin{bmatrix} 2 & 1 & 1 \\ 1 & 2 & 1 \\ 1 & 1 & 2 \end{bmatrix} - \begin{bmatrix} 3 & 0 & 0 \\ 0 & 3 & 0 \\ 0 & 0 & 3 \end{bmatrix}\right\}$

$= \frac{1}{2}\begin{bmatrix} -1 & 1 & 1 \\ 1 & -1 & 1 \\ 1 & 1 & -1 \end{bmatrix} \quad \ldots(i)$

For A^{-1}
$a_{11} = (-1)^2 (-1) = -1$
$a_{12} = (-1)^3 (-1) = 1$
$a_{13} = (-1)^4 (1) = 1$
$a_{21} = (-1)^3 (-1) = 1$
$a_{22} = (-1)^4 (-1) = -1$
$a_{23} = (-1)^5 (-1) = 1$
$a_{31} = (-1)^4 (1) = 1$
$a_{32} = (-1)^5 (-1) = 1$
$a_{33} = (-1)^5 (-1) = -1$

$\therefore A^{-1} = \begin{bmatrix} -1 & 1 & 1 \\ 1 & -1 & 1 \\ 1 & 1 & -1 \end{bmatrix}'$

$= \begin{bmatrix} -1 & 1 & 1 \\ 1 & -1 & 1 \\ 1 & 1 & -1 \end{bmatrix} \quad \ldots(ii)$

From (i) and (ii),
$$\frac{1}{2}[A^2 - 3I] = A^{-1}.$$

28. (c) $\frac{\sqrt{3}}{2}$

Explanation :
$\Delta = \begin{vmatrix} \cos 15° & \sin 15° \\ \sin 15° & \cos 15° \end{vmatrix}$

$= \cos^2 15° - \sin^2 15°$
$= \cos 2 \times 15° = \cos 30°$
$= \frac{\sqrt{3}}{2}.$

29. (c) $-a^3 - b^3 - c^3 + 3abc$

Explanation :
$\Delta = \begin{vmatrix} a & b & c \\ b & c & a \\ c & a & b \end{vmatrix}$

$= a(bc - a^2) - b(b^2 - ac) + c(ab - c^2)$
$= abc - a^3 - b^3 + abc + abc - c^3$
$= -a^3 - b^3 - c^3 + 3abc.$

30. (c) $a^2 + b^2 + c^2 + d^2$

Explanation :
$\Delta = \begin{vmatrix} a+ib & c+id \\ c+id & a-ib \end{vmatrix}$

$= (a+ib)(a-ib) - (c+id)(-c+id)$
$= (a^2 - i^2b^2) - (-c^2 + i^2d^2)$
$= a^2 + b^2 + c^2 - i^2d^2$
$= a^2 + b^2 + c^2 + d^2.$

31. (c) A

Explanation : Since,
$$A^2 = I$$
then $\quad A \cdot A = I$
or $\quad A^{-1}(A \cdot A) = A^{-1}I$
$\Rightarrow \quad (A^{-1}A)A = A^{-1}$
$\Rightarrow \quad IA = A^{-1}$
$\Rightarrow \quad A^{-1} = A.$

32. (c) $x - 5y + 17 = 0$

Explanation : If A, B and C are collinear, then area of triangle formed is zero.

$\therefore \quad \frac{1}{2}\begin{vmatrix} 3 & 4 & 1 \\ -7 & 2 & 1 \\ x & y & 1 \end{vmatrix} = 0$

$\Rightarrow 3(2 - y) - 4(-7 - x) + 1(-7y - 2x) = 0$
$\Rightarrow 6 - 3y + 28 + 4x - 7y - 2x = 0$
$\Rightarrow \quad 2x - 10y + 34 = 0$
$\Rightarrow \quad x - 5y + 17 = 0.$

33. (c) 5

Explanation : Since the points A(3, -2), B(k, 2) and C(8, 8) are collinear.

Then, area of triangle formed is 0.

$$\frac{1}{2}\begin{vmatrix} 3 & -2 & 1 \\ k & 2 & 1 \\ 8 & 8 & 1 \end{vmatrix} = 0$$

∴
$$\Rightarrow 3(2-8) + 2(k-8) + 1(8k-16) = 0$$
$$\Rightarrow -18 + 2k - 16 + 8k - 16 = 0$$
$$\Rightarrow 10k - 50 = 0$$
$$\Rightarrow k = 5.$$

34. (c) 13

Explanation :
$$M_{23} = [10-(-3)]$$
$$= 10 + 3 = 13.$$

35. (a) Assertion and reason is correct and R is the correct explanation A.

Explanation :
$$\Delta = \begin{vmatrix} a^2+x^2 & ab-cx & ac+bx \\ ab+cx & b^2+x^2 & bc-ax \\ ac-bx & bc+ax & c^2+x^2 \end{vmatrix}$$

∴
$$\Delta^c = \begin{vmatrix} a^2+x^2 & cx+ab & ac-bx \\ ab-cx & b^2+x^2 & ax+bc \\ ac+bx & bc-ax & c^2+x^2 \end{vmatrix}^T$$

$$= \begin{vmatrix} a^2+x^2 & ab-cx & ac+bx \\ cx+ab & b^2+x^2 & bc-ax \\ ac-bx & ax+bc & c^2+x^2 \end{vmatrix} = \Delta^2$$

$$= \begin{vmatrix} x & c & -b \\ -c & x & a \\ b & -a & x \end{vmatrix}^2$$

36. (a) Both (A) and (R) are true and R is the correct explanation A.

Explanation :
$$\text{Let } f(\theta) = \begin{vmatrix} \cos(\theta+\alpha) & \cos(\theta+\beta) & \cos(\theta+\gamma) \\ \sin(\theta+\alpha) & \sin(\theta+\beta) & \sin(\theta+\gamma) \\ \sin(\beta-\gamma) & \sin(\gamma-\alpha) & \sin(\alpha-\beta) \end{vmatrix}$$

$$\therefore f'(\theta) = \begin{vmatrix} -\sin(\theta+\alpha) & -\sin(\theta+\beta) & -\sin(\theta+\gamma) \\ \sin(\theta+\alpha) & \sin(\theta+\beta) & \sin(\theta+\gamma) \\ \sin(\beta-\gamma) & \sin(\gamma-\alpha) & \sin(\alpha-\beta) \end{vmatrix}$$

$$+ \begin{vmatrix} \cos(\theta+\alpha) & \cos(\theta+\beta) & \cos(\theta+\gamma) \\ \cos(\theta+\alpha) & \cos(\theta+\beta) & \cos(\theta+\gamma) \\ \sin(\beta-\gamma) & \sin(\gamma-\alpha) & \sin(\alpha-\beta) \end{vmatrix}$$

$$+ \begin{vmatrix} \cos(\theta+\alpha) & \cos(\theta+\beta) & \cos(\theta+\gamma) \\ \sin(\theta+\alpha) & \sin(\theta+\beta) & \sin(\theta+\gamma) \\ 0 & 0 & 0 \end{vmatrix}$$

$$= 0 + 0 + 0 = 0$$
$$f'(\theta) = 0 \Rightarrow f(\theta) = c$$

37. (a) Assertion and reason is correct and reason is corect explanation A.

Explanation :
$$\because \frac{d}{dx} f(x) g(x) = f(x) \frac{d}{dx} g(x) + g(x) \frac{d}{dx} f(x)$$

$$\Rightarrow \frac{d}{dx} f(x) g(x) \neq \frac{d}{dx} f(x) \frac{d}{dx} g(x)$$

$$\Rightarrow \Delta(x) = \begin{vmatrix} f_1(x) & f_2(x) \\ g_1(x) & g_2(x) \end{vmatrix}$$

$$= f_1(x) g_2(x) - f_2(x) g_1(x)$$

$$\therefore \frac{d}{dx} \{\Delta(x)\} = \{f_1(x) g_2'(x) + g_2'(x) f_1(x)\}$$

$$- \{f_2(x) g_1'(x) + g_1(x) f_2'(x)\}$$

$$\Delta'(x) = \begin{vmatrix} f_1'(x) & f_2'(x) \\ g_1(x) & g_2(x) \end{vmatrix} + \begin{vmatrix} f_1(x) & f_2(x) \\ g_1'(x) & g_2'(x) \end{vmatrix}$$

$$\neq \begin{vmatrix} f'(x) & f_2'(x) \\ g_1'(x) & g_2'(x) \end{vmatrix}$$

38. (a) Assertion and reason is correct and reason is correct explanation A.

Explanation :
$$\because \quad \Delta x = \begin{vmatrix} f(x) & g(x) \\ a & b \end{vmatrix}$$

$$= bf(x) - ag(x)$$

$$\therefore \int \Delta(x) \, dx = \int \{bf(x) - ag(x)\} \, dx$$

$$= b \int f(x) \, dx - a \int g(x) \, dx$$

$$= \begin{vmatrix} \int f(x) \, dx & \int g(x) \, dx \\ a & b \end{vmatrix}$$

39. (d) A is incorrect, R is correct.

Explanation :
$$\Delta = \begin{vmatrix} a-1 & a & a+1 \\ b-1 & b & b+1 \\ c-1 & c & c+1 \end{vmatrix}$$

$C_1 \to C_1 + C_3$

$$\Delta = \begin{vmatrix} 2a & a & a+1 \\ ab & b & b+1 \\ 2c & c & c+1 \end{vmatrix}$$

$$= 2\begin{vmatrix} a & a & a+1 \\ b & b & b+1 \\ c & c & c+1 \end{vmatrix}$$

$$= 0$$

∵ 0 is not even natural number.
So A is incorrect.
So A is false but R is true.

40. (a) A is correct, R is correct, R is correct explanation of A.

Explanation :
Here, matrix

$$A = \begin{vmatrix} 2 & 3 & -1/2 \\ 7 & 3 & 2 \\ 3 & 1 & 1 \end{vmatrix}$$

$|A| = 2(3-2) - 3(7-6) - \dfrac{1}{2}(7-9)$

$ = 2 - 3 + 1$

$ = 0.$

41. (a) Both A & R true & R is correct explanation of A.

    Explanation:
    As $(adj\ A) = 49$
    then $|adj\ A| = |A|^{3-1}$
    (As order of matrix is 3)
    $49 = |A|^2$
    $\Rightarrow |A| = 7.$

42. (c) A is true, R is false.

    Explanation:
    A matrix is singular, if $|A| = 0$.

    Now for matrix $\begin{bmatrix} 2 & 1 & 0 \\ 0 & 1 & 2 \\ 1 & -2 & x \end{bmatrix}$

    $|A| = 0$
    $\therefore 2(x+4) - 1(0-2) + 0 = 0$
    $\Rightarrow 2x + 8 + 2 + 0 = 0$
    $\Rightarrow x = -5.$

43. (c) Both A & R is false.

    Explanation:
    Minor of element 6 is
    $H_{13} = (1-4)$
    $\phantom{H_{13}} = -3.$

44. (b) Both A & R is true, but R is not correct explanation of A.

    Explanation:
    $|2AB| = 2^3 |A| |B|$
    $ = 8 \times 3 \times -4$
    $ = -96.$

45. (a) Both A & R true, R is correct explanation of A.

    Explanation:
    $A\ (adj\ A) = \begin{bmatrix} 5 & 0 \\ 0 & 5 \end{bmatrix}$

    $= 5^2 \begin{bmatrix} 1 & 0 \\ 0 & 1 \end{bmatrix}$

    $= 25I$

    Here $|A| = \begin{vmatrix} 5 & 0 \\ 0 & 5 \end{vmatrix} = 25$

    $A\ (adj\ A) = |A| I.$

46. (d) A is false, R is true.

    Explanation:
    Area of triangle with vetices (1, 1), (0, 2), (k, 0) is 3 units.

$\dfrac{1}{2} \begin{vmatrix} 1 & 1 & 1 \\ 0 & 2 & 1 \\ k & 0 & 1 \end{vmatrix} = 3$

$\Rightarrow 1(2-0) - 1(0-k) + 1(0-2k) = 6$
$\Rightarrow 2 + k - 2k = 1$
$\Rightarrow -k = 6 - 2$
$\Rightarrow k = -1$

$\therefore$ Value of k is -4.

47. (i) (b) Let, length = x m, breadth = y m
    then, area = $xy = A_1$
    If length is decreased by 50 m and breadth is increased by 50 m then
    new area = $(x-50)(y+50) = A_2$
    Given that
    $A_1 = A_2$
    $xy = (x-50)(y+50)$
    $ = xy - 50x - 50y + 2500$
    $50x - 50y = 2500$
    $x - y = 50$ ...(i)
    Now, if length is decreased by 10 m and breadth is decreased by 20 then
    Area = $(x-10)(y-20)$
    $ = xy - 20x - 10y + 200 + 5300$
    $ = xy - 20x - 10y + 5500 = A_3$
    Given $A_1 = A_3$
    $xy = xy - 20x - 10y + 5500$
    $20x + 10y = 5500$
    $2x + y = 550$ ...(ii)
    Hence correct option is (b).

(ii) (a) Matrix equation
    $\begin{bmatrix} 1 & -1 \\ 2 & 1 \end{bmatrix} \begin{bmatrix} x \\ y \end{bmatrix} = \begin{bmatrix} 50 \\ 550 \end{bmatrix}$

(iii) (c) $A = \begin{bmatrix} 1 & -1 \\ 2 & 1 \end{bmatrix}$

$|A| = 1 + 2 = 3$

Adj. $A = \begin{bmatrix} 1 & +1 \\ -2 & 1 \end{bmatrix}$

$A^{-1} = \dfrac{1}{3} \begin{bmatrix} 1 & 1 \\ -2 & 1 \end{bmatrix}$

$X = A^{-1} B$

$= \dfrac{1}{3} \begin{bmatrix} 1 & 1 \\ -2 & 1 \end{bmatrix} \begin{bmatrix} 50 \\ 550 \end{bmatrix}$

$\begin{bmatrix} x \\ y \end{bmatrix} = \dfrac{1}{3} \begin{bmatrix} 50 + 550 \\ -100 + 550 \end{bmatrix}$

$= \dfrac{1}{3} \begin{bmatrix} 600 \\ 450 \end{bmatrix}$

$$= \begin{bmatrix} 200 \\ 150 \end{bmatrix}$$

$x = 200, y = 150$

Length of rectangle = 200 m.

(iv) (a) Length of breadth = 150.

(v) (b) Area of rectangle = $xy = 200 \times 150$
= 30,000 sq. m.

48. (i) (b) According to the question, we get
$x + y + z = 6, y + 3z = 11$
and $x + z = 2y \Rightarrow x - 2y + z = 0$

In matrix form, this system of equations can be written as
$$AX = B \qquad ...(i)$$
where, $A = \begin{bmatrix} 1 & 1 & 1 \\ 0 & 1 & 3 \\ 1 & -2 & 1 \end{bmatrix}, X = \begin{bmatrix} x \\ y \\ z \end{bmatrix}$ and B

$$= \begin{bmatrix} 6 \\ 11 \\ 0 \end{bmatrix}$$

(ii) (a) Here, $|A| = \begin{vmatrix} 1 & 1 & 1 \\ 0 & 1 & 3 \\ 1 & -2 & 1 \end{vmatrix}$

$= 1(1 + 6) - 1(0 - 3) + 1(0 - 1)$
[expanding along R_1]
$= 7 + 3 - 1 = 9 \neq 0$

Since, $|A| \neq 0$, so the inverse of A exists.

Now, cofactors corresponding to each element of $|A|$ are

$C_{11} = (-1)^{1+1} \begin{vmatrix} 1 & 3 \\ -2 & 1 \end{vmatrix} = 1 + 6 = 7$

$C_{12} = (-1)^{1+2} \begin{vmatrix} 0 & 3 \\ 1 & 1 \end{vmatrix} = -(0 - 3) = 3$

$C_{13} = (-1)^{1+3} \begin{vmatrix} 0 & 1 \\ 1 & -2 \end{vmatrix} = 0 - 1 = -1$

$C_{21} = (-1)^{2+1} \begin{vmatrix} 1 & 1 \\ -2 & 1 \end{vmatrix} = -(1 + 2) = -3$

$C_{22} = (-1)^{2+2} \begin{vmatrix} 1 & 1 \\ 1 & 1 \end{vmatrix} = 0$

$C_{23} = (-1)^{2+3} \begin{vmatrix} 1 & 1 \\ 1 & -2 \end{vmatrix} = -(-2 - 3) = 3$

$C_{31} = (-1)^{3+1} \begin{vmatrix} 1 & 1 \\ 1 & 3 \end{vmatrix} = 3 - 1 = 2$

$C_{32} = (-1)^{3+2} \begin{vmatrix} 1 & 1 \\ 0 & 3 \end{vmatrix} = -(3 - 0) = -3$

$C_{33} = (-1)^{3+3} \begin{vmatrix} 1 & 1 \\ 0 & 1 \end{vmatrix} = 1 - 0 = 1$

Then, adj (A) $= \begin{bmatrix} 7 & 3 & -1 \\ -3 & 0 & 3 \\ 2 & -3 & 1 \end{bmatrix}^T$

$= \begin{bmatrix} 7 & -3 & 2 \\ 3 & 0 & -3 \\ -1 & 3 & 1 \end{bmatrix}$

Thus, $A^{-1} = \dfrac{1}{|A|}$ adj(A)

$= \dfrac{1}{9} \begin{bmatrix} 7 & -3 & 2 \\ 3 & 0 & -3 \\ -1 & 3 & 1 \end{bmatrix}$

(iii) (a) 1

Now, the solution of Eq. (i) in Q. (i) is given by
$$X = A^{-1}B \qquad ...(ii)$$

On putting the values of A^{-1} and B in R.H.S. Eq. (ii), we get

$X = \dfrac{1}{9} \begin{bmatrix} 7 & -3 & 2 \\ 3 & 0 & -3 \\ -1 & 3 & 1 \end{bmatrix} \begin{bmatrix} 6 \\ 11 \\ 0 \end{bmatrix}$

$= \dfrac{1}{9} \begin{bmatrix} 7 \times 6 - 3 \times 11 + 2 \times 0 \\ 3 \times 6 + 0 \times 11 - 3 \times 0 \\ -1 \times 6 + 3 \times 11 + 1 \times 0 \end{bmatrix}$

$= \dfrac{1}{9} \begin{bmatrix} 42 - 33 + 0 \\ 18 + 0 - 0 \\ -6 + 33 + 0 \end{bmatrix} = \dfrac{1}{9} \begin{bmatrix} 9 \\ 18 \\ 27 \end{bmatrix} = \begin{bmatrix} 9/9 \\ 18/9 \\ 27/9 \end{bmatrix} = \begin{bmatrix} 1 \\ 2 \\ 3 \end{bmatrix}$

$\Rightarrow \begin{bmatrix} x \\ y \\ z \end{bmatrix} = \begin{bmatrix} 1 \\ 2 \\ 3 \end{bmatrix}$

On comparing both sides, we get
$x = 1, y = 2$ and $z = 3$
which are the required numbers.

(iv) (b) $y = 2$

(v) (c) $z = 3$

49. (i) (b) According to the question, we have
$x + y + z = 6000,$ ...(i)
$x + 0y + 3z = 111000$ ...(ii)
and $x + z = 2y \Rightarrow x - 2y + z = 0$ ...(iii)

Let $A = \begin{bmatrix} 1 & 1 & 1 \\ 1 & 0 & 3 \\ 1 & -2 & 1 \end{bmatrix}, X = \begin{bmatrix} x \\ y \\ z \end{bmatrix}$

and $B = \begin{bmatrix} 6000 \\ 11000 \\ 0 \end{bmatrix}$

Then, the matrix equation is AX = B.

(ii) (a) Now, $A = \begin{vmatrix} 1 & 1 & 1 \\ 1 & 0 & 3 \\ 1 & -2 & 1 \end{vmatrix}$

$$= 1(0+6) - 1(1-3) + 1(-2)$$
$$= 6 + 2 - 2 = 6 \neq 0$$

∴ A^{-1} exists.

Now, the cofactors of the elements of $|A|$ are given by

$C_{11} = \begin{vmatrix} 0 & 3 \\ -2 & 1 \end{vmatrix} = 6, C_{12} = -\begin{vmatrix} 1 & 3 \\ 1 & 1 \end{vmatrix} = 2,$

$C_{13} = \begin{vmatrix} 1 & 0 \\ 1 & -2 \end{vmatrix} = -2;$

$C_{21} = -\begin{vmatrix} 1 & 1 \\ -2 & 1 \end{vmatrix} = -3, C_{22} = \begin{vmatrix} 1 & 1 \\ 1 & 1 \end{vmatrix} = 0,$

$C_{23} = -\begin{vmatrix} 1 & 1 \\ 1 & -2 \end{vmatrix} = 3;$

$C_{31} = \begin{vmatrix} 1 & 1 \\ 0 & 3 \end{vmatrix} = 3, C_{32} = -\begin{vmatrix} 1 & 1 \\ 1 & 3 \end{vmatrix} = -2,$

$C_{33} = \begin{vmatrix} 1 & 1 \\ 1 & 0 \end{vmatrix} = -1$

∴ $(\text{Adj } A) = \begin{bmatrix} 6 & 2 & -2 \\ -3 & 0 & 3 \\ 3 & -2 & -1 \end{bmatrix}^T$

$= \begin{bmatrix} 6 & -3 & 3 \\ 2 & 0 & -2 \\ -2 & 3 & -1 \end{bmatrix}$

$\Rightarrow A^{-1} = \dfrac{1}{|A|} (\text{adj } A) = \dfrac{1}{6} \begin{bmatrix} 6 & -3 & 3 \\ 2 & 0 & -2 \\ -2 & 3 & -1 \end{bmatrix}$

(iii) (d) $\quad X = A^{-1}B = \dfrac{1}{6} \cdot \begin{bmatrix} 6 & -3 & 3 \\ 2 & 0 & -2 \\ -2 & 3 & -1 \end{bmatrix} \begin{bmatrix} 6000 \\ 11000 \\ 0 \end{bmatrix}$

$\Rightarrow X = \dfrac{1}{6} \cdot \begin{bmatrix} 36000 - 33000 + 0 \\ 12000 + 0 + 0 \\ -12000 + 33000 - 0 \end{bmatrix} = \dfrac{1}{6} \begin{bmatrix} 3000 \\ 12000 \\ 21000 \end{bmatrix}$

$\Rightarrow \begin{bmatrix} x \\ y \\ z \end{bmatrix} = \begin{bmatrix} 500 \\ 2000 \\ 3500 \end{bmatrix}$

$\Rightarrow x = 500, y = 2000$ and $z = 3500$.

(iv) (b) $y = 2000$

(v) (a) $z = 3500$

❏❏

Chapter 5

Continuity and Differentiability

1. Check whether the function $f(x) = 3x - 5$ is continuous at $x = 0, x = -5$ and at $x = 3$.
   (a) $f(x)$ is continuous at $x = 0$
   (b) $f(x)$ is not continuous at $x = 0$
   (c) $f(x)$ is not continuous at $x = -5$
   (d) $f(x)$ is not continuous at $x = 3$

2. Find the continuity of $f(x) = x$ at $x = k$, k be any positive value:
   (a) $f(x)$ is continuous at $x = k$
   (b) $f(x)$ is not continuous at $x = k$
   (c) $f(x)$ is continuous at $x = 0$
   (d) None of the above

3. Find the continuity of $f(x) = \dfrac{x^2 - 16}{x + 4}$, $x \neq -4$ at $x = k$, k be any positive value:
   (a) $f(x)$ is not continuous at $x = k$
   (b) $f(x)$ is continuous at $x = k$
   (c) $f(x)$ is continuous at $x = -4$
   (d) $f(x)$ is not continuous at $x = -4$

4. Find all points of discontinuous of f, where f is defined by
   $$f(x) = \begin{cases} x+3, & \text{if } x \leq 3 \\ x-3, & \text{if } x > 3 \end{cases}$$
   (a) f is discontinuous at $x = 3$
   (b) f is continuous at $x = 3$
   (c) f is continuous at $x = -3$
   (d) f is discontinuous at $x = -3$

5. Find all points of discontinuity of f, where f is defined by
   $$f(x) = \begin{cases} x^2+3, & \text{if } x \leq 3 \\ x^2-3, & \text{if } x > 3 \end{cases}$$
   (a) f is discontinuous at $x = -3$
   (b) f is discontinuous at $x = 3$
   (c) f is continuous at $x = -3$
   (d) f is continuous at $x = 3$

6. Find all points of discontinuity of f, where f is defined by
   $$f(x) = \begin{cases} x^2+x+3, & \text{if } x < 3 \\ 0, & \text{if } 0 \leq x \leq 1 \\ x^2-x+3, & \text{if } x > 1 \end{cases}$$
   (a) f is discontinuous at all points of c
   (b) f is continuous at all points of c
   (c) f is discontinuous at $x = 0$
   (d) f is continuous at $x = 0$

7. Find all points of discontinuous of f, where f is defined by
   $$f(x) = \begin{cases} 3, & \text{if } x \leq -1 \\ 3x, & \text{if } -1 < x \leq 1 \\ 3, & \text{if } x > 1 \end{cases}$$
   (a) f is discontinuous at all points of c
   (b) f is continuous at all points of c
   (c) f is discontinuous at $x = 0$
   (d) f is continuous at $x = 0$

8. The function $f(x) = 2 - 3x$ is:
   (a) Increasing
   (b) Decreasing
   (c) Neither increasing nor decreasing
   (d) None of these

9. The function $f(x) = e^{|x|}$ is:
   (a) Continuous everywhere but not differentiable at $x = 0$
   (b) Continuous and differentiable everywhere
   (c) Not continuous at $x = 0$
   (d) None of the above

10. The function $f(x) = \begin{cases} 1, & \text{if } x \neq 0 \\ 2, & \text{if } x \neq 0 \end{cases}$ is not continuous at:
    (a) $x = 0$ (b) $x = 1$
    (c) $x = -1$ (d) None of these

11. The point of discontinuity of the function $f(x) = \begin{cases} 2x+3, & \text{if } x \leq 2 \\ 2x-3, & \text{if } x > 2 \end{cases}$ is:
    (a) $x = 0$ (b) $x = 1$
    (c) $x = 2$ (d) None of these

12. If $f(x) = \begin{cases} \lambda(x^2 - 2x), & \text{if } x \leq 0 \\ 4x+1, & \text{if } x > 0 \end{cases}$, then which one of the following is correct:
    (a) $f(x)$ is continuous at $x = 0$ for any value of l
    (b) $f(x)$ is discontinuous at $x = 0$ for any value of l

(c) $f(x)$ is discontinuous at $x = 1$ for any value of l
(d) None of the above

13. The function $f(x) = \cot x$ is discontinuous on the set:
(a) $\{x = n\pi : n \in Z\}$
(b) $\{x = 2n\pi : n \in Z\}$
(c) $\{x = (2n + 1)\frac{\pi}{2}; n \in Z\}$
(d) $\{x = \frac{n\pi}{2}; n \in Z\}$

14. The function defined by $g(x) = x - [x]$ is discontinuous at:
(a) all rational points
(b) all irrational points
(c) all integral points
(d) None of the above

15. The function $f(x) = \begin{cases} \frac{k\cos x}{\pi - 2x}, & \text{if } x \neq \frac{\pi}{2} \\ 3, & \text{if } x = \frac{\pi}{2} \end{cases}$ is continuous at $x = \frac{\pi}{2}$, when k equals:
(a) -6
(b) 6
(c) 5
(d) -5

16. The number of points at which the function $f(x) = \frac{1}{x - [x]}$ [.] denotes the greatest integer function is not continuous is: [NCERT Exemplar]
(a) 1
(b) 2
(c) 3
(d) None of these

17. If $f(x) = \begin{cases} \frac{\sqrt{1+kx} - \sqrt{1-kx}}{x}, & \text{for } -1 \leq x < 0 \\ 2x^2 + 3x - 2, & \text{for } 0 \leq x \leq 1 \end{cases}$ is continuous at $x = 0$, then k is equal to:
(a) -4
(b) -3
(c) -2
(d) -1

18. If $f(x) = 2x$ and $g(x) = \frac{x^2}{2} + 1$, then which of the following can be discontinuous functions?
(a) $f(x) + g(x)$
(b) $f(x) + g(x)$
(c) $f(x) \cdot g(x)$
(d) $\frac{g(x)}{f(x)}$

19. The set of points, where the function f given by $f(x) = |2x - 1| \sin x$ is differentiable is: [NCERT Exemplar]
(a) R
(b) $R - \{\frac{1}{2}\}$
(c) $(0, \infty)$
(d) None of these

20. The differential coefficient of $\sin(\cos(x^2))$ with respect to x is:
(a) $-2x \sin x^2 \cos(\cos x^2)$
(b) $2x \sin(x^2) \cos(x^2)$
(c) $2x \sin(x^2) \cos(x^2) \cos x$
(d) None of these

21. If $y = \sqrt{3x+2} + \frac{1}{\sqrt{2x^2+4}}$, then $\frac{dy}{dx}$ is equal to:
(a) $\frac{3}{2\sqrt{3x+2}} - \frac{2x}{(2x^2+4)^{3/2}}$
(b) $\frac{3}{2\sqrt{3x+2}} - \frac{2x}{(2x^2+4)^{3/2}}$
(c) $\frac{3}{2\sqrt{3x+2}} - \frac{2x}{(2x^2+4)^{3/2}}$
(d) None of the above

22. Let $f(x) = \begin{cases} (x-1)\sin\frac{1}{(x-1)}, & \text{if } x \neq 1 \\ 0, & \text{if } x = 1 \end{cases}$. Then, which of the following is true?
(a) f is differentiable at $x = 1$ but not at $x = 0$
(b) f is neither differentiable at $x = 0$ nor at $x = 1$
(c) f is differentiable at $x = 0$ and $x = 1$
(d) f is differentiable at $x = 0$ but not $x = 1$

23. The derivative of $2x + 3y = \sin y$ is:
(a) $\frac{2}{\cos y}$
(b) $\frac{2}{\cos y + 3}$
(c) $\frac{2}{\cos y - 3}$
(d) None of these

24. If $x + \sin y = \log x$, then $\frac{dy}{dx}$ is equal to:
(a) $\frac{1-x}{x \sin y}$
(b) $\frac{1-x}{x \cos y}$
(c) $\frac{1+x}{x \cos y}$
(d) None of these

25. If $2x + 3y = \sin x$, then $\frac{dy}{dx}$ is equal to:
(a) $\frac{\cos x + 2}{3}$
(b) $\frac{\cos x - 2}{3}$
(c) $\cos x + 2$
(d) None of these

26. If $y = \sqrt{\sin x + y}$, then $\frac{dy}{dx}$ is equal to:
(a) $\frac{\cos x}{2y - 1}$
(b) $\frac{\cos x}{1 - 2y}$
(c) $\frac{\sin x}{1 - 2y}$
(d) $\frac{\sin x}{2y - 1}$

27. If $\cos y = x \cos(a + y)$ with $\cos a = 1$, then $\frac{dy}{dx}$ is equal to:

(a) $\dfrac{\sin^2(a+y)}{\sin a}$ (b) $\dfrac{\cos^2(a+y)}{\sin a}$

(c) $\sin^2(a+y)\sin a$ (d) None of these

28. If $y = \sin^{-1}\left(\dfrac{2x}{1+x^2}\right)$, then $\dfrac{dy}{dx}$ is equal to:

(a) $\dfrac{1}{1+x^2}$ (b) $\dfrac{2}{1+x^2}$

(c) $\dfrac{2}{1-x^2}$ (d) $\dfrac{-2}{1+x^2}$

29. If $y = \tan^{-1}\left(\dfrac{3x-x^3}{1-3x^2}\right), -\dfrac{1}{\sqrt{3}} < x < \dfrac{1}{\sqrt{3}}$, then $\dfrac{dy}{dx}$ is:

(a) $\dfrac{3}{1+x^2}$ (b) $\dfrac{1}{1+x^2}$

(c) $\dfrac{-3}{1+x^2}$ (d) $\dfrac{3}{1-x^2}$

30. If $y = \sin^{-1} x + \sin^{-1}\sqrt{1-x^2}$, $-1 \le x < 1$, then $\dfrac{dy}{dx}$ in equal to:

(a) 0 (b) 1
(c) 2 (d) 3

31. Derivative of $\cot^{-1}\left[\dfrac{\sqrt{1+\sin x} - \sqrt{1-\sin x}}{\sqrt{1+\sin x} - \sqrt{1-\sin x}}\right], 0 < x < \dfrac{\neq}{2}$ is:

(a) $\dfrac{1}{2}$ (b) 1
(c) 2 (d) None of these

32. If $y^x = e^{y-x}$, then $\dfrac{dy}{dx}$ is equal to:

(a) $\dfrac{1+\log y}{y\log y}$ (b) $\dfrac{(1+\log y)^2}{y\log y}$

(c) $\dfrac{1+\log y}{(\log y)^2}$ (d) $\dfrac{(1+\log y)^2}{\log y}$

33. If $x = e^{x-y}$, then $\dfrac{dy}{dx}$ is equal to:

(a) $\dfrac{x-y}{x\log x}$ (b) $\dfrac{y-x}{\log x}$

(c) $\dfrac{y-x}{x\log x}$ (d) $\dfrac{x-y}{\log x}$

34. If $x = at^2$ and $y = 2at$, then $\dfrac{dy}{dx}$ is equal to:

(a) t (b) $\dfrac{1}{t}$

(c) $\dfrac{-1}{t^2}$ (d) None of these

35. If $x = a(\cos\theta + \theta\sin\theta)$ and $y = a(\sin\theta - \theta\cos\theta)$, then $\dfrac{dy}{dx}$ is equal to:

(a) $\tan\theta$ (b) $\cos\theta$
(c) $\sin\theta$ (d) $\cos\theta$

36. The derivative of $\cos^{-1}(2x^2-1)$ w.r.t. $\cos^{-1}x$ is:

(a) 2 (b) $\dfrac{-1}{2\sqrt{1-x^2}}$

(c) $\dfrac{2}{x}$ (d) $1-x^2$

37. The derivative of $\sin^2 x$ with respect to $e^{\cos x}$ is:

(a) $\dfrac{2\cos x}{e^{\cos x}}$ (b) $-\dfrac{2\cos x}{e^{\cos x}}$

(c) $\dfrac{2}{e^{\cos x}}$ (d) None of these

38. If $y = \cos^{-1} x$, then the value of $\dfrac{d^2y}{dx^2}$ in terms of y alone is:

(a) $-\cot y\,\text{cosec}^2 y$ (b) $\text{cosec}\, y\cot^2 y$
(c) $-\cot y\,\text{cosec}\, y$ (d) None of these

39. The function $f(x) = \tan x$ is discontinuous on the set

(a) $\{x = n\pi : n \in Z\}$ (b) $\{x = 2n\pi : n \in Z\}$
(c) $\left\{x = (2n+1)\dfrac{\pi}{2}; n \in Z\right\}$ (d) $\left\{x = \dfrac{n\pi}{2}; n \in Z\right\}$

40. The function $f(x) = e^{|x|}$ is:

(a) $f'(0) = 1$ (b) $f'(0) = -1$
(c) $f'(0) = 0$ (d) $f'(0)$ does not exist

41. If $f(x) = x\sin\dfrac{1}{x}$, where $x \ne 0$, then the value of the function f at $x = 0$, so that the function is continuous at $x = 0$, is:

(a) 0 (b) -1
(c) 1 (d) none of these

42. If $f(x) = \begin{cases} mx+1, & \text{if } x < \dfrac{\pi}{2} \\ \sin x + n, & \text{if } x > \dfrac{\pi}{2} \end{cases}$, is continuous at $x = \dfrac{\neq}{2}$, then

(a) $m = 1, n = 0$ (b) $m = \dfrac{n\pi}{2} + 1$

(c) $n = \dfrac{m\pi}{2}$ (d) $m = n = \dfrac{\pi}{2}$

43. Let $f(x) = |\sin x|$. Then

(a) f is everywhere differentiable
(b) f is everywhere continuous but not differentiable at $x = n\pi, n \in Z$

(c) f is everywhere continuous but not differentiable at $x = (2n+1)\dfrac{\pi}{2}, n \in Z$.

(d) none of these

Choose the correct option :
(a) Both (A) and (B) are true and R is the correct explanation A.
(b) Both (A) and (R) are true but R is not correct explanation of A.
(c) A is true but R is false.
(d) A is false but R is true.

44. **Assertion (A) :** The function $f(x) = |x|$ is discontinuous at $x = 0$.
    Reason (R) : The function $f(x) = |x|$ is non-differentiable at $x = 0$

45. **Assertion (A) :** $f(x) = \dfrac{1}{\{x\}}$ is discontinuous for integral values of x, where $\{\}$ denotes the fractional part function.
    Reason (R) : For integral values of x, $f(x)$ is not defined.

46. **Assertion (A) :** The function $f(x)$ in the figure is differentiable at $x = a$.

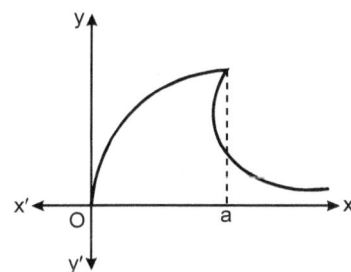

    Reason (R) : The function $f(x)$ is continuous at $x = a$

47. **Assertion (A) :** $f(x) = \sqrt{(x-2)} + \sqrt{(2-x)}$ is continuous at $x = 2$
    Reason (R) : $f(x)$ is a point function.

48. **Assertion (A) :** The function
$$f(x) = \begin{cases} [x] + \sqrt{x - [x]}, & x \geq 0 \\ \sin x, & x < 0 \end{cases}$$
    where [ ] denotes the greatest integer function, is continuous everywhere.
    Reason (R) : $f(x)$ is a periodic function

49. **Assertion (A) :** The function $f(x) = \{x\}$, where $\{\}$ denotes the fractional part function, is discontinuous at $x = 1$.
    Reason (R) : $\lim\limits_{x \to 1^-} f(x) \neq \lim\limits_{x \to 1^+} f(x)$

50. **Assertion (A) :** The function
$$f(x) = \dfrac{(27 - 2x)^{1/3} - 3}{9 - 3(243 + 5x)}$$
    is continuous eveywhere is $f(0) = 2$.

    Reason (R) : For continuous function
    $f(0) = \lim\limits_{x \to 0} f(x)$

51. **Assertion (A) :** If $f(x)$ is continuous, then $|f(|x|)|$ is also continuous.
    Reason (R) : If $|f(x)| \leq |x| \ \forall \ x \in R$, then $|f(x)|$ is continuous at $x = 0$.

52. **Assertion (A) :** $f(x) \begin{cases} x^2 \sin\left(\dfrac{1}{x}\right), & x \neq 0 \\ 0, & x = 0 \end{cases}$ is continuous at $x = 0$
    Reason (R) : Both $h(x) = x^2$, $g(x) = \begin{cases} \sin\left(\dfrac{1}{x}\right), & x \neq 0 \\ 0, & x = 0 \end{cases}$
    are continuous at $x = 0$.

53. **Assertion (A) :** $f(x) = x\left(\dfrac{1 + e^{1/x}}{1 - e^{1/x}}\right) (x \neq 0), f(0) = 0$ is continuous at $x = 0$.
    Reason (R) : A function is said to be are continuous at a if both limits are exists and equal to $f(a)$.

54. **Consider the following values.**
    $x = a \cos^3 \theta, y = a \sin^3 \theta$
    On the basis of above information, answer the following questions:

    (i) $\left.\dfrac{dx}{d\theta}\right|_{\theta = \frac{\pi}{4}} =$
    (a) $\dfrac{3a}{2\sqrt{2}}$ (b) $\dfrac{-3a}{2\sqrt{2}}$
    (c) $\dfrac{4\sqrt{2}}{3a}$ (d) $\dfrac{-1}{\sqrt{3}}$

    (ii) $\left.\dfrac{dy}{d\theta}\right|_{\theta = \frac{\pi}{4}} =$
    (a) $\dfrac{3a}{2\sqrt{2}}$ (b) $\dfrac{-3a}{2\sqrt{2}}$
    (c) $\dfrac{4\sqrt{2}}{3a}$ (d) $\dfrac{-1}{\sqrt{3}}$

    (iii) $\dfrac{dy}{dx} =$
    (a) $\tan \theta$ (b) $-\tan \theta$
    (c) $\cot \theta$ (d) $-\cot \theta$

    (iv) $\left.\dfrac{dy}{dx}\right|_{\theta = \frac{\pi}{6}} =$
    (a) $\dfrac{3a}{2\sqrt{2}}$ (b) $\dfrac{-3a}{2\sqrt{2}}$
    (c) $\dfrac{4\sqrt{2}}{3a}$ (d) $\dfrac{-1}{\sqrt{3}}$

(v) $\dfrac{d^2y}{dx^2} =$

(a) $\dfrac{3a}{2\sqrt{2}}$ (b) $\dfrac{-3a}{2\sqrt{2}}$

(c) $\dfrac{4\sqrt{2}}{3a}$ (d) $\dfrac{-1}{\sqrt{3}}$

55. The derivative of f at $x = c$ is defined by

$$f(x) = \lim_{h \to 0} \dfrac{f(c+h) - f(c)}{h}$$

A function is said to be differentiable at a point c if left hand derivative at $x = c$ is equal to the right hand derivative at $x = c$.

Similarly, a function is said to be differentiable in an interval (a, b) if it is differentiable at every point of (a, b).

Based on the above information, answer the following questions:

(i) Derivative of $f(x) = \cos(\sqrt{x})$ is:

(a) $-\sin(\sqrt{x})$ (b) $\dfrac{-\sin(\sqrt{x})}{2\sqrt{x}}$

(c) $\sin(\sqrt{x})$ (d) $\dfrac{1}{2}\sin(\sqrt{x})$

(ii) If $y = a \sin t$, $x = a \cos t$ then $\dfrac{dy}{dx}$ is:

(a) $\cos t$ (b) $-\tan t$
(c) $-\cot t$ (d) $\sin t$

(iii) $f(x) = |x|$ is:

(a) Differentiable at all points $x \in R$
(b) Differentiable at all points $x \in R - \{0\}$
(c) Not Differentiable at $x = 1$
(d) None of these

(iv) Derivative of function $f(x) = \sin(x^2)$ is:

(a) $2\cos(x^2)$ (b) $2x\cos(x^2)$
(c) $2x^2 \sin(x)$ (d) $2\cos(x)$

(v) If $y + \sin y = \cos x$ then $\dfrac{dy}{dx}$ is:

(a) $\dfrac{-\sin x}{1 + \cos y}$ (b) $\dfrac{\cos x}{1 + \sin y}$

(c) $\dfrac{\cos y}{1 + \sin x}$ (d) $\dfrac{-\cos x}{1 + \sin y}$

56. A function is continuous at $x = c$, if the function is defined at $x = c$ and if the value of the function at $x = c$ equals the limit of the function at $x = c$

i.e., $\lim\limits_{x \to c} f(x) = f(c)$

Based on the above information answer the following questions:

(i) The relationship between a and b so that the below function is continuous at $x = 3$,

$$f(x) = \begin{cases} ax + 1; & x \le 3 \\ bx + 3; & x > 3 \end{cases}$$

(a) $a = b + 2$ (b) $a + b = \dfrac{2}{3}$

(c) $a = b + \dfrac{2}{3}$ (d) None of these

(ii) $f(x) = \begin{cases} kx^2; & x \le 2 \\ 3; & x > 2 \end{cases}$ is continuous at $x = 2$ then k is:

(a) $k = 0.25$ (b) $k = 3$
(c) $k = 0.75$ (d) $k = 1$

(iii) If $f(x)$ and $g(x)$ is continuous at $x = c$ then:

(a) $f \pm g$ is continuous at $x = c$
(b) $f \pm g$ is continuous at $x = c$
(c) $f \pm g$ may or may not continuous
(d) None of these

(iv) $f(x) = \begin{cases} 2x; & x < 2 \\ x - 1; & x > 6 \end{cases}$ at $x = 6$:

(a) Continuous
(b) Discontinuous
(c) May or may not continuous
(d) None of these

(v) $f(x) = \begin{cases} \dfrac{|x|}{x}; & x \ne 0 \\ 0; & x = 0 \end{cases}$ at $x = :$

(a) Continuous
(b) Discontinuous
(c) May or may not continuous
(d) None of these

Solutions

1. (a) $f(x)$ is not continuous at $x = 3$
   Explanation:
   $f(x) = 3x - 5$
   At $x = 0$,
   $f(0) = 3 \times 0 - 5 = -5$
   $\lim\limits_{x \to 0^+} f(x) = \lim\limits_{x \to 0}(3x - 5) = 3 \times 0 - 5$
   $= -5$

   $\therefore \lim\limits_{x \to 0^+} f(x) = f(0)$

   Therefore, f is continuous at $x = 0$.
   At $x = -5$,
   $f(-5) = 3 \times (-5) - 5 = -20$
   $\lim\limits_{x \to 5^-} f(x) = \lim\limits_{x \to 5}(3x - 5) = 3 \times (-5) - 5$
   $= -20$

∴ $\lim_{x \to -5} f(x) = f(-5)$

Therefore, f is continuous at $x = -5$.
At $x = 3$, $f(3) = 3 \times (3) - 5 = 4$
$$\lim_{x \to 3^+} f(x) = \lim_{x \to 3} (3x - 5)$$
$$= 3 \times (3) - 5 = 4$$
∴ $\lim_{x \to 3} f(x) = f(3)$

Therefore, f is continuous at $x = 3$.

2. (a) $f(x)$ is continuous at $x = k$
   Explanation :
   The given function is,
   $$f(x) = x$$
   At $x = 0$,
   $$f(k) = k$$
   $$\lim_{x \to k} f(x) = \lim_{x \to k} (x) = k$$
   ∴ $\lim_{x \to k} f(x) = f(k)$

   ∴ $f(x)$ is continuous at $x = k$.

3. (b) $f(x)$ is continuous at $x = k$
   Explanation :
   The given function is, $f(x) = \dfrac{x^2 - 16}{x + 4}$
   At $x = k$,
   $$f(k) = \dfrac{x^2 - 16}{k + 4} = \dfrac{(k+4)(k-4)}{k+4} = k - 4$$
   $$\lim_{x \to k} f(x) = \lim_{x \to k} \left(\dfrac{x^2 - 16}{x + 4} \right) = \dfrac{(k+4)(k-4)}{k+4} = k - 4$$
   ∴ $\lim_{x \to k} f(x) = f(k)$.

4. (a) f is discontinuous at $x = 3$
   Explanation :
   The given function f is
   $$f(x) = \begin{cases} x + 3, & \text{if } x \leq -1 \\ x - 3, & \text{if } x > 1 \end{cases}$$

   (i) $c < 3$
   (ii) $c = 3$
   (iii) $c > 3$
   where c be a point on the real line. Then these three cases are valid
   Case (i) : $c < 3$
   then
   $$f(x) = x + 3$$
   $$f(c) = c + 3$$
   $$\lim_{x \to c} f(x) = \lim_{x \to c} (x + 3) = c + 3$$
   $$\lim_{x \to c} f(x) = f(c)$$

   Therefore, f is continuous at all points x, such that $x < 3$
   Case (ii) : $c = 3$
   then
   $$f(x) = x + 3$$
   $$\lim_{x \to c} f(x) = \lim_{x \to c} (x + 3) = 3 + 3 = 6$$

   The value of the function f at $c = 3$ is 6.
   Case (iii) : $c > 3$
   then
   $$f(x) = x - 3$$
   $$f(c) = c - 3$$
   $$\lim_{x \to c} f(x) = \lim_{x \to c} (x - 3) = c - 3$$
   $$\lim_{x \to c} f(x) = f(c)$$

   The given function f is discontinuous at point $c = 3$.

5. (b) f is discontinuous at $x = 3$
   Explanation :
   The given function f is
   $$f(x) = \begin{cases} x^2 + 3, & \text{if } x \leq 3 \\ x^2 - 3, & \text{if } x > 3 \end{cases}$$

   (i) $c < 3$
   (ii) $c = 3$
   (iii) $c > 3$
   where c be a point on the real line. Then these three cases are valid
   Case (i) : $c < 3$
   then
   $$f(x) = x^2 + 3$$
   $$f(c) = c^2 + 3$$
   $$\lim_{x \to c} f(x) = \lim_{x \to c} (x^2 + 3) = c^2 + 3$$
   $$\lim_{x \to c} f(x) = f(c)$$

   Therefore, f is continuous at all points x, such that $x < 3$
   Case (ii) : $c = 3$
   then
   $$f(x) = x^2 + 3$$
   $$\lim_{x \to c} f(x) = \lim_{x \to c} (x^2 + 3)$$
   $$= 3^2 + 3 = 12$$
   The value of the function f at $c = 3$ is 12.
   Case (iii) : $c > 3$
   then
   $$f(x) = x^2 - 3$$
   $$f(c) = c^2 - 3$$
   $$\lim_{x \to c} f(x) = \lim_{x \to c} (x^2 - 3) = c^2 - 3$$
   $$\lim_{x \to c} f(x) = f(c)$$

   The given function f is discontinuous at point $c = 3$.

6. (a) f is discontinuous at all points of c
   Explanation :
   The given function f is
   $$f(x) = \begin{cases} x^2 + x + 3, & \text{if } x < 0 \\ 0, & \text{if } 0 \leq x \leq 1 \\ x^2 - x + 3, & \text{if } x > 1 \end{cases}$$

(i) $c < 0$
(ii) $c > 1$
(iii) $0 \leq c \leq 1$
where c be a point on the real line. Then these three cases are valid.

Case (i) : $c < 0$
then
$$f(x) = x^2 + x + 3$$
$$f(c) = c^2 + c + 3$$
$$\lim_{x \to c} f(x) = \lim_{x \to c} (x^2 + x + 3) = c^2 + c + 3$$
$$\lim_{x \to c} f(x) = f(c)$$

Therefore, f is continuous at all points x, such that $x < 0$

Case (ii) : $c > 1$
then
$$f(x) = x^2 - x + 3$$
$$\lim_{x \to c} f(x) = \lim_{x \to c} (x^2 - x + 3) = c^2 - c + 3$$

Therefore, f is continuous at all points x, such that $x > 1$.

Case (iii) : $0 \leq c \leq 1$
then
$$f(x) = 0$$
$$f(c) = 0$$
$$\lim_{x \to c} f(x) = \lim_{x \to c} (x^2 - x + 3) = c^2 - c + 3$$
$$\lim_{x \to c} f(x) = f(c)$$

Therefore, f is continuous at all points x, such that $0 \leq x \leq 1$.
But, the given function f is discontinuous at all points of c.

7. (a) f is discontinuous at all points of c
   Explanation :
   The given function f is
   $$f(x) = \begin{cases} 3, & \text{if } x \leq -1 \\ 3x, & \text{if } -1 \leq x \leq 1 \\ -3, & \text{if } x > 1 \end{cases}$$

   (i) $c \leq -1$
   (ii) $c > 1$
   (iii) $-1 < c \leq 1$
   where c be a point on the real line. Then these three cases are valid.

   Case (i) : $c \leq -1$
   then
   $$f(x) = 3$$
   $$f(c) = 3$$
   $$\lim_{x \to c} f(x) = \lim_{x \to c} 3 = 3$$
   $$\lim_{x \to c} f(x) = f(c)$$

   Therefore, f is continuous at all points x, such that $x \leq -1$

   Case (ii) : $c > 1$
   then
   $$f(x) = -3$$
   $$\lim_{x \to c} f(x) = \lim_{x \to c} -3 = -3$$

   Therefore, f is continuous at all points x, such that $x > 1$.

   Case (iii) : $-1 < c \leq 1$
   then
   $$f(x) = 3x$$
   $$f(c) = 3c$$
   $$\lim_{x \to c} f(x) = \lim_{x \to c} (3x) = 3c$$
   $$\lim_{x \to c} f(x) = f(c)$$

   Therefore, f is continuous at all points x, such that $-1 < c \leq 1$.
   But, the given function f is discontinuous at all points of c.

8. (b) Decreasing
   Explanation :
   $$f(x) = 2 - 3x$$
   $$f'(x) = -3 < 0$$
   Hence, function is strictly decreasing.

9. (a) Continuous everywhere but not differentiable at $x = 0$
   Explanation :
   $$f(x) = e^{|x|} = \begin{cases} e^x, & x \geq 0 \\ e^{-x}, & x < 0 \end{cases}$$
   $$f'(x) = \begin{cases} e^x, & x \geq 0 \\ -e^{-x}, & x < 0 \end{cases}$$
   $$f(0) = e^0 = 1$$
   $$\text{RHL} = \lim_{x \to 0^+} e^x = e^0 = 1$$
   $$\text{LHL} = \lim_{x \to 0^+} e^{-x} = e^{-0} = 1$$
   If $x = 0$
   $$f(x) = \text{LHL} = \text{RHL}$$
   $\therefore f(x)$ is continuous at $x = 0$
   $$\text{LHD} = \lim_{x \to 0^-} f'(x) = \lim_{x \to 0^-} -e^{-x}$$
   $$= -e^{-0} = -1$$
   $$\text{RHD} = \lim_{x \to 0^+} e^x = e^0 = 1$$
   $$\text{LHD} \neq \text{RHD}$$
   $\therefore f(x)$ is not differentiable at $x = 0$.

10. (a) $x = 0$
    Explanation :
    $$\lim_{x \to 0^-} f(x) = 1 \; \lim_{x \to 0^+} f(x) \neq f(0) = 2$$

11. (c) $x = 2$
    Explanation :
    $$\lim_{x \to 2^-} f(x) = 7 \text{ and } \lim_{x \to 2^+} f(x) = 1$$

12. (b) $f(x)$ is discontinuous at $x = 0$ for any value of l
    Explanation :
    $$\lim_{x \to 0^-} f(x) = 0 \text{ and } \lim_{x \to 0^+} f(x) = 1$$

Continuity and Differentiability | 301

13. (a) $\{x = n\pi : n \in \mathbb{Z}\}$

Explanation :

We know that, $f(x) = \cot x$ is continuous in $\mathbb{R} - \{n\pi : n \in \mathbb{Z}\}$

Since, $f(x) = \cot x = \dfrac{\cos x}{\sin x}$ [since, $\sin x = 0$ at $n\pi$, $n \in \mathbb{Z}$]

Hence, $f(x) = \cot x$ is discontinuous on the set $\{x = n\pi : n \in \mathbb{Z}\}$

14. (c) all rational points

Explanation :

$f(x) = [x]$ is discontinuous at every integer.

15. (b) 6

Explanation :

We have, $f(x) = \begin{cases} \dfrac{k \cos x}{\pi - 2x}, & \text{if } x \neq \dfrac{\pi}{2} \\ 3, & \text{if } x = \dfrac{\pi}{2} \end{cases}$

$f(x)$ is continuous at $x = \dfrac{\pi}{2}$

$\therefore \quad \lim\limits_{x \to \frac{\pi}{2}^-} \dfrac{k \cos x}{\pi - 2x} = 3$

$\Rightarrow \lim\limits_{h \to 0} \dfrac{k \cos\left(\dfrac{\pi}{2} - h\right)}{\pi - 2\left(\dfrac{\pi}{2} - h\right)} = 3$

$\Rightarrow \lim\limits_{h \to 0} \dfrac{k \sin h}{2h} = 3$

$\therefore \quad \dfrac{k}{2} = 3 \Rightarrow k = 6$

16. (d) None of these

Explanation :

$x - [x] = 0$ when x is an integer, so that $f(x)$ is discontinuous for all $x \in I$ i.e., $f(x)$ is discontinuous at infinite number of points.

17. (c) -2

Explanation :

$\text{LHL} = \lim\limits_{x \to 0^-} \dfrac{\sqrt{1+kx} - \sqrt{1-kx}}{x}$

$= \lim\limits_{x \to 0^-} \dfrac{2kx}{x(\sqrt{1+kx} + \sqrt{1-kx})} = k$

$\text{RHL} = \lim\limits_{x \to 0^+} (2x^2 + 3x - 2) = -2$

$f(0) = -2$

$\because$ If is given that $f(x)$ is continuous at $x = 0$.

$\therefore \quad \text{LHL} = \text{RHL} = f(0) \Rightarrow k = -2$.

18. (d) $\dfrac{g(x)}{f(x)}$

Explanation :

We know that, if f and g are continuous functions, then

(a) $f + g$ is continuous

(b) $f - g$ is continuous

(c) fg is continuous

(d) $\dfrac{f}{g}$ is continuous at these points, where $g(x) \neq 0$.

Here, $\dfrac{g(x)}{f(x)} = \dfrac{\dfrac{x^2}{2} + 1}{2x} = \dfrac{x^2 + 2}{4x}$

which is discontinuous at $x = 0$.

19. (b) $\mathbb{R} - \left\{\dfrac{1}{2}\right\}$

Explanation :

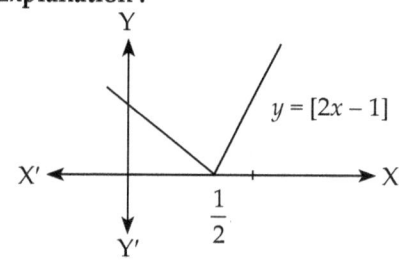

Let $u(x) = \sin x$
$v(x) = |x|$
$f(x) = v \circ u(x) = v[u(x)]$
$= v(\sin x)$
$= |\sin x|$

$\because u(x) = \sin x$ is a continuous function and $v(x) = |x|$ is a continuous function.

$\therefore f(x) = v \circ u(x)$ is also continuous everywhere but $v(x)$ is not differentiable at $x = 0$.

$\Rightarrow f(x)$ is not differentiable where $\sin x = 0$

$x = n\pi, n \in \mathbb{Z}$

Hence, $f(x)$ is continuous everywhere but not differentiable at $x = n\pi, n \in \mathbb{Z}$.

$\because$ At $x = \dfrac{1}{2}$, curve have two tangents at that point, therefore from the graph it is clear that $y = |2x - 1|$ is not differentiable at $x = \dfrac{1}{2}$.

$\therefore f(x) =$ is differentiable in $\mathbb{R} - \left\{\dfrac{1}{2}\right\}$.

20. (a) $-2x \sin x^2 \cos(\cos x^2)$

Explanation :

$y = \sin(\cos x^2)$

Therefore, $\dfrac{dy}{dx} = \dfrac{d}{dx} \sin(\cos x^2)$

$= \cos(\cos x^2) \dfrac{d}{dx}(\cos x^2)$

$$= \cos(\cos x^2)(-\sin x^2)\frac{d}{dx}(x^2)$$
$$= -\sin x^2 \cos(\cos x^2)(2x)$$
$$= -2x \sin x^2 \cos(\cos x^2)$$

21. (a) $\dfrac{3}{2\sqrt{3x+2}} - \dfrac{2x}{(2x^2+4)^{3/2}}$

Explanation :

Let $y = \sqrt{3x+2} + \dfrac{1}{\sqrt{2x^2+4}}$

$= (3x+2)^{1/2} + (2x^2+4)^{-1/2}$

Therefore,

$\dfrac{dy}{dx} = \dfrac{1}{2}(3x+2)^{\frac{1}{2}-1} \cdot \dfrac{d}{dx}(3x+2)$

$\quad + \left(-\dfrac{1}{2}\right)(2x^2+4)^{-\frac{1}{2}-1} \cdot \dfrac{d}{dx}(2x^2+4)$

$= \dfrac{1}{2}(3x+2)^{-\frac{1}{2}} \cdot (3) - \left(\dfrac{1}{2}\right)(2x^2+4)^{-\frac{3}{2}} \cdot 4x$

$= \dfrac{3}{2\sqrt{3x+2}} - \dfrac{2x}{(2x^2+4)^{\frac{3}{2}}}$

22. (d) f is differentiable at $x = 0$ but not $x = 1$

Explanation :

We observe that,

$\lim\limits_{x \to 1} \dfrac{f(x)-f(1)}{x-1} = \lim\limits_{x \to 1} \dfrac{(x-1)\sin\left(\dfrac{1}{x-1}\right)}{x-1}$

$= \lim\limits_{x \to 1} \sin\left(\dfrac{1}{x-1}\right)$

= An oscillating number between -1 and 1

$\therefore \lim\limits_{x \to 1} \dfrac{f(x)-f(1)}{x-1}$ does not exist.

$\Rightarrow f(x)$ is not differentiable at $x = 1$.

and $= \lim\limits_{x \to 0} \dfrac{f(x)-f(0)}{x-0}$

$= \lim\limits_{x \to 0} \dfrac{(x-1)\sin\left(\dfrac{1}{x-1}\right) - \sin 1}{x}$

$= \lim\limits_{x \to 0} \dfrac{x\sin\left(\dfrac{1}{x-1}\right)}{x} - \lim\limits_{x \to 0} \dfrac{\sin\left(\dfrac{1}{x-1}\right) + \sin 1}{x}$

$= -\sin 1 - \lim\limits_{x \to 0} \dfrac{2\sin\dfrac{x}{2(x-1)}\cos\left\{\dfrac{2-x}{2(x-1)}\right\}}{\left\{\dfrac{x}{2(x-1)}\right\}2(x-1)}$

$= -\sin 1 + \cos 1$

$\therefore f(x)$ is differentiable at $x = 0$.

23. (c) $\dfrac{2}{\cos y - 3}$

Explanation :

Given, $2x + 3y = \sin y$

On differentiating both sides w.r.t. x, we get

$\dfrac{d}{dx}(2x+3y) = \dfrac{d}{dx}(\sin y)$

$\Rightarrow 2 + 3\dfrac{dy}{dx} = \cos y \dfrac{dy}{dx}$

$\Rightarrow 3\dfrac{dy}{dx} - \cos y \dfrac{dy}{dx} = -2$

$\Rightarrow (3 - \cos y)\dfrac{dy}{dx} = -2$

$\Rightarrow \dfrac{dy}{dx} = \dfrac{2}{\cos y - 3}$

24. (b) $\dfrac{1-x}{x \cos y}$

Explanation :

$\sin y + x = \log x$

on differentiale with respet to x, we get

$\cos y \dfrac{dy}{dx} + 1 = \dfrac{1}{x}$

$\cos y \dfrac{dy}{dx} = \dfrac{1}{x} - 1$

$\cos y \dfrac{dy}{dx} = \dfrac{1-x}{x}$

$\dfrac{dy}{dx} = \dfrac{1-x}{x \cos y}$

25. (b) $\dfrac{\cos x - 2}{3}$

Explanation :

Given, $2x + 3y = \sin x$

On differentiating both sides w.r.t.x, we get

$\dfrac{d}{dx}(2x+3y) = \dfrac{d}{dx}(\sin x)$

$2 + 3\dfrac{dy}{dx} = \cos x$

$3\dfrac{dy}{dx} = \cos x - 2$

$\dfrac{dy}{dx} = \dfrac{\cos x - 2}{3}$

26. (a) $\dfrac{\cos x}{2y - 1}$

Explanation :

$\because \quad y = (\sin x + y)^{1/2}$

$\therefore \quad \dfrac{dy}{dx} = \dfrac{1}{2}(\sin x + y)^{-1/2} \dfrac{d}{dx}(\sin x + y)$

[by chain rule derivative]

$$\Rightarrow \quad \frac{dy}{dx} = \frac{1}{2}\cdot\frac{1}{(\sin x + y)^{1/2}}\cdot\left(\cos x + \frac{dy}{dx}\right)$$

$$\Rightarrow \quad \frac{dy}{dx} = \frac{1}{2y}\left(\cos x + \frac{dy}{dx}\right) \quad [\because (\sin x + y)^{1/2} = y]$$

$$\Rightarrow \frac{dy}{dx}\left(1 - \frac{1}{2y}\right) = \frac{\cos x}{2y}$$

$$\therefore \quad \frac{dy}{dx} = \frac{\cos x}{2y}\cdot\frac{2y}{2y-1} = \frac{\cos x}{2y-1}$$

27. (b) $\dfrac{\cos^2(a+y)}{\sin a}$

Explanation :

Given, $\cos y = x \cos (a + y)$

$$\Rightarrow \quad x = \frac{y}{\cos (a+y)}$$

$$\frac{dx}{dy} = \frac{d}{dy}\left\{\frac{\cos y}{\cos(a+y)}\right\}$$

$$= \frac{\cos(a+y)(-\sin y) - \cos y[-\sin(a+y)1]}{\cos^2(a+y)}$$

$$= \frac{\sin (a+y-y)}{\cos^2(a+y)} = \frac{\sin a}{\cos^2 (a+y)}$$

[$\because$ sin (A – B) = sin A cos B – cos A sin B]

$$\therefore \quad \frac{dx}{dy} = \frac{1}{\frac{dx}{dy}} = \frac{\cos^2(a+y)}{\sin a}$$

28. (b) $\dfrac{2}{1+x^2}$

Explanation :

Put $\quad x = \tan\theta$

$$y = \sin^{-1}\left(\frac{2\tan\theta}{1+\tan^2\theta}\right)$$

$$= \sin^{-1}(\sin 2\theta)$$

$$y = 2\theta = 2\tan^{-1} x$$

$$\therefore \quad \frac{dy}{dx} = \frac{2}{1+x^2}$$

29. (a) $\dfrac{3}{1+x^2}$

Explanation :

$$y = \tan^{-1}\frac{3x - x^3}{1 - 3x^2}$$

$$= 3\tan^{-1} x$$

$$\frac{dy}{dx} = \frac{3}{1+x^2}.$$

30. (a) 0

Explanation :

Put $\sin^{-1}\sqrt{1-x^2} = \cos^{-1} x$

$$\therefore \quad y = \sin^{-1} x + \cos^{-1} x$$

$$= \frac{\pi}{2}$$

$$\therefore \quad \frac{dy}{dx} = 0$$

$$\Rightarrow \quad \log x = \frac{x}{y}$$

31. (a) $\dfrac{1}{2}$

Explanation :

$$\cot^{-1}\frac{\sqrt{1+\sin x} - \sqrt{1-\sin x}}{\sqrt{1+\sin x} + \sqrt{1-\sin x}}$$

$$y = \cot^{-1}\left[\left(\cos\frac{x}{2} + \sin\frac{x}{2}\right) + \left[\cos\frac{x}{2} - \sin\frac{x}{2}\right]\right]$$

$$y = \cos\frac{x}{2} + \sin\frac{x}{2} - \left(\cos\frac{x}{2} - \sin\frac{x}{2}\right)$$

$$y = \cos^{-1}\frac{2\cos\frac{x}{2}}{2\sin\frac{x}{2}} = \cot^{-1}\cot\frac{x}{2}$$

$$= \frac{x}{2}$$

$$\frac{dy}{dx} = \frac{1}{2}.$$

32. (d) $\dfrac{(1+\log y)^2}{\log y}$

Explanation :

We have, $\quad y^x = e^{y-x}$

Taking log both sides, we get

$$x \log y = y - x$$

$$\Rightarrow \quad x(\log y + 1) = y$$

$$\Rightarrow \quad \frac{y}{1+\log y} = x$$

On differential with respect to x, we get

$$\left(\frac{(1+\log y) - \left(\frac{1}{y}\right)y}{(1+\log y)^2}\right) = \frac{dy}{dx} = 1$$

$$\frac{\log y}{(1+\log y)^2}\frac{dy}{dx} = 1$$

$$\Rightarrow \quad \frac{dy}{dx} = \frac{(1+\log y)^2}{\log y}$$

33. (a) $\dfrac{x-y}{x\log x}$

Explanation :

Given that, $x = e^{x/y}$

Taking log on both sides, we get

$$\log x = \frac{x}{y}.\log e = \frac{x}{y}$$

$\Rightarrow \quad x = y \log x$

Now, differentiating w.r.t. x, we get

$\Rightarrow \quad 1 = y \cdot \dfrac{1}{x} + \log x \cdot \dfrac{dy}{dx}$

$\Rightarrow \quad \dfrac{dy}{dx} = \dfrac{x-y}{x \log x}$

34. (b) $\dfrac{1}{t}$

Explanation :
Given that, $x = at^2,\ y = 2at$

So $\quad \dfrac{dx}{dt} = 2at$

and $\quad \dfrac{dy}{dt} = 2a$

Therefore, $\dfrac{dy}{dx} = \dfrac{\frac{dy}{dt}}{\frac{dx}{dt}} = \dfrac{2a}{2at} = \dfrac{1}{t}$

35. (a) $\tan\theta$

Explanation :
Given, $x = a(\cos\theta + \theta\sin\theta),\ y = a(\sin\theta - \theta\cos\theta)$
On differentiating w.r.t. θ, we get

$\dfrac{dx}{d\theta} = a\dfrac{d}{d\theta}(\cos\theta + \theta\sin\theta)$

$= a\left\{\dfrac{d}{d\theta}(\cos\theta) + \dfrac{d}{d\theta}(\theta\sin\theta)\right\}$

$= a\{-\sin\theta + (\theta\cos\theta + \sin\theta \cdot 1)\}$

$= a\theta\cos\theta$

[using product rule in $\dfrac{d}{d\theta}(\theta\sin\theta)$]

and $\dfrac{dy}{d\theta} = a\dfrac{d}{d\theta}(\sin\theta - \theta\cos\theta)$

$= a\left\{\dfrac{d}{d\theta}(\sin\theta) - \dfrac{d}{d\theta}(\theta\cos\theta)\right\}$

$= a[\cos\theta - \{\theta(-\sin\theta) + \cos\theta \cdot 1\}]$

$= a\theta\sin\theta$

[using product rule in $\dfrac{d}{d\theta}(\theta\sin\theta)$]

$\Rightarrow \quad \dfrac{dy}{dx} = \dfrac{\frac{dy}{d\theta}}{\frac{dx}{d\theta}} = \dfrac{a\theta\sin\theta}{a\theta\cos\theta} = \tan\theta$

36. (a) 2

Explanation :
Let $u = \cos^{-1}(2x^2 - 1)$ and $v = \cos^{-1}x$

$\therefore \dfrac{du}{dx} = \dfrac{1}{\sqrt{1-(2x^2-1)^2}} \cdot 4x = \dfrac{-4x}{\sqrt{1-(4x^4+1-4x^2)}}$

$= \dfrac{-4x}{\sqrt{-4x^4+4x^2}} = \dfrac{-4x}{\sqrt{4x^2(1-x^2)}} = \dfrac{-2}{\sqrt{1-x^2}}$

and $\dfrac{dv}{dx} = \dfrac{-1}{\sqrt{1-x^2}}$

$\therefore \dfrac{du}{dv} = \dfrac{du/dx}{dv/dx} = \dfrac{-2/\sqrt{1-x^2}}{-1/\sqrt{1-x^2}} = 2$

37. (b) $-\dfrac{2\cos x}{e^{\cos x}}$

Explanation :
Let $u(x) = \sin^2 x$ and $v(x) = e^{\cos x}$. We want to find

Thus $\dfrac{du}{dv} = \dfrac{du/dx}{dv/dx}$. Clearly, $\dfrac{du}{dx} = 2\sin x \cos x$ and

$\dfrac{dv}{dx} = e^{\cos x}(-\sin x) = -(\sin x)e^{\cos x}$

$\dfrac{du}{dv} = \dfrac{2\sin x \cos x}{-\sin x\, e^{\cos x}} = -\dfrac{2\cos x}{e^{\cos x}}$

38. (a) $-\cot y \csc^2 y$

Explanation :
Given, $\quad y = \cos^{-1}x$

$\Rightarrow \quad x = \cos y$

On differentiating w.r.t. y, we get

$\dfrac{dx}{dy} = -\sin y$

$\Rightarrow \quad \dfrac{dy}{dx} = -\csc y$ ...(i)

Again, differentiating w.r.t. x, we get

$\dfrac{d^2y}{dx^2} = \dfrac{d}{dx}(-\csc y) = -(-\csc y \cot y)\dfrac{dy}{dx}$

$= \csc y \cot y(-\csc y) = -\cot y \cdot \csc^2 y$

[from Eq. (i)]

39. (a) $(2n+1)\dfrac{\pi}{2}$

Explanation :
when $\tan(2x+1)\dfrac{\pi}{2}$

$\tan\left(n\pi + \dfrac{\pi}{2}\right) = -\cot n\pi$

It is not defined at the integral points ($n \in z$)

Hence $f(x)$ discontinous at $(2x+1)\dfrac{\pi}{2}$

40. (d) $f'(0)$ does not exist

Explanation :

$f(x) = \begin{cases} e^x & x \leq 0 \\ e^{-x} & x < 0 \end{cases}$

$\text{RHD} = \lim_{h \to 0}\dfrac{e^h - f(0)}{h}$

$\lim_{h \to 0}\dfrac{e^h - 1}{h} = 1$

$$\text{LHD} = \lim_{h\to 0}\frac{e^{-h} - f(0)}{-h}$$

$$\lim_{h\to 0}\frac{e^{-h} - 1}{-h} = -1$$

Since, RHD ≠ LHD

that implies f is not differentiable at $x = 0$

$f'(0)$ does not exist.

41. (a) 0

Explanation :

We have $f(x) = x\sin\frac{1}{x}$, where $x \neq 0$.

Since, $f(x)$ is continuous at $x = 0$,

We must have $\lim_{x\to 0} x\sin\frac{1}{x} = f(0)$

∴ $f(0) = 0 \times$ [an oscillating value between -1 and 1]

∴ $f(0) = 0$

42. (c) $n = \frac{m\pi}{2}$

Explanation :

We have, $f(x) = \begin{cases} mx + 1, & \text{if } x \leq \frac{\pi}{2} \\ \sin x + n, & \text{if } x > \frac{\pi}{2} \end{cases}$, is continuous

at $x = \frac{\pi}{2}$

∴ L.H.L. $= \lim_{x\to \frac{\pi}{2}^-}(mx + 1) = \lim_{h\to 0}\left[m\left(\frac{\pi}{2} - h\right) + 1\right]$

$= \frac{m\pi}{2} + 1$

and R.H.L.

$= \lim_{x\to \frac{\pi}{2}^+}(\sin x + n) = \lim_{h\to 0}\left[\sin\left(\frac{\pi}{2} + h\right) + n\right]$

$= \lim_{h\to 0}[\cos h + n] = 1 + n$

We must have L.H.L. = R.H.L.

⇒ $\frac{m\pi}{2} + 1 = n + 1$

∴ $n = \frac{m\pi}{2}$

43. (b) f is everywhere continuous but not differentiable at $x = n\pi, n \in Z$

Explanation :

We have, $f(x) = |\sin x|$

We know that $|x|$ and $\sin x$ are continuous for all real x.

So, $|\sin x|$ is also continuous for all real x.

$|x|$ is non-differentiable at $x = 0$

So, $|\sin x|$ is non-differentiable when $\sin x = 0$

or $x = n\pi, n \in Z$

Hence, $f(x)$ is continuous everywhere but not differentiable at $x = n\pi, n \in Z$.

44. (b) Assertion and reason are correct but reason is not the correct explanation of reason.

Explanation :

It is clear from the figure $f(x)$ is continuous at $x = 0$ but non-differentiable at $x = 0$.

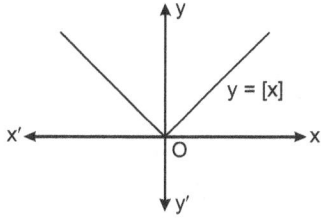

45. (a) Assertion and reason are correct and reason is the correct explanation of assertion.

Explanation :

If $x \in I$, then $\{x\} = 0$

∵ $0 \leq \{x\} < 1$ or $\{x\} = x - \{x\} = 0$

⇒ $x = [x]$ (for $x \in I$)

46. (d) Assertion is false, reason is correct.

Explanation :

At $x = a$, two tangents can be drawn. Hence, $f(x)$ is non-differentiable at $x = a$ but continuous at $x = a$.

47. (d) Assertion is false, reason is correct.

Explanation :

$\sqrt{x-2}$ is defined for $x \geq 2$

and $\sqrt{(2-x)}$ is defined for $x \leq 2$

∴ $f(x)$ is defined only when at $x = 2$

∴ $f(2) = 0$

Hence, $f(x)$ is discontinuous at $x = 2$

And $f(x)$ is a point function.

[∵ domain and range consist of one value only]

48. (c) Assertion is true, reason is false.

Explanation :

Hence, $f(x)$ is continuous everywhere but non-periodic function.

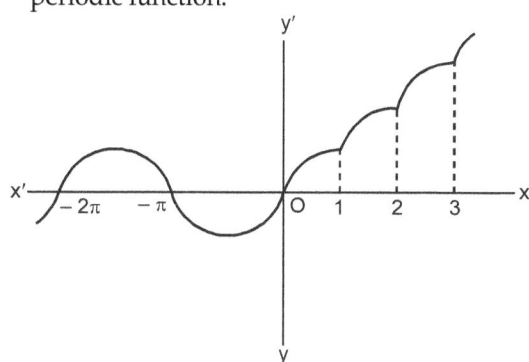

49. (a) Both (A) and (R) are true and R is the correct explanation A.

Explanation :

It is clear from figure

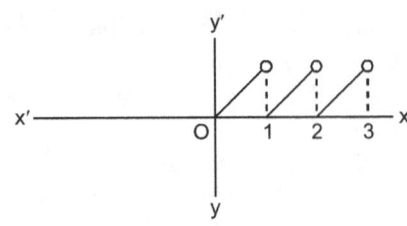

$f(x)$ is discontinuous at $x = 1$

∵ $\lim\limits_{x \to 1^-} f(x) \ne \lim\limits_{x \to 1^+} f(x)$

50. (a) Both (A) and (R) are true and R is the correct explanation A.

Explanation :

$f(0) = \text{RHL} = \lim\limits_{x \to 0^+} f(x) = \lim\limits_{x \to 0} f(h)$

$= \lim\limits_{h \to 0} \dfrac{(27-2h)^{1/3} - 3}{9 - 3(243+5h)^{1/5}}$

$= \dfrac{1}{3} \lim\limits_{h \to 0} \dfrac{\dfrac{(27-2h)^{1/3} - (27)^{1/3}}{(27-2h) - 27} \times (-2h)}{\dfrac{(243)^{1/5} - (243+5h)^{1/5}}{243 - (243+5h)} \times (-15h)}$

$= \dfrac{1}{3} \cdot \dfrac{2}{5} \cdot \dfrac{\dfrac{1}{3}(27)^{-2/3}}{\dfrac{1}{5}(243)^{-4/5}}$

$= \dfrac{2}{15} \cdot \dfrac{5}{3} \cdot \dfrac{3^{-2}}{3^{-4}} = \dfrac{2}{9} \cdot 9 = 2$

51. (a) Both (A) and (R) are true and R is the correct explanation A.

Explanation :

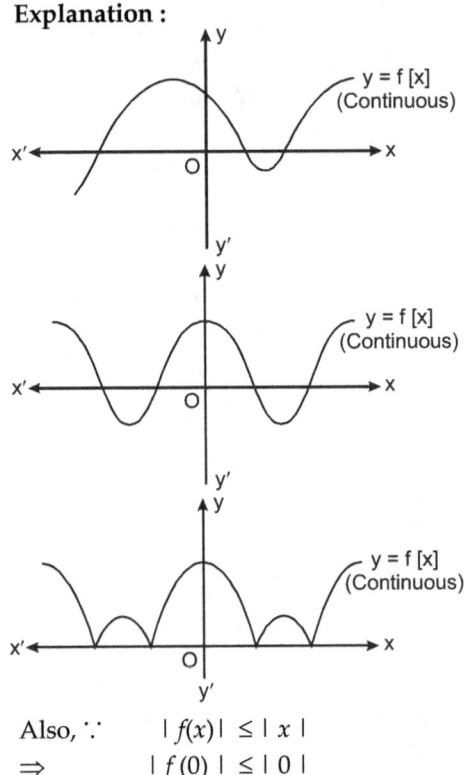

Also, ∵ $|f(x)| \le |x|$

⇒ $|f(0)| \le |0|$

⇒ $|f(0)| \le 0$

∴ $|f(0)| = 0$

⇒ $f(0) = 0$

∵ $|f(x)| \le |x|$

$\lim\limits_{x \to 0} |f(x)| \le \lim\limits_{x \to 0} |x|$

⇒ $\lim\limits_{x \to 0} |f(x)| \le 0$

But $\lim\limits_{x \to 0} |f(x)| \ge 0$

∴ $\lim\limits_{x \to 0} |f(x)| = 0 = |f(0)|$

RHL = V.F.

Hence, $|f(x)|$ is continuous at $x = 0$.

52. (c) A is true but R is false.

Explanation :

Option is (c) A is true but R is false.

Assertion

$f(0) = 0$

$\lim\limits_{x \to 0} x^2 \sin\left(\dfrac{1}{x}\right) = 0^2 \times \text{(finite value)}$

$= 0$

∴ It is continuous at $x = 0$

Reason: $h(x) = x^2$ is continuous but $g(x)$ is not continuous

$\lim\limits_{x \to 0} \sin\left(\dfrac{1}{x}\right) = $ not defined (value oscillates)

$\lim\limits_{x \to 0} \sin\left(\dfrac{1}{x}\right) \ne 0$

∴ It is not continuous at $x = 0$.

53. (a) Both (A) and (R) are true and R is the correct explanation A.

Explanation :

Correct option is (a) Both A and R are true and R is the correct explanation of A.

Assertion:

$f(x) = x\left(\dfrac{1+e^{1/x}}{1-e^{1/x}}\right) (x \ne 0)$

L.H.L. $= \lim\limits_{x \to 0^-} f(x) = \lim\limits_{x \to 0} x\left(\dfrac{1+e^{1/x}}{1-e^{1/x}}\right)$

$= \lim\limits_{h \to 0}(-h)\left(\dfrac{1+e^{1/x}}{1-e^{1/x}}\right) = 0$

R.H.L. $= \lim\limits_{x \to 0^-} f(x) = \lim\limits_{x \to 0^+} x\left(\dfrac{1+e^{1/x}}{1-e^{1/x}}\right)$

$= \lim\limits_{h \to 0} h\left(\dfrac{1+e^{1/h}}{1-e^{1/h}}\right) = \lim\limits_{h \to 0} h\left(\dfrac{e^{-1/h}+1}{e^{-1/h}-1}\right) = 0$

Given $f(0) = 0$

So, LHL = RHL = $f(0)$

Hence, $f(x)$ is continuous at $x = 0$

Also, reason is true.

54. (i) (b) $x = a\cos^3\theta$

$\therefore \quad \dfrac{dx}{d\theta} = a(3\cos^2\theta)(-\sin\theta)$

$\qquad = -3a\cos^2\theta\sin\theta$

$\dfrac{dx}{d\theta}\bigg|_{\theta=\frac{\pi}{4}} = -3a\cos^2\dfrac{\pi}{4}\sin\dfrac{\pi}{4}$

$\qquad = -3a\left(\dfrac{1}{\sqrt{2}}\right)^2\left(\dfrac{1}{\sqrt{2}}\right) = \dfrac{-3a}{2\sqrt{2}}$

(ii) (a) $y = a\sin^3\theta$

$\therefore \quad \dfrac{dy}{d\theta} = a(3\sin^2\theta\cos\theta)$

$\qquad = 3a\sin^2\theta\cos\theta$

$\therefore \quad \dfrac{dy}{d\theta}\bigg|_{\theta=\frac{\pi}{4}} = 3a\sin^2\dfrac{\pi}{4}\cos\dfrac{\pi}{4} = 3a\left(\dfrac{1}{\sqrt{2}}\right)^2\left(\dfrac{1}{\sqrt{2}}\right)$

$\qquad = \dfrac{3a}{2\sqrt{2}}$

(iii) (b) $\dfrac{dy}{dx} = \dfrac{\dfrac{dy}{d\theta}}{\dfrac{dx}{d\theta}} = \dfrac{3a\sin^2\theta\cos\theta}{-3a\cos^2\theta\sin\theta} = -\tan\theta$

(iv) (d) $\dfrac{dy}{dx}\bigg|_{\theta=\frac{\pi}{6}} = -\tan\dfrac{\pi}{6} = \dfrac{-1}{\sqrt{3}}$

(v) (c) $\dfrac{d^2y}{dx^2} = \dfrac{d}{dx}\left(\dfrac{dy}{dx}\right)$

$\qquad = \dfrac{d}{dx}(-\tan\theta)$

$\qquad = -\sec^2\theta \times \dfrac{d\theta}{dx}$

$\qquad = -\sec^2\theta \times \dfrac{1}{-3a\cos^2\theta\sin\theta}$

$\qquad = \dfrac{1}{3a}\sec^4\theta\, \text{cosec}\,\theta$

$\therefore \quad \dfrac{d^2y}{dx^2}\bigg|_{\theta=\frac{\pi}{4}} = \dfrac{1}{3a}(\sqrt{2})^4(\sqrt{2}) = 4\dfrac{\sqrt{2}}{3a}$

55. (i) (b) $y = \cos\sqrt{x}$

$\dfrac{dy}{dx} = \dfrac{-\sin\sqrt{x}}{2\sqrt{x}}$

(ii) (c) $x = a\cos t$

$y = a\sin t$

$\dfrac{dx}{dt} = -a\sin t$

$\dfrac{dy}{dt} = a\sin\theta$

$\dfrac{dy}{dx} = \dfrac{\dfrac{dy}{dt}}{\dfrac{dx}{dt}}$

$\qquad = \dfrac{-a\sin t}{a\cos t} = \dfrac{-\sin t}{\cos t}$

$\qquad = -\cot t.$

(iii) (b) $f(x) = (x)$

R.H.D.

$f'(x) = \lim\limits_{h\to 0}\dfrac{f(0+h) - f(0)}{h}$

$\qquad = \lim\limits_{h\to 0}\dfrac{(0+h) - 0}{h}$

$\qquad = \lim\limits_{h\to 0}\dfrac{h}{h}$

$\qquad = 1$

Left hand derivative

$\qquad = \lim\limits_{h\to 0}\dfrac{f(0-h) - f(x)}{-h}$

$\qquad = \lim\limits_{h\to 0}\dfrac{|-R|}{h}$

$\qquad = \lim\limits_{h\to 0}\dfrac{-h}{h}$

$\qquad = -1$

$\because$ LHD $\neq$ RHD

$\Rightarrow f$ is not differentiable at $x = 2$.

(iv) (b) $f(x) = \sin x^2$

$f'(x) = \cos x^2\,\dfrac{d(x^2)}{dx}$

$\therefore \quad f'(x) = \cos x^2 \times 2x$

$\qquad = 2x\cos x^2.$

(v) (a) $y + \sin y = \cos x$

$\dfrac{dy}{dx} + \cos y\,\dfrac{dy}{dx} = -\sin x$

$\dfrac{dy}{dx}[1 + \cos y] = -\sin x$

$\dfrac{dy}{dx} = \dfrac{-\sin x}{1 + \cos y}.$

56. (i) (b) $f(3) = 3(t)$

RHL

$\lim\limits_{x\to 3^+} f(x) = \lim\limits_{h\to 0} f(3+h)$

$\qquad = \lim\limits_{h\to 0} a(3+h) + 1$

$\qquad = 3a + 3h + 1$

$\qquad = 3a + 1$

LHL

$\lim\limits_{x\to 3^+}(x) = \lim\limits_{h\to 0} f(3-h)$

$$= \lim_{h \to 0} b(3-h) + 3$$
$$= 3b + 3$$
∴ f is continous at x = 3 then
$$3a + 1 = 3b + 3$$
$$3a + 1 = 3b + 3$$
$$3a - 3b = 2$$
$$3(a - b) = 2$$
$$a - b = \frac{2}{3}$$
or $\quad a = b + \frac{2}{3}.$

(ii) (c) The given function is
$$f(x) = \begin{cases} kx^2, & \text{if } f(x) \le 2 \\ 3, & \text{if } x > 2 \end{cases}$$

The given function f is continuous at x = 2.
$$\lim_{x \to 2} f(x) = \lim_{x \to 2} f(x) = f(2)$$
$$\Rightarrow \lim_{x \to 2}(kx^2) = \lim_{x \to 2}(3) = 4k$$
$$\Rightarrow k \cdot 2^2 = 3 = 4k$$
$$\Rightarrow 4k = 3$$
$$\Rightarrow k = \frac{3}{4} = 0.75$$

(iii) (a) $f(x)$ and $g(x)$ are continuous at $x = 0$.
So, $(f + g), (f - g)$ are continuous.

(iv) (b) Discontinuous
$$f(x) = \begin{cases} 2x, & x < 6 \\ x - 1, & x \ge 6 \end{cases}$$
$$f(6) = 6 - 1 = 5$$
RHL
$$\lim_{x \to 6^+} f(x) = \lim_{h \to 0} f(6 + h)$$
$$= \lim_{h \to 0}(6 + h - 1)$$
$$= \lim_{h \to 0}(5 + h)$$
$$= 5$$

LHL
$$\lim_{x \to 6^-} f(x) = \lim_{h \to 0} f(6 - h)$$
$$= \lim_{h \to 0} 2(6 - h) = 12$$
∴ $\quad f(6) = \text{RHL} \ne \text{LHL}$
$\Rightarrow$ function is not continuous at $x = 6$.

(v) (b) Discontinuous
Case I : When $x = 0$
$f(x)$ is continuous at $x = 0$
If $\quad$ LHL = RHL = $f(0)$
If $\quad \underset{x \to 0^-}{\text{Lt}} f(x) = \underset{x \to 0^+}{\text{Lt}} f(x) = f(0)$

LHL at $x \to 0$
$$\underset{x \to 0^-}{\text{lt}} f(x) = \underset{h \to 0}{\text{lt}} f(0 - h)$$
$$= \underset{h \to 0}{\text{lt}} f(-h)$$
$$= \underset{h \to 0}{\text{lt}} \frac{|-h|}{-h}$$
$$= \underset{h \to 0}{\text{lt}} \frac{-h}{-h}$$
$$= \underset{h \to 0}{\text{lt}} -1$$
$$= -1$$

RHL at $x \to 0$
$$\underset{x \to 0^+}{\text{lt}} f(x) = \underset{h \to 0}{\text{lt}} f(0 + h)$$
$$= \underset{h \to 0}{\text{lt}} f(h)$$
$$= \underset{h \to 0}{\text{lt}} \frac{|h|}{h}$$
$$= \underset{h \to 0}{\text{lt}} \frac{h}{h}$$
$$= \underset{h \to 0}{\text{lt}} 1$$
$$= 1$$
∴ $\quad$ LHL ≠ RHL.

Chapter 6: Applications of Derivative

1. The abscissa of the point on the curve $3y = 6x - 5x^3$, at which the normal passes through origin is:
   (a) 1
   (b) $\frac{1}{3}$
   (c) 2
   (d) $\frac{1}{2}$

2. The two curves $x^3 - 3xy^2 + 2 = 0$ and $3x^2y - y^3 = 2$:
   (a) touch each other
   (b) cut at right angle
   (c) cut at an angle $\frac{\pi}{3}$
   (d) cut at an angle $\frac{\pi}{4}$

3. The tangent to the curve given by $x = e^t \cdot \cos t$, $y = e^t \cdot \sin t$ at $t = \frac{\pi}{4}$ makes with x-axis an angle:
   (a) π
   (b) $\frac{\pi}{4}$
   (c) $\frac{\pi}{3}$
   (d) $\frac{\pi}{2}$

4. The equation of the normal to the curve $y = \sin x$ at $(0, 0)$ is:
   (a) $x = 0$
   (b) $y = 0$
   (c) $x + y = 0$
   (d) $x - y = 0$

5. The point on the curve $y^2 = x$, where the tangent makes an angle of $\frac{\pi}{4}$ with x-axis is
   (a) $\left(\frac{1}{2}, \frac{1}{4}\right)$
   (b) $\left(\frac{1}{4}, \frac{1}{2}\right)$
   (c) $(4, 2)$
   (d) $(1, 1)$

6. The angle of intersection of the curves $y^2 = x$ and $x^2 = y$ at $(1, 1)$ is:
   (a) $\tan^{-1}\left(\frac{4}{3}\right)$
   (b) $\tan^{-1}\left(\frac{3}{4}\right)$
   (c) Positive
   (d) None of these

7. The interval on which the function $f(x) = 2x^3 + 9x^2 + 12x - 1$ is decreasing is: [NCERT Exemplar]
   (a) $[-1, \infty)$
   (b) $[-2, -1]$
   (c) $(-\infty, -2]$
   (d) $[-1, 1]$

8. If $y = x(x-3)^2$ decreases for the values of x given by: [NCERT Exemplar]
   (a) $1 < x < 3$
   (b) $x < 0$
   (c) $x > 0$
   (d) $0 < x < \frac{3}{2}$

9. The function $f(x) = \tan x - x$: [NCERT Exemplar]
   (a) always increases
   (b) always decreases
   (c) never increases
   (d) sometime increase and sometimes decreases

10. The function $f(x) = 4\sin^3 x - 6\sin^2 x + 12\sin x + 100$ is strictly: [NCERT Exemplar]
    (a) increasing in $\left(\pi, \frac{3\pi}{2}\right)$
    (b) decreasing in $\left(\frac{\pi}{2}, \pi\right)$
    (c) decreasing in $\left[\frac{-\pi}{2}, \frac{\pi}{2}\right]$
    (d) decreasing in $\left[0, \frac{\pi}{2}\right]$

11. Which of the following function is decreasing on $\left(0, \frac{\pi}{2}\right)$? [NCERT Exemplar]
    (a) $\sin 2x$
    (b) $\tan x$
    (c) $\cos x$
    (d) $\cos 3x$

12. The curve $y = x^{1/5}$ has at $(0, 0)$: [NCERT Exemplar]
    (a) a vertical tangent (parallel to Y-axis)
    (b) a horizontal tangent (parallel to X-axis)
    (c) an oblique tangent
    (d) not tangent

13. If $x + y = K$ is normal to $y^2 = 12x$, then K is:
    (a) 3
    (b) 9
    (c) -9
    (d) -3

14. If the curve $ay + x^2 = 7$ and $x^3 = y$, cut orthogonally at $(1, 1)$, the the value of a is:
    (a) 1
    (b) 0
    (c) -6
    (d) 6

15. The points at which the tangents to the curve $y = x^3 - 12x + 18$ are parallel to X-axis are: [NCERT Examplar]
    (a) $(2, -2), (-2, -34)$
    (b) $(2, 34), (-2, 0)$
    (c) $(0, 34), (-2, 0)$
    (d) $(2, 2), (-2, 34)$

16. If x is real, then the minimum value of $x^2 - 8x + 17$ is:
    (a) -1
    (b) 0
    (c) 1
    (d) 2

17. The function $f(x) = 2x^3 - 3x^2 - 12x + 4$, has :
    (a) two points of local maximum
    (b) two points of local minimum
    (c) one maxima and one minima
    (d) no maxima or minima

18. The maximum slope of curve :
    $y = -x^3 + 3x^2 + 9x - 27$ is :
    (a) 0   (b) 12
    (c) 16   (d) 32

19. The function $f(x) = x^x$ has a statinoary point at :
    (a) $x = e$ (b) $x = \dfrac{1}{e}$
    (c) $x = 1$ (d) $x = \sqrt{e}$

20. A right circular cylinder which is open at the top and has a given surface area, will have the greatest volume, if its height h and radius r are related by :
    (a) $2h = r$ (b) $h = 4r$
    (c) $h = 2r$ (d) $h = r$

21. The equation of tangent to the curve $(1 + x^2) = 2 - x$, where it crosses x-axis is :   [NCERT Exemplar]
    (a) $x + 5y = 2$ (b) $x - 5y = 2$
    (c) $5x - y = 2$ (d) $5x + y = 2$

22. The tangent to the curve $y = e^{2x}$ at the point (0, 1) meets x-axis at :   [NCERT Exemplar]
    (a) (0, 1)   (b) $\left(-\dfrac{1}{2}, 0\right)$
    (c) (2, 0)   (d) (0, 2)

23. What is the slope of the tangent to the curve $y = \dfrac{2x}{(x^2 + 1)}$ at (0, 0) ?
    (a) 0   (b) 1
    (c) 2   (d) 3

24. What will be the differential function of $\sqrt{(x^2 + 2)}$?
    (a) $x\sqrt{(x^2 + 2)}$ (b) $\dfrac{x}{\sqrt{(x^2 + 2)}}$
    (c) $\dfrac{x}{\sqrt{(x^2 - 2)}}$ (d) $\dfrac{-x}{\sqrt{(x^2 + 2)}}$

25. What is the derivative of $\log (x^2 + 4)$?
    (a) $\left(\dfrac{2x}{x^2 + 4}\right)$ (b) $\dfrac{2x}{(x^2 - 4)}$
    (c) $\dfrac{-2x}{(x^2 + 4)}$ (d) $\dfrac{-2x}{(x^2 - 4)}$

26. What is the nature of function of $(x) = 7x - 4$ on R ?
    (a) increasing
    (b) decreasing
    (c) strictly increasing
    (d) increasing and decreasing

27. Find the interval in which function $f(x) = x^2 - 4x + 5$ is increasing :
    (a) $(2, \infty)$ (b) $(-\infty, 2)$
    (c) $(3, \infty)$ (d) $(-\infty, \infty)$

28. Find the interval in which function, $f(x) = \sin x + \cos x$, $0 \le x \le 2\pi$ is decreasing :
    (a) $\left(\dfrac{\pi}{4}, \dfrac{5\pi}{4}\right)$ (b) $\left(\dfrac{-\pi}{4}, \dfrac{5\pi}{4}\right)$
    (c) $\left(\dfrac{\pi}{4}, \dfrac{-5\pi}{4}\right)$ (d) $\left(\dfrac{-\pi}{4}, \dfrac{\pi}{4}\right)$

29. The minimum value of the function, $y = 2x^3 - 21x^2 + 36x - 20$ is :
    (a) -120 (b) -126
    (c) -128 (d) None of these

30. Let l be the length and b be the breadth of a rectangle such that $l + b = k$. What is the minimum area of rectangle ?
    (a) $2k^2$ (b) k^2
    (c) $\dfrac{k^2}{2}$ (d) $\dfrac{k^2}{4}$

31. The critical point and nature for the function $f(x, y) = x^2 - 2x + y^2 + 2y - 2$ is :
    (a) (1, 1) Max.   (b) (1, -1) Max.
    (c) (1, 1) Min.   (d) (1, -1) Min.

32. What is the maximum area of a triangle that can be inscribed in a circle of radius 'a' ?
    (a) $\dfrac{3a^2}{4}$ (b) $\dfrac{a^2}{2}$
    (c) $\dfrac{3\sqrt{3}a^2}{4}$ (d) $\dfrac{\sqrt{3}a^2}{4}$

33. The greatest value of $5 \sin^2 x + 7 \cos^2 x - 4 \sin x \cos x$ will be :
    (a) $6 - \sqrt{5}$ (b) $6 + \sqrt{5}$
    (c) $-6 + \sqrt{5}$ (d) $-6 - \sqrt{5}$

34. Which one of following is corect in respect of the function, $f(x) = x^3 \sin x$?
    (a) It has local maximum at $x = 0$
    (b) It has local minimum at $x = 0$
    (c) It has neither maximum nor minimum at $x = 0$
    (d) It has maximum value as 1

Choose the correct option :
(a) Both (A) and (B) are true and R is the correct explanation A.
(b) Both (A) and (R) are true but R is not correct explanation of A.
(c) A is true but R is false.
(d) A is false but R is true.

35. **Assertion (A)** : The points of contact of the vertical tangents to $x = 2 - 3 \sin \theta$, $y = 3 + 2 \cos \theta$ are $(-1, 3)$ and $(5, 3)$.

Reason (R) : For vertical tangent, $\dfrac{dx}{d\theta} = 0$.

36. **Assertion (A) :** If $y^2 = 3 + 2x - x^2$ then, at $(3, 0)$ and $(-1, 0)$ tangent is perpendicular to x-axis.

    Reason (R) : At $(3, 0)$ and $(-1, 0)$, $\dfrac{dy}{dx} = \infty$.

37. **Assertion (A) :** The points on the curve $y^2 = x + \sin x$ at which the tangent is parallel to x-axis lie on a striaght line.

    Reason (R) : Tangent is parallel to x-axis, then
    $\dfrac{dy}{dx} = 0$ or $\dfrac{dy}{dx} = \infty$.

38. **Assertion (A) :** Equation of tangents to the curve $f(x) = x^2$ at the point where slope of tangent is equal to functional value of the curve is $4x - y - 4 = 0, y = 0$.

    Reason (R) : $f'(x) = f(x)$, at functional value of curve.

39. An architect designs a building for a multi-national company. The floor consists of a rectangular region with semicircular ends having a perimeter of 200 m as show below :

    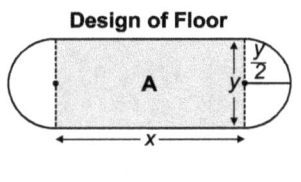
    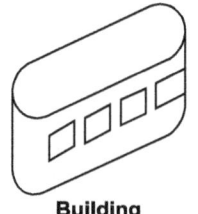

    Give the answers of the following questions :

    (i) If x and y represents the length and breadth of the rectangular region, then the relation between the variables is :
    (a) $x + \pi y = 100$ (b) $2x + \pi y = 200$
    (c) $\pi x + y = 50$ (d) $x + y = 100$

    (ii) The area of the rectangular region A expressed as a function of x is :
    (a) $\dfrac{2}{\pi}(100x - x^2)$ (b) $\dfrac{1}{\pi}(100x - x^2)$
    (c) $\dfrac{x}{\pi}(100 - x)$ (d) $\pi y^2 + \dfrac{2}{\pi}(100x - x^2)$

    (iii) The maximum value of area A is :
    (a) $\dfrac{\pi}{3200}$ m^2 (b) $\dfrac{3200}{\pi}$ m^2
    (c) $\dfrac{5000}{\pi}$ m^2 (d) $\dfrac{1000}{\pi}$ m^2

    (iv) The CEO of the multi-national company is interested in maximizing the area of the whole floor including the semi-circular ends. For this to happen the value of x should be :
    (a) 0 m   (b) 30 m
    (c) 50 m   (d) 80 m

    (v) The extra area generated if the area of the whole floor is maximized is :
    (a) $\dfrac{3000}{\pi}$ m^2

    (b) $\dfrac{5000}{\pi}$ m^2
    (c) $\dfrac{7000}{\pi}$ m^2
    (d) No change both areas are equal

40. A new township is to be constructed along the curve $y = x^3 - 11x + 5$. Two attraction point i.e., amusement park and shopping mall is to be made on the this curve. At a point $(1, -5)$ on the curve amusement park is to be constructed and on another point shopping mall is to be constructed at which tangent has the equation $y = x - 11$.

    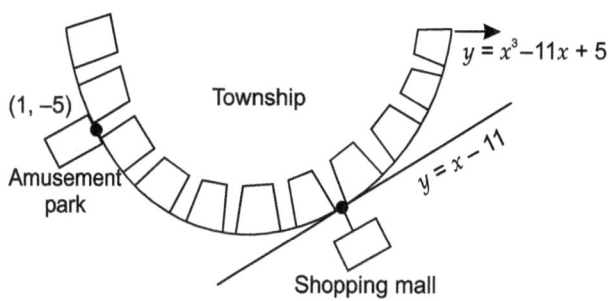

    Give the answers of the following questions :

    (i) Find the slope of the normal to the curve at $(1, -5)$ on which amusement park is to be constructed ?
    (a) $\dfrac{1}{8}$ (b) 8
    (c) -8 (d) $\dfrac{-1}{8}$

    (ii) Find the equation of normal to the curve along which amusement park is to be constructed ?
    (a) $8y - x - 41 = 0$ (b) $8y + x = 41$
    (c) $8y + x + 41 = 0$ (d) $8y - x + 41 = 0$

    (iii) Find the point of x where curve along which township is parallel to X-axis ?
    (a) $\pm\sqrt{\dfrac{11}{3}}$ (b) $\pm\dfrac{11}{3}$
    (c) ± 4 (d) ± 2

    (iv) Find the points on the curve at which tangent $y = x - 11$ is given ?
    (a) $(-2, 19)$ (b) $(2, -9)$
    (c) $(-2, 9)$ (d) $(2, -19)$

    (v) What is the slope of tangent at the curve ?
    (a) 3   (b) 1
    (c) -1 (d) $\dfrac{1}{2}$

41. A new room is to be constructed in a house to increase the living area into it. A window is to be opened on one of the walls of the room in shape of rectangle surmounted by an equilateral triangle. If

the perimeter of window is 12 m and they want to bring maximum light from the window.

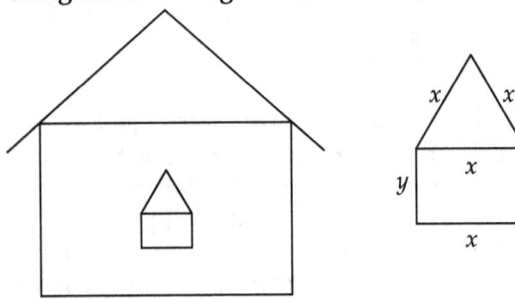

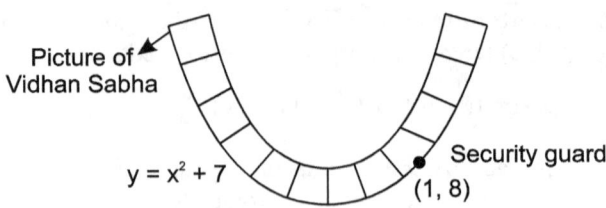

Give the answers of the following questions :

(i) Express y in terms of x :
(a) $y = 6 - \dfrac{3}{2}x$
(b) $y = 3x - 6$
(c) $y = \dfrac{3}{2}x - 12$
(d) $y = \dfrac{3}{2}x - 6$

(ii) If A represent the area of window, what is the function of in terms of x ?
(a) $A = \dfrac{x - 3x^2 + \sqrt{3}x^2}{4}$
(b) $A = \dfrac{3x^2}{2} - \dfrac{\sqrt{3}}{4}x^2 - 6x$
(c) $A = 6x - \dfrac{3x^2}{2} + \dfrac{\sqrt{3}}{4}x^2$
(d) $A = \left(\dfrac{3 + \sqrt{3}}{4}\right)x^2 + 6x$

(iii) For what value of x, the area will be maximum ?
(a) $\dfrac{12}{6 + \sqrt{3}}$
(b) $\dfrac{12}{6 - \sqrt{3}}$
(c) $\dfrac{18 - 6\sqrt{3}}{6 - \sqrt{3}}$
(d) $\dfrac{6 - \sqrt{3}}{12}$

(iv) Write the breadth of window :
(a) $\dfrac{6 + \sqrt{3}}{12}$
(b) $\dfrac{6 - \sqrt{3}}{12}$
(c) $\dfrac{12}{6 + \sqrt{3}}$
(d) $\dfrac{18 - 6\sqrt{3}}{6 - \sqrt{3}}$

(v) What is the maximum area of triangular part of window ?
(a) $\dfrac{63\sqrt{3}}{39 - 17\sqrt{3}}$
(b) $\dfrac{36\sqrt{3}}{39 - 12\sqrt{3}}$
(c) $\dfrac{39 - 12\sqrt{3}}{36\sqrt{3}}$
(d) $\dfrac{36\sqrt{3}}{39 + 12\sqrt{3}}$

42. Vidhan Sabha is situated in Delhi along the curve $y = x^2 + 7$. A security guard is standing at a point (1, 8) on the curve who keeps his eyes horizontally and vertically on the people for security purposes. Security guard has a doubt on a person who is standing at a point (3, 7). He catches the person after a while.

Give the answers of the following questions :

(i) Find the slope of tangent at given points :
(a) 2
(b) $-\dfrac{1}{2}$
(c) $\dfrac{1}{2}$
(d) -2

(ii) Find the slope of normal to the curve at given point :
(a) 2
(b) $-\dfrac{1}{2}$
(c) $\dfrac{1}{2}$
(d) -2

(iii) Find the equation of tangent to the given curve :
(a) $y = 2x - 6$
(b) $y = x + 6$
(c) $2y = x - 6$
(d) $y = 2x + 6$

(iv) Find the equation of normal to the curve :
(a) $x + 2y = 17$
(b) $x - 2y = 17$
(c) $x - 2y + 17 = 0$
(d) $x + 2y + 7 = 0$

(v) How much distance covered by security guard to catch that person ?
(a) $\dfrac{1}{\sqrt{5}}$
(b) 5
(c) $\sqrt{5}$
(d) 4

43. After the lockdown period of Covid-19, it is difficult to restart the business of Touring Agency. A tour operator charges ₹ 200 per passenger for 50 passengers. He is giving a discount of ₹ 5 for each 10 passenger in excess of 50. He wants to maximise his earning during this pandemic period.

Give the answer of the following questions :

(i) Let x be the number of passengers and y is the earning per passenger of the operator. Write the function of y in terms of x.
(a) $y = 225 - \dfrac{x}{2}$
(b) $y = \dfrac{x}{2} - 225$
(c) $y = 200 + \dfrac{x}{2}$
(d) $y = 200 - \dfrac{x}{2}$

(ii) Give the slope of that earning function.
(a) $\dfrac{-1}{5}$
(b) $\dfrac{1}{10}$
(c) $\dfrac{1}{2}$
(d) $\dfrac{-1}{2}$

(iii) What is the total earning function ?
(a) $225 - \dfrac{x}{2}$
(b) $225x - \dfrac{x^2}{2}$

Applications of Derivative | 313

(c) $220 - \dfrac{x}{2}$ (d) $220 - \dfrac{x^2}{3}$

(iv) At what value of x he can have the maximum amount ?

(a) 200   (b) 225
(c) 175   (d) 220

(v) What is his maximum amount of earning ?

(a) 225   (b) 175
(c) 25000   (d) 25312·50

Solutions

1. (a) 1

Explanation :
Let (x_1, y_1) be the point on the given curve $3y = 6x - 5x^3$ at which the normal passes through the origin. Then we have $\left(\dfrac{dy}{dx}\right)_{(x_1, y_1)} = 2 - 5x_1^2$.

Again, the equation of the normal of (x_1, y_1) passing through the origin gives $2 - 5x_1^2 = \dfrac{-x_1}{y_1}$

$= \dfrac{-3}{6 - 5x_1^2}$.

Since $x_1 = 1$ satisfies the equation.

2. (b) cut at right angle

Explanation :
From first equation of the curve, we have

$3x^2 - 3y^2 - 6xy \dfrac{dy}{dx} = 0$

$\Rightarrow \dfrac{dy}{dx} = \dfrac{x^2 - y^2}{2xy} = (m_1)$ say

and second equation of the curve gives

$6xy + 3x^2 \dfrac{dy}{dx} - 3y^2 \dfrac{dy}{dx} = 0$

$\Rightarrow \dfrac{dy}{dx} = \dfrac{-2xy}{x^2 - y^2} = (m_2)$ say

Since $m_1 \cdot m_2 = -1$.
So, both curves are orthogonal.

3. (d) $\dfrac{\pi}{2}$

Explanation :
$\dfrac{dx}{dt} = -e^t \cdot \sin t + e^t \cos t$, $\dfrac{dy}{dt} = e^t \cos t + e^t \sin t$

$\therefore \left(\dfrac{dy}{dx}\right)_{t = \frac{\pi}{4}} = \dfrac{\cos t + \sin t}{\cos t - \sin t} = \dfrac{\sqrt{2}}{0} = \infty$

$\tan \theta = \infty$

$\theta = \tan^{-1} \infty$

$\theta = \dfrac{\pi}{2}$

So the correct option is (d).

4. (c) $x + y = 0$

Explanation :
Here $y = \sin x$

$\dfrac{dy}{dx} = \cos x$.

$\therefore$ Slope of normal $= \left(\dfrac{-1}{\cos x}\right)_{x = 0} = -1$.

Hence, the equation of normal is

$y - 0 = -1(x + 0)$

or $x + y = 0$.

5. (b) $\left(\dfrac{1}{4}, \dfrac{1}{2}\right)$

Explanation :

$\dfrac{dy}{dx} = \dfrac{1}{2y}$

Also tangent makes an angle of $\dfrac{\pi}{4}$ with x-axis.

$\therefore \dfrac{dy}{dx} = \tan \dfrac{\pi}{4} = 1$

$\Rightarrow 1 = \dfrac{1}{2y}$

$\Rightarrow y = \dfrac{1}{2} \Rightarrow x = \dfrac{1}{4}$

6. (b) $\tan^{-1}\left(\dfrac{3}{4}\right)$

Explanation :
Given, equation of curves are

$y^2 = x$ and $x^2 = y$

$\therefore x^4 = x$

$\Rightarrow x^4 - x = 0$

$\Rightarrow x(x^3 - 1) = 0$

$\Rightarrow x = 0, x = 1$

At $x = 0, y = 0, x = 1, y = 1$

$\therefore$ Points of intersection are (0, 0) and (1, 1).

Now, $y^2 = x$ and $y = x^2$

$2y \dfrac{dy}{dx} = 1$ and $\dfrac{dy}{dx} = 2x$

$\dfrac{dy}{dx} = \dfrac{1}{2y}$

$\Rightarrow m_1 = \dfrac{1}{2}$ and $m_2 = 2$

$\therefore \tan \theta = \left|\dfrac{m_2 - m_1}{1 + m_1 m_2}\right|$

$$= \left|\frac{2 - \frac{1}{2}}{1 + \frac{1}{2} \times 2}\right| = \frac{\frac{3}{2}}{2}$$

$$\Rightarrow \quad \tan\theta = \frac{3}{4}$$

$$\Rightarrow \quad \theta = \tan^{-1}\frac{3}{4}$$

7. (b) $[-2, -1]$
   Explanation :
   We have, $f(x) = 2x^3 + 9x^2 + 12x - 1$
   $\therefore \quad f'(x) = 6x^2 + 18x + 12$
   $\quad\quad\quad = 6(x^2 + 3x + 2) = 6(x + 2)(x + 1)$
   So, $f'(x) \leq 0$, for decreasing.
   On drawing number lines as below

   ```
   +ve        −        +ve
   ←——————+———————+——————→
          −2       −1
   ```

   We see that $f'(x)$ is decreasing in $[-2, -1]$.

8. (a) $1 < x < 3$
   Explanation :
   We have, $y = x(x-3)^2$
   $\therefore \quad \dfrac{dy}{dx} = x \cdot 2(x-3) \cdot 1 + (x-3)^2 \cdot 1$
   $\quad\quad = 2x^2 - 6x + x^2 + 9 - 6x$
   $\quad\quad = 3x^2 - 12x + 9$
   $\quad\quad = 3(x^2 - 3x - x + 3) = 3(x - 3)(x - 1)$

   ```
      +        −        +
   ←——+————————+———————→
      1        3
   ```

   So, $y = x(x-3)^2$ decreases for $(1, 3)$.
   [Since, $y' < 0$ for all $x \in (1, 3)$, hence y is decreasing on $(1, 3)$].

9. (a) always increases
   Explanation :
   We have, $\quad f(x) = \tan x - x$
   $\therefore \quad\quad f'(x) = \sec^2 x - 1$
   $\Rightarrow \quad\quad f'(x) \geq 0, \forall\, x \in R$
   So, $f(x)$ always increases.

10. (b) decreasing in $\left(\dfrac{\pi}{2}, \pi\right)$

    Explanation :
    We have,
    $\quad f(x) = 4\sin^3 x - 6\sin^2 x + 12\sin x + 100$
    $\therefore \quad f'(x) = 12\sin^2 x \cdot \cos x - 12\sin x \cdot \cos x$
    $\quad\quad\quad\quad + 12\cos x$
    $\quad\quad = 12[\sin^2 x \cdot \cos x - \sin x \cdot \cos x + \cos x]$
    $\quad\quad = 12\cos x\,[\sin^2 x - \sin x + 1]$
    $\Rightarrow \quad f'(x) = 12\cos x\,[\sin^2 x + (1 - \sin x)] \quad\ldots(i)$
    $\because\ 1 - \sin x \geq 0$ and $\sin^2 x \geq 0$
    $\therefore\ \sin^2 x + 1 - \sin x \geq 0$

    Hence, $f'(x) > 0$, when $\cos x > 0$ i.e., $x \in \left(-\dfrac{\pi}{2}, \dfrac{\pi}{2}\right)$
    So, $f(x)$ is increasing when $x \in \left(-\dfrac{\pi}{2}, \dfrac{\pi}{2}\right)$ and
    $f'(x) < 0$, when $\cos x < 0$ i.e., $x \in \left(\dfrac{\pi}{2}, \dfrac{3\pi}{2}\right)$
    Hence, $f(x)$ is decreasing when $x \in \left(\dfrac{\pi}{2}, \dfrac{3\pi}{2}\right)$
    Since $\left(\dfrac{\pi}{2}, \pi\right) \in \left(\dfrac{\pi}{2}, \dfrac{3\pi}{2}\right)$
    Hence, $f(x)$ is decreasing in $\left(\dfrac{\pi}{2}, \pi\right)$

11. (c) $\cos x$
    Explanation :
    In the interval $\left(0, \dfrac{\pi}{2}\right)$, $f(x) = \cos x$
    $\Rightarrow \quad f'(x) = -\sin x$
    which gives $f'(x) < 0$ in $\left(0, \dfrac{\pi}{2}\right)$
    Hence, $f(x) = \cos x$ in decreasing in $\left(0, \dfrac{\pi}{2}\right)$.

12. (a) a vertical tangent (parallel to Y-axis)
    Explanation :
    We have, $\quad y = x^{1/5}$
    $\Rightarrow \quad \dfrac{dy}{dx} = \dfrac{1}{5} x^{\frac{1}{5} - 1} = \dfrac{1}{5} x^{-4/5}$
    $\therefore \quad \left(\dfrac{dy}{dx}\right)_{(0,0)} = \dfrac{1}{5} \times (0)^{-4/5} = \infty$
    So, the curve $y = x^{1/5}$ has a vertical tangent at $(0, 0)$, which is parallel to Y-axis.

13. (a) 9
    Explanation :
    We have, $\quad y^2 = 12x$
    $\Rightarrow \quad 2y\dfrac{dy}{dx} = 12$
    $\Rightarrow \quad \dfrac{dy}{dx} = \dfrac{6}{y}$
    Let $x + y = K$ be normal to $y^2 = 12x$ at point $P(x_1, y_1)$, then
    $\left(\dfrac{-1}{dy/dx}\right)_{\text{at } p} = $ (Slope of the line $x + y = K$)
    $\Rightarrow \quad -\dfrac{y_1}{6} = -1$
    $\Rightarrow \quad y_1 = 6$
    Since (x_1, y_1) lies on $y^2 = 12x$, therefore
    $\quad\quad y_1^2 = 12x_1$

$\Rightarrow \qquad 12x_1 = 36$

$\Rightarrow \qquad x_1 = 3$

Also $P(x_1, y_1)$ lies on $x + y = K$, therefore

$\qquad x_1 + y_1 = K$

$\Rightarrow \qquad K = 9.$

14. (d) 6

Explanation :

We have, $\quad ay + x^2 = 7$ and $x^3 = y$

On differentiating w.r.t. x in both equations, we have

$$a \cdot \frac{dy}{dx} + 2x = 0 \text{ and } 3x^2 = \frac{dy}{dx}$$

$\Rightarrow \qquad \frac{dy}{dx} = -\frac{2x}{a}$ and $\frac{dy}{dx} = 3x^2$

$\Rightarrow \qquad \left(\frac{dy}{dx}\right)_{(1,1)} = \frac{-2}{a} = m_1$

and $\qquad = 3 \cdot 1 = 3 = m_2$

Since, the curves are orthogonally at (1, 1).

$\therefore \qquad m_1 \cdot m_2 = -1$

$\Rightarrow \qquad \left(\frac{-2}{a}\right) \cdot 3 = -1$

$\therefore \qquad a = 6.$

15. (d) (2, 2), (– 2, 34)

Explanation :

The given equation of curve is

$\qquad y = x^3 - 12x + 18$

$\therefore \qquad \frac{dy}{dx} = 3x^2 - 12$

[on differentiating w.r.t. x]

So, the slope of line parallel to the X-axis.

$\therefore \qquad \left(\frac{dy}{dx}\right) = 0$

$\Rightarrow \qquad 3x^2 - 12 = 0$

$\Rightarrow \qquad x^2 = \frac{12}{3} = 4$

$\therefore \qquad x = \pm 2$

For $x = 2$, $\quad y = 2^3 - 12 \times 2 + 18 = 2$

and for $x = -2$, $y = (-2)^3 - 12(-2) + 18$

$\qquad = 34$

So, the points are (2, 2) and (– 2, 34).

16. (c) 1

Explanation :

Let $\quad f(x) = x^2 - 8x + 17$

$\therefore \quad f'(x) = 2x - 8$

So, $\quad f'(x) = 0$, gives $x = 4$

Now, $\quad f''(x) = 2 > 0, \forall\ x$

So, $x = 4$ is the point of local minima.

$\therefore$ Minimum value of $f(x) =$ at $x = 4$.

$\qquad f(4) = 4 \times 4 - 8 \times 4 + 17$

$\qquad = 1.$

17. (c) one maxima and one minima

Explanation :

We have $\quad f(x) = 2x^3 - 3x^2 - 12x + 4$

$\therefore \qquad f'(x) = 6x^2 - 6x - 12$

Now, $\quad f'(x) = 0$

$\Rightarrow \quad 6(x^2 - x - 2) = 0$

$\Rightarrow \quad 6(x + 1)(x - 2) = 0$

$\Rightarrow \qquad x = -1$ and $x = +2$

On number line for $f'(x)$, we get

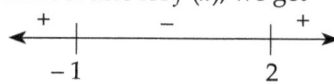

Hence $x = -1$ is point of local maxima and $x = 2$ is point of local minima.

So, $f(x)$ has one maxima and one minima.

18. (b) 12

Explanation :

We have, $\quad y = -x^3 + 3x^2 + 9x - 27$

$\therefore \qquad \frac{dy}{dx} = -3x^2 + 6x + 9 =$ Slope of the curve

and $\qquad \frac{d^2y}{dx^2} = -6x + 6 = -6(x - 1)$

$\therefore \qquad \frac{d^2y}{dx^2} = 0$

$\Rightarrow \quad -6(x - 1) = 0$

$\Rightarrow \qquad x = 1 > 0$

Now, $\quad \frac{d^3y}{dx^3} = 6 - < 0$

So, the maximum slope of given curve is at $x = 1$.

$\therefore \left(\frac{dy}{dx}\right)_{(x=1)} = -3 \cdot 1^2 + 6 \cdot 1 + 9 = 12.$

19. (b) $x = \dfrac{1}{e}$

Explanation :

We have, $\quad f(x) = x^x$

Let $\qquad y = x^x$

and $\qquad \log y = x \log x$

$\therefore \qquad \frac{1}{y} \cdot \frac{dy}{dx} = x \cdot \frac{1}{x} + \log x \cdot 1$

$\Rightarrow \qquad \frac{dy}{dx} = (1 + \log x) \cdot x^x$

$\therefore \qquad \frac{dy}{dx} = 0$

$\Rightarrow \quad (1 + \log x) \cdot x^x = 0$

$\Rightarrow \qquad \log x = -1$

$\Rightarrow \qquad \log x = \log e^{-1}$

$\Rightarrow \qquad x = e^{-1}$

$\Rightarrow \qquad x = \dfrac{1}{e}$

Hence $f(x)$ has a sationary point at $x = \dfrac{1}{e}.$

20. (d) $r = h$

Explanation :
Surface area, $S = 2\pi rh + \pi r^2$ ...(i)
and $V = \pi r^2 h$ ...(ii)

From Eq. (i), $h = \dfrac{S - \pi r^2}{2\pi r}$

From Eq. (ii), $V = \dfrac{r}{2}(S - \pi r^2)$

$\Rightarrow \dfrac{dV}{dr} = \dfrac{1}{2}(S - 3\pi r^2) = 0$

$\Rightarrow S - 3\pi r^2 = 0$
$\Rightarrow S = 3\pi r^2$

On putting the value of S in Eq. (i), we get
$3\pi r^2 = 2\pi rh + \pi r^2$
$\Rightarrow r = h.$

21. (a) $x + 5y = 2$

Explanation :
We have, equation of the curve $y(1 + x^2) = 2 - x$
It is given that the curve crosses x-axis.
Putting $y = 0$ in equation (i), we get
$\therefore \quad 0(1 + x^2) = 2 - x$
$\Rightarrow \quad x = 2$

So, the curve passes through the point (2, 0).
Now differentiating equation (i) w.r.t. x, we get

$\therefore \quad y \times (0 + 2x) + (1 + x^2) \cdot \dfrac{dy}{dx} = 0 - 1$

$\Rightarrow \quad \dfrac{dy}{dx} = \dfrac{-1 - 2xy}{1 + x^2}$

$\therefore \quad \left(\dfrac{dy}{dx}\right)_{(2,0)} = \dfrac{-1 - 2 \times 0}{1 + 2^2} = -\dfrac{1}{5}$

= slope of tangent to the curve

$\therefore$ Equation of tangent of the curve passing through (2, 0) is

$y - 0 = -\dfrac{1}{5}(x - 2)$

or $5y + x = 2.$

22. (b) $\left(-\dfrac{1}{2}, 0\right)$

Explanation :
The given equation of curve is
$y = e^{2x}$

$\therefore \quad \dfrac{dy}{dx} = 2 \cdot e^{2x}$

$\therefore \quad \left(\dfrac{dy}{dx}\right)_{(0,1)} = 2 \cdot e^{2.0}$

$= 2$
= Slope of tangent to the curve

$\therefore$ Equation of tangent is
$y - 1 = 2(x - 0)$
or $y = 2x + 1$

Above tangent line meets the x-axis, where $y = 0$.
$\therefore \quad x = -\dfrac{1}{2}$

So, the required point is $\left(\dfrac{-1}{2}, 0\right)$

23. (c) 2

Explanation :
Given, $y = \dfrac{2x}{x^2 + 1}$

$\therefore \quad \dfrac{dy}{dx} = \dfrac{(x^2 + 1) \times 2 - 2 \times (2x)}{(x^2 + 1)^2}$

$= \dfrac{2x^2 + 2 - 4x^2}{(x^2 + 1)^2}$

$= \dfrac{-2x^2 + 2}{(x^2 + 1)^2}$

$\left(\dfrac{dy}{dx}\right)_{(0,0)} = \dfrac{2}{1} = 2.$

24. (b) $\dfrac{x}{\sqrt{(x^2 + 2)}}$

Explanation :
$y = \sqrt{x^2 + 2}$

$\dfrac{dy}{dx} = \dfrac{1}{2} \times \dfrac{1}{\sqrt{x^2 + 2}} \times 2x$

$= \dfrac{x}{\sqrt{x^2 + 2}}$

$\therefore \quad dy = \dfrac{x}{\sqrt{x^2 + 2}} dx$

25. (a) $\left(\dfrac{2x}{x^2 + 4}\right)$

Explanation :
Let $f(x) = \log(x^2 + 4)$

$\therefore \quad f'(x) = \dfrac{1}{x^2 + 4} \times 2x$

$\Rightarrow \dfrac{dy}{dx} = \dfrac{2x}{x^2 + 4}$

$\Rightarrow dy = \left(\dfrac{2x}{x^2 + 4}\right) dx$

26. (c) strictly increasing

Explanation :
Let x_1 and x_2 be any two numbers in R.
Then, $x_1 < x_2$
$\Rightarrow 7 \times 1 < 7 \times 2$
$\Rightarrow 7 \times 1 - 4 < 7 \times 2 - 4$
As $f(x_1) < f(x_2)$. Thus, function f is strictly increasing on R.

27. (a) $(2, \infty)$

Explanation :
Here, $f(x) = x^2 - 4x + 5$

Then, $f'(x) = 2x - 4$
∴ $f'(x) = 0$
Then, $x = 2$
Now, point $x = 2$ divides the line into two disjoint intervals and the interval namely $(2, \infty)$ is increasing on $f(x)$.

28. (a) $\left(\dfrac{\pi}{4}, \dfrac{5\pi}{4}\right)$

    Explanation :
    $$f(x) = \sin x + \cos x$$
    $$f'(x) = \cos x - \sin x$$
    Now, $f'(x) = 0$ gives
    $$\sin x = \cos x,$$
    which gives that $x = \dfrac{\pi}{4}, \dfrac{5\pi}{4}$ as $0 \le x \le 2\pi$.

29. (a) -120

    Explanation :
    $$y = f(x) = 2x^3 - 21x^2 + 36x - 20$$
    $$f'(x) = 6x^2 - 42x + 36$$
    $$f''(x) = 12x - 42$$
    For maxima/minima point, $f'(x) = 0$
    $$6x^2 - 42x + 36 = 0$$
    $\Rightarrow$ $x^2 - 7x + 6 = 0$
    $\Rightarrow$ $(x - 6)(x - 1) = 0 \Rightarrow x = 6, 1$
    ∴ $f''(6) = 72 - 42 = 30 > 0$
    $f''(1) = 12 - 42 = -30 < 0$
    ∴ Minimum point is 6.
    and minimum value is
    $$f(6) = 2(6)^3 - 21(6)^2 + 36(6) - 20$$
    $$= 432 - 756 + 216 - 20 = -128.$$

30. (d) $\dfrac{k^2}{4}$

    Explanation :
    Here, $l + b = k$
    or $l = k - b$
    Area $= l \times b = (k - b)b$
    $= kb - b^2$
    ∴ $\dfrac{dA}{db} = k - 2b$
    For maximum area, $\dfrac{dA}{db} = 0$
    $\Rightarrow$ $k - 2b = 0$
    $\Rightarrow$ $b = \dfrac{k}{2}$
    $\dfrac{d^2A}{db^2} = -2 < 0$ (maximum area)
    ∴ Area $= (k - b) \times b$
    $= \left(k - \dfrac{k}{2}\right) \times \dfrac{k}{2} = \dfrac{k^2}{4}$

31. (b) $(1, -1)$ Max.

    Explanation :
    $$f(x, y) = x^2 - 2x + y^2 + 2y - 2$$
    Partial derivatives
    $$f'(x) = 2x - 2$$
    and $f'(y) = 2y + 2$
    ∴ For critical points
    $$f'(x) = 0$$
    $\Rightarrow$ $x = 1$
    and $f'(y) = 0$
    $2y + 2 = 0$
    $\Rightarrow$ $y = -1$
    So, critical points $(1, -1)$.
    Now, $f''(x) = 2 > 0$ and $f''(y) = 2 > 0$
    So at $(1, -1)$.
    $(f_x'' \times f_y'') - f_x' f_y' = 2 \times 2 - 0 = 4 > 0.$

32. (c) $\dfrac{3\sqrt{3}a^2}{4}$

    Explanation : Area of equilateral triangle
    $= \dfrac{\sqrt{3}}{4} \times \text{side}^2$
    ∴ Radius, OA $=$ OB $=$ OC $= a$
    Here OD $= \dfrac{a}{2}$
    As O is centroid of $\triangle$ABC.
    ∴ BD $= \sqrt{OB^2 - OD^2}$
    $= \sqrt{a^2 - \dfrac{a^2}{4}} = \dfrac{\sqrt{3}a}{2}$
    Now, BC $= 2$BD $= \sqrt{3}a$
    So, area $= \dfrac{\sqrt{3}}{4} \times (\sqrt{3}a)^2$
    $= \dfrac{3\sqrt{3}}{4} a^2.$

33. (b) $6 + \sqrt{5}$

    Explanation :
    $y = 5 \sin^2 x + 7 + \cos^2 x - 4 \sin x \cos x$
    $= (2 \sin x - \cos x)^2 + \sin^2 x + 6 \cos^2 x$
    $= (2 \sin x - \cos x)^2 + (\sin^2 x + \cos^2 x) + 5 \cos^2 x$
    $y_{\max} = (\sqrt{2^2 + (1)^4}) + 1 + 5$
    $= 6 + \sqrt{5}$

34. (b) It has local minimum at $x = 0$

    Explanation :
    Given $f(x) = x^3 \sin x$
    ∴ $f'(x) = x^3 \cos x - 3x^2 \sin x$
    Now, $f''(x) = -x^3 \sin x + 3x^2 \cos x - 3x^2 \cos x - 6x \sin x$
    For critical points, $f'(x) = 0$
    $\Rightarrow$ $x^3 \cos x - 3x^2 \sin x = 0$
    $\Rightarrow$ $x^2 (x \cos x - \sin x) = 0$
    ∴ $x = 0$

At $x = 0$
$\Rightarrow \quad f''(x) = 0$
$\Rightarrow$ Function has local min. at $x = 0$.

35. (a) Both (A) and (R) are true and R is the correct explanation of A.
    Explanation :
    For vertical tangent $\dfrac{dx}{d\theta} = 0$
    $\therefore \quad -3\cos\theta = 0 \Rightarrow \cos\theta = 0$
    $\Rightarrow \quad \theta = \pi/2,\ 3\pi/2$
    At $\theta = \pi/2;\ x = 2 - 3 = -1,\ y = 3 + 0 = 3$ i.e., $(-1, 3)$
    and At $\theta = 3\pi/2;\ x = 2 + 3 = 5$ and $y = 3 + 0 = 3$
    i.e., $(5, 3)$.

36. (a) Both (A) and (R) are true and R is the correct explanation A.
    Explanation :
    $2y\dfrac{dy}{dx} = (2 - 2x)$
    $\Rightarrow \quad \dfrac{dy}{dx} = \left(\dfrac{1-x}{y}\right)$
    $\left.\dfrac{dy}{dx}\right|_{(3, 0)} = \infty$ and $\left.\dfrac{dy}{dx}\right|_{(-1, 0)} = \infty$
    i.e., tangents makes an angle $\dfrac{dy}{dx}$ with x-axis.

37. (d) A is true but R is false.
    Explanation :
    $\because \quad y^2 = x + \sin x$ ...(i)
    $\therefore \quad 2y\dfrac{dy}{dx} = 1 + \cos x = 0 \quad \left[\because \dfrac{dy}{dx} = 0\right]$
    $\therefore \quad \cos x = -1$,
    then $\sin x = 0$
    From equation (i), $y^2 = x$ (Parabola).

38. (a) Both (A) and (R) are true and R is the correct explanation A.
    Given $\quad f'(x) = f(x)$
    $\Rightarrow \quad 2x = x^2$
    $\Rightarrow \quad x = 0, 2$
    at $x = 0,\ y = 0$
    and at $x = 2,\ y = 4$
    So we have to find equation of tangents at $(0, 0)$ and $(2, 4)$.
    At $(0, 0),\ f'(0) = 0$ and at $(2, 4),\ f'(2) = 4$
    $\therefore$ Tangents are $y - 0 = 0(x - 0)$ and $y - 4 = 4(x - 2)$
    i.e., $y = 0$ and $4x - y - 4 = 0$.

39. (i) (b) Perimeter = 200 m
    $\Rightarrow \quad 2x + 2\pi\left(\dfrac{y}{2}\right) = 200$
    $\Rightarrow \quad 2x + \pi y = 200$.

    (ii) (a) Area of rectangular region
    $= l \times b$

    $\Rightarrow \quad A = xy = x\left(\dfrac{200 - 2x}{\pi}\right)$ [From (i)]
    $\therefore \quad A = \dfrac{2}{\pi}(100x - x^2)$

    (iii) (c) $\dfrac{dA}{dx} = \dfrac{2}{\pi}(100 - 2x)$
    Put $\dfrac{dA}{dx} = 0$
    $\Rightarrow \quad x = 50$
    $\dfrac{d^2A}{dx^2} = \dfrac{2}{\pi}(-2) < 0$
    $\therefore$ A is maximum when $x = 50$
    $\therefore$ Maximum area $= \dfrac{2}{\pi}(5000 - 2500)$
    $= \dfrac{5000}{\pi}$ m^2

    (iv) (a) Area of whole floor
    $= xy + \pi\left(\dfrac{y}{2}\right)^2$
    $= \dfrac{(200 - \pi y)y}{2} + \dfrac{\pi y^2}{4}$
    $= 100y - \dfrac{\pi y^2}{2} + \dfrac{\pi y^2}{4}$
    $A_1 = 100y - \dfrac{\pi y^2}{4}$
    $\Rightarrow \quad \dfrac{dA_1}{dy} = 100 - \dfrac{2\pi y}{4}$
    $\Rightarrow \quad \dfrac{dA_1}{dy} = 0$
    $\Rightarrow \quad 200 = \pi y$
    $\Rightarrow \quad y = \dfrac{200}{\pi}$
    $\Rightarrow \quad \dfrac{d^2A_1}{dy^2} = -\dfrac{\pi}{2} < 0$
    $\therefore A_1$ is maximum when
    $y = \dfrac{200}{\pi}$ and $x = \left[\dfrac{200 - \pi\left(\dfrac{200}{\pi}\right)}{2}\right] = 0$
    $\Rightarrow \quad x = 0$.

    (iv) (d) When the whole area is maximized, there will be no further increase in area.

40. (i) (a) Given equation of curve is
    $y = x^3 - 11x + 5$
    $\dfrac{dy}{dx} = 3x^2 - 11$ at $(1, -5)$

$$\frac{dy}{dx} = 3(1)^2 - 11 = -8$$

Slope of normal to the curve is $\frac{1}{8}$.

$\therefore$ Slope of normal $= \dfrac{-1}{\frac{dy}{dx}} = \dfrac{1}{8}$.

(ii) (d) Equation of normal is

$$y - y_1 = \frac{-1}{\frac{dy}{dx}}(x - x_1)$$

$$y + 5 = \frac{1}{8}(x - 1)$$

$$8y + 40 = x - 1$$
$$8y - x + 41 = 0.$$

(iii) (a) For curve parallel to X-axis slope i.e.,

$$\frac{dy}{dx} = 0$$

$$3x^2 - 11 = 0$$

$$x^2 = \frac{11}{3}$$

$$x = \pm\sqrt{\frac{11}{3}}$$

(iv) (b) Slope of tangent = Slope of curve

$$3x^2 - 11 = 1$$
$$3x^2 = 12$$
$$x^2 = 4$$
$$x = \pm 2$$

If $x = 2, y = -9$, if $x = -2, y = 19$

But $(-2, 19)$ does not lie on the tangent.

(v) (b) Slope of tangent is

$$y = x - 11$$
$$\frac{dy}{dx} = 1.$$

41. (i) (a) $P \Rightarrow 3x + 2y = 12$

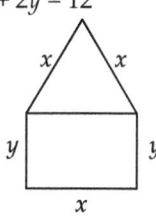

$$2y = 12 - 3x$$
$$y = \frac{12 - 3x}{2}$$
$$= 6 - \frac{3}{2}x.$$

(ii) (c) $A = xy + \dfrac{\sqrt{3}}{4}x^2$

$$A = x\left(6 - \frac{3}{2}x\right) + \frac{\sqrt{3}}{4}x^2$$

$$A = 6x - \frac{3}{2}x^2 + \frac{\sqrt{3}}{4}x^2$$

(iii) (b) Differentiating A w.r.t. x,

$$\frac{dA}{dx} = 6 - 3x + \frac{\sqrt{3}}{2}x$$

Put $\dfrac{dA}{dx} = 0$,

$$6 + x\left(\frac{\sqrt{3}}{2} - 3\right) = 0$$

$$x\left(\frac{\sqrt{3}}{2} - 3\right) = -6$$

$$x = \frac{6}{3 - \frac{\sqrt{3}}{2}}$$

$$x = \frac{12}{6 - \sqrt{3}}.$$

(iv) (d) $\dfrac{d^2A}{dx^2} = -3 + \dfrac{\sqrt{3}}{2} = -\text{ve}$

$\therefore$ Area is maximum.

$\therefore$
$$y = 6 - 3\left(\frac{12}{6 - \sqrt{3}}\right)$$

$$= \frac{36 - 6\sqrt{3} - 18}{(6 - \sqrt{3})}$$

$$y = \left(\frac{18 - 6\sqrt{3}}{6 - \sqrt{3}}\right) \text{m}.$$

(v) (b) Area of triangular part of window

$$= \frac{\sqrt{3}}{4}x^2 = \frac{\sqrt{3}}{4}\left(\frac{12}{6 - \sqrt{3}}\right)^2$$

$$= \frac{\sqrt{3}}{4} \times \frac{144}{36 + 3 - 12\sqrt{3}} = \frac{36\sqrt{3}}{39 - 12\sqrt{3}} \text{ sq. unit}.$$

42. (i) (a) Given equation of curve $y = x^2 + 7$ at $(1, 8)$

Slope of tangent $\dfrac{dy}{dx} = 2x$

$$\frac{dy}{dx} = 2 \times 1 = 2$$

(ii) (b) Slope of normal to the curve is

$$= \frac{-1}{\frac{dy}{dx}} = \frac{-1}{2}$$

(iii) (d) Equation of tangent at $(1, 8)$ with slope 2 is

$$y - y_1 = \frac{dy}{dx}(x - x_1)$$

$$y - 8 = 2(x - 1)$$
$$y - 8 = 2x - 2$$
$$y = 2x + 6$$

(iv) (a) Equation of normal at (1, 8) is

$$y - y_1 = \frac{-1}{\frac{dy}{dx}}(x - x_1)$$

$$y - 8 = \frac{-1}{2}(x - 1)$$

$$2y - 16 = -x + 1$$
$$2y + x = 17$$

(v) (c) Distance $= \sqrt{(y_2 - y_1)^2 + (x_2 - x_1)^2}$

$$= \sqrt{(7-8)^2 + (3-1)^2}$$
$$= \sqrt{1+4} = \sqrt{5} \text{ unit}$$

43. (i) (a) **Let** x be no. of passenger and y be the amount of earning per passenger.

$$y = 200 - \frac{5}{10}(x - 50)$$
$$= 200 - \frac{1}{2}x + 25$$
$$y = 225 - \frac{1}{2}x \qquad \textbf{Ans.}$$

(ii) (d) Slope $= \frac{-1}{2}$

(iii) (b) Total earning = rate × no. of passenger

$$TE = \left(225 - \frac{x}{2}\right)x$$

$$\Rightarrow \qquad TE = 225 - \frac{x^2}{2}$$

(iv) (b) $\qquad TE = 225x - \frac{x^2}{2}$

$\qquad TE'(x) = 225 - x$

Put $\qquad TE'(x) = 0$

$\qquad x = 225$

Thus, for $x = 225$ he can have the maximum amount.

(v) (d) $\qquad TE''(x) = -1$

∴ Maximum at $x = 225$

and total earning is

$$225 \times 112 \cdot 50 = ₹ \; 25312 \cdot 50.$$

Chapter 7

Linear Programming

1. In an LPP, if the objective function $z = ax + by$ has the same maximum value on two corner points of the feasible region, then the number of points at which Z_{max} occurs is : [CBSE – 2020]
   (a) 0
   (b) 2
   (c) finite
   (d) infinite

2. The graph of the inequality $2x + 3y > 6$ is : [CBSE – 2020]
   (a) half plane that contains the origin
   (b) half plane that neither contains the origin nor the points of the line $2x + 3y = 6$
   (c) whole XOY–plane excluding the points on the line $2x + 3y = 6$
   (d) entire XOY plane.

3. Which of the following types of problems cannot be solved by linear programming methods?
   (a) Transportation problem
   (b) Manufacturing problems
   (c) Traffic signal control
   (d) Diet problems

4. The optimal value of the objective function is attained at the points:
   (a) Corner points of the feasible region
   (b) Any point of the feasible region
   (c) on x-axis
   (d) on y-axis

5. An optimisation problem may involve finding :
   (a) maximum profit
   (b) minimum cost
   (c) minimum use of resources
   (d) All of the above

6. The condition $x \geq 0, y \geq 0$ are called :
   (a) restrictions only
   (b) negative restrictions
   (c) non-negative restrictions
   (d) None of the above

7. The feasible region for the an LPP is shown in this following figure. Then, the minimum value of Z = $11x + 7y$ is

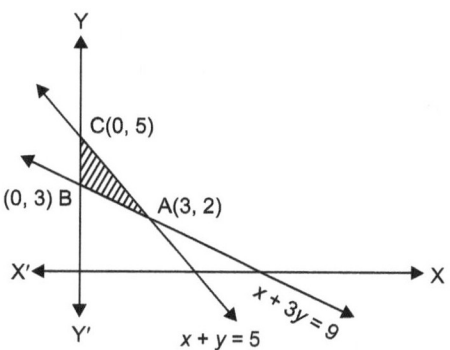

   (a) 21
   (b) 47
   (c) 20
   (d) 31

8. The maximum value of $Z = 4x + 3y$, if the feasible region for the an LPP is shown below :

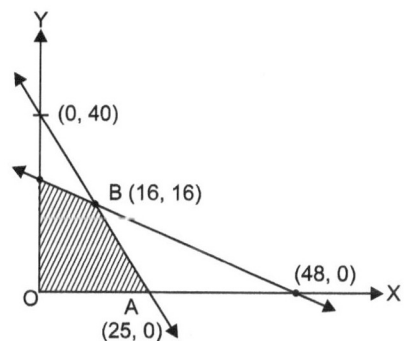

   (a) 112
   (b) 100
   (c) 72
   (d) 110

9. In which of the following problems (s), linear programming can be used :
   (a) manufacturing problems
   (b) diet problems
   (c) transportation problems
   (d) All of these

10. Corner points of the feasible region for an LPP are (0, 2), (3, 0), (6, 0), (6, 8) and (0, 5).
    Let $F = 4x + 6y$ be the objective function. The minimum value of F occurs at :
    (a) (0, 2) only
    (b) (3, 0) only
    (c) the mid-point on the line segment joining the points (0, 2) and (3, 0) only
    (d) any point on the line segment joining the points (0, 2) and (3, 0)

11. The corner points of the feasible region determined by the following system of linear inequalities $2x + y \leq 10$, $x + 3y \leq 15$, $x, y \geq 0$ are $(0, 0)$, $(5, 0)$, $(3, 4)$ and $(0, 5)$. Let $Z = px + qy$, where $p, q > 0$. Condition on p and q, so that the maximum of Z occurs at both $(3, 4)$ and $(0, 5)$ is:
    (a) $p = q$ (b) $p = 2q$
    (c) $p = 3q$ (d) $q = 3p$

12. The variable x and y in a linear programming problem are called:
    (a) decision variables (b) linear variables
    (c) optimal variables (d) None of these

13. The linear inequalities or equations or restrictions on the variables of a linear programming problem are called:
    (a) linear relations (b) constraints
    (c) functions (d) objective functions

14. The objective function of an LPP is:
    (a) a constraint
    (b) a function to be optimised
    (c) a relation between the variables
    (d) None of the above

15. Which of the term is not used in a linear programming problem?
    (a) Optimal solution (b) Feasible solution
    (c) Concave region (d) Objective function

16. Which of the following sets are not convex?
    (a) $(x, y) : 2x + 5y < 7$ (b) $(x, y) : x^2 + y^2 \leq 4$
    (c) $(x|x|) = 5$ (d) $(x, y) : 3x^2 + 2y^2 \leq 6$

17. The optimal value of the objective function is attained at the point is:
    (a) given by intersection of inequations with axes only
    (b) given by intersection of inequations with X-axis only
    (c) given by corner points of the feasible region
    (d) None of the above.

18. The feasible solution for a LPP shown in Fig. Let $Z = 3x - 4y$ be the objective function. Minimum of Z occurs at:

    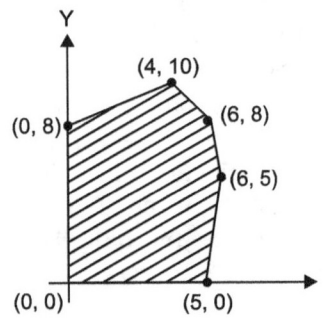

    (a) $(0, 0)$ (b) $(0, 8)$
    (c) $(5, 0)$ (d) $(4, 10)$

19. Refer to Question 18. Maximum of Z occurs at:
    (a) $(5, 0)$ (b) $(6, 5)$
    (c) $(6, 8)$ (d) $(4, 10)$

20. Refer to Question 18. (Maximum value of Z + Minimum value of Z) is:
    (a) 13 (b) 1
    (c) -13 (d) -17

21. Feasible region in the set of points which satisfy:
    (a) The objective functions
    (b) Some the given functions
    (c) All of the given constraints
    (d) None of these

22. The region of feasible solution in LPP graphic method is called.
    (a) Infeasible region (b) unbounded region
    (c) Infinite region (d) feasible region

23. In equation $3x - y \geq 3$ and $4x - 4y > 4$:
    (a) Have solution for positive x and y
    (b) Have no solution for positive x and y
    (c) Have solution for all x
    (d) Have soluton for all y

24. The corner point of the feasible region determined by the system of linear constraints are $(0, 0)$, $(0, 30)$, $(20, 40)$, $(60, 20)$, $(50, 0)$. The objective function is $Z = 4x + 3y$. Compare the quantity in Column A and Column B:

Col. A	Col. B
Max Z	340

    (a) Quantity in column A is greater
    (b) Quantity in column A is greater
    (c) Two quantities are equal
    (d) Relationship cannot be determined and the basis of information supplied

25. In a LPP, the objective function is always:
    (a) cubic (b) quadratic
    (c) linear (d) constant

26. Maximise, $Z = -x + 2y$, subject to the constraints $x \geq 3$, $x + y \geq 5$, $x + 2y \geq 6$, $y \geq 0$:
    (a) Max, $Z = 12$ at $(2, 6)$
    (b) Z has no max. value
    (c) Max., $Z = 10$ at $(2, 6)$
    (d) Max., $Z = 14$ at $(2, 6)$

27. A linear programming problem is one that is concerned with:
    (a) finding the upper limits of a linear function of several variables
    (b) finding the lower limit of a linear function of several variables
    (c) finding the limiting values of a linear function of several variables
    (d) finding the optimal value (max or min) of a linear function of several variables

28. Objective function is expressed in terms of the ....
    (a) Numbers (b) Symbols
    (c) Decision variables (d) None of these

29. In a transportation problem, with 4 supply point and 5 demand points how many number of contraints required in its formulation :
    (a) 20 (b) 1 (c) 0 (d) 9
30. The feasible region (shaded) for a LPP is shown in the figure. The max. Z = 5x + 7y is :

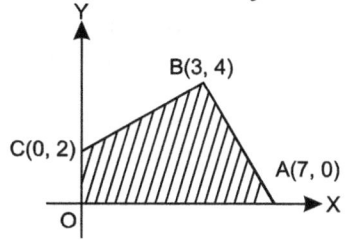

    (a) 43 (b) 47 (c) 45 (d) 49
31. The position of points O(0, 0) and P(2, – 2) in the region of graph of inequation 2x – 3y < 5, will be :
    (a) O inside and P outside
    (b) O and P both inside
    (c) O and P both outside
    (d) O outside and P inside
32. Let Z = ax + by is a linear objective function variables x and y are called .... variables.
    (a) Independent (b) Continuous
    (c) Decision   (d) Dependent
33. Infeasibility means that the number of solutions to the linear programming models that satisfies all constraints is :
    (a) At least   (b) An infinite number
    (c) Zero   (d) At least 2

    Choose the correct option :
    (a) Both (A) and (B) are true and R is the correct explanation A.
    (b) Both (A) and (R) are true but R is not correct explanation of A.
    (c) A is true but R is false.
    (d) A is false but R is true.

34. **Assertion (A)** : The region represented by the set $\{(x, y) : 4 \leq x^2 + y^2 \leq 9\}$ is a convex set.
    Reason (R) : The set $\{(x, y) : 4 \leq x^2 + y^2 \leq 9\}$ represents the region between two concentric circles of radii 2 and 3.
35. **Assertion (A)** : If a L.P.P. admits two optimal solutions then it has infinitely many optimal solutions.
    Reason (R) : If the value of the objective function of a LPP is same at two corners then it is same at every point on the line joining two corner points.
36. A furniture dealer deals in only two items—tables and chairs. He took a loan of ₹ 50,000 from the bank to invest in this business. He took a room on rent for the storage of furniture which has a storage space of at most 60 pieces. A table costs ₹ 2500 while a chair costs ₹ 500. He estimates that from the sale of one table, he can make a profit of ₹ 250 and that from the sale of one chair a profit of ₹ 75. Find the number of tables and chairs he should buy from the available money so as to maximize his total profit, assuming that he can sell all the items which he buys.

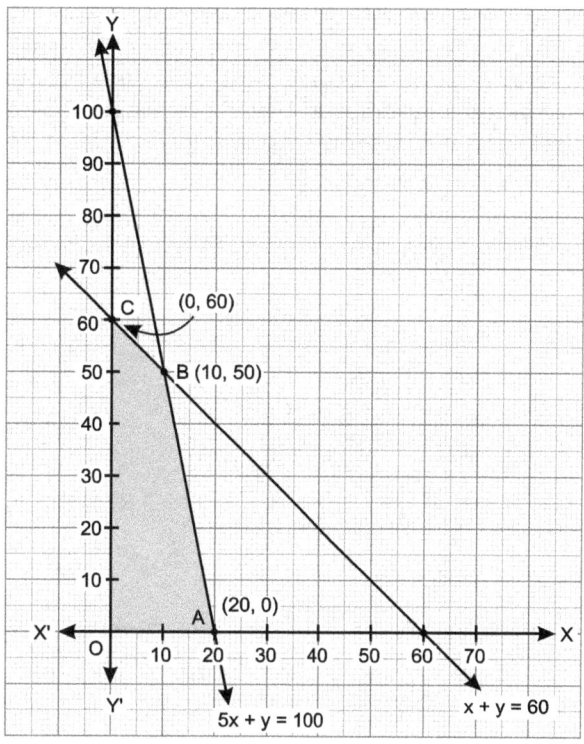

Fig.
Graphical representation of optimization problem

Based on the above information answer the following :
(i) Which constraint shows the linear objective function using decision variables x and y ?
    (a) Z = 250x + 75y   (b) Z = 250x – 75y
    (c) Z = 275x – 50y   (d) Z = 75x – 250y
(ii) Which equation shows that "he can store only 60 pieces of chairs and tables" ?
    (a) x + y ≥ 60   (b) x – y ≥ 60
    (c) x – y = 60   (d) x + y ≤ 60
(iii) Choose correct investment constraint by furniture dealer :
    (a) 2500x + 500y ≤ 50000
    (b) 2500x – 500y ≤ 50000
    (c) 500x – 2500y ≤ 50000
    (d) 500x + 2500y ≤ 50000
(iv) In which case total profit would be ₹ 6250 ?
    (a) 10 tables and 50 chairs
    (b) 50 tables and 10 chairs
    (c) 5 tables and 55 chairs
    (d) 20 tables and 40 chairs
(v) Due to this storage space maximum of 60 pieces, his investment is limited to a maximum of :
    (a) ₹ 55000   (b) ₹ 50000
    (c) ₹ 58000   (d) ₹ 45000

37. A cooperative society of farmers has 50 hectare of land to grow two crops X and Y. The estimation of income from crops per hectare is 10,500 and 9,000 respectively. To control weeds, a runny herbicide has used for both crops at rates of 20 litres and 10 litres per hectare. Additionally, no more than 800 litres of herbicide should be used for protecting fish and natural world using a fishpond which collect drainage from this ground.

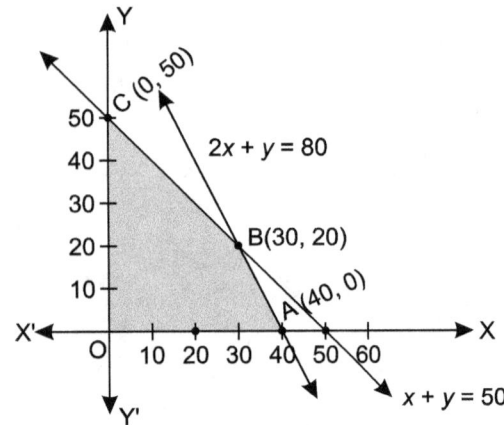

Fig. : Graph of OABC is the feasible region (shaded)

Corner Point	Z = 10500x + 9000y
O(0, 0)	0
A(40, 0)	420000
B(30, 20)	495000
C(0, 50)	450000

Based on the above information answer the following questions :

(i) What is the objective function of given problem ?
 (a) Z = 9000x + 10500y (b) Z = 10500x + 9000y
 (c) Z = 8000x + 10500y (d) Z = 10500x − 9000y

(ii) Which equation shows the constraint related to land ?
 (a) $x + y \geq 50$ (b) $x - y \geq 50$
 (c) $x + y \leq 50$ (d) $x - y \leq 50$

(iii) What is the characteristics of the feasible region OABC ?
 (a) Unbounded (b) Bounded
 (c) Both (a) and (b) (d) None of these

(iv) The maximum income would be got by people is :
 (a) ₹ 4,95,000 (b) ₹ 4,90,000
 (c) ₹ 4,85,000 (d) ₹ 4,80,000

(v) How much ground should be billed to each crops so as to maximize the total income of the people ?
 (a) 30 hectare for crop x and 20 hectare from crop y
 (b) 20 hectare for crop x and 30 hectare from crop y
 (c) 20 hectare for crop x and 40 hectare from crop y
 (d) 40 hectare for crop x and 20 hectare from crop y

38. There are three machines installed in a factory, machines I, II and III. Out of these three machines, machines I and II are capable of being operated for at most 12 hours in a day whereas machine III must be operated for at least 5 hours a day. In factory they produce only two types of toys namely, M and N each of them requires the use of all the three machines. The number of hours taken by M and N on each of the three machines are given in the table below :

Items	Number of hours required on machines		
	I	II	III
M	1	2	1
N	2	1	1.25

The amount of profit she makes on per price of toy M is ₹ 600 and on toy N is ₹ 400.

Corner point	Z = 600x + 400y	
(5, 0)	3000	
(6, 0)	3600	
(4, 4)	4000	← Maximum
(0, 6)	2400	
(0, 4)	1600	

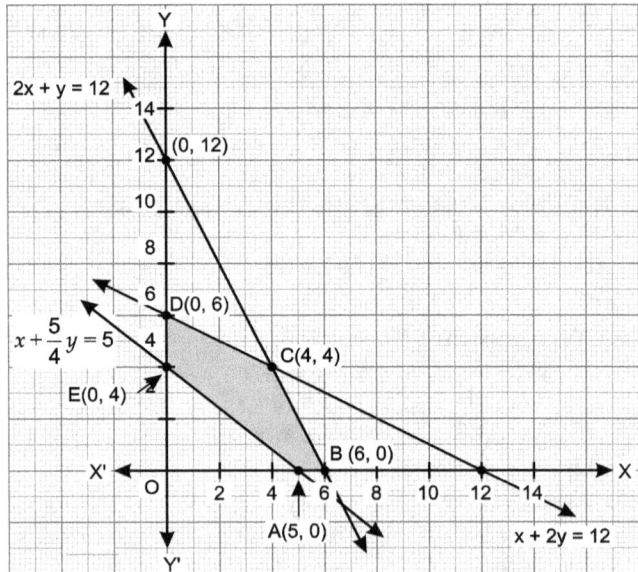

Fig.

Graph of ABCDE is the feasible region (shaded)

Based on the above information answer the following :

(i) How many of each type of toys should she produce so as to maximize her profit assuming that she can sell all the toys that she produed ? What will be the maximum profit ?
 (a) 4 units, ₹ 4000 (b) 4 units, ₹ 6000
 (c) 5 units, ₹ 3600 (d) 5 units, ₹ 5600

(ii) Select the equation of the total profit on production :
(a) $Z = 600x - 400y$
(b) $Z = 600x + 400y$
(c) $Z = 600x \times 400y$
(d) None of these

(iii) Choose the correct constraint of Machine I :
(a) $x + 2y \geq 12$
(b) $x + 2y \leq 12$
(c) $x + 2y = 12$
(d) $x + 2y \leq 12$

(iv) According to above figure 1, constraint on Machine II is :
(a) $2x + 2y \leq 12$
(b) $2x + y \leq 12$
(c) $x + 2y \leq 12$
(d) $x + 2y \leq 21$

(v) Tick on correct constraint on Machine III is :
(a) $x + \dfrac{5}{4}y \geq 5$
(b) $x + \dfrac{5}{4}y \leq 5$
(c) $x + \dfrac{3}{4}y \leq 5$
(d) $x + \dfrac{3}{4}y \geq 5$

39. Corner points of the feasible region for an LPP are (0, 3), (5, 0), (6, 8), (6, 8). Let $z = 4x - 6y$ be the objective function.
Based on the above information, answer the following questions :

(i) The minimum value of z occurs at :
(a) (6, 8)
(b) (5, 0)
(c) (0, 3)
(d) (0, 8)

(ii) Maximum value of z occurs at :
(a) (5, 0)
(b) (0, 8)
(c) (0, 3)
(d) (6, 8)

(iii) Max z – min z =
(a) 58
(b) 68
(c) 78
(d) 88

(iv) The corner points of the feasible region determined by the system of linear in equalities as :

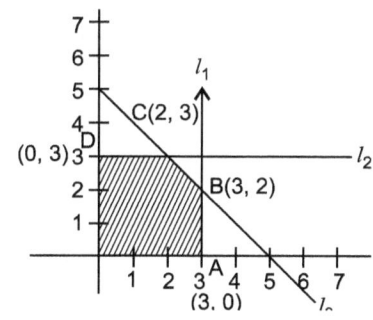

(a) (0, 0), (– 3, 0), (3, 2), (2, 3)
(b) (3, 0), (3, 2), (2, 3), (0, – 3)
(c) (0, 0), (3, 0), (2, 3), (3, 2), (0, 3)
(d) None of these

(v) The feasible solution of LPP belongs to :
(a) First and second quadrant
(b) First and third quadrant
(c) Only second quadrant
(d) Only first quadrant

40. Linear programming is a method for finding the optimal values (maximum or minimum) of quanties subject to the constraints when relationshp is expressed as linear equation or inequalities. Based on the above information, answer the following questions :

(i) The optimal value of the objective function is attainted at the points :
(a) x-axis
(b) on y-axis
(c) which are corner points of the feasible region
(d) none of these

(ii) The graph of the inequality $3x + 4y \leq 12$ is
(a) Half plane that contains the origin
(b) Half plane that neither contains the origin nor the points one the line $3x + 4y = 12$
(c) Whole XOY plane excluding the points on the line $3x + 4y = 12$
(d) None of these

(iii) The feasible region for an LPP is shown in the figure. Let $z = 2x + 5y$ be the objective function maximum of z occurs at

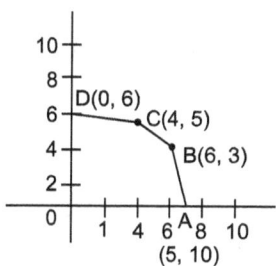

(a) (7, 0)
(b) (6, 3)
(c) (0, 6)
(d) (4, 3)

(iv) The corner points of the feasible region determined by the system of linear constraints are (0, 10), (5, 5), (15, 15), (0, 20). Let $z = px + qy$, where $p, q > 0$ condition on p and q so that the maximum of z occurs at botht he points (15, 15) and (0, 20) is :
(a) $p = q$
(b) $p = 2q$
(c) $q = 2p$
(d) $q = 3p$

(v) The corner points of feasible region determined by the system of linear constraints are (0, 0), (0, 40), (20, 40), (60, 20), (60, 0). The objective function is $z = 4x + 3y$. Compare the quantity in Column A and Column B :

Column A	Column B
Max Z	325

(a) The quantity in column in A is greater
(b) The quantity in column in B is greater
(c) The two quantities are equal
(d) None of these

Solutions

1. (d) infinite
2. (b) half plane that neither contains the origin nor the points of the line $2x + 3y = 6$
   Explanation :
   As the required region is not forwards the origin.
3. (c) Traffic signal control
   Explanation :
   It does not have constraints.
4. (a) Corner points of the feasible region
   Explanation :
   By putting the corner points in objective function, we get the optimal value.
5. (d) All of the above
   Explanation :
   An optimisation problem may involve finding maximum profit, minimum cost or minimum use of resources etc.
6. (c) non-negative restrictions
   Explanation :
   The conditions $x \geq 0$, and $y \geq 0$ are called non-negative restrictions.
7. (a) 21
   Explanation :
   The values of Z at the corner points are given by

Corner point	Value of Z
(3, 2)	47
(0, 3)	21 (Minimum)
(0, 5)	35

   From the above table, we see that the minimum value of Z is 21.
8. (a) 112
   Explanation :
   Since, the feasible region is bounded. Therefore, maximum of Z must occur at the corners points of the feasible region.

Corner point	Value of Z
O(0, 0)	4(0) + 3(0) = 0
A(25, 0)	4(25) + 3(0) = 100
B(16, 16)	4(16) + 3(16) = 112 (Maximum)
O(0, 24)	4(0) + 3(24) = 72

   Hence, the maximum value of Z is 112.
9. (d) All of these
   Explanation :
   By definitions of L.P.P.
10. (d) any point on the line segment joining the points (0, 2) and (3, 0).
    Explanation :

Corner point	F = 4x + 6y
(0, 2)	12
(3, 0)	12
(6, 0)	24
(6, 8)	72
(0, 5)	30

    The minimum value of F is 12 at (0, 2) and (3, 0).
    ∴ The minimum value of F occurs at any point on the line segment joining the points (0, 2) and (3, 0).
11. (d) $q = 3p$
    Explanation :
    The maximum value of Z is unique.
    It is given that the maximum value of Z occurs at two points (3, 4) and (0, 5). Value of Z at (3, 4) = Value of Z at (0, 5).
    $\Rightarrow \quad p(3) + q(4) = p(0) + q(5), 3p + 4q = 5q$
    $\Rightarrow \quad 3p = q$ or $q = 3p$.
12. (a) decision variables
13. (b) constraints
14. (b) a function to be optimised
15. (c) Concave region
16. (c) $(x|x|) = 5$
    Explanation :
    $|x| = 5$ is not a convex set at any two points from negative positive x-axis of joined will lie not in set.
17. (c) given by corner points of the feasible region
18. (b) (0, 8)
    Explanation :

Corner Points	Corresponding value of Z = 3x – 4y
(0, 0)	0
(5, 0)	15 (Maximum)
(6, 5)	– 2
(6, 8)	– 14
(4, 10)	– 28
(0, 8)	– 32 (Minimum)

    Hence, the minimum of Z occurs at (0, 8) and its minimum value is (– 32).
19. (a) (5, 0)
    Explanation :
    Refer to solution 18, maximum of Z occurs at (5, 0).
20. (d) – 17
    Explanation :
    Refer to solution 18, maximum value of Z + minimum value of Z = 15 – 32 = – 17.
21. (c) All of the given constrainsts

22. (d) feasible region
23. (a) Have solution for positive x and y
    Explanation :
    As both the inequalities are greater.
24. (b) Quantity in column A is greater
    Explanation :

Corner Points	$Z = 4x + 3y$
(0, 0)	0
(0, 30)	90
(20, 40)	200
(60, 20)	300 — Max.
(50, 0)	200

    ∴ Column A < Column B.
25. (c) linear
    Explanation :
    In a LPP, the objective function is always linear.
26. (b) Z has no max. value
    Explanation :
    Here, $Z = -x + 2y$
    Given constraints are $x \geq 3$, $x + y \geq 5$, $x + 2y \geq 0$, $y \geq 0$

Corner points	$Z = -x + 2y$
D(6, 0)	– 6
A(4, 1)	– 2
B(3, 2)	1

    Here, the open half plan has points in common with the feasible region.
    ∴ Z has no more value.
27. (d) Finding the optimal value (max or min) of a linear function of several variables
    Explanation :
    By definition.
28. (c) Decision variables
    Explanation :
    As it involves decision variables, for which function need to minimized or minimised.
29. (d) 9
    Explanation :
    Given, $m = 4, n = 5$
    No. of constraints $= m + n = 4 + 5 = 9$.
30. (a) 43
    Explanation :

Corner Points	$Z = 5x + 7y$
A(7, 0)	35
B(3, 4)	43 — Max.
C(0, 2)	14

31. (a) O inside and P outside
    Explanation :

    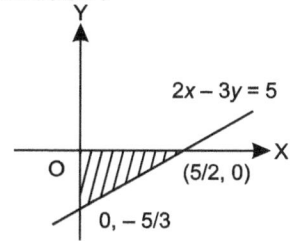

32. (c) Decision
    Explanation :
    Variables x and y are decision variables, which helps to decide the min. and max. value of Z.
33. (c) Zero
    Explanation : As not all the constraints are satisfied. That is why, no solution exist or is infeasible.
34. (a) (A) is incorrect, (R) is correct.
    Explanation :
    As it represents a concave set.
35. (a) (A) is correct, (R) is correct, (R) is correct explanation of (A).
36. (i) (a) The linear objective function using decision variables x and y is :
        $Z = 250x + 75y$
    (ii) (d) Following equation shows that "he can store only 60 pieces of chairs and tables :
        i.e., $x + y \leq 60$
    (iii) (a) Correct investment constraint by furniture dealer is :
        $2500x + 500y \leq 50000$
    (iv) (a) He may choose to buy 10 tables and 50 chairs, as he can store only 60 pieces. Total profit in this case would be ₹ (10 × 250 + 50 × 75), i.e., ₹ 6250.
        i.e., 10 tables and 50 chairs
    (v) (b) Due to his storage space maximum of 60 pieces, his investment is limited to a maximum of ₹ 50000.
37. (i) (b) Objective function is
        $Z = 10500x + 9000y$
    (ii) (c) The equation for land is :
        i.e., $x + y \leq 50$.
    (iii) (b) Bounded is the characteristics of the feasible section (covered).
    (iv) (a) The people will get the maximum income of ₹ 4,95,000 (by table).
    (v) (a) Ground should be allocated to each crop so as to maximize the total income of the people.
        i.e., 30 hectare for crop x and 20 hectare from crop y.
38. (i) (a) According to table the point (4, 4) is giving the maximum value of Z. Hence, the manufacturer has to produce 4 units of each item to get the maximum profit.
    (ii) (b) The equation of the total profit on production : $Z = 600x + 400y$.
    (iii) (c) The correct constraint of Machine I : $x + 2y \leq 12$.
    (iv) (b) According to above table, constraint on Machine II is : $2x + y \leq 12$.

(v) (a) Constraint on Machine III is : $x + \dfrac{5}{4}y \geq 5$.

39. (i) (d)

S. No.	Corner Point	Min Z
1.	(0, 3)	−18
2.	(5, 0)	20
3.	(5, 8)	−24
4.	(0, 8)	−48

∴ Min value = −48

So min value of z occurs at (0, 8).

(ii) (a) Max. value = 20 at (5, 0)

So max. value of z occurs at (5, 0).

(iii) (b) Max. z − min z = 20 − (−48)
= 20 + 48
= 68.

(iv) (c) [(0, 0), (3, 0), (3, 2), (2, 3), (0, 3)]

(v) (d) Only first quadrant.

40. (i) (c)

(ii) (c)

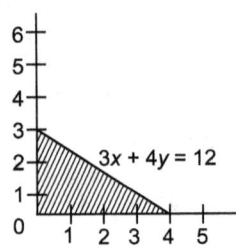

From the above graph inequality lies in whole XOY plane excluding the points on the line $3x + 4y = 12$.

(iii) (d)

S. No.	Corner Point	Z
1.	O(0, 0)	0
2.	A(7, 0)	14
3.	B(6, 3)	27
4.	C(4, 5)	(33) Max z
5.	D(0, 6)	30

∴ Max value = 33

So max z occurs at (4, 5).

(iv) (d) Max value of z at (15, 15)
$15p + 15y$ ...(i)
Max value of z at (0, 20) is
$20q$ ...(ii)

∴ Max value occurs at two points so their objective function are equal.

Hence eq. (i) and eq. (ii),
$15p + 15q = 20q$
$15p = 5q$
$q = 3p.$

(v) (b)

S. No.	Corner Point	Z
1.	(0, 0)	0
2.	(0, 40)	120
3.	(20, 40)	200
4.	(60, 20)	(300) Max
5.	(60, 0)	240

∴ Max value = 300

Hence, quantity in column B is greater.

❏❏